X USER TOOLS

B

D1534660

O'Reilly & Associates, Inc.

X USER TOOLS

Linda Mui and Valerie Quercia
with other authors, including Ian Darwin,
David Flanagan, Tim O'Reilly,
and Norm Walsh

O'Reilly & Associates, Inc.

X User Tools

by Linda Mui and Valerie Quercia, and other contributors
(See the Preface for a complete list of contributors)

Editor: Tim O'Reilly

Production Editor: Mary Anne Weeks Mayo

Printing History:

September 1994:   First Edition.

August 1996:   Minor corrections.

ISBN 1-56592-019-8

ISBN: 1-56592-019-8

Table of Contents

Part Four: Window Managers

Chapter 12:   The twm Window Manager   229

Chapter 14: The olwm Window Manager   309

Part Five: The User Environment

Chapter 16: Simple Startup Scripts   375

Chapter 17: Configuring Applications   383

Chapter 23: Screen Dumps   533

Chapter 24: Drawing and Viewing Pictures   545

Part Seven: System Administration

Chapter 27: Tools for Administrators   625

Chapter 28: Configuring the X Display Manager 637

Figures

Tables

How to Use This Book

Article Number

The first two digits indicate what chapter the article is in, the last two digits indicate the number of the article within that chapter. The article number is used to refer to this article in all cross references throughout the book.

Dictionary-style Headers

As in a dictionary, we show you the entry that starts and ends each page, in case the article heading isn't visible. On a left-hand page, the number of the first article on that page (which may be continued from a previous page) is shown in the upper-left corner. On a right-hand page, the number of the last article on that page is shown in the upper-right corner.

CD-ROM

If you don't want to type this script into a file yourself, or if we're talking about a program that isn't shown, you can install it from the CD-ROM that comes with this book. Give the install program the name listed under the icon. See Article 31.08 for complete installation instructions.

Author's Initials

The author's full name is listed in the Preface.

Cross-reference

If you want to know more about the topic in the gray type, read the article whose number appears between the parentheses immediately following the terms in gray.

Footer

The chapter title appears in the footer near the inside margin of the right-hand page, so you can always see the general topic of the chapter.

Glossary Reference

When a word or phrase appears in gray without a corresponding article number, it means that the topic is covered in the glossary.

6.04

6.03 More Root Window Decorations

The *xcsetroot* client can do most everything *xsetroot (6.02)* can do, plus a bit more. *xcsetroot* accepts all but one of *xsetroot's* options (-cursor_name). *xcsetroot* also lets you specify graphics in two additional formats: GIF and X Window dump *(23.01)*.

To create a root window made up of tiles of a window or screen-dump file, use the syntax:

```
% xcsetroot -xwd dump_file
```

To decorate with tiles of a GIF file, you'd use a line similar to:

```
% xcsetroot -gif bear.gif
```

Whenever you run *xcsetroot*, the program returns a message giving copyright information and statistics about the graphic you've specified. For instance, when I ran the preceding command, *xcsetroot* echoed:

```
XCsetroot, written by Thomas Wu and Davor Matic (c) 1990, MIT Fishbowl
bear.gif is 640x480, 8 bits per pixel, non-interlaced, 256 colors.
```

Since there are quite a few interesting GIF files floating around, *xcsetroot* can be a lot of fun. I was happy to be able to display one of my favorite GIFs: an ad for a 1974 Volkswagon convertible, complete with three photos of the bug, posted to the Internet. For the surrounding text, the enterprising owner used a background color close to the color of the car.

Many GIF files will tax the average server's color mapping and swapping capabilities. If *xcsetroot* cannot allocate sufficient colors to render an image, it may compensate by using some colors multiple times. The average eye should not notice these variations. (If you are bionic, you'll have to live with it.)

—*VQ*

6.04 A Wider Selection of Root Window Graphics

Both *xloadimage (24.85)* and *xv (24.96)* allow you to display images of several different types on your root window. Use *xloadimage* with the *-onroot* option and *xv* with the *-root* option.

The advantage of using *xloadimage* or *xv* over *xsetroot (24.86)* or *xcsetroot (24.86)* is that these programs can handle additional graphic file formats. Both *xloadimage* and *xv* allow you to display: X bitmaps; portable bitmaps, pixmaps, and graymaps; Sun rasterfiles; and GIFs. (See Article 22.01 for more information about graphic file formats.)

xloadimage additionally can handle: X window dumps, X pixmaps, Sun icon files, Fuzzy bitmap images, CMU WM raster files, FaceSavers, MacPaint files, and Group 3 FAX images. *xv* adds: JPEG format, TIFF files, and the OPEN

Preface

It All Started ...

Once upon a time, there was a book called *UNIX Power Tools*, which was chock full of tips and tricks about using UNIX. The book was written in article format by multiple authors, whose different ideas and viewpoints made the whole a little richer. But the most innovative part of *UNIX Power Tools* was that it was written as "hypertext-in-print": using cross references throughout the book, could open it up anywhere and read something interesting, and if readers didn't understand some underlying concept, the cross reference was right there, pointing them to the appropriate article. The book was accompanied by a CD-ROM containing publicly available software for the most popular UNIX platforms.

UNIX Power Tools was both fun to write and immensely successful. So in the spirit of Hollywood, we decided to expand the formula to other topics, and one of the first topics that came to mind was the X Window System.

Thus *X User Tools*: tips, tricks and software for X.

Why "User Tools"?

Some people will have you believe that to get anything out of using X, you have to understand all its complications from the internals up. We don't buy this. In fact, we have co-workers who use X effectively every day, for a variety of purposes, without understanding it at all. To get going, all those users needed was to have someone show them a tip, such as what to put in their startup script or in their resource file. This book collects those tips in one place, so you can get X to work for you without having to become an expert first.

Of course, it always helps to know the gritty details of how things work. Not everyone needs handholding. So we've also included plenty of tips for users who are comfortable with the more subtle and intricate aspects of using X.

Don't Forget the Software!

If we think of users, then we have to think of software. Let's face it, a computer is only as useful as the software that runs on it. For X, there's a plethora of software available, all (or most) of it free and yours for the taking. But first you need to find it, build it for your platform, and figure out how to use it. So we got all the best software packages for X, wrote articles about them, built them for the most popular UNIX platforms, and put them on the accompanying CD. We might have missed a few programs; if so, just drop us a line, and we'll put it on the list for our second edition.

program
name

An article about a program or file that's on the CD will have an icon next to it with the program name (see left). To get one of these programs, just insert the CD into your CD-ROM drive and then use our *install* script *(31.08)*. That cross reference means that the *install* script is described in Article 8 in Chapter 31.

Using Cross References

As we mentioned, there are cross references sprinkled throughout this book. It might take a little getting used to, but once you get the hang of it, you'll see that cross-referenced text appears in a gray font, and the article number it refers to is shown within parentheses, in bold text. If a cross reference is to a single word, for example, a client name like this: *xclock (3.02)*, the cross reference is probably to an article that introduces that client. Cross references to phrases, like this: use a GIF file as your root background *(6.04)* are to an article that explains more about the concept or problem highlighted with the same gray font.

Glossary entries use a different type of cross reference; they do not have a number reference and appear simply in the darker font.

Cross references don't necessarily give a complete list of all articles about a topic. We've tried to pick one or a few articles that give the best information. For a more complete list, use the Index.

How This Book Is Organized

While most books are organized from A to Z, we begin with the ABCs and then switch to an alphabet soup. Specifically, Part 1 tells you some basics about X Window System architecture and how to get started. Then we plunge right into the applications we think you'll find useful. We give you tips on how to configure things later on, but first we want to make sure you know what you want to configure! Our goal has been to present information in the order we think you'll find most interesting. We hope we've succeeded.

Here's a run-down of the contents:

Part 1

The Basics. This part of the book helps the new user get his or her feet wet.

Part 2

The X Desktop. This section outlines programs for organizing your daily workday.

Part 3

Working with Applications. We include X applications such as mailers, editors, games, and more than you ever wanted to know about *xterm*.

Part 4

Window Managers. This part of the book documents the most popular window managers: how to use them, and how to configure them. We cover the usual suspects (*twm*, *mwm*, and *olwm*), but also go into great detail with the latest darling of the window manager family, *fvwm*.

Part 5

The User Environment. This section demonstrates how to write simple startup scripts, configure resources easily, and deal with remote clients. The more advanced chapters towards the end of this section discuss more complicated topics concerning resources and startup environments.

Part 6

Graphics. We cover programs that work with the X graphics formats, including conversion and drawing programs.

Part 7

System Administration. This last section presents applications for administrators, as well as some friendly configuration tips for the X display manager. We also describe how to write your own tools and tell you how to install programs from the accompanying CD.

Font and Character Conventions

Italic

is used for new concepts when they are defined; command names and command-line options; client, directory, filenames and hostnames and annotations in some code examples.

`Courier`
> indicates directives, functions, resources, and shell variables, as well as sample code fragments and examples. A reference to a code example or code fragment within text is also shown in Courier.

`Courier Bold`
> denotes text that should be typed verbatim.

`Courier Italic`
> indicates variables within code examples and fragments for which a context-specific substitution should be made. (The variable `filename`, for example, would be replaced by an actual filename.)

Helvetica
> denotes buttons, keys, key sequences, and menu items.

name(n)
> refers to a manual page in Section *n* of the UNIX programmer's manual. For example, *getopt(3)* refers to a page called *getopt* in Section 3.

`%`   is the C shell prompt.

`$`   is the Bourne shell prompt.

. . .
> stands for text (usually computer output) that's been omitted for clarity or to save space.

CTRL
> starts a control character. To create CTRL-D, for example, hold down the "control" key and press the "D" key. Control characters are not case sensitive; "D" refers to both the uppercase and lowercase letter.

The Authors

Each article in the book is signed by initials, indicating who wrote it. Most of the articles were written by one of the two main authors, Linda Mui and Valerie Quercia, but other authors contributed their expertise. All are listed below with their corresponding initials:

AN	Adrian Nye
AO	Andy Oram
DJF	David Flanagan
EAP	Eric Pearce
IFD	Ian Darwin
JP	Jerry Peek

LM	Linda Mui
MEO	Miles O'Neal
NW	Norm Walsh
TOR	Tim O'Reilly
VQ	Valerie Quercia

If we could do one thing differently in this book, we would have used more "voices" from around the X community. As it is, we're saving that for a second edition. So send us email if you have ideas for new articles: we want to hear from you! Which brings us to...

We'd Like to Hear From You

We have tested and verified all of the information in this book to the best of our ability, but you may find that features have changed (or even that we have made mistakes!). Please let us know about any errors you find, as well as your suggestions for future editions, by writing:

> O'Reilly & Associates, Inc.
> 103 Morris Street, Suite A
> Sebastopol, CA 95472
> 1-800-998-9938 (in the US or Canada)
> 1-707-829-0515 (international/local)
> 1-707-829-0104 (FAX)

You can also send us messages electronically. To be put on the mailing list or request a catalog, send email to:

> *info@ora.com*   (via the Internet)
> *uunet!ora!info*   (via UUCP)

To ask technical questions or comment on the book, send email to:

> *bookquestions@ora.com* (via the Internet)

Acknowledgments

First of all, we have to thank all the authors who allowed us to use their material. We're especially grateful to David Flanagan, who gave us many of the *xterm* and *twm* tips he has collected over the years (some of which were published in the *Sun Observer* magazine, albeit in a different form). Thanks also to Ian Darwin, who let us use material he had written on OPEN LOOK; without Ian, we were up a creek on *olwm*.

Next, we have special thanks to the in-house authors who volunteered to write articles on topics that they were experts on (or at least, knew more than we did!). Thanks to Andy Oram for his article on *emacs*, to Jerry Peek for writing on *xmh* and *exmh*, and to Norm Walsh for his material on Tcl/Tk.

Many thanks to Tim O'Reilly, who originally conceived the idea and framework for this kind of book. Tim also served as editor, providing context, organization, and, best of all, some thoughtful articles with his unique point of view.

Miles O'Neal acted as a reviewer and also gave us many useful suggestions. One of Miles' crusades is having well-crafted resource files for many of his favorite programs. Miles submitted those to us for the CD-ROM and wrote about them for the book: Miles, we thank you, and we think our readers will thank you, too!

The book was reviewed by several persons, who did admirable jobs considering how little time we gave them. In addition to Miles, thanks to Ollie Jones, Dinah McNutt, Eric Pearce, Dave Curry, and Werner Klauser for their reviews.

Thanks also to all of the authors of the software packages we wrote about and included on the CD-ROM. Without their efforts, we wouldn't have had anything to write about; without their generosity in making their software free in the first place, we wouldn't be able to distribute hundreds of megabytes of software for the price of a book.

Ready-to-Run Software packaged up all the software for the disk, porting it to the major UNIX platforms and making it easy to install. Thanks to Jeff Moscow and the rest of the Ready-to-Run staff.

Edie Freedman created the original design for our Tools series, and Jennifer Neiderst tweaked the design for the needs and peculiarities of this book. Lenny Muellner wrote the macros and tools for printing the book in *troff*. But first the book was converted into (gasp) SGML by Lenny and Norm Walsh, to ensure that the book will survive the online revolution.

Mary Anne Weeks Mayo was the copyeditor/project manager who made sure that everything came together. If you think that's hard enough with one author making little tweaks all the time over the phone, imagine what it's like with two authors just down the hall! Thanks also to Nicole Gipson, Ellen Siever, and Kismet McDonough for their efforts in the final production stages.

Chris Tong wrote the index. Although most of the illustrations are screen dumps generated by the authors, Chris Reilley was responsible for cleaning them up and giving them the O'Reilly Seal of Approval.

Extra special thanks to Frank Willison, who valiantly read our drafts and gave us the support we needed to make this into a book.

Part One

The Basics

This book is for the impatient reader. We know most people don't want to know how a television works; they just want to turn it on.

For that reason, we've tried to keep this section of the book short and sweet. For users who are absolutely new to X, the two chapters in this section try to teach the bare minimum you need to know about X to get working.

—LM

1

Welcome to X

1.01 Introduction

Many users of the X Window System are programmers or seasoned UNIX professionals who are comfortable with having to figure something out before they can use it. But an increasing number of people using X today are end users who just need to get a job done. This book is for the X end user.

So who are these end users? Well, let me look around my office. We have some managers who spend a lot of time in email and composing memos. We have a production department that prepares books for publishing using both UNIX-based markup languages and X-based WYSIWYG software. We have our sales department using a database application to get customer information. We have system administrators who need to monitor the performance of multiple machines.

Not all of these people understand X, and few of them should have to. And for the most part, our administrators have done a great job of making the system "transparent" to the end users. But none of these users are using X to its full potential, and that's what this book is about: how to get the most out of X without first getting a master's degree.

I doubt that X can ever make your UNIX system look like a Macintosh. But this book will show you that it doesn't have to be a no-frills system with function and no form.

This book is organized as a series of articles, loosely grouped together by subject. The idea is that you can browse through for articles that interest you and ignore the ones that don't. If an article mentions a concept you may not be familiar with, we include a (hopefully unintrusive) pointer to the article that explains it. The result is that you only have to read what's appropriate for your level. People just interested in getting something to work for them can ignore references to more complicated topics, and people who need to know what's "under the hood" can follow the pointers to their heart's content.

Both the beauty and the bane of X is that it is designed as just a tool, leaving many of its bells and whistles as add-ons. This makes it a monster to use if you don't know how to configure it, but a joy if you want to tinker with it to your liking.

Since X leaves so many gaps in its implementation, there's also a plethora of X software out there that's publicly available, available to anyone who can find the source code, build it for their platform, and figure out how to use the program. One of the intentions of this book is to make that software instantly available to anyone on one of our supported platforms with a CD-ROM drive.

I like to compare X to a restaurant that serves everything a la carte. If you can't identify anything on the menu, then it's possible that you'll have a bland, unsatisfying meal. But given a little instruction in how to order, you can choose one from column A and one from column B, and end up with a seven-course culinary delight. This book is like a menu that explains how to order X. And it'll also tell you the ingredients, but only if you really want to know.

As you'd expect from a first chapter, this introduction explains a lot of the groundwork for the rest of the book. Read this chapter if you prefer to learn things in a sequential manner; but the rest of you might want to jump ahead and start browsing through the rest of the book.

This chapter tells you the basics of how X works. This discussion goes fairly quickly; we just want to define a few terms and provide a conceptual background for the rest of the book.

Although you can read this book straight through, we think you'll get the most out of it by just turning to random pages and discovering something that you find interesting or that might make your life easier.

—LM

1.02 Servers and Clients

The most important two words you need to understand if you're working with X are *client* and *server*. In layman's terms, the X application programs are generally called clients, and the software that manages your keyboard and monitor is called the server.

X is a little easier to understand if we go into a little bit of background. The problem is that there are dozens of workstation manufacturers, each of which has designed its own hardware. Each of these workstations needed graphic programs to be specially written for them, because the commands for drawing on one workstation's display wouldn't work on another. This meant that even though all these workstations had similar operating systems, programmers still needed to work on porting the graphics requests if they wanted their applications to run on a different platform.

X simplifies this by separating the graphics requests from the actual hardware. The idea is that each hardware platform has a program written for it that accepts a standardized set of commands and translates that into its own hardware-specific graphics requests. Applications don't try to communicate directly with the display, but with the intermediary program. Since this intermediary program accepts requests from any number of applications, it is called the server and the applications are called clients.

So the server essentially contributes the user's monitor as an output device for X clients and the user's keyboard and mouse (or pointer) as input devices. The word server is sometimes used to refer to the hardware itself, but technically, the X server is only the software that manages the monitor, keyboard and pointer device.

A request made by a client may be to display something on your monitor, or it might be a request for information (such as the dimensions of the monitor, if a certain font is available, etc.). Meanwhile, when the user types on the keyboard or moves the mouse, the server intercepts these actions as *events* to inform clients about.

The language the client and server communicate in is the *X Protocol*. The X Protocol can run on a local machine, or over the TCP/IP or DECnet network protocols. The important point here is that clients and servers can communicate over a network. This means that a machine might only run a server and not be able to run any client applications at all, and the user sitting at the desk would never know the difference. Even though most client applications are written using the UNIX operating system, an X server can be written for your machine and you can run X programs as long as you have a graphic display.

So people use X not only on UNIX workstations, but also on Macintoshes, PCs, and (most importantly) on *X terminals*, which are designed specifically for running X servers. We have a few workstations at our office, but most users have X terminals and run their X clients from a Sun multiprocessor over TCP/IP. This way we give a graphical interface to each of our users without having to buy a workstation for each of them.

Client/server technology as used by X may seem backwards to some people. We are used to servers being remote, massive machines, such as file servers, news servers, mail servers, etc. For X, however, the server is the local machine that receives requests from client programs running anywhere on the network.

—LM

1.03 Starting an X Session

A working X environment requires a server running at your desk and at least one client program displaying to your server. This poses a few logistical problems when starting an X session.

An X server without clients displays a blank *root window* screen. There is no window manager running. There are no *xterm* *(2.02)* windows available for starting new clients. There's often no way to quit the X server. Similarly, an X client cannot start up without a server to connect to. That would be like starting a phone conversation before the other end picks up.

So starting an X session involves two steps: starting the X server itself locally and then starting at least one client either locally or remotely.

There is no generic way to start an X session, however. X servers can run on workstations, X terminals, or PCs. A machine may be dedicated to the X server, or it may need to have the server explicitly started. X clients might run locally, or they may need to be executed from a remote system. The user may or may not have already supplied a password and logged in.

So the most appropriate method for starting your X session is usually dependent on what sort of server you use. If you have an X terminal, your administrator should have set you up to use the X Display Manager (*xdm*) *(28.02)*. Under *xdm*, your X server is already running, and you should see either a login box to provide a user name and password, or a chooser box to choose a machine to log in to. When you log in, some initial clients are executed to help you get started.

Some workstation users might be set up to use *xdm*, but many workstation users might also use the *xinit* or *startx* command, or even a vendor-specific command (such as *openwin* for Sun OpenWindows). Under these methods, your workstation is not running an X server, but just a large console window *(27.02)*. You need to log in as you would on a terminal emulator, and then type in the command that starts both the X server and some initial clients.

If you have a PC- or Macintosh-based X server, you may use yet another startup method built into your server software.

Most startup methods also give some facility for setting up your environment and starting a set of clients automatically. They may have a default environment for accounts with generic or unpersonalized configurations, but they also permit you to customize your startup environment. See Article 2.09 for a very simple example of a customized startup script, or Chapters 17 and 21 for more details about writing startup scripts.

—*LM*

1.04 GUIs and X

One confusing feature of X is that it can be "dressed" in different ways. In other window systems (such as the Macintosh operating system, or Microsoft Windows), the graphical user interface, or GUI, is built into the system. On a Macintosh, for example, all windows have a certain familiar decoration, and can all be moved and closed in the same way. Applications may do different things, but there are a few features you can depend on, e.g., Command-Q to quit an application or double clicking on filenames to open them.

X, on the other hand, is more of a concept than an integrated window system. I like to think of it as a car assembly that might be used in several different models. The engine that Toyota turns into a Corolla might become a Geo Prism for Chevrolet. Each cars may have a different "look and feel," and they might be sold by different companies, but they're the same engine under-neath, and parts for one car might easily be used in the other. This might be a way to consider the relationship of the GUI to X: X is the engine under the hood of several GUIs, including Motif and OPEN LOOK.

The result is that five different people might be running X, but their windows and applications may look completely different.

A large component of any GUI is how windows are moved and resized. In X, this is accomplished via a special client program called a *window manager*. By making the window manager a client, each vendor can provide its own window manager on top of X.

In most cases, users run the window manager sold by their vendor, which is integrated into a complete seamless environment with other applications that work under the same GUI. This is sort of like buying a Geo Prism and getting all your parts and service from the dealer. However, it is possible to mix and match window managers with applications from different GUIs—sort of like getting a replacement hubcap from a junkyard. The hubcap may fit your tire rim, but may not resemble the hubcaps on the other three wheels.

There are many different window managers for X, and which one you use depends partly on preference and partly on availability. The window manager that comes with most every version of X is *twm*; there are several other win-dow managers available, both commercial and free. Other than *twm*, the most popular window managers are *mwm* and *olwm*. Many users are also migrat-ing towards an environment called HP Vue, which is an integrated window manager and session manager.

For many users, what window manager they use is preconfigured for them by a vendor or by their system administrator, and is therefore something they never think about. As far as they are concerned, their particular environment *is* X. This is just fine, since there are few instances when it really matters which one you use.

—LM

1.05 Libraries, Toolkits, Widgets, and GUIs

It's very uncommon to write an X application from scratch. Instead, programmers are likely to use *toolkits*. You may see mention of a certain application being OPEN LOOK-based, Athena-based, or Motif-based; these terms refer to the toolkit used to write the application.

The X Protocol *(1.02)* is the language used to communicate between client and server. In general, however, only programmers writing servers need to use the X Protocol directly. For writing clients, programmers use *libraries*, which are archives of commonly used functions.

Xlib is the lowest-level library for writing client applications for X. It is basically an interface to the X Protocol, with a one-to-one correspondence between X protocol requests and library functions. Writing a program in Xlib is time consuming and laborious, however (kind of like rolling your own phyllo dough to make baklava). Instead, programmers use toolkits that are written on top of Xlib. Toolkits are a set of programming libraries and *widgets* for programming in X. A widget is best described as a graphical component, such as a menu, command button, dialog box, or scrollbar. Programmers use toolkits not only because it's easier than writing from scratch, but also so their applications have a uniform look and feel with other applications.

Popular toolkits for X11 are the Athena toolkit, which was developed by the X Consortium; OSF/Motif, developed by the Open Software Foundation; OLIT, developed by AT&T; and XView, developed by Sun. Both OLIT and XView are implementations of the OPEN LOOK GUI specification.

Although it defines a certain look and feel, a toolkit does not an environment make. The idea is for vendors who license the toolkit to design their own environments on top of it. Examples of such environments are Sun OpenWindows (based on XView) and products such as SCO Open Desktop and HP Vue (both based on OSF/Motif).

Many of the popular window managers are associated with a toolkit, and have a design that's consistent with that toolkit. The window manager distributed with X11 is *twm*, written with the Athena toolkit. The "sample" window manager for OSF/Motif is *mwm*. *olwm* is the OPEN LOOK window manager. Occasionally, applications are written that assume one window manager or another. For example, many OpenWindows-based applications give you no way to close windows because they assume you'll be running the OPEN LOOK window manager *olwm*. (*olwm* includes a facility to close windows nicely.) Another possible problem may be dialog boxes that don't work properly with an incompatible window manager. Usually, however, these applications are still usable under your window manager of choice; they just look a little out of place since you may be mixing multiple designs.

The competition among the various graphical user interfaces, known as the "GUI wars," may come to an end with the emergence of a standard interface called the Common Desktop Environment (CDE). The CDE is one component of the proposed Common Open Software Environment, or COSE (pronounced "cozy"), currently being developed by a consortium of UNIX industry leaders, including Sun, Hewlett-Packard, DEC, IBM, USL, SCO, and Univel. COSE is intended to define common specifications and technologies to help UNIX compete in an increasingly PC-dominated market.

Expected to be released in 1994, the Common Desktop Environment will provide a window manager and several desktop tools, such as a file manager, mail utility, etc. The CDE will also allow for several virtual desktops on which you can spread out your windows (and your work). The CDE, as proposed, will blend user environment components and styles from several participating vendors, including OSF/Motif's window manager, HP Vue and the HP Encapsulator, Sun's DeskSet and ToolTalk, USL's System V Release 4.2 Desktop, and IBM's CUA and Workplace Shell.

Once the CDE is finalized, vendors should begin releasing CDE-based commercial desktop products. Presuming the standard is created and vendors comply, the CDE will provide all X users with a single look and feel, presuming they want one, regardless of the platform. Of course, users who are happy with their current hybrid environments may continue to pick and choose among window managers and desktop utilities.

—*LM, VQ*

1.06 *What Are Resources?*

X applications use variables called *resources* for defining the default behavior of a client. Resources came about because the design of X makes configuring an application a little harder than on other window systems. X applications generally run on multiuser systems, so you can't just configure all applications on the system level. Different users might want different defaults. System administrators should define some defaults at the system level, but individual users also need to be able to set their own preferences.

X is also set up so that a user might run an application on multiple types of displays. That same user might want different defaults depending on whether he or she has color support or how big their monitor is. So X has to provide a way to specify defaults depending on the display being used. Furthermore, on today's networks it's likely that you'll have several diskless machines running the same binaries and configuration files. You might want different defaults for each machine.

Resources are a way of managing defaults at each of these levels. Resources can be set at the user level, system level, server level, and client level. The advantage is that you can configure applications any number of ways.

For details on using resources, see Chapters 17 and 20.

—*LM*

2

Starting Clients
on a UNIX System

2.01 No One Told Me This Book Was About UNIX!

Surprise!

X is operating system-independent. But to start up X programs on any given operating system, you have to deal with the peculiarities of that OS. Most X users work on some flavor of the UNIX operating system, and all programs on a UNIX system have to start within a UNIX shell.

Now, you might set up your environment so that you can run all your favorite programs automatically and never have to sully your hands with the UNIX command line. But even if you do that, a shell is eventually called for each client that you start. The upshot is this: if you work on UNIX, then you really can't ignore the shell. The good news is that despite everything you heard, UNIX doesn't have to be very difficult: there are just a few issues you need to be aware of.

In this chapter, we discuss how to start and stop clients in UNIX, and we talk about the influence of the UNIX shell on X programs. We also introduce you to the idea of a startup script (although we don't talk about startup scripts in detail until Chapter 16). In later chapters, we'll talk about other ways to start clients, such as configuring your window manager's root menu *(12.22, 13.19, 14.27, and 15.23)*, and application launchers like *bricons (21.17)*.

—LM

2.02 Starting Clients with the xterm Client

X is a graphical environment, but the most commonly used type of client is still a *terminal emulator*. A terminal emulator is a program that runs a UNIX shell, giving you command-line access to a UNIX system. There are many terminal emulators available both from vendors and as freeware, but the most common is *xterm*, if only because it's the one included in the X Consortium's X distribution. Because *xterm* is the closest thing to a "standard" terminal emulator across all flavors of X, X users (and writers!) often say "xterm" when referring to any X-based terminal emulator.

Most X users have at least one terminal emulator like *xterm* open at all times. Often, users will have several. Die-hard UNIX users still do most of their work within *xterm* windows, and for them, the primary advantage of X is to have several such windows open at once. Other users might do most of their work in other X applications, but they're also likely to have at least one *xterm* window running, for starting new applications if for nothing else.

When an *xterm* window first opens, you should see a *shell prompt*. The shell prompt may be configured any number of ways, but it usually includes your user name and the name of the host you're working on. The prompt often ends with a percent sign (%) or dollar sign ($). For example, my prompt on a machine called *ruby* looks like:

```
lmui@ruby %
```

At this prompt, you can type any UNIX command installed on your host. To start a new X client, you can usually just type the client name at the prompt with an ampersand (&) appended, and press **Return**. For example, to run a client called *xclock* (3.02), I type in the text shown in bold type:

```
lmui@ruby % xclock &
[1] 8653
lmui@ruby %
```

If the command is successful, the shell returns a message you can ignore (containing the *job control* ID and process ID). The *xclock* client appears on your display. Your prompt then reappears, ready for another command (unless you forget the ampersand—see Article 2.03).

Figure 2-1 shows what this might actually look like within an *xterm* window.

This is far from the last you'll hear about the *xterm* client. We use it for examples sprinkled throughout the book, and we even devoted the entirety of Chapter 11 to tips and tricks about using *xterm*.

—*LM*

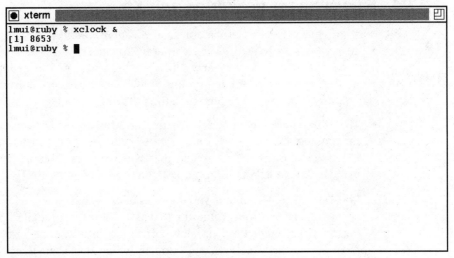

Figure 2-1: Running a command in an xterm window

2.03 Putting Commands in the Background

If you run an X client from the command line, you generally have to put an ampersand (&) at the end of the command line. This runs the command in the background, and returns your shell prompt so that you can run another command simultaneously. If you don't use the ampersand, then you can't use that terminal shell again until the X client quits.

Occasionally, I forget to type the ampersand. If you neglected to put the command in the background in a shell that supports job control, type **CTRL-Z** to suspend the command and then use the *bg* command to place it in the background.

```
% xterm
        (xterm window appears normally)
^Z
Stopped
% bg
[1]     xterm &
```

If the system you're on does not support job control, interrupt the process using the appropriate key sequence (**CTRL-C** on many systems) and start over. You can also kill the window *(2.08)*, but always try to kill programs as "nicely" as you can.

— *VQ*

2.04 Environment Variables and X

UNIX programs use special variables called *environment variables*, and X programs on UNIX systems are no exception. You need to know about environment variables because they may affect the behavior of your clients, and may even affect whether your client works at all! The most important environment variables for running X programs are the following:

- The PATH environment variable is the most important environment variable for running any programs on a UNIX system (not just X programs). If PATH is not set correctly, it's possible that you won't be able to run any commands. Article 2.05 talks about PATH in more detail.

- The DISPLAY environment variable identifies which X server to display the client on, and a wrong value for DISPLAY will result in a client not appearing on your server (and possibly appearing on someone else's!) Luckily, most people have DISPLAY set correctly when they start their X session— see Article 19.08 if you have problems.

Other environment variables also affect X programs. Most clients use a set of environment variables for determining what resources *(1.06)* to read (Chapter 20 talks about each of these in detail). In addition, many clients set up their own environment variables, or use already established UNIX environment variables, such as MANPATH *(5.02)* (where your manpages are), PRINTER (what printer you want to use), HOME (your home directory), and USER (your user name).

Many of the environment variables used by a program are listed on the manpage. But many are not, because the program doesn't call them directly. An example is the TZ environment variable, which is used by the *ctime(3)* routines to find out what time zone you're in. The *xclock* manpage doesn't list TZ on the manpage, but *xclock* certainly uses it (see Article 3.12).

In the C shell, you can set an environment variable using the *setenv* command. For example, to set my PRINTER environment variable, I might do:

```
% setenv PRINTER ibis
```

In the Bourne shell, you have to do this in two steps: set the variable and then *export* it:

```
$ PRINTER=ibis
$ export PRINTER
```

Any printing commands from now on will send the request to the printer called *ibis*.

—*LM*

2.05 Your Search Path

When you call a program within a UNIX shell, it looks for a program by that name in its *search path*. A shell's search path is the value of the PATH environment variable *(2.04)*, which is set to a list of colon-separated directories. For example, my search path might be as follows:

```
/bin:/usr/bin:/usr/bin/X11:/usr/ucb:/etc:/usr/lib:/usr/local/bin:
/usr/local/frame/bin:/home/lmui/bin:.
```

When I run a program like *xterm*, the shell looks for an executable program called *xterm* in each of those directories, in order. When it finds a program by that name, it executes it. If there are two programs called *xterm* in different directories in your search path, the one in the directory that is listed first is the one that is executed.

So if you try running an X program and get the following error message:

```
% xterm &
xterm: Command not found.
```

Then either the program does not exist, or something is wrong with your search path. What you need to do is find out what directory *xterm* lives in and then make sure that directory is in your search path.

On our system (as on many systems), *xterm* is installed in */usr/bin/X11*. So I need to add */usr/bin/X11* to my path. Under the Bourne or Korn shell:

```
$ PATH=$PATH:/usr/bin/X11
$ export PATH
```

Under the C shell, the path shell variable is propagated to the PATH environment variable, but not vice-versa. So you generally change the path shell variable using the *set* command:

```
% set path=($path /usr/bin/X11)
```

Now the *xterm* command can run in this shell. To set up */usr/bin/X11* in your search path permanently, put the command in your shell startup file, i.e., *.profile* or *.cshrc*.

—*LM*

2.06 Environment Variables for OpenWindows

If you work on Sun OpenWindows, you need to set a few environment variables before you can work properly. OpenWindows users generally have to set the following three environment variables:

```
% setenv OPENWINHOME /usr/openwin
% set path = ($path $OPENWINHOME/{bin,demo} )
% setenv LD_LIBRARY_PATH $OPENWINHOME/lib:/usr/lib
```

The OPENWINHOME environment variable should be set to whatever directory your OpenWindows distribution is installed into. Usually it's installed in */usr/openwin*, but some sites might choose to install it in */usr/local/openwin* or somewhere else non-standard.

The user's search path then needs to be changed to include directories containing OpenWindows executables. These executables are generally installed into */usr/openwin/bin* and */usr/openwin/demo*.

Finally, the LD_LIBRARY_PATH environment variable needs to be set. This variable defines where OpenWindows programs need to look for shared libraries. Many OpenWindows programs will not work if they can't find their shared libraries.

—*LM*

2.07 *Inheritance of Environment Variables*

An important feature of environment variables *(2.04)* is that programs inherit them from their parents, but not the other way around. In other words, environment variables for any given program are read from the UNIX shell that started it. If you set a new environment variable in an *xterm* window and then start a new *xterm* from that shell:

```
% setenv PRINTER ibis
% xterm &
```

The new *xterm* window will inherit the new value of PRINTER from its parent shell. This matters quite a lot, especially when it comes to the value of PATH. Since many programs need to start new programs themselves, it's important that they inherit an appropriate PATH. For example, the mailer client *xmh (7.06)* is just a front-end to the MH mail handler programs, and will fail miserably if the MH executables aren't found in its search path. Window managers *(1.04)* are often configured to start new programs *(12.22, 13.19, 14.27, and 15.23)* but they won't work if they aren't started with the right directories in their search paths.

However, there's no way to pass an environment variable back to its parent shell. So if you reset the PRINTER environment variable to another value in the new *xterm* shown above, it won't affect the value in the parent *xterm*.

—*LM*

2.08 *Removing a Window*

Once you have a client running, how do you get rid of it?

Depending on the client, there may be several ways to close a window. As a rule, you should try to use the "gentlest" method available. Some exit methods give the client a chance to perform clean-up duties (such as saving your work!) before quitting. So if you want to get rid of a window, try things in (roughly) the following order:

1. Some clients provide the means to exit cleanly, and you should try these methods first. In many cases, a **Quit**, **Close**, or **Exit** button will scream out at you. If the client has pull-down menus, look there as well; often a **Quit** item appears on a **File** menu. If a client's escape hatch isn't obvious, check the manpage. (For example, *xcalc* quits when you type q or **CTRL-C**, but you'll only find that out if you look at the manpage.)

2. Sometimes a client doesn't provide an obvious way to quit, or won't respond to its own quit command. *oclock* .XET N .XE1 "oclock command" ./XET and *xclock* .XET N .XE1 "xclock command" ./XET *(3.02)* are renegades, providing no exit method. When quitting isn't an option, the next thing to try is to give the client a gentle shove, usually using the window manager.

   • If you use *twm*, select the Delete item on the Twm menu *(12.31)*. (You can also configure *twm* to have its own Close button *(12.18)*.)

   • If you use *olwm*, use the **Close** item on the Window menu *(14.08)*.

   • The *fvwm* Window Ops menu *(15.12)* also has a **Delete** item.

   • If you're using *mwm*, closing a window is fairly easy for you, but may or may not be easy on the client process. There are two fairly reliable exit methods: the **Close** item on the Window Menu *(13.07)* and a double-click on the **Window** command button. Both of these methods invoke *mwm*'s f.kill function.

     Whether this function allows the client to exit cleanly, however, depends on how the client is programmed to respond to some precautionary routines that are built into f.kill. Figuratively speaking, the f.kill sheriff asks a client if it wants to go peaceable-like, and if the client understands and says "Yep," it'll go quietly and no harm done. But if the client doesn't understand or isn't talking, things could get ugly.

     How do you know which case you're up against? Basically, you don't. Unless you happen to have written the client's code yourself—in which case I suggest you add an exit function—my advice is to shoot first and ask questions later. Aren't you glad you asked?

3. If these (marginally) friendly means don't work, it's time to call in the real muscle. There are a few ways to kill a client window. When you kill a client, the process exits and the associated window is removed. Here are the deadly methods:

- If you're using *twm,* use the Kill item on the Twm menu *(12.31).*

- *fvwm* provides a **Destroy** function on the **WindowOps** menu *(15.12)*; the standard GoodStuff module *(15.10)* also has a **Kill** button.

- You can also remove a stubborn window using the *xkill* client. On the command line of an *xterm* window, type:

  ```
  % xkill
  ```

  The pointer changes to a draped-box symbol, and you are instructed to "Select the window whose client you wish to kill with button 1." Click on the window you want to kill with the first mouse button. Be very careful or you could zap the wrong window!

- The UNIX *kill* command. First, find the process id (PID) for the client. For example, to determine the PID number for *xclock,* go to an *xterm* window and type:

  ```
  % ps -aux | grep xclock | grep -v grep
  ```

  at a system prompt. Under System V, type:

  ```
  % ps -e | grep xclock | grep -v grep
  ```

  at a system prompt. The resulting display should look something like this:

  ```
  128  p0  0:00  xclock
  ```

  The number in the first column is the process ID. Then type:

  ```
  % kill 128
  ```

  The *xclock* display will be removed, and you will get the message:

  ```
  Terminated  xclock
  ```

- For removing *xterm* windows only: the **Send KILL Signal** item on the client's **Main Options** menu. Article 11.14 describes the *xterm* menus.

— VQ

2.09 *A Glimpse at Startup Scripts*

When you first start your X session, what you see depends on what level of user configuration is supported at your site. You might see an elaborate array of windows and utilities. You might see a single terminal emulator window without even a window manager to adorn it. To be honest, you might see nothing: your X session might be totally hosed due to a faulty *startup script.*

A startup script is basically a *batch file,* or a series of commands lumped together to save having to type the same sequence of commands every day. It is usually a UNIX shell script that is run when you first log on under X.

Without a startup script, you'll still have a workable X environment that you can start your favorite clients from, but why do something manually when you can get the computer to do the work for you?

In order to use a startup script to its full potential, you need to know a bit more about X than you might at this point. But we want to give you a taste of startup scripts now so that you know that the facility exists. Chapter 16 describes a few more basics about startup scripts, and Chapter 21 talks about startup scripts in even more detail.

For now, let's just walk through a simple example. Every time I log in I like to load some resources *(17.03)*, start up a window manager, open a few *xterm* *(11.01)*, windows; and start a mail application *(7.02)*, a clock *(3.02)*, and a calculator *(5.05)*. For this, I created the following start-up script:

```
#!/bin/sh

xrdb -merge $HOME/.Xresources

xterm -geometry -1-1 &
xterm -geometry -1+1 &
xclock -geometry +1-1 &
xmail &
xcalc -iconic &


twm
```

This script is run using the Bourne shell, */bin/sh*. The first thing it does is load my resources into the server using the *xrdb* client. I want to make sure this command is run before any other clients because the resources need to finish in order for those clients, in turn, to start up.

When *xrdb* is finished loading, I start up a few of my favorite clients. The only thing important to remember is to start these clients in the background so they can run concurrently. I also specify certain positions using the *–geometry* command-line option *(17.10)* so the windows don't overlap each other more than they have to, and I start one of my windows iconified.

My last client is *twm*, my window manager. I start *twm* in the foreground so that when I log out of the window manager, my entire X session exits. It is very important to have one client in the foreground; otherwise your X session exits immediately after it starts. See Article 16.03 for more information.

The full X session might resemble Figure 2-2.

You can use this simple startup script as a basis for your own X session. Just type in a script modelled after this one.

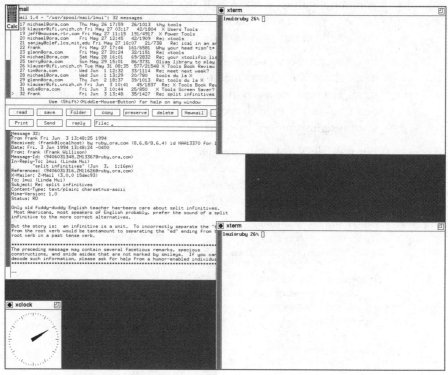

Figure 2-2: A start-up environment

If you use a workstation and use *xinit* to start your X session, you can type in this script as *$HOME/.xinitrc*. If you use *xdm* to start up your X session, you should call it *$HOME/.xsession* and make it executable:

```
% chmod +x $HOME/.xsession
```

If you use remote execution to start your X session (as you might with a PC or Mac X server or from some X terminals), call this script whatever you like and then set up your X server to execute it upon startup (as documented by your X server's vendor).

—LM

2.10 Why Can't I See Files That Start with a Dot (.)?

A UNIX tradition is to name some files with an initial period, or *dot*. These are called *dot files*, and are used primarily for configuring applications or saving data used by an application. For example, your shell startup file may be named *.cshrc* or *.profile*. Other UNIX programs may use dot files, such as *.exrc* for *vi*, *.emacs* for *emacs (9.02)*, etc.

In addition, many X programs use this convention. Your startup script *(2.09)* is usually called either *.xsession* or *.xinitrc*. Window managers can be configured using files such as *.mwmrc (13.09)* and *.twmrc (12.11)*. The *plan (4.05)* program uses a file called *.dayplan*. *xpostit (4.12)* uses a whole directory called *.postit-notes*.

Each of these files is installed into your home directory. But if you list your home directory with the *ls* command, you may not see them:

```
% ls $HOME
Mail  TUTORIAL
```

This is because dot files are not listed by *ls* unless you explicitly ask for them. The idea is that most users don't want to know about configuration files, so they are usually hidden to the *ls* command. However, they are definitely there:

```
% ls $HOME/.cshrc
/home/lmui/.cshrc
```

If you call *ls* with the *−a* option, then you should see them:

```
% /bin/ls -a $HOME
.                       .cshrc~            .xsession
..                      .gopherrc          .xsession-errors
.Xauthority             .login             Mail
.cshrc                  .mailrc            TUTORIAL
```

Note that you also see the files . and ... These are special files used by UNIX, representing the current directory and its parent directory. You should just ignore them (and don't try to remove them!)

—LM

Part Two

The X Desktop

What's a desktop?

Desk accessories are precisely what they sound like. On your desk, you might have a clock, a calculator, a notepad, a Rolodex, a calendar, etc. You might also keep a book or two within reach, such as a dictionary or other reference material. These are things you don't use all the time, but keep handy because you might want them at any time.

Desk accessories follow the same model. They are small programs to keep around for immediate access—to schedule an appointment, to make a quick calculation, etc.—but which are unlikely to be the focus of your work. They help to make your workday a little easier (or just a little more entertaining).

Browse through this section to see which accessories you should include on *your* desktop.

—*LM*

3

Clocks and More Clocks

3.01 A Whole Chapter About Clocks?!?

Yes, this entire chapter is about clock applications. Why? Well, you might as well ask why there are so many clocks.

One reason, of course, is that clock programs are easy to write. *xclock* was one of the first clients supplied with X, and has been built on almost every platform (even under the Mac OS). A lot of the publicly available software available for X consists of programs that were written as an exercise by someone who was learning X programming and used *xlock* as their guide.

But just because there are so many clock programs, does this book need to cover them all? Obviously, no. But we've chosen to cover most of them anyway. There are tons of clocks, and each user chooses just one. But the clock you choose to run gives you a chance to express your personality on an otherwise functional desktop. We considered supplying just one of these clocks, but we realized that it was sort of like a men's store carrying just one style of tie.

So browse through these clocks. Some of them are both useful and attractive, and you'll want to start using them today. Some of them are marginally useful but interesting in concept. Some of them are amusing but totally impractical for daily use. Let's face it, some of these are downright bizarre, but we just had to include them.

—LM

3.02 The Standard Clocks

Before we get into the fun stuff, let's introduce you to the Old Standbys. The standard X distribution comes with two clock applications: *xclock* and *oclock*.

xclock is the most popular clock application, but this is mostly because of availability, not originality. By default, it shows an analog clock in a square window (see Figure 3-1).

Figure 3-1: Standard xclock window

xclock supports a couple of command-line options that are worthy of note. The *–chime* option says to chime every half-hour. You can also use the options *–digital* or *–d* to show a digital clock (see Figure 3-2).

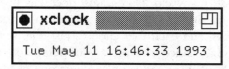

Figure 3-2: Digital xclock window

In general, however, *xclock* is pretty darn boring.

oclock is the X distribution's other clock. It shows a round clock instead of a square clock, using the SHAPE extension (see Figure 3-3).

A cool thing to do with *oclock* is to call it with the *–transparent* option, so that the background of the window shows through the clock (although this may be a performance hit on slower X servers). Article 3.11 shows an example using *–transparent*. Another favorite thing is to elongate the clock by just changing the size of the window (see Figure 3-4).

—LM

fP is t... r clock a
stly be... ability,
, it shows ...log clock in

ps "" "" ...oscale
ard xcl...
fP supp... of commar
orthy o...
ime\fP o... to chime
-hour.

Figure 3-3: Standard oclock window

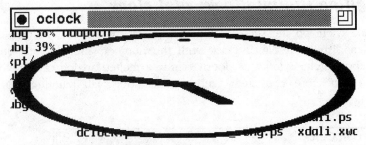

Figure 3-4: Elongated oclock window

3.03 A Digital Alarm Clock

If you want something slightly different, try out the *dclock* program. *dclock* also has the added advantage of a primitive alarm system.

dclock

dclock shows a digital clock that scrolls when changing digits, just like the numbers on some older clock radios. You can use a *–date* option to have a date shown beneath the clock, using special % symbols. The manpage lists the full range of symbols. For example:

```
% dclock -date "Today is %W, %M %d, %Y" &
```

Shows you the window shown in Figure 3-5.

Figure 3-5: The dclock application

dclock also has a built-in alarm. For example:

```
% dclock -alarm -alarmTime 17:30 &
```

This means that at 5:30 P.M., the clock will flash five times and your display will beep, just in time for Happy Hour.

If you like *dclock*, then try out the resources distributed on the CD *(20.23)* for an example of how to customize it to show the date, to set an alarm, etc.

If you need more elaborate reminders, take a look at the calendar programs in Chapter 4.

—LM

3.04 *Melting Digital Clock: xdaliclock*

xdaliclock

While we're on the subject of digital clocks, we should mention *xdaliclock*, which displays a digital clock with the numbers melting into one another. (Unfortunately, *xdaliclock* doesn't show a melted analog clock, which would be much more consistent with the Salvador Dali painting that its name evokes.)

Figure 3-6: xdaliclock

If you have a color server, try the *–cycle* command-line option. The colors used by *xdaliclock* change continuously. You might also try this with the *–shape* command-line option, which uses the SHAPE extension so that the numbers seem to float on top of your other windows (although if you use *twm (12.01)* as your window manager, you should be sure to suppress the titlebar *(12.16)* on the *xdaliclock* window, or your window manager will become very confused).

Although *xdaliclock* is pretty, you might find it slows down your server tremendously. There are command-line options to change the frequency that it updates the clock, but that takes away a lot of its charm. So *xdaliclock* is one of those apps you're likely to show off to people but never actually use.

—LM

3.05 Night and Day

sunclock

sunclock shows the portion of the Earth that has daylight. The line at the bottom of the window shows the current time and date, as well as the time and date for Greenwich Mean Time (aka UTC).

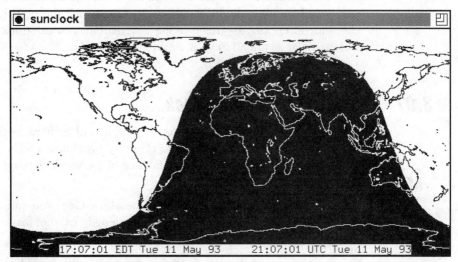

Figure 3-7: The sunclock application

The portion of the Earth that's shown as black on white is currently illuminated by the Sun; the portion in reverse video is in night. If you iconify *sunclock*, you get a tiny version of it as the icon (which may be good enough for most people, and certainly uses up less screen real estate).

According to the manpage, *sunclock* uses an algorithm published in Jean Meeus' *Astronomical Formulae for Calculators*. The caveat (as noted in the manpage) is that "The illuminated area shown is the area which would be sunlit if the Earth had no atmosphere. The actual illuminated area is larger because of atmospheric refraction and twilight." So basically, *sunclock* shows us what parts of the Earth would be lit by the Sun if the Earth were in a vacuum.

—*LM*

3.06 An X Sundial

xMoveIt

xMoveIt is a clever little program for moving a window around your screen like an hour hand. Just call *xMoveIt*:

```
% xMoveIt &
[2] 3936
```

```
%          ====> Please select the window
           ====> you wish to have moved
           ====> change by clicking the
           ====> pointer in that window.
```

and then point at the window you want to use as your hour hand. If you consider the center of your screen to be the center of a clock, then the window is moved to the position on your screen in which the hour hand would appear. With an enormous stretch of the imagination, you can think of *xMoveIt* as a way to have a sundial in your air-conditioned office.

—LM

3.07 *The Coolest Analog Clock*

swisswatch

swisswatch is an analog clock application that advertises itself as the "mother of all X toolkit clocks." It justifies this claim by providing a trillion (approximate) resources, for configuring every nuance of the clock. Among the configurable features are:

- The appearance of the marks around the clock face. You can change the number of marks. You can change the length of the marks. You can change the position of the marks.

- The appearance of the hands. You can change their width, their shape, whether they're filled or outlined, and a multitude of other details.

As you can see, *swisswatch* is well named because it's the X clock application for the very precise. In its default configuration, it looks like Figure 3-8.

Figure 3-8: Default swisswatch window

The app-defaults file *(20.12)* for *swisswatch* also has several built-in package configurations for different types of clocks. You can access these using the *—name* option. For example, try out the *swissclock* look:

```
% swisswatch -name swissclock
```

The resulting clock is shown in Figure 3-9.

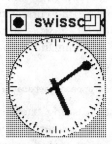

Figure 3-9: swissclock configuration

(A Swiss reviewer assures us (with patriotic zeal) that this is what the clocks in Swiss train stations look like.)

—*LM*

3.08 Time in the Titlebar (xcuckoo)

xcuckoo

One cool thing is to put the current time in your titlebar. You can do this using an application called *xcuckoo* (a somewhat bizarre name, having something to do with laying eggs on another window. *xcuckoo* seems like a misnomer since it doesn't have much to do with a traditional cuckoo clock).

By default, *xcuckoo* tries to put the current time in the titlebar of the *twm* Icon Manager window.

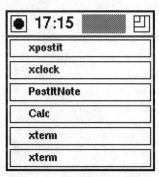

Figure 3-10: xcuckoo on a twm Icon Manager window

This is obviously inappropriate if you don't use the Icon manager, or if you don't use *twm* at all. You can change *xcuckoo* to use the titlebar of another window using the *–window* option:

```
% xcuckoo -window xterm
```

You can also set up *xcuckoo* to use the output of a command (instead of the current time) as text to place in the window's titlebar. And you can use the *−mode* option to tell *xcuckoo* not to actually replace the current titlebar text, but to append or prepend it. The *−separator* string tells it what string to use to separate the titlebar text from the current time or command output. The following command line combines some of these features:

```
% xcuckoo -window xterm -command 'fortune' -mode append -separator ": " &
```

This command gives you a titlebar consisting of the string "xterm: " followed by a fortune. You might use the *−command* option to alter the format of the date used, e.g., I use options to the UNIX *date* (3.17) command to have the date shown in 12-hour format, with seconds shown. Since it doesn't make sense to have seconds without having the time updated more frequently, I also have *xcuckoo* update every five seconds (the default is 60 seconds).

```
% xcuckoo -command "date '+%r'" -update 5 &
```

—LM

3.09 A Clock That Chimes

If you have a Sun4 series workstation, you can try out a version of *oclock* (3.02) that supports sounds. You can set up *oclock*++ to play specified sounds at the quarter-hour, half-hour, and hour.

oclock++

By default, *oclock*++ plays no sounds and behaves just like standard *oclock*. Set the hourSound resource or use the *−hoursound* command-line option to have it use a particular sound every hour:

```
% oclock++ -hoursound BigBen.au
```

Sound files for Sun4 machines usually have an *.au* suffix. *oclock*++ comes with these sounds: *BigBen.au*, *CuckooClock.au*, *GrandfatherClock.au*, *MetalAlarm.au*, and *TowerClock.au*. You can also use any other *.au* sound file you happen to have lying around. (Be warned that hearing the entire James Bond theme every hour may become irritating after a while.)

There are similar resources and command-line options for setting the sound to use on the half-hour, at quarter-past, and at quarter-to. The chimeSound resource and *−chimesound* command-line option can be used to set a sound to use as a chime every hour. This sound is repeated according to the hour, e.g., at 10 A.M., it will chime 10 times.

By default, these sounds are played at 75% volume capacity. If you find that this is too loud (or too soft), you can use the *−volume* command-line option (or the volumeSound resource) to set it to another value:

% oclock++ -chimesound JamesBrown.au -volume 100

—LM

3.10 Clocks in Different Languages

Here's a different kind of clock: *xticktalk* is a clock that displays the time as
written words. Figure 3-11 shows an *xticktalk* clock.

Figure 3-11: xticktalk in English

xticktalk

xticktalk doesn't have a manpage, but it does have several command-line
options you can see by typing `xticktalk -help`. In addition to the usual Xt
options, *xticktalk* has a command-line option to print time after the half-hour
relative to the next hour (e.g., "Ten to four"), another option to turn off printing "am" and "pm", and an option to regulate how often the display updates.

Now the fun part of *xticktalk*. You can use the *–language* option to *xticktalk*
to print the time in different languages. Among the more common supported
languages are English, French, Spanish, Japanese, German, Swedish, Norwegian, Italian, Finnish, Vietnamese, Dutch, and Afrikaans. Some of these languages also have command-line options for using different character sets (e.g.,
–kanji for Japanese and *–latin1* for Swedish and Norwegian). Figure 3-12
shows *xticktalk* in German:

Figure 3-12: xticktalk in German

But *xticktalk* doesn't just end there. It also supports some languages that are
slightly more...obscure. For example, pig Latin:

Figure 3-13: xticktalk in pig Latin

xticktalk can also give you what it calls "baby talk". (We recommend this with
the *–noampm* command-line option.)

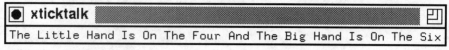

Figure 3-14: Baby talk

And the very latest version of *xticktalk* now supports the language spoken on the planet Klingon:

Figure 3-15: xticktalk in Klingon

Obviously this will come in useful if you are captured by renegade Klingons who are desperate to know the correct time. *BIyaj'a?* [*]

xticktalk also comes with an ASCII-based version, *ticktalk*, which just sends the current time to standard output:

```
% ticktalk -language french
Seize Heures Trente-Deux
```

—LM

3.11 Transparent oclocks: The Better to See You with . . .

If you have access to some interesting bitmaps, it's fun to specify an image as the root window background *(6.02)* and then place a transparent *oclock (3.02)* over it. Nasty copyright laws prevent us from showing you the X version of the Mickey Mouse watch, but here's a combination we like.

The happy guy is our editor and boss, Tim O'Reilly. I created the bitmap from a FaceSaver file *(25.02)* using utilities from the Portable Bitmap Toolkit *(25.01)*. I can place a bevy of bosses (gulp) on my root window using the *xsetroot* .XET N .XE1 "xsetroot command" .XE2 "setting background bitmap via" ./XET *(6.02)* client.

```
% xsetroot -bitmap /home/val/bitmaps/tim
```

Then I run a transparent *oclock*. (I also specify reverse video *(17.08)*, because the white clock shows up better.)

```
% oclock -transparent -rv &
```

---

[*] I don't claim to be fluent in Klingon (God forbid!), but according to my sources, this means "Understood?" Okrand, Marc: *The Klingon Dictionary*, 1985, Pocket Books.

Notice that I've suppressed any window manager decoration *(12.16)* on the oclock and resized *(12.17)* it to suit the man.

Figure 3-16: On the boss' time

Since it's after five and I'm still here, Tim is smiling.

—VQ

3.12 *Different Time Zones*

Most of us live in one time zone and are happy with that. But if you work with people overseas, you might be interested in having clocks for different time zones.

One easy way to do it is to temporarily change the TZ environment variable *(2.04)* before starting your clock application. If you use the C shell (or some derivative thereof), you can do this in a subshell:

```
% (setenv TZ PST8PDT; xclock &)
```

or if you use the Bourne or Korn shell:

```
$ TZ=PST8PDT xclock 2> /dev/null &
```

If you keep multiple clocks hanging around, each with different time zones, it's a good idea to give them titlebars so you know which is which. So you might have the following lines in your *.xsession*:

```
#!/bin/sh
        ...
        (other commands)
        ...
TZ=PST8PDT xclock -name "California" 2> /dev/null &
TZ=EST5EDT xclock -name "Boston" 2> /dev/null &
```

```
TZ=JST xclock -name "Tokyo" 2> /dev/null &
TZ=GMT xclock -name "London" 2> /dev/null &
   ...
```

You can then get a nice little news room-style display of the time in different parts of the world, as shown in Figure 3-17.

Figure 3-17: Clocks for different time zones

—LM

3.13 Different Time Zones (Again!)

Well, I thought I was clever getting my multiple *xclocks* in different timezones (as shown in Article 3.12). Then, as usual, I found out that someone else was much more clever than I was.

xchrono

xchrono is a program that can show you a whole series of clocks for different cities throughout the world. Supported cities are Boston, New York, Chicago, Denver, Los Angeles, Hawaii, Tokyo, Sydney, London, Paris, Frankfurt, and Rio de Janeiro. (Quick quiz: which one of these isn't a city?) In addition, Greenwich Mean Time (GMT) is always shown.

For example, *xchrono –boston* shows the time for Boston, *xchrono –london*, shows the time for London, etc.

Figure 3-18 shows you what you get if you use the suggested application defaults. You end up with a window that shows each of the supported cities.

Note a few nice features: *xchrono* tells you what the date is in each of these cities, and whether it's A.M. or P.M. An asterisk after "AM" or "PM" means that the time zone is currently honoring daylight savings time.

—LM

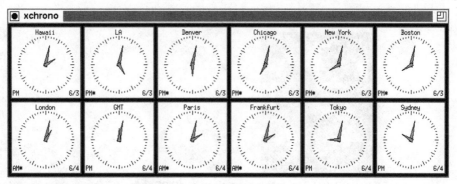

Figure 3-18: Clocks for different time zones, take 2

3.14 A Color Clock: xchrom

xchrom

If you have a color display, you might enjoy *xchrom*. *xchrom* displays the time in the chromachron format. The dial has a background segmented (like a pie) into twelve colors, displaying a twelfth of the background at a time. On top of the color pie sits a black disk with a 1/12 segment cut out. The disk moves around the pie, displaying portions of the background color segments.

So how do you tell the time on a chromachron clock? Well, the idea is that on exact hours, the pie segment shown through the cut segment of the disk is a single color. For example, at 12:00, the portion of the pie that's shown is all yellow. As we get closer to 1:00, the segment moves over to show a little bit of orange (the next color), until finally at 1:00 the entire orange segment is shown.

If this seems a little confusing to you, look at Figure 3-19, which shows an *xchrom* window at approximately 12:25. (Forgive us for the monochrome figure; just take our word for it that each pie segment is a different color.)

xchrom updates the time every minute. Among the resources that are supported are `twelveOClock` for specifying the color for 12:00, `oneOClock` for specifying the color for 1:00, and so on.

—*LM*

3.15 The Weirdest Clock

t3d

Did you ever think a clock might make you seasick? *t3d* is a bizarre three-dimensional clock that twists, turns, throbs, and pulsates, with the questionable aim of telling you the time. The clock face is composed of spheres that float around, and the entire clock face rotates from left to right. Figure 3-20

Figure 3-19: A chromachron clock at 12:25

shows *t3d*; you'll have to imagine its constant movement yourself.

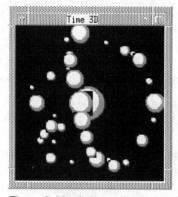

Figure 3-20: A three-dimensional clock

This is a clock?

Now use your imagination. The current time is 11:28 and 40 seconds. You can sort of see a big hand and little hand, and maybe even a second hand if you look real hard. Val says it looks to her like soda pop. To me, it looks more like a lava lamp come alive.

Obviously, *t3d* is meant more as a conversation piece than anything useful. Trying to figure out the time with *t3d* usually isn't worth the trouble (not when you could just as easily look at your wristwatch!), but I think it might win the award for the most unusual clock idea.

—*LM*

3.16 Kitty Clock

Okay, ready for something very cute? *mxclock* is a Motif-based version of *xclock* that includes a *–cat* option. Without *–cat*, *mxclock* resembles our boring-yet-reliable *xclock* (3.02). However, with *–cat*, you get a black cat with a swinging tail and eyes that move back and forth, as shown in Figure 3-21. (Well, you can't see the motion in the figure, but use your imagination.)

mxclock

Figure 3-21: Dinner time

This clock should remind you of the "Kit-Cat" plastic wall clock sold in many novelty stores.

—LM

3.17 The UNIX date Command

You'll notice that none of these clocks provide features for setting the time. That's because they all rely on the underlying system clock, which is set by the UNIX *date* command. You typically have to be the superuser to use *date* to set the time, though anyone can use it to display the time. Heck, here's the simplest X clock of all: in your *xterm*, at the UNIX shell prompt, type:

```
% date
Thu May 12 14:02:43 PDT 1994
```

— TOR

3.18 So What's the Best Clock?

So now that you've seen the clocks available, which one is the best? Of course, that's up to you. But if you must have an opinion....

Val's favorite is *mxclock* *(3.16)*, because it reminds her of her beloved cat Minx. (Boy, won't Minx be surprised when Val tries to put that bow tie around his neck.) It's also much more entertaining than many of the other clocks.

Our editor Tim tells us his favorite is the digital clock you get from *xclock –d* *(3.02)*. His main reason is that it takes up the least amount of space on his screen. (Although it's possible that *xcuckoo (3.08)* is even better, since it puts the date in the titlebar of an already existing window.)

Our reviewer Miles O'Neal speaks the virtues of *xdaliclock (3.04)* with the *–shape* and *–cycle* command-line options. The result is that numbers float on the screen, changing colors continuously.

As for me: don't faint, but my favorite is the clock I bought at a discount department store and hung on my wall.

—LM

4

Office Management

4.01 Calendars and Reminders

A friend of ours recently told us his life was stolen. He had lost a suitcase at the airport, containing his passport, medicine, and a camera. All those things were replaceable; but when he said his life was stolen, he was talking about his little leather-bound book. This book contained a calendar, addresses, phone numbers, and pages upon pages of random notes and reminders. Without that notebook, our friend felt uprooted.

This chapter is about X software for managing your life (Personal Information Managers, as they say in the PC world). These programs aren't as flexible as a book you can carry in your back pocket, but since you probably spend most of the workday in front of your X server, they can become very useful. You can have X programs remind you about appointments. You can use X programs to maintain phone numbers and addresses. You can use X programs to post to-do lists on your screen. You can even use a program to help you keep track of your time as you go through the day, so you can remember later on what it was you did.

—LM

4.02 A Monthly Calendar: xcalendar

xcalendar

xcalendar is a simple calendar application that shows you a monthly calendar and allows you to edit a list of items for each day. Start up *xcalendar* to see a listing for the current month, as in Figure 4-1.

If you now select a date on the calendar, a window appears in which you can enter or edit a message for that day, as shown in Figure 4-2.

When you're done, just press **Done** or **Save**. To edit the next day, press the right arrow button; to get to the previous day, press the left arrow button.

Figure 4-1: xcalendar window

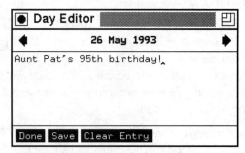

Figure 4-2: xcalendar day editor

On the main *xcalendar* window, you can also use the right and left arrow buttons to see the next and previous months (respectively). For help (actually, just the manpage), press the question mark in the lower right corner. To quit, press **Q** in the lower-left corner.

xcalendar also takes arguments for alternate months or years on the command line. For example, to come up initially for the month of September this year, enter:

```
% xcalendar 9
```

For June of 1965, type:

```
% xcalendar 6 1965
```

(Much to my disappointment, *xcalendar* does not do the right thing with September 1752, when the change over to the Gregorian calendar left out a few days. Try the UNIX command *cal 9 1752* to see what it *should* look like!)

—LM

4.03 A Simple Scheduling Program: ical

ical is a calendar program that's perfect for anyone who just wants to schedule appointments and get warnings when they approach.

ical is written in Tcl/Tk *(30.01)*. Using *ical*, you can set appointments, repeat them on a regular basis, and be reminded as the appointed time rolls around. *ical* also allows you to share your calendar with several other users, so co-workers can keep track of each other's schedules.

ical

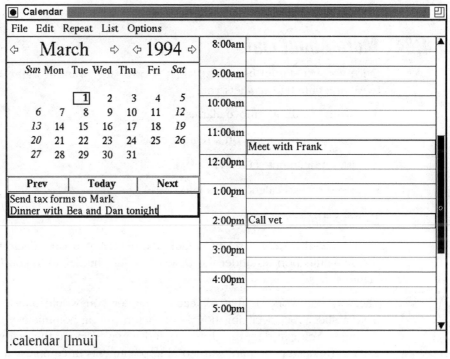

Figure 4-3: ical calendar

Figure 4-3 shows a sample *ical* calendar window. In the upper left of the window is the current month, with today's date highlighted. (You can select a different day by just clicking on it.) On the right side of the screen is a list of time slots for today's appointments.

To set an appointment, just click on a time slot and type away. You can change the time of an appointment by dragging it with the second mouse button, and you can stretch out the length of an appointment using the third mouse button. When the time for an appointment nears, *ical* pops up reminders at specified intervals before the actual appointment.

You can also set up general reminders for a given day by typing them at the bottom left of the *ical* window. You might use this area to list birthdays or to remind yourself that your rent is due on the first of each month.

If you need a different month (or different year!), you can use the arrows around the name of the month and year to move around. As shortcuts, *ical* also provides **Prev**, **Today**, and **Next** buttons for getting around quickly.

That should be enough to get you up and running. For more information about *ical*, see Article 4.04.

—LM

4.04 *More About ical*

Once you get started using *ical (4.03)*, you probably want to figure out how to tweak it a little bit. *ical* lets you:

- Change, add, or remove alarms.

- Repeat appointments on a regular basis.

- List appointments quickly.

- Merge several calendar files into one.

Setting Alarms

Under *ical*, there are a set of default alarms that you can redefine using the **Default Alarms** pop up under the **Options** menu. The default menu is shown in Figure 4-4.

The way this works is that for each reminder you would like to have, you have a slider for specifying how soon before the appointment you want the reminder. You can drag the slider up and down to move the warning later or earlier. By default, you are warned of appointments three times: at 20 minutes before the appointment, at 10 minutes before, and again at the actual appointment time. If you want more warnings, press **Add Alarm** to get a fourth slider; if you think this is overkill (as I do), press **Remove Alarm** to remove the rightmost slider. When you're happy with the current settings, press **Done**.

If you want to change the alarms for a specific appointment only, you can pull down the **Change Alarms** window from the **Edit** menu. This works exactly as **Default Alarms**, but it only affects the highlighted appointment.

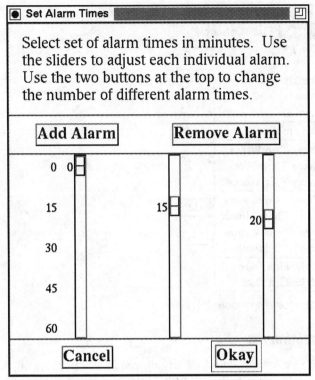

Figure 4-4: Changing default alarms

Repeating Appointments

Some appointments might be repeated on a regular basis. To set up an appointment to repeat, pull down the **Repeat** menu (as shown in Figure 4-5).

(The default behavior is not to repeat at all.) Most of the items here are pretty self-explanatory. The only items that might require a bit of explanation are **Make First Date** and **Make Last Date**. Selecting these for a repeating item means that the currently selected date is the first or last of the series of appointments.

Here's a neat feature of *ical*: occasionally you might want to change something in a repeating entry for just one time. If you want to do that, you can just select **Make Unique** under the **Edit** menu. Now any changes to that entry won't affect any other repeating occurrences of the same entry. This might come in handy if a regular meeting is cancelled or changed one week.

Figure 4-5: ical repeating menu

Listing Appointments

Some people might be irritated by having reminders pop up on their screens all day, and may prefer to have all their day's appointments shown at once. For them, *ical* supports a listing feature. If you call *ical* with a *–list* command-line option, you'll get a listing of today's appointments on standard output. No X window is opened when you use *–list*, which makes it handy for users who are dialing in on a terminal emulator to check in for appointments. For users on X servers, another alternative is the *–popup* option, which prints a list of appointments in a pop-up window that your rent is due (again, without opening an actual *ical* calendar window).

Usually, only appointments from today or tomorrow are shown in a *–list* or *–popup* listing. You can change this by selecting the **Default Listings** menu under the **Options** menu, or use the *–show* command-line option to extend the number of days that you want appointments listed. For example, to see the week's appointments:

```
% ical -list -show +7
```

You can also use the **List** menu to change listing behavior, or the **List Item** menu under the **Edit** menu for a single appointment.

One thing you might want is to have your appointments mailed to you every day. For that, you might use *cron* (or *tkcron* *(27.08)*), or you might just add the appropriate line in your startup script *(2.09)*. For example, to mail my daily listings to myself (*lmui*), I might include the following line in my startup script:

```
ical -list | mail lmui
```

Calendar Files

By default, *ical* uses a file in your home directory called *.calendar* for storing appointments. (You can specify a different file using the *–calendar* command-line option or by setting the CALENDAR environment variable *(2.04).*) However, you can also set up *ical* to read in external calendar files, so that several people can share a central calendar in addition to their personal one. This way, appointments for an entire department might be stored in one group-writable file.

To source in an external calendar, select the **Include Calendar** item under the **File** menu. You can later remove an external calendar using **Remove Include**. (You cannot remove your main calendar, e.g., *$HOME/.calendar*.)

When using multiple calendar files, you can move items from one calendar to another using the **Move Item To** menu under the **Edit** menu.

—*LM*

4.05 *Schedule Your Workday with plan*

plan is a calendar program that lets you write in appointments and sends you reminders about them. It's got all the features of *ical (4.03)*, plus a few more that make it slightly more powerful. *plan* may not as easy to use as *ical*, but it has an excellent online help system.

plan

Before starting *plan*, you should start the *pland* daemon. *plan* can work without it, but *pland* is the program responsible for sending pop-up reminders to your display.

```
% pland
```

Because you need to have *pland* running in order to receive messages, it's common to start it in your startup script *(2.09)* so that it's automatically running whenever you're logged in. (Actually, if you start *plan* running without a *pland* already running, you will be prompted to start it anyway.)

Once you have *pland* running, you can start the *plan* program.

```
% plan
```

(The *plan* program spawns a child process and exits, so you don't need to start it in the background.) A window displaying the current month appears. Figure 4-6 shows the initial *plan* window.

Figure 4-6: Initial plan window

One caveat about *plan*: it only understands dates after January 1, 1970. This shouldn't be a problem if the space/time continuum remains stable, but be aware of it anyway.

—LM

4.06 Configuring Your plan Environment

If you want to use *plan* *(4.05)*, one of the first things you'll want to do is to reconfigure it to use your preferred date conventions. *plan* defaults to European date conventions: I prefer 12-hour time; I like to use Sunday as the beginning of a week; and I want to specify dates as month-day-year (rather than day-month-year, which is the European preference). I do all this via the **Config** pull-down menu.

To access the **Config** menu, just hold the first mouse button down on the word **Config** at the top of the *plan* window. You can also use Meta-C (or Alt-C) to access the menu. The **Config** menu appears in Figure 4-7.

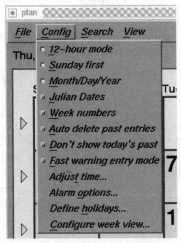

Figure 4-7: Setting some plan preferences

The first three items are the ones I want to select for "American" preferences. Select these for now so you can start using *plan* effectively right away; the only other configuration that you might need immediately is to set the time correctly by selecting **Adjust Time** . . . . This gives a small window allowing you to set the time; usually you can just let it **Guess** and the time will be set correctly for you.

You may have noticed that a few holidays appear on the **Month** display. These holidays are kept in a file in your home directory called *.holiday*. Holidays can be edited via the **Config** menu, but *plan* is also distributed with several "sample" holiday files for different countries or cultures. I installed the *holiday_us* sample file (for U.S. holidays). Other available holiday files are for German, Dutch, Canadian, French, Swiss, and British users.

You might want to edit your holiday file, because although many useful days are included (such as Thanksgiving, Memorial Day, etc.), there are also some less popular holidays listed, such as Bill of Rights Day, Wright Brothers' Day, and World Poetry Day.

You don't need to configure *plan* every time you log in; your preferences are saved in your *$HOME/.dayplan* file, so they will not only take effect immediately but also remain in effect the next time you start the *plan* program.

—*LM*

4.07 Using plan

The *plan* (4.05) program lets you schedule appointments easily and then set warnings, repeat appointments, etc. This article covers what most people want to use a scheduling calendar program for. See Article 4.08 for details of some of the more advanced features of *plan.*

Scheduling an Appointment

To set up an appointment, click on the day to see a **Schedule** window. The **Schedule** window consists of one appointment per line; each line has a field for **Date**, **Time**, **Length**, and **Note**. There are also columns to press for additional data. For example, suppose I want to register a lunch appointment tomorrow (Thursday) afternoon at 1:00 P.M. I press on the date (January 13) and then click in the first empty **Date** column, as shown in Figure 4-8.

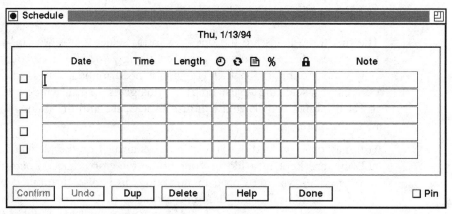

Figure 4-8: The plan Schedule window

Here, you can type in a date and press **Return**. You can also press **Return** without typing in a date and *plan* assumes the selected date (i.e., the date you clicked on to access the **Schedule** window). The date may be specified as *Month/Day* or as *Day/Month*, depending on how you specified it on the Config menu (4.06).

After pressing **Return**, you're placed in the **Time** column. You can type in a time in in the 24-hour convention (aka European or military time), or with an appended **a** or **p** to signify A.M. or P.M., again, depending on how you specified it on the **Config** menu. Press **Return** after specifying a time. If you press **Return** without specifying a time, midnight is assumed; this is appropriate for reminders that aren't tied to a particular time (e.g., "Aunt Pat's birthday").

Next, you're in the **Length** column. Here, you can type in how long you think this appointment will take. If you press **Return** without specifying a length of time, the field becomes 0:00. My experience is that this is fine for most appointments. *plan* isn't smart enough to use the **Length** field to warn you against scheduling conflicting appointments; it only uses this field for displaying **Week** views, as shown later in this article.

Once you press **Return** in the **Length** field, you jump ahead over several columns to the **Note** field at the end. Here, you can type in a short message describing the appointment. When you press **Return**, the appointment is confirmed. (You can also press the **Confirm** button on the bottom left of the window.) When the appointment is confirmed, the square to the left of the note is darkened (or turns red, on a color display), and the appointment appears on the main *plan* calendar window. A completed **Schedule** might look like Figure 4-9.

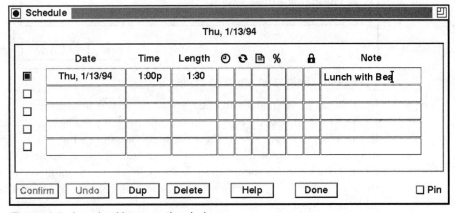

Figure 4-9: Lunch with my mother-in-law

If you start a **Note** with a dash (–) or equal sign (=), the note will not appear on the calendar, but only on the schedule listings. You may want to do this if you don't like cluttering your display with reminders that aren't associated with a particular day.

The **Note** column of the **Schedule** window gives you a quick way to jot down what the appointment is. But you can also click on the column containing a text icon to write a longer message.

Warnings

Now for the nifty features. We skipped over several columns between the **Length** and **Note** fields in the *plan* **Schedule** window. The first of these columns is represented by a small clock icon; this is the "warning" column. By clicking on this column, you get a small window asking you when you want to be warned about this appointment. A reminder to make a phone call probably doesn't need any advance warning (which is the default), but a reminder to go for a dentist's appointment across town might need a half-hour warning. Some reminders might need two warnings, for example, you might need to be reminded an hour in advance that you have a meeting coming up, and then be reminded again 10 minutes in advance. The Advance Warnings window appears in Figure 4-10.

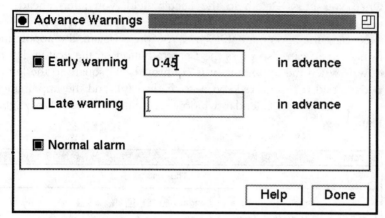

Figure 4-10: Setting up warnings in plan

In addition to **Normal alarm** (i.e., an alarm at the actual time of the appointment), you can specify two other alarms: an **Early warning** and a **Late warning**. If you click on either of these, the small square to the left is darkened (or turns red, on a color display) and the default value is inserted. For example, when I click on (or near) **Early warning**, I see the default of 45 minutes, as shown in the figure. A clock appears in the column to show that there are additional warnings.

"Recycling" Appointments

Another nice feature is that you can set up appointments to repeat on a given schedule. This is very useful for weekly meetings or for monthly reminders. To reuse (or recycle) an appointment, click on the column headed by a "recycle" icon to bring up a **Schedule Recycler** window, shown in Figure 4-11.

plan gives you a lot of flexibility for repeating appointments. You can have the same appointment repeated on a given day of the month, or on a given day of the week, etc. In the figure, I've set up a weekly Friday meeting. I can also use the recycler to remind me to turn in a time sheet on the 1st and 16th of each month, or to remind me about street cleaning on my street on the second Wednesday of each month.

Being Notified

When you're done entering a message, you can actually exit *plan* if you wish. As you change configurations and add new appointments, *plan* writes the new data in a file in your home directory called *.dayplan*. The *pland* daemon

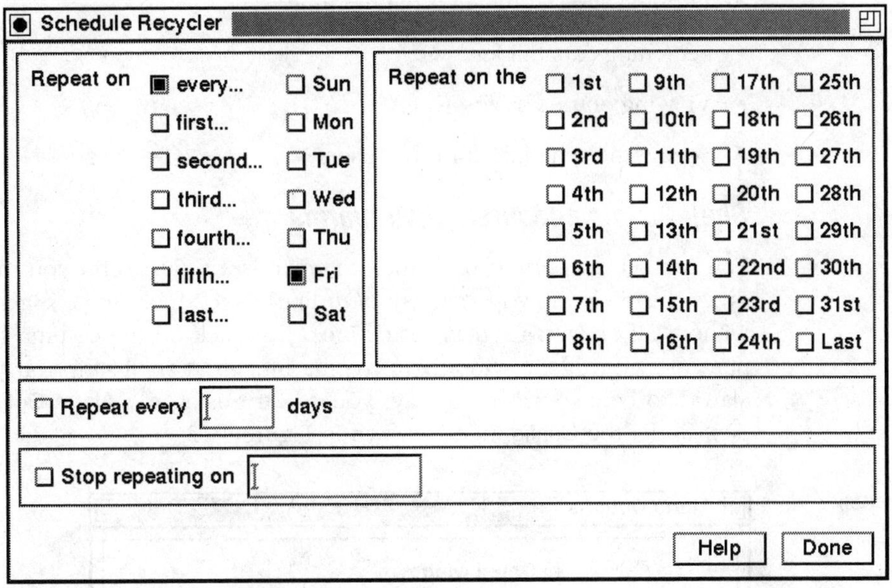

Figure 4-11: Setting appointments to repeat in plan

regularly checks *$HOME/.dayplan* to know when appointments are coming up. So as long as the *pland* daemon is still running, you will still be reminded of appointments. When the appointment comes up (or when its time for an advance warning), *pland* calls a separate program called *notifier* that pops a window to your display.

Other Scheduler Buttons

The buttons on the bottom of the display can be used to Confirm an entry, to Undo an entry that is not yet confirmed, to Duplicate the selected entry, and to Delete an entry. The Help button brings up online help, and the Done entry removes the Scheduler window when you're done entering and changing appointments.

The Pin button says to keep this appointment window around (rather than recycling it the next time an appointment window is requested).

—LM

4.08 "Advanced" plan

Now for the heavy-duty stuff. The *plan (4.05)* program has a bunch of features that may not be useful to everyone, but for those few people who need them, these features could be indispensible. These features include:

- Running shell scripts at a regular time.

- Searching capabilities.

- Viewing entries by the week.

- Seeing the schedule for other users.

Shell Scripts and Alternative Alarms

You can set up *plan* to run other commands, not just send you message windows. In this way, you can use *plan* like the UNIX *cron* command *(27.08)*, but without all of *cron*'s syntax restrictions. Just click on the column headed by a percent sign to get a window for typing in a short shell script. If you want all alarms to behave a certain way, you can try using the **Alarm Options ...** window under the **Config** menu, shown in Figure 4-12.

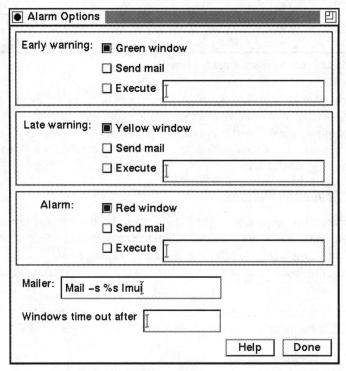

Figure 4-12: Setting up different alarms

You can use this to have mail sent to you instead of a pop-up alarm window or to specify a shell script you want run at the appropriate time.

The Search Menu

Clicking on a date isn't the only way to get a **Scheduler** window. You can also use the **Search** pull-down menu to see all appointments for today, for tomorrow, for this week, for next week, or next month, or all appointments for all time (!). Another neat feature is that you can do a keyword search; so if all you remember is that you made an appointment with Peter sometime in the spring, you can just search for "Peter" and find it.

Viewing Weeks and Years

The default view is the **Month** view, but you can use the **View** pull-down menu to select a **Year** or **Week** view window. The **Year** view isn't that interesting, but the **Week** view is worth looking at since it tries to give you a listing of the week's appointments at a glance, as shown in Figure 4-13.

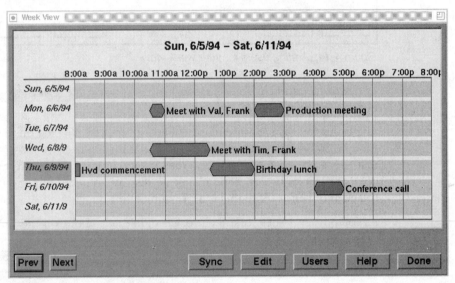

Figure 4-13: A week of appointments

Schedules of Other Users

Now look at the buttons at the bottom of the **Week** window. The **Week** window has the ultra-nifty feature that lets you view the appointments of other users as well as your own. Specify the other users by pressing the **Users** button; this button brings up a new window letting you add and delete other users. In this example, I add users *sue* and *val*, as shown in Figure 4-14.

I wrote in the names *sue* and *val* in the **User** column, and pressed return. The square to the left of the entry is darkened to to indicate that the entry is in effect. The other thing I need to do is edit the **Home** field to point *plan* to the correct home directory. *plan* needs this information to find the other user's

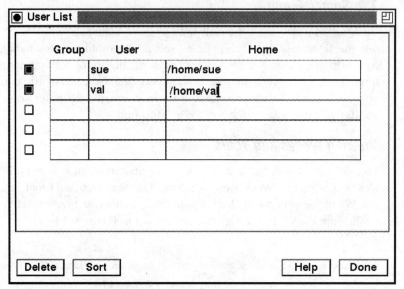

Figure 4-14: Adding users for your week view

.dayplan file, and for some reason it doesn't parse the UNIX *passwd* information correctly on its own.

The **Group** field is most useful on color displays. By clicking on the **Group** box for a given user, you can select a color code for the user. This color is used for that user's appointments on the **Week** view window. There are eight distinct colors available, but on a monochrome display you can only see two of them (black and white). Still, this is a pretty nice feature.

As for privacy issues: one feature we didn't talk about on the **Schedule** window was the column headed by a lock icon. Clicking on this button places the entry in a separate *.dayplan* file, called *.dayplan.priv*, which is readable only by the owner. The result is that you can lock out other users from any private appointments.

Also on the **Week** window are buttons for switching to the previous or next week. You can also re-synchronize (i.e., reread everyone's *.dayplan* files so that the **Week** view is up-to-date), re-edit your own week's appointments, or call up **Help**. Dismiss the **Week** window using the **Done** button.

—LM

4.09 Using xmessage to Create Reminder Notes

xmessage is an application that just prints a message in a window. For example:

```
% xmessage "Call Tim about book outline"
```

xmessage

results in the window shown in Figure 4-15.

Figure 4-15: xmessage display

You can leave this message up as a reminder of something to do before you log out. To dismiss the message, just press the **Okay** button.

As an alternative to *xmessage*, you can also try using *xpostit* (4.12).

(The version of *xmessage* on the CD-ROM is one that includes a scrollbar (11.02) if needed.)

—*LM*

4.10 xmessage for To-Do Lists

The *xmessage* (4.09) program supports a *–file* option to have the message read from a file. Using this feature, you can set up *xmessage* to run from your startup script (2.09) and call a file containing today's to-do list.

```
xmessage -file $HOME/.todo -title "`date +'%a, %h %d'`" &
```

(Note that I use the *date* command (3.17) to set the titlebar to the current date, using a standard Xt option, *–title*.) The resulting window might resemble that in Figure 4-16.

At the end of each day, you can edit the file to create a new to-do list for tomorrow. You can even automate this process, by putting an *xedit* command (9.03) at the very end of your startup script.

—*LM*

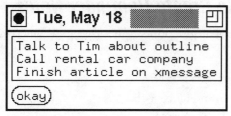

Figure 4-16: A to-do list with xmessage

4.11 Using at and xmessage for an Alarm

Here's a poor man's calendar program: you can use the *xmessage (4.09)* client with the standard UNIX *at* command to simulate an alarm:

```
% at 12:30
at> xmessage "Production meeting."
at> ^D <EOT>
job 15510 at Mon May 17 12:30:00 1993
```

This way, the *xmessage* program pops up the message at the specified time. It's not a rigorous calendar program like *ical (4.03)* or *plan (4.05)*, but it works.

—*LM*

4.12 Sticky Notes

You can use *xmessage (4.09)* to post reminders to yourself on your screen. But if you want to do this a bit more elegantly, try *xpostit*.

Before you start *xpostit* for the first time, you should create a *$HOME/.postitnotes* directory.

```
% mkdir ~/.postitnotes
% xpostit &
```

xpostit

When you start *xpostit*, a small plaid-patterned box appears. Figure 4-17 shows the *xpostit* control panel.

Figure 4-17: The xpostit control box

If you press down the third mouse button in this window, a pop-up menu appears, as in Figure 4-18.

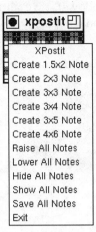

Figure 4-18: The xpostit pop-up menu

From this menu, you can create a new note of a specified size. For example, if you pull down **Create 1.5x2 Note**, you get a window of approximately that size. You can type your message in this window as in Figure 4-19. (You can also "tear off" a note by holding down the first mouse button on the control panel and then dragging it off the control panel.)

Figure 4-19: A post-it note

When you're done, you can resize the window (the text will wrap accordingly) and place it elsewhere on your screen using your window manager. Then if you press **Save**, the note is saved in the *$HOME/.postitnotes* directory.

The *$HOME/.postitnotes* directory not only contains the text for the notes, it also contains its geometry *(17.10)*. That means that if the messages are all saved, you can log out today and when you start up *xpostit* tomorrow, all the notes are right where you left them.

You can use the **Erase** button to erase a note or the **Destroy** button to get rid of it for real. On the control panel, you can raise (or lower) all notes (so you don't have to go searching for them behind windows), save all the notes, or exit the program entirely. Note that if you don't explicitly save the notes before you exit, they're gone for good.

The default title for notes is **PostItNote** *#n*. You can change the title by pressing the **Title** button. Pressing this button brings up a window as shown in Figure 4-20.

Figure 4-20: Changing the title for a post-it note

xpostit is blatantly and unashamedly patterned after the brand-name Post-It Notes marketed (and invented) by 3M Company. Users with color displays will appreciate the homage of the red-plaid control box and the canary-yellow text windows.

—LM

4.13 A Poor Man's Postitnote

With the *–sv* option, *xpostit* *(4.12)* is supposed to save all notes to disk when you exit. On my system, though, this didn't appear to be all that robust. (I live out in the country, and especially in the winter, we are subject to power outages.)

Rather than battling with *xpostit*, I decided to use a program I knew did a good job of saving its contents on abnormal termination: the good old *vi* text editor. *xpostit* is a nice program, but I realized that for my purposes, I could do everything it does and more simply by running *vi* with *xterm –e* *(11.25)*.

Here's what I put in my startup script *(2.09)*:

```
xterm -title POSTITNOTES -g 33x33+580+0 -bg '#ffff95' -e vi $HOME/.postit &
```

I generally only need one *xpostit* window, but I like it to be long and tall, not one of the standard *xpostit* sizes. I keep my to-do list there, and even my taller window usually isn't big enough, but since I've got a full-fledged text editing window there (not just a fixed-size *xpostit* window), my text *can* grow longer than the visible portion of the window.

One other thing: I couldn't figure out the exact bright yellow color that Dave Curry used for his original *xpostit* application, but I experimented with *xcoloredit* *(26.16)* until I found something that seemed close enough. I specified that on the command line as the background color of the window.

—TOR

4.14 *Organizing Addresses*

A while back, the famed *twm* author Tom LaStrange challenged X hackers everywhere to come up with the best publicly available application based on the Rolodex cardholder system.

xrolodex

One of the products of that challenge was *xrolodex*. *xrolodex* is a (relatively) simple application for organizing names and addresses.

Start up *xrolodex* with the name of a rolodex file. You can name the rolodex file anything you want, but a convention is to place it in your home directory with a *.xrolo* suffix (for example, *$HOME/my.xrolo*).

```
% xrolodex my.xrolo
```

If the rolodex file does not exist yet, *xrolodex* comes up with an empty entry window. To start adding entries, just type in the window and press New/Ins (see Figure 4-21).

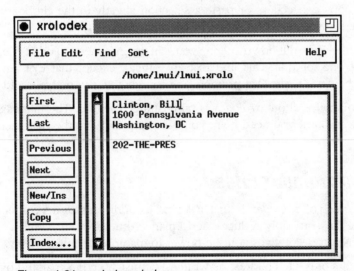

Figure 4-21: xrolodex window

When you have several entries, you can use *xrolodex* to search them easily. You can move to the first entry by pressing First and then page forward by pressing Next. Or you can go backwards by pressing Last and Previous. The order in which the entries appear may not be ideal; you can pull down the Sort menu and select Ascending or Descending to sort the entries. (Since *xrolodex* doesn't understand first names vs. last names, it's a good idea to list all your entries last name first.)

To find a particular entry, you can press **Index** to see a listing of the first lines of each entry (usually the person's name). Or you can pull down the **Find** menu and select **Find Entry** to specify a string to search for, as shown in Figure 4-22.

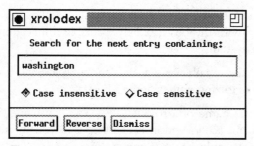

Figure 4-22: xrolodex find window

Using the **Edit** pull-down menu, you can copy or delete an entire entry. You can also specify that an entry should be appended to the list (by default, they are inserted before the first entry). For editing within the text window, you can press the third mouse button to access a pop-up window allowing you to cut or copy a selection, or paste a selection already in the clipboard. You can also perform a search and replace within the entry.

Under the **File** pull-down menu, you can open a new rolodex file, save the current one, or quit. **Quit** and **Exit** are similar, except that **Exit** automatically saves the entry while **Quit** prompts you for whether the entry should be saved.

Everything else about *xrolodex* is fairly straightforward. The manpage is close to useless, but if you need help, you can just pull down the **Help** menu.

—LM

4.15 *Using xrolodex Files*

One feature of *xrolodex* is that it keeps its addresses in a very simple ASCII format. This probably reduces performance, but if you're familiar with standard UNIX tools, it gives you the power to manipulate entries easily.

xrolodex stores each address as written, with each entry separated by a special string. By default, the separator string is ####. (Although you can change the separator string by setting the XRolodex*entryDelimiter resource, we don't recommend it for consistency's sake).

How do you use this information? Well, here's an example. When I first discovered *xrolodex*, I already had addresses written into a single-line format (so that I could just *grep* for a keyword). My entries read:

```
Adrienne Nordstrom, 46 East Davis Blvd., St. Louis, MO  63108
Alan King, 333 University Road, Fresno, CA  94705
Andy Rooney, 909 Park Avenue, NY, NY  10011
       ...
```

Once I discovered *xrolodex*, I wanted to use it but I didn't want to type all these addresses in again. Instead, I wrote a *sed* script to convert them into an *xrolodex* form:

```
% sed '/^$/d\
i\\
####\
s/, */\\
/g' address_list >> my.xrolo
```

My *sed* script removes empty lines. Then for each remaining line, it inserts the #### delimiter, and then converts each comma (and any spaces following a comma) into a newline.

(Now, it would be ideal if the entries could be converted into a last-name-first format. I'll leave that as an exercise for the reader....)

Here's another situation in which you'd run commands on the *xrolodex* source file itself. If you want a listing of all addresses, you can just print the text file. But sometimes you might want to only see a selected number of the entries (for example, only people living in a particular zip code). I'm not much of a *perl* programmer, but I wrote up a *perl* script called *xrolomatch* as a sort of general-purpose pattern searcher.

xrolomatch

xrolomatch takes two arguments: the regular expression string to search for, and the filename. For example, for all addresses with a zip code of either 02138 or 02139, I might do:

```
% xrolomatch '0213[89]' my.xrolo
```

The regular expression should be placed within single quotes to prevent the shell from trying to interpret it.

xrolomatch takes any regular expression string that might appear in an entry. For example, if you want to find someone named either "Allen" or "Alan", you might type:

```
% xrolomatch 'Al*[ea]n' my.xrolo
```

—*LM*

4.16 Pegboard

It's the end of December, and around this time of year we're deluged with email from our co-workers announcing that they'll be out all next week, or will be available only by email, etc. *xpeg* is a program for maintaining that sort of information. It's an X-based pegboard that you can use to make your whereabouts known to your co-workers.

xpeg

The syntax for *xpeg* is to specify the name of a pegboard file, and your name as it appears in the file. *xpeg* is distributed with a sample file, and the *README* suggests you test the program by opening the sample file under the name of the author:

```
% xpeg sample_pegfile "Ken Nelson"
```

The first argument identifies the name of the *xpeg* file to use. The second argument identifies the user's name as it appears in the sample file. The sample window appears in Figure 4-23.

● xpeg						囝
Xpeg						
The Engineers Of Software Systems Design, Inc.						
XPeg, a tool for the 90's.						
about	quit	update	save	new	group	Your Username: Ken Nelson
Ken Nelson	Fri Aug 24 08:48:0	I wrote Xpeg, ssdken@jarthur.claremo
Lee Jensen	Thu Aug 23 18:25	Not in yet
Doug Pollard	Thu Aug 23 18:25	Here but not "in" yet
Bruce Crabtree	Thu Aug 23 18:26	Porting to HP, phone (555)–555
George Marschalk	Thu Aug 23 18:28	At desk, phone 555–2322
Tom Radi	Fri Aug 24 08:50:2	At Coporate Headquarters
Tippy	Fri Aug 24 10:03:1	In the corporate doghouse.

Figure 4-23: xpeg sample file

Each person has a line with their name, the time that their entry was last updated, and a message identifying what they're up to today.

Now for the problems with *xpeg*. Your *xpeg* username is taken from the command line (as shown above), or from an XPEG_USER environment variable *(2.04)*. This is used to determine whether you can edit an entry: you can only edit entries matching your user name. There are two problems here: one is that you might mistype your user name; the other is that if the whole idea is to provide some security against people editing other peoples' entries, it's easily circumvented by just specifying someone else's name. (Then again, this may also be an advantage, since you can call in sick to have someone edit your entry.)

The *xpeg* pegboard file is taken from the command line, as shown in the example. It can also be specified in an XPEG_FILE environment variable. But this relies on users knowing where this file is located.

—*LM*

4.17 Front-ends to xpeg

pegboard

I like the potential of *xpeg*, but I wasn't happy with its interface. We also have too many people for a single pegboard for the entire company; instead, we would need multiple pegboards for different groups. So I wrote a front-end shell script for use at our office, called *pegboard*. When I call *pegboard* for the writer's group, for example, I do:

```
% pegboard writers &
```

and I might see a window resembling Figure 4-24.

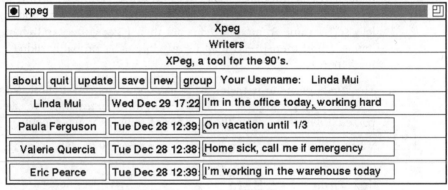

Figure 4-24: Writer's pegboard

Grab this script off the CD-ROM and adapt it for your own office. Undoubtedly you'll have different groups, you may prefer to just use user names (in the USER environment variable *(2.04)*) instead of bothering to find their full name, and you might also need to make some other system-specific changes (e.g., if you don't have NIS you might search */etc/passwd* directly instead of using *ypcat passwd*). But if you want to use *xpeg*, I recommend some sort of front-end like this to reduce the chance of user error.

I also wrote a quickie script for changing your entry. This script is called *changepeg*, and it replaces the message for your entry with the text specified

changepeg

on the command line. *changepeg* is smart enough to find your entry and change them in all pegboard files you appear in:

```
% changepeg Going fishing, be back tomorrow.
```

It also changes the date for the entry, so that everyone knows they have the most up-to-date information about your whereabouts. If you appear in several pegboard files and want to change only one of them, then just specify the group name as the first argument.

xpeg obviously needs a lot of work before it can become ready for prime time on its own. But with a few front-ends, it's not a bad little tool.

—*LM*

4.18 *Managing Timesheets*

Contractors frequently have several different projects going on at once, and need to keep track of how much time they spend on each. They might spend a few hours on one project, a portion of an hour on another, take lunch, and then spend the afternoon on a third project. Unless they've been writing down their activities throughout the day, they may end up having to reconstruct timesheets at the end of the day, involving a little bit of guesswork. ("Well, let's see, I came in around 9:30, but then I got coffee and chatted for a few minutes, and then I read mail for a while, so I probably didn't start working until 10 or so . . . ")

The *timex* program is meant to help contractors stay honest. When you start working on a given project, just select it in the *timex* window; as each minute passes, *timex* increments the number of minutes you've spent on that project.

timex

When you first start *timex*, it gives you a window as shown in Figure 4-25.

Figure 4-25: The initial timex window

Press the **Add** button to add a new project. An **addpopup** window appears as in Figure 4-26. Type in the name of your new project and press **OK**.

This is only a beta version of *timex*, so it's a bit dumb about expanding the size of its text window to accommodate a longer project name. But it saves the project names so that the next time you start up *timex*, you should see all your projects listed (see Figure 4-27).

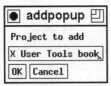

Figure 4-26: The timex add window

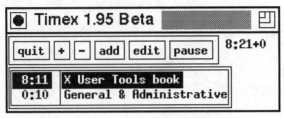

Figure 4-27: timex in action

Just select each project as you start work on it. When you go to lunch, press **pause**, which keeps everything as is until you return. If you need to make adjustments, press the + and - buttons to increment or decrement five minutes, or press **edit** to edit the actual project name or to more carefully fine-tune the amount of time spent on a particular project.

At the top-right corner of the *timex* window is the total number of hours you've been working today, along with the number of hours you've added or subtracted to your *timex*-calculated hours.

timex saves all its information in the *$HOME/.timex/* directory. (You can override this using the TIMEXDIR environment variable.) The *projectlist* file contains a list of all your projects. And each day that you've used *timex* has a file associated with it (in the form *YYYY-MM-DD*).

At the end of a week, you might want to add up your hours. For that, use the *sumtimex* script that's distributed with *timex*. *sumtimex* defaults to telling you your hours for the previous week (assuming that you run it on a Monday rather than a Friday), but you can just specify the week number to *sumtimex*. You have to calculate the week number yourself, but luckily *sumtimex* tells you what the previous week number was, and you can just add one. On a Friday evening, I might add up my hours as follows (knowing that this is week number 23 of the year):

```
% sumtimex 23
No file for day 1994-06-11
No file for day 1994-06-12
Linda Mui
Hours worked for week 23 1994
```

Project	TOT!	Mon	Tue	Wed	Thu	Fri	Sat	Sun
Date	!	6/6	7/6	8/6	9/6	10/6	11/6	12/6
===
General & Administrative	1.4!	0.2		0.7	0.3	0.2		
X User Tools book	40.3!	8.1	9.6	5.2	9.2	8.2		
===
Total	41.7!	8.3	9.6	5.9	9.5	8.3	0.0	0.0
	0.0							

sumtimex shows the amount of time billed to each project for the entirety of last week.

One little caveat: *sumtimex* depends on finding the *weekno.perl* script, which it assumes to reside in the current directory. This means you either need to run the script in that directory, or alter the *sumtimex* script to point to the absolute pathname of the *weekno.perl* script. (*sumtimex* is written in *perl*).

—*LM*

4.19 *A Spreadsheet Program*

They say that the "killer app" that got PCs into every office was the spreadsheet. There are commercial spreadsheets for X, but before you invest in one of those, take a look at *xspread*.

xspread is a simple X port of a character-based spreadsheet for UNIX, *sc*. Like other spreadsheets, you have rows and columns, and each cell can contain numbers, strings, or formulas.

xspread

Figure 4-28 shows you an empty *xspread* worksheet.

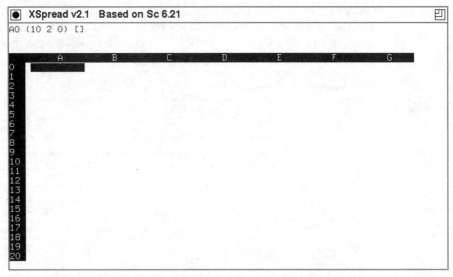

Figure 4-28: An X-based spreadsheet

To be honest, I'm totally ignorant about spreadsheets, so I can't tell you much more. But if you're familiar with spreadsheets, then you should be able to pick up *xspread* and start crunching along.

—*LM*

5

The Reference Desk

5.01 Facts at Your Fingertips

I have a bookshelf filled with computer books and quick references. But sometimes nothing quite compares to getting my information online.

This chapter is about reference applications—little programs for getting snippets of information quickly. There are manual pages *(5.02)*, a calculator *(5.05)* (and an abacus *(5.08)*), as well as programs for seeing the periodic table *(5.07)*, ASCII charts *(5.06)*, and even dictionary definitions *(5.04)*.

In addition to the clients listed in this chapter, be sure to check out Chapter 8, which covers reference clients that work over the Internet.

—*LM*

5.02 Manual Pages

xman

One of the core set of clients in the X distribution is *xman*, a client for reading UNIX manual pages (aka manpages).

When you start *xman*, you're presented with a small Manual Browser window (see Figure 5-1). The manual browser includes buttons labelled **Help**, **Quit**, and **Manual Page**.

The **Manual Page** button gives you online documentation for *xman* and provides pull-down menus under the **Options** and **Sections** buttons. (The **Help** button also gives you the online documentation, but not much else, so I never touch the **Help** button.)

xman uses the MANPATH environment variable *(2.04)* to find manpages. MANPATH is set to a colon-separated list of directories that are expected to have subdirectories entitled *man1*, *man2*, and so on (up to *man8*), as well as *manl* and *mann*. If MANPATH is not defined, *xman* defaults to */usr/man*.

Figure 5-1: xman Manual Browser window

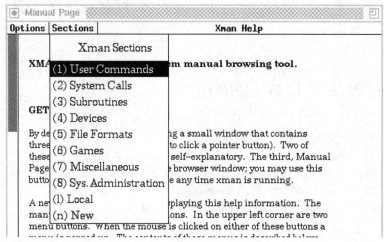

Figure 5-2: Sections menu

Options	Sections	Xman Help	
24to8	AUFS	DOC-19.22	
FvwmIdentify	FvwmInitBanner	FvwmModuleDebugger	
FvwmNoClutter	FvwmSaveDesktop	GoodStuff	
Intro	List	Mail	
Pnews	Rnmail	a2p	
acctcom	adb	addbib	
addftinfo	adjacentscreens	admin	
adpcm_dec	adpcm_enc	aedplot(g)	
afm2tfm	afmtodit	agrep	
ali	alias	align_equals	
anno	anytopnm	appres	
apropos	ar(v)	arch	
archie	areacode	as	

Figure 5-3: Directory list

You can use the **Sections** menu (see Figure 5-2) to display all the manpages of a certain type and then select the one you want to see.

Note that when you select the *man1* manpages, *xman* folds together *all* the *man1* files in each of the directories listed in MANPATH. Figure 5-3 shows a portion of a window with a directory listing.

When you select a manpage, *xman* first reformats it (if necessary) and then displays it in the same window. If *xman* reformats a manpage, it asks you if it should save the new formatted manpage; always say "yes" unless you think you may be low on disk space. This will save *xman* and the standard UNIX *man* command from having to reformat the same manpage the next time around.

Figure 5-4 shows an *xman* window with a manual page displayed.

A manpage is easier to read and browse through using *xman* than it is using standard *man*.

Another very useful feature of *xman* is the search feature. To use this, select **Search** from the **Options** menu. A small search window pops up as shown in Figure 5-5. Type in the string that you want to search for.

The search can work in two ways: either it can bring up a manpage named after the specified string, or it can search for the string via *apropos(1)*. If you press **Return**, it looks for the manpage. This method of finding a manpage is useful because you don't have to think about what directory you think it might be in, and it usually comes up with the one you want.

There is no manpage for printer, so in this example I press **Apropos**. If you press **Apropos**, you get a listing of all manpages that make references to the string.

My main problem with *xman* is that I find its menu structure to be misleading and mostly unnecessary. But all in all, it is useful for people who are always looking at manpages (like me!) Furthermore, you can change much of *xman*'s behavior using resources. Try out the resources for *xman* that are distributed on the CD-ROM *(20.23)*.

—*LM*

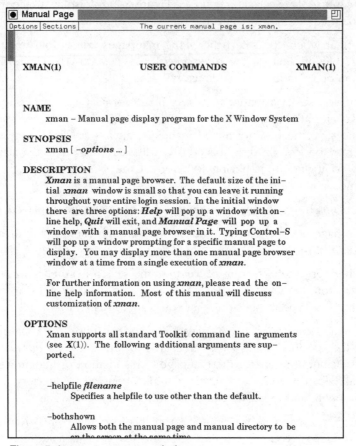

Figure 5-4: xman manpage window

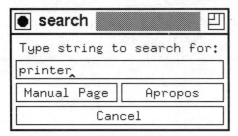

Figure 5-5: Search window

5.03 Another Manpage Browser: tkman

tkman is the neatest manpage viewer (with the possible exception of some commercial offerings, such as Sun's Answerbook, IBM's InfoExplorer, and SGI's Iris Insight. It depends on *wish*, the Tcl/Tk shell (see Article 30.01), but since it has Tk and Tcl available:

tkman

- Click on any word in the displayed manual pages and it appears in the text-pattern window, so you can click on the **Man** or **Apropos** button.

- Double-click on a word and you go straight to its manpage.

- A menu of all the sections in the current manpage, so you can jump to any one.

- A history of the last dozen or so manpages you've seen.

Figure 5-6 shows *tkman* in all its glory.

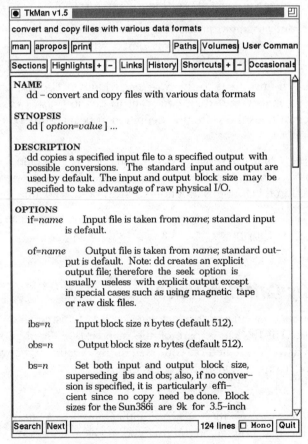

Figure 5-6: Manual pages in tkman

Get it. Explore it. Use it. Keep a copy running and iconified.

Alas, because it's a script, it can be slow. Slow to start up, and slow to format manpages. So be it; it's still a great tool.

—*IFD*

5.04 A Dictionary Client

I have a NeXT computer that comes with an online dictionary, Webster. I've set things up so other users at our company can use my dictionary, by installing a daemon that accepts requests for definitions across the network. My NeXT workstation thus acts as a Webster server.

If you don't have a licensed Webster server at your site, this article won't be useful to you. Although you might be tempted to ask around for someone on the Internet who will let you use theirs, note that this is completely illegal. And not all NeXT computers can run the Webster server daemon. But if you do have a Webster server legally available to you, read on.

xwebster

xwebster is a client program for querying a Webster site and returning the dictionary definition (see Figure 5-7). At my office, where our business is writing and editing books, we use it all the time.

There are three distinct areas to the *xwebster* window. Use the one-line box in the middle to specify the string you want to define (in this case, "cat"). If the Webster server finds the word, the definition appears in the bottom area of the window.

If *xwebster* doesn't find the word, it assumes that it's a misspelling and gives a listing of possible correctly spelled words in the top area of the *xwebster* window. Each word in this listing is a button you can press to define that word.

If you have a NeXT-based Webster server, the **Thesaurus** button can be used to give you a list of synonyms instead of a direct definition.

—*LM*

5.05 A Scientific Calculator: xcalc

xcalc

xcalc is a scientific calculator that emulates a Texas Instruments TI-30 or a Hewlett-Packard HP-10C. It is part of the standard X distribution, so you should already have it installed on your system. By default, *xcalc* works like a TI-30 calculator. To run *xcalc* in this mode, enter:

```
% xcalc &
```

There are two ways to use the calculator: either press the buttons on the calculator using the first pointer button, or type in the numbers or symbols on

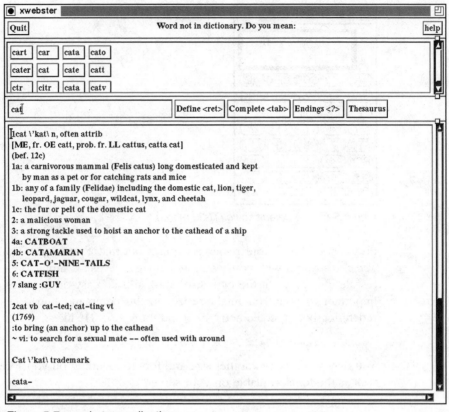

Figure 5-7: xwebster application

the keyboard. (To use the keyboard, *xcalc* must be the active window.) Some of the calculator keys do not have obvious keyboard equivalents. See the manpage for the proper shortcuts.

The values punched on the calculator and the results of the calculations are displayed in the long horizontal display along the top of the *xcalc* window. Figure 5-8 shows *xcalc*.

You can also operate the calculator in Reverse Polish Notation (as an HP-10C calculator operates), by entering:

```
% xcalc -rpn &
```

In Reverse Polish Notation the operands are entered first, then the operator. For example, 5 * 4 = would be entered as 5 Enter 4 *. This entry sequence is designed to minimize keystrokes for complex calculations.

You can exit the calculator by typing q, Q, or **CTRL-C**. On the TI calculator, you can also press the **AC** key with the third mouse button. On the HP calculator, press the **ON** key with the third mouse button.

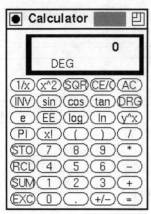

Figure 5-8: The default xcalc (TI-30 mode)

Please note: one of our reviewers points out that if you want a different-sized *xcalc*, resizing it with your window manager reveals a limitation—*xcalc* won't rescale the text to fit the new size buttons. If an easy-on-the-eyes calculator is important to you, you might resize on the command line or via resources, redefining both the geometry *(17.13)* and font *(17.14)*. He likes:

```
xcalc -geometry 740x320 -fn helvr24
```

You may want to try another size and font, depending on your preferences, as well as the fonts available on your server.

— VQ, LM

5.06 *ASCII Chart*

xascii

Here's a handy reference tool: *xascii* is a client that displays the ASCII chart in decimal, hexadecimal, or octal.

We know that some of you have already memorized the ASCII charts, but the rest of us mortals are continually picking through the appendices of our old language manuals to find out what the octal representation of **DEL** is. Sure, we can look on the *ascii(7)* manpage or cruise through */usr/pub/ascii*, but the *xascii* client is so much nicer.

By default, *xascii* comes up showing decimal notation (see Figure 5-9). Just press **Octal** to see octal notation or **Hex** to see hexadecimal.

Well, there's not much more to it, but *xascii* is one of those programs that's very simple yet continuously useful.

— LM

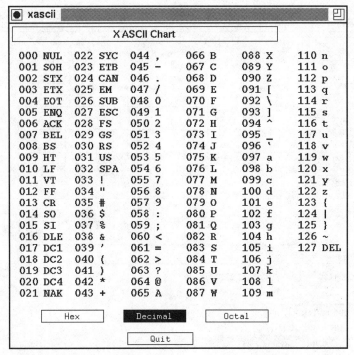

Figure 5-9: xascii window

5.07 The Periodic Table

xelem

Every now and then, you just *have* to know the melting point of magnesium. For that, we offer *xelem*, a Tcl-based *(30.01)* program for displaying (and plotting!) information about your favorite elements, in a handy periodic table format (see Figure 5-10).

Each element is shown properly on a periodic table, along with its atomic number. (I was temporarily thrown by the presence of deuterium, since as a high school student I always respected the privacy of hydrogen in the upper-left corner of the table. But my local chemistry buff assures me that this is a legitimate isotope of hydrogen and it *is* in its proper place, although it's a little puzzling why it was included over all the other hard-working isotopes.)

Now here's the cool part. The traditional periodic table includes each element's atomic number. *xelem* allows you to break from the crowd: imagine impressing your co-workers with your knowledge of an element's melting point. Select **Show** from the **Options** pull-down menu and you'll get a pop up allowing you to select another property of each element to display. A line at the lower-left corner of the window indicates you what property is currently being shown (see Figure 5-11).

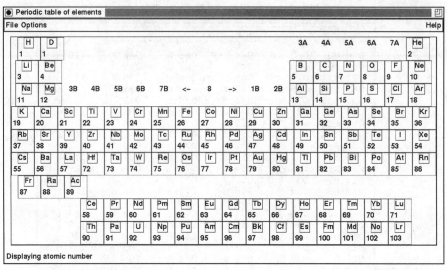

Figure 5-10: *xelem periodic table*

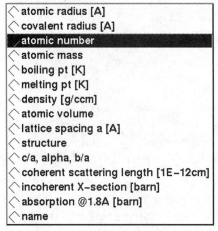

Figure 5-11: *Choosing an element property*

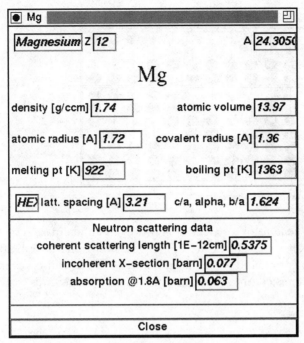

Figure 5-12: Magnesium in a nutshell

Another nice feature of *xelem* is that you can get loads of information about each element by clicking on the element symbol. For example, Figure 5-12 shows everything you ever wanted to know about magnesium.

Anyway, I'm not a chemist, and I couldn't identify radium if I sat on it (at least not right away), but I think *xelem* may come in useful for some readers.

—LM

5.08 *An Abacus?!?*

Yes, this is almost the 21st century, and we're using computers to simulate an abacus. This is sort of like using a television to show still photographs (apologies to Kodak).

xabacus

Now that I've maligned it, I must admit *xabacus* is pretty cool, if only because it shows you the sum in decimal (as shown in Figure 5-13). Using *xabacus* for a few minutes, I quickly learned how abacuses work.

To use the abacus, just slide the counters by holding down the first mouse button. The decimal output is automatically updated.

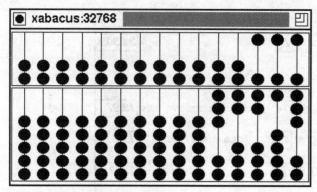

Figure 5-13: An X-based abacus

Here's another feature of *xabacus*: it comes with an alternate resource file for simulating a Korean abacus. (The Chinese version is the default abacus.) The Korean abacus is rumored to be faster, but since *xabacus* users aren't likely to be all that interested in speed, I'm not sure whether this has any non-academic value.

—LM

6

Decorating Your Display

6.01 Decorations and Conversation Pieces

Do you ever wish you had a "fun" computer? Are you irritated by Macintosh users who brag about their latest screen saver or system beep? I don't mean to disparage UNIX and X, but if they were giving an award for Cutest Computer, your RS/6000 workstation probably wouldn't win.

So this chapter is about decorating your display. You can animate your background, or change the behavior of your cursor. We also provide a few programs you can use as screensavers, so that you can have a pretty picture show up on your display when you're not there. Many of the programs in this chapter are close to useless, but they make nice conversation pieces the next time your Macintosh friends start taunting you about your boring X workstation.

—LM

6.02 Decorating the Root Window

In the X environment, your screen background is known as the root window. The standard root window background for most X servers is a black-and-white dotted pattern called appropriately *root weave*. (The "weave" is tight: it basically looks gray.)

There are several programs that will let you change the root-window background. Among the standard clients, *xsetroot* lets you set the background to another pattern or to a solid color.

Four basic *xsetroot* options allow you to specify the root window decoration:

1. The option *–gray* (or *–grey*) provides a slightly lighter gray background than the default.

2. Use the *–solid* option to set the color of the root window to a solid color.

For example, the command:

```
% xsetroot -solid lightblue
```

creates a light-blue root window. You can use a name from a color name database *(26.04)* or a numeric color specification *(26.11)*.

3. The option *–modu* takes two options (*x y*), and creates a plaid-like grid where *x* and *y* are the horizontal and vertical dimensions of each grid square in pixels. Both of the dimensions must be between 1 and 16 pixels. The command:

```
% xsetroot -mod 16 16
```

creates the largest possible grid squares. Vary the dimensions as you like. You can also specify foreground and background colors, as described for *–bitmap* below.

4. The *–bitmap* option covers the root window in a series of tiles featuring the specified bitmap. For example, the command:

```
% xsetroot -bitmap /home/val/bitmaps/tim
```

covers the root window with a tiling of the bitmap */home/val/bitmaps/tim*. Tim, in this case, is Tim O'Reilly, my editor and technically speaking (ahem), my boss.

Keep in mind that you can spice up a bitmap pattern by specifying alternative foreground and/or background colors *(26.02)*. The following command creates a root window Andy Warhol would be proud of:

```
% xsetroot -bitmap /home/val/bitmaps/tim -fg yellow -bg hotpink
```

Without options, *xsetroot* provides the default *root_weave* pattern. Since this gray is actually a stipple pattern of black and white pixels, it works on monochrome screens too.

Though *xsetroot* provides a reasonable number of screen decors, it is somewhat limited in the types of images it can display. Sometimes it's nice to be able to branch out. For instance, though a screenful of bitmap bosses can be a fine incentive, sometimes I'd prefer to look at a GIF of my new (mortgaged) home, to remind myself that time is money.

Since *xsetroot* can't display GIF files, I need to use another client for this purpose. Among the publicly available graphics clients are several that expand the list of possible root-window patterns. Check out *xcsetroot (6.03)*, *xloadimage (6.04)*, and *xv (6.04)*.

—*VQ*

6.03 More Root Window Decorations

xcsetroot

The *xcsetroot* client can do most everything *xsetroot (6.02)* can do, plus a bit more. *xcsetroot* accepts all but one of *xsetroot*'s options (*–cursor_name*). *xcsetroot* also lets you specify graphics in two additional formats: GIF and X Window dump *(23.01)*.

To create a root window made up of tiles of a window or screen-dump file, use the syntax:

```
% xcsetroot -xwd dump_file
```

To decorate with tiles of a GIF file, you'd use a line similar to:

```
% xcsetroot -gif bear.gif
```

Whenever you run *xcsetroot*, the program returns a message giving copyright information and statistics about the graphic you've specified. For instance, when I ran the preceding command, *xcsetroot* echoed:

```
XCsetroot, written by Thomas Wu and Davor Matic (c) 1990, MIT Fishbowl
bear.gif is 640x480, 8 bits per pixel, non-interlaced, 256 colors.
```

Since there are quite a few interesting GIF files floating around, *xcsetroot* can be a lot of fun. I was happy to be able to display one of my favorite GIFs: an ad for a 1974 Volkswagon convertible, complete with three photos of the bug, posted to the Internet. For the surrounding text, the enterprising owner used a background color close to the color of the car.

Many GIF files will tax the average server's color mapping and swapping capabilities. If *xcsetroot* cannot allocate sufficient colors to render an image, it may compensate by using some colors multiple times. The average eye should not notice these variations. (If you are bionic, you'll have to live with it.)

— *VQ*

6.04 A Wider Selection of Root Window Graphics

Both *xloadimage (24.05)* and *xv (24.06)* allow you to display images of several different types on your root window. Use *xloadimage* with the *–onroot* option and *xv* with the *–root* option.

The advantage of using *xloadimage* or *xv* over *xsetroot (24.05)* or *xcsetroot (24.06)* is that these programs can handle additional graphic file formats. Both *xloadimage* and *xv* allow you to display: X bitmaps; portable bitmaps, pixmaps, and graymaps; Sun rasterfiles; and GIFs. (See Article 22.02 for more information about graphic file formats.)

xloadimage additionally can handle: X window dumps, X pixmaps, Sun icon files, Fuzzy bitmap images, CMU WM raster files, FaceSavers, MacPaint files, and Group 3 FAX images. *xv* adds: JPEG format, TIFF files, and the OPEN

LOOK–specific PM format. (*xv*'s strength actually lies more in the variety of operations it can perform.)

So, I can fill my root window with an X pixmap of a tapir, a gentle animal that looks like a cross between a pig and an anteater:

```
val@ruby 17% xloadimage -onroot tapir.xpm
```

Figure 6-1 shows a tapir, which despite its pig-gone-awry appearance is actually a relative of the horse and rhino. Linda says a tapir looks like an animal a kid might make up using spare parts. Tapirs are native to tropical America, Malaysia, and Sumatra, and are as gentle in temperament as they are whimsical in appearance.

Figure 6-1: Pixmap of a tapir—one woman's root-window background

— *VQ*

6.05 *Changing Your Background Slowly*

floatbg

Can't decide what color to use for your root window *(6.02)*? Try out *floatbg*, which starts out with a randomly chosen color and then slowly changes it. In fact, it changes so slowly you shouldn't notice it. The color is changed every 10 seconds by the smallest, tiniest increment.

I started *floatbg* half an hour ago, and it was lavender. Now it's a shade that I can best describe as spring green.

—LM

6.06 *Let It Snow*

xsnow

Run the *xsnow* client and you'll be working in a winter wonderland. OK, I admit it: I'm a sap for this program. But give it a chance: you may be too. *xsnow* decorates your root window *(6.02)* with the cutest little green fir trees, then it starts an ever-so-gentle snowfall, which over time will pile up on top of your windows and icons. (In this case, refreshing your screen *(6.13)* is better than using a snowblower.) But my favorite part is Santa's sleigh, pulled by six tiny reindeer, cruising the sky. Due to popular demand, a recent patch provides one of the lead deer with a red nose.

You can specify a background color for all this activity by running *xsnow* with the *–bg* option. The default is a dullish gray. On my color screen, I run *xsnow* with a slate blue background—my idea of a night sky. The less impressive black-and-white image is shown in Figure 6-2.

xsnow also lets you specify the color of the trees (*–tc color*), the snow (*–sc color*), and the sleigh (*–slc color*). (A monochrome monitor really does not do *xsnow* justice.) Another interesting option is *–santa santa_size*, which lets you specify a small (*0*), medium (*1*), or large (*2*) Saint Nick. The default Santa is the middle-of-the-road size (*1*). With the jolly old man, I tend to think the bigger the better and always opt for *–santa 2*. When you set Santa size, the sleigh and reindeer are automatically resized proportionally. (Wouldn't want to tire the little guys out, after all.) It's difficult to appreciate Rudolf's nose at any but the largest size (full power!). You can also set *–santaspeed*; typical speeds are *1*, *2*, and *4*, which are the default speeds for santa size *0*, *1*, and *2*, respectively. (Admittedly, this is a little confusing.)

If you want to get fancy, you can regulate the speed and style of the snowfall, whether snow piles up on screen objects and how high. You can also specify *–notrees*, *–nosanta*, and *–norudolf*, though I wouldn't go without them. See the online manpage for more about options.

A Scroogey system administrator might take issue with the resources Santa requires. If you get into one of these sticky situations, keep in mind that a strong "Humbug!" goes a long way.

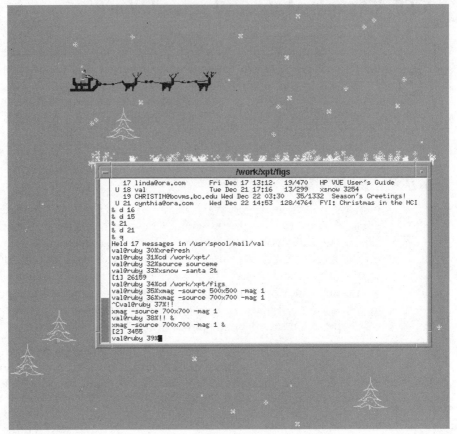

Figure 6-2: xsnow covers your windows while Santa covers the sky

To complete my little Christmas scene, I specify the star cursor as my root window pointer *(6.14)*:

```
% xsetroot -cursor_name star
```

Then I can leave it in the sky, or as my friend Clairemarie brilliantly suggested, place it on the top of one of the little trees. "May your days be merry and bright . . . . "

— VQ

6.07 *Where Your Mouse Goes a Cat Follows: oneko*

oneko is one of my favorite programs: a little cat that runs all over your screen chasing (what else) your mouse. To add to the realism, the root window pointer looks just like a little mouse. As soon as you move it, the kitty goes scrambling after.

oneko

The sensitive of heart should not be concerned. This cat and mouse game is just about as harmless as it could be. There's no "Wild Kingdom" moment where cat swallows mouse in the great outdoors. The very cute kitty simply runs where ever you drag the mouse and sits attentively nearby. If the pointer stays in one place for a few moments, the kitty gets bored and grooms himself. More than a few moments and the kitty yawns and falls asleep, complete with zzzzzz's. When you move the mouse again, the kitty shakes himself back to action and goes padding after. You can specify a striped cat using the *–tora* option (both neko and tora-neko are Japanese words to describe our feline friends). Figure 6-3 shows some of the action.

Figure 6-3: Screen kitty chases the mouse—to a point

The latest version of *oneko* attempts political correctness through species neutrality. In other words, if you'd prefer, you can have a dog chasing a bone. I think the bone cursor looks like a tiny dumbbell, but the dog is pretty cute. Use *–dog* to try it out. (I don't know what happened to the Japanese word for dog.) Figure 6-4 shows a satisfied pooch, with bone in sight.

Figure 6-4: Happy dog catches up with bone cursor

A minor caution: This program is too much fun to care a lot about system resources, but your system administrator might care a bit. Also, if you're obsessive about screen activity and run *oneko* and *xroach* (6.08) at the same time, the cat (or dog) will cripple the roaches, and the system will suffer a little more.

—VQ

6.08 The Electric Roaches

xroach

The *xroach* program lets you experience the joy of roach infestation in the comfort of your own screen. Watch as a small army of bitmap bugs scurry for cover behind windows and icons. Moving windows is the equivalent of turning on the kitchen lights; the roaches scramble for cover again.

The latest and (ahem) greatest version of *xroach* allows you to smush the little buggers using your pointer—if that's your idea of fun and if you can catch them. They run like the devil. To make them smushable, use the *–squish* option. To make them catchable, set a slower speed than the default 20, say 10.

```
% xroach -squish -speed 10 &
```

Click on a roach and you'll stop it dead in its tracks, and leave a savory little stain of "roach guts" to boot. In Figure 6-5, our crunchy little friend didn't make it to safety.

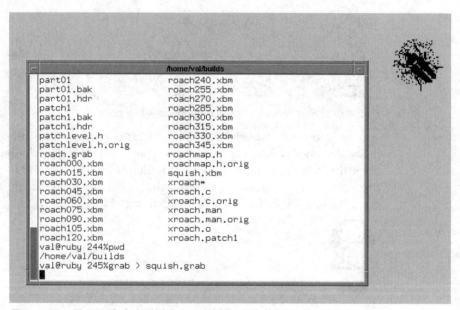

Figure 6-5: Roadkill on the information highway

The default colors for both the roaches and their (yuk) innards are black. To increase the quease factor, you can specify colors using *–rc* (roach color) and the memorable *–rgc* (roach-gut color). The program's creator, J.T. Anderson, recommends yellowgreen for the latter. Personally I'm in no hurry to test it.

xroach did come in handy recently for a particularly unappetizing joke, or so I hear. Here's the story: A friend of ours had scanned in some menus from local restaurants, saving us the terrible inconvenience of having to get out of our chairs to order lunch. Around this time, another (less fortunate) friend, let's call her Donna Woonteiler, encountered some flesh-and-blood roaches at one of these same local eateries. Well, someone, I can't quite remember who, sent this poor, already traumatized woman a GIF of the menu and then overran it with *xroach*. What some people won't do for a laugh. Ieeesh.[*]

— VQ

6.09 Phases of the Moon

xphoon

One of the earliest X exercises was *xphoon*, for showing the phase of the moon on your root window *(6.02)* as shown in Figure 6-6.

If you take a careful look, you'll see the dark side of the moon isn't completely black. This is because *xphoon* tries to calculate in the reflection from the Earth. You can disable the reflection using the *–b* command-line option.

Usually, *xphoon* will just display the moon on your root window and exit. If you use the *–t* option, however, *xphoon* continues running and updates the moon at a specified interval (in seconds). For example:

```
% xphoon -t 300 &
```

Starts *xphoon* running in the background, updating the root window every five minutes.

When I feel like being really silly, I combine *xphoon* with the *xancur* .XET N .XE1 "xancur command" ./XET .XET N .XE1 "animation" .XE2 "of cursor" ./XET cursor animator client *(6.16)*. *xancur* comes with a Star Trek animation, which shows the U.S.S. Enterprise shooting photon torpedos. Then I move my cursor around so that the Enterprise orbits the moon of Sol3.

— LM

6.10 Hello, World

xearth

Here's a nifty one. Just as *xphoon* *(6.09)* turns your root window into a picture of the moon, *xearth* turns your root window into a picture of the Earth (see Figure 6-7). It shows the portion of the Earth that's currently lit by the Sun, updating every five minutes.

You might think of *xearth* as showing what you would see if you were standing on the Sun.

---

[*] Since the roaches only run on the root window *(6.02)* proper, you would need to display the GIF file using *xloadimage (24.05)*, *xcsetroot (6.03)*, or a comparable program. The standard *xsetroot (6.02)* cannot handle GIF files.

Figure 6-6: Phase of the moon on the root window

Now, you may not always want to see the portion of the earth that's lit. Being an American, I can't come to terms with the idea of other parts of the Earth having sunlight when we don't (can't we just buy them off?). I'd rather just see my own fixed part of the world, darn it. So *xearth* also supports *–pos* command-line option, for specifying the latitude and longitude of a point that becomes the center of the display. Seeing how I must have skipped school when we learned basics about longitude and latitude, I got someone else to tell me that our latitude and longitude here in Boston are 42 and –72 respectively. So I tried:

```
% xearth -pos 42 -72
```

This gives me a pleasant picture of the world with me smack in the center of it, just the way I like it.

—LM

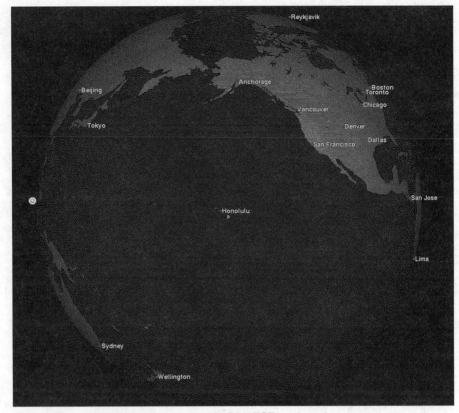

Figure 6-7: xearth at approximately 5:45 P.M. EST on June 9

6.11 Go Fish

If you have color and a lot of cycles to burn up, then you will probably go crazy over *xfishtank*. *xfishtank* turns your root window into an undersea utopia. Your screen takes on the hue of aquamarine, and little fish start swimming around (peacefully coexisting with your X windows). Bubbles float around in the deep blue sea.

xfishtank

Figure 6-8 shows a portion of the *xfishtank* background.

If you're a fan of After Dark (a popular screensaver *(6.18)* for unmentionable Other Operating Systems), then *xfishtank* will make you feel right at home.

— LM

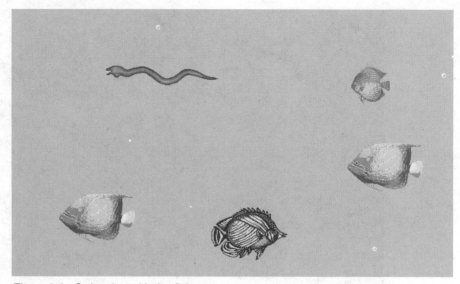

Figure 6-8: Swimming with the fishes

6.12 Flipping Out

xflip

Here are two of the classics. *flip* and *meltdown* are two programs that have always been popular among pranksters. *flip* literally flips your server across a vertical axis and then back again, with backwards characters on your windows and everything. *meltdown*, meanwhile, melts the windows on your server and then restores them.

These programs are most useful for running on someone else's display, and then watching them become horrified as they see their work being melted down before them. Of course, this only works if you have server access control *(19.12)* disabled....

—*LM*

6.13 Refreshing Your Screen

Sometimes it happens that a window (or maybe your entire root window) gets corrupted. This is common on workstations if the user hasn't used *xterm –C* or *xconsole (27.02)* to divert console messages. It's also likely to happen when running buggy or older clients. If this happens to you, try running the *xrefresh* command.

```
% xrefresh
```

This will redraw your screen and clean up any leftover debris. Many window managers also have a **Refresh** item on their root menu.

—LM

6.14 *Changing the Root Window Pointer*

Sick of moving the pointer across your root window *(6.02)* and seeing that same old tired X symbol? Longing to try something else, anything else, even if it's just another letter, say a nice Q? Well, *xsetroot* .XET N .XE1 "xsetroot command" .XE2 "changing root window pointer via" ./XET *(6.02)* can help.

You can change the shape of the root window pointer to one of the standard X cursor shapes or to any bitmap, using these options:

```
-cursor_name standard_cursor_name
-cursor cursorfile maskfile
```

The first option allows you to set the root window pointer to one of the standard cursor symbols. To view these symbols, you can display the cursor font using *xfd*, the X font displayer:

```
xfd -fn cursor &
```

The file *cursorfont.h* (generally found in the directory */usr/include/X11*) lists the names that correspond to the characters in the cursor font. To specify a standard cursor on a command line or in a resource file, strip the XC_ prefix from the name. Thus, to set the root window pointer to the pirate cursor symbol (a skull and crossbones!), you would enter:

```
% xsetroot -cursor_name pirate
```

The second *xsetroot* option:

```
-cursor cursorfile maskfile
```

allows you to set the root window pointer to a bitmap, perhaps one you create. The parameters *cursorfile* and *maskfile* are bitmaps. The *cursorfile* is the bitmap used for the pointer shape. In effect, the *maskfile* is placed behind the *cursorfile* bitmap to set it off from the root window.

For the *cursorfile*, you can use any of the standard bitmaps (generally found in */usr/include/X11/bitmaps*) or you can create a bitmap of your own using the *bitmap* editor *(22.03)*.

Every standard cursor has an associated mask, which appears next to it when you display the cursor font. If you are using your own bitmap as the *cursorfile*, you need to create a *maskfile* *(22.12)* to go with it.

Once you have the components of the cursor, a bitmap, and maskfile, you can specify it as the new pointer symbol. Here we have a cat cursor:

```
% xsetroot -cursor cat cat.mask
```

—VQ

6.15 *Hide That Pesky Cursor*

unclutter

Here's an unusual application that I've become a bit attached to: *unclutter* is based on the idea that sometimes your cursor gets in your way. For example, if you're editing in a window and you have to move your mouse to see what character it's hiding. What *unclutter* does is that it checks every few seconds to see if you've moved your mouse; if not, it makes it "invisible." The cursor comes back immediately when you move or click your pointer again.

—LM

6.16 *Cursor Animation*

Bored by the big "X" in your root window *(6.02)*? *xancur* is one of our all-time favorites: a cursor animator. It takes a set of bitmaps *(22.01)* and makes a movie out of it to replace your cursor. It also comes with a set of sample animations that are particularly amusing: my favorite is the smiley face sticking its tongue out.

Each animation is composed of a series of bitmap files. These bitmap files are listed in a simple script file that you invoke on the *xancur* command line. Each bitmap must have an accompanying mask file *(22.12)* (though these are not listed in the script).

xancur

To try out one of the existing animations, look at one of the sample animation directories, such as *happy2* in which the smiley face resides. Each animation directory contains bitmaps, masks, and scripts for running the animation (the scripts have the uninventive name *Script*). Make sure *xancur* is in your search path *(2.05)* and call one of the scripts. For example, I might do:

```
% xancur -script /usr/local/lib/X11/xancur/happy2/Script &
```

Your root window cursor should be a smiley face sticking its tongue out at you—over and over. (Admittedly, this can get tired.)

—LM

6.17 Making Your Own Cursor Movie

If you have the patience and inclination, you can create your own bitmap movie and use it as your root cursor using *xancur* (6.16). You can do this from scratch using the *bitmap* editor (22.03), but it's no small task to create a reasonable sequence of bitmap and mask files (22.12). Though you probably don't aspire to the same heights, Disney has an entire staff for jobs like this.

If you want a head start, you can appropriate a series of publicly available bitmaps from Anthony Thyssen's *AIcons* collection (22.17). His *movies* directory contains sequences of bitmaps that lend themselves to animation using *xancur*. Unfortunately, he does not provide mask files, so you'll still need to do some bitmap editing.

eyeball

We took a sequence of files showing an eyeball walking forward, to the left, backward, and to the right and put them in their own directory. In sequence, it seems like the eye-guy is dancing in a circle. Here's where the work comes in. There are 24 bitmaps in the series, so we created 24 mask files to match! (This is easier than it sounds.) Then we put the bitmap filenames in a *Script* file, in the following format:

```
# Cursor: dancing eyeball guy

eye_f1.xbm
eye_f2.xbm
eye_f3.xbm
eye_f4.xbm
eye_f5.xbm
eye_f6.xbm
eye_l1.xbm
eye_l2.xbm
eye_l3.xbm
eye_l4.xbm
eye_l5.xbm
eye_l6.xbm
eye_b1.xbm
eye_b2.xbm
eye_b3.xbm
eye_b4.xbm
eye_b5.xbm
eye_b6.xbm
eye_r1.xbm
eye_r2.xbm
eye_r3.xbm
eye_r4.xbm
eye_r5.xbm
eye_r6.xbm

# Eof
```

(The first and last lines are comments; the blank lines are for readability.) To get that eyeball going, run *xancur* with the *–script Script* command-line option. We can't do justice to this animation in our static illustrations, but here are four images, one from each segment of the eye-guy's dance:

Figure 6-9: Animated eyeball cursor

To shut the eyeball, you have to kill the process.

One caveat: We showed this program to some co-workers who use X terminals, and our system administrator came bounding in because of all the network traffic that *xancur* produces. If you run *xancur* over a network, remember that it produces continuous traffic and may clog things up for the rest of your site.

— VQ

6.18 *The Built-In Screensaver*

There are screensavers and there are screensavers. Way back in the no-frills days of computers, a screensaver just turned your screen blank. The idea was to prevent images from "burning in" on your screen overnight.

How naive we were. Commercial screensavers now make up an enormous share of the software market for Macintosh and PC computers. The commercial screensavers show amusing animated pictures on your screen, such as fish, flying toasters, cartoon characters, etc., clearly more entertaining than the blank screen. Although images remain on the screen, they move around enough to prevent burning in. This sort of screensaver may not actually prevent burn-in as well as just dimming the screen would, but you can't argue with success.

X has some programs you can use as screensavers, such as *xlock* (6.19), *xnlock* (6.20), and *xscreensaver* (6.22). However, your X server also has its own built-in screensaver, which usually just blanks your screen when it's been idle for a certain amount of time. If all you're interested in is in saving your precious phosphors, then the built-in screensaver is probably good enough—all you have to do is to make sure it's enabled.

You can control the server's built-in screensaver using the *xset* command with the s keyword. The screensaver is usually on by default, but if not, you can turn it on using the following command:

```
% xset s on
```

You can also change the timeout: the amount of time that the server should be idle before the screensaver activates. For example, to have the screensaver come on after a five-minute timeout instead of the default 10 minutes (300 seconds instead of 600 seconds), type:

```
% xset s 300
```

The screensaver also supports using a pattern instead of just a blank screen. However, the pattern is one that's built into the server; it isn't one the user has any control over. For most X servers, the pattern is the X logo symbol. To use the logo as your screensaver (against the background of your root window), type:

```
% xset s noblank
```

The pattern cycles every 10 minutes (600 seconds); that is, every 10 minutes it'll switch patterns. However, since the X logo is the only pattern it knows, all you get is the logo in a different size and position.

You can change the frequency that the pattern is changed by specifying a second number after the timeout. For example, the following line asks for a patterned screensaver to come on after five minutes and then cycle every minute:

```
% xset s noblank s 300 60
```

If you really miss having an animated picture, you can try setting a really low cycle (e.g., one second) and then watch the little X logo jump around like mad.

If you want to see your current *xset* settings, run it with the *q* keyword. In addition to the screensaver, *xset* also controls various other server parameters, such as keyboard and pointer control *(18.02, 18.03, 18.04)*, the bell sound *(6.24)*, etc. Look for the section on the screensaver:

```
% xset q
    ...
Screen Saver:
  prefer blanking: yes   allow exposures: yes
  timeout: 600   cycle:  600
    ...
```

To get back to the default settings, use *xset s default*.

—*LM*

6.19 xlock: Lock Your Server

xlock is an application you can use when you leave your desk or go to lunch. The idea is for it to prevent anyone from walking up to your server while you're away to read personal files, change your password, or send nasty messages to your boss. It also functions as a screensaver, preventing your precious pixels from burning out.

xlock

To start up *xlock*, just start it on the command line:

```
% xlock
```

xlock assumes you are using the local server (e.g., unix:0, or localhost:0). If you are using an X terminal or other remote server, you'll have to use the *–remote* command-line option:

```
% xlock -remote
```

The server is taken over by a screensaver. By default, the screensaver is *life*, which is based on Conway's game of life but just looks like a bunch of logos to the uneducated eye. You can change the screensaver using the mode resource, or using the *–mode* command-line option. There's a Pyro-type fireworks screensaver, a *swarm* mode, a *worm* mode, etc.

The screensavers are pretty cool, but my preference is "blank" (especially when I'm using a remote server, since network traffic and the load on machines being used by other people may be a concern).

```
% xlock -mode blank
```

To make this a default, I use the mode resource:

```
XLock.mode: blank
```

The screensaver continues to run until a key is pressed or the pointer is clicked. You are then prompted to type your password and **Return** to unlock the screen. If the password isn't typed within 30 seconds, *xlock* re-enables the screensaver. You can also start it again immediately by pressing on the icon to the left of the password prompt. By default, the key you use to get to the password prompt is ignored; you can use the *–usefirst* command-line option or usefirst resource to tell *xlock* to accept the first key you press as the first key of your typed password.

If you like, you can set up *xlock* to just act as a screensaver and not actually lock the screen, by using the *–nolock* command-line option.

Now for the caveats of *xlock*. *xlock* uses host-based access control (19.12) to disable connection from all hosts, restoring the previous list only when your password is entered and the lock is disabled. This means that if *xlock* is killed inelegantly, your host access control list isn't restored. It also means that if you have a server that won't allow remote clients to change the access control list (like most MIT-derived servers), you won't be able to use *xlock* remotely unless you use the *–allowaccess* command-line option or `allowaccess` resource, which disables *xlock*'s use of host-based access control. (Personally, I believe *xlock* should stay out of the access control business altogether, so I like to use *–allowaccess*.)

By default, *xlock* doesn't show anything as you type in your password. You can use the *–echokeys* command-line option or `echokeys` resource to have it show question marks (?) for each character you type. Beware that this may be considered a security risk (since anyone looking over your shoulder might see how many characters your password is, I suppose).

You can configure *xlock* to accept *root*'s password as well as your own using the *–allowroot* command-line option or `allowroot` resource. If you're comfortable with the idea of supplying your *root* password to a freeware program, then this gives your administrator a way to break your lock, without killing the program completely. However, some administrators may feel uneasy about supplying their *root* password in these circumstances. (For example, I could alter the *xlock* sources to email me the *root* password if supplied, and then run the altered version until an administrator finally falls for it.)

—LM

6.20 *Lock Your Server and Leave a Message: xnlock*

xnlock is another screen-locking program (like *xlock* (6.19)). The reason to use *xnlock* rather than *xlock* is if you want to leave a message on your screen.

xnlock

When you call up *xnlock*, the screen goes blank and a little cartoon character appears and starts walking around. Occasionally messages are shown (which are meant to be funny, with variable success). When you type a key or press the mouse button, you are prompted for your password; if you don't type the password correctly in 30 seconds, the prompt disappears and the little guy continues his meandering across your screen. A "countdown" shows you how many seconds you have left to type your password.

By default, *root*'s password may be typed instead of yours, so that an administrator might get ahold of your server in case of an emergency. You can override the default behavior by using the *–noar* command-line option or `xnlock.acceptRootPasswd` resource. As with *xlock*, however, administrators are likely to be wary of using the *root* password with *xnlock* (or should be).

If you like, you can set up *xnlock* as a screensaver only. If you use the *–ip* (ignore password) command-line option, pressing a key or mouse button stops *xnlock* without prompting for a password.

If you want to leave a particular message on the screen, you can specify it on the command line. This message is used instead of *xnlock*'s built-in witticisms.

You might use it to tell people looking for you that you're in a meeting:

```
% xnlock "I'm in the conference room"
```

You can also use the *–filename* command-line option for *xnlock* to take its message text from a particular file.

```
% xnlock -filename my.whereabouts
```

If no file is specified, the *–filename* option tells *xnlock* to read a message from *$HOME/.msgfile*.

Something I do is set up *xnlock* to tell people what time I left.

```
% echo "Left for lunch at 'date +%M:%M'" > ~/.msgfile
% xnlock -filename ~/.msgfile
```

You can make an alias for these commands, or enter them as a command to run from your window manager's root menu. (See Article 6.21 for an example.)

If you prefer, you can have the output of a program shown. This might be useful if you're just waiting for a particular event before you continue working. For example, if I'm waiting for a file to print, I might have *xnlock* check the print queue intermittently. This is much easier than stopping *xnlock* just to run *lpq* and then start *xnlock* again.

```
% xnlock -prog lpq
```

—LM

6.21 Different xnlock Messages

I have a *$HOME/.msgs* directory with my common *xnlock (6.20)* messages in it. To start *xnlock* with these messages, I created a window manager menu to call *xnlock* with the appropriate command-line options. Here is a simplified version my *twm* submenu *(12.24)* for *xnlock*:

```
Menu "NoseLock"
{
        "NoseLock"      !"xnlock -fg magenta -ar 'Nobodys home' &"
        "At Lunch"      !"xnlock -fg green -ar -f $HOME/.msgs/lunch &"
        "Conference"    !"xnlock -fg cyan -ar -f $HOME/.msgs/conf &"
        "Meeting"       !"xnlock -fg orange -ar -f $HOME/.msgs/mtg &"
        "Unavailable"   !"xnlock -fg blue -ar -f $HOME/.msgs/not_in &"
        "Vacation"      !"xnlock -fg red -ar -f $HOME/.msgs/vac &"
}
```

In addition to using the *–f* command-line option to call a different message for each situation, I also use different colors to help differentiate them (using the *–fg* command-line option *(17.06)*).

—MEO

6.22 A "Real" Screensaver

My complaint about programs like *xlock* and *xnlock* is that you have to call the program explicitly. I have a hard enough time remembering to bring my wallet when I go to lunch. I'm unlikely to remember to run a command every time I leave my desk.

xscreensaver

xscreensaver is another program that puts up a pretty picture when you go away. What puts *xscreensaver* a notch above the rest is that the screensaver automatically kicks in when you've been idle for a specified amount of time (say, 10 minutes or so). It can also be set up to lock your screen while you're away.

xscreensaver does this magic using a special server extension called XIDLE. If you don't have the XIDLE extension, then *xscreensaver* does it the hard way: by checking your keyboard and mouse for input, and activating when they've both been idle. Yes, this means network overhead, but it's effective. (A real screensaver extension is reportedly in the works, but *xscreensaver* doesn't use it yet.)

The first thing *xscreensaver* does is disable your server's built-in screensaver (6.18). A small icon might appear at the upper-left corner of your display; if so, you're in luck. We'll discuss the *xscreensaver* icon below.

Now just work as normal. When you leave your X server idle for a while (10 minutes usually), a pattern starts moving across your screen. The pattern changes after a specified cycle time (usually 10 minutes again). When you move your mouse or type a key, the pattern goes away and *xscreensaver* returns to dormant mode.

You can change the timeout (i.e., how long the server should be idle before the screensaver activates itself) using the *-timeout* command-line option or the timeout resource. You can also change the cycle time (i.e., how frequently *xscreensaver* switches to the next pattern) using the cycle command-line option.

If you want to lock the screen, use the *-lock* command-line option, or set the lock resource. Then when you try to disable the screensaver by pressing a key or moving the mouse, you're asked to type in your password instead.

Some users might see a small icon at the upper-left corner of their display while *xscreensaver* is dormant. This feature can't always be relied on, but if you see it, then you can use it to control *xscreensaver*. For example, you can "blank" or lock the screen immediately by clicking on the icon with the left or right mouse button. You can also use the middle mouse button to bring up a control menu for locking the screen, blanking, changing the timeout, etc.

Each of the screensaver modules are programs in their own right; they are built and installed as individual programs, and then the command-lines used to execute them are installed as resources. This means you can change what screensaver modules you use by setting some resources. The programs resource can be used to specify screensaver commands used by all machines, and then there are also the colorPrograms and monoPrograms resources for specifying screensavers for use on color or monochrome machines only. Each of these resource can have multiple commands listed (which will be cycled through by *xscreensaver*).

```
*programs:      qix -root                                              \n\
                attraction -root -mode splines -segments 300           \n\
                pyro -root                                             \n\
                rorschach -root -offset 7                              \n\
                slidescreen -root                                      \n\
                decayscreen -root                                      \n\
                flame -root                                            \n
```

Each line must call a command to run on the root window, and then end with \n, with another trailing backslash (\) for all but the last command. If you just copy the application defaults *(20.12)* file for *xscreensaver*, you should get the idea.

In my opinion, *xscreensaver* is the crème de la crème as far as X screensavers go. My biggest complaint is that the manpage is misleading (some might say wrong); it lists many command-line options that aren't supported yet, and gives the wrong application class name *(20.05)* (it should be XScreenSaver).

—*LM*

6.23   *The Best Screensaver of All*

A screensaver is great if you go away from your desk for a coffee break, but if you're going away overnight, it's usually better to turn your display off. The display is one of the biggest power consumers in any computer. If you care about the environment, don't waste that power showing pretty pictures to an empty room.

—*TOR*

6.24   *Controlling the Bell*

An audio bell—a beep sound that programs can use to warn users about anything from "end of file" to "you have new mail"—is standard equipment in X servers. The bell can be controlled through the *xset* command, using the *b* keyword.

The bell is on by default in most cases, but if you need to turn it on, type:

    % xset b on

To turn it off:

    % xset b off

On some servers, the volume of the bell can be altered. You might also be able to change the pitch and the duration of the bell. Three numbers are accepted as parameters to *xset b*:

    xset b *volume pitch duration*

The volume can be given on a scale of 0 to 100, with 0 equivalent to turning the bell off. The pitch is specified in terms of Hz, and the duration is specified in milliseconds. For each of these values, the special value *–1* can also be specified, which means to return to the default. If you only want to change the volume, you can omit the other numbers:

    xset b 75

To see your current settings, use *xset q*. In addition to the audio bell, *xset* also controls various other server parameters, such as keyboard and pointer control *(18.02, 18.03, 18.04)* and the server's built-in screen saver *(6.18)*. Look for the line concerning the bell parameters:

    % xset q
        ...
        bell percent: 50   bell pitch: 400   bell duration: 100
        ...

—*LM*

6.25 *Playing Audio CDs*

If you have a CD-ROM drive attached to your workstation, then check out *xmcd*. *xmcd* is a program for driving audio compact disks on your CD-ROM drive. You can then use earphones to listen to the CD. (Sorry, there's no way to play them over your workstation's speakers—not yet, at least.)

xmcd

Installing *xmcd* requires a little bit of work. First of all, *xmcd* needs to be installed by *root* in order to be able to mount and read the CD. Next, you need to configure it with some information about your CD-ROM drive. If you know nothing about CD-ROM drives (like me!), don't fret, in many cases all you need is a make and model number, or at least a good guess.

The features that *xmcd* supports depend on your CD-ROM drive. However, most CD-ROM drives will allow it to play CDs, stop, rewind and fast forward, use repeat play, shuffle play, sampling, and eject. You can also press the keypad button, which brings up a small window allowing you to select a track by number. The *xmcd* window appears in Figure 6-10.

Figure 6-10: Playing an audio CD

There are a few other X-based CD players out there, but what I like about *xmcd* is that it looks (to me) like a automotive CD panel. However, *xmcd* is also considerate enough to display English labels rather than icons over the buttons (just press the upper-left button, with the letter A). This comes in very useful for people like me, who are not particularly gifted in icon recognition.

Now here's my favorite part. If you looked carefully at Figure 6-10, you might notice that the title of the CD appears beneath the track display. This information comes from a special "CD Database" maintained by *xmcd* (with a little help from you, of course). If you press the button that looks like a file cabinet, you bring up the CD Database entry for the current CD (if any). Figure 6-11 shows an example database entry.

The way this works is that *xmcd* calculates an identification string for each CD pressing (in hexadecimal, it seems), and then looks for a file in the database describing it. Using this feature, you can enter the artist, title, and names of the tracks for any of your favorite CDs, and *xmcd* maintains this information for you.

xmcd_cddb

In fact, if you want to be lazy about it, you can start by downloading the *cddb* database that is distributed alongside *xmcd*. This database contains hundreds of CDs already entered into database format by other users. Even I found a few of my CDs listed, and I have weird taste.

If the database doesn't recognize your CD immediately (in which case all the titles come up as question marks), try pressing the **Link** button on the database window (which appears shaded in the figure). *xmcd* will let you browse through the database entries (mercifully showing you only likely candidates, i.e., other CDs with the same number of tracks). If you find your CD and select it, then *xmcd* automatically links the entry and installs it under the new name as well as the old one.

If you don't find your CD, you can look on the back of the CD case and type in the title and tracks. You can also enter additional information about each track or about the CD in general (by pressing the **Ext Info...** buttons). Press **Save** when you're happy with the CD database information, and you're all set.

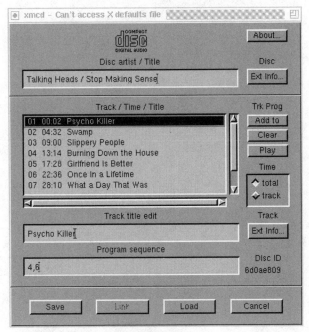

Figure 6-11: A CD database entry

xmcd will recognize the CD from now on, as soon as you pop it into the CD-ROM drive. Not only does the main *xmcd* window show the CD title and track name, you can also use the Database window to select tracks, by just double-clicking on the name of the song. (It's much easier when you don't have to remember that "Here Comes the Sun" is track number 7 on *Abbey Road*.)

And now here's the neat part: you can program the CD by either writing in comma-separated track numbers in the **Program Sequence** window, or just selecting tracks in and pressing the **Add to** button. This program can then be saved in the database file, so that every time you listen to the CD, you can listen to just the songs you like. Just bring up the database window again and press the **Play** button there. This way, you can avoid "Mary, Queen of Arkansas" every time you listen to your otherwise-favorite Springsteen CD.

—LM

Part Three

Working with Applications

Read any computer magazine and you'll see industry leaders talking about open systems, distributed computing, threads, MIS, API, RISC, SPARC, MIPS, and other popular industry buzzwords. But ask users what they want, and you'll find out that all most people care about is having applications that work.

We want to emphasize that this is an X book for users. So once you're reasonably competent in X, we want to make sure you know what you could be using it for.

—LM

7

X-Based Mailers

7.01 Email on a UNIX System

If you ask people what they use a computer for, practically everyone will include email on their list of things they use every day. Many X users continue to use text-based mailers for email, but that's more a function of habit rather than opportunity: there are many X-based mailers available, many of which are publicly available. This chapter not only covers X-based mail programs, but also what we call mail accessories (like *xbiff (7.10)*).

Before we talk about X-based mailers, though, it helps to hear some background on how email works on a UNIX system.

On UNIX, incoming email is directed to a file named after your login name, in a systemwide spool directory such as */usr/spool/mail* or */var/spool/mail*. For example, my login name is *lmui*, and my incoming mail folder is */usr/spool/mail/lmui*. As new mail comes in for me, the mail is appended to the spool file. This file is also called your system mailbox, and is readable and writable only by you. It is an ASCII file —that is, you can open it with an editor or use commands like *more* to look at it (although if you use an editor, make sure not to write the file!).

Mail is managed by a systemwide daemon that processes new mail and distributes them to the correct mail folders. The program used on most sites is called *sendmail*, but you should never have to deal with it (and be thankful for that!)

To read your mail, most systems have a basic, no-frills mailer installed as */bin/mail*. This is the original mailer from Very Old UNIX, and it's pretty hideous. You can recognize it from its question-mark prompt (?) and general unfriendliness. Many systems, then, have another version of *mail* installed, which is based on Berkeley (BSD) mail. This mailer is sometimes installed under the name *mailx, Mail*, and often just as */usr/ucb/mail* (*ucb* stands for

University of California at Berkeley). BSD *mail* is more powerful than /bin/mail, and can be recognized from its ampersand prompt (&).

Then there are other mail programs, mostly from the public domain—such as *mush* and *elm*. What these programs have in common with original *mail* and BSD *mail* is that they are monolithic: you enter the program, read your mail, and then have to quit out of it before you return to your shell prompt. When you enter the program, it reads the system mail folder, and when you quit, it rewrites the mail folder (noting which messages you had read, deleted, etc.) To avoid overwriting mail messages that came in while you were reading your mail, some of these programs are smart enough to monitor your mail file and submit new messages to you as they come in, and others are just careful not to overwrite new messages when you quit.

Another publicly available mailer program is distributed under the name MH. MH is not just a single program, however, but a set of programs that run independently. The idea is that you can read, delete, save, and forward messages directly from the command line, without having to quit out of a mailer to access the command line for other purposes. MH reads files from your system mail file, but then it doesn't return them there, but saves them in a subdirectory of your home directory (usually *$HOME/Mail*).

We're telling you all this because each of the X mailers we include here is really just a front-end to other UNIX mail programs. For example, *xmail* (7.02) and *xmailtool* (7.03) are front-ends to BSD mail. *xmh* (7.06) and *exmh* (7.07) are front-ends to MH.

—LM

7.02 A Simple Mail Application: xmail

xmail is a program for reading and sending mail messages. It's not as polished as some commercial mail readers, but it gets the job done.

xmail

As seen in Figure 7-1, *xmail* gives you a listing of your messages in the top half of the window, with individual messages in the bottom half of the window. In between are *command buttons* for reading, saving, or sending messages. You can use scrollbars to move among screenfuls of message headers or to browse through a long mail message.

At first glance, *xmail* looks like a no-frills mailer, with few functions. However, if you hold down the third mouse button on each of the command buttons, a menu comes up with alternate options. For example, if you press the **read** button with the first mouse button, then the selected message appears in the bottom field of the window. However, if you hold down the third mouse button

```
  xmail                                                                    
  xmail 1.4 - "/usr/spool/mail/lmui": 20 messages 1 unread
      5 len@ruby.ora.com     Fri Apr  9 12:41    29/1223   rcsoelim "bug," not reall
      6 eap@ora.com          Thu May  6 13:20    26/780    Re:  internet talk radio
      7 eap@ora.com          Fri May 28 17:03    59/2004   cd procedure
      8 tim@ora.com          Sat May 29 10:41   137/5689   Sales Department Reorgani
      9 len@ora.com          Tue Jun  1 15:51    29/860    gsed vs sed what? oi!
     10 len@ora.com          Tue Jun  1 16:37    28/634    more on gsed failure
     11 afx@ibm.de           Fri Jun 11 14:20    42/1736   Re: X Power Tools book
     12 ahmed@asc.slb.com    Fri Jun 11 19:31    52/2064   Question on X Administrat
     13 jerry@ora.com        Sun Jun 13 11:10    47/1611   Change to getXheads scrip
     14 eap@ora.com          Mon Jun 14 13:41    20/642    UPT CD
     15 john@ora.com         Mon Jun 14 14:37    47/1956   Re:  Vol8 purchasers
     16 jerry@ora.com        Mon Jun 14 16:44    24/635    File to fix
     17 lark                 Mon Jun 14 17:28    78/2898   Online Internet Resource
     18 jeff@mousse.rtr.COM  Tue Jun 15 17:15    36/1387   Re: MH?
     19 eap@ora.com          Tue Jun 15 18:15    18/563    zmail
  >  20 root                 Wed Jun 16 08:39    22/668    editor saved ``articles/0

                Use <Shift><Middle-Mouse-Button> for help on any window

   [ read ]    [ save ]   [ Folder ]  [ copy ]  [ preserve ]  [ delete ]  [ Newmail ]  [ quit ]

   [ Print ]   [ Send ]   [ reply ]   [ File: _                                              ]

  Message 20:
  From root Wed Jun 16 08:39:09 1993
  Return-Path: <root>
  Received: by ora.com (5.65c/Spike-2.1)
          id AA00494; Wed, 16 Jun 1993 08:39:08 -0400
  Date: Wed, 16 Jun 1993 08:39:08 -0400
  From: root (The Great Humongous)
  Message-Id: <199306161239.AA00494@ora.com>
  Subject: editor saved ``articles/0092''
  Apparently-To: lmui
  Status: RO

  You were editing the file "articles/0092"
  at <Tue Jun 15 18:26> on the machine ``ruby''
  when the system went down.

  You can retrieve most of your changes to this file
  using the "recover" command of the editor.
  An easy way to do this is to give the command "vi -r articles/0092".
  This method also works using "ex" and "edit".

  "ex" and "edit".
```

Figure 7-1: Reading mail with xmail

on **read**, you see a menu giving you a choice between the next message, the previous message, and seeing the full header of the current message (see Figure 7-2).

The menu also tells you how to access the item without bringing up the entire menu, e.g., if you hold down the **Shift** key while you click the first mouse button on **read**, this is equivalent to pulling down **next** under **read**.

Most commands also have keystroke equivalents as well. You can get this listing by pressing the question mark.

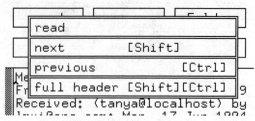

Figure 7-2: The read menu under xmail

a	REPLY to all recipients	A	REPLY to all included
c	COPY a message	C	COPY to Author file
d	DELETE the message	u	UNDELETE a message
f	READ with full headers	F	FORWARD a message
m	MAIL a message	M	REPLY to a message
i	incorporate NEW MAIL	N	retrieve NEW MAIL
p	read PREVIOUS message	P	PRINT a message
r	READ the message	R	REPLY included
s	SAVE current message	S	SAVE to author
n	read the NEXT message	w	WRITE current message
q	QUIT, committing changes	x	EXIT, no commits
?	DISPLAY this help info	>LF>	REMOVE this help info

To compose a new message, press the **Send** button, or press reply to reply to the currently selected message. This gives you an *xterm* window *(2.02)* running *vi* for composing a message. If you prefer to use an editor other than *vi* for your messages (and who wouldn't!), you can set the editorCommand resource, or use the *–editorCommand* command-line option. The editorCommand resource is written as a command string, but with *sprintf*-style %s codes that *xmail* substitutes with the display name and the name of the temporary mail edit buffer (respectively). For example, if I wanted to use *xedit*, I might define the following resource:

```
XMail*editorCommand:    xedit -display %s %s
```

When you're done editing a mail message, *xmail* presents you with the message header to edit, as shown in Figure 7-3. You can use this window to change the **To:** line, **Subject:** line, **Cc:** line, or **Bcc:** line. You can press **ReEdit** to edit the message body again before you send it. When you're satisfied with the message, press **Send**; you might also press **Cancel** to cancel the message. (The message body is saved in *$HOME/dead.letter*).

If you iconify *xmail*, the icon shows a closed mailbox with the flag down. When new mail arrives, a beep sounds and the icon changes to an open mailbox with the flag up and a letter poking out. When you open *xmail* again, the **Newmail** button is highlighted. You can press it to read the new message.

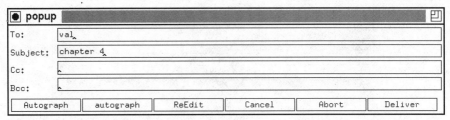

Figure 7-3: xmail send window

xmail automatically updates the mail folder if you quit *xmail*, if you switch to another folder, or if you just iconify the *xmail* window. To quit without saving your changes, pull down the quit menu using the third mouse button and select exit (or just hold down the Shift key while clicking on the quit window).

—LM

7.03 A Mailer Based on BSD Mail: xmailtool

xmailtool is similar to *xmail (7.02)*, but it is a little more powerful (in my opinion). Like *xmail*, *xmailtool* has a split-window display: the top of the window shows the list of messages, the bottom of the window shows the message text, and in between is a series of action buttons.

xmailtool

At the top of the *xmailtool* window is a set of four buttons representing what action to take when a message is selected (see Figure 7-4). When *xmailtool* starts up, the default action is to show the message, which is what you usually want.

To display the message text, just select it and the message body appears in the bottom half of the window.

If you press on Delete Message, Save Message, or Preserve Message as the action, then any messages you select will be (you guessed it) deleted, saved, or preserved. This is easier than *xmail* for dealing with multiple messages, e.g., if you wanted to delete several messages in *xmail*, you would have to repeatedly press Delete and then select the message you want to delete. With *xmailtool*, you can do it this way using the delete button in the middle of the window, but if you select the default mouse action to Delete Message then you can just quickly click on messages you want to get rid of.

(Notice that this might also become a problem if you get confused and delete messages you were hoping to read. Just press undelete to restore the previous deleted message. You can press undelete repeatedly until no messages are left to be restored.)

You can scroll through messages and select them to show, delete, save, or preserve. You can also do searches by pressing CTRL-S to bring up the search

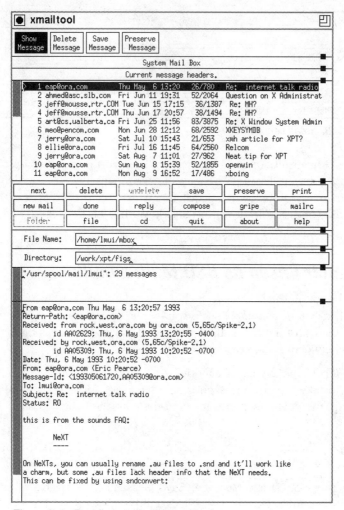

```
┌───────────────────────────────────────────────────────────────┐
│ ● xmailtool                                                  ▣ │
│ ┌─────┐┌──────┐┌──────┐┌────────┐                              │
│ │Show ││Delete││Save  ││Preserve│                              │
│ │Message││Message││Message││Message│                          │
│ └─────┘└──────┘└──────┘└────────┘                              │
│                      System Mail Box                           │
│                   Current message headers.                     │
│ ▷  1 eap@ora.com      Thu May  6 13:20   26/780   Re:  internet talk radio │
│    2 ahmed@asc.slb.com Fri Jun 11 19:31  52/2064  Question on X Administrat │
│    3 jeff@mousse.rtr.COM Tue Jun 15 17:15 36/1387 Re: MH?      │
│    4 jeff@mousse.rtr.COM Thu Jun 17 20:57 38/1494 Re: MH?      │
│    5 art@cs.ualberta.ca Fri Jun 25 11:56  83/3875 Re: X Window System Admin │
│    6 meo@pencom.com    Mon Jun 28 12:12  68/2592  XKEYSYMDB    │
│    7 jerry@ora.com     Sat Jul 10 15:43  21/653   xmh article for XPT? │
│    8 ellie@ora.com     Fri Jul 16 11:45  64/2560  Relcom       │
│    9 jerry@ora.com     Sat Aug  7 11:01  27/962   Neat tip for XPT │
│   10 eap@ora.com       Sun Aug  8 15:39  52/1855  openwin      │
│   11 eap@ora.com       Mon Aug  9 16:52  17/486   xboing       │
│ ┌──────┐┌──────┐┌────────┐┌──────┐┌────────┐┌──────┐          │
│ │ next ││delete││undelete││ save ││preserve││print │          │
│ └──────┘└──────┘└────────┘└──────┘└────────┘└──────┘          │
│ ┌──────┐┌──────┐┌──────┐┌────────┐┌──────┐┌──────┐            │
│ │new mail││done ││reply ││compose ││gripe ││mailrc│            │
│ └──────┘└──────┘└──────┘└────────┘└──────┘└──────┘            │
│ ┌──────┐┌──────┐┌──────┐┌────────┐┌──────┐┌──────┐            │
│ │Folder││ file ││  cd  ││  quit  ││about ││ help │            │
│ └──────┘└──────┘└──────┘└────────┘└──────┘└──────┘            │
│ File Name:   /home/lmui/mbox                                   │
│                                                                │
│ Directory:   /work/xpt/figs                                    │
│                                                                │
│ "/usr/spool/mail/lmui": 29 messages                            │
│                                                                │
│                                                                │
│ From eap@ora.com Thu May  6 13:20:57 1993                      │
│ Return-Path: <eap@ora.com>                                     │
│ Received: from rock.west.ora.com by ora.com (5.65c/Spike-2.1)  │
│       id AA02629; Thu, 6 May 1993 13:20:55 -0400               │
│ Received: by rock.west.ora.com (5.65c/Spike-2.1)               │
│       id AA05309; Thu, 6 May 1993 10:20:52 -0700               │
│ Date: Thu, 6 May 1993 10:20:52 -0700                           │
│ From: eap@ora.com (Eric Pearce)                                │
│ Message-Id: <199305061720.AA05309@ora.com>                     │
│ To: lmui@ora.com                                               │
│ Subject: Re:  internet talk radio                              │
│ Status: RO                                                     │
│                                                                │
│ this is from the sounds FAQ:                                   │
│                                                                │
│       NeXT                                                     │
│       ----                                                     │
│                                                                │
│ On NeXTs, you can usually rename .au files to .snd and it'll work like │
│ a charm, but some .au files lack header info that the NeXT needs. │
│ This can be fixed by using sndconvert:                         │
└───────────────────────────────────────────────────────────────┘
```

Figure 7-4: Reading mail with xmailtool

window, entering a string, and pressing **Search**. The next message containing the specified string is displayed in the message box. The **search** window remains open, so you can just keep pressing the **Search** button to view all messages on a particular topic, or all messages from a single sender.

The buttons directly underneath the header listing are self-explanatory (literally). By placing the pointer on top of a command button, a help message appears near the top of the window. If this annoys you as much as it does me, you can turn it off using the +*autoHelp* command-line option, or setting the autoHelp resource to False.

Many of the buttons have **Shift** equivalents. That is, when you hold down the **Shift** key, the button takes a new meaning. Some of these new meanings are meant to parallel behavior in BSD mail, such as for the **reply** button. If you hold down the **Shift** key, the **reply** button toggles between responding to the sender or responding to all recipients. Similarly, holding down **Shift** on the **compose** button changes it to **forward**; holding down **Shift** on the **next** button changes it to **prev**; holding down Shift on the **quit** button changes it to **abort**, which means to quit without saving; and holding down Shift on the **save** button makes it **Save** (we'll explain more about this last one in Article 7.04).

—*LM*

7.04   *Using Folders in xmailtool*

In your *$HOME/.mailrc* file, you can set a `folder` variable to a directory containing mail folders. For example, I use *$HOME/Mail*, so I enter the following line into *$HOME/.mailrc*:

```
set folder=Mail
```

(The folder is assumed to be relative to your home directory.)

If the `folder` variable is set, I can get a listing of that directory in *xmailtool* (7.03) by pressing the **Folder** button. Once in this listing, I can save the current message to a file by holding down the **Shift** key while selecting a filename. I can change the mailbox file name to this file by holding down the **CTRL** key while selecting a filename. This is useful if you intend to save several messages to the same file, since it means you don't have to bring up the **Folder** window every time (this can take a while if you have a large folder directory like mine).

If you just select the filename without either the **Shift** or **CTRL** key pressed, the current mail folder is saved, and the selected file is taken as the new mail folder. You can switch back by pressing the **Return To System Folder** button at the top of the **Folder** window.

Underneath the command buttons are input fields for specifying a filename and directory name. The filename is used for the default mailbox file (generally *$HOME/mbox*), in which messages are placed if you select **save** via the command buttons. You can also press the **file** button to switch the folder to the mailbox file (and then toggle back again by pressing **file** a second time). This is useful for quickly examining saved messages.

Using the directory field is another way you might work with folders. For example, instead of using *$HOME/mbox* as a catch-all message file, I like to save mail messages in a *$HOME/Mail* directory, in folders named after the topic or after the person who sent the mail. What I do is set the directory to

/home/lmui/Mail and then press **cd** to change to that directory. After that, I can save messages by placing the filename in the **File Name:** field and pressing **Save**.

The **Save** button (which you get by pressing **Shift** on the **Save** button) places messages in a file named after the person who sent the mail. If you have a large folder directory (like I do), this is faster than bringing up the folder window for saving files. (This feature depends on your BSD mailer supporting the **Save** functionality.)

—*LM*

7.05 *Composing Messages in xmailtool*

One of the ways that *xmailtool (7.03)* exceeds *xmail (7.02)* is in sending messages. In composing a new message or replying to someone else's message, *xmailtool* puts you in an editor buffer containing *To:*, *Subject:*, and *Cc:* fields, and your *.signature* file appended. It uses the editor specified in your EDITOR variable in *$HOME/.mailrc* (*not* the EDITOR environment variable). The best part is that if you don't have EDITOR specified in *$HOME/.mailrc*, then *xmailtool* uses the standard text widget, which is just fine for most mail messages, and certainly easier for new users. The initial composition window is shown in Figure 7-5.

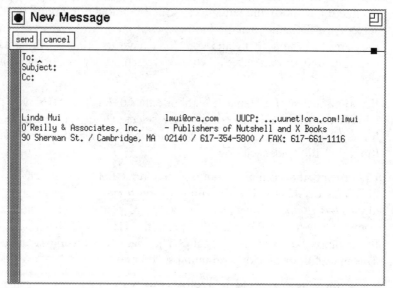

Figure 7-5: Editing a new message in xmailtool

When you're done editing the message, you can just press **send**, or, if you reconsider sending the message, **cancel**. This is much easier and more intuitive than the way *xmail* handles new messages. If you have EDITOR set in

$HOME/.mailrc, then you finish by exiting your editor as usual; you are then presented with a text buffer asking you to confirm the text (and edit as needed).

From the text window, you can start a line with some of the `tilde` escapes supported by BSD mail *(7.01)*. For example, you can enter ~f (for forward) and have the body of the current message inserted. You can enter ~v to enter *vi*.

One more thing: by default, *xmailtool* assumes that if you specify your own editor, it's a text-based editor and needs to be started within an *xterm (2.02)* window. This is what you want if your editor is *vi* or regular *emacs*, but not if your editor is *xedit (9.03)* or some other X-based editor. If you want to use an X-based editor, you'll need to set the `edit_needs_xterm` variable to 0 in *$HOME/.mailrc*:

```
set edit_needs_xterm=0
```

There are more features, but that should do it for now to get you interested in *xmailtool*.

—*LM*

7.06 *Why Use xmh for Your Email?*

The mail agent called *xmh* comes with the X distribution from the X Consortium; there's a good chance that it's on your system. But the email package underneath *xmh*, called MH, isn't installed on a lot of systems.[*] Also, MH stores email in a different way than most mail agents do: MH stores each message in a separate file. Once you start using MH, you can't switch back to another mailer without doing a little work.

"Hmmm," you're probably asking now, "should I bother with *xmh*?" I was hoping you'd ask. :-)

Do you get a lot of email and need powerful mail-handling features? Do you want to be able to do nontraditional things with your email, such as combining it with an appointment system, using it as a database, or processing it automatically?

MH lets you do that. The *xmh* interface gives you access to a lot of MH features and lets you define new buttons to run custom commands. (If you need MH features that aren't available from *xmh*, you can run them in an *xterm (2.02)* window.)

MH is a modular email system. Instead of One Big Program, MH is a group of separate programs. One program lists the messages in a mail folder, another program moves messages between folders, and so on. Each of those

---

[*] If your system doesn't have MH, your system administrator can get it by anonymous FTP from *ftp.ics.uci.edu* in the directory *pub/mh*.

programs can be configured, or replaced with your own version written as a UNIX shell script, Perl or C program, or other executable. If there isn't an MH command to do what you want, you can write a new one. You can handle your mail exactly the way you need to; you don't need to put up with an email system that doesn't do quite what you want.

You don't need to customize *xmh* before you use all of its built-in features, though. In fact, *xmh* hides the MH commands from you with a normal-looking X interface of buttons and menus. But the flexibility and power are there if you need them.

I won't try to cover all of the *xmh* features in this article. For nitty-gritty details on MH, try the Nutshell Handbook *MH & xmh: E-mail for Users & Programmers* by Jerry Peek (O'Reilly & Associates Inc.). Your online *xmh*(1) manpage also has a lot of information.

I'll start with a diagram of the main *xmh* window. See Figure 7-6. Next, let's look at a few of the *xmh* (and MH) features you won't find in most other mailers.

Folders and Subfolders

Most mail systems let you separate mail messages into folders. In those mail systems, people with lots of mail can get a confusing mess of hundreds of folders: when a user wants to find a folder, she has to read through a really long list of folder names. To reduce the number of top-level folders, *xmh* lets you divide your folders into subfolders. (MH lets you make sub-subfolders, and sub-sub-subfolders, and so on. *xmh* stops at one level of subfolders, which is enough for almost everyone!)

For example, let's say you manage ten computer systems and you want to keep mail folders about the errors on each system. Instead of making ten top-level mail folders, you could make a top-level folder named *syserrs* and a subfolder for each of the ten systems. Figure 7-7 shows the top part of the *xmh* main window, the buttons for four top-level folders, and the menu that drops down when a folder has subfolders. (Showing all ten subfolders is a little wasteful, so I just show four.)

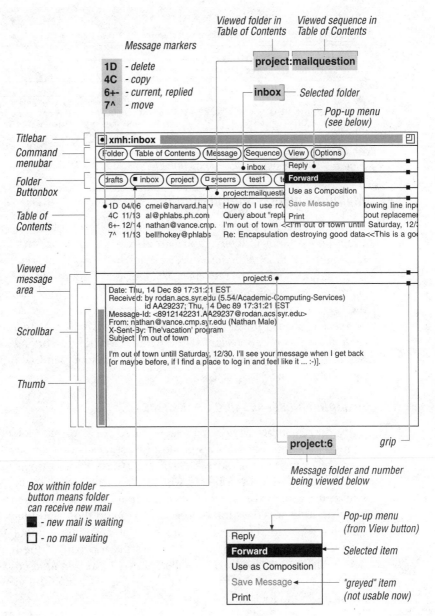

Figure 7-6: Anatomy of xmh

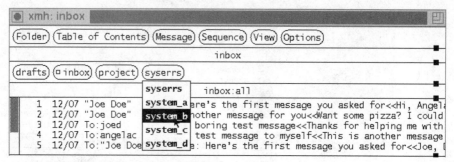

Figure 7-7: The syserr folder and subfolders

Multiple Folders, Multiple Drafts

If you need to use messages from two or more mail folders at the same time, that's no problem in *xmh*. You can also work on more than one outgoing message at a time. For instance, you might be working on a status report, hunting and combining messages from several folders. In the middle of the status report, you realize that you also need to reply to a message in one of the folders you're viewing. No sweat: just pop up a second composition window. If you don't finish the draft messages, *xmh* will save them for you in its draft folder; you can restart *xmh* anytime and keep working on the drafts. Figure 7-8 shows a draft message, the draft folder window, and two other open folder windows.

Grouping Messages into Sequences

xmh can remember certain messages in each of your mail folders and give a name to those messages. This group of messages is called a *sequence*. Whenever you want to find those messages, just ask *xmh* to open that sequence; the window's table of contents will list only the messages in the sequence. You can keep many sequences in each folder. The sequences are saved between *xmh* sessions for as long as you keep those messages in the folder (though you can remove the sequences at any time without removing the messages themselves). Figure 7-9 shows the top part of the main *xmh* window with its **Sequence** menu pulled down. The *mailquestions* sequence is active (notice the check mark), but I'm about to change the view to show all messages in the folder.

An especially easy way to make sequences is with the **Pick** window explained in the next section.

Figure 7-8: Multiple compositions

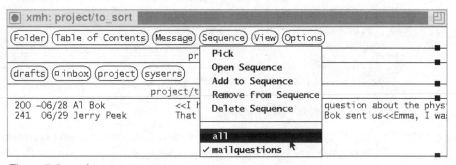

Figure 7-9: xmh sequence menu

Searching for Messages

Some mailers let you search through folders to find a message from a particular user, or a message containing some particular word. *xmh* uses the powerful MH *pick* command. You can search by any header (To:, Subject:, and many more) or search entire messages. The messages Pick finds are added to a sequence (see the previous section of this article).

Take a look at Figure 7-10. I'm looking for messages from John to Alison, or from Mona to Zelda. *xmh* will add the messages it finds to the sequence named *temp*. The **Skip** buttons let you negate a search (find messages that don't match something). The **Or** buttons let you choose more possible matches.

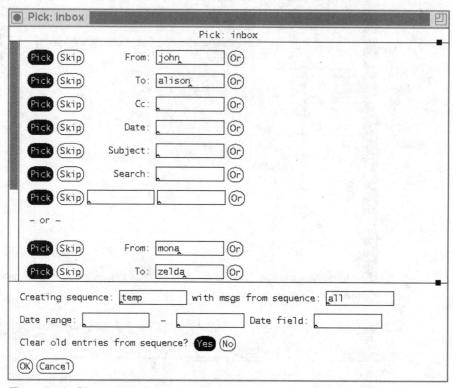

Figure 7-10: Pick and choose messages

Using Custom Commands

xmh lets you make one or many new buttons and bind commands to them. The commands can be *xmh* commands or any UNIX command. To get started, you add an entry like this to your X resource file *(17.03)*:

```
Xmh*CommandButtonCount:5
```

That says "make five new buttons" and gives them the boring names **button1**, **button2**, etc. (Of course, you can change the names on the buttons.) The buttons go under the table of contents, as you can see in Figure 7-11.

Maybe you have a FAX system on your computer, and you'd like to be able to send mail messages to your Miami office by FAX. You could add a new button labeled **FAX Miami**. When you click on it with mouse button 1 (for example), it will run the UNIX command `sendfax 1-305-555-2368`. The full pathnames of

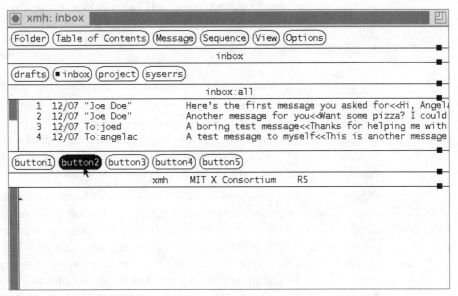

Figure 7-11: Newly created buttons

the message(s) you select in the table of contents will be added to the end of the command. Just add the following lines to your X resource file:

```
Xmh*CommandButtonCount:1
Xmh*commandBox.button1.label: FAX Miami
Xmh*commandBox.button1.translations: #override\
  <Btn1Down>,<Btn1Up>: XmhShellCommand(sendfax 1-305-555-2368) unset()
```

—*JP, from the Nutshell Handbook* MH & xmh: E-mail for Users & Programmers

7.07 *Another MH Mailer: exmh*

Do you get a lot of email? Want a more powerful email program? Since the early 1980s, UNIX users who need an extremely flexible email system have chosen MH. But the MH command-line interface isn't always easy to use. *xmh* *(7.06)*, a user interface to MH, comes in the X distribution. The *xmh* interface is limited, though, and can be hard to customize.

exmh

A hot new program, *exmh*, has a window that looks something like *xmh*. But *exmh* has many more great features.

- MIME multimedia mail: rich text, sound, graphics and video. A graphical interface to the MH folder system (see Figure 7-13 below) makes it easy to find folders, subfolders, sub-subfolders....

- A Preferences menu to customize many *exmh* features.

- Mail folder processing can be much faster under *exmh*. *exmh* saves its state: when you restart, you'll be back where you left off.

- and much more.

exmh is written in Tcl/Tk *(30.01)*, and it has been designed to be easily customized by users. It supports a per-user library of customized Tcl routines, and per-user definitions of buttons and menus via X resources. So it's easy to customize. And if you can't make *exmh* do something (for example: combining your email with an appointment system, using email as a database, processing it automatically) you can make it happen by writing standard UNIX scripts (shell, Perl, cron *(27.08)*, and so on) to interface with plain MH.

Figure 7-12 shows *exmh* version 1.3 handling a folder with sample MIME messages. The top pane has a button for each of your top-level mail folders; nested folders have a drop shadow. The middle pane is a summary of the folder contents. The bottom pane shows a message. This multipart MIME message has rich text (notice the Italic font), an external body part (a graphic that exmh can fetch with anonymous FTP) and an audio message. After clicking the third mouse button next to the audio part, a new menu of choices appears. (The graphic isn't shown here.)

One of my favorite MH features is that its mail folders can be nested, just as the UNIX file system can nest directories. *xmh* can't display more than the first layer of subfolders, but *exmh* can.

Figure 7-13 shows the top pane of the *exmh* display. Click the second mouse button on the top-level project folder to display its subfolders named for years. Clicking on the *1991* subfolder brings up its subfolders. When you find the one you want, the first button opens the folder.

exmh is designed to work well with systems that presort arriving mail into different folders based on keywords in the mail headers. You can use your own external agent, like *procmail*, or let *exmh* periodically sort mail for you using the MH mail-delivery mechanism. When folders get new mail, their label is highlighted in the display, and unseen messages in a folder are highlighted so you can quickly see what's new. When you are at the end of a folder, the "Next message" command automatically takes you to the next folder with new messages.

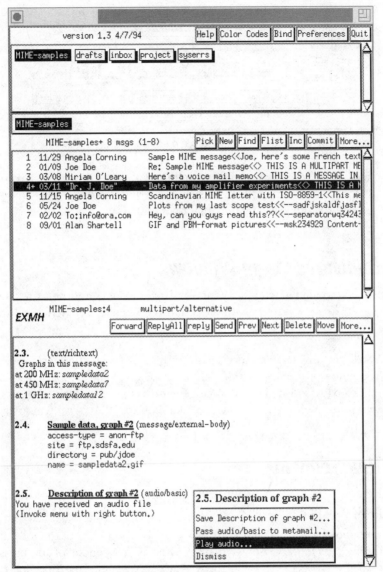

Figure 7-12: Interface for exmh version 1.3

For nitty-gritty details on MH, try the Nutshell Handbook *MH & xmh: Email for Users & Programmers* by Jerry Peek (O'Reilly & Associates Inc.).

I've just scratched the surface here. *exmh* is evolving rapidly; version 1.4 should be out by the time this book is printed. If you want a publicly available and very flexible graphical interface to your email (with, probably, a few

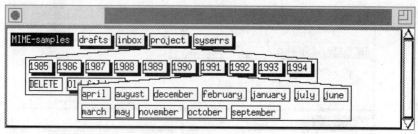

Figure 7-13: exmh folder-choosing pane shows nested folders

minor bugs and glitches until development slows down), try *exmh*. I've used MH for years because I haven't seen a GUI interface that gives me the power I need, but *exmh* just might change my mind.

—JP

7.08 Dedicated xterm Windows

If you're really attached to your text-based mailers and news readers, you can use the *–e* option to *xterm (11.25)* to start up a mailer in a dedicated window:

```
% xterm -e mailx
```

You'll get an *xterm* window with your text-based *mailx* application running. The name of the application, *mailx*, appears in the titlebar. You can use any other text-based mailer in place of *mailx*, such as *mush*, *elm*, or even (sigh) */bin/mail*. When you exit your mailer, you exit the *xterm* window.

—LM

7.09 Read-only Mailer

Here's a cute little program that's actually quite useful. It's a read-only "crippled" mail program called *xmailbox*.

xmailbox

xmailbox comes up with a list window, showing each of the messages in your mailbox. *xmailbox* shows you the name of the sender of the message, along with the subject line (or if there is no subject line, the first line of the message), as shown in Figure 7-14.

If you click on one of these messages with the first mouse button, a message window appears showing the mail message, as shown in Figure 7-15.

From here, you can only move to the next message, move to the previous message, or dismiss the message window. You can't reply to the message, you can't forward it to anyone else, you can't save it anywhere, and you can't delete it.

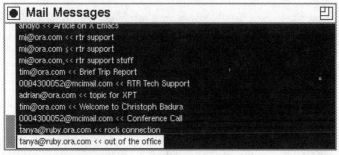

Figure 7-14: xmailbox list window

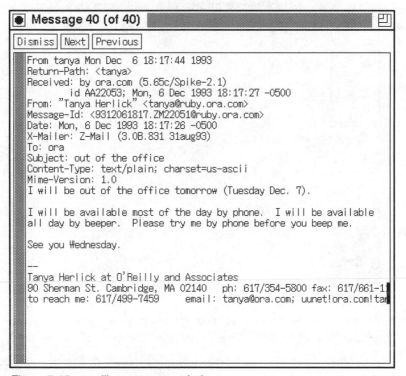

Figure 7-15: xmailbox message window

So what's the point?

Well, here's an example. I never exit my mailer, but occasionally I might log in somewhere else, e.g., on someone else's X terminal. I may want to monitor my mail, but if I start a real mailer, I run the risk of accidentally overwriting my system mailbox *(7.01)*. It's always a bad idea to have a file open for writing by more than one program. By using *xmailbox*, there's no danger that I'll overwrite my mail file.

xmailbox also has another window: an *xbiff*-type *(7.10)* window that just indicates if you have new mail. You can switch back and forth between the list window and the biff window by pressing the **Shift** key while you press the third mouse button.

—*LM*

7.10 The X Version of "you have new mail."

xbiff

The *xbiff* program is a simple application for indicating new mail in your system mailbox *(7.01)*. You can use it with any mailer program you choose; it just keeps an eye on your incoming mail file and notifies you when new messages arrive. *xbiff* just contains a bitmap of a mailbox with a flag, as shown in Figure 7-16.

Figure 7-16: Initial xbiff window

When you have new mail, *xbiff* beeps, goes into reverse video *(17.08)*, and the mail flag pops up, as shown in Figure 7-17.

Figure 7-17: xbiff with new mail

After you've read your mail, you can click on the window to return it to normal, or just wait a minute and it will return to normal automatically.

For those of you who haven't heard this bit of UNIX folklore yet: the *xbiff* program gets its name from the UNIX *biff* program, which in turn gets its name from the name of the programmer's dog. Like all self-respecting canines, Biff the dog barked whenever the mailman came to the door, thus alerting the programmer that he had new mail.

—*LM*

7.11 xbiff With Sounds

xbiff++

xbiff++ is a client meant for SPARCstations with audio support. It's similar to *xbiff (7.10)*, but it's much more fun. Its most important extension to *xbiff* is that it allows you to play different sounds according to who sends you email.

xbiff++ works by looking at the mail headers and checking those against sound bindings that you've set up either on the command line or in a resource file. You can set up what sounds to get under what circumstances by using the *–soundBindings* command-line option, or by defining the soundBindings resource. Each binding consists of a pattern, a vertical bar separator, and the path of the sound file to use when the pattern is matched. The patterns should include the header type—one of To:, From:, Cc:, or Subject:—followed by the string .* and whatever name, alias, or subject you want to match. Several sound bindings can be listed, separated by a comma. For example, I set the soundBindings resource as follows:

```
XBiff++*soundBindings: From:.*val|/usr/demo/SOUND/sounds/cuckoo.au,\
From:.*tim|/work/xpt/src/lib/sounds/whip.au,\
From:.*Mailer-Daemon|/usr/demo/SOUND/sounds/crash.au,\
To:.*jokers@ora.com|/usr/demo/SOUND/sounds/laugh.au,\
From:.*root|/usr/demo/SOUND/sounds/computer.au
```

Since my resource specification takes up several lines, I use backslashes (\) at the end of each line to make sure the specification is continued. Note that I can't insert whitespace for formatting purposes, since it would be taken as part of the pattern string.

At the risk of offending a few people, I've set up my *xbiff++* so that I hear a cuckoo when I get mail from Val, and I hear a whip when I get mail from my boss Tim. (Hi Tim!) When the mailer daemon returns my mail, I hear a crash. When the mail is from a "joker's" mailing list (fictional, in this case), I hear laughter. And when *root* is sending me mail, I hear a computer sound.

Some sound files are included in the standard SunOS distribution of */usr/demo/SOUND/sounds*, and *xbiff++* comes with a few more sounds. But if you have a microphone for your workstation, you can also record sounds if you *really* want to personalize *xbiff++*. At minimum, you might record yourself speaking the names of the people you get the most mail from, so that when you get mail you know immediately who it's from without having to remember if a rooster crow means Tim or Val:

```
XBiff++*soundBindings: From.*tim|/home/lmui/sounds/tim.au\
From.*val|/home/lmui/sounds/val.au
```

You can also set up a sound for all other messages that aren't matched. For this, use the *–sound* command-line option or sound resource:

```
XBiff++*sound:    /usr/demo/SOUND/sounds/splat.au
```

You can press the third mouse button in the *xbiff++* window at any time, to check your new mail and play any appropriate sounds. If you have no new messages, *xbiff++* can play a sound as specified using the *–noMailSound* command-line option, or the noMailSound resource. *xbiff++* is distributed with a sound file named *NoMail.au* for this purpose. A somber and sincere voice tells you, "Sorry, no mail."

```
XBiff++*noMailSound:       /usr/local/lib/sounds/NoMail.au
```

Another feature of *xbiff++* is that in the same way you set up sound bindings, you can also set up what they call face bindings. If you happen to have pictures of your best email buddies (and who doesn't!), you can set up *xbiff++* to turn the familiar mailbox bitmap into your friend's face. Like sound bindings, face bindings can be set using the *–faceBindings* command-line option or by setting the faceBindings environment variable:

```
*faceBindings: From.*val|/home/val/bitmaps/gumby.xbm,\
From.*tim|/home/val/bitmaps/tinytim,\
From.*paul|/home/val/bitmaps/faces/face.paul
```

(Unfortunately, this doesn't work for anything but simple bitmaps yet. It's also supposed to work for GIF images, but that feature hasn't been implemented either.)

—*LM*

7.12 tkpostage

Here's one of my favorite alternatives to *xbiff* (7.10).

tkpostage

tkpostage is an adorable Tcl/Tk (30.01)-based program that shows the number of messages in your mailbox. The cute part is that it resembles a metered U.S. stamp, with a count of your messages in place of the price of the postage. Figure 7-18 shows a *tkpostage* window.

If you click on the *tkpostage* window, another window appears showing headers from all your messages.

There are various ways of configuring *tkpostage*. You can have it use a different system mailbox (7.01) other than the one in */usr/spool/mail* if you use the *–mailDrop* command-line option, mailDrop resource, or MAILDROP environment variable. By default, it checks the mail file every two seconds, but you can change this using the *–delay* command-line option or delay resource. (two seconds seems a bit extreme to me.) When new mail arrives, it generally goes

Figure 7-18: Five messages

into reverse video *(17.08)*, you can disable this using the *–flip* command-line option or by setting the *flip* resource to `False`.

You can also set up *tkpostage* to beep when you get new mail. Usually, I find this annoying, but if you like to be beeped, use the *+beep* command-line option or set the `beep` resource to TRUE.

There's plenty more. You can twiggle the fonts, number offsets, etc. But I think *tkpostage* works just great as shipped.

—LM

7.13 *Seeing Subject Lines with xlbiff*

Yes, another version of *biff*. The most obvious gimmick for this one is that it shows you the subject lines of your mail messages. But probably the best part about *xlbiff* is that you can set it up to remain hidden until you actually have new messages. *xlbiff* also enough flexibility so that you can use it to monitor events other than new mail.

xlbiff

xlbiff is designed to work with MH *(7.06)*, but can also work with other mailers (with just a small change in its resources). The `scanCommand` resource defines what command should be used to find the headers of new messages. The default command is *scan* (the command for MH users); but BSD mail *(7.01)* users can also change the resource as needed.

To help you create robust scan commands, you can use parameters to specify the name of your mail file and the width, or number of columns, that you want shown. (The window usually shows 80 columns, but you can change this with the *–columns* command-line option or `columns` resource.) For example, the scan command for an MH user might read:

```
XLbiff*scanCommand:     scan -file %s -width %d
```

Here, the `%s` string is substituted with the name of your mail file, and the `%d` string is substituted with the number of columns. Because of the flexibility of the MH *scan* command itself, you can easily alter this command to fit your needs.

I'm not a MH user, so I use the BSD mail command shown here:

```
XLbiff*scanCommand:      echo 'x' | /usr/ucb/mail | grep '^.[UN]'
```

(In this case, I needed to supply the full pathname of BSD mail on my system. Your results may vary.) When I have new messages, a window similar to the one in Figure 7-19 pops up at the lower left corner of my display.

```
●  xlbiff                                                                   ▣
>N 43 lmui@ora.com        Mon Jul 18 10:57   16/577   Great job!
 N 44 bug-reports@ora.com Mon Jul 18 11:00   21/801    Re: INTER2-PROD/248: miss
 N 45 val                 Mon Jul 18 11:21   10/366   You deserve a raise!
```

Figure 7-19: xlbiff window

Only new and unread messages are shown.

When you click on the *xlbiff* window, it disappears, only to reappear when you have new mail again. You can also set up *xlbiff* to disappear on its own. I prefer doing it this way, since I'm usually too impatient to even take a second away from whatever else I'm doing. To do this, call *xlbiff* with the *–fade* command-line option or fade resource:

```
% xlbiff -fade 10 &
```

Now the *xlbiff* window automatically disappears 10 seconds after popping up. This is usually long enough for me to glance at the new message and decide if it's worth looking at right away.

The way *xlbiff* works is that it checks to see if your incoming mail file has changed, and if it has, it pops up a new window. In its default configuration, it checks for new mail every 15 seconds, but you can alter this using the *–update* command-line option or update resource.

The most interesting feature of *xlbiff* is that you can use it for monitoring files other than your mail file. For example, suppose I like to monitor the */usr/adm/messages* file. I can use the *–file* command line option (or file resource) to specify a different file other than my incoming mail file *(7.01)*, and I can use the *–scanCommand* command-line option mentioned previously to specify what I want to see when the file has changed. So I could run the following command:

```
% xlbiff -file /usr/adm/messages -scanCommand "tail %s" &
```

Whenever a change happens to the *messages* file, *xlbiff* pops up a window showing the last 10 lines of the file. (Notice that I use the %s code to tell the UNIX *tail* command which file to use—in this case, */usr/adm/messages.*)

You can also change the command that *xlbiff* uses to check if the file has changed. Usually, it just checks the file size, but you might want to use your own script instead. Use the *–checkCommand* command-line option or check-Command resource to change the command used to determine whether *xlbiff* needs to rescan.

—LM

8

Network Utilities

8.01 So You're on the Internet

It's a common saying that the world is split into the haves and have-nots. You might build on that by adding that the "haves" are split into those who take advantage of it and those who don't.

The Internet is something many people have access to, but not everyone knows how to use. Our company has been on the Internet for years, but I bet only about 10 percent of us are comfortable with finding and using its resources. And many of us are only comfortable to a limit. I was confused the first few times I tried using Gopher and WAIS, so I tend to stay away from them, but I use anonymous *ftp* almost every day.

What X can provide is an interface to the Internet, to make it easy to find and then retrieve the information you want. This chapter covers X interfaces to FTP *(8.02)*, Gopher *(8.08)*, and WAIS *(8.09)* , as well as Mosaic *(8.10)*, an elegant World Wide Web browser for viewing documents and graphics all over the Internet. We also cover a Usenet news reader *(8.05)* and *talk (8.06)*-like programs for just communicating with other users over the network.

If you're not on the Internet...well, our apologies. These utilities will be of limited use to you. But if you are on the Internet, this chapter can show you how the Internet can become your own personal playground.

— LM

8.02 Retrieving Files with xftp

Before there was Gopher or WAIS or the World Wide Web, there was anonymous FTP (file transfer protocol). Using FTP, a site can make some of its files available to the public without extending access to their entire file system.

When you connect to a remote site via FTP, there are a limited number of commands you can run: just enough commands to let you find a file that interests you and then copy it over to your system.

moxftp

xftp is an X front-end to FTP. A sample connection with *xftp* is shown in Figure 8-1.

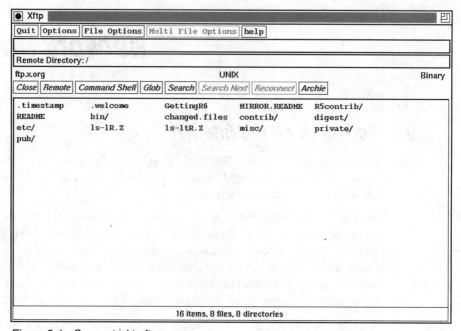

Figure 8-1: Connected to ftp.x.org

xftp starts up unconnected to an FTP site. To connect to a site, you need to press the **Login** button, and a connection box appears as shown in Figure 8-2.

In the figure, you see that several hosts appear for me to select from. *xftp* gets this list of hosts from either the file called *.netrc* or the file called *.moxftprc* in my home directory. See below for more information on configuring these files.

If you don't have a *.netrc* or *.moxftprc* file, or if you want to connect to a different host, then edit the fields in the connection box. At minimum, you should type in the name of the host, your login name on that host (usually *anonymous*), and the password to use. As a shortcut, you could just type in the name of the host and then pull down the **Anonymous Login** menu. The menu lets you choose between three types of passwords: Guest, Mail Address, and Login Name. Most anonymous FTP sites request your mail address as your password.

You might also specify what directory to connect to, and what local directory to use. If you know what remote directory you want to connect to, I

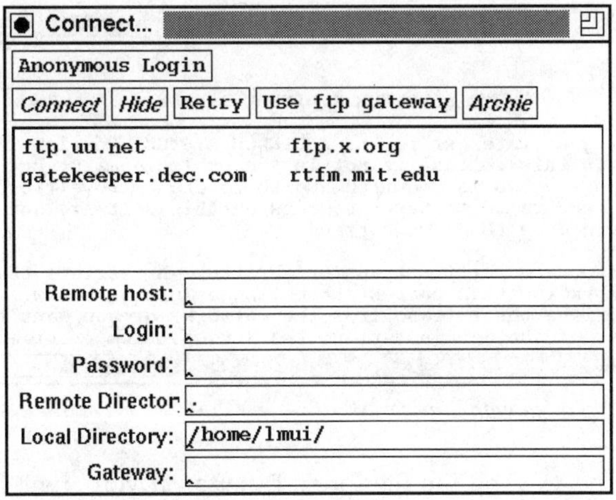

```
┌──────────────────────────────────────────────────┐
│ ● Connect...  ▓▓▓▓▓▓▓▓▓▓▓▓▓▓▓▓▓▓▓▓▓▓▓▓▓▓▓  ▣ │
│ ┌────────────────┐                                 │
│ │Anonymous Login │                                 │
│ └────────────────┘                                 │
│ ┌───────┐┌────┐┌─────┐┌──────────────┐┌──────┐    │
│ │Connect││Hide││Retry││Use ftp gateway││Archie│    │
│ └───────┘└────┘└─────┘└──────────────┘└──────┘    │
│  ftp.uu.net          ftp.x.org                     │
│  gatekeeper.dec.com  rtfm.mit.edu                  │
│                                                    │
│                                                    │
│      Remote host: [                            ]   │
│           Login: [                            ]    │
│        Password: [                            ]    │
│  Remote Director [.                           ]    │
│  Local Directory: [/home/lmui/                ]    │
│         Gateway: [                            ]    │
└──────────────────────────────────────────────────┘
```

Figure 8-2: xftp connection box

recommend that you specify it here since that will save you some time. The local directory is usually the directory you ran *xftp* from. When you copy files from the remote system, this is the directory that files will be copied into, so you may want to change it before connecting to the remote site. If you always use the same local or remote directories, you can specify them in a file in your home directory called *.moxftprc*, as shown below.

On some sites, you can't connect to external hosts directly via FTP but must first connect to a gateway machine. If you have to use a gateway, you can specify that as well in the **Connect** window.

When you're ready, press **Connect** to connect to the remote host. Then wait while *xftp* initiates the connection and lists top-level directory (or the remote directory you specified in the Connect box), as we showed in Figure 8-1.

Once connected, a directory listing automatically appears (you can suppress this under the **Options** menu). You can *cd* to a directory by selecting it and then selecting **Cd** from the **File Options** menu, or go up a directory level by selecting **Up** from the same menu.

To copy a file to your local machine, select the file in the directory listing and then select **Get** from the **File Options** menu.

Here's one of my favorite features of *xftp*. If you want to read a file without copying it over, you can select it and then select **Veiw** from the **File Options** menu. (No, that's not our typo: it says "Veiw" on the menu, not "View.") The file is copied to *tmp* and then a **View File** window appears. If the file is compressed (i.e., has a *.Z* suffix), *xftp* is smart enough to uncompress it before showing it to you (although it's confused with files that have a *.gz* suffix). A sample **View File** window is shown in Figure 8-3.

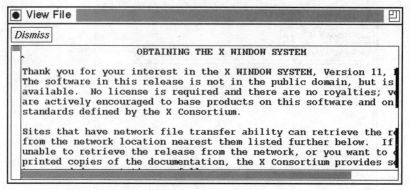

Figure 8-3: Viewing a file with xftp

When you're done viewing the file, press **Dismiss**. If you aren't familiar with using standard UNIX *ftp*, then take my word for it that viewing files can be tedious, and *xftp* makes this much easier for you.

In large directories, you might appreciate *xftp*'s searching features. For example, if looking for all files with the string "FAQ" in its name, you might press the **Search** button to bring up a small window allowing you to specify a search string, shown in Figure 8-4. In the figure, we specify it using UNIX regular expression syntax and then press the **Regular exp** button. *xftp* highlights a file matching the expression. You can continue pressing **Search Next** to bounce around to each of the files in the directory that match the string.

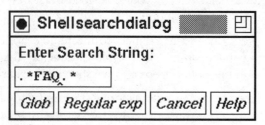

Figure 8-4: Specifying a search string

Another thing that *xftp* helps out with is dealing with multiple files. If you select more than one file, you can get all the files at once by selecting **Get Selected Files** from the **Multi File Options** menu. You can select multiple files by just clicking on them in turn, or you can use the **Glob** button, which works much like the **Search** feature except that each of the files matching the string is automatically selected.

The **Remote** button toggles between showing you the local and remote directories. The **Close** button disconnects from the remote site, and the **Reconnect** button reconnects to the previous host if you were timed out (which happens to me all the time).

The **Command Shell** button gives you direct access to the underlying *ftp* shell. This is most useful for sites that have commands not supported by *xftp* (such as the indispensible *index* and *locate* commands on *gatekeeper.dec.com*).

The **Archie** button gives you a window for conducting an Archie search. It isn't as flexible as *xarchie*, but it's a nice feature nonetheless.

If you connect to the same sites all the time, you can set up your *$HOME/.netrc* or *$HOME/.moxftprc* file to make *xftp* a bit easier to use. For example, my *.netrc* reads as follows:

```
machine ftp.x.org login anonymous password lmui@ora.com
machine ftp.uu.net login anonymous password lmui@ora.com
machine gatekeeper.dec.com login anonymous password lmui@ora.com
machine rtfm.mit.edu login anonymous password lmui@ora.com
```

If you include a password for any of your sites (as I do), your *.netrc* has to be readable only by you or you won't be connected. Note that this is necessary even if it's for anonymous FTP. (Even though this feature is supposed to provide security against other users surreptitiously reading your password, it's still a bad idea to put any real passwords in your *.netrc* file anyway.)

In addition, *xftp* lets you configure a *$HOME/.moxftprc* file. The syntax is the same as for *.netrc*, except that it accepts some special keywords. The new keywords are `remote_dir`, `local_dir`, and `note`. My extended *.moxftprc* might read as follows:

```
machine ftp.x.org login anonymous password lmui@ora.com
remote_dir /contrib local_dir /work/xpt/src/export note X Sources
machine ftp.uu.net login anonymous password lmui@ora.com remote_dir /pub
machine gatekeeper.dec.com login anonymous password lmui@ora.com
note comp.sources.x is here
machine rtfm.mit.edu login anonymous password lmui@ora.com remote_dir
/pub/Usenet local_dir /home/lmui/misc note all FAQ's, all the time
```

If you want to know more about *xftp*, there's extensive help available by pressing the **Help** button.

There are actually three incarnations to *xftp*: a Motif version (*mftp*), an OPEN LOOK version (*oftp*), and the standard Athena version (*xftp*). This is why the package is distributed under the name *moxftp*.

—LM

8.03 Getting a Single File With xgetit

In writing this book, I found myself spending a lot of time connected to *ftp.x.org* so I could download software from their *contrib* area. I kept on getting timed out. And I kept on feeling guilty for monopolizing a valuable connection to a very popular and valuable FTP site.

xgetit

xgetit is a very simple tool for getting programs the quick 'n easy way. It depends on your primary selection buffer *(11.05)* containing the name of the site you want to *ftp* from, and the full pathname of the file you want. For example, your primary selection buffer might contain:

```
/pub/book.catalog.Z@ftp.ora.com
```

To make it easy for me to get files on the fly, I copied a listing of all the files in the *contrib* directory into a file on my local machine. The lines in the file resembled:

```
-rw-r--r--  1 ftp     867 May 20 1992 xgetit.README
-rw-r--r--  1 ftp   17023 Apr 22 1992 xgetit.tar.Z
-rw-rw-rw-  1 ftp   20014 Sep 12 1991 xgks-widget.tar.Z
-rw-rw-rw-  1 ftp  768569 Apr 23 1991 xglobe.tar.Z
-rw-r--r--  1 ftp   19561 Dec  3 1992 xgopher.1.2.README
-rw-r--r--  1 ftp  183754 Dec  3 1992 xgopher.1.2.tar.Z
    ...
```

I edited each line to include the full pathname and the site name.

```
-rw-r--r--  1 ftp     867 May 20 1992 /contrib/xgetit.README@ftp.x.org
-rw-r--r--  1 ftp   17023 Apr 22 1992 /contrib/xgetit.tar.Z@ftp.x.org
-rw-rw-rw-  1 ftp   20014 Sep 12 1991 /contrib/xgks-widget.tar.Z@ftp.x.org
-rw-rw-rw-  1 ftp  768569 Apr 23 1991 /contrib/xglobe.tar.Z@ftp.x.org
-rw-r--r--  1 ftp   19561 Dec  3 1992 /contrib/xgopher.1.2.README@ftp.x.org
-rw-r--r--  1 ftp  183754 Dec  3 1992 /contrib/xgopher.1.2.tar.Z@ftp.x.org
    ...
```

I keep one window open viewing the file. Now, when I want to get a package, I can just select the last word of a line and start up *xgetit*. The name of the file I want will be in the primary selection.

```
% xgetit &
```

When the *ftp* transfer is done, a window appears indicating whether or not the retrieval worked:

The file is downloaded into the same directory that you run *xgetit* from.

—*LM*

```
┌─────────────────────────────xgetit──────────────────────────┐
│ ┌──────┐                                                     │
│ │ done │                                                     │
│ └──────┘                                                     │
│Getting file xgetit.tar.Z from path /contrib at host export.x.org...│
│Connected to ftp.x.org.                                       │
│220 ftp.x.org FTP server (NEWS-OS Release 4.1C) ready.        │
│331 Guest login ok, send ident as password.                  │
│230 Guest login ok, access restrictions apply.               │
│200 Type set to I.                                            │
│Interactive mode on.                                          │
│250 CWD command successful.                                   │
│200 PORT command successful.                                  │
│150 Opening data connection for xgetit.tar.Z (binary mode) (17023 bytes).│
│226 Transfer complete.                                        │
│local: xgetit.tar.Z remote: xgetit.tar.Z                      │
│17023 bytes received in 4.5 seconds (3.7 Kbytes/s)            │
│221 Goodbye.                                                  │
│ÿ                                                             │
└──────────────────────────────────────────────────────────────┘
```

Figure 8-5: xgetit response window

8.04 *Finding Files with Archie*

Now, one of the questions that FTP access brings up is: how do you know where you can find a particular file to retrieve?

The answer is Archie. Archie is a service that keeps an updated index of all anonymous FTP sites and what files they have available there. The no-frills way of accessing Archie is via Telnet to one of the Archie servers, but since this is X, there's a better way.

xarchie

xarchie is a program that basically does it all for you: it tells you where you can find a certain archive, and then it lets you *ftp* it right off. When you first start up *xarchie*, type in a string identifying what you are looking for in the **Search Term** box. This string should be in the filename of the archive. Then you can press **Return** or select **Query Item** from the **Query>** menu, as shown in Figure 8-6.

By default, *xarchie* will look for a file matching your query *exactly*. You can change that by setting another **Search Type**, under the **Settings>** menu as shown in Figure 8-7. You should take some care in determining what your query type is, since a very precise query may miss many (if not all) matches, but an imprecise query may take a Very Long Time.

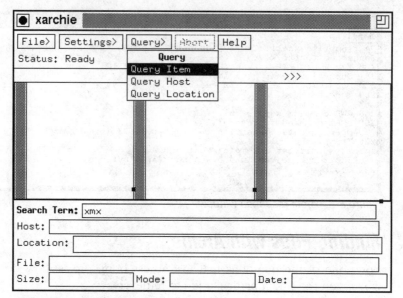

Figure 8-6: xarchie query

Figure 8-7: Changing the query type

Other settings you can specify are a sort method and a Nice Level (options are Nice, Nicer, Very Nice, Extremely Nice, and Nicest). If you're unfamiliar with this terminology, it lets you set a lower priority for your query, so that other people with more important queries on the Archie host can go first. You can access all the settings via the **Settings Panel**, available by bringing up **Other...** on the **Settings>** menu.

In my case, I'm looking for *xmx* (27.09), chosen because I don't expect it to be available at very many sites. *xarchie* queries the configured Archie host for the specified file. The default Archie host can be specified using the archieHost resource. You can also use the **Archie Host** menu under the **Settings>** menu, but you should usually restrict yourself for the Archie host that's nearest.

Now be prepared to wait. A long time.[*] There are only 11 Archie hosts in the world, and they get a megaton of traffic. If you grow impatient, you can press the **Abort** button and be shown the matches up to the time of the abort. *xarchie* tells you how many matches it's made so far on the status line (with the message "Receiving..." followed by the number of matches already made), so you might just abort the search if you have a reasonable number of matches already.

When the search is completed (or aborted), all sites with matching files are listed in the left-most field of the *xarchie* window. If you select one of the sites, directories containing matching files are displayed in the middle field. Selecting one of the directories displays the filename(s) in the third field, as shown in Figure 8-8. (If there is only one site or only one directory on a given site, their contents are automatically displayed.) The fields at the bottom of the screen are filled with the name of the host, the location of the file, and the filename, along with its size, permissions, and date.

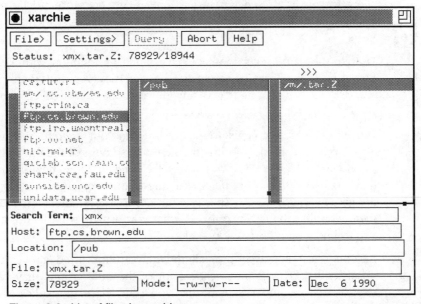

Figure 8-8: List of files in xarchie

From the pathname alone, you can often tell whether this is the file you want. For example, the copy of *xmx* that appears in the file called */lude-crim/xmx-1.0/run/crim/sun4.1_sparc/bin/xmx* on *clouso.crim.ca* is likely to be an executable for a SPARCstation running SunOS 4.1, which will be useless

---

[*] If the wait is ridiculously long, you might try another Archie site. Although you're encouraged to use the one closest to you, you might find that it's unbearably slow and you'd have better results elsewhere. Also, it's better to wait until very early or very late in the day to start an Archie query.

to you if you work on an HP machine. Also, it's generally Good Manners to use the site that is geographically closest to you.

Once you have determined which file you want, you can have *xarchie* connect to the remote site and get the file for you by selecting **Get** on the **File>** menu. The list display is temporarily shaded and the **Status:** line shows the progress of the file transfer. The file is retrieved and placed in the directory you started *xarchie* in. (Alternatively, you can change the local *ftp* directory using the **Other Settings** window.)

For an idea of some sample resource customization for *xarchie*, try out the resources on the CD-ROM *(20.23)*.

—LM

8.05 Reading News

xrn

There are many news readers out there, but only a couple for X. *xrn* is a client for reading Usenet news. Usenet news does not strictly rely on your being on the Internet, but it's being tied to the Internet increasingly over the years.

Despite the name, *xrn* does not have much in common with *rn*. When you first start it up, *xrn* connects to the NNTP server and then checks your *$HOME/.newsrc* file. It rejects any newsgroups that it thinks are bogus and reports these rejections to standard error.

If there are any new newsgroups not listed in your *.newsrc*, *xrn* window then pops up in Add mode and lists the new newsgroups at the top of the window, as shown in Figure 8-9. You can select one or more newsgroups and add them to the top of your *.newsrc*, to the bottom, or after another group (you are given a dialog box to specify what group to add after). You can also add them "unsubscribed." Since this is what you usually want to do, it will please you to know that this is the default.

As you select a newsgroup, all the newsgroups listed above it are added unsubscribed. This is nice, since a lot of the new groups may be not be of interest to you, and it means that you don't have to explicitly unsubscribe them (as you do with other news readers).

When you're done with Add mode, press **Quit**. You'd think this would quit you from *xrn*, but it doesn't, it just takes you out of Add mode and puts you in Newsgroup mode. Any newsgroups that you haven't explicitly subscribed to are added unsubscribed.

In Newsgroup mode, a listing of all newsgroups with unread news appears in the top half of the window (see Figure 8-10). Select a newsgroup and press **Read** to scan the group. You can also do many other things, such as subscribe

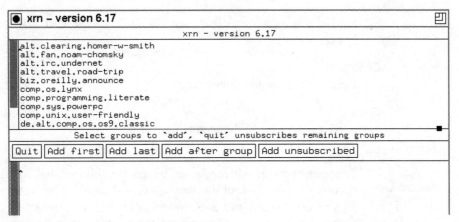

Figure 8-9: Top of xrn Add mode

to the group, rescan the group, etc. (*xrn* tells you what the button does as your pointer hovers over it).

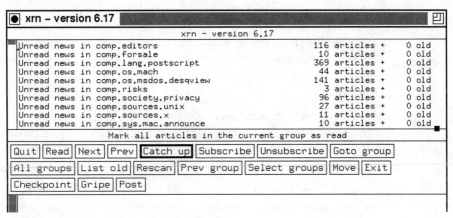

Figure 8-10: Top of xrn Newsgroup mode

Among the more interesting functions in Newsgroup mode are:

Catch up

> Mark all the articles in the selected group as read. This comes in useful when you don't have the time today for *rec.arts.startrek.current* (it's amazing that anyone ever does!), but don't want to completely unsubscribe right away.

List old

> List *all* newsgroups you subscribe to, regardless of whether there's new news there or not. You might want to do this to access the group for posting or unsubscribing.

Rescan

Fold in any new news that came in since you started *xrn* (or since you last rescanned).

Checkpoint

Update your *.newsrc* immediately.

Gripe

Send a complaint to the maintainers of *xrn*.

All groups

This puts you in All mode, in which the bottom half of the window becomes a listing of all the newsgroups available. The Newsgroup mode buttons are shaded and thus unselectable. You can use this mode to subscribe to other groups or to change the order of the groups.

Pressing **Quit** quits you from *xrn*, updating your *.newsrc* file. Pressing **Exit** quits *xrn*, but doesn't write your *.newsrc*. (Be careful here, since you almost always want your *.newsrc* updated.)

When you select a newsgroup and press **Read**, you're placed in Article mode. The unread articles in the newsgroup are shown at the top of the window, and the current article is shown at the bottom of the window. You can move through the articles sequentially by pressing **Next** or **Next unread**; or you can select an article before pressing one of the **Next** buttons and see that article instead.

My favorite way to read articles is to just select the article by clicking it with the second mouse button: the article automatically appears below (see Figure 8-11). As you read articles, a plus sign (+) appears to the left of the article list at the top of the window, to let you know you've already read the article.

In Article mode, you can mark individual articles as read or unread, catch up on the entire newsgroup (i.e., mark everything as read), and also perform many of the functions available at the Newsgroup level. (One of my favorite buttons is **Fed up**, which is like **Catch up** except that it brings you directly to the next newsgroup whereas **Catch up** brings you back to Newsgroup mode.) Article mode also lets you set up "kills"; that is, it lets you set up all articles pertaining to a particular subject as read. You can also set up author kills, so you don't have to read any more articles by a particularly obnoxious poster.

At the bottom of the *xrn* window, below the actual article field, are several buttons with actions you can take for the article. You can **Save** the article in a file, **Reply** to the sender, **Forward** the article to a friend (or enemy), post a **Followup** to the newsgroup, or **Cancel** the article (only allowed if you were the one who posted it).

Figure 8-11: xrn Article mode

Occasionally you may come across an article that looks like gibberish (especially in the humor groups); this is often because the article is written in Rotation 13. Under this scheme, each letter is replaced with the letter that is 13 characters before or after it in the alphabet. For example: "a" and "n" trade places, "b" and "o" trade places, etc. This makes the article deliberately difficult to read without pressing the **Rot-13** button to translate the letters back. Be warned that this strategy is most frequently used for jokes that are in poor taste, the idea being that if you press **Rot-13** then you asked for it and can't complain that you were caught unawares.

The header of an article is the portion that shows who posted it, when it was posted, to what groups, what path it took to get to your site, etc. The times that you care about this are few and far between, so you can use the **Toggle header** button to suppress the headers, or press it again to see the full headers once more.

To print an article, press **Print**.

Now for the confessions of an *xrn* convert. For the past few years, I've been trying *xrn* upon occasion and then rejecting it in disgust. My impression was that it's ugly, unintuitive, etc. And then one day my regular news reader became unavailable because of an incompatibility with our new news-server software, and I was stuck with *xrn* for a week. I began to realize that I'd been giving *xrn* a bum deal, because once you get the hang of it, it's pretty nice. When my regular news reader came back, I found myself missing many of *xrn*'s features, and I've never turned back. So give *xrn* a chance, it just may surprise you.

Also, the CD-ROM includes a few resources for *xrn* that help make it a little more palatable. See Article 20.23 for more information.

—LM

8.06 Can We Talk?

xtalk

The *xtalk* client lets you have an interactive conversation with another user who may be working locally or in another hemisphere. The other user just needs be logged in on another machine on the network with a compatible *talk* daemon.

The big limitation of *xtalk* is that it only works for systems supporting the Berkeley 4.3 *talkd* daemon. The 4.3 *talkd* is incompatible with 4.2 *talkd*. Note that one of the most popular UNIX platforms, SunOS, is still using the 4.2 *talkd*, so if you're on SunOS you're out of luck, or you should try *xbchat (8.07)* instead.

If your system uses 4.3 *talkd*, you can try *xtalk*. If you call up *xtalk* without specifying a username, you're asked to supply a name.

If you want to talk to someone on another machine, type in their name as *name@machine*, as you would for an email address. (You can also use *host!name*, *host:name*, or *host.name*, but I prefer *user@host* since it's so much more intuitive.)

In my case, I want to talk to Val, so I supply her name as *val@opal.ora.com* and press **Ok**. Val has to have a shell active (e.g., have a terminal emulator like

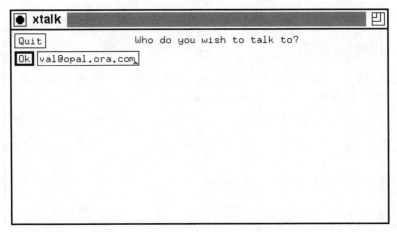

Figure 8-12: Initiating a talk request

xterm running) and she also has to be accepting messages on that shell. (The UNIX *mesg* command controls whether messages are accepted for your shell; the default is yes.)

Before the actual talk connection starts, the *xtalk* program checks the remote machine for a *talk* daemon and it asks the other person (Val) to respond. Val sees a message like:

```
Message from Talk_Daemon@opal at 17:02 ...
talk: connection requested by lmui@opal.
talk: respond with: talk lmui@opal
```

Val can respond using either the UNIX *talk* program or using an *xtalk* program on her own machine. Or she can totally ignore me. (Or she may not be there at all!) Until she responds, I get the message "Waiting for your party to respond.", with the opportunity to quit if I get impatient.

When Val finally responds, the "Waiting…" message now says "Talking". Val and I can now have a conversation (see Figure 8-13).

The big advantage of *xtalk* over regular *talk* is that the program shows the sequence of the conversation. The UNIX *talk* program gives you a *curses*-based split screen, which lets you see what the other person says but not in relation to what you're saying. If you look at a *talk* window at the end of a conversation, it's difficult to figure out who said what first. *xtalk*, on the other hand, shows you the conversation in sequence.

Using a program like *xtalk* is a good way to communicate with someone immediately if you can't use a telephone (or aren't comfortable communicating with other humans without a keyboard in between).

—LM

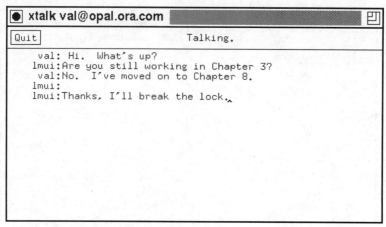

Figure 8-13: An xtalk conversation

8.07 Can We Chat?

Most people at our office use a version of SunOS, so we can't use *xtalk* *(8.06)* since it depends on a different *talk* protocol. Instead, we use *xhchat*.

xhchat

xhchat is a very simple variation of *xtalk*. It doesn't use the *talk* mechanism, but instead just opens another window on a remote server. To start an *xhchat* conversation, specify the remote server on the command line:

```
% xhchat opal:0
```

Since *xhtalk* opens the remote window directly, it's dependent on the remote server allowing access from your account. You may get the following error message:

```
% xhchat opal:0
Xlib: connection to "opal:0.0" refused by server
Xlib: Client is not authorized to connect to Server
Cannot open display opal:0
```

This means that server access control *(19.12)* is preventing you from accessing the remote server, and you're out of luck. See Article 19.13 for information on how to get the other user to extend access control to you.

Assuming you are allowed to access the remote server, a window appears resembling Figure 8-14. Note that unlike *xtalk*, the remote user does not have a chance to give permission for the connection—you just barrel right in. (This might be considered rude in some circles.)

This window is similar to a split-screen *talk* window. The advantage over *talk* is that *xhchat* supports some editing functions: you can select a position in your half of the "chat" window and edit away. This sort of editing is a nice

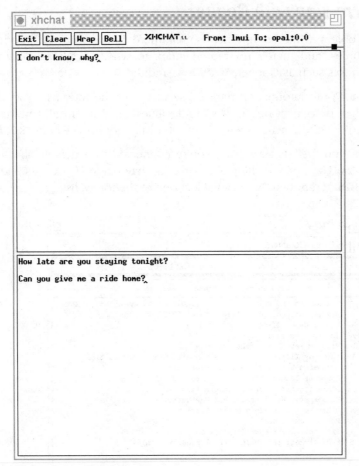

Figure 8-14: Chatting away

advantage over *talk* and *xtalk*, where bad typing can make any conversation impossible to follow. When your discussion exceeds a screenful of text, *xhchat* gives you a scrollbar so you can still backtrack easily.

One disadvantage is that many people (for example, me!) prefer the play-by-play type display of *xtalk*, to keep better track of who said what when. And of course, *xhchat* requires that you relax your security enough to let other users in. Still, if you can't use *xtalk*, *xhchat* isn't a bad alternative.

—LM

8.08 *Burrowing with Gopher*

A problem with the Internet is that there is a wealth of information and resources, and there's no central index to what's available. That's changing with tools such as Gopher, WAIS *(8.09)*, and the World Wide Web *(8.10)*.

Gopher is an information retrieval service over the Internet. The idea behind Gopher is to provide "hooks" to facilities on both local and remote sites, regardless of the actual methods of retrieval. *xgopher* is Gopher's X interface.

xgopher

When you first start *xgopher*, you're connected to a default directory, in this case the University of Illinois at Urbana-Champaign (UIUC), as shown in Figure 8-15. From here, you can select one of the topics listed.

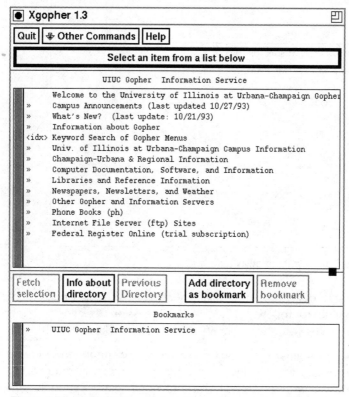

Figure 8-15: A Gopher query in action

Some items are preceded by markings signifying what sort of selection it is. A topic with greater-than signs (>>) preceding it is another directory of topics. A topic preceded by the `<idx>` string will allow you to do a WAIS search—for example, **Keyword Search of Gopher Menus** gives you a search of all Gopher topics matching a particular string. A topic preceded by `<tel>` means that it will give you a Telnet window (e.g., to the Library of Congress LOCIS server).

A topic preceded by <img> is an image that *xgopher* will attempt to show via *xloadimage* (by default). A topic without a marking is linked to a text file; selecting the topic will open a window displaying the text via *ftp*.

If you click on a topic and then press the **Info about selection** button, you'll find out what sort of connection it is, and to what site. Since Gopher is just a pointer to these facilities, you can take note of the sites and what method to connect with (e.g., TELNET or Gopher), so you can connect to it directly in the future and cut out the Gopher middleman.

To select the item, double-click on the selection or press **Fetch selection**. To return to the previous menu, press **Previous Directory**.

"Bookmarks" are hooks to particular directories in the service. This is an easy way to get back to a point in the directory structure without having to negotiate all these menus. If you press **Add selection as bookmark**, the directory will appear in the bottom half of the *xgopher* screen, under **Bookmarks**. To return to that point, just double-click on its bookmark listing.

xgopher is nice enough to tell you when it's waiting for information (so you don't think it's just hung), and it also has occasional tips via a cute little gopher guy, as shown in Figure 8-16.

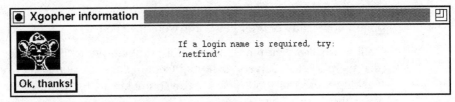

Figure 8-16: Cute little gopher—say thanks!

—LM

8.09 *Getting Information Using WAIS*

WAIS is an information retrival service (what, another one?!) Gopher *(8.08)* and WAIS are often lumped together, but they're conceptually very different ways of accessing information. I think of Gopher as the Internet's Table of Contents, and WAIS as its Index.

xwais

To understand the power of WAIS, start it up and press the **New** button under **Questions**. Then press the **Add Source** button and select one of the listed *.src* files (see Figure 8-17). Each of these files is a WAIS database.

Probably the best place to start is with the *directory-of-servers.src* database. You might browse through the list of servers for something interesting, but the best way to see how WAIS works is to know what you're looking for and then ask the directory of servers what WAIS servers can help you.

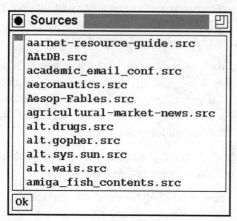

Figure 8-17: xwais source list

To query a WAIS database, go to the **Tell me about:** box and enter a series of keywords. Now, you might think that you should be as specific as possible, but WAIS isn't as smart as you think. All it knows is keywords. At this point, you have to figure out what sort of databases might help you, and what words they might use to describe themselves. Then include as many keywords as you can, since *xwais* will search for all of them and then "rate" them according to how many of your keywords were matched.

Well, it's hallowe'en time, so I want a pumpkin-pie recipe. Since it's unlikely that there are any servers dedicated to pumpkins, I use the keywords recipes, cooking, desserts, food, and I throw pumpkin in for good measure. Next, I press the **Search** button.

xwais searches through each of the servers and then returns the ones that have anything remotely matching my keywords, as shown in Figure 8-18.

The first number in each listing is the score of the match for that item. A match of 1000 means that this is a pretty safe bet; the lower the score, the less likely a match it is. You can find out about each of these servers by selecting them and them pressing **View**. Now, I have no idea how WAIS makes these determinations, since a tropical archaeobotany database isn't likely to have pumpkin-pie recipes, but it turns out that a keyword for the tropical archaeobotany database is "food." One of the other low-scoring sites, *cool.src*, turns out to be about cultural and artistic conservation, but one of its topics is "Food, drink, and insects"—YUM. *usdacris.src* turns out to be the U.S. Department of Agriculture's reporting system for agriculture, food, and nutrition, and forestry research in the United States. Again, not exactly what I was looking for.

However, *recipes.src* and *usenet-cookbook.src* sound like good bets.

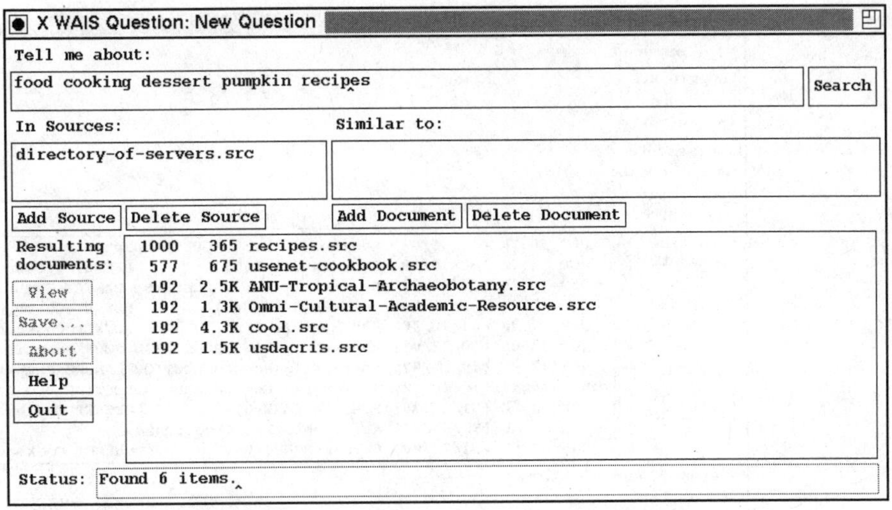

```
┌────────────────────────────────────────────────────────────────────────┐
│ ● X WAIS Question: New Question  ▓▓▓▓▓▓▓▓▓▓▓▓▓▓▓▓▓▓▓▓▓▓▓▓▓▓▓▓▓▓▓▓   🗗    │
│ Tell me about:                                                           │
│ ┌────────────────────────────────────────────────────────┐  ┌────────┐ │
│ │ food cooking dessert pumpkin recipes                     │  │ Search │ │
│ └────────────────────────────────────────────────────────┘  └────────┘ │
│ In Sources:                      Similar to:                             │
│ ┌──────────────────────────────┐ ┌──────────────────────────────────┐  │
│ │ directory-of-servers.src     │ │                                  │  │
│ │                              │ │                                  │  │
│ └──────────────────────────────┘ └──────────────────────────────────┘  │
│ ┌───────────┐┌───────────────┐   ┌──────────────┐┌─────────────────┐    │
│ │Add Source ││ Delete Source │   │ Add Document ││ Delete Document │    │
│ └───────────┘└───────────────┘   └──────────────┘└─────────────────┘    │
│ Resulting   1000   365 recipes.src                                       │
│ documents:   577   675 usenet-cookbook.src                               │
│ ┌──────────┐ 192  2.5K ANU-Tropical-Archaeobotany.src                    │
│ │ View     │ 192  1.3K Omni-Cultural-Academic-Resource.src               │
│ ┌──────────┐ 192  4.3K cool.src                                          │
│ │ Save...  │ 192  1.5K usdacris.src                                      │
│ ┌──────────┐                                                             │
│ │ Abort    │                                                             │
│ ┌──────────┐                                                             │
│ │ Help     │                                                             │
│ ┌──────────┐                                                             │
│ │ Quit     │                                                             │
│ └──────────┘                                                             │
│ Status: ┌─────────────────────────────────────────────────────────────┐ │
│         │ Found 6 items.                                                │ │
│         └─────────────────────────────────────────────────────────────┘ │
└────────────────────────────────────────────────────────────────────────┘
```

Figure 8-18: A directory search

Now you can make your actual query. You can open up a new **Question** window, or you can reuse the one you already have open. Since I like to leave one window dedicated to the directory of servers, I generally open a second **Question** window. In the new window, press **Add Source** to get to the source list (as you did before), and add *recipes.src* to the **In Sources:** listing. Do the same for *usenet-cookbook.src*. If you make a mistake, you can select a database and press **Delete Source** to remove it from the list of sources.

Now go back to the **Tell me about:** button and type in keywords for pumpkin pie, e.g., pumpkin and pie. Then press **Return** or press the **Search** button. You will see a screen much like Figure 8-19.

The top five listings are clearly pumpkin-pie recipes, and I grab those quickly. I'm not quite sure how cheese soup got in there, but I'm happy with what I have. Figure 8-20 shows one of the recipes (chosen only because of its brevity, so I hope no one else is offended that theirs wasn't chosen).

If you want to save the recipe on local disk, press **Save To File**.

Now, you might notice that the question boxes have a **Save** button. Suppose you wanted to check every week whether there were any new pumpkin-pie recipes. Rather than starting a new question every week by repeating the same sources and question, you could save the question when quitting. When you press the **Quit** button, a window appears for saving the question. Type in the name of the question (or use the default name, **New Question**), and press **Save&Quit**. The question now appears in the main *xwais* window, as shown in Figure 8-21.

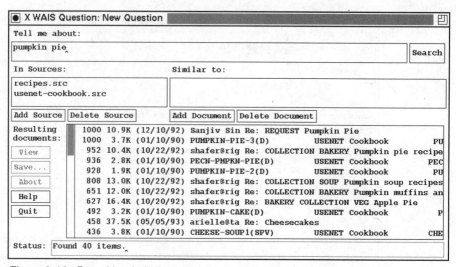

Figure 8-19: Pumpkin-pie listings

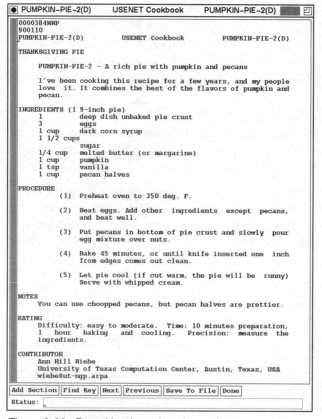

Figure 8-20: Pumpkin-pie recipe via xwais

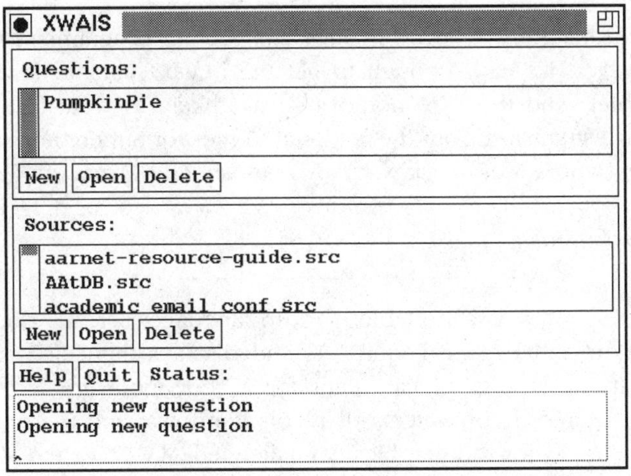

```
┌─────────────────────────────────────────────────┐
│ ● XWAIS ░░░░░░░░░░░░░░░░░░░░░░░░░░░░░░░░░    [⊡]  │
│ ┌───────────────────────────────────────────────┐│
│ │ Questions:                                     ││
│ │ ┌─────────────────────────────────────────────┐│
│ │ │ PumpkinPie                                  ││
│ │ │                                             ││
│ │ └─────────────────────────────────────────────┘│
│ │ [New] [Open] [Delete]                          ││
│ │                                                ││
│ │ Sources:                                       ││
│ │ ┌─────────────────────────────────────────────┐│
│ │ │ aarnet-resource-guide.src                   ││
│ │ │ AAtDB.src                                   ││
│ │ │ academic email conf.src                     ││
│ │ [New] [Open] [Delete]                          ││
│ │                                                ││
│ │ [Help] [Quit]  Status:                         ││
│ │ ┌─────────────────────────────────────────────┐│
│ │ │ Opening new question                        ││
│ │ │ Opening new question                        ││
│ └─────────────────────────────────────────────────┘
└─────────────────────────────────────────────────┘
```

Figure 8-21: xwais main window with new question

You'd want to save a question if it's one you will ask frequently and is exceed-ingly laborious to enter. The pumpkin-pie question is a pretty simple one, but suppose you had a more complicated question, e.g., suppose you wanted to find out whether there was any way to connect your Macintosh machine to the printer on your NeXT machine. You'd be searching for mac, next, printers, networks, cables, and who knows what else, and you'd be using a variety of sources, such as the *NeXT.FAQ.src*, the *mac.FAQ.src*, *macintosh-tidbits.src*, and *macintosh-news.src*. This is complicated enough to save so that you don't have to spend 10 minutes reconstructing the question every week.

xwais is a bit buggy. The **Question** window hangs easily, and the built-in source list is woefully out of date. However, someone recently asked me if the lyrics for Arlo Guthrie's "Alice's Restaurant" are online anywhere, and I found not just one but multiple versions via *xwais*.

—*LM*

8.10 An Introduction to Mosaic and WWW

Whenever anyone sees Mosaic for the first time, their reaction is almost always, "Wow!" Mosaic is a tool that's part hypertext, part information retrieval. To risk overhyping it, it has to be seen to be believed.

Mosaic is an interface to the World Wide Web (WWW). WWW, aka "the Web," is a client/server system for distributing documents across the Internet in hypertext. Based on a protocol called HTTP, it incorporates a markup language on designated servers that can be interpreted by any number of Web clients across a network. Mosaic is one of these clients.

> **Note:** Unfortunately, we can't include the Mosaic program on our CD-ROM. However, it's easy enough to get the newest version if you're on the Internet (and if you're not, you're not likely to want it!). You can get the latest version from the National Center for Supercomputing Applications (where Mosaic for X, the Macintosh, and Microsoft Windows were all born). Use anonymous FTP *(8.02)* to get Mosaic from *ftp.ncsa.uiuc.edu.*

On one level, WWW is a portable markup language: it reads documents in a special markup language called HTML, and displays them according to your interface. Mosaic is a graphical client for X, but there are also versions of Mosaic for Macintosh computers, Microsoft Windows, and there's a character-based client (*lynx*) for the graphically challenged. WWW, or the Web, does for text what X does for graphics.

WWW is network-based. So, like *xgopher (8.08)* or *xwais (8.09)*, the links are to files that might be anywhere on the Internet, and the cool part is that you don't need to know where they are, you just ask for them and you get them.

On another level, WWW is a *hypertext* system. Sprinkled among the text are links to other files. We call this book "hypertext in print": when we mention something from another article or chapter, we tell you the section number so you can refer to it easily. An online hypertext system takes out the step where you have to actually turn the pages: just click on the reference and the other section appears, and when you're done, return to the previous section by just pressing a button.

A superset of hypertext is *hypermedia*. WWW is a hypermedia system because you can place pointers not just to HTML-formatted text files, but also to audio files and graphic images. Of course, this is dependent on your having the hardware to play audio and display graphics in a supported format. But assuming you have the correct set-up, you might display a GIF image or play a Sun *.au* sound file from a remote site.

In addition to everything else, WWW is an information-retrieval service. It not only links to other HTML-formatted files, it can also Telnet to other sites, start up Gopher *(8.08)* or WAIS *(8.09)* connections, and FTP files to display on your machine in text (i.e., non-HTML) format. You can even use Mosaic to read Usenet news *(8.05)*. Basically, if you have Mosaic, you may not need any of the other tools such as *xgopher* or *xwais*, or even a news reader like *xrn*. Mosaic even has a facility for reading manpages, so you may not even need *xman* *(5.02)*. One tool does it all.

The best way to learn about Mosaic is to start it up and click away. By default, when you open Mosaic you're connected to NCSA at UIUC, home of

Mosaic. This is called your home page, configurable via the `homeDocument` resource, by specifying another home page on the command line, or via the WWW_HOME environment variable. The syntax for specifying a home page is somewhat complicated, but usually it follows the form:

> `http:` *//site/pathname*

For example:

> `http://nearnet.gnn.com/gnn/GNNhome.html`

This uses the HTTP protocol on *nearnet.gnn.com*, accessing file *gnn/GNNhome.html*. This is called a Universal Resource Locator, or URL. Although HTTP is the preferred access method, you can also connect to Web home pages via *ftp*, or using the pathname of local files. (See Figure 8-22 for a view of the GNN home page.)

If you're interested in a topic that's underlined, click on it and it brings you to the specified link. Dashed lines mean that you've already looked at this link. This is a very nice feature, since otherwise you might really get lost in the jungle of WWW! (On color displays, dashed links also appear in a different color.)

Due to the nature of Mosaic, it is probably the best self-documenting program available today; just start it up and look for **Internet Starting Points** under the **Navigate** menu. If you want to learn still more about Mosaic, look for *The Mosaic Handbook for the X Window System* by Dale Dougherty, Richard Koman, and Paula Ferguson, published by O'Reilly & Associates Inc.

The collection of sample resource files on the CD-ROM *(20.23)* not only has some resources for Mosaic, it also has some resources for editing HTML files using the *asedit* client *(9.06)*.

—*LM*

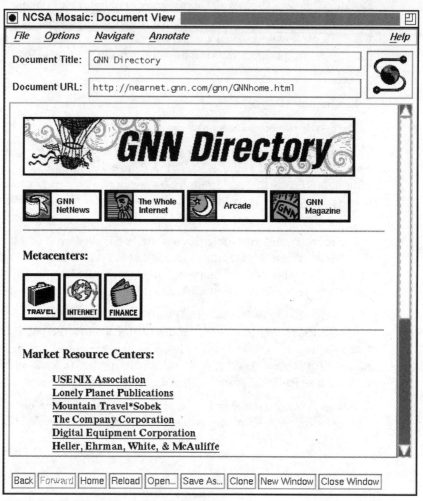

Figure 8-22: A Web home page in Mosaic

9

Editing and Viewing Files

9.01 Editing Files in X

I remember the day I first saw UNIX. My job was editing files online, so I came to the office and was told to start up *vi*. I was too young to question it, but as time wore on, I started to wonder if there was an alternative to learning a complicated editor before I could even start to do my work.

Well, it's too late for me: I'm now a *vi* master and proud of it. But there's still time to save yourselves. That's what this chapter is about: X-based editors for the faint of heart.

To be honest, if you're a "power user" who wants a full-fledged editor, you're likely to be disappointed. Most of these editors are pretty lame. We write this with the knowledge that those of you who use an *xterm* window *(2.02)* and *vi* will probably continue to work that way (like me!). But if you're an *emacs (9.02)* user, then you may be thrilled to switch over to the X version. And many of you with simpler editing needs will be happy to use one of the other X-based editors, thus avoiding the frightening initiation to the worlds of *vi* and *emacs*.

In addition to *vi* and *emacs*, this chapter also covers other commands for just viewing or comparing files. We cover *xless (9.07)* for viewing files, and *xp (9.08)* for a split-screen comparison of files.

—LM

9.02 emacs for X Users

If you're an experienced *emacs* user, sporting overdeveloped muscles in the little finger of your left hand, you'll think that the X version is mostly bells and whistles. Most of its features offer longer ways of doing what you're already used to accomplishing with a few keystrokes. Some typical GUI features have

emacs

been pasted on to an application that achieved incredible power long before graphical interfaces existed. But a few features make life easier, and we'll explore those here.

This article is not for *emacs* novices. My advice to those of you who don't know *emacs* is: run the tutorial, start editing files, and play around with the mouse and pull-down menus. There are some neat features in the X version of *emacs* that will be easier for you than the conventional key-based commands. These features include:

- Using the first mouse button to move point

- Choosing buffers from the **Buffers** menu

- **Undo** and **Spell** in the **Edit** menu

- Describe **Key** in the **Help** menu

- **Search** and **Search Back** in the **Move** menu when you're reading mail

- The whole **Summary** and **Classify** menus when you're reading mail

- Using the scrollbar to figure out where you are in a document, and to move around

(This article assumes that you're using Version 19 of *emacs*.)

Setting Up Your X Session

First, let's get off to the right start. I could tell you to invoke *emacs* at the command line (the X version will automatically start up if you're on an xterm), but that's just for experimental use. Instead, install this as your *.xsession* file:

```
twm &
xterm -ls -iconic -geometry 81x50+1+1 &
emacs -geometry 81x60+200+50
```

This sets up your X session the way a hard-core *emacs* user likes it. *twm* happens to be my window manager; you can substitute another if you like. The *xterm* command gives you a little icon you can click on if you want to leave *emacs* and, say, run a *curses*-based program. The final command establishes you right in the middle of an *emacs* session, where you'll stay for your entire workday; when you exit *emacs* you will log out of X.

Give yourself a couple menu options and buttons to start up new *emacs* sessions and you'll be all set to run *emacs* conveniently whenever you want. Now log in and see what you get (see Figure 9-1).

For now, ignore the top of the window (which in *emacs* is called a frame). We'll try a few of its menus later. The bottom of the frame looks normal, with a status line and a minibuffer. Find a file (C-x C-f) to get yourself oriented; might as well find a long one, so we can play with the scrollbar.

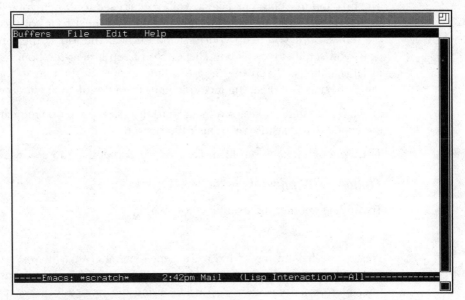

Figure 9-1: A basic emacs session

The Scrollbar

On the right side of the screen is the scrollbar. Some people respond positively to it and some don't. If you try it out and decide you don't need it, put this in your *.emacs* file to suppress it (it says "If I'm running on an X terminal, turn off the scrollbar"):

```
(if (getenv "DISPLAY")
    (scroll-bar-mode -1))
```

In the window containing the scrollbar, the background color represents the size of your whole document. The foreground color—the actual bar—represents the amount of the buffer you can currently see.

The scrollbar will be near the top when start editing (where it says Top in your mode line), and as you move down, the bar will move down too. So if the scrollbar is one-tenth the length of the window and is half-way down, you are looking at one-tenth of the document, in the middle.

Now move around using the scrollbar. Go down to the bottom by clicking the second mouse button at the bottom of the scrollbar window. Go back to the top by clicking the second button at the top. The window represents the whole document; wherever you click the second button is where you'll end up.

The first and third buttons take a while to get used to. When you click the first button in the scrollbar window, the line that it is next to it goes to the top of the frame. So if you keep your first mouse near the top of the scrollbar window, you scroll slowly as you click; if you keep it near the bottom, you scroll in large chunks. Keep the mouse a little above the bottom if you want the same effect as **C-v** (keeping a couple lines from the original window visible).

Similarly, the third mouse scrolls upward. It goes slow if you're near the top of the window and fast if you're near the bottom.

That's enough for the scrollbar. Let's look at something more powerful.

Frames (X Windows)

Try finding another file using the command:

```
C-x 5 b filename
```

Presto, you have a new window, except remember that in *emacs* we call it a frame. It can be nice to create new frames so you have large buffers for all your files, and convenient if you like using the mouse to move around from one top-level X window to another.

What you have now is two frames looking at the same edit session. If you make a change in one frame, then look at the same buffer in the other, the change will be reflected there. The two frames have access to exactly the same buffers all the time.

Don't use **C-x C-c** to get rid of the new frame! That would end your whole *emacs* session. Instead, use **C-x 5 0**.

For fun, try **C-x 5 m**. That starts a new frame for writing a mail message. Unfortunately, after you send the mail message, the frame remains. To make the frame go away, you have to put the following hack in your *.emacs* file:

```
(setq mail-setup-hook
    '(lambda ()
        (setq send-mail-function
            '(lambda ()
                (sendmail-send-it)
                (delete-frame)))))
```

delete-frame is the function bound to **C-x 5 0**.

There are other commands affecting frames, but I'll let you look at the *emacs* documentation for them. Increasingly, in this article, I'll be giving you just a hint of what's available, and you'll need to either experiment or read the documentation to find out the rest.

Cutting and Pasting in emacs and Between Windows

In Version 19, *emacs* works very smoothly with *xterm* and other applications to share selected text. Say you've got a directory listing like that in Figure 9-2.

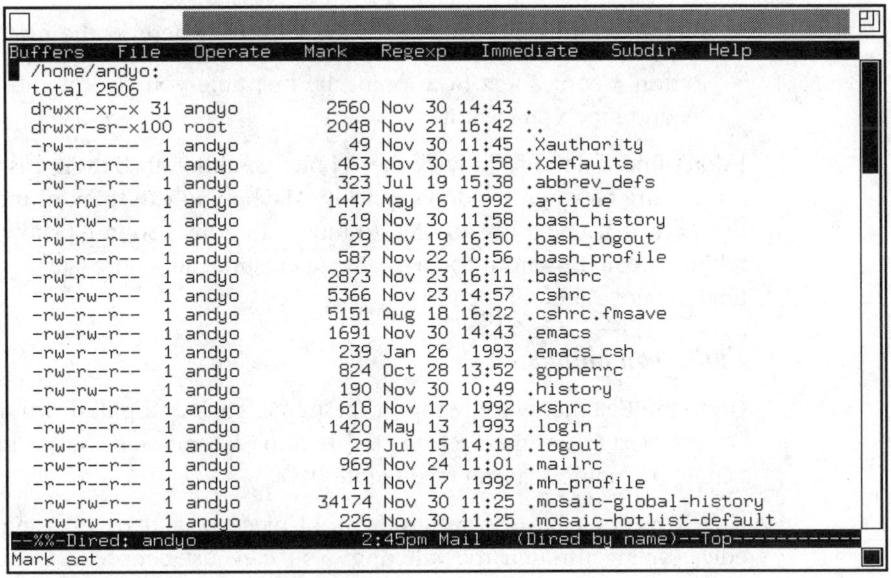

```
┌─┐                                                                    ┌─┐
│ │█████████████████████████████████████████████████████████████████│ │
└─┘                                                                    └─┘
Buffers   File    Operate    Mark    Regexp    Immediate   Subdir    Help
█ /home/andyo:
  total 2506
  drwxr-xr-x 31 andyo        2560 Nov 30 14:43 .
  drwxr-sr-x100 root         2048 Nov 21 16:42 ..
  -rw-------  1 andyo          49 Nov 30 11:45 .Xauthority
  -rw-r--r--  1 andyo         463 Nov 30 11:58 .Xdefaults
  -rw-r--r--  1 andyo         323 Jul 19 15:38 .abbrev_defs
  -rw-rw-r--  1 andyo        1447 May  6  1992 .article
  -rw-rw-r--  1 andyo         619 Nov 30 11:58 .bash_history
  -rw-r--r--  1 andyo          29 Nov 19 16:50 .bash_logout
  -rw-r--r--  1 andyo         587 Nov 22 10:56 .bash_profile
  -rw-r--r--  1 andyo        2873 Nov 23 16:11 .bashrc
  -rw-rw-r--  1 andyo        5366 Nov 23 14:57 .cshrc
  -rw-r--r--  1 andyo        5151 Aug 18 16:22 .cshrc.fmsave
  -rw-rw-r--  1 andyo        1691 Nov 30 14:43 .emacs
  -rw-r--r--  1 andyo         239 Jan 26  1993 .emacs_csh
  -rw-r--r--  1 andyo         824 Oct 28 13:52 .gopherrc
  -rw-rw-r--  1 andyo         190 Nov 30 10:49 .history
  -r--r--r--  1 andyo         618 Nov 17  1992 .kshrc
  -rw-r--r--  1 andyo        1420 May 13  1993 .login
  -rw-r--r--  1 andyo          29 Jul 15 14:18 .logout
  -rw-r--r--  1 andyo         969 Nov 24 11:01 .mailrc
  -r--r--r--  1 andyo          11 Nov 17  1992 .mh_profile
  -rw-rw-r--  1 andyo       34174 Nov 30 11:25 .mosaic-global-history
  -rw-rw-r--  1 andyo         226 Nov 30 11:25 .mosaic-hotlist-default
--%%-Dired: andyo         2:45pm Mail   (Dired by name)--Top-----------
Mark set                                                              ■
```

Figure 9-2: An emacs directory listing

Man! What a lot of pull-down menus! I'll let you explore those on your own, because they offer the same functions as the keys in Dired mode.

Back to cutting and pasting: choose a directory and copy the name (you can use M-w; later we'll show how to use the mouse). Now go to your xterm, type ls with a space following it, and click the second button. Your directory is pasted in.

Now pretend you want to save a part of your xterm. Click the first button in it and drag it across some text. Go back to your emacs session and type C-y. You'll yank what you selected from the xterm. Uuch, looks pretty ugly, doesn't it? That's OK, just type C-w, and it gets killed again. That's because point and mark were set around the text when you pasted it in.

So the *emacs kill* and *yank* commands are completely integrated with the X selection buffer. But you can kill and yank using a mouse as well as the traditional commands. Try a kill right now. Put the mouse at the start of the text and press the first button. Put it at the end and press the third. You've just copied the text into your kill ring (the equivalent of M-w). Click the third button again, and the text is cut. Now click the second button to put it back.

So this is what the buttons do in your editing buffer:

- Button 1 sets point. In some later versions, you can also use it to select words or lines; just double-click or triple-click with it, or drag it across the text you want to select.

- Button 2 yanks the contents of the kill ring wherever the mouse is placed.

- Button 3 copies text from point the first time you click it and cuts text the second time you click it.

I don't find a need for any of these buttons, although Button 1 is kind of nice for moving between windows quickly. Maybe you can think of more powerful functions that you'd like to bind to mouse buttons. Soon I'll show you how to rebind them. But now for a really interesting cut-and-paste experience; it's time to take a look at menus.

Pull-down Menus

Go to the **Edit** menu at the top of the frame, click and pull down till you get to **Choose Next Paste**, then release the button. A temporary buffer pops up containing the entire kill ring (see Figure 9-3).

Now you don't have to retrieve an old piece of text by pressing **M-y** repeatedly, cycling through the kill ring. You can just choose it from this listing. Then press **C-y** in your document and there it is. The whole kill ring rotates when you select one item.

To tell you the truth, this is about the only thing that's really new in the pull-down menus. Most of them just give access to functions that you could perform with one or two keystrokes. For instance, it's your subjective opinion which is faster:

- Press **C-x C-b**, move to *Buffer List* window, move point down to desired buffer, and press the first mouse button.

- Place mouse over the **Buffers** menu, click, move down to the desired buffer, and release.

Not to mention the brute-force method:

- Press **C-x b**, type in the first few characters of the buffer name, press the space bar and **RETURN** key.

But if you use a feature only once in a while, you may find the menus convenient. For instance, if you want to save a mail message from RMAIL to a UNIX file, and you aren't used to doing so, it's easier to use the **Classify** menu than to remember the key sequence.

A recent addition to *emacs* you might want to check out is bookmarks, which are available both through the **File** menu and through standard commands.

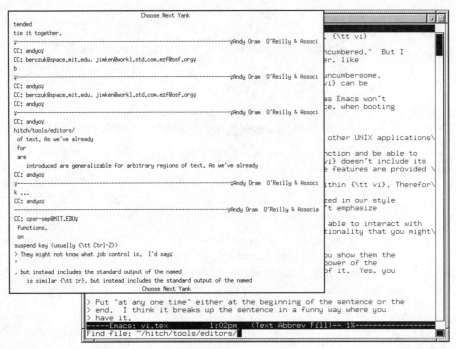

Figure 9-3: A kill ring

Bookmarks preserve a buffer and the current position of point. So you can save your place and go back to it in a future *emacs* session.

The RMAIL, Dired, and Shell modes have special pull-down menus you can explore. If you get tired of them and decide not to use menus anymore, put in your *.emacs* file:

```
(if (getenv "DISPLAY")
    (menu-bar-mode -1))
```

Rebinding Mouse Buttons

Version 19 of *emacs* makes this easy. Let's say that for some reason you want to click the second button to reply to a mail message. In other words, you want the second button to be bound to the rmail-reply function when you're in RMAIL mode. The *.emacs* entry to do this is:

```
(define-key rmail-mode-map [mouse-2] 'rmail-reply)
```

You can put any combination of shift, control, and meta key together with a button. (But the **Escape** key cannot substitute for Meta.) For instance, this entry causes you to forward a mail message when you hold down the Shift key and press the second button:

```
(define-key rmail-mode-map [S-mouse-2] 'rmail-forward)
```

And either of the following specifies a combination of the Shift key, the CTRL key, and the second button:

```
(define-key rmail-mode-map [C-S-mouse-2] 'rmail-forward)
(define-key rmail-mode-map [S-C-mouse-2] 'rmail-forward)
```

Features Documented in the Manual

In this article, I've mostly described things that aren't well documented in the *emacs* manual. Writing about a graphical program is hard! In particular, none of the menus are documented in the *emacs* manual.

But some things are well described, including how to customize things like fonts and colors. So read the *emacs* manual or online info. The O'Reilly Nutshell handbook *Learning GNU Emacs* also has a useful chapter on the X version, although currently it covers Version 18, and therefore is only partly applicable to Version 19.

—AO

9.03 Editing With xedit

The basic editing tool for X is *xedit*. I'm not a very big fan of *xedit*, but it is the most common X-based editor. It's basically a wrapper around the Athena text widget.

xedit

The *xedit* window (see Figure 9-4) is divided into four parts:

- A commands section, which features three command push buttons (Quit, Save, and Load) and an area to their right in which a filename can be entered.

- A message window, which displays messages from the client and can also be used as a scratch pad.

- The filename display, which shows the name of the file being edited and the read/write permissions for the file.

- The edit window, in which the text of the file is displayed and in which you issue the editing commands.

The three push buttons in the commands section have the following functions:

Figure 9-4: Test file displayed in edit window

Quit

Exits the current editing session and closes the window. If changes have not been saved, *xedit* displays a warning in the message window and does not exit, thus allowing the user to save the file.

Save

Writes the file. If file backups are enabled (using the `enableBackups` resource), *xedit* first stores a copy of the unedited file with a *.BAK* suffix and then overwrites the original file with the contents of the edit window. The filename used is the text that appears in the area immediately to the right of the **Load** button.

Load

Loads the file displayed immediately to the right of the button into the edit window. If a file is currently being displayed and has been modified, a warning message will ask the user to save the changes, or to press **Load** again.

This interface has at least two serious pitfalls. First, if you're working on a file that has unsaved changes and you try to load a second file, it's possible to overwrite the second file. This is how it happens. In order to load a second file, you must enter the name of the file in the area next to the **Load** button; then press **Load**. If you try to load a second file while editing a file with unsaved changes, *xedit* warns you to save or press **Load** again. If you press **Save** the current file will be saved—but as the name to the right, the second file you intended to load.

If backups are not enabled, this action will overwrite the file you wanted to load. If backups are enabled, the first file will be saved under the name of the second file with a *.BAK* extension and the second file will not be overwritten. Because of this potential problem, it's a good idea to set the resource `enableBackups` to `on` before using *xedit*.

A second problem can occur after you've loaded a file by entering the name in the window next to the **Load** button. Suppose you've been editing the file for some time, but haven't saved the changes. If you go to save the changes and accidentally double-click on **Load** (not that difficult to do), you'll reload the version of the file before you made the edits. The changes are lost!

Although *xedit* can come in useful for simple editing tasks (e.g., within a mailer such as *xmail (7.02)*), I don't recommend using it as your primary text editor. The program is somewhat buggy and its behavior can be erratic. For example, it's fairly easy to overwrite files inadvertently, as explained in the discussion of the **Load** button above. The redraw command (**CTRL-L**) causes text in the window to scroll so as to reposition the cursor in the center of the editing window—not a welcome surprise. Some of the commands to create a new paragraph may also inadvertently copy preceding text. These are just a few of *xedit*'s inconvenient features.

xedit recognizes various **CTRL** and Meta keystroke combinations that are bound to a set of commands similar to those provided by the *emacs (9.02)* text editor.

—VQ

9.04 The axe Text Editor

axe is another X-based editor, and is presumed to be much better than *xedit* *(9.03)*. You be the judge. What I like about *axe* is that you don't need to learn any new keystrokes for serious editing (as you do for *xedit*); you can do most of what you want via pull-down menus. So users can get up-to-speed with *axe* very quickly. When users become frustrated with having to use the menus, they can start learning the key bindings (which are conveniently patterned after *emacs* (9.02) key mappings. Well, convenient for *emacs* users at least; us *vi* holdouts are still left out in the cold).

When you first start *axe*, a small control box appears, as shown in Figure 9-5. You use this box to create new windows, to get help, and to quit the *axe* application entirely.

aXe

Figure 9-5: The axe control box

Press the axe-patterned **Edit** box to get a new text window, as shown in Figure 9-6.

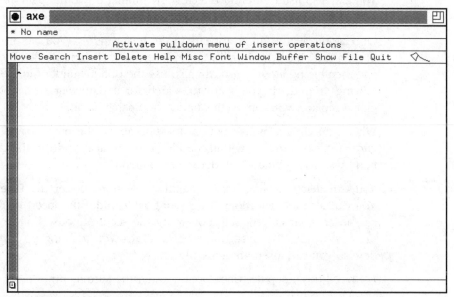

Figure 9-6: An axe text box

The row immediately above the text buffer (which is currently empty) shows a series of pull-down menus (and a cute little axe). As your cursor hovers over a menu, the buffer on top of the menus shows what its function is.

To open a file, use the **File** pull-down menu to select **Load**. The **file load** window appears, with a listing of your current directory. If you want to open a file in a different directory, you can type its pathname. The **fileload** window appears in Figure 9-7.

Figure 9-7: Loading a file with axe

You can also list a different directory by pulling down the **path** menu to move to a parent directory or to your home directory.

Once you select a file, it appears in the text window. You can now edit it by placing the I-bar where you want to insert text, clicking the left mouse button, and then typing at will. You can also use the options under the **Move** menu for moving around. If you want to search for a particular string or perform a global replace, you can do this under the **Search** menu.

When you click a mouse button, the line above the menu bar displays your current cursor position within the file. You can also find out the current position by selecting **Where?** under the **Misc** menu.

You can delete words, lines, or entire selections under the **Delete** window. You can also cut selections, for pasting later under the **Insert** menu. You can also insert your current selection using the second mouse button (as you can in *xterm*) *(11.05)*. The **Insert** menu also allows you to bring up a pop-up window so you can insert an entire file.

For boo-boos, keep the **Undo** option under the **Misc** menu in mind.

A text file in an *axe* text window appears in Figure 9-8.

There's plenty more to talk about. Since you can open several editing windows under *axe*, the **Window**, **Buffer** and **Show** menus are all for juggling different files that are currently open. The **File** and **Quit** menus are for saving and closing files and *axe* in general. The **Font** menu gives you the opportunity to

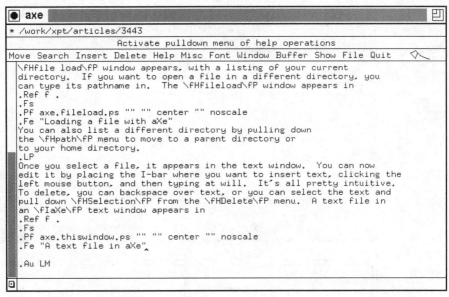

Figure 9-8: A text file in axe

choose larger fonts if you want. You can set some user preferences under the **Misc** menu and also format or center text (useful for titles or if you write poetry on the computer). And if you ever get stuck or just want to know more, there's a plethora of online help under the **Help** menu.

—LM

9.05 *A Kinder, Gentler Editor: asedit*

asedit is yet another editor, but this one is prettier and friendlier. It's Motif-based, so it's got pretty menus and is easy to use. It's also got an elaborate online help system and a built-in spell checker. *asedit* is still limited as far as powerful editing goes, but at least it looks nice.

asedit

asedit actually reminds me a lot of working on a Macintosh. When you first start it up, it opens you up into a new empty file called *NoName1* (reminiscent of the Macintosh "Untitled" files). At the top are four menus with Mac-like commands. Figure 9-9 shows the **File** menu.

You can open a file by choosing **Open** and then selecting a file. Under the **Edit** menu you can copy and paste; under the **Search** menu are commands for searching and replacing; and under the **Tools** menu are various functions such as running a spell checker, sorting text, changing case, reformatting text, and also user-definable filters. To use items under the **Tools** menu, first select the text in question and then select the spell checker, *sort* command, etc. Figure 9-10 shows *asedit* with text selected for use with the **Double Space** filter.

Figure 9-9: The asedit file menu

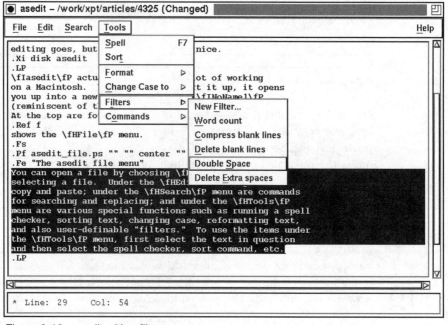

Figure 9-10: asedit with a filter

One oddity about *asedit*: it uses your **Backspace** key to erase text preceding your cursor, but your **Delete** key to erase text *after* your cursor. This feature makes it easier to edit without having to use your mouse to position your cursor as much, but it can be surprising, especially if you don't have a Backspace key mapped *(18.07)*.

—LM

9.06 asedit Translations for HTML

If you edit files in the HTML markup language *(8.10)*, then check out these translation tables *(20.29)* for *asedit (9.05)*, supplied by our generous friend and reviewer
Miles O'Neal. HTML is used to format files for the World Wide Web. Like most
markup languages, it's extremely powerful, but laborious to enter. These translations make HTML files a little easier to code.

See Article 20.23 for information about installing these resources.

Once the resources are installed, when you start *asedit* you should be able to
use some new control sequences to insert useful strings. For example, **CTRL-B**
inserts the string <b> (which starts bold text in HTML), and **Alt-B** inserts the
string </b>.

—LM

9.07 Viewing Files with xless

xless

Here's an X program based on *less*, a popular lookalike for the *more* program.
To use *xless*, specify the file on the command line:

```
% xless ch08.xless
```

The resulting window appears in Figure 9-11.

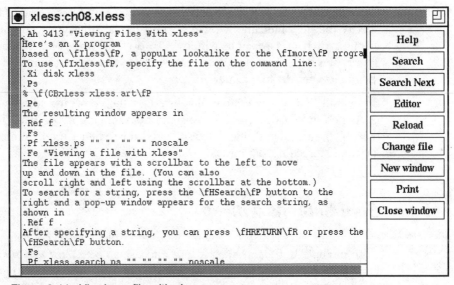

Figure 9-11: Viewing a file with xless

The file appears with a scrollbar to the left to move up and down in the file. (You can also scroll right and left using the scrollbar at the bottom.) To search for a string, press the **Search** button to the right and a pop-up window appears for the search string, as shown in Figure 9-12. After specifying a string, you can press **Return** or press the **Search** button.

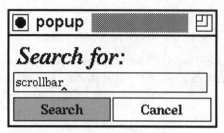

Figure 9-12: Searching for a string

You can continue searching for the same string using the **Search Next** button.

If you'd like to edit the file, you can press the **Editor** button. An *xterm* window appears, using the editor specified in your EDITOR environment variable. If you're using an X-based editor such as *xedit (9.03)* or *xemacs (9.02)*, (i.e., one which doesn't require an *xterm*), set the editorDoesWindows resource to True.

You can use the **Reload** button to reexamine the current file.

To change the file in the current window, you can press **Change file** and then specify the new filename. However, *xless* can also let you view multiple files at once, each in a separate window. To do that, press **New window** and then specify the new filename. **Close window** closes the current window. **Print** sends the file to your default printer via *lpr.*

If you call *xless* with multiple files listed on the command line, then each file is opened in its own window. This can be annoying if you want to list many files on the command line. (I discovered this when I tried running *xless* * in its source directory. Big mistake.)

—LM

9.08 Split Screens with xp

xp is a cute program for viewing files in a split screen. Of course, you can open multiple buffers in *xemacs (9.02)*, and using *axe (9.04)* or *asedit (9.05)*, you can just have several editing windows open. But *xp* allows you to *more* multiple files at once, without taking up all the real estate required to open several files in *xless (9.07)*. It also lets you use regular expressions in searches.

xp

For example, you can start using *xp* by comparing two files:

```
% xp Makefile Makefile.bak
```

The initial window shows the first file listed (with the standard Athena scrollbar to the left), as shown in Figure 9-13.

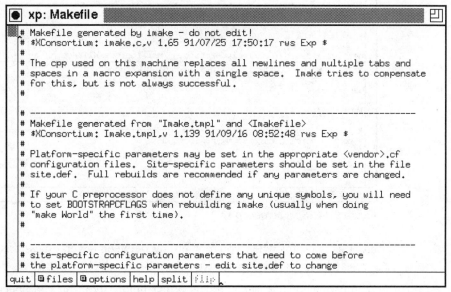

Figure 9-13: xp showing an initial file

You can now press the **split** button. The screen is split at the top of the window, with two independent scrollbars. The separator line has a black square to the far right; to enlarge the top portion (and decrease the bottom portion), just drag this square down. At this point, the same initial file appears in both halves of the screen.

To get to the second file for comparison, press the **files** button. Each time you press **files**, it will bring up the next file listed on the command line. Although I only specified two files on the command line, you can specify as many as you want (although you can only view two at a time). One limitation of *xp* is that you can't backtrack on the **files** listing; once you get to the last file, that's it.

In this example, I wanted to compare two *Makefile* s *(31.16)*. I press **files** and the *Makefile.bak* file appears in the bottom window. The top window remains unchanged. Now I can scroll the two halves and compare the two files. In this case, the only difference is that the new *Makefile* has dependencies added by *makedepend* at the end of the file; Figure 9-14 shows where the files start to differ.

By pressing **flip**, you can put the contents of the first window on top and the contents of the second on bottom. Since new files always replace the bottom

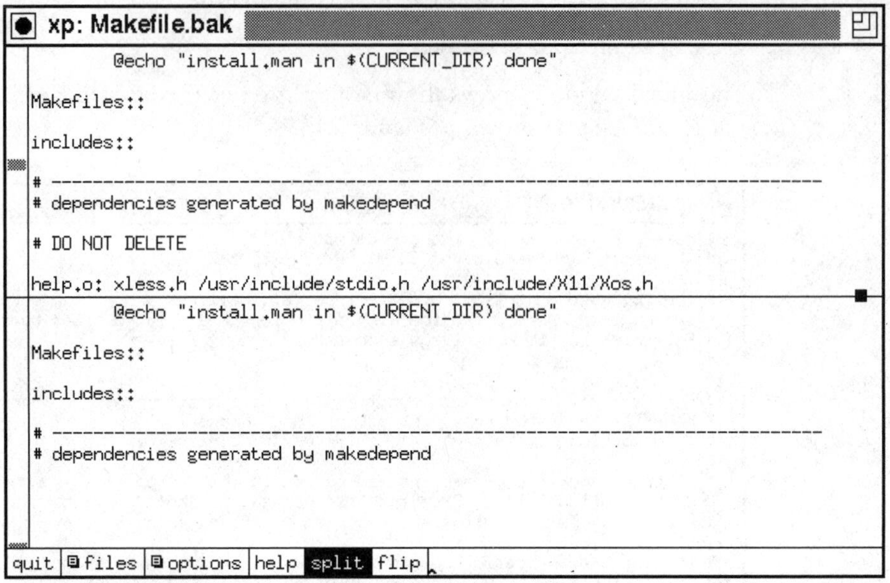

```
┌──────────────────────────────────────────────────────────────────┐
│ ● xp: Makefile.bak ▓▓▓▓▓▓▓▓▓▓▓▓▓▓▓▓▓▓▓▓▓▓▓▓▓▓▓▓▓▓▓▓▓▓▓▓▓       ⌸ │
├──────────────────────────────────────────────────────────────────┤
│            @echo "install.man in $(CURRENT_DIR) done"              │
│                                                                    │
│  Makefiles::                                                       │
│                                                                    │
│  includes::                                                        │
│                                                                    │
│▒ #  ------------------------------------------------------------   │
│  # dependencies generated by makedepend                            │
│                                                                    │
│  # DO NOT DELETE                                                   │
│                                                                    │
│  help.o: xless.h /usr/include/stdio.h /usr/include/X11/Xos.h     ■ │
│            @echo "install.man in $(CURRENT_DIR) done"              │
│                                                                    │
│  Makefiles::                                                       │
│                                                                    │
│  includes::                                                        │
│                                                                    │
│  #  ------------------------------------------------------------   │
│  # dependencies generated by makedepend                            │
│                                                                    │
│▒                                                                   │
├──────────────────────────────────────────────────────────────────┤
│ quit │⊟ files │⊟ options │ help │ split │ flip                     │
└──────────────────────────────────────────────────────────────────┘
```

Figure 9-14: Split screen in xp

file, this is useful when you're shuffling between several files. It is also useful for searching, as described below.

To the right of the **flip** button is a text field. Here you can specify a search string (using regular expressions, if you like). For example, I could type /install:: and press **Return**, and the bottom window scrolls until the string "install::" appears in the middle of the window (with the string highlighted). Press **Return** again and the string is searched for again. Although the search is only performed in the bottom window, you can then press **flip** and search again in the other file.

If no files are specified on the command line, then standard input is used. You can also use standard input by specifying "–" as a filename. This makes it possible to compare a file against standard input. For example, the following command line compares the */etc/passwd* file against the NIS *passwd* database:

```
% ypcat passwd | xp /etc/passwd -
```

—LM

10

Just For Fun

10.01 Work Isn't Everything

For many of us, our first computer experience was playing a game. I remember when we first saw a Macintosh computer, and spent hours playing multiplayer games like MacYahtzee and PhaseCraze, adventure games (anyone else remember Radical Castle?), and solitaire games like Klondike and Concentration. I still have a Macintosh at home, and every year for Christmas I buy my husband the latest game and then say goodbye because I won't see him again until he gets sick of it.

Let's face it, there's something inherently sinful about games. Not just because you should be working; also because there's that little voice inside your head complaining that you're wasting time playing games when you could be outdoors doing something healthy or productive. Games are pretty low on the recreation totem pole: there's this new "fun ethic" that says you should be spending your spare time climbing mountains or reading up on the Peloponnesian Wars.

Be that as it may, some of us are just addicted to games and that's all there is to it. So we'll wait until everyone's gone for the day and then shamefacedly start up a game, and guiltily slink home ninety minutes later (if we're lucky). There are plenty of games out there, but the ones that I'm addicted to are goal-oriented solitaire games (like *spider* (10.06), *xmahjongg* (10.07), and *ishido* (10.08)). Other people (like my husband) are more interested in arcade-type games like *xasteroids* (10.11) and *xmris* (10.12). And *everyone* loves *tetris* (10.02).

And then there are those people just aren't interested in games and think that those of us who play games are slothful idiots. And maybe they're right. But if you're a gameplayer, then this is the chapter for you.

—LM

10.02 Tetris!

tetris

A computer without *tetris* is like a car without a stereo: it does what it's supposed to, but it isn't nearly as much fun. *tetris* runs on every platform, and was one of the first games ported to X. Since then, *tetris* has evolved from the no-frills version in X11R3 to the Ultra version we present here.

If you've never played *tetris* before, the idea is that shapes come raining down from the top of the screen. The standard shapes are shown in Figure 10-1.

Figure 10-1: Tetris shapes

As the shapes come down, your mission is to place them in such a way so that rows going across get filled up. When a row is filled, it disappears. As a piece falls to the bottom, you can use the l key to move it to the right, the j key to move it to the left, and the k key to rotate it. Once the piece hits the bottom, it can't be moved anymore. Once you have it placed, you can press the space bar for the piece to drop the rest of the way down in its current position; this gives you extra points, and also saves you from getting bored when you're still at a lower speed. (See Figure 10-2 for a look at Tetris in action.)

(If these keys seem non-intuitive, then you might prefer to use your arrow keys instead: right arrow for right, left arrow for left, up arrow to rotate, and down arrow to drop.)

As the pieces come down faster and faster, it becomes harder and harder to position pieces so that rows are completed. The rows start piling up, and before you know it you're in Big Trouble.

tetris is a game that appeals to our innate sense of organization. Just place the pieces neatly and you do just fine. You get in trouble when the game starts going faster and you end up leaving blank areas; the pieces don't have so far to fall, you run out of time to place pieces, and the game ends when the pieces have no where to go. One useful feature (in my experience) is to use Alt-N when you start getting in trouble. This gives you a "next" box, so you'll always know what piece is coming next and can plan accordingly. You get fewer points, but you'll last longer.

One special detail about this version of *tetris* is that when the game reaches the highest speed (9), you enter "bonus mode." Unusual, mutated, hard-to-

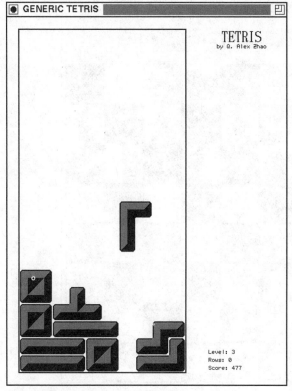

Figure 10-2: Tetris in action

place shapes start appearing in bonus mode, adding a new level of complexity to the game.

—LM

10.03 *A Chess Program*

xboard

xboard is an X-based chess program. It's actually just a front-end to GNU Chess. To install *xboard*, you first have to install the GNU Chess binary for interacting with the *xboard* client (*gnuchessx*). Then start up *xboard* to have a fully functional chess program, as shown in Figure 10-3.

Just drag the pieces to where you want to go. Then watch the computer wipe you out. As you'd expect from a GNU product, *xboard* is impressively robust and supports literally dozens of command-line options and resources. I'll just mention the more important features, and let you explore the rest.

By default, *xboard* gives you a five-minute clock for 40 moves (that is, if you move 40 times in five minutes, the clock will be reset, otherwise you lose). You can change this using the *–mps* and *–tc* options which alter the number of

Figure 10-3: The Xboard chess program

gnuchess

moves per session or the amount of time, respectively. For example, to have it ask for just one move each 30 seconds, try:

```
% xboard -mps 1 -tc 0:30 &
```

You can also turn off the clock completely using the *–clock* command-line option:

```
% xboard -clock False &
```

If you're playing with a clock, remember that you can always select **Pause** under the **Mode** menu if you want to take a break and actually do some work. A faster way to pause the game is to press the **P** button near the top right of the board.

You can control how many moves ahead the computer player will look when making a move with the *–sd* command-line option, and how much time the computer player thinks for each move using the *–st* command-line option.

You can save your game so you might restart from it later. This is useful if your administrator is inconsiderate enough to reboot the system in the middle of a game. You can also save just the current position, so you can test out different strategies.

By selecting **Edit Game** under the **Mode** menu, you can control both sides of the board. Select **Machine Black** to have the computer take over again (or **Machine White** if you want to switch sides). You can also select **Edit Position** to edit the board. This lets you move pieces wherever you want, remove them entirely, add new pieces, etc. I found out that I can actually beat the computer if I just give myself a dozen or so queens.

There are also a series of options for specifying what colors to use for the pieces or for the board squares. If you don't want to play with a computer but prefer to interface with (gasp) humans, then try running *xboard* with the Internet Chess Server or with its mail interface.

In its simplest incarnation, *xboard* is designed to work with one human player against one computer player (GNU Chess) However, *xboard* also lets you specify a different computer program or pit two programs against each other.

Using the Internet Chess Server

The Internet Chess Server (ICS) is a meeting place for chess players around the world, each one aching to play a game with a faceless stranger (i.e., you). If this doesn't scare you, then you can try it out by running *xboard* with the *–ics* command-line option, and run *xboard* in the foreground:

```
% xboard -ics

**** Welcome to the Internet Chess Server at ics.uoknor.edu ****

This program was written and is maintained by Daniel Sleator
<sleator@cs.cmu.edu> (aka Darooha). Direct general questions about the
chess server -- as well as comments about bugs and features -- to him.

Other people are in charge of various specific aspects of this system,
such as: the local host, rules and etiquette, client programs (giics,
xboard, etc), and registration. Type "help people" upon logging in to
see who to contact for specific purposes.

Type the name you wish to use:
```

The graphical *xboard* window comes up, while a character-based Telnet session to the remote site is initiated. Once you've found an opponent, you can use the *xboard* window as your interface to the game. You should become a registered user if you intend to use the ICS on a regular basis, but you can still try it out without registering.

Playing Chess by Email

Another way to use *xboard* is through its mail interface. *xboard* is distributed with a program called *cmail*. Using *cmail*, you can play a game via email. To start a game in email, run *cmail* in place of *xboard*:

```
% cmail
cmail 2.10, Copyright (C) 1993 Free Software Foundation, Inc.
cmail comes with ABSOLUTELY NO WARRANTY; for details type `cmail -w'.
cmail is free software, and you are welcome to redistribute it
under certain conditions; type `cmail -c' for details.

Chess directory </home/lmui/Chess> does not exist. Create it? [y/q]:
```

cmail prompts you with several questions, such as the email address of the other player. Then it starts *xboard*. Play your first move and then select **Mail Move** under the **File** menu. Then go off and work until you get mail from your opponent.

When you receive mail from your opponent specifying their move, run the mail message through *cmail*. Depending on what mailer program you use, you may be able to pipe the message directly, or you may have to save the message and then call *cmail* from the command line:

```
% cmail < chessmail
```

If the game window is already open, *cmail* is smart enough to use it instead of starting *xboard* all over again.

—LM

10.04 Blackjack

xblackjack

Blackjack, or "Twenty-One," is probably the easiest, fastest, and most addictive of card games. *xblackjack* is a casino blackjack game for X11.

In this casino version of blackjack, you start off with $200. Before each "hand," you make a bet by holding down the first mouse button on the "money bar" and sliding it to the amount you want to bet. When you release the first mouse button, the bet is registered and the hand is dealt. (A typical *xblackjack* window is shown in Figure 10-4.)

There is only one other player: the dealer (aka, the computer), who has one card turned face-down. Once the hand is dealt, you can press one of the buttons on the panel to the left of the "table" to **Hit** or **Stand**. A **Hit** means that you want another card dealt to your hand, and **Stand** means that you will keep the current hand. (If you have 21, *xblackjack* assumes that you want to stand.) The computer's suggestion is highlighted, using the same counting algorithm as the dealer uses.

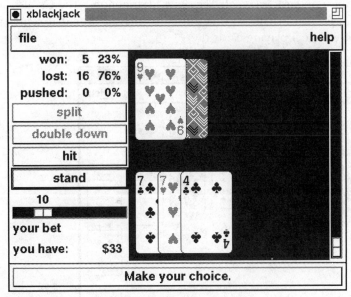

Figure 10-4: A typical xblackjack window

A few special features are:

- "Insurance," which you're offered via a dialog box if the dealer has an ace showing at the beginning of the hand. Insurance means that you're now betting that the dealer has blackjack, i.e., that the hidden card has a value of 10. If so, your original bet loses, but you're paid 2 to 1 on the insurance.

- "Double down," where you can double your bet.

- "Split," which you can do if you have two of the same card. You can now play two hands in succession against the same dealer.

The panel to the left of the table shows how well you're doing. (As you see from Figure 10-4, I'm not doing all that well.) When 52 cards have been dealt, the dealer reshuffles, and you keep on playing. To end a game, select **Quit** from the **File** menu.

—LM

10.05 *Standard Solitaire: klondike*

klondike is a Tcl *(30.01)*-based solitaire game. It's a bit slow and has some annoying error messages, but it's fun.

klondike might be considered the standard solitaire game for computers. (See Figure 10-5 for a typical *klondike* game board.) It's the solitaire game you get

klondike

with the standard Microsoft Windows distribution. There's also a shareware version for the Macintosh that I used to play. I hear that some people even play it with real playing cards (!).

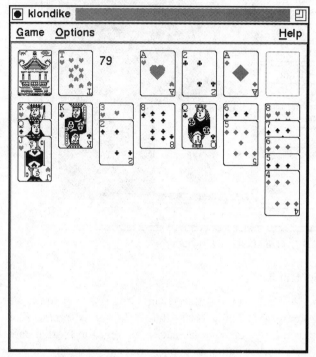

Figure 10-5: klondike game board

I should confess that I didn't play this version of *klondike* thoroughly enough to figure out the scoring. But according to the online help, you're incremented five points when you add cards to the tableau and 10 points when you place cards on their foundations. You're decremented two points every 15 seconds. You're also decremented points when you move cards from the foundation back to the tableau, and when you move a single card at the bottom of a block to another column. Also, when turning cards over three at a time, you're allowed only three free trips through the deck; after that they cost you 25 points. When turning cards over one at a time, you're only allowed one free pass, and after that you lose (gulp) 100 points per pass.

Although this game can be slow, I found it to be entertaining enough to waste a good hour on it, determined to win. I did not win. So all in all, I give it a thumbs up.

—LM

10.06 *An Awesome Solitaire Game*

If anyone ever asks you what you can do using X that you can't do on another window system, just point them to *spider*. This is one of my favorite games, and as far as I know it doesn't exist on any other platform. PCs and Macintoshes have solitaire games, but those don't hold a candle to *spider*. (See Figure 10-6 for a typical *spider* game.)

Why this love-fest for *spider*? Because it's difficult. It's maddening. It lets you cheat, and you still lose.

spider

The way *spider* works is that there are two decks of cards, shuffled together. Click on the deck the first time and 10 columns are each filled with four or five face-down cards covered by one card that's face up.

The rules are actually very simple on paper. You can move any card on the bottom of a stack onto a card of a higher number, regardless of the suit. But you can move several cards as a group only if they all have the same suit.

As you move a card, you uncover the card underneath. If you don't like it, you can press u to undo the move with no penalty except an audio beep and the word "Cheater!" at the bottom of the screen. (This hasn't been a big deterrent against cheating.)

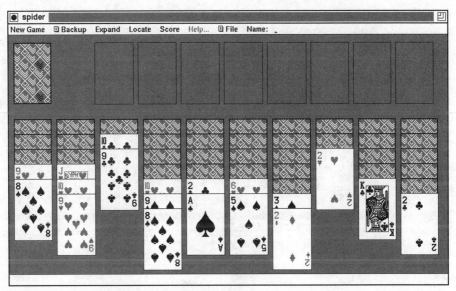

Figure 10-6: A spider game in action

You don't have to actually drag cards; in most cases you can just click on them, and they will move to the smartest place. (There are some circumstances when *spider*'s idea of a smart move conflicts with your strategy.)

If you empty out an entire column, you can put any card on the empty spot. This becomes invaluable for shuffling cards around to get them into moveable groups of a single suit.

When you've done all you can for that hand, click on the deck or press **d**, and another hand is dealt, one card on each column. There are five hands in all.

If you get an entire King through Ace of a single suit, you can click on it and move it to the "bank" above. But you actually get more points if you manage to arrange all the suits without moving a column out of the way. This is exceedingly difficult but also very satisfying. The only way to get a perfect score is to uncover all the cards and arrange them in suits without having to remove any off the board, as shown in Figure 10-7.

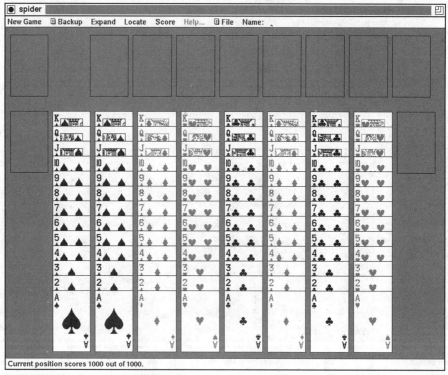

Figure 10-7: A spider victory

—*LM*

10.07 Mah Jongg

xmahjongg

If you feel like burning out your eyes for hours on end, try *xmahjongg*. *xmahjongg* is a tile-based solitaire game in which the object is to remove all the tiles on the board. The *xmahjongg* board resembles that in Figure 10-8.

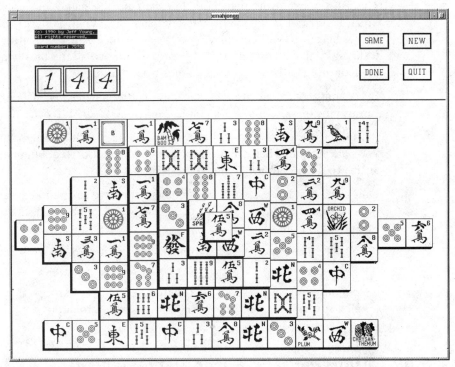

Figure 10-8: An initial xmahjongg window

It's sort of hard to tell from the picture, but some tiles are positioned on top of others. Only the ones at the edges can be removed from the board. The tiles have different patterns and characters, and in order to remove pieces, you need to match two tiles by selecting them with your first mouse button. A match means both the character *and* pattern need to be the same, with the exception of the special tiles with the names of flowers and the seasons; all flowers match each other, and all seasons match each other.

The numbers at the top left corner of the board tell you how many tiles you still need to remove. There are 144 tiles in all. Note that for many board configurations, it is literally impossible to remove all the tiles. As you remove tiles, your score decreases by 2; your goal is to get down to a score of 0 tiles.

If you press the **Done** button, a message appears telling you how many matches are currently available on the board, and your score is frozen. If you have more matches available, you can continue to play but your score doesn't continue to decrement. You will be playing just for the honor of finishing, but you won't have the satisfaction of ending up with a 0 score. Note that the number of matches left does not correspond to the number of moves you have left, since removing tiles often uncovers new matches.

The rules aren't really that hard. Just start up the game and you'll catch on. You'll soon start developing your own strategy. When you do, please let me know, because I've been playing this game since I first saw it for the Macintosh, and I'm still lousy at it. (Is it better to remove all the tiles lying on top of the board or is it better to remove tiles from the edges?)

By default, colors are used to distinguish different layers. If you prefer, you can use the *−c* option to have colors corespond to the tile pattern.

If you get stuck on a board but think a different strategy might have helped, you can press the **Same** button to start the same board configuration all over again. To get a completely new board, press **New**.

One piece of advice: to play *xmahjongg*, you have to spend extended periods of time searching a screen of tiles that are difficult to distinguish. Try to remember to blink.

If you like tile games, have a color display, and want to try something a bit more complex, try out *ishido (10.08)*.

A complication with *xmahjongg* is that before you can use it, you need to install a special font. See Article 31.13 for more information.

—*LM*

10.08 *A Different Tile-Based Game: ishido*

If you have a color monitor, then you might want to try *ishido*. *ishido* is a tile-based game like *xmahjongg (10.07)*, but that's where the comparisons end. Whereas the idea in *xmahjongg* is to remove tiles, *ishido* is based on adding tiles to a board.

ishido

The *ishido* board is shown in Figure 10-9.

From the figure, you can see squares with different designs on the board. There are six different designs in all: maple leaf, smiley face, sickle, star, dollar sign, and circle. What you can't tell is that the squares also have six different colors. At the right of the board is the control panel, where the next tile is shown. The idea is to place the new tile on the board, adjacent to another piece that's either the same color or the same design. Just click on a square to place it there. Keep on placing tiles until you can't move any longer. There are 72 tiles in all.

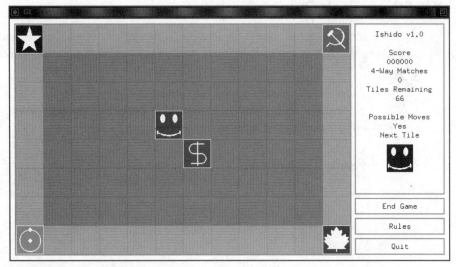

Figure 10-9: The ishido tile game

This probably seems stupid, but there's actually a lot of strategy involved. It's not that hard to place tiles when you only need to match the tiles on a single side, since you only need to match a single design or a single color. It gets a bit hairy, though, when the board becomes crowded and you have to match tiles on two sides, or on three sides, or on (gasp) four.

To match two sides, you need to match by shape on one side and by color on the other. To match three sides you have to match two colors and one shape or two shapes and one color. And to match four sides, you have to match two colors and two shapes. You get an increasing number of points depending on the number of sides you match. (If you press the **Rules** button, you'll see the full rules for the game).

So the strategy is how to place the tiles to set up the most four-way matches.

I'm very fond of *ishido*. The only reason I'm not a total addict is that I don't have a color monitor. Even so, I played for quite a while on my lowly grayscale monitor, never understanding it completely until I finally saw it in color.

—*LM*

10.09 A Tank Game

cbzone

If strategic games aren't your type of thing, you might try *cbzone*. *cbzone* is just the sort of game for people who like to blow things up. Seriously, it's not half bad. It's a faithful version of the arcade game *battlezone*.

cbzone comes up with a screen showing you the view from a tank. Your mission is simple: find and destroy the other tanks before they find you. A *cbzone* window appears in Figure 10-10.

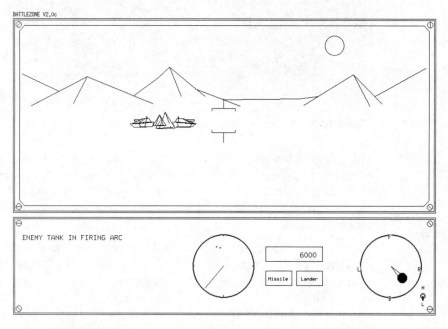

Figure 10-10: Sighting the enemy in cbzone

At first glance, *cbzone* requires a lot of imagination to truly envision the danger of the menacing stick figures approaching you on the screen. But after a while, it becomes pretty engaging, and you really want to destroy those nasty suckers.

One thing about *cbzone* is that it takes over the entire screen and grabs your server. If you want to stop playing for a few minutes (e.g., to do some work!), press the space bar or the letter i to have it pause and iconify.

—LM

10.10 Capture the Flag

capture

"Capture the flag" is a two-player board game. Like chess, there are two sides starting out on each end of the board. Each side has 40 pieces, and each piece has an assigned ranking. You move pieces one square at a time, and when two opposing pieces meet each other, the one with the highest ranking wins. The piece is hidden from the other player, so there's no way to know what ranking the opponent piece is until you attack it. The goal is to be the first player to capture the flag. (See Figure 10-11 for a view of a *capture* board.) This game is Chinese in origin, but is similar to the American game Stratego.

To start *capture*, specify the name of the server your opponent is using. (If you don't specify a second display, both windows appear on your server, which doesn't make for a very compelling game.) For example:

```
% capture ncd14:0.0
```

One window appears on your screen, and your opponent's window appears on ncd14:0.0. Note that this requires that the remote server extends its access control to you *(19.13)*.

When the game starts up, the 40 pieces have been randomly placed in position. Before you start the game, you may switch the position of any two pieces by clicking on them with the first mouse button.

Placing the pieces is probably the most important part of the game. I don't play this game, so I can't say much about the strategy, but one way to go about it might be to place the flag as far out of the way as possible and then place the six bombs to protect the flag. Then again, you might put the bombs in other random places just to confuse your opponent. Some people might put their infantry (i.e., lower-ranked pieces) in front, and generals in back; whereas others might put some higher-ranked pieces in front for easy attacks. Honestly, this can turn into a very complex game, and if anyone knows a sure-fire way to win, please tell me!

When you're done placing your pieces, press the **Done** bar and your opponent is notified that you're ready to begin play. Note that after placement mode, flags and bombs can no longer be moved.

Once the game begins, you can start moving pieces across the board. Each piece can move only one square at a time, with the exception of the scout pieces. You cannot move onto a square already occupied by one of your pieces. You can't move across the lakes in the middle of the board. If you try to move onto an opponent's square, this is an attack, and the lower ranking piece is removed from the board. (If two equally ranked pieces meet, they are both removed.)

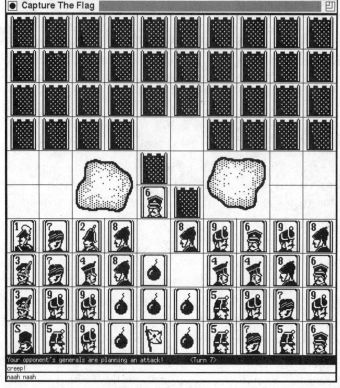

Figure 10-11: A capture board

When a piece attacks a bomb, the bomb explodes, and the piece is removed from the board. The one exception is the miner, which can defuse bombs by removing them from the board.

capture also provides two talk buffers at the bottom of the screen. The intention of these boxes is "so that the two players can insult each other" (according to the manpage).

To quit *capture*, press **CTRL-Q**. Press **CTRL-N** to start a new game, and **CTRL-L** to refresh your display.

—*LM*

10.11 Asteroids

xasteroids

One of the classic video games from way back when was *asteroids*. In *xasteroids*, you're a star ship in the middle of an asteroid belt, and you have to avoid them or destroy them or else you die (see Figure 10-12 for a view of *xasteroids*). Use the **e** key to rotate left, the **r** key to rotate right, and the **p** key to fire. If you need to move, **o** gives you a thrust in the current direction. The backquote key (`) puts on your shields (you only have a limited amount of shielded time, so use it wisely). The space bar puts you in hyperspace. ESCAPE pauses the game.

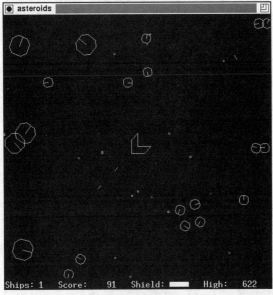

Figure 10-12: xasteroids game

When your ship is destroyed, press **s** to get a new ship in the middle of the screen (noting that if there are asteroids there, you will be destroyed immediately).

—LM

10.12 *Apples Don't Fall Far from Trees, You Know*

Here's an arcade game that looks pretty good even if you don't play arcade games. The *xmris* is an X version of a video-arcade game called "Mr. Do." Or so the manpage says; since I don't hang out in video arcades, I couldn't say. What I can tell you is that *xmris* is great fun.

xmris

The idea behind *xmris* is that you're a little elf guy trying to pick up points and escape these blue meanies. There are little cherries around for you to pick up (points!) and big apples that can drop down and crush things. In a lot of ways, it's similar to Pacman. The idea is to scurry around avoiding the meanies. You can move right and left using the **z** and **x** keys, and up and down using the apostropher and slash keys. Each of these keys is redefinable by specifying keysyms with the associated X resources, such as Xmris.Right, Xmris.Left, and so on. You can kill meanies by maneuvering them so that the apples fall on them, or by throwing a ball at them (using the space bar, also redefinable via the Xmris.Space resource).

You can pause *xmris* by pressing p or by just removing focus from the *xmris* game. When the game is paused, the little elf guy goes to sleep, as shown in Figure 10-13.

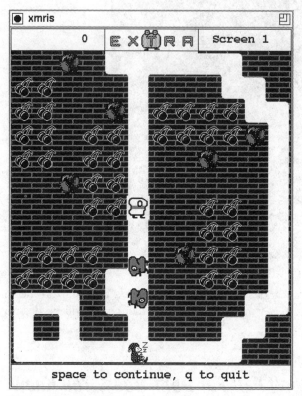

Figure 10-13: xmris taking a snooze

If you're interested, you can get a slightly different sprite by specifying the *–gender "female"* command-line option. This gives you what the manpage calls a more "modern" elf protagonist. Personally, I don't see much of a difference between the male and female sprites, but I appreciate the effort regardless.

—LM

11

Getting the Most out of xterm

11.01 Working with xterm

So far in this book we've bounced around the net looking at many clients that may be new to you. Think of it as having been sort of an out-of-body vacation. Now, for better or worse, it's time to come home.

You should believe us by now that there are tons of X clients available. And in theory, you should be able to spend your entire workday without once using an *xterm* window. But who does that? *xterm* is still by far the most commonly used X client, and it's likely to remain so for quite some time. So we've devoting an entire chapter to this single client.

xterm gives you a window with your standard shell prompt (as specified in your *passwd* entry). You can use this window to run any command-line oriented UNIX program, or to start up additional X applications. (Val uses *xterm* to read mail and news too, but then again she likes *vi*.) Article 2.02 shows a picture of an uncustomized *xterm* window, while that article and the remainder of Chapter 2 describe how to use *xterm* to start other clients.

The uncustomized *xterm* window should be sufficient for most users' needs. Certainly you can do anything in this *xterm* window that you can from a character-based terminal. But *xterm* also has special features you can use, and since you spend so much time in *xterm*, you might as well use them.

This chapter gives you a set of tricks and tips about using *xterm*, including:

- Specifying and using a scrollbar *(11.02, 11.03, 11.04)*

- Copying and pasting text selections *(11.05, 11.07)*

- Modifying text selection behavior *(11.08, 11.09)*

- Printing the current directory in the *xterm* titlebar *(11.12)*.

- Dynamically changing fonts and other features *(11.15, 11.14)*.

- Mapping keys to specified functions *(11.19)*.

For a world of clever things you can do in an *xterm*, see *UNIX Power Tools* (O'Reilly & Associates Inc. and Random House).

—*LM, VQ*

11.02 *Working with Scrollbars*

One of my favorite *xterm* features is the scrollbar. Using the scrollbar, you can reexamine the output or error from a command, select previous text to supply in another command line or to paste into a file, or to hide your current screen from a nosy co-worker.

There are many ways to start up the scrollbar. You can specify the *–sb* option on the command line:

```
% xterm -sb &
```

or you can set the scrollBar resource to true:

```
XTerm*scrollBar: true
```

or for a window that's already running, you can call up the **VT Options** menu by holding down the CTRL key and the center mouse button, and select **Enable Scrollbar**.

A scrollbar appears on the left side of the *xterm* window, as shown in Figure 11-1.

—*LM*

11.03 *How Many Lines to Save?*

If you use the scrollbar in *xterm (11.02)*, you'll find that by default the scrollbar retains only 64 previous lines of text. You can change this by using the *–sl* command-line option:

```
% xterm -sb -sl 200 &
```

or by setting the saveLines resource:

```
XTerm*saveLines: 200
```

You don't want to go crazy with the number of saved lines, though. Too many lines saved may crunch on virtual memory and also make it hard to scroll.

—*LM*

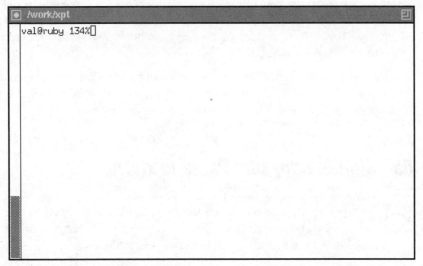

Figure 11-1: xterm window with scrollbar

11.04 More About Scrollbars

If you use the scrollbar in *xterm* *(11.02)*, you'll soon notice that the scroll region jumps back to the bottom as soon as you either type into the window or when output is sent to that window. This can become annoying when you're trying to copy text repeatedly from earlier in this shell session, or when you're trying to look at previous messages on the console but more keep scrolling down. As you might imagine, you can control this (at least a little bit) using command-line options or resources.

You can use the *−si* command-line option or scrollTtyOutput resource (also called scrollInput before X11R5) to disable repositioning to the bottom of the screen on output. This comes in handy when you're trying to examine the output or error stream from a command without waiting for it to finish. The caveat is that although you aren't returned to the very bottom of the buffer anymore, your position is still moved, so it remains a certain number of lines from the bottom. So if four lines are printed to your screen, you aren't brought to the very bottom, but you are brought four lines down. (Another trick is to use **CTRL-S** to stop the tty output while you browse through text, and then **CTRL-Q** to continue tty output.)

Also, try the *+sk* command-line option or scrollKey resource to disable repositioning to the bottom of the screen when you press a key. You might want to do this when you want to apply information from previous screens to your current command line. (Then again, some of us have gotten used to just pressing a key to bring the scrollbar back down to the bottom.)

Another feature you might like is *jump scroll*. When jump scroll is enabled, *xterm* scrolls more than one line at a time, thus speeding up the scrolling process. This feature is particularly helpful when you're scrolling large amounts of text.

Jump scroll is available on the VT Options menu *(11.14)*, through the *–j* command-line option, and through the jumpScroll resource. (See the *xterm* manpage for a complete list of options and resources.)

—LM

11.05 *Simple Copy and Paste in xterm*

You can select text to copy and paste within the same *xterm* window or between *xterm* windows using the pointer. You don't need to be in a text editor to copy and paste. You can also copy or paste text to and from the command line, between the command line and a file, etc.

There are several ways to select (copy) text; all require you to use the pointer. You can select a passage of text, or you can select text by individual words or lines.

When you select text, it becomes highlighted and is copied into global memory from which you can paste it into any *xterm* window. Regardless of the number of *xterm* windows you're running, you can only store one selection in memory at a time. You can paste that selection as many times as you like. When you make another selection, the new text replaces the previous selection in memory.

Table 11-1 summarizes all of the text selection methods.

Table 11-1: Button Combinations to Select Text for Copying

To select	Do this
Passage	Click the first button at the start of the selection and the third button at the end of the selection. Or: At the beginning of the selection, hold down the first button; drag the pointer to the end of the desired text; and release the button.
Word	Double-click the first button anywhere on the word.
Line	Triple-click the first button anywhere on the line.

To clear the highlighting, move the pointer off the selection and click the first button anywhere else in the window. Note, however, that the text still remains in memory until you make another selection.

Of the two methods for selecting a passage, the first is generally easier. Hypothetically, you can select a passage of any length, but we've found there to be limitations in practice. The size of the window limits the amount of text you can highlight in one action. You can extend a selection *(11.07)* beyond the parameters of a window. Copying an extremely long selection, however, doesn't seem to work reliably. Also, when pasting a long selection, the text can become garbled.

You can paste text into any *xterm* window, either onto the command line or into a text file you're editing. In both cases, move the pointer into the window and click the second button. The text will be pasted; in other words, it will appear on the screen, just as if you typed it in. Note that to paste into an open text file, the editing program must be in insert mode.

— *VQ*

11.06 The Trouble with Tabs

Complications can arise if you're copying text that includes tabs. With the current implementation of the copy-and-paste feature, tabs are saved as spaces. If you're copying a large amount of text with many tabs from one text file to another, having tabs converted to spaces can create problems.

Tabs aren't the only control characters that have problems. Other control characters (for example, **CTRL-G**) appear on the screen with a carat and the corresponding ASCII character (for example, ^G).

A possible workaround is to change all tabs in the first file to some unique character or string (using a global command provided by your text editor); copy and paste the text into the second file; and then convert the unique strings back to tabs in both files using your text editor.

— *VQ*

11.07 Extending a Text Selection

Regardless of how you make a text selection *(11.05)*, you can extend that selection to encompass more text, using any of a number of simple pointer actions. Most of the methods to extend a selection involve using the third pointer button. All of the methods are summarized in Table 11-2.

Table 11-2: Button Combinations to Extend a Text Selection

To select	Do this
Passage	Move the pointer to the place in the text to which you want the selection to extend; click the third button. Or: Hold down the third button; move the pointer to the end of the text you want to include; release the button.

Table 11-2: Button Combinations to Extend a Text Selection (continued)

To select	Do this
Word	Move the pointer to the word to which you want the selection to extend (either to the left or right of the previous selection); click the third button anywhere on the word. Or: Hold down the third button; drag the pointer onto the last word you want to include (either to the left or right of the previous selection); release the button. Or: After double-clicking the first button anywhere on the word to select it, continue to hold the button down and drag the pointer to the left or right. The selection will be extended by word. When you've included the words you want, release the button.
Line	Move the pointer to the line to which you want the selection to extend (either above or below the previously selected line); click the third button anywhere on the line. Or: Hold down the third button; drag the pointer onto the last line you want to include (either above or below the previously selected line); release the button. Or: After triple-clicking the first button anywhere on the line to select it, continue to hold the button down and drag the pointer up or down. The selection will be extended by line. When you've included the lines you want, release the button.

The easiest way to extend a selection is just to move the pointer away from the selected (highlighted) words, to the left or right, to encompass additional text. Then click the third pointer button. A new selection will be made that extends from the previous selection to the pointer's location.

For instance, suppose you've highlighted the second half of a line of text. You might then move the pointer over a few words to the left, towards the beginning of the line, and click the third pointer button to include the additional words in the selection.

Alternatively, you can press and hold down the third pointer button; drag the pointer to extend the selection; and release the pointer button.

Remember that an extension always begins from the previous selection. By moving the pointer up or down, or to the right or left of the last selection, you can select part of one line or add or subtract several lines of text.

If the previous selection was by word or line (by double- or triple-clicking), when you extend it, the extension is automatically by word(s) or line(s). There are a few ways of extending a selection made by word or line.

First, if you hold the button down after double- or triple-clicking (rather than releasing it) and move the pointer, you will select additional text by words or lines at a time. Then release the button to end the selection.

More commonly you will probably decide to extend the selection after making it (and releasing the first pointer button). For example, suppose you select a single word by double-clicking the first pointer button. You can extend the selection to include the next word to the right on the same line by placing the pointer on any part of the word and clicking the third button. Use the same method to extend the selection by several words at once.

If you originally selected an entire line by triple-clicking the first pointer button, moving the pointer to another line and clicking the third button extends the selection to encompass that new line and all lines in between.

As an alternative, you can also extend a word or line selection by pressing and holding down the third pointer button, dragging the pointer, and releasing the third button. The extension still increments by word or line as appropriate.

To select text that fills more than one screen, select the first screenful. Use the scrollbar to view the additional text. Then use the third pointer button to extend the selection. The original selection does not need to be in view; clicking the third button will extend it to the point you choose.

— *VQ*

11.08 *Defining What Makes Up a Word for Selection Purposes*

You probably already know how to select text *(11.05)* in an *xterm*, and you've probably discovered that double-clicking will select the entire word around the pointer. What you may not know is that it is possible to change what defines a "word."

xterm maintains a table of all the ASCII characters and their *character classes*. Any sequence of adjacent characters of the same class is treated as a word. Numbers, letters, and the underscore are in class 48 (which is the ASCII code for the character 0) and Space and Tab are in class 32 (the ASCII code for Space). By default, all the other characters are in classes by themselves.

For UNIX users, this isn't really the most useful default; it would be better if you could select filenames, Internet addresses, resource specifications, etc., as single words even though they contain punctuation characters.

You can modify the character class table with *xterm*'s charClass resource variable *(1.06)*. The value this resource accepts is a comma-separated list; each item on the list is an ASCII character code or range of characters, followed by a colon, followed by the character class that the character should be added to. I set the charClass resource as follows:

```
xterm*charClass: 33:48, 37:48, 42:48, 45-47:48, 63-64:48, 126:48
```

This tells *xterm* to treat !, %, *,-, ., /, ?, @ and ˜ as characters of the same class as numbers and letters.

—DJF

11.09 Selecting Command-Line Text

If you've used double-clicking to select words, you've probably also used triple-clicks to select whole lines *(11.05)* from an *xterm*. I often find that I want to select a command without the prompt that precedes it and without the newline that follows it, so that I can paste the command and then append to it.

You can get *xterm* to behave this way with two resources: cutToBeginningOfLine, which controls whether *xterm* begins the selection at the mouse or at the beginning of the line, and cutNewline, which controls whether *xterm* selects the newline. Turn off both of these resources, as follows:

```
xterm*cutToBeginningOfLine: False
xterm*cutNewline: False
```

You can also use the command-line option equivalents: *−cb* turns off cutting to the beginning of the line, and *−cn* turns off cutting the newline.

In an X11R4 *xterm*, when a single long line wraps onto multiple *xterm* lines, and you select it, newlines are inserted where the line wraps. This means that you cannot correctly paste it all at once into another *xterm*. This has been fixed in X11R5.

—DJF

11.10 Wrapping Backwards

By default, when your command wraps onto the next line in *xterm*, you can't backspace to the previous line. The *xterm* resource reverseWrap can be set to change this behavior.

reverseWrap controls whether a backspace at the beginning of a line will bring you to the end of the previous one. If set to true, reverseWrap will allow you to backspace back to the previous line when typing a long command that has wrapped onto multiple lines.

This is exceedingly useful, since the long commands are the ones you're least likely to want to retype.

—DJF

11.11 Using Bold Text

Like most terminals and terminal emulators, *xterm* responds to certain escape sequences that are sent to it. The following command, for example, will make your *xterm* display everything that follows in bold characters:

```
% echo "^[[1m"
```

and this one will restore text to the normal font:

```
% echo "^[[0m"
```

(The sequence ^[is generated by pressing the **Escape** key, or **CTRL-[**.)*

Rather than have all text bold, I use these sequences in my *.cshrc* file to make my command-line prompt stand out from the surrounding text:

```
if ( xterm =~ $TERM ) then
    set prompt="^[[1m${host}:${user} \!% ^[[0m"
endif
```

I can also replace the number "1" in the bold escape sequence with the number "4" for underlined text, or with "7" for text in reverse video. In any of these cases, the sequence "^[[0m" will restore your *xterm* to normal text.

Note that on a *terminfo*-based system, you can use the *tput* command to generate these sequences more easily:

```
% tput bold    (turn on bold)
% tput sgr0    (turn off bold)
```

On a *termcap*-based system, you might get the publicly available program called *tc* or *tcap* (also available on the O'Reilly & Associates' *UNIX Power Tools* CD) and use that instead:

```
% tc md    (turn on bold)
% tc me    (turn off bold)
```

In order for this to work with an X11R4 *xterm*, you must have specified a bold font (with the *–fb* command-line option or the xterm*boldFont resource).

---

* If you are using file completion, then you may get a beep or nothing when you type the **Escape** key. In that case, you have to type **CTRL-V** before the **Escape** character. In a text editor, you will also have to issue some kind of quote-next-character command to insert an actual escape character.

In X11R5, *xterm* will automatically overstrike its normal font to produce bold if the bold font isn't specifically set.

—*DJF, LM*

11.12 *Setting the Titlebar and Icon Text*

Under most modern window managers, most windows, including *xterm*, are displayed with a titlebar. You can change the text used in the titlebar using the following *xterm* escape sequence:

```
^[]2;string^G
```

(Note that this sequence has a close bracket following the **Escape**, not an open bracket, and ends with a **CTRL-G** character, not a caret followed by a "G.")

I use this sequence to display my current working directory and directory stack in the titlebar, where they are visible but unobtrusive. I do this by adding a few lines to my *.cshrc*:

```
if ( xterm =~ $TERM ) then
    alias settitle 'echo "^[]2;`dirs`^G"'
    alias cd 'chdir \!*; settitle'
    alias pushd 'pushd \!*; settitle'
    alias popd 'popd \!*; settitle'
    settitle                    initialize the titlebar
endif
```

Each command I use for changing directories uses my *settitle* alias to reset the string in the titlebar. I also call *settitle* directly, to set the titlebar the first time.

If you change the number "2" in the escape sequence to "1," it will set the text that appears in the *xterm*'s icon instead of the titlebar. If you change it to "0," it will set the text for both the icon and the titlebar. If you use and iconify a number of *xterms*, you may find these sequences useful.

If you use *tcsh*, you can use the special alias *cwdcmd* in your *.tcshrc* or *.cshrc* file. This special alias is run automatically whenever the directory is changed. So the above sequence of aliases can be replaced by a single one:

```
if ( xterm =~ $TERM ) then
    alias cwdcmd 'echo "^[]2;`dirs`^G"'
endif
```

—*DJF*

11.13 The Simple Way to Pick a Font

X font names make the Rosetta Stone look like bedtime reading. Those hardy souls who want to experiment with fonts or access fonts on remote machines must take the high road and learn the X font naming conventions *(17.18)* anyway. But if you just want to locate some fonts to use with *xterm* and other clients, you can use the predefined aliases for some of the constant-width fonts that should be available on most systems.

Figure 11-2 lists the aliases for some constant-width fonts that should be appropriate for most of the standard clients, including *xterm*. To give you an idea of the range of sizes, each alias is written in the font it identifies.

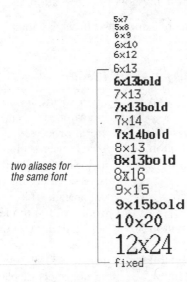

```
              5x7
              5x8
              6x9
              6x10
              6x12
            ─ 6x13
              6x13bold
              7x13
              7x13bold
              7x14
              7x14bold
              8x13
              8x13bold
 two aliases for ─    8x16
 the same font        9x15
              9x15bold
              10x20
              12x24
            ─ fixed
```

Figure 11-2: Miscellaneous fonts for xterm and other clients

In these cases, the aliases refer to the dimensions in pixels of each character in the font. (For example, "10×20" is the alias for a font with characters 10 pixels wide by 20 pixels high.) Note, however, that an alias can be virtually any character string.

The default font for many applications, including *xterm*, is a 6×13 pixel font that has *two* aliases: "fixed" and "6×13." Many users consider this font to be too small. If you have enough screen space, you might want to use the 10×20 font for *xterm* windows:

```
% xterm -fn 10x20 &
```

You can make this font the default for *xterm* by specifying it as the value for the font resource variable *(17.14)*:

```
XTerm*font: 10x20
```

— *VQ*

11.14 *The xterm Menus*

xterm has four different menus, each providing items that serve different purposes. You display a menu by placing the pointer on the window and simultaneously pressing the **CTRL** (keyboard) key and a pointer button. When you're using a window manager that provides a titlebar or frame, the pointer must rest within the window proper *not* on any window decoration.

The following table describes the menus and how to display them:

Table 11-3: The xterm Menus

Menu Title	Display by Holding	Use To
Main Options	CTRL, pointer button 1	Enter secure mode; interrupt, stop, etc., the xterm process.
VT Options	CTRL, pointer button 2	Toggle user preferences, including scrollbar, reverse video, margin bell; toggle Tektronix/VT100 mode.
VT Fonts	CTRL, pointer button 3	Select alternative display font.
Tek Options	CTRL, pointer button 2, on Tektronix window	Toggle VT100/Tektronix mode; select display font.

As shown in Figure 11-3, three of the four *xterm* menus are divided into sections separated by horizontal lines. The top portion of each divided menu contains various modes that can be toggled. (The one exception is the **Redraw Window** item on the **Main Options** menu, which is a command.) A check mark appears next to a mode that is currently active. Selecting one of these modes toggles its state.

The items on the **VT Fonts** menu change the font in which text is displayed in the *xterm* window. Only one of these fonts can be active at a time. To turn one off, you must activate another. See Article 11.15 for information on using the **VT Fonts** menu.

When you display an *xterm* menu, the pointer becomes the arrow pointer and initially appears in the menu's title. Once the menu appears, you can release any keyboard key. The menu will remain visible as long as you continue to hold down the appropriate pointer button. (You can move the pointer off the menu without it disappearing.) To toggle a mode or activate a command, drag the pointer down the menu and release the pointer button on the item you want.

If you decide not to select a menu item after the menu has appeared, move the pointer off the menu and release the button. The menu disappears and no action is taken.

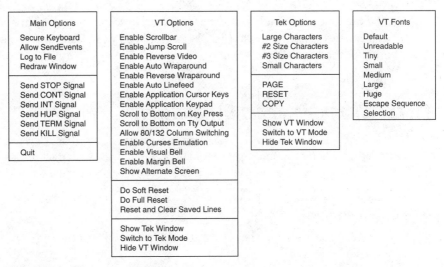

Figure 11-3: The xterm menus

You probably won't use the *xterm* menus too often. You can set most mode entries using command-line options when invoking *xterm* or by entries in a resource file *(17.01)*. See the *xterm* manpage for a complete list of options and resource variables.

The various modes on the menus are very helpful if you've set (or failed to set) a particular mode on the command line and then decide you want the opposite characteristic. For instance, say you've run *xterm* without a scrollbar *(11.02)* and then decide you want one. You can toggle the scrollbar on from the **VT Options** menu.

The sections below the modes portion of each menu contain various commands. Selecting one of these commands performs the indicated function. Many of these functions can be invoked only from the *xterm* menus. However, some functions can be invoked in other—often more convenient—ways. For example, you can remove the *xterm* window using several of the items on the Main Options menu, but it's probably simpler to type exit or logout, or use a window manager menu or button. Of course, the *xterm* menus can be very helpful when other methods to invoke a function fail. And some functions (such as Secure Keyboard) are not available in any other way—unless you do a little customizing.

Most people will probably tend to use the mode toggles on the VT Options menu (that allow you to turn features like the scrollbar on and off) and the items on the VT Fonts menu (that allow you to change the display font once the client is running). If you're concerned about security, you may want to invoke secure keyboard mode *(11.17)* from the Main Options menu before typing passwords and other sensitive information.

Note that a Release 5 patch has eliminated *xterm*'s logging capability for security reasons. If this patch has been applied, your Main Options menu will not offer the Log to File option.

—*VQ*

11.15 *Changing Fonts Dynamically*

Ideally you want to set up your environment so that *xterm* windows (and other clients) come up automatically with the characteristics you prefer, including the display font. I use the very large 10×20-pixel font *(11.13)* for all my *xterm* windows by specifying the resource variable *(17.01)*:

```
XTerm*font: 10x20
```

But if you start an *xterm* and then decide you want a different font, you do have an option.

The *xterm* VT Fonts menu *(11.14)* allows you to change a window's font on the fly, a very handy capability. You can change the font any number of times to accommodate a variety of uses. You might choose to use a large font for text editing. You could then change to a smaller font while a process is running since you don't need to be reading or typing in that *xterm*. Since *xterm*'s dimensions are determined by the number of characters wide by the number of lines high, changing the font also changes the size of the window.

When the focus is on an *xterm*, you display the menu by pressing CTRL and then the third pointer button. The default menu is shown in Figure 11-4.

The items on the VT Fonts menu are toggles, each of which provides a different size display font. If you have not toggled any items on this menu, a check mark will appear next to Default, which is the font specified when the *xterm* was run. This font could have been specified on the *xterm* command line or in a resource file. Whatever the case, this font remains the Default for the duration of the current *xterm* process.

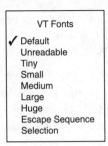

Figure 11-4: xterm's VT Fonts menu lets you change fonts dynamically

By default, the **Unreadable**, **Tiny**, **Small**, **Medium**, **Large**, and **Huge** menu choices toggle the following constant-width fonts:

Table 11-4: VT Fonts Menu Defaults

Menu Item	*Default Font*
Unreadable	nil2
Tiny	5×7
Small	6×10
Medium	7×13
Large	9×15
Huge	10×20

Bring up the **VT Fonts** menu and toggle some of these fonts to see what they look like. The second choice is not called **Unreadable** for nothing, but it does have a practical use. See the article on active icons *(11.16)* for more information.

You can specify your own **Unreadable**, **Tiny**, **Small**, **Medium**, **Large**, and **Huge** fonts using the *xterm* resource variables font1, font2, font3, font4, font5, and font6. You might want to specify bold alternatives to some of the default fonts. For example, 7×13 bold is somewhat more readable than the standard **Medium** font.

Enabling Escape Sequence and Selection

When you first run an *xterm* window, the final two choices on the **VT Fonts** menu, **Escape Sequence** and **Selection**, are not functional. (They will appear in a lighter typeface than the other selections.) The average user may not care about these items, but if you're experimenting with fonts, they are sometimes useful.

To enable **Selection**, you first have to select a font name. You can do this simply by highlighting a font name with the pointer, as you would any text selection *(11.05)*, but it's more likely you'll use **Selection** in concert with the *xfontsel* client *(17.19)*. Once you've selected a font name, you can toggle it using the

Selection menu item. A serious limitation: **Selection** tries to use the last selected text as a font name. If the last selected text was not a valid font name, toggling **Selection** will get you nothing more than a beep. When there is no PRIMARY text selection in memory, the menu item becomes grayed out again.

The **Escape Sequence** item is a little more complicated, but once set up will be available for the duration of the *xterm* process. To make it available you first need to change the font by a more primitive method, using a literal escape sequence that you send to the *xterm* using the UNIX *echo* command:

```
val@ruby 181% echo "Esc]50;7x13boldControl-G"
```

These are the literal keys you type to change the font to 7×13bold. But pressing **Escape** actually generates the symbol ^[and **CTRL-G** appears as ^G, so you'll get a line that looks like this:

```
val@ruby 181% echo "^[]50;7x13bold^G"
```

I've used a short fontname alias *(11.13)*, but you could use a full name or a name with wildcards *(17.15)*. Once you've changed the font in this manner, you can toggle it using the **Escape Sequence** menu item. If you change the font again using the literal escape sequence, that font will be available via the menu item.

— VQ

11.16 *An Active Icon*

The **Unreadable** item on the VT Fonts menu *(11.14)* toggles a font called *nil2*. If you select the **Unreadable** font, your *xterm* window becomes very tiny, almost the size of some application icons. Though you cannot read the actual text in a window this size, the window is still active and you *can* observe if additional output, albeit minuscule, is displayed. An *xterm* window displaying text in such a small font can, in effect, serve as an *active icon*. These pseudo-icons can help you monitor whether information is being output, in cases where you don't have to read it. Figure 11-5 shows an *xterm* window using the **Medium** font (7×13) from the VT Fonts menu and also an active icon.

— VQ

11.17 *Secure Keyboard Mode*

Because the client-server model leaves some pretty sizeable security holes, *xterm* provides a way to safeguard passwords and other potentially sensitive information. Generally, input events (such as the keys you type in an *xterm* window) are made available via the server to other clients. Hypothetically, an adept system hacker could access this information. A fairly serious breach of security could easily occur, for instance, if someone were able to find out a

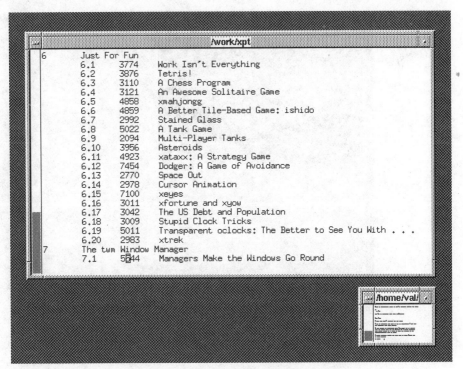

```
                                          /work/xpt
6        Just For Fun
         6.1    3774    Work Isn't Everything
         6.2    3876    Tetris!
         6.3    3110    A Chess Program
         6.4    3121    An Awesome Solitaire Game
         6.5    4858    xmahjongg
         6.6    4859    A Better Tile-Based Game: ishido
         6.7    2992    Stained Glass
         6.8    5022    A Tank Game
         6.9    2094    Multi-Player Tanks
         6.10   3956    Asteroids
         6.11   4923    xataxx: A Strategy Game
         6.12   7454    Dodger: A Game of Avoidance
         6.13   2770    Space Out
         6.14   2978    Cursor Animation
         6.15   7100    xeyes
         6.16   3011    xfortune and xyow
         6.17   3042    The US Debt and Population
         6.18   3009    Stupid Clock Tricks
         6.19   5011    Transparent oclocks: The Better to See You With . . .
         6.20   2983    xtrek
7        The twm Window Manager
         7.1    5344    Managers Make the Windows Go Round
```

/home/val/

Figure 11-5: An xterm using a medium font and an active icon

user's password or the *root* password. Enabling **Secure Keyboard** mode causes all user input to be directed *only* to the *xterm* window itself. You may want to activate **Secure Keyboard** mode before you type a password or other important text in an *xterm* window and then disable it again.

To toggle secure mode:

1. Display *xterm*'s Main Options menu *(11.14)* (press the **CTRL** key and the first pointer button);

2. Select **Secure Keyboard** from the menu.

When you enable **Secure Keyboard** mode, the *xterm* window will switch to reverse video *(17.08)* (as if you had enabled the **Reverse Video** mode from the **VT Options** menu). Figure 11-6 shows an *xterm* in secure mode.

When you disable **Secure Keyboard** mode, the colors will be switched back.

Be aware that only one X client at a time can secure the keyboard. Thus, if you have enabled **Secure Keyboard** mode in one *xterm*, you will not be allowed to enable it in another *xterm* until you disable it in the first. If **Secure Keyboard** mode is not available when you request it, the colors will not be switched and a bell will sound.

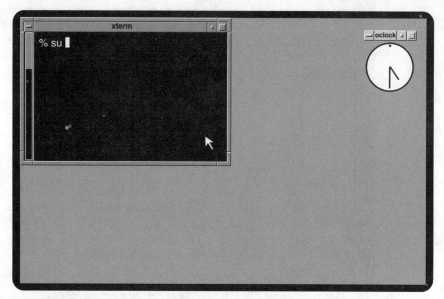

Figure 11-6: Reverse video is enabled when the keyboard is secure

If you request **Secure Keyboard** mode and are not refused, but the colors are *not* exchanged, be careful: you are not in secure mode! If this happens, there's a good chance that someone has tampered with the system. If the application you're running displays a prompt before asking for a password, it's a good idea to enable **Secure Keyboard** mode before the prompt is displayed and then verify that the prompt is displayed in the proper colors. Before entering the password, you can also display the **Main Options** menu again and verify that a check mark appears next to **Secure Keyboard** mode.

Be aware that **Secure Keyboard** will be disabled automatically if you iconify the *xterm* window, or start *twm* *(12.01)*, *mwm* *(13.01)* or another window manager that provides a titlebar or other window decoration. (You can enable **Secure Keyboard** mode once the window manager is running, though.) This limitation is due to the X protocol. When the mode is disabled, the colors will be switched back and the bell will sound to warn you.

Naturally, this level of security is not necessary in every environment: if the nature of the work is in no way sensitive, if the system administrator has taken pains to secure the system in other ways, etc.

Though intended to counteract a security weakness, the **Secure Keyboard** mode toggle can also be used to get around a weakness of the Motif window manager *(13.08)*. If *mwm* dies, it's possible that the focus can be lost; i.e., the focus is no longer directed to any application window. Selecting **Secure Keyboard** mode for any *xterm* should cause that window to grab the focus again.

—VQ

11.18 Translations to Enter xterm Commands with Function Keys

Among the more useful translations *(20.29)* you can specify for *xterm* are function key mappings that allow you to enter frequently used commands with a single keystroke. This sort of mapping involves an action called string, which passes a text string to the shell running in the *xterm* window.

The translation table syntax for such a function key mapping is fairly simple. The following line maps the text string "lpq –Pprinter1" (the BSD 4.3 command to check the queue for the printer named printer1) to the **F1** function key:

```
<Key>F1:    string("lpq -Pprinter1")
```

Notice the quotes surrounding the text string. If the argument to string includes spaces or non-alphanumeric characters, the whole argument must be enclosed in one pair of double quotes.

The translation table would be:

```
*VT100.Translations:  #override\
    <Key>F1:          string("lpq -Pprinter1")
```

This sample translation causes lpq –Pprinter1 to be passed to the command line in the active *xterm* window when you press the **F1** function key, as in Figure 11-7.

Notice, however, that the command is not invoked because the sample translation does not specify a carriage return. You can add a return as the argument to another string action within the same translation.

To specify the **Return** (or any) key, use the hexadecimal code for that key as the argument to string. (Use the *xmodmap* client *(18.07)* to determine keycodes.) The letters "0x" signal a hexadecimal key code. If you want to enter a key as an argument to string, use "0x" followed by the specific code. For my keyboard, the code for the **Return** key is "d" or "0d."* The following

---

* The command xmodmap -pk returns a long listing of all keycodes. The codes have either of the following forms:

```
0xffab
0x00ab
```

where *ab* represents two alphanumeric characters. To specify a key as an argument to string, you can omit the "ff" or "00" in the *xmodmap* listing.

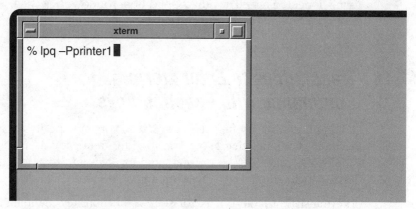

Figure 11-7: Pushing F1 passes command text to xterm shell

translation table specifies that pressing **F1** passes the line lpq -Pprinter1 followed by a carriage return to an *xterm* window:

```
*VT100.Translations: #override\
    <Key>F1:        string("lpq -Pprinter1") string(0x0d)
```

Remember, you can list several translations in a single table. The following table maps function keys **F1** through **F3**:

```
*VT100.Translations: #override\
    <Key>F1:    string("lpq -Pprinter1") string(0x0d)\n\
    <Key>F2:    string("cd ~/news;ls") string(0x0d)\n\
    <Key>F3:    string("xterm -display harry:0.1 &") string(0x0d)
```

According to these translations, pressing **F2** inserts the command string cd ~/news;ls, which changes directory to ~/*news* and then lists the contents of that directory. Notice that you can issue multiple commands (*cd*, *ls*) with a single key by separating them with a semicolon (;). Pressing **F3** opens an *xterm* window on my alternate screen *(27.11)*.

Keep in mind that all the translations for an application can appear in the same table. For example, we can combine the *xterm* translations to use *xclipboard (11.21)* with the translations to map function keys.

```
*VT100.Translations:    #override\
    Button1 <Btn3Down>: select-end(PRIMARY,CUT_BUFFER0,CLIPBOARD)\n\
    !Shift <Btn2Up>:    insert-selection(CLIPBOARD)\n\
    ~Shift ~Ctrl ~Meta <Btn2Up>:   insert-selection(PRIMARY,CUT_BUFFER0)\n\
    <Key>F1:        string("lpq -Pprinter1") string(0x0d)\n\
    <Key>F2:        string("cd ~/news;ls") string(0x0d)\n\
    <Key>F3:        string("xterm -display harry:0.1 &") string(0x0d)
```

The order of the translations is not important. However, it is necessary to end all but the final line with the sequence "\n\" to make the resource a continuous string. See Article 20.29 for more information on translation table syntax.

—VQ

11.19 Sets of Keymappings for Special Situations

Article 11.18 describes how to use translations *(20.29)* in order to define keyboard shortcuts that enter command lines. But what if you want to use different shortcuts when you're running different programs in an *xterm* window? If you're like me, you use *xterm* in a number of different contexts (running *vi*, *dbx*, *rn*, etc.) and want to define different sets of keyboard shortcuts for these situations. Well, as foresight would have it, *xterm* actually provides a way to switch between sets of keyboard mappings.

You customize *xterm* to do this using the keymap() action, which dynamically installs a set of new translations *(20.29)*. keymap takes a single argument, *name*, and installs the translation table described by the resource Keymap.

For example, I have a specialized set of mappings I use when I'm running the *dbx* debugger program within an *xterm* window. I press **F9** to get the dbxKeymap mappings. When I'm done running *dbx*, I press **F8** to get the standard set again.

```
xterm*VT100.translations: #override\
    <Key>F9: keymap(dbx)     install the dbx macros below

xterm*VT100.dbxKeymap.translations:\     dbx macros; note no \n here.
    <Key>F1: string("print ") insert-selection(PRIMARY) string("\n")\n\
    <Key>F2: string("next\n")\n\
    <Key>F3: string("list\n")\n\
    <Key>F8: keymap(None)    un-install
these macros
```

—DJF

11.20 Translations to Scroll from the Keyboard

By default, *xterm* binds **Shift-PgUp** and **Shift-PgDown** to the scroll-back and scroll-forw actions to scroll up and down *(11.02)*. My Sun3 keyboard doesn't have these keys, so I add translations *(20.29)* that make the shifted arrow keys do this scrolling.

```
xterm*VT100.translations: #override\
    Shift <Key>Up: scroll-back(1, halfpage)\n\\011
    Shift <Key>Down: scroll-forw(1, halfpage)\n
```

—DJF

11.21   xterm Translations to Use xclipboard

You can copy text from an *xterm* window and paste it into the *xclipboard* window *(11.22)* using the same pointer commands used between *xterm* s *(11.05)*, but you'd be underestimating *xclipboard*. With a little work up front, you can send text selections automatically to *xclipboard*, and also paste them from the clipboard to another window without having to copy again.

In order for text you copy from an *xterm* to be pasted automatically into *xclipboard*, the text must be made the CLIPBOARD selection. You set this up to happen by specifying a few translations *(20.29)* for *xterm*. [*] Here are the translations I use to coordinate *xterm* with *xclipboard*:

```
*VT100.Translations:        #override\
    Button1 <Btn3Down>: select-end(PRIMARY,CUT_BUFFER0,CLIPBOARD)\n\
    !Shift <Btn2Up>:    insert-selection(CLIPBOARD)\n\
    ~Shift ~Ctrl ~Meta <Btn2Up>:  insert-selection(PRIMARY,CUT_BUFFER0)
```

These translations set up *xterm* to work with the clipboard using the pointer commands described in Article 11.22. Read that article to get working.

—VQ

11.22   Working with xclipboard

The *xclipboard* client does exactly what you might think: it allows you to save multiple text selections *(11.05)* and copy them to other windows. You can have text you copy from an *xterm* window made the CLIPBOARD selection (and thus automatically appear in the *xclipboard* window). To set this up, you first need to customize *xterm* using resources. [†] If you specify resources like those we explain in Article 11.21, you'll be able to send *xterm* text to the *xclipboard* window by highlighting it using the first pointer button, and then, while holding that button, clicking the third.

In order to allow you to store multiple text selections, the seemingly tiny *xclipboard* actually provides multiple screens, each of which can be thought of as a separate buffer. Each time you use the pointer to make text the CLIP-BOARD selection, the *xclipboard* advances to a new screen in which it

---

[*] If you're using a terminal emulator other than *xterm*, the program should also allow this sort of customization. See the client manpage for the actions (the equivalents of `select-end` and `insert-selection`) to include in the translation table.

[†] Since there can be only one CLIPBOARD selection at a time, you can only run one *xclipboard* per display.

displays and stores the text. If you make a long selection, it might take up more than one screen, but the clipboard still considers it a single buffer. When you make a selection that extends beyond the bounds of the *xclipboard* window (either horizontally, vertically, or both), scrollbars *(11.02)* will be activated in the window to allow you to view the entire selection.

To the right of the command buttons is a tiny box that displays a number corresponding to the selection currently in the *xclipboard* window. Once you have saved multiple selections, you can click on the client's **Next** and **Previous** command buttons to move forward and backward among these screens of text.

If you've coordinated *xterm* with *xclipboard* using the guidelines outlined in Article 11.21, you paste the CLIPBOARD selection in an *xterm* window by holding down the **Shift** key and clicking the second pointer button. When you paste the CLIPBOARD selection, you get the selection that's currently being displayed in the *xclipboard* window. Here's where the client really comes in handy. Suppose you send four selections to *xclipboard* and you want to paste #2. Just go back to selection #2 using the **Prev** command button; then when you use the pointer command to paste the CLIPBOARD selection, selection #2 is pasted. In Figure 11-8, we've pasted selection #2 into a new file. (Notice that the text is too wide for the *xclipboard* window and that a horizontal scrollbar has been provided so we can view the entire selection.)

A selection remains available in *xclipboard* until you **Quit** the program or use the **Delete** button to erase the current buffer.

Use the **Save** command button to to save the text in the current buffer to a file. A dialog will ask you to **Accept** or **Cancel** the save to a file with the default name *clipboard*. You can change the filename using Text widget *(9.03)* commands. If you want to save multiple selections, you'll need to change the filename each time, or you'll overwrite the previous save.

You can edit text you send to the *xclipboard* using Text widget commands. When you edit a screenful of text, the *xclipboard* continues to store the edited version, until you delete it or exit the program.

— VQ

11.23 *Problems with Large Selections*

If you experiment making large selections with *xclipboard*, you may discover what seems to be a bug in the program. Though in most circumstances, making a new selection causes the screen to advance and display the new text, this does not happen reliably after a selection vertically spanning more than one screenful. In these cases, the new selection *is* saved in the *xclipboard* (and the number in the small box is incremented to indicated this); however,

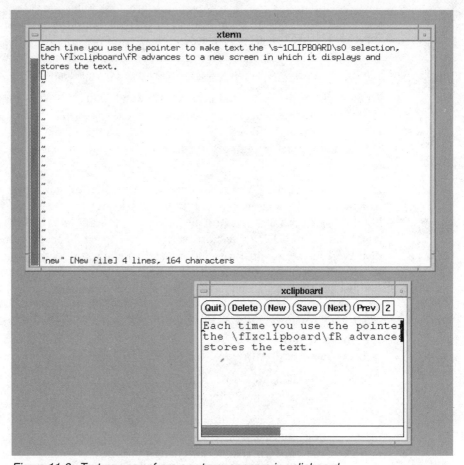

Figure 11-8: Text you copy from an xterm appears in xclipboard

the *xclipboard* window does not automatically advance to show you the new current selection. Instead, the previous long selection is still displayed. (For example, though the box says "5," indicating that a fifth selection has been saved, the window is still displaying selection #4.) This is a bit of *xclipboard* sleight of hand. The new selection has been successfully made, but the appearance of the window belies this fact. The **Next** button will probably add to your confusion; it will not be available for selection, suggesting that the text in the window is the last selection saved. This is not the case.

In order to get around this problem and display the actual current selection, press the **Previous** button. The same long selection (which is, in actuality, the **Previous** selection) will again be displayed. (The small box will flip back to display the preceding number as well.) Then the **Next** button will be enabled, and you can click on it to display the actual current selection. The selection displayed in the window and the number in the small box will correspond.

— *VQ, from the* X Window System User's Guide

11.24 *Pasting from emacs to xterm*

If you are an *emacs (9.02)* user, you may have had difficulty pasting text from *emacs* into an *xterm*. Unlike *xterm*, GNU *emacs* is not a sophisticated X application, and it still uses cut buffers rather than selections for cut and paste. You can run into problems transferring text between applications that communicate using these two different mechanisms.

By default, to paste text into an *xterm* window *(11.05)*, you click the second pointer button. *xterm* maps this input activity (the click) to a particular action (in its translation table *(20.29)*):

```
insert-selection(PRIMARY, CUT_BUFFER0)
```

This line specifies that when you paste text into an *xterm* window (i.e., perform the action called `insert-selection`), by default you paste text from the PRIMARY selection; only when the selection is empty are the contents of the cut buffer pasted. Herein lies the dilemma in copying text from an *emacs* window.

emacs can store text *only* in the cut buffer. If you've previously selected text in an *xterm* window, that text is stored in the PRIMARY selection. When you go to paste the text you copied from the *emacs* window—the text in the cut buffer—into an *xterm*, you get the PRIMARY selection instead!

One possible workaround is to change the way that text copied from an *xterm* is stored. You can add a translation that ignores the PRIMARY selection and always pastes from the cut buffer.

```
xterm*VT100.translations: #override\n\\011
    Shift <Btn2Up>: insert-selection(CUT_BUFFER0)\n
```

This modification is really for serious *emacs* users. If you're also going to coordinate *xterm* with *xclipboard (11.22)*, you'll have to make sure all your translations *(11.21)* work well together.

—*DJF, VQ*

11.25 Running a Single Command with xterm -e

The *–e* option to *xterm* is useful for running a single command before exiting. For example, if you just want to run a character-based mail program:

```
% xterm -e mail
```

When you quit the *mail* program, the *xterm* window exits.

The *–e* option needs to be the last *xterm* option on the command line. The remainder of the command line is assumed to be part of the command to be executed by *xterm*. The new window has the command name in its titlebar.

One use for *xterm –e* is for running remote *xterm* s *(19.04)*. To run remote clients for real, you need to put the hostname in your .XET N .XE1 ".rhosts file" "rhosts file" ./XET *.rhosts* file *(19.06)*, which is a potential security hole. Instead, you might run a command like the following:

```
% xterm -e rlogin
hostname &
```

The *xterm* process runs on the local system, but immediately logs you into the remote machine. You are prompted for a password before you can log in to the remote system. This isn't as convenient as a true remote client, but it's far more secure.

You can use *–e* to create a makeshift X display for any character-based programs you like to run. For example, you might want to keep track of messages sent to the console, but you can't run *xterm –C (27.02)* because you aren't actually logged in on the console. You might run something like this:

```
% xterm -e tail -f /usr/adm/messages &
```

—LM

11.26 Don't Quote Arguments to xterm -e

Being a belt-and-suspenders kind of guy, I've gotten in the habit of quoting arguments to commands. This makes good sense with lots of UNIX shell commands, but it can get you in trouble with *xterm –e*. For example, when I wanted to set up my poor man's *xpostit (4.13)*, I at first used the command:

```
xterm ... -e 'vi .postit' &
```

only to receive the perplexing message:

```
Can't execvp vi .postit
```

in the resulting window.

The quotes caused the entire string to *xterm* as an argument, and it apparently parsed it as a single command name, rather than a command plus argument. Removing the quotes solved the problem.

— TOR

11.27 *When Resizing Causes Problems*

When you run *xterm*, the client sets the appropriate environment variables *(2.04)* to reflect the dimensions of the window. Many programs use this information to determine the physical dimensions of output to the window.

If you resize an *xterm* window, the shell must be notified so that programs that rely on this information can work with the correct dimensions. If the underlying operating system supports terminal resizing capabilities (e.g., the SIGWINCH signal in systems derived from BSD 4.3), *xterm* will use these facilities to notify programs running in the window whenever it is resized. However, if your operating system does not support terminal resizing capabilities, you may need to request explicitly that the environment variables be updated to reflect the resized window.

The *resize* client sends a special escape sequence to the *xterm* window and *xterm* sends back the current size of the window. The results of *resize* can be redirected to a file that can then be sourced to update the TERMCAP environment variable (on *termcap* systems) or the LINES and COLUMNS environment variables (on *terminfo* systems).

To update the appropriate variables to match a window's changed dimensions using the Bourne shell, enter:

```
$ resize > filename
```

and then execute the resulting shell command file:

```
$ . filename
```

The variable(s) will be updated and the dimensions of the text within the window will be adjusted accordingly.

If you use the C shell, you *source* the shell command file:

```
% source filename
```

However, in the C shell, it's preferable to define this alias for *resize*:

```
alias rs 'set noglob; eval `resize`; unset noglob'
```

Then use rs to update the variable(s) to reflect a window's new dimensions.

Note that even if your operating system supports terminal resizing capabilities, *xterm* may have trouble notifying programs running in the window that the window has been resized. On some older systems (based on BSD 4.2 or earlier), certain programs, notably the *vi* editor, cannot interpret this information. If you resize a window during a *vi* editing session, *vi* will not know the new size of the window. If you quit out of the editing session and start another one, the editor should know the new window size and operate properly.

— *VQ*

Part Four

Window Managers

If you've worked in the X environment for a while, you know the importance of a window manager program. A window manager lets you move windows, resize them, convert them to icons and back again, remove them, and perform all sorts of sleight-of-hand. You can run X without a window manager, but that's a little like running a puppet show without strings.

You probably know the basics of using at least one window manager. This section reviews the fundamentals for some of the more popular programs (*mwm*, *olwm*, and *twm*); more importantly, it describes how to configure these window managers to make your work easier.

Finally, this section focuses on our favorite of the several publicly available window managers, *fvwm*.

—VQ

12

The twm Window Manager

12.01 An Old Reliable Way to Manage Windows

In the atmosphere of the GUI wars, *twm* has declared permanent neutrality. It's the window manager that comes with the standard version of X, and it looks it. *twm* isn't one of these fancy, dressed-up programs that decorate your windows like they're going to hang in the Louvre. It's basic, providing each window with no more than a simple border and titlebar. However, despite the bare-bones appearance, you can perform pretty much every window management task you need to using *twm*.

If you've ever worked with *twm*, you know that you focus input on a window by moving the pointer into it. *twm* isn't as versatile in this regard as some other window managers that let you choose an alternate focus policy. The Motif window manager *(13.01)* can be configured to use either pointer or explicit (click-to-type) focus, for instance. But *twm* does mimic click-to-type focus for a single window (see Article 12.07).

More importantly, many *twm* features *are* customizable, including menus *(12.22)*, key and pointer bindings, the Icon Manager *(12.09)*, behaviors like auto-raise *(12.13)*, and the appearance of window manager components. I've chosen to use *twm* when I've had fancier window managers at hand because I like the simplicity, and I've found it has plenty of power and versatility, as well. Try it, you may like it too.

If you like the look and feel of *twm*, you can have all that and virtual screen capability too with the *tvtwm* window manager *(12.10)*. Check it out.

— *VQ*

12.02 Once Around the twm Environment

twm is one of the less elaborate window managers, both in the level of decoration it provides and the number of operations available by default. You'll actually have to do a little simple customization to activate some of the more useful features. As with most window managers, customization centers around a startup file, called *.twmrc* *(12.11)*.

The current article describes a slightly modified *twm* environment, which includes a must-have customization, the Icon Manager *(12.09)*. However, regardless of the amount of customization you're interested in doing, I think you'll find that *twm* has plenty of power and versatility.

Figure 12-1 shows a screen being managed by *twm*.

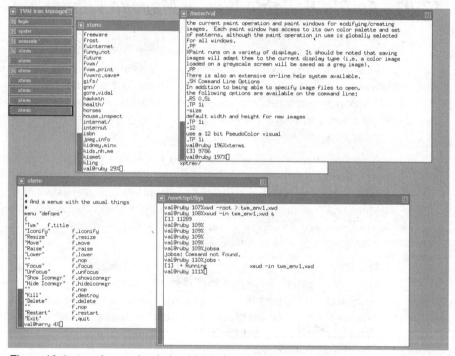

Figure 12-1: twm has a simple but highly functional look and feel

My sample display has four active *xterm* windows. The only other visible feature is the Icon Manager window in the upper-left corner of the display.

In the default *twm* environment, when you run a new window, you have to place it on the screen manually, using the pointer. You might want to make automatic window placement *(12.12)* one of your first modifications.

twm's default focus policy is pointer focus. In other words, in order to type or invoke commands in a window, you first have to move the pointer into it. When a window has the input focus, the middle region of the titlebar is high-lighted. Since only one window can receive input at any time, only one window on your screen can be highlighted. If the pointer is resting on the root window, you can't enter text or commands in a client window. (However, there is a way to direct focus to a window regardless of pointer location *(12.07)*.)

Let's take a closer look at the Icon Manager. This small, menu-like window contains one entry for each client window running—regardless of whether that window is currently iconified. Each client name is enclosed in a rectangle. If the client is currently iconified, the name is preceded by a small letter X. On the sample display, five windows are currently iconified.

You can iconify and deiconify any window on the display by clicking on its entry in the Icon Manager window. (The X preceding the client's name lets you track what state the window is in.) You can also use the Icon Manager to direct the input focus to a particular window. Article 12.09 shows you these and other Icon Manager powers.

I've customized *twm* to bring up the Icon Manager automatically *(12.15)*, and make it work efficiently (e.g., to serve in place of traditional icon symbols). Keep in mind that without these customizations, the environment would be noticeably different.

If you don't use an Icon Manager, iconifying a window causes a small icon symbol to appear on the screen. These tiny icon symbols can really clutter the display. (In our slightly modified *twm* environment, the only evidence that a client window has been iconified—besides its absence, of course—is a neat little X before its Icon Manager entry.) It's also easy to lose icons under active windows. Article 12.08 simulates the sheer heck of working without an Icon Manager.

So make the customizations necessary to set up the Icon Manager *(12.15)*. But as an interim measure, you can call up an Icon Manager once *twm* is running by using the Twm root menu *(12.04)*. (Note, however, that unless you modify your *.twmrc* startup file, you'll get icon symbols *in addition to* the Icon Manager. Still potentially a bit of a mess.)

Besides icon management, *twm* naturally provides all the basic window management functions *(12.03)*, including moving, resizing, raising, lowering, etc. The easiest way to perform most functions is by using the pointer on various parts of the *twm* titlebar, which spans the top of each window on the display. (It looks like the only decoration *twm* provides is the titlebar. Actually there's a skeletal frame around the entire window, but the titlebar is the only useful part.) Article 12.03 reviews the pointer commands on the titlebar.

When a window's titlebar is obscured by other features on the screen, you'll need to access window manager functions using either key/pointer button shortcuts *(12.05)* or the Twm menu *(12.04)*. Article 12.31 provides an overview of all the default *twm* functions.

— *VQ*

12.03 *Basic Window Management Functions Using the Pointer*

As with most window managers, *twm* provides simple pointer commands for most functions. Many of these commands are performed on the titlebar, the components of which are detailed in Figure 12-2.

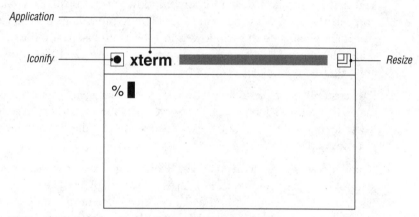

Figure 12-2: *Click on the titlebar to perform simple window managment functions*

The bar contains the name of the application (e.g., *xterm*), two command buttons (used to iconify and resize the window) and a region that is highlighted when the window has the input focus.

When you move the pointer onto either one of the command buttons, the pointer symbol changes to a small hand cursor, indicating that you can push the button. If you move the pointer onto any other part of the titlebar, it becomes an arrow cursor.

Table 12-1 summarizes the pointer actions to perform various window management functions. Many of those are performed on a window's titlebar; some on an icon, and on the Icon Manager *(12.09)*. The Twm menu *(12.04)* is posted (i.e., displayed) on the root window.

Table 12-1: Pointer Commands for twm Functions

Function	Pointer Location	Action
Move	Titlebar	First pointer button down, drag, release
Move	Icon	First pointer button down, drag, release
Raise	Titlebar	First or second pointer button click
Lower	titlebar	Second pointer button click
Resize	Resize ("nested squares") titlebutton	Hold any pointer button down, cross desired border, drag, release.
Iconify	Iconify ("dot") titlebutton	Any pointer button click
Iconify	Icon Manager entry	First or second pointer button click
Deiconify	Icon or Icon Manager entry	First or second pointer button click
Focus input	Window	Place pointer on window.
Focus input	Icon Manager entry	Place pointer there to focus input on corresponding window.
Post Twm menu	Root window	Press first pointer button.

For keyboard accelerators for most functions, see Article 15.06.

Most of these functions are very simple—and also rudimentary. If you've been using *twm* for even a short time, you're probably an old hand at iconifying, moving, raising, etc. Window manager jocks can now exit this article, stage left (presuming you've even bothered to come this far). For true beginners, here's a closer look at a couple of the less obvious functions.

To move a window, place the pointer on the titlebar (not the command buttons), hold down the first pointer button, drag the outline to the new location, and release. Figure 12-3 shows a window being moved.

When you use the pointer to move a window, the pointer rests in the titlebar; if you don't move the pointer subsequently, input should be focused on the window you've moved. Moving a window also raises it to the top of the window stack.

Resizing is probably the trickiest basic function, but you should catch on with a little practice. With *twm*, a client window becomes nearly as flexible as a

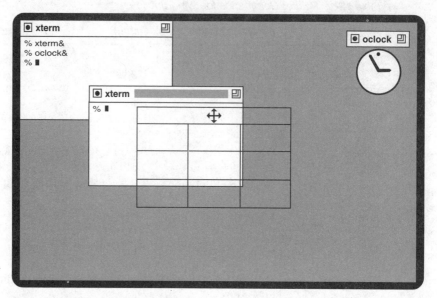

Figure 12-3: Moving a window

rubber band. You can resize a window horizontally, vertically, or simultaneously in both directions.

Regardless of the way you want to resize a window, you begin by pressing any pointer button on the resize command button. The resize button is in the right corner of the titlebar, and is decorated with a set of nested squares.

Then drag the pointer across *any* border or corner of the window and stretch it in whatever direction you want. (You may have to move the pointer slightly outside the window, even if you want to drag a border or corner *in* to create a smaller window.) An outline will show you how you're resizing the window.

At the same time, a small box displaying the window's changing dimensions will appear in the upper-left corner of the screen. (For most clients, dimensions are measured in pixels. *xterm* is an exception—its dimensions are measured in characters wide by lines high. See Article 17.11.) When the window is the size you want, release the pointer button. Figure 12-4 illustrates a window being "stretched" from the lower-left corner.

— VQ

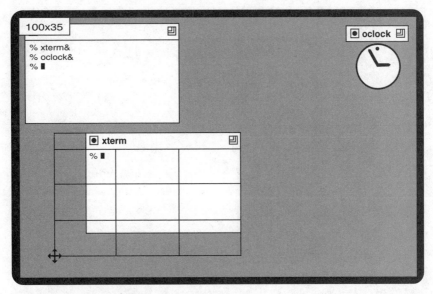

Figure 12-4: Resizing a window from the corner

12.04 The Twm Menu

You should be able to perform most window management functions by clicking the pointer on the *twm* titlebar *(12.03)* or by using a ckey/pointer shortcut *(12.05)*. For cases in which the titlebar is covered, the Twm menu gives you another form of access to these functions, as well as providing some additional functions.

In the standard version of *twm*, you bring up the Twm menu by moving the pointer to the root window and holding down the first pointer button. The pointer becomes an arrow with which you can point at menu items. The default Twm menu appears in Figure 12-5.

Then, to select a menu item: continue to hold down the first button and drag the pointer down the menu to the desired item. Notice that a horizontal band, or *highlighting bar*, follows the pointer. When you've highlighted the desired menu item, select it by releasing the button.

Rather than run down the menu items in order, we'll first consider the ones you can't perform using either the frame or a key/pointer shortcut.

Figure 12-5: Twm menu

Focus

When you select **Focus**, the pointer becomes the dot cursor. Move the pointer to the window you want to be the focus window and click the first button. The window retains the input focus, regardless of where you move the pointer. Article 12.07 describes this process in greater detail.

Unfocus

To recover pointer focus, select this item.

Show Icon Manager

Brings up the Icon Manager *(12.09)* window (generally in the upper-left corner of the screen). See Article 12.15 to learn how to set up the Icon Manager to appear automatically when *twm* is started.

Hide Icon Manager

Makes the Icon Manager go away.

Delete

When you select **Delete**, the pointer becomes a skull and crossbones. Click on the window you want to remove gently.

Kill When you select **Kill**, the pointer becomes a skull and crossbones. Click on the window you want to kill *(2.08)*.

Restart

Stops and restarts the *twm* window manager. Windows are redrawn without titlebars; icons are converted back to windows. When *twm* is restarted, titlebars are put back and windows that were previously iconified are re-iconified. You must restart *twm* to activate any window manager customizations *(12.11)*.

Exit

Stops the window manager. Windows are redrawn without titlebars; icons are converted back to windows. Pointer focus is in effect.

Here are the remaining **Twm** menu items and a few quick tips on how to use them.

Iconify

When you select **Iconify**, the pointer becomes the dot cursor. Move the pointer to the window you want to iconify and click the first button.

Resize

When you select **Resize**, the pointer becomes the cross-arrow cursor. Move the cross arrow to the window you want to resize; press and hold the first pointer button; resize; release the pointer button.

Move

When you select **Move**, the pointer becomes the cross arrow cursor. Place the cross arrow anywhere on the window you want to move; press and hold down the first pointer button; drag to the new location; release the pointer button.

Raise

When you select **Raise**, the pointer becomes the dot cursor. Move the pointer to the window you want to raise and click the first button.

Lower

When you select **Lower**, the pointer becomes the dot cursor. Move the pointer to the window you want to lower and click the first button.

All of the window management functions are customizable. You can add items to or delete items *(12.22)* from the **Twm** menu and even define new menus *(12.23)* by modifying the *.twmrc* startup file *(12.11)*.

—*VQ*

12.05 Key and Pointer Button Shortcuts

When a window's titlebar is covered by other windows, you can still perform most of the important *twm* functions using a key and pointer button combination. There are shortcuts to iconify, move, raise, and lower. All of the shortcuts require you to place the pointer somewhere in the window, hold down the so-called Meta key, and perform some pointer action. (Meta is the name of a function, not an actual physical key. On many keyboards, the Alt key acts as "Meta." See Article 18.14 for more information.)

Table 12-2: twm Key/Pointer Shortcuts on Windows

Function	What You Do
Iconify	Meta key, second pointer button click
Move	Meta key, first or third pointer button down, drag, release
Raise	Meta key, third pointer button click
Lower	Meta key, first pointer button click

Note that there's no shortcut to resize a window. You have to raise the window (Article 12.13) to get at the resize titlebutton; or use the Resize item on the Twm menu *(12.04)*. For an overview of all functions, see Article 12.31.

—VQ

12.06 Placing and Sizing a New Window

When you first start using *twm*, chances are it will be set up so that you have to place new windows manually using the pointer. I'm sure you've been this route: you run a window, the pointer changes to a corner symbol, you move the corner to the place you want, and then click the first button. The new window is displayed.

Interactive placement can be a hassle and you may choose to modify *twm* to place windows automatically. (See Article 12.12 for instruction.) However, if you don't mind manual placement, it does offer one advantage: you can specify the size of the window at the same time. The second pointer button allows you to size the window interactively. The third pointer button specifies a window of maximum height for your screen.

Of course, you might be happy with automatic placement and then manual resizing *(12.03)*, or you might want to use the *–geometry* option *(17.10)* to specify both size and position. But interactive sizing is a *twm* feature that few users know about, and it can come in handy.

Sizing a New Window Using the Second Button

To see how this works, try running an *xterm* with no options. As usual, the pointer becomes the upper-left corner cursor to allow you to place the window. Move the corner to the place you want. Now rather than simply clicking the first pointer button, press and hold down the second button. A window outline is displayed and the pointer is redisplayed as the cross-arrow cursor in the center of the outline, as in Figure 12-6.

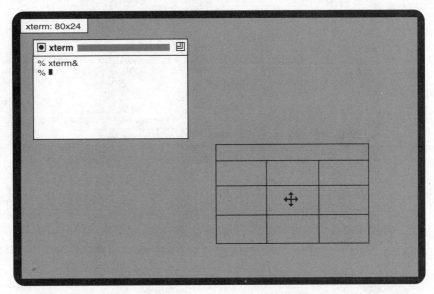

Figure 12-6: Placing and sizing a new window using the second pointer button

The resize box, which tracks the window's dimensions, is also displayed in the upper-left corner of the screen. (Most applications have dimensions in pixels; *xterm* is an exception: it is some number of characters wide by some number of lines high, 80×24 by default. See Article 17.11.)

To size the window, you move the cross-arrow cursor towards any border (or corner) of the outline and drag it out; or cross the border and drag it back in to make a smaller window. (If you want, you can monitor the exact dimensions by reading the resize box.) Once you have the outline the size you want, release the second pointer button. The outline and the resize box disappear. The window is displayed in the location and size you specified.

Specifying Maximum Height Using the Third Button

Again, let's run an *xterm* with no options. Move the corner cursor to the place you want the upper-left corner to be; then click the *third* pointer button. The resulting window will be the maximum height possible for your screen, given the upper-left corner location you selected, as in Figure 12-7.

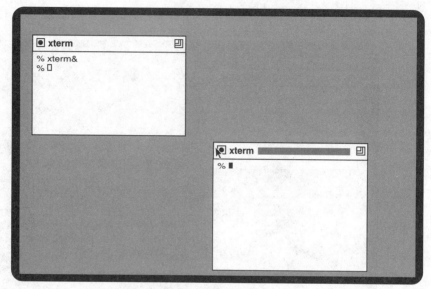

Figure 12-7: Clicking the third pointer button specifies maximum height

— *VQ*

12.07 *Keeping the Focus on One Window*

twm doesn't offer a choice of focus policies, but you can temporarily direct focus to a particular window and keep it there. The **Focus** item on the **Twm** menu temporarily disables pointer focus and directs input to whatever window you select. When you select **Focus**, the pointer becomes the dot cursor. Move the pointer to the window you want to be the focus window and click the first button. The window retains the input focus, regardless of where you move the pointer.

Focusing on one window can be useful when you're going to be working in that window for an extended period. If I expect to be writing for a while, I direct focus to the terminal window I'm using and move the pointer aside. Once the focus is set in this way, there's no danger of my knocking the pointer out of the window I'm typing in and losing my keystrokes in the bargain.

The **Focus** item remains in effect until you turn it off. To recover pointer focus, just select **Unfocus** from the **Twm** menu.

—*VQ*

12.08 *When Icons Ruled the Earth*

Many years ago, when I was hiking alone through the old country (Tennessee), I met a gypsy barroom queen in Memphis. She told me many things. She told me that I would meet my true love in line at the convenience store where Elvis shops. She told me never to cross over running water, unless there is a public restroom on the other side. And she told me one other thing—a warning—that I will share with you: never run *twm* without an Icon Manager *(12.09)*, or you will become a hair-sprouting, moon-obsessed wolf creature.

I cannot verify that this is so. But I can honestly tell you, I have never taken the risk.

As a rule, of course, iconifying is a very good thing. It gets big ugly windows out of the way, so you can look at little ugly windows, or vice versa. It lets you hide the personal mail you're sending, the game you're playing, or the bitmap picture of your boss you're defacing. So, you definitely want to make iconifying as uncomplicated and pleasant as possible.

Without an Icon Manager, iconifying windows means ending up with tiny little icon symbols all over the place. It means losing the tiny little icons under other windows. Even if you don't sprout fangs, it means moving your windows around and around like a stupid jerk, cussing under your breath, and wanting to throw a brick through your stupid screen. Or maybe it's just me. I am half Italian. And then, of course, there's the howling and the bloodbaths.

But if the thousands of dollars you will save on therapy (not to mention hair removal) isn't enough to get you to set up the Icon Manager *(12.15)*, a quick look at the alternative should be.

The default environment is not exactly friendly to the user bent on iconifying. Converting a window to an icon is the easy part: just click on the iconify title-button *(12.03)*.

But here's where the trouble starts. The icon is displayed at the same coordinates the window was. But the icon is—much smaller! Figure 12-8 gives you an idea of the scale of these little monsters.

So you can easily lose it under other windows. Deiconifying is easy—in theory. You just click on the icon and the window is redisplayed in the position it appeared before it was iconified. The tricky part is finding the icon.

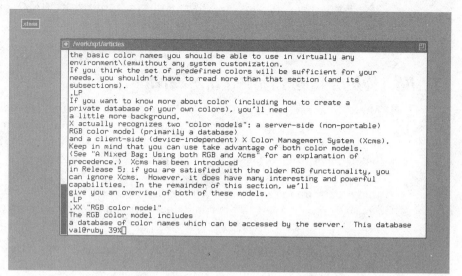

the basic color names you should be able to use in virtually any
environment\(emwithout any system customization.
If you think the set of predefined colors will be sufficient for your
needs, you shouldn't have to read more than that section (and its
subsections).
.LP
If you want to know more about color (including how to create a
private database of your own colors), you'll need
a little more background.
X actually recognizes two "color models": a server-side (non-portable)
RGB color model (primarily a database)
and a client-side (device-independent) X Color Management System (Xcms).
Keep in mind that you can use take advantage of both color models.
(See "A Mixed Bag: Using both RGB and Xcms" for an explanation of
precedence.) Xcms has been introduced
in Release 5; if you are satisfied with the older RGB functionality, you
can ignore Xcms. However, it does have many interesting and powerful
capabilities. In the remainder of this section, we'll
give you an overview of both of these models.
.LP
.XX "RGB color model"
The RGB color model includes
a database of color names which can be accessed by the server. This database
val@ruby 39%

Figure 12-8: An icon can hide itself under your windows like a roach under the stove

Once you iconify a window, you can move the icon around on the display
and the new location becomes the default location for the icon. In other
words, next time you iconify the window, the icon won't be displayed at the
same coordinates as the window, but at the place you moved the icon to
before. This environment begs for the Icon Manager.

Now, the *twm* afficionado can tell you that the Icon Manager is not the only
icon organizing alternative. You can specify what's known as an *icon region*.
The thing is, setting up an icon region requires specifying where on the screen
you want the icons and how you want them to be arranged there, which is
just what the Icon Manager will do for you. Personally, I'd stick with the Icon
Manager.

The only case in which you might want to trouble with an icon region is if
you're attached to having icon symbols hanging around. Maybe you even
want to specify your own bitmaps in place of the simple icon symbols *twm*
provides, or the fancier pixmaps some clients may provide. Admittedly, however, this is fairly esoteric stuff. For more information, see the IconRegion and
Icons resource variables *(1.06)* on the *twm* manpage.

—*VQ*

12.09 Using the Icon Manager

You may notice that icons can easily get lost behind windows on the display. And you can spend a foolish amount of time searching for them. By selecting the Show Iconmgr item on the Twm menu, you can bring up a window called the Icon Manager, from which you can iconify and deiconify any window on the display. To configure *twm* to bring up the Icon Manager automatically at startup, see Article 12.15.

As described in Article 12.02, the Icon Manager window contains a menu-like list of each client window running on the display—regardless of whether a window is currently iconified. Each client name is enclosed in a rectangle. If the client is currently iconified, the name is preceded by a small letter X.

In Figure 12-9, an *oclock* (3.02) and two *xterm* windows are iconified. In addition to these iconified windows, two active *xterm* windows appear on the screen. These windows are also represented by rectangles in the Icon Manager; however, no X symbol precedes the names. Notice that the rectangle representing the window with the input focus is highlighted.

By default the Icon Manager is displayed in the upper-left corner of the screen. When you run an additional client, an entry is added to the Icon Manager window. When a client exits, its entry is removed from the window.

The Icon Manager makes iconifying and deiconifying windows simple. To convert a window to an icon, you just click on the Icon Manager rectangle that corresponds to the window in question. Unless you've suppressed the icon symbols *(12.15)* (a good idea), an icon will be displayed on the corresponding Icon Manager rectangle (near the place you clicked).

Note that if you iconified the window *before* bringing up the Icon Manager, when you click on the titlebar's iconify button *(12.03)*, the icon will instead be displayed at the same coordinates the window was! If this happens, drag the icon onto the Icon Manager; this will become the default location for the icon. Then you can iconify the window by any method you like (by clicking on the iconify command button, for instance), and the icon will be displayed on the Icon Manager. With a little window manager customization, you can avoid this problem entirely, as we'll explain later.

The Icon Manager really comes in handy when you want to deiconify a window (i.e., convert an icon back to a window). Just click on the Icon Manager rectangle that corresponds to the window in question. (There should be an X to the left of the client name, indicating that it is currently iconified.) The window is deiconified and displayed in its previous location.

If you have several windows with the same name (for example, "xterm"), it may be hard to tell which rectangle corresponds to which window. If you click on the wrong rectangle (and convert the wrong icon back to a window),

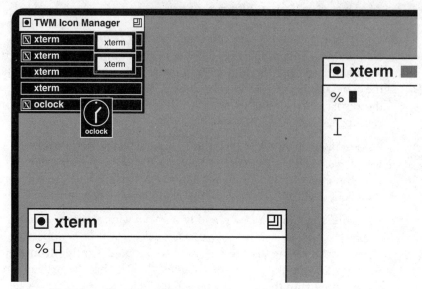

Figure 12-9: Icon Manager with three windows iconified

just click a second time to iconify the window again. However, if you find repeat client names too confusing, you can specify an alternative using the *–name* option *(20.04)*, which most applications recognize.

In addition to iconifying and deiconifying, the Icon Manager lets you direct the input focus. Just place the pointer on the Icon Manager rectangle corresponding to the window and it will become the focus window. Note that when AutoRaise *(12.13)* is in effect, focusing in this way also raises the window to the top of the window stack.

You can move, resize, raise, lower, and even iconify the Icon Manager just like any other window. You can also kill the Icon Manager window, though this is NOT a good idea. You can hose *twm* in the process. Luckily, *twm* is smart enough not to let you remove the Icon Manager using either the Kill or Delete items on the Twm menu *(12.04)*. But if you're trying to *xkill (2.08)* another window, remember to give the Icon Manager a wide berth.

The only serious limitation to using the default configuration of the Icon Manager is that you can still have icons obscuring your screen. Article 12.15 describes how to: customize *twm* so that icons aren't created; specify that the Icon Manager is brought up automatically when you log in; and set a different location for the Icon Manager window.

—VQ

12.10 tvtwm: twm with a Virtual Desktop

tvtwm

The *tvtwm* window manager (Tom's virtual *twm*) extends the basic capabilities of *twm* by extending the area of your screen. Rather than being limited to your screen's literal dimensions, *tvtwm* creates a virtual desktop of any size you specify. Basic window management functions are the same as for *twm*, but you have a lot more screen real estate on which to spread out your windows.

Figure 12-10 shows the upper-left screenful of a *tvtwm* virtual desktop. This particular desktop is the size of three screenfuls by three screenfuls. (Edit your *.twmrc* file *(12.11)* to provide the dimensions *(12.30)*.) The small window in the lower-right corner, labeled "Virtual Desktop," is called the *panner*. The panner mirrors the entire space and helps you navigate it.

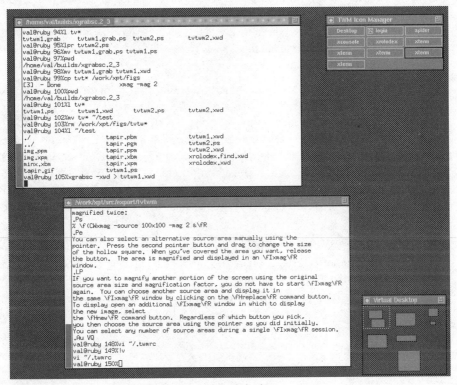

Figure 12-10: tvtwm provides a large virtual desktop

Notice that I've already customized *twm* to provide an Icon Manager window *(12.15)*, which is extremely useful with a large desktop.

Figure 12-11 shows a close-up of the panner.

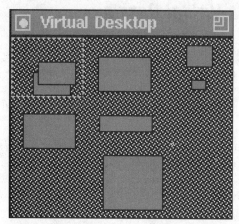

Figure 12-11: The panner shows the entire desktop and helps you get around

The panner is what is known as a "sticky" window. It is, in effect, stuck to the screen; it's visible in the lower-right corner of the monitor, regardless of the part of the desktop you're viewing.

The panner shows you the entire desktop in miniature, so you can keep track of what's going on in this large space. The window reveals a tiny representation of each application you run. However, the panner window is not mirrored in itself. (Sticky windows do not appear in the panner.) Small windows like the initial *xman* window *(5.02)* and *xpostit (4.12)* will be fairly hard to spot in miniature, but a blip representing them is there if you look closely. In our figure, several windows of varying sizes are running. I have an idea what each of them is from memory, but labeling would be a nice addition to the program code.

Notice the dotted outline surrounding the upper-left part of the panner. This outline surrounds the part of the desktop that is currently being displayed on your screen. You can move this outline to reveal another portion of the desktop by holding down the first pointer button, dragging the outline to another part of the panner, and releasing the pointer button. The screen will be updated to show the area you've chosen. (If you become a *tvtwm* enthusiast, there's a way to specify shortcuts for getting around the desktop. See Article 12.30 for details.)

Whatever changes you make to a window on the desktop will be mirrored in the miniature version in the panner. Likewise, you can move the miniature versions, and the actual windows will be moved. To do this, hold the second pointer button down on the miniwindow, drag it to any place on the desktop, and release. Of course, if you drag the window outside the panner's outline, you will no longer be able to see it on screen.

Notice that the panner has a titlebar with buttons to iconify and resize *(12.03)*, just like any application. Resizing the panner changes the size of the desktop! This function can come in very handy when space gets tight. However, keep in mind that if you specify the initial dimensions of the desktop *(12.30)* in screenfuls, and then set up shortcuts to jump from screen to screen *(12.30)*, resizing the panner can throw the whole environment off.

So, in such a large environment, where does a new window go when you start it? If automatic window placement *(12.12)* is specified, a new window may be placed relative to the entire desktop, or relative to the part of the desktop you're viewing. It depends on how the particular client communicates with *tvtwm*. More sophisticated programs should place the window on the current screenful.

There are some even less obvious reprecussions of using *tvtwm*, which occur due to the presence of the virtual root window. First, because of the way the virtual root window is implemented, you cannot simply make a window dump with *xwd (23.01)*. The X window dumper treats everything on a particular screenful of the desktop as a single window. To capture an application window proper, use *xgrabsc* or *xgrab (23.05)* instead.

A second ramification of having the virtual root window is that you cannot use *xsetroot (6.02)* or *xcsetroot (6.03)* to decorate it. Both of those programs decorate only the actual root window. To decorate the virtual root window, use *xloadimage (24.05)* or *xv (24.06)*.

tvtwm also provides a few variables that allow you to specify background and foreground colors and patterns for the virtual desktop and the panner window. For example, you can specify a color for the root window background using the `VirtualDesktopBackground` variable in your *.twmrc* file. See the online *tvtwm* manpage for a complete list of variables, and the discussion of color window manager features *(12.26)* for guidelines on implementing them.

You can run *tvtwm* by adding a single line to your *.twmrc* file *(12.11)*, exiting *twm*, and then starting a *tvtwm* process. The line in question specifies the size of your desktop; we recommend that you make a few more modifications to your *.twmrc* file in order to use *tvtwm* more effectively. See Article 12.30 for details.

If the idea of a virtual desktop appeals to you and you're not married to *twm*, you might also check out the somewhat more sophisticated *fvwm* window manager *(15.01)*.

—VQ

12.11 How Can I Change twm?

The default version of *twm* will let you perform all of the standard window manager operations in fairly convenient ways. But every user has different needs and you might like to adapt *twm* to suit them. The default operation of *twm* is largely controlled by a systemwide file, called *system.twmrc*, which sets the contents of the Twm menu *(12.04)*, how menu functions are invoked, what key/button shortcuts *(12.05)* can be used for window management functions, etc.

You customize the window manager by editing a copy of the *system.twmrc* file in your home directory. (Your personal file should be called *.twmrc*.) Once you edit your *.twmrc* file, you activate the changes by restarting *twm*. If you forget to restart the window manager, none of your changes will take effect.

Your Twm menu should offer a **Restart** option. When you select it, there will be a flurry of activity as window manager decorations go away and icons are converted back to windows. When *twm* is restarted, titlebars are put back, windows that were previously iconified are re-iconified; more importantly, your customizations should be implemented (presuming you've used the correct syntax, etc.).

If your Twm menu doesn't have a **Restart** option, you can always kill the window manager process and run it again. However, be sure that *twm* is not your session's controlling process *(16.03)* or, you'll be bumped out of X.

Among the possible *twm* customizations, you can:

- Set up the Icon Manager to come up automatically and to serve in place of the icon symbols (Article 12.15).

- Change the Twm menu and define your own menus (Articles 12.22 and 12.23).

- Bind functions to keyboard key/pointer button combinations (Article 12.23).

- Issue command strings to the shell (Article 12.23).

We strongly recommend that you:

- Configure the Icon Manager *(12.15)*.

- Specify the RandomPlacement variable *(12.12)*, which saves you from having to place every new window manually.

These basic customizations will make almost anyone's life easier. In some environments, they may even have been done for you in the *system.twmrc*. (The downside of RandomPlacement is that it prohibits interactive sizing *(12.06)*. If you like this feature, you may want to stick with manual placement.)

In addition to these basic customizations, you might also consider specifying:

- The `AutoRaise` variable *(12.13)*, which automatically raises a window when you focus on it.

- The `NoTitleFocus` variable *(12.27)*, which compensates for a minor *twm* bug that can cause keystrokes to be lost.

`AutoRaise` is particularly powerful. Unfortunately, if you also specify `NoTitleFocus`, the power is more limited. See Article 12.27 for an explanation.

Suppressing the titlebar *(12.16)* can sometimes improve aesthetics. If you're interested in additional customizations, you can find further instructions later in this chapter.

— VQ

12.12 *Automatic Window Placement*

The single most irritating feature of the default configuration of *twm* may be that you have to place new windows manually. You know the story. You run a client, you wait a second, the pointer changes to an upper-left corner symbol; then you move the pointer to the screen location you want and click to position the new window. (Whew.) And unless you have the perspective and coordination of a Leonardo, you'll probably have to move the damn thing again anyway.

If you're like me (at least in one way), you don't want to go to all this trouble. As an alternative, you can leave issues of placement up to *twm*. To configure *twm* to place new windows randomly on the screen, just add the following variable to your *.twmrc* file:

```
RandomPlacement
```

(Then restart *twm* *(12.11)* to activate the change.) Once a new window is displayed, it's simple to move it to the exact location you want.

twm's idea of random is actually somewhat predictable. New windows will be positioned at increasingly greater distances from the upper-left corner of the screen.

The only obvious advantage to sticking with the default manual placement is that you can also interactively size the new window. See Article 12.06 for more information. Of course, all of this placement and sizing business becomes irrelevant if you run a client with the *–geometry (17.10)* option.

— VQ

12.13 Raising Windows: Manual or Automatic?

If you arrange your windows in a tiled *(21.19)* fashion (that is, without overlapping), raising windows won't be an issue. However, those of us in the window-overlapping crowd need a way to change the stacking order so that we can access "buried" clients.

Without any customization, *twm* lets you raise a window to the top of the window stack simply by clicking on the titlebar. This action is easy to perform and easy to remember, but there are situations in which it isn't entirely practical. For instance, if you work with a lot of windows like I do, titlebars are often buried, and where does that leave you?

When you can't get at a window's titlebar, there are three other "manual" methods to raise the window. The first method is quick, but not particularly intuitive: while holding down the so-called Meta key *(18.14)* (often **Alt**), click the third pointer button anywhere in the window.

The second method is a bit of a trick. You can click twice on the Icon Manager rectangle corresponding to the window. The first click iconifies the window. The second click deiconifies the window, which is redisplayed at the top of the window stack.

The final method is more laborious: the Twm menu's *(12.04)* **Raise** item. Pop up the menu by holding down the third pointer button on the root window. Drag the pointer down and release on **Raise**. The pointer changes to a dot symbol. You then click on the window you want to raise. Admittedly, using the menu is not as simple or automatic as clicking on the titlebar or as fast as the key-pointer shortcut, but it can come in handy in a pinch.

If you want to avoid the problem, you can customize *twm* so that windows are raised automatically whenever you place the pointer anywhere on them. Just add `AutoRaise` to the variables section of your *.twmrc* file *(12.11)* and restart the window manager. Note, however, that you must specify the list of clients to be raised as an argument to the `AutoRaise` variable. For example, I use the following line:

```
AutoRaise { "XTerm" "Xmh" }
```

to specify that all *xterm (2.02)* and *xmh (7.06)* windows will be raised automatically when I move the pointer into them. (Notice that I use the application class names *(20.05)* to specify all instances of *xterm* and *xmh*.) I still need to raise all other application windows manually. If you're inclined to use many different applications and to stack them up, you may want to specify several arguments to `AutoRaise`. (For those who change their environment frequently, `AutoRaise` may not be practical.)

Keep in mind that, if you're using the Icon Manager *(12.09)*, AutoRaise changes your environment in an additional way. Generally, when you place the pointer on an Icon Manager entry, the corresponding window takes over the input focus.* If you've specified AutoRaise, placing the pointer on an Icon Manager entry that corresponds to an active window both focuses input on the window and raises it.

Another complication can arise if one of your applications pops up a dialog box. If the dialog appears on top of the application window, you can move the pointer onto the dialog without changing the stacking order (see window stack). However, if you move the pointer off the dialog without making a selection (i.e., back on to the application window), you will raise the window and bury the dialog in the process. If you get into a situation like this, move the window aside to get at the dialog.

If you decide to use AutoRaise, you may be made a little dizzy by the shuffle of windows when you move your pointer across the screen or across the Icon Manager, but I think it generally saves time and energy.

— VQ

12.14 *Iconifying with a Function Key*

If you like to rely on the keyboard more than the pointer, you can configure *twm* to iconify when you press a key. The following binding from my *.twmrc* file *(12.11)* lets me iconify a window by pressing the **F8** function key:

```
"F8"    = : all : f.iconify
```

The "all" means the function is valid when the pointer rests in any of the valid contexts (window, titlebar, icon, root window, and Icon Manager *(12.09)*). However, since f.iconify doesn't make sense with the pointer on the root window, nothing happens when you press **F8** in that context.

Note that f.iconify is a toggle. Thus, you can use the **F8** function key both to iconify a window and to deiconify it. (The pointer needs to rest on the icon symbol or Icon Manager entry to deiconify.)

— VQ, DJF

12.15 *Setting Up the Icon Manager*

To specify that the Icon Manager *(12.09)* is brought up automatically when the window manager is started, include the following variable in your *.twmrc* file *(12.11)*:

```
ShowIconManager
```

---

* If you've also specified NoTitleFocus *(12.27)*, this isn't the case.

However, without further customization, you'll still have icon symbols on your screen. Since having the Icon Manager makes the symbols unnecessary (and they can get in the way), it's a good idea to suppress them. You can specify that icons not be created simply by adding the variable IconifyByUnmapping to your *.twmrc* file. Then the only evidence that a window is iconified is the X before its entry in the Icon Manager window.

Where Have All the Icons Gone?

Keep in mind that a somewhat confusing situation can arise if you specify IconifyByUnmapping and then select **Hide Iconmgr** from the Twm menu *(12.04)*. The latter action "unmaps" the Icon Manager window: it is no longer displayed. If you then iconify a window, it will simply seem to disappear! Because of IconifyByUnmapping, no icon will be displayed. And you won't have access to the iconified application through the Icon Manager. In such a circumstance, in order to deiconify the application, you would have to select **Show Iconmgr** from the **Twm** menu and then click on the appropriate Icon Manager partition.

Placing the Icon Manager

Another useful variable is IconManagerGeometry, which allows you to specify the initial size and location for the Icon Manager window. IconManagerGeometry requires as an argument the standard *geometry* string (which is also supplied to the *–geometry* toolkit option *(17.10)*):

```
widthxheight±xoff±0yoff
```

The *width* and *height* are interpreted as pixels. It actually doesn't make much sense to specify the dimensions, since the default size is based on the number of client windows running, but there's a somewhat compelling reason to do so. We've found that if we omit the dimensions (and simply specify position), *twm* can interpret the x and y coordinates in unexpected ways. The dimensions:

```
160x160
```

are slightly greater than the defaults, to make the window more readable. (Note that if you specify another font for the Icon Manager, using the IconManagerFont resource variable *(17.01)*, these dimensions may not suffice.)

Then you can specify whatever coordinates you want, using the same guidelines as those described for the *–geometry* option. For example, the following line places the left side of the Icon Manager window flush against the left side of the screen and the bottom edge of the window 150 pixels above the bottom edge of the screen:

```
IconManagerGeometry "160x160+0-150"
```

As you start additional applications, entries are added to the bottom of the Icon Manager window. This position leaves 150 pixels of room on the screen for new entries. (If you start more applications than will fit in this space, of course, you can move the window.)

An Icon Manager of a Different Shape?

For the more exacting *twm* user, the IconManagerGeometry variable also takes an optional second argument that specifies a number of columns. Keep in mind that specifying columns can create an Icon Manager window that takes up more room horizontally and less vertically. Depending on the layout of your screen, this can be an advantage. You should adjust the width factor in the geometry string to accommodate the number of columns you want. Selecting the dimensions is largely a guessing game. I find 240 pixels of width provides plenty of room for three icons and their application names:

```
IconManagerGeometry "240x240-0+0" "3"
```

The previous line creates an Icon Manager three columns wide in the upper-right corner of the screen, as in Figure 12-12.

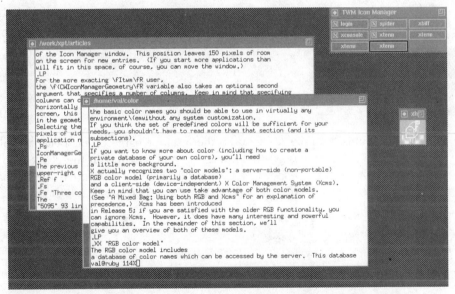

Figure 12-12: Three columns give the Icon Manager a horizontal orientation

You may also want to use the SortIconManager variable, which causes windows in the Icon Manager to appear alphabetically by application name, rather than in the order in which the applications are run.

For information about other variables to control the Icon Manager, see the *twm* manpage.

—VQ

12.16 *Suppressing the twm Titlebar*

There will probably be times when you'd like to run a client window without the *twm* titlebar *(12.03)*. Luckily, *twm* makes it fairly easy to suppress the titlebar for a particular application. Simply add `NoTitle` to the variables section of your *.twmrc* file *(12.11)* followed by the names of the clients (and then restart the window manager).

The following line says that *oclock (3.02)* windows should have no titlebars. (We think this is a much neater look. An *oclock* with a titlebar seems to float below the bar.)

```
NoTitle { "oclock" }
```

`NoTitle` can take an argument in the form of a list. To suppress the titlebar for multiple clients:

```
NoTitle { "oclock" "xclock" "xeyes" }
```

As an alternative, you can place each client on its own line with the braces before and after:

```
NoTitle
{
    "oclock"
    "xclock"
    "xeyes"
}
```

In this example, we've used the instance name of each client. This will work for all instances of the application, unless you run the client with the *—name* option *(20.04)* to specify an alternate name. To suppress the titlebar for these cases as well, you can instead use the application class names *(20.05)*:

```
NoTitle
{
    "Clock"
    "XClock"
    "XEyes"
}
```

Having no titlebar may look nice, but the downside is that it complicates window management.

—VQ

12.17 Managing a Window Without a Titlebar

If you suppress *twm*'s titlebar *(12.16)* for a client window, it becomes a little harder to move the window, resize it, etc. Basically, you have to rely on the Twm pop-up menu *(12.04)* or a keyboard/pointer shortcut *(12.05)*.

The default **Twm** menu provides items that let you **Resize, Move, Raise,** and **Lower** any window—regardless of whether it has a titlebar. *twm* also provides a few key and pointer button shortcuts for simple functions. (There's no shortcut for resizing; you'll have to use the menu.)

Suppose you have an *oclock (3.02)* without a titlebar and you want to move it. What can you do? There are a couple of options:

* Select the **Move** item from the **Twm** menu. Move the cross-arrow pointer to the window. (Since there is no titlebar, you must place the pointer on the window proper.) Press and hold any pointer button, drag the window outline to the location you want, and release the button.

* Press the Meta key *(18.14)*; then press and hold down the third pointer button (you can release the key); drag the window outline to the new location; finally, release the pointer button.

—VQ

12.18 Adding a Close Button to the Titlebar

twm doesn't offer any really quick method to close a window. You can use the **Delete** or **Kill** items on the Twm menu *(12.04)*, but then you have to display the menu, etc. The advantage of these methods is that you have to be deliberate about removing a window, making an accident unlikely.

But if you're willing to risk accidentally closing a window, you can add a button for that purpose to the titlebar. The following lines in the bindings section of your *.twmrc* file will move the iconify button to the right, next to the resize button, and create an entirely new close button in the upper-left corner, as in Figure 12-13.

```
LeftTitleButton ":xlogo" = f.delete
RightTitleButton ":dot" = f.iconify
RightTitleButton ":resize" = f.resize
```

In order to override the default titlebar buttons, you also have to add the variable NoDefaults to your *.twmrc* file. If you try this new button arrangement without specifying NoDefaults, you'll actually get titlebars with five buttons each: the two default buttons and the three you specify! (Keep in mind, however, that NoDefaults may change some of the ways you're used to *twm* working and you may end up needing additional customizations to compensate.)

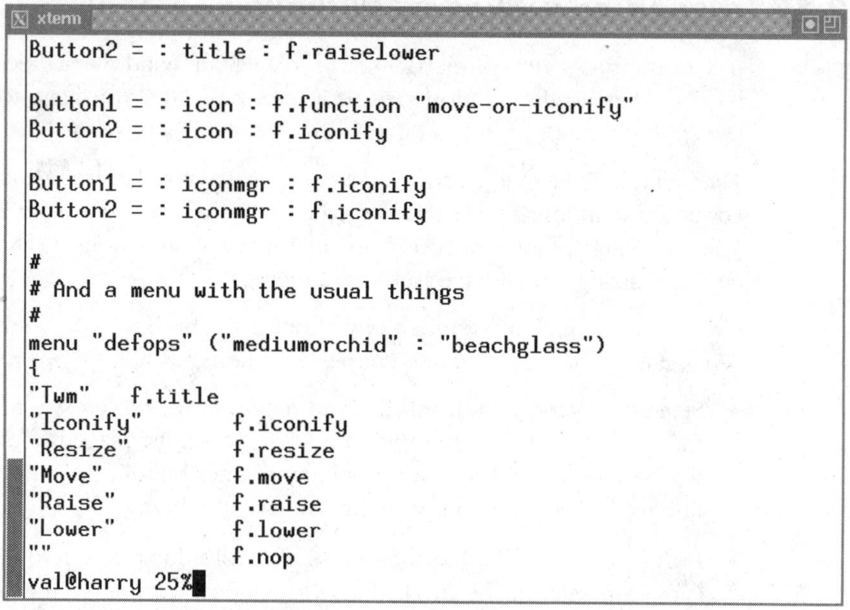

```
Button2 = : title : f.raiselower

Button1 = : icon : f.function "move-or-iconify"
Button2 = : icon : f.iconify

Button1 = : iconmgr : f.iconify
Button2 = : iconmgr : f.iconify

#
# And a menu with the usual things
#
menu "defops" ("mediumorchid" : "beachglass")
{
"Twm"      f.title
"Iconify"        f.iconify
"Resize"         f.resize
"Move"           f.move
"Raise"          f.raise
"Lower"          f.lower
""               f.nop
val@harry 25%
```

Figure 12-13: Reorganizing the titlebar and adding a close button

The new close button is decorated with the "X" symbol (*xlogo*) and it invokes
f.delete, a gentle way to remove a window. The close button is particularly
useful for removing windows like *xclock* (3.02). Some applications may not
respond to f.delete, and you may need to kill them. *twm* provides a function
called f.destroy that does just that. You can invoke it using the Kill item on
the Twm menu. See Article 2.08 for other ways to kill a window.

As we've suggested, the liability with having a close button is that you'll nuke
a window by mistake. This is bad. As an alternative, you might consider specifying key bindings that invoke f.delete and f.destroy. Map these functions to
key combinations you're not likely to hit by mistake. The following lines map
delete and destroy/kill to combinations involving the Meta key and function
keys on my Sun-3 keyboard:

```
"F33" = m : all : f.delete
"F35" = m : all : f.destroy
```

If you go the titlebutton route, you may want to know more about the bitmap
images that appear on buttons and how to specify alternatives. Article 12.20
discusses the standard set of bitmaps *twm* recognizes and also shows you how
to invoke your own images.

— VQ, DJF

12.19   Adding a Maximize Button to the Titlebar

Most standard versions of *mwm* and *fvwm* offer shortcuts that let you maximize a window. Though you have to tweak *twm* to provide the same powers, the customization is fairly easy to do. *twm* also offers several flavors of maximizing. It has a function that lets you maximize in the most general sense (so that the window fills the screen). But it also provides functions to maximize a window only vertically or horizontally, or only from a single window border.

Admittedly, these are more ways than you'll probably care about. I personally never use the standard maximizing function, regardless of the window manager. I just find an application window the size of the root window to be a waste of space. I much prefer the option of resizing only in the vertical direction, so I have more room to read and write.

I can add a titlebar button that lets me maximize vertically using *twm*'s f.zoom function. I add the following line to the bindings section of my *.twmrc* file:

```
RightTitleButton ":menu" = f.zoom
```

which creates a maximize button in the right corner of the titlebar, to the left of the resize button (see Figure 12-14.) The resize button is decorated with nested squares.

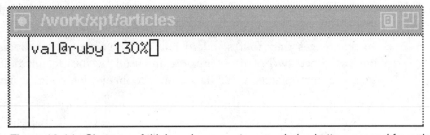

Figure 12-14: Close-up of titlebar shows custom maximize button, second from right

To decorate our the new maximize button, I've chosen a small bitmap that looks a little bit like a traffic light. The second column in the sample *.twmrc* file entry above gives the name of this bitmap file, which somewhat confusingly is *menu*. Don't let that throw you. This is simply the name of the image file. The bitmap image doesn't determine the functionality of the command button; it merely decorates the button.

The *menu* bitmap file is one of only five images *twm* can call upon by default. The name *menu* is something of a misnomer given the way we're using the bitmap. The image itself is not very suggestive of a particular meaning; it takes on meaning when paired with a *twm* function. You may want to come up with a more appropriate visual image. Article 12.20 describes the default images and how to create and use additional ones, including a suggested bitmap for our maximize button.

—VQ

12.20 *Decorations For New Titlebar Buttons*

twm provides five standard bitmap images that can be used to decorate the command buttons on the titlebar. The default titlebar uses two of these images: the dot inside the iconify button and the nested squares inside the resize button. (See Article 12.03 for a look.) The bitmap image of the dot has two valid names: *dot* or *iconify*. The image on the resize button is called simply *resize*.

In addition to these two images are: the *xlogo* bitmap, which looks like a small X (and is also called *delete*); the *menu* bitmap, which looks a bit like a tiny traffic light; and the *question* bitmap, which is no more than a small question mark.

I used the *xlogo* bitmap for the close button *(12.18)* I added to the titlebar; and the *menu* bitmap for my maximize button *(12.19)*. (If you're up to doing the work, there are probably better choices for the latter, as we'll see.)

The question-mark bitmap image is intended more for *twm*'s use than for yours. The window manager uses this image if it can't find a bitmap you specify in your *.sqrc* file. More about this later.

So that leaves only four standard images for you to use to decorate titlebar buttons. Since two of those images are used by the default buttons, if you stick with the defaults, you'll have only two images left over for new buttons.

Now, granted, you're not going to want to clutter up the titlebar with buttons anyway. But even if you want to add only a single additional button, it would be nice if the bitmap image decorating it gave some visual clue to its function.

The xlogo (or delete) image works OK for our new close button *(12.18)*, though a little skull or income tax form might be better. But the default bitmaps offer nothing even in the ballpark for our custom maximize button *(12.19)*. We settled on the *menu* bitmap image, which doesn't have much obvious significance, at least to me.

If you're interested enough in aesthetics, you may want to come up with a slightly better image to decorate this button, We did just that using the *bitmap* editor *(22.03)*. Article 22.14 shows you the new and improved maximize bitmap, official filename *max*, which depicts a small window being stretched to a tall one. (Well, vaguely, anyway. I'm no Leonardo.)

In order to use our own bitmap in the *.twmrc* file, we need to tell *twm* where it can find the image, and then we need to reference the image in the line defining the button. The `bitmapFilePath` resource variable *(17.01)* lets you specify a pathname in which *twm* searches for bitmap files:

```
*bitmapFilePath: /home/val/bitmaps
```

Then we supply the name of the bitmap file (*max*) on the line defining the maximize button *(12.19)*.

```
RightTitleButton "max" = f.zoom
```

When you supply a bitmap file of your own, you *do not* precede the filename with a colon. You only use a colon before the name of one of *twm*'s internal bitmap images; the colon is the signal that the image is local to the window manager.

Figure 12-15 shows an *xterm* window with the latest version of the maximize button, complete with our own (semi-meaningful) bitmap.

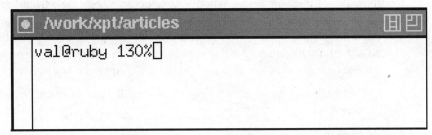

Figure 12-15: Decorating a maximize titlebutton with our own bitmap image

— VQ

12.21 How a Menu Is Defined

The third section of the *system.twmrc* file *(12.11)* contains lines that define the Twm menu *(12.04)*. If you want to edit that menu or create other menus, you do so in the third section of your own *.twmrc* file.

Menu definitions have the format:

```
menu  "menu_name" {
"item_name"  action
          .
          .
          .

}
```

You must provide a *menu_name* in the first line of the menu definition. You also use that *menu_name* elsewhere in the file to specify how the menu is to be displayed. You might display a menu using a pointer or key/pointer command, or you might access a menu via another menu. Regardless of how you set it up, you must pair the *menu_name* with the predefined *twm* function f.menu.

In the case of the default **Twm** menu, the *menu_name* is defops. You display the **Twm** menu by holding the first pointer button on the root window. This display method is specified in the second section of the *system.twmrc* file, which binds *twm* functions to pointer button or button/key commands:

```
.ta  .9i 1.15i 2.4i 3.5i
Button1 =                 : root : f.menu  "defops"
```

The previous line specifies that when pointer button one is held in the context of the root window, the f.menu function is activated and the menu displayed is the one associated with the name defops. When you define your own menus, you can set them up to be displayed in a variety of ways.

Now let's look at an individual line in the menu definition. Each *item_name* is the label of a menu item. When you select the *item_name* from the menu, the corresponding *action* is performed. You can specify one of *twm*'s predefined functions as the action; or you can actually supply a command line that you would normally enter in an *xterm* window. In order to invoke a command from a menu, the action must be prefixed by an exclamation point (!).

The standard **Twm** menu (pictured in Article 12.04) uses only predefined actions:

```
menu "defops"
{
"Twm"             f.title
"Iconify"         f.iconify
"Resize"          f.resize
"Move"            f.move
"Raise"           f.raise
"Lower"           f.lower
""                f.nop
"Focus"           f.focus
"Unfocus"         f.unfocus
"Show Iconmgr"    f.showiconmgr
"Hide Iconmgr"    f.hideiconmgr
""                f.nop
"Kill"            f.destroy
"Delete"          f.delete
""                f.nop
"Restart"         f.restart
"Exit"            f.quit
}
```

The *twm* manpage describes all the available actions.

You can change the Twm menu *(12.22)* by editing the menu definition.

— *VQ*

12.22 Changing the Twm Menu

You can change the 259 Twm menu *(12.04)* by editing the lines defining it in your *.twmrc* file *(12.11)*. Typically you might want to add a command that you execute frequently. You can execute a shell command from a *twm* menu by prefacing the command with an exclamation mark. You pair the command with an item name. In the following example, we've added a menu item that brings up *xcalc (5.05)* to the **Twm** menu:

```
menu "defops"
{
"Twm"                f.title
"Iconify"            f.iconify
"Resize"             f.resize
"Move"               f.move
"Raise"              f.raise
"Lower"              f.lower
""                   f.nop
"Calculator"         !"xcalc &"
""                   f.nop
"Focus"              f.focus
"Unfocus"            f.unfocus
"Show Iconmgr"       f.showiconmgr
"Hide Iconmgr"       f.hideiconmgr
""                   f.nop
"Kill"               f.destroy
"Delete"             f.delete
""                   f.nop
"Restart"            f.restart
"Exit"               f.quit
}
```

Notice that we've also added a blank line before the **Calculator** item, to separate it from the other menu offerings:

```
""      f.nop
```

When you add a command to a *twm* menu, the command must be in your search path *(2.05)*. In most environments, the standard X clients will be found in the directory */usr/bin/X11*, which should be part of virtually any search path. It's easy to add *xcalc* to our **Twm** menu because it lives in */usr/bin/X11*.

However, problems can arise when you want to run a command that resides in an atypical place. For example, I happen to have my own *bin* of goodies under my *home* directory. Among my favorite programs is *oneko (6.07)*, which provides a cat to chase your mouse. If I want to be able to start *oneko* from my **Twm** menu, the command has to be in my search path; or I have to use its full pathname in my *.twmrc* file:

```
"Cat and Mouse"  !"/home/val/bin/oneko &"
```

If you add a command that isn't in your search path, you won't be able to execute it from your menu. Rather than having to enter full pathnames for all commands, you're probably better off configuring your X session so that your search path is set properly *(16.04)*.

In adding items to the **Twm**, you are not limited to system commands. You can also add items that invoke predefined *twm* functions. The function `f.identify` provides various information (name, class name *(20.05)*, geometry *(17.10)*, border width, depth) about any window you select. To add this function to a menu, you might include a line similar to:

```
"Get wininfo"    f.identify
```

(When you invoke `f.identify`, the pointer changes to a dot cursor and you click on the window about which you want information. See Article 20.08.)

If you want to access several additional items via menu, you might not want to clutter the **Twm** menu. You can also create separate menus (see Article 12.23) and/or submenus (see Article 12.24).

—VQ

12.23 *Creating a Separate Menu*

Rather than add item upon item to the **Twm** menu, you might want to create an entirely separate menu of your own commands. To specify a new menu, you have to come up with the menu definition, and also specify how the new menu is going to be displayed.

The following lines in my *.twmrc* file *(12.11)* define a new menu I'll name "mycommands." (This name is arbitrary, but you also use it in the line that specifies how the menu is to be displayed.) I'll use the more friendly title **Utilities** as the first item. You would place the lines defining the menu somewhere in the menu section of your *.twmrc* file, probably right after the **Twm** menu definition *(12.21)*.

```
menu "mycommands"
{
"Utilities"            f.title
"New Window"           !"xterm &"
"Mailbox"              !"xbiff -geometry -10+145 &"
"Clock"                !"oclock -geometry -0+0 &"
"Calculator"           !"xcalc -geometry -0+250&"
"Read News"            !"xterm -e /usr/local/bin/vn &"
"Give wininfo"         f.identify
""                     f.beep
"Spider"               !"/home/val/bin/spider &"
"Ishido"               !"/home/val/bin/ishido &"
}
```

On this menu I've tried to include some general-purpose utilities and games. The f.title function simply creates a menu title line, in this case displaying the tag "Utilities." The **New Window** item runs another *xterm*. (Note the exclamation mark to preface a shell command.) The **Mailbox, Clock, Calculator** menu items also execute system commands, in each case bringing up a desktop client. The **Read News** item runs a temporary *xterm* shell in which a news reader is running. (When you're done reading, the *xterm* goes away.)

Give wininfo invokes a predefined *twm* function that provides statistics (such as geometry, depth, etc.) about a window you select. (See Article 20.08.)

Spider and **Ishido** run a solitaire *(10.06)* and matching game *(10.08)*, repectively. I've set these fun items off from the more utilitarian functions using a blank line. If you select the blank item, you should hear a beep (assuming the keyboard bell is audible *(6.24)*).

A minor issue: You may notice that for some of the commands (*vn, spider,* and *ishido*) I've used full pathnames. This is just to call attention to the fact that these commands are found in somewhat atypical directories, which may not be included in the average search path *(2.05)*. In my environment, using these particular pathnames works fine. However, using full pathnames is not the optimal solution to search path problems. For instance, one complication that can arise is that a command will need to access another command that is also extraneous to your search path! Ideally, you want to run your X session with your path set properly. See Article 16.04 for more information.

In addition to the lines defining the menu, you must also specify how the menu is to be displayed. There are a couple of ways to do this. You can create an entirely separate menu by specifying a unique button binding in the key/button bindings section of the .twmrc file. The following line says that you press pointer button 2 on the root window to display the Utilities menu:

```
Button2 = : root : f.menu "mycommands"
```

You might instead want to access a new menu, such as Utilities, from another menu (maybe Twm). To set up Utilities as a submenu of Twm, see Article 12.24.

Keep in mind that you can define multiple menus, but each needs to be displayed in a unique way.

— *VQ*

12.24 Creating a Submenu

Once you define a menu of your own *(12.23)*, you might want to make it accessible from another menu. Or you might not. The downside of a submenu is that you need a fairly steady hand to display it. I'm a little too klutzy for submenus. I'm always slipping off the "parent" menu in the wrong place to access the submenu. Heck, I never even get to see the thing.

But if you're more coordinated and the idea of a submenu appeals to you, it's easy to set one up. Just add a line of the following format to the parent menu:

```
"item_name"      f.menu    submenu_name
```

For instance, suppose you want to add a submenu to the **Twm** menu. We can do that with the **Utilities** menu we created in Article 12.23:

```
menu "mycommands"
{
"Utilities"              f.title
"New Window"             !"xterm &"
"Mailbox"                !"xbiff -geometry -10+145 &"
"Clock"                  !"oclock -geometry -0+0 &"
"Calculator"             !"xcalc -geometry -0+250&"
"Read News"              !"xterm -e /usr/local/bin/vn &"
"Give wininfo"           f.identify
""                       f.beep
"Spider"                 !"/usr/bin/X11/spider &"
"Ishido"                 !"/usr/bin/X11/ishido &"
}
```

Notice that **Utilities** is the title of the menu; the "name" that *twm* knows it by is actually "mycommands." In order to access the **Utilities** menu from the **Twm** menu, you would add the following line to the Twm menu definition *(12.22)*:

```
"Utilities..."  f.menu "mycommands"
```

Notice the syntax we've used to connect the submenu to the **Twm** menu. First, we've specified an *item_name* suitable to be the title of the submenu. Then we've paired this name with the function f.menu, followed by the actual *menu_name* ("mycommands") that is used in the submenu definition.

When you highlight the **Utilities** item on the **Twm** menu, the corresponding submenu is displayed. You can select an item from the submenu simply by dragging the pointer down the menu and releasing on the item you want. When you select an item, both the **Twm** menu and the submenu will disappear.

—VQ

12.25 *A Preferences Menu*

You might want to create a *twm* menu that lets you set user preferences, such as bell volume *(6.24)*, mouse speed *(18.02)*, keyclick volume *(18.04)*, etc. The **Preferences** menu shown below offers several items that invoke *xset* with a number of different options.

```
menu "Preferences" {
"Bell Loud"      !"xset b 80&"
"Bell Normal"    !"xset b on&"
```

```
"Bell Off"      !"xset b off&"
"Click Loud"    !"xset c 80&"
"Click Soft"    !"xset c on&"
"Click Off"     !"xset c off&"
"Mouse Fast"    !"xset m 4 2&"
"Mouse Normal"  !"xset m 2 5&"
"Mouse Slow"    !"xset m 1 1&"
}
```

Of course, you need to set up some method for displaying this menu. If you want to access it directly from the root window, see Article 12.23. To set it up as a submenu, see Article 12.24.

— VQ

12.26 Color Window Manager Features

Maybe you work in a monochrome world and expect no more. But if you have a color machine, you might want to jazz up your window manager components. *twm* does provide a default set of colors, but they're the fairly drab combination of maroon and gray. (Apologies to the MIT football team.)

You can specify other colors for menus, borders, titlebars, backdrop shadows, information boxes, icons, the Icon Manager *(12.09)*, etc., in your *.twmrc* file *(12.11)*. You specify most colors in the variables section of the file. There are two exceptions, which are specified in the menus section:

- The menu highlighting bar

- Individual menu items you want to appear in colors other than the defaults

twm recognizes 18 color variables, which are detailed on the manpage. The default colors for menus and other components are set using these variables. Note that they can only be used within a Color or Monochrome list in the variables section of the *.twmrc* file. A Color list tells *twm* what scheme to use on a color machine and has the format:

```
Color
{
    variable "color"
    variable "color"
    variable "color"
                    .
                    .
                    .

}
```

I use the color scheme:

```
Color
{
    BorderColor "slategrey"
    DefaultBackground "darkorchid2"
```

```
DefaultForeground "gray85"
TitleBackground "mediumorchid"
TitleForeground "gray85"
MenuBackground "mediumorchid"
MenuForeground "gray70"
MenuTitleBackground "gray70"
MenuTitleForeground "mediumorchid"
IconBackground "mediumorchid"
IconForeground "gray85"
IconBorderColor "gray85"
IconManagerBackground "mediumorchid"
IconManagerForeground "gray85"
}
```

Take a look at a *.twmrc* file to get a better idea.

You have to specify colors for a menu's highlighting bar within the menu definition. In the following example, the foreground and background colors of the bar are white smoke and hot pink.

```
menu "mycommands" ("WhiteSmoke" : "HotPink")
{
"Utilities"     f.title
"New Window"    !"/usr/bin/X11/xterm &"
"Mailbox"       !"/usr/bin/X11/xbiff -geometry -10+145 &"
"Clock"         !"/usr/bin/X11/oclock -geometry -0+0 &"
                      .
                      .
                      .
```

You specify the default colors for individual menu items using the variables MenuForeground and MenuBackground. To override the defaults for a particular menu item, edit the menu definition like this:

```
menu "mycommands" ("WhiteSmoke" : "HotPink")
{
"Utilities"     f.title
"New Window"      ("blue" : "gray")  !"/usr/bin/X11/xterm &"
"Mailbox"       !"/usr/bin/X11/xbiff -geometry -10+145 &"
"Clock"         !"/usr/bin/X11/oclock -geometry -0+0 &"
                      .
                      .
                      .
```

The **New Window** item will appear in blue text on a gray background.

— VQ

12.27 Some of My Keystrokes Are Missing

If you are running *twm* on a slow system, you may notice that the system can't keep up with the movement of the pointer. When you move the pointer from one window to another and begin typing, you may find that your first few characters were entered into the original window, dropped into intervening windows, or "lost" on the root window.

This annoying problem happens because the window manager and X server can't always keep up with the pointer. It is unlikely to be fixed in the near future, but *twm* provides a workaround: adding NoTitleFocus to the variables section of your *.twmrc* file *(12.11)* (and then restarting *twm*) should keep the bug from popping up.

Note, however, that setting this variable changes the way you focus input to a window—in a way that leads to some drawbacks. NoTitleFocus means that a window does not have the input focus when the pointer rests on the titlebar. Since you typically raise a window by clicking on the titlebar (or move it by dragging from the titlebar), setting NoTitleFocus means you must move the pointer a second time—off the titlebar and into the window proper—in order to enter text.

If you're using the Icon Manager *(12.09)*, this change in focusing has still another implication. Normally, when you place the pointer on an Icon Manager entry that corresponds to an active window, that window takes over the focus. However, the way this happens is that the titlebar is highlighted. So, if you specify NoTitleFocus, placing the pointer on the Icon Manager entry will highlight the corresponding window's titlebar, but you won't be able to enter text!

If you're in the habit of using the Icon Manager to focus (particularly in concert with AutoRaise *(12.13)*), think carefully before specifying NoTitleFocus. But if you routinely lose keystrokes because of system lag, it's probably worth setting the variable anyway. Just be aware of the changes in focusing and make the best of it.

—*VQ*

12.28 Switching the Focus Using Keystrokes

If you get tired of moving the pointer from window to window, you can customize *twm* to transfer the input focus using keystrokes. The f.warpto function causes the pointer to jump or "warp" to the application whose name follows it. In my *.twmrc* file *(12.11)*, I bind my Sun3 function keys to switch between windows:

```
"F1"    = : all : f.warpto "emacs"
"F2"    = : all : f.warpto "xterm"
```

```
"F3"     = : all : f.warpto "manualBrowser"
"F4"     = : all : f.warpto "gxditview"
```

For the keystroke column, you need to use the keysym name. Article 18.12 describes how to use the *xev* client to determine keysyms. *xev* returns both a keysym number in hex (e.g., 0xffff) and a corresponding name (e.g., Delete). In your *.twmrc* file, use the keysym name. Don't forget to put it in quotes or *twm* will not be able to interpret it.

With this setup, I rarely need to touch the mouse. It helps that I only use one *xterm* and one *emacs* window. If you use multiple instances of the same application and you want to switch between them with f.warpto, you've got to give the windows different names, using the *–name (20.04)* option. You might name them according to the system they're on or what you use them for. If you're not too concerned with practicality, you can come up with more creative names. I know a guy who names his *xterm*s after famous golf courses.

Since you're transferring the focus without moving the pointer, it's probably a good idea to raise the focus window automatically too. Article 12.13 describes how.

By default, f.warpto ignores iconified windows. To have f.warpto deiconify an iconified window and warp the pointer to it, add WarpUnmapped to the variables section of your *.twmrc* file. (Don't forget to restart the window manager.)

As a complement to this setting, you might also want to specify the WarpCursor variable, which causes the pointer to be warped into any window you deiconify. You can limit the applications this is valid for by supplying a list argument. See the *twm* manpage for more information.

—DJF, VQ

12.29 *Switching Between Screens Using Keystrokes*

My workstation is set up to use a dual frame buffer *(27.11)*. It has two virtual screens (one color, one monochrome) on the same monitor. I can set up *twm* to switch the pointer between these two screens using the f.warptoscreen function:

```
"F9"     = : all : f.warptoscreen "next"
```

Pressing **F9** swaps the pointer to the other screen. Since the alternative is dragging the pointer off either horizontal edge of the screen, this is a great shortcut.

—VQ

12.30 Preparing to Run tvtwm

In order to run *tvtwm* (12.10), you'll need to make at least one modification to your *.twmrc* file (12.11), to specify the size of the virtual desktop. You can supply the dimensions in pixels (22.01) if you like (3000 pixels wide by 2000 high is a reasonable size), or you can specify the dimensions in screenfuls. The latter is simpler and also more logical. The following line creates a desktop that is the equivalent of a space three screens wide by three screens high:

```
VirtualDesktop: 3x3
```

This is the size of the desktop described in Article 12.10, and provides quite a bit of space. Once you add this line to your *.twmrc* file, you're ready to go. You can exit *twm* and start *tvtwm*. You don't need to make any further customizations, but there are a few simple ones it's good to have.

First, if you haven't already done so, customize your *.twmrc* file to use the Icon Manager (12.15). Working without an Icon Manager (12.08) is even more harrowing on a large virtual desktop than on a discrete screen.

Then make the Icon Manager a sticky window (12.10), so that it stays in sight no matter what part of the desktop you're viewing:

```
Sticky { "TWM Icon Manager" "xbiff" }
```

I've made my *xbiff* mail notifier program (7.10) sticky as well. You might want to classify other desktop applications as sticky too, but be careful not to clutter the screen with sticky windows. The all-important panner window (12.10) is sticky automatically.

The StickyAbove variable makes sticky windows remain on top of other windows on the display. Since you don't want to lose sight of the panner, this variable is also good to have.

If you specify StickyAbove, you can also specify PannerOpaqueScroll. Normally, the screen is updated after you move the dotted outline in the panner. PannerOpaqueScroll causes the screen to be updated as you move the panner. This is useful, but slows the process of moving the view around (scrolling).

Navigating the desktop is a lot easier if you specify shortcuts using four *tvtwm* functions intended for that purpose: f.scrollleft, f.scrollright, f.scrollup, and f.scrolldown. You map these functions to reasonable keys on your keyboard. In addition, you need to specify the distance to be scrolled. Use the variables ScrollDistanceX and ScrollDistanceY, which determine how far you scroll in the horizontal and vertical directions, respectively.

To scroll a screenful at a time, specify 100 for 100%. Add these lines to the variables section of your *.twmrc* file:

```
ScrollDistanceX 100
ScrollDistanceY 100
```

Then map the scroll functions to logical keys in the key/button bindings section of the *.twmrc* file. The following lines map the arrow keys on the right keypad of my Sun3 keyboard to the appropriate scrolling functions:

```
"Left" = : all : f.scrollleft
"Right" = : all : f.scrollright
"Down" = : all :. f.scrolldown
"Up" = : all : f.scrollup
```

The combination of the ScrollDistance variable settings and these keymappings allow me to pan to a new screenful of the desktop using arrow keys. The word "all" refers to the *context* in which the function works, that is, where the pointer has to be. I want to be able to switch to another screenful of the desktop regardless of where the pointer is, so I've specified that these functions work in all contexts.

— VQ

12.31 *A Summary of twm Functions*

Table 12-3 summarizes the window management functions you can perform using the titlebar *(12.03)*, keys/buttons *(12.05)*, and the Twm menu *(12.04)*. The first column lists the desired function; the second, the pointer location; and the third, the required action (button-key combination, menu item, etc.). In this column, "click" means to press and immediately release the specified pointer button; "down" means to press and hold the pointer button; and "drag" means to move the pointer while holding down the pointer button. In all cases, you can let go of the keyboard key as soon as you have pressed the appropriate pointer button.

Note that these key bindings can be changed in your *.twmrc* file *(12.11)*. The combinations described in the table are valid for the default configuration of *twm*, as specified in the *system.twmrc* file.

Table 12-3: Summary of Window Manager Functions

Function	Pointer Location	Action
Move	Titlebar	First pointer button down, drag
Move	Window or icon	Meta key, third pointer button down and drag
Move	Twm menu	Select Move item, any pointer button down, drag

Table 12-3: Summary of Window Manager Functions (continued)

Function	Pointer Location	Action
Resize	"nested squares" titlebutton	Any pointer button down, cross desired border, drag, release
Resize	**Twm** menu	Select **Resize** item; any pointer button down, cross desired window border, and drag
Raise	Titlebar	First pointer button click
Raise	Window or icon	Meta key, third pointer button click
Raise	**Twm** menu	Select **Raise** item, any pointer button click
Lower	Titlebar	Second (middle) pointer button click
Lower	Window or icon	Meta key, first pointer button click
Lower	**Twm** menu	Select **Lower** item, any pointer button click
Iconify	"dot" titlebutton	Any pointer button click
Iconify	Window	Meta key, second pointer button click
Iconify	**Twm** menu	Select **Iconify** item, any pointer button click
Iconify	Icon Manager entry	First or second pointer button click on rectangle corresponding to window
Deiconify	Icon	First or second pointer button click
Deiconify	Icon Manager entry	First or second pointer button click on rectangle corresponding to window
Focus input	Window	Place pointer in window to focus input there
Focus input	Icon Manager entry	Place pointer there to focus input on corresponding window
Twm menu	Root	First pointer button down
Focus	**Twm** menu	Select **Focus** item; click any pointer button on target
Unfocus	**Twm** menu	Select **Unfocus** item; click any pointer button on target
Display Icon Manager	**Twm** menu	Select **Show Icon Manager** item

Table 12-3: Summary of Window Manager Functions (continued)

Function	Pointer Location	Action
Remove Icon Manager	Twm menu	Select **Hide Icon Manager** item
Remove window (gently)	Twm menu	Select **Delete** item; click any pointer button on target
Remove window	Twm menu	Select **Kill** item; click any pointer button on target
Restart window manager	Twm menu	Select **Restart** item
Stop window manager	Twm menu	Select **Exit** item

— VQ

13

The Motif Window Manager

13.01 1001 Ways to Manage Windows

The Motif window manager went into the GUI wars and KO'd the competition. There's a lot of weight behind those frames. *mwm* provides more ways to perform window manager operations than any other program. And *mwm* is also more versatile and more configurable. You want pointer focus *(13.14)*, you got it. Different key bindings, no problem. Different frame features for different applications *(13.17)*, additional menus *(13.21)*, auto-raise *(13.15)*, an icon box *(13.11)*, screen-specific characteristics *(13.10)*, you name it.

However, the very power and versatility of *mwm* can also be a liability. The number and nature of the configurable features can be fairly confusing. The following chapter should steer you towards some of the more useful customizations, as well as reviewing some of the basic features.

— VQ

13.02 Working with mwm

The Motif window manager provides more decoration and more ways to access its functions than virtually any other window manager. This article should orient you to a basic *mwm* environment. It does not attempt to deal with the truly vast number of possible customizations *(13.09)*. However, even if your flavor of *mwm* is very different from the version described here, the basic principles should be the same.

If you hear someone talk about a "Motif environment," they probably mean an environment in which both *mwm* and Motif-based applications are running. Motif applications are programs that have been written using the Motif toolkit. *mwm* and other Motif clients have a distinctive look and feel. For instance, the *mwm* Window Menu *(13.04)* probably looks and operates very much like a pull-down menu provided by any Motif client.

Understanding *mwm* will definitely help you use other Motif applications. However, you should also be aware that the types of menus, command buttons, and other feature *mwm* offers are merely a subset of those another Motif client might have. Our current discussion is limited to the window manager.[*]

Figure 13-1 shows a screen on which *mwm* is running.

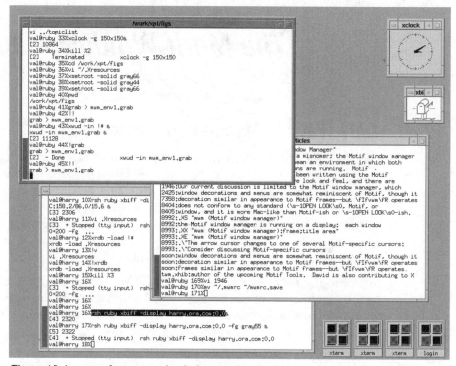

Figure 13-1: mwm frames each window on the display

My sample display has three active *xterm* windows, an *xclock* window (3.02), an *xbiff* mailbox window (7.10), and four icons, in the lower-right corner.

The most distinguishing feature of *mwm* is the frame it places around all windows on the display. Notice that the application windows on our typical display are surrounded by this frame. (If you run a non-rectangular window, such as *oclock* (3.02), you'll see an exception; rather than a frame, a titlebar appears to "float" above the window.) By clicking a mouse or other pointing device on various parts of the window frame (or titlebar, if that's what's available), you can perform management functions on the window (13.03).

---

[*] For more information about the features common to Motif applications, see Volume Three, *X Window System User's Guide, Motif Edition*, also published by O'Reilly & Associates, Inc.

In addition to pointer commands, *mwm* provides two default menus, the Window Menu *(13.04)* and Root Menu *(13.05)*, which provide other methods to access some of the basic functions, as well as some additional commands. The Window Menu is a pull-down menu that is displayed on a window or icon, while the Root Menu is a popup menu that is displayed on the root window. For users who don't like to use a pointer, there are also keyboard shortcuts, or accelerators *(13.06)*, for many *mwm* functions.

mwm provides more decoration than the average window manager. Notice the three-dimensional appearance of buttons, titlebars, icons, etc. This effect is achieved using subtle shading. The icon symbols generated by *mwm* are typically somewhat large and elaborate. Although it's certainly hard to lose icons of this size, and you may find them aesthetically pleasing, they're also liable to clutter up your screen. There are four icons on my sample screen—a manageable number. Still, it's generally a good idea to customize *mwm* to provide an icon box *(13.11)*, which can store and organize a large number of icons in a small window.

In the default *mwm* environment, when you run a new window, it is placed automatically on the screen. The new window also automatically takes over the input focus, so you can enter text or commands immediately.

For most people, automatic window placement is the best method. For those rare individuals who would prefer to place new windows manually, set the clientAutoPlace resource variable to false in your resource file *(17.03)*. Article 13.09 describes the basic procedures for modifying *mwm*. See the online *mwm* manpage for more information about clientAutoPlace and other available resources.

mwm's default focus policy is explicit, or click-to-type, focus. In other words, in order to type or invoke commands in a window, you first have to click the pointer on it. (You can customize *mwm* to make the focus follow the pointer's movement using the KeyboardFocusPolicy resource variable *(13.14)*.) When a window has the input focus, its frame will appear in a different color or pattern than other windows on the display.

An icon can also have the input focus. When an icon has the focus, you can display the Window Menu and invoke the menu's functions or use keyboard accelerators *(13.06)* for various functions to affect the icon. As is the case when a window has the focus, an icon with the focus changes in appearance; it takes on a different color, and the label along its bottom edge becomes broader.

In most cases, you'll use simple pointer commands to perform window management functions. Keep in mind, however, that both of *mwm*'s menus can be useful in certain circumstances. For instance, the Window Menu can be useful when parts of the window frame are obscured by another window. It's fairly simple to add items to the Root Menu *(13.19)*, you might want to add menu items to start some of the applications you use regularly. You might choose to combine some of your own commands on a submenu *(13.22)*, or create an entirely separate menu *(13.21)*, accessed in a different way.

Article 13.24 provides a summary of all the default *mwm* functions.

— VQ

13.03 *Managing Windows Using the Pointer*

The frame *mwm* provides and several features of it are tools that allow you to manage a window using the pointer, as described in Figure 13-2.

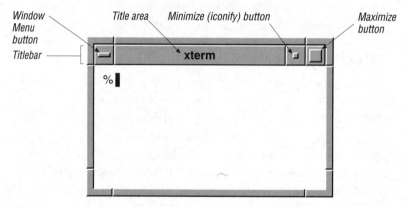

Figure 13-2: Manage a window by using the pointer on its frame

The wider top edge of the frame is the titlebar. The titlebar is composed of several parts including a title area (displaying the name of the application) and three command buttons (**Minimize**, Maximize, and Window Menu *(13.04)*). Notice that whenever you move the pointer into the titlebar, the pointer changes to the arrow cursor.

The outer part of the frame (outside of the titlebar) is divided by small lines into eight sections: four long borders (two horizontal and two vertical) and four corners. You can resize a window using the pointer on these sections, which are labeled in Figure 13-3.

Table 13-1 summarizes the pointer actions to perform various window management functions. Many of those are performed on a window's frame, some are performed on an icon, and others on the icon box *(13.11)*. The Root Menu *(13.19)* is posted (i.e., displayed) on the root window.

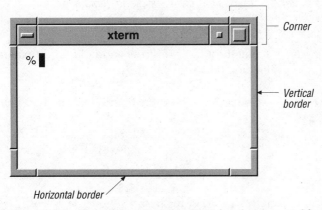

Figure 13-3: Outer frame is divided into four borders and four corners for resizing

Table 13-1: Pointer Commands for mwm Functions

Function	Pointer Location	Action
Move	Titlebar	First pointer button down, drag, release
Move	Icon	First pointer button down, drag, release
Raise window	Frame (not including titlebuttons)	First pointer button click
Raise window	Window	First pointer button click (`Key-boardFocusPolicy` *(13.14)* must be explicit; `FocusAutoRaise` *(13.15)* must be true; both are defaults.)
Raise window	Icon box	Double-click first pointer button on icon corresponding to active window you want to raise.
Raise icon	Icon	Click first pointer button. (This action also posts the **Window Menu**. Click on the root window to remove the menu.)
Iconify	**Minimize** command button	First pointer button click
Deiconify	Icon or icon box entry	Double-click first pointer button.
Post Root Menu	Root window	Third pointer button down
Post Window Menu	**Window Menu** titlebutton	Click first pointer button; or press and hold third pointer button.

Table 13-1: Pointer Commands for mwm Functions (continued)

Function	Pointer Location	Action
Post Window Menu	Frame (not in-cluding titlebut-tons)	Press and hold third pointer but-ton.
Post Window Menu	icon	Press and hold third pointer but-ton.
Focus input	Window	Click on window (default). You can also specify pointer focus *(13.14)*.

For keyboard accelerators for most functions, see Article 15.06.

Most of these functions are very simple, and also rudimentary. If you've been using *mwm* for even a short time, you're probably an old hand at iconifying, moving, raising, etc. Window manager jocks can now exit this article, stage left (presuming you've even bothered to come this far). For true beginners, there are some subtleties that might take some getting used to.

For instance, a single click on an icon posts the **Window Menu** *(13.04)*, while a double-click converts the icon back to a window. When deiconifying, between the first and second clicks, you'll notice that the **Window Menu** is dis-played for an instant above the icon. If you pause too long between the two clicks in deiconifying a window, the second click will not be interpreted and the icon will not be converted back to a window. Instead the **Window Menu** will remain on the screen, as in Figure 13-4.

If you get stuck on the **Window Menu** by mistake, you can convert the icon to a window by clicking the first pointer button on the **Restore** menu item, or pressing the space bar or the **Return** key. (Either of these keys invokes the boxed/highlighted menu item, in this case **Restore**.)

If you want to remove the menu without invoking a command, simply move the pointer off the icon and menu and click the first pointer button.

What are some of the other nuances to the basic *mwm* functions? Well, the maximize command button (on the titlebar) is a toggle. Maximizing a window generally means enlarging it to the size of the root window. (In some cases, a client application may specify its own maximum window size and maximizing will produce a window of this size.) The Maximize command button lets you toggle between a window's original size and its maximized size. (The **Restore** item on the **Window Menu** will also switch a maximized window back to its original size.)

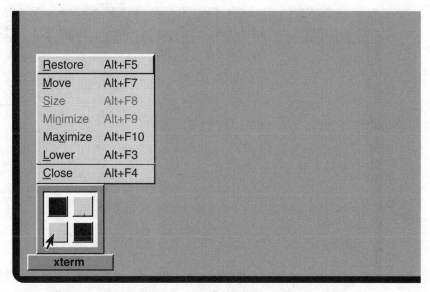

Figure 13-4: Window Menu being displayed over an icon

Another less than obvious feature: when you're using the default explicit (click-to-type) focus policy, operations like raising or moving a window also direct the input focus to that window.

What else? When you're moving a window, you may notice that a small, rectangular box appears in the center of the screen. This box displays the location of the window as you move it, in terms of its x and y coordinates on the screen. The discussion of the *–geometry* option *(17.10)* explains how screen locations are interpreted.

Like virtually any window manager, *mwm* lets you resize a window horizontally, vertically, or simultaneously in both directions. There is one basic action you perform to resize; how the dimensions are changed depends on the part of the outer frame you grab with the pointer and how you move it.

If you place the pointer within a window and then move it into one of the long horizontal or vertical borders, you'll notice the pointer changes to a new shape: an arrow (pointing toward the window border), with a short line perpendicular to it. This short line represents the window border. Try moving the pointer in this fashion in one of the windows on your display to get a better idea of what the pointer looks like. If you move the pointer from within a window into the outer border at one of the corners, the pointer will become an arrow pointing diagonally at a small corner symbol (see Figure 13-5).

Figure 13-6 shows all of the possible resize pointers.

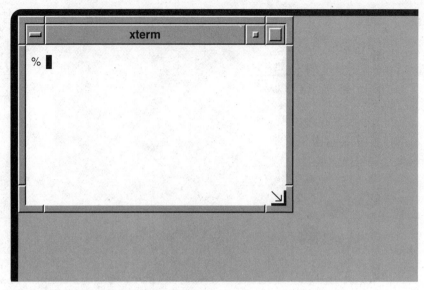

Figure 13-5: Window with resizing pointer

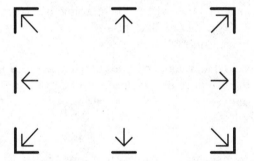

Figure 13-6: Resizing pointer symbols

Once the pointer changes to one of these shapes, you can move the border or corner of the window. Resizing from one of the long borders only allows you to change one dimension of the window: a horizontal border can only be moved up or down, changing the height; a vertical border can only be moved left or right, changing the width. You can move a corner in any direction you choose, changing both dimensions of the window if you want.

Note that resizing an *xterm* window will not change the dimensions of the text currently in the window. If you make the window smaller, for instance, some of the text may be obscured. On most operating systems, this should not be a problem. As you continue to work, the text will be adjusted to display in the newly sized window. If you resize during a text-editing session, it's possible that the text-editing program will not know about the window's new size and will operate incorrectly. To solve this problem, simply quit out of the editor and start another session.

— VQ

13.04 Review of Window Menu Functions

You can display the Window Menu from either a window or an icon (the menu offerings are slightly different). There are several ways to display the menu from a window. The easiest way is to click the first pointer button on the Window Menu command button. Figure 13-7 shows the default Window Menu.

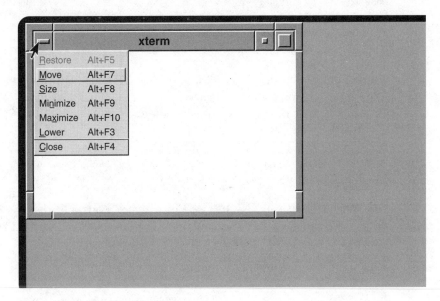

Figure 13-7: The Window Menu

You can also display the menu by placing the pointer anywhere else on the frame (other than the command buttons) and holding down the third button. If you don't want to use the pointer, the keyboard shortcuts Shift-Escape and Meta-space bar toggle the menu on and off for the focus window. *

Each item can be invoked in a number of ways: clicking on it; typing the underlined mnemonic abbreviation; or using a keystroke combination (or keyboard accelerator), which works on the focus window without the menu being posted. You can invoke the boxed selection by hitting Return or the space bar.

---

* Meta is a function that is mapped to a physical key; you won't find a key labeled Meta on your keyboard. The *xmodmap* client *(18.07)* will help you identify the Meta key *(18.14)*.

Table 13-2 lists each item, what it does, and the shortcuts to use it. (*mwm* considers the Alt and Meta keys to be equivalent.)

Table 13-2: Window Menu Items When Displayed on a Window

Item	Function	Mnemonic	Accelerator
Restore	Deiconifies a window or changes a maximized window back to its normal size	r	Alt+F5
Move	Moves the window or icon	m	Alt+F7
Size	Resizes the window	s	Alt+F8
Minimize	Iconifies a window	n	Alt+F9
Maximize[a]	Converts a window to the maximum size allowed by the client (often the size of the root window)	x	Alt+F10
Lower	Moves the window or icon to the bottom of the stack	l	Alt+F3
Close	Kills the process and closes the window	c	Alt+F4

[a] If your keyboard does not have an **F10** function key, the **Maximize** item will not appear on the **Window Menu** without some customization. Since you'll probably use this item infrequently, if at all, you may not miss it. If you want to use it, however, Article 13.18 provides instructions.

The **Window Menu** can also be used to manage icons. To display the menu, place the pointer on the icon and click the first button. Article 13.03 shows the **Window Menu** displayed over an icon. You can also press and hold down the third button; or you can use either of these keyboard shortcuts: **Shift-Escape** or Meta-space bar.

Table 13-3 summarizes the **Window Menu** functions when invoked from an icon. (To use a keyboard accelerator, the icon must have the input focus.)

Table 13-3: Window Menu Items When Displayed on an Icon

Item	Function	Mnemonic	Accelerator
Restore	Converts the icon back to a window (in its previous state)	r	Alt+F5
Move	Moves the icon on the display	m	Alt+F7
Size	Not available for selection	n/a	n/a
Minimize	Not available for selection	n/a	n/a
Maximize	Converts an icon to a window the size of the root window	x	Alt+F10
Lower	Sends an icon to the bottom of the window/icon stack	l	Alt+F3

Table 13-3: Window Menu Items When Displayed on an Icon (continued)

Item	Function	Mnemonic	Accelerator
Close	Exits the client, removing the icon	c	Alt+F4

If you're using an icon box *(13.11)*, you can display the **Window Menu** on an icon in the box or on the icon box itself. When the menu is displayed on the icon box, the menu items apply to the box, as if it were any window; however, the **Close** item is replaced with an item called **Pack Icons**, which lets you optimize the layout of icons in the box. The **Pack Icons** item has the mnemonic abbreviation "p", and the keyboard accelerator **Shift+Alt+F7**.

— VQ

13.05 *The Root Menu Revisited*

While pointer commands *(13.03)* and the Window Menu *(13.04)* provide most of the functions you'll need to manage windows and icons, the **Root Menu** offers commands to control the overall display. To post the **Root Menu**, move the pointer to the root window and press and hold down the third pointer button. The default **Root Menu** appears in Figure 13-8.

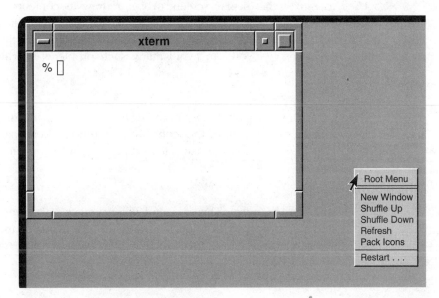

Figure 13-8: The mwm Root Menu

When you display the **Root Menu**, the pointer changes to the arrow pointer. As you can see, the default **Root Menu** offers only six items. To select an item, drag the pointer down the menu to the desired item. Notice that a rectangular box surrounds the item you're pointing at. To select the boxed item, simply release the pointer button.

The functions performed by the default **Root Menu** are described below.

New Window

Runs an *xterm* window on the display specified by the DISPLAY environment variable *(19.09, 19.10)* generally the local display. When you create a new window (by using the menu or typing the command in an *xterm*), the new window automatically becomes the active window.

Shuffle Up

Moves the bottom window or icon in the window stack to the top (raises it). (It's generally simpler to raise a window or icon by placing the pointer on it and clicking the first button, but this item is useful when an object is entirely obscured.)

Shuffle Down

Moves the top window or icon in the window stack to the bottom (lowers it).

Refresh

Used to *refresh* the display screen, that is, redraw its contents. **Refresh** is useful if system messages appear on the screen, overlaying its contents. (The *xrefresh* client *(6.13)* can be used to perform the same function. If you own the "console," you can avoid many such problems by running the *xconsole* client *(27.02)*.)

Pack Icons

If you are using an icon box *(13.11)* to organize icons on the display, this item optimizes the layout of the icons within the box. Note that the Window Menu *(13.04)* provides the same item when displayed on the icon box window.

Restart...

Stops and restarts *mwm*. This is useful when you've edited the *.mwmrc* configuration file *(13.09)*, which specifies certain *mwm* features, and want to activate the changes. Since this function is potentially more dangerous than the other **Root Menu** options, it is separated from the other options by a horizontal line.

The ellipse (...) following the **Restart** item signals that you will be queried for confirmation. When you select **Restart**, a dialog box appears in the center of the screen with command buttons asking you to either **OK** the restart process or **Cancel** the request, as in Figure 13-9.

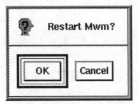

Figure 13-9: Dialog box to confirm or cancel restart procedure

Click on the appropriate command button using the first pointer button. (In most cases, you should also be able to select the highlighted button simply by pressing **Return** or hitting the space bar.)

If you select **OK**, the window manager process is stopped. The screen will momentarily go blank. The new *mwm* process will be started immediately. While the new *mwm* process is starting, an hourglass symbol is displayed in the center of the otherwise blank screen. The hourglass appears to be filling up with sand until the window manager is running and the windows again are displayed on the screen.

Keep in mind that you can add, change, or remove Root Menu items *(13.19)* by editing the *.mwmrc* configuration file *(13.09)* in your home directory. If you'd like, you can also create submenus *(13.22)*, known in the Motif environment as *cascading menus.*

— VQ

13.06 *Taking Advantage of Keyboard Accelerators*

It's possible to perform most window management functions without taking your hands off the keyboard. Article 13.04 describes the keyboard accelerators for **Window Menu** items, which allow you to perform the most common functions, including iconifying, moving, and resizing.

But before you can perform one of these functions on a window or icon, it must have the input focus. If you are running the default version of *mwm* (which assumes the click-to-type focus policy and focusAutoRaise *(13.15)*), you can cause the focus to circulate from window to window (including iconified windows) within the window stack using either of the key combinations that appear in Table 13-4.

Table 13-4: Key Combinations to Change Focus Window (Explicit Focus Only)

Key Combination	Action
Meta-Tab[a]	Move focus to next window in stack.
Meta-Shift-Tab	Move focus to previous window in stack.

[a] Since *mwm* considers the Meta key and the Alt key interchangeable, these actions should also work if you substitute Alt for Meta.

You won't find a key labeled Meta on your keyboard, rather Meta is a symbolic key function *(18.14)* that is mapped to an actual physical key. The key combination Meta-Tab refers to whatever key on your keyboard performs the Meta function and the key labeled Tab. This combination circulates the focus from the current top of the stack to the bottom. What this means is that the top window in the stack is moved to the bottom; the second highest window becomes the top window and gets the input focus.

The key combination Meta-Shift-Tab circulates the focus from the current bottom of the stack to the top. In other words, the lowest window in the stack is moved to the top and given the input focus.

How would these shortcuts help you in practice? Suppose you want to focus on an *xterm* window buried beneath two others. You would hit the Meta-Tab combination twice to uncover and focus on the window. Then you could work in the *xterm* or perform any of the actions available on the Window Menu using their keyboard accelerators. For example, to iconify the window, you'd use Alt-F9 (Meta-F9). To deiconify, Alt-F5 (Meta-F5).

If you can't remember the Window Menu shortcuts, you can post the menu using keyboard shortcuts as well. Once you focus on the window/icon, post the menu using either of the combinations listed in Table 13-5. (These keystroke combinations also remove the menu, if you don't want to invoke an action.)

Table 13-5: Key Combinations to Post/Remove the Window Menu

Key Combination	Action
Meta-space bar	Display/remove Window Menu.
Shift-Escape	Display/remove Window Menu.

If pointer focus is in effect, you can't rely solely on the keyboard to perform window management functions. You can still use the accelerators for Window Menu actions, but you have to move the pointer to transfer focus first. However, you can change the stacking order using keystrokes, regardless of the focus policy. The key combinations in Table 13-6 shuffle the window stack, but they don't transfer the focus.

Table 13-6: Key Combinations to Change the Stacking Order

Key Combination	Action
Meta-Escape	Move top window to bottom of stack.
Meta-Shift-Escape	Move bottom window to top of stack.

The only difference between these keystroke combinations is the direction in which they reorder the windows.

The key combination Meta-Escape moves the window currently at the top of the stack to the bottom. (The second highest window becomes the top window.)

The key combination Meta-Shift-Escape moves the window currently at the bottom of the stack to the top. (The second lowest window becomes the bottom window.)

— VQ

13.07 *One Way to Remove a Stubborn Window*

The command button on the left side of the titlebar brings up the **Window Menu**, which provides seven items that manage the window and its icon. This command button also provides a shortcut for killing a client process. Double-clicking the first pointer button on the **Window Menu** command button kills the client program and closes the window. The "double" is important: it minimizes the chance of removing a window by mistake. However, it's not impossible to do this, so you should be careful around the **Window Menu** command button.

Also be aware that like other methods of "killing" a program, double-clicking on the **Window Menu** button can adversely affect underlying processes. It's generally a good idea to try client-specific methods of stopping the process first. See Article 2.08 for a discussion of gentle, and not so gentle, elimination methods.

You can customize *mwm* so that double-clicking performs no function by setting the resource variable wMenuButtonClick2 to false. See the *mwm* manpage for more information.

— VQ

13.08 *What to Do if mwm Dies and the Focus Is Lost*

If you're using the Motif window manager and for some reason it dies, you may find yourself unable to enter text in any window! *mwm* has a bug that makes it possible to lose the focus entirely when the window manager dies. Without complications, the focus policy should revert to pointer focus. To restart the window manager, you should simply be able to move the pointer into an *xterm* window and enter the *mwm* command. However, if the focus is lost, restarting the window manager becomes a big problem.

If *mwm* dies and no window retains the focus, you can restore focus to an *xterm* window using the Secure Keyboard item *(11.17)* of the *xterm* client's Main Options menu *(11.14)*. To display this menu, place the pointer in the window, hold the **CTRL** key and press the first pointer button. (Once the menu is displayed, you can release the **CTRL** key, but continue to hold the pointer button.) Then drag the pointer down the menu to highlight **Secure Keyboard** and release the button to select the item.

This action places the *xterm* in **Secure Keyboard** mode, which is useful for entering passwords and other privileged information. To indicate that this mode is in effect, the *xterm* displays in reverse video and (more importantly in our predicament) takes over the keyboard focus. (See Article 11.17 for more information about **Secure Keyboard** mode.) Now that keyboard input is focused on an *xterm*, you can enter the *mwm* command or any other command you like. When you restart the window manager, **Secure Keyboard** mode is turned off, and you're back in business.

If you're using a terminal emulator that doesn't offer a secure keyboard mode, you can always log on at someone else's terminal and then start *mwm* on your display. Use the *–display* option *(19.08)* and your display name as an argument.

—*VQ*

13.09 How Can I Change mwm?

Most people will probably be satisfied with the default configuration of *mwm*, which provides fairly convenient tools for performing standard window manager operations. However, if you want to change *mwm*, virtually every feature is customizable.

The default operation of *mwm* is largely controlled by a file called *system.mwmrc*, which establishes the contents of the Root Menu *(13.05)* and the Window Menu *(13.04)*, how menu functions are invoked, and what key and button combinations can be used to manage windows. To modify the behavior of *mwm*, you can edit a copy of this file (call it *.mwmrc*) in your home directory.

In addition to the flexibility provided by the *.mwmrc* startup file, *mwm* has dozens of application resources *(1.06)* you can put in your *.Xresources* or *.Xdefaults* file *(17.03)*. *mwm* resources fall into roughly three categories:

* *Component appearance resources* set the characteristics of *mwm*'s component features, such as the window frame *(13.03)*, menus *(13.02)*, dialog boxes, and icons *(13.02)*.

- *mwm-specific appearance and behavior resources* determine characteristics of the window manager client, such as focus policy, what sets of key and button bindings are valid, and so forth. .

- *Client-specific resources* set the appearance and behavior of a particular client or class *(20.05)* of clients. (You can also specify them for all clients.)

Some of these resources are potentially helpful to a wide number of users; other resources are extremely esoteric. If anything, Motif errs on the side of having too many configurable features.

Regardless of how you modify *mwm*—by editing the *.mwmrc* file, specifying resources, or both—your customizations will not take effect automatically. You must restart *mwm* to activate the changes. If you edit your resources file, you must make sure the new resource specifications are being read. Article 17.03 explains the two simplest methods of making resources available.

Once you've loaded any new resource settings, you can restart *mwm*. Your Root Menu *(13.05)* should offer a **Restart** option. When you select it, you will be prompted as to whether you want to proceed or cancel the operation. (Article 13.05 includes an illustration of the dialog box *mwm* provides.) If you OK the restart procedure, there will be a flurry of activity as window manager decorations go away and icons are converted back to windows. When *mwm* is restarted, frames are put back, windows that were previously iconified are re-iconified; more importantly, your customizations should be implemented. Of course, the success of your customizations presumes you've used the correct syntax in the *.mwmrc* file and/or the resource specifications, and that you've loaded any new resources properly. When *mwm* has been restarted, it should reflect any changes made to both *.mwmrc* and resource files.

If your **Root Menu** doesn't have a **Restart** option, you can always kill *(2.08)* the window manager process and run it again. However, be sure that *mwm* is not your session's controlling process *(21.11)*, or you'll be bumped out of X.

Among the possible *mwm* customizations, you can:

- Set up an icon box *(13.11)* to come up automatically; the icon box helps you organize icons on the display and also provides some window management functions.

- Change the focus policy *(13.14)*; explicit (click-to-type) is the default.

- Specify whether the focus window is automatically raised. (See Article 13.15.)

- Change the Root Menu *(13.19)* and the Window Menu *(13.18)* and define your own menus *(13.21)*.

- Bind functions to keyboard keys, pointer buttons, or key/pointer combinations.

- Change the window manager decorations; you can alter frames, menus, dialogs, etc., for individual applications, application classes, or across the board. Suppressing window decoration *(13.17)* can preserve the aesthetics of clients like *oclock (3.02)*.

The only recommendation we make is that you use an icon box; without one, the large Motif icons can really get in the way. Any other changes are purely discretionary, but take a look at some of the other articles in this chapter to get an idea of some of the things you can do.

—VQ

13.10 *Running mwm on a Multiscreen Display*

My (old, reliable) Sun 3/60 color workstation is configured to use dual frame buffers *(27.11)*. This means there are two virtual screens accessible from a single physical monitor; screen 0 is color, and screen 1 is monochrome. I "scroll" between them by moving the pointer off either side of the monitor.

By default, *mwm* manages only screen 0. To let *mwm* know it needs to manage all screens in the display, I set the following resource *(17.02)*:

```
Mwm*MultiScreen:        True
```

Once you've specified that *mwm* should manage all screens within the display, you can specify different resources for each screen, with a few limitations. (A caveat: there are enough customizable features that you could fiddle with them as effectively as Nero.) First, you need to give the screens names that can be used in resource specifications. I specify the names using the Screens resource variable, as in the following line:

```
Mwm*Screens:    color mono
```

Note that both this step and the preceding one can also be accomplished on the *mwm* command line:

```
% mwm -multiscreen -screens color mono
```

But it's easier to specify the resources and forget about them.

Now I've specified that *mwm* is going to manage all (in this case both) screens and named them color and mono. The next step is to add screen-specific lines to my resource file. You can make a resource specification apply to one screen by adding the screen name after Mwm.

Suppose I want to use an icon box on both screens, but put them in different locations. I can provide an IconBoxGeometry for both the color and mono screens:

```
Mwm*UseIconBox: True
Mwm*color*IconBoxGeometry:        2x2-0-0
Mwm*mono*IconBoxGeometry:         2x2+0+0
```

In the preceding example, the first line specifies that both screens will use an icon box. The second line says that on the screen named color (screen 0) the box will be two icons square and be located at coordinates -0-0 (the lower-right corner of the screen). The third line specifies an icon box of the same size on the screen named mono, but places it at coordinates +0+0 (the upper-left corner).

Some resources won't lend themselves to screen-specific values. The most serious limitation we encountered was that *mwm* won't let you specify different focus policies for different screens. The following lines *should* specify explicit focus on screen 0 and pointer focus on screen 1.

```
Mwm*color*KeyboardFocusPolicy:  explicit
Mwm*mono*KeyboardFocusPolicy:   pointer
```

In practice, however, only one focus policy can apply per display and the default explicit focus is used.

Remember: once you've specified your resources properly, you still need to restart *mwm* (13.09) in order to activate the changes.

— *VQ*

13.11 *Using an Icon Box*

It's easy to set up *mwm* to provide an icon box (see Figure 13-10), which helps you organize icons and also provides a few window management functions. Just set the following resource (17.03):

```
Mwm*UseIconBox:  True
```

Then when you start (or restart) *mwm*, your display will have an icon box. By default, the icon box is six icons wide by one icon high and is located in the lower-left corner of the display.

Each window you run is represented by an icon in the box, regardless of whether that window is active or iconified. (Without an icon box, only iconified windows are represented by icons.) In the icon box, an icon corresponding to a window currently on the display appears flatter and less defined than the image of an iconified window. The icon box in Figure 13-10 contains two iconified windows (the first *xterm* and *xclock*) and four icons representing windows currently visible on the display.

The icon box can hold more icons than will fit in one window. You can view icons that extend beyond the visible bounds of the icon box by using the horizontal and vertical scrollbars.

Figure 13-10: An icon box

By clicking the first pointer button on icons in the icon box, you can perform some window management functions. With a single click on any icon image, you can display the Window Menu *(13.04)* and use its functions on the icon or corresponding active window. Depending on whether you click on an iconi-fied window or an icon representing an active window, different menu items are available for selection. (Displaying the **Window Menu** from an icon repre-senting an active window on the display is not particularly useful.)

- When you double-click on an iconified window, the icon is converted back to a window (and is raised to the top of the window stack).

- When you double-click on an icon representing an active window, the cor-responding window is raised to the front of the display. (The icon box retains the input focus.)

If you're trying to double-click (to deiconify or raise a window), and you pause too long between the two clicks, the action will fail, and you'll get stuck on the **Window Menu**. If you were trying to deiconify a window, you can com-plete the action by selecting the **Restore** menu item. If you were trying to raise an active window, the **Window Menu** won't help. Move the pointer onto the root window and click to get rid of the menu. Then try double-clicking again. (In the last ditch, you can raise the window itself using the pointer *(13.03)*.)

When you display the **Window Menu** from the icon box, you can use the menu commands to affect the box itself (which is actually a window). The **Pack Icons** item rearranges the icons in the box to fill in empty slots. This is useful when icons are removed from the box (i.e., when a window is closed) or the box is resized *(13.13)*. If you don't want to use **Pack Icons**, you can move the icons into adjacent empty slots manually using the pointer.

— VQ

13.12 Alternate Size and Position for the Icon Box

You can specify alternate dimensions for the icon box by setting the variable iconBoxGeometry. For example, if you want an icon box three icons wide by two icons high, use the specification:

```
Mwm*iconBoxGeometry:   3x2+0-0
```

which creates a box of the desired size in the lower-left corner of the display. (This is the default location; you could omit the +0-0 from the geometry string and get the same result.)

The following specification creates an icon box four icons wide by three icons high in the lower-right corner of the display:

```
Mwm*iconBoxGeometry:   4x3-0-0
```

— VQ

13.13 Resizing the Icon Box

When you resize the icon box, you'll notice the resize action has a tendency to jump the width or height of an icon at a time. *mwm* only allows the box to be resized exactly to fit a number of icons wide and a number high, though there are no obvious limitations as to the numbers. Basically, you can have an icon box of any size, even one icon high and wide, and display the other icons using the scrollbars.

As you resize the box, the small rectangular window in the center of the screen assists you: it shows the dimensions in the number of icons wide by the number of icons high.

If you don't want the default icon box of six icons wide by one icon high, Article 13.12 describes how to specify geometry *(17.10)*.

— VQ

13.14 Setting the Focus Policy

If you don't like the default click-to-type focus policy, you can specify pointer focus using the *mwm* resource variable, keyboardFocusPolicy. Specify the following resource *(17.03)*:

```
Mwm*KeyboardFocusPolicy:      pointer
```

Besides pointer, this resource variable accepts the value explicit, which signifies click-to-type focus.

The focusAutoRaise variable *(13.15)* is closely related. If this variable is set to be true, the focus window is automatically raised to the front of the display.

Keep in mind that when you're using pointer focus, auto-raise may cause a distracting shuffling effect.

— *VQ*

13.15 *Automatically Raising the Focus Window*

focusAutoRaise is a resource that when true causes the focus window to be raised to the top of the window stack. When the focus policy is explicit (click-to-type), focusAutoRaise is true for all clients by default. When the focus policy is pointer (real-estate-driven), focusAutoRaise is false for all clients by default.

These defaults are very sensible. If you are using the default click-to-type focus, focusAutoRaise is clearly very desirable. You click on a window to focus input and the window is raised to the top of the stack so that you can work with it easily. However, if you change the focus policy to pointer focus, turning focusAutoRaise on can make the display seem chaotic.

When pointer focus is active as you move the pointer across the display, the focus changes from window to window based on the location of the pointer, often a desirable feature. However, if focusAutoRaise is set to be true, each time the pointer moves into a window, the window will be moved to the front of the display. Simply moving the pointer across a screenful of windows can create a distracting shuffling effect! If you set the focus policy to pointer, we suggest you leave focusAutoRaise set to false. (Of course, if you use a tiled window layout *(21.19)*, in which there's no overlapping, focusAutoRaise is irrelevant.)

Of course, using pointer focus without focusAutoRaise is just my preference. You may want to experiment awhile to see how you like working with it.

Hypothetically, you *can* turn autoFocusRaise behavior on or off only for particular clients, but this is not necessarily desirable, with either focus policy. For instance, say you're using the default *mwm* settings so that explicit focus is in effect and focusAutoRaise is true for all clients. You can suppress the auto-raise feature only for the class of *xterm* windows by specifying:

```
Mwm*XTerm*focusAutoRaise: false
```

But what is the point? In most cases, you want to raise the focus window so that you can work with it more easily.

When pointer focus is in effect, setting focusAutoRaise differently for different clients can have tedious and unnecessary complications. It becomes fairly easy to "bury" one window beneath another inadvertently. For example, say focusAutoRaise is turned on for *xterm* windows only, and turned off for *xbiff*. If an *xbiff* window appears on top of an *xterm* and you move the pointer into the *xterm*, the *xterm* is raised automatically, covering the *xbiff* window.

You can send the *xterm* to the back using the **Lower** item of the **Window Menu**. Although the *xterm* retains the focus, it is not raised. `focusAutoRaise` specifies that a window is raised when the focus is moved to a window (retaining the focus is a different matter). However, if you move the pointer to another window and back to the *xterm*, the *xbiff* window will be buried again. In order to avoid such a situation, you would have to arrange all windows so that a part of the frame is exposed at all times. No window should ever appear entirely on top of another.

Given the limitations and potential problems, we discourage setting `focusAutoRaise` differently for different applications, regardless of the focus policy.

— *VQ*

13.16 *Changing How mwm Looks*

The Motif window manager provides features that can be thought of as components: client window frames, menus, icons, and what are known as *feedback* or *dialog boxes*. An example of a feedback box is the box that appears so that you can confirm or cancel a **Restart** command from the **Root Menu**, as illustrated in Article 13.05.

Certain resources *(1.06)* allow you to specify the appearance of one or all of these *mwm* component features. In specifying the resource setting, you can use the name of one of the features as part of the resource name. For example, one of the most useful component appearance resources is `background`, which specifies the background color *(17.06)*. You can specify a resource that sets the background color of any of the *mwm* components. The following resource specification sets the background color of all client window frames to light blue:

```
Mwm*client*background:     lightblue
```

Table 13-7 summarizes the resource name that corresponds to each of the *mwm* components.

Table 13-7: Resource Names Corresponding to mwm Components

Component	Resource Name
Menu	menu
Icon	icon
Client window frame	client
Feedback/dialog box	feedback
Titlebar	title

Thus, to set the background color of feedback boxes to sea green, you'd use the following resource:

```
Mwm*feedback*background:  seagreen
```

In keeping with resource naming syntax *(20.15)*, if you omit any specific component from the resource specification, it applies to *all* components. Thus, the following specification sets the background color of all window frames, feedback boxes, icons, and menus to light gray:

```
Mwm*background:   lightgray
```

Since the titlebar is actually part of the client window frame, the title resource is a special case. The title resource allows you to specify characteristics for the titlebar alone (including the command buttons), while you can specify characteristics for the rest of the frame (the resize border) using client. Thus, you might have the resource specifications:

```
Mwm*client*title*background:    lightblue
Mwm*client*background:          aquamarine
```

These lines would create two-tone window frames with aquamarine borders and light blue titlebars (perhaps too vivid a combination). (Note that these colors do not apply to the active (focus) window. To change these characteristics for the focus window, you would need to specify the activeBackground resource. See the online *mwm* manpage for more information.)

Similarly, you can specify resources for individual menus, by using the menu component with the menu name, as in the following example:

```
Mwm*menu*UtilitiesMenu*background:   seagreen
```

This line gives the Utilities Menu a sea green background.

— VQ

13.17 *Suppressing Motif Window Manager Decoration*

The *mwm* frame is a handy tool, but you may not want all of the windows on your screen to be framed. Or you may be happy with a partial frame. (I never use the Maximize button, for instance.) As you might expect, *mwm* allows a lot of flexibility in frame specification.

In Article 12.16 we show how to suppress the *twm* titlebar for applications like *oclock (3.02)* that look better without the bar. You might want to suppress the *mwm* window frame for the same reason. If you're a *twm* user, you make such a modification by editing the *.twmrc* startup file *(12.11)*; *mwm* users control such features with resource variables *(17.03)*.

mwm also offers more flexibility in controlling the level of window decoration. You can suppress the frame if you want, but you can also opt for a simplified frame. This can be useful when you aren't inclined to use certain parts of the frame, such as the Maximize button *(13.03)*. A simplified frame can also be a good idea on a small application, such as *xbiff (7.10)* or *xcalc (5.05)*. And if you're running several applications, *mwm* frames can actually make the screen seem crowded.

You control how much of a frame an application has using *mwm*'s clientDecoration resource variable. (This is a client-specific resource *(13.09)*, which means that it can be applied to particular applications.) The clientDecoration resource has a somewhat complicated syntax. It accepts a list of options, each of which corresponds to a part of the client frame.

The options are: maximize (button); minimize (button); menu (the **Window Menu** button); border; title (titlebar); resizeh (resize handles); all, which encompasses all decorations previously listed (this is the default); and none, which specifies that no decorations are used.

Some decorations require the presence of others; if you specify such a decoration, any decoration required with it will be used automatically. Specifically, if any of the command buttons is specified, a titlebar is also used; if resize handles or a titlebar is specified, a border is also used.

By default, a client window has all decoration. To specify only certain parts of the default frame, you can use one of two syntaxes: with the first syntax, you disable certain frame features (all other default features are still used); with the second syntax, you enable only certain features.

You supply clientDecoration with a list of options to be enabled or disabled. If the first item is preceded by a minus sign, the features in the list are disabled. (Any option not listed remains enabled.)

If the first item is preceded by a plus sign (or no sign is used), only those features listed are enabled.

For example, the following resource specification:

```
Mwm*XBiff*clientDecoration: -minimize maximize menu
```

removes the three command buttons from *xbiff* window frames. (The window will still have the titlebar, resize handles, and border.)

The following line specifies the same characteristics using the alternate syntax:

```
Mwm*XBiff*clientDecoration: title resizeh border
```

I can get rid of the Maximize button for all clients using the following line:

```
Mwm*clientDecoration: -maximize
```

—VQ

13.18 Eek! My Window Menu Has No Maximize Item!

The default *mwm* offers a variety of ways to maximize a window: a command button on the frame, the **Maximize** item on the **Window Menu**, and the keyboard shortcut for the menu item, to name most of them. For some people this may be several ways too many. Personally, I never use the maximize function. In fact, I've even customized *mwm* so that frames don't offer a maximize command button at all. Then I can't click on it and make the window really huge by mistake when I'm actually trying to make it small. If you'd like to get rid of this feature too, skip to Article 13.17 right now. (Eh, whenever.) But if you are an open (or even a closet) maximizer, the current article holds important information for you.

The default keyboard shortcut for the **Maximize** menu item is **Alt-F10**. By typing **Alt-F10**, you can maximize a window in a flash. Such keyboard shortcuts are one of the strengths of *mwm*. The only problem with this particular shortcut is that some keyboards don't have an **F10** function key. My Sun3 keyboard doesn't, for instance. Luckily, I don't care. But if your keyboard doesn't have an **F10** and you have the need (the drive even) to maximize, you may find yourself up a creek. You may long to type **Alt-F10**—maybe your life is dull, maybe you are strange, maybe you like big windows, I don't know—but no dice. What's more, when you display the **Window Menu**, you will not be able to find the **Maximize** item. You can look all you want. You can display the menu again and again in the vain hope. But you will come up empty, as in Figure 13-11.

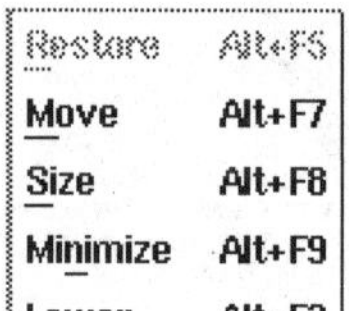

Figure 13-11: Maximize is missing! (How can I sleep?)

A possible workaround is to edit the line defining the **Maximize** menu item in your *.mwmrc* file *(13.09)*. Here's the default menu definition:

```
Menu DefaultWindowMenu
{
        Restore _R        Alt<Key>F5        f.restore
        Move    _M        Alt<Key>F7        f.move
        Size    _S        Alt<Key>F8        f.resize
        Minimize_n        Alt<Key>F9        f.minimize
        Maximize_x        Alt<Key>F10       f.maximize
        Lower   _L        Alt<Key>F3        f.lower
        no-label                            f.separator
        Close   _C        Alt<Key>F4        f.kill
}
```

To make the **Maximize** item available on your **Window Menu**, try changing the F10 to F2:

```
Menu DefaultWindowMenu
{
        Restore _R        Alt<Key>F5        f.restore
        Move    _M        Alt<Key>F7        f.move
        Size    _S        Alt<Key>F8        f.resize
        Minimize_n        Alt<Key>F9        f.minimize
        Maximize_x        Alt<Key>F2        f.maximize
        Lower   _L        Alt<Key>F3        f.lower
        no-label                            f.separator
        Close   _C        Alt<Key>F4        f.kill
}
```

When you restart the window manager *(13.09)*, the **Window Menu** should include **Maximize**, with the **Alt-F2** accelerator, as in Figure 13-12.

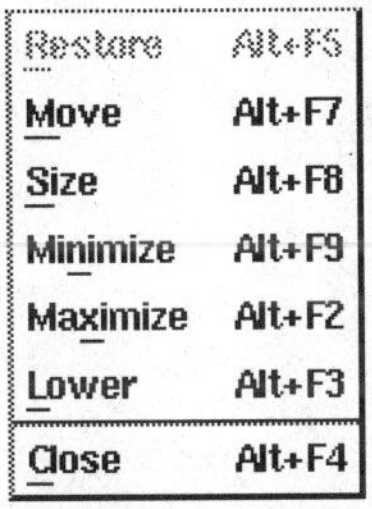

Figure 13-12: Maximize and the Window Menu, together again for the first time

I don't know about you, but this is a load off my mind.

— *VQ*

13.19 *Customizing the Root Menu*

You can add items to the *mwm* Root Menu *(13.05)* simply by adding lines of the format:

"label"   function

within the menu definition section of your *.mwmrc* file *(13.09)* (and then restarting the window manager).

The f.exec function allows you to execute system commands from a menu. In the default **Root Menu**, the **New Window** command uses the f.exec function to execute the system command xterm &, as shown below:

```
# Root Menu Description
Menu DefaultRootMenu
{
        "Root Menu"                     f.title
        "New Window"                    f.exec "xterm &"
        "Shuffle Up"                    f.circle_up
        "Shuffle Down"                  f.circle_down
        "Refresh"                       f.refresh
        "Pack Icons"                    f.pack_icons
    !   "Toggle Behavior..."            f.set_behavior
        no-label                        f.separator
        "Restart..."                    f.restart
    !   "Quit..."               f.quit_mwm
}
```

To create a menu item labeled **Clock** that opens an *xclock* window on your display, simply add a line to your *.mwmrc* file, as shown here:

```
# Root Menu Description
Menu DefaultRootMenu
{
        "Root Menu"                     f.title
        "New Window"                    f.exec "xterm &"
        "Clock"                         f.exec "xclock &"
        "Shuffle Up"                    f.circle_up
        "Shuffle Down"                  f.circle_down
        "Refresh"                       f.refresh
        "Pack Icons"                    f.pack_icons
    !   "Toggle Behavior..."            f.set_behavior
        no-label                        f.separator
        "Restart..."                    f.restart
    !   "Quit..."                       f.quit_mwm
}
```

In most cases, the label is a text string, but you can use a bitmap image *(13.20)* instead, if you like.

You can also edit (or remove) existing menu items. Two items (**Toggle Behavior** and **Quit**) are commented out by an exclamation mark at the beginning of the line. **Toggle Behavior** invokes f.set_behavior, which toggles between your own customized version of *mwm* and the standard version for your environment. You can also invoke this function using a keystroke combination *(13.23)*.

The **Quit** menu item causes the window manager to exit (it is not restarted). You might invoke **Quit** before starting another window manager, such as *twm*.

However, be careful that *mwm* is not the controlling process *(21.11)*, or you'll shut down X in the bargain.

To add either **Toggle Behavior** or **Quit** to the **Root Menu**, just delete the initial exclamation mark and restart the window manager, as usual.

You might also want to change what an existing menu item does. Say you want to run the *hpterm* terminal emulator (developed by Hewlett-Packard) rather than *xterm*. You would edit the **New Window** line in your menu specification to look like this:

```
# Root Menu Description
Menu DefaultRootMenu
{
        "Root Menu"             f.title
        "New Window"            f.exec "hpterm &"
        "Clock"                 f.exec "xclock &"
        "Shuffle Up"            f.circle_up
        "Shuffle Down"          f.circle_down
        "Refresh"               f.refresh
        "Pack Icons"            f.pack_icons
    !   "Toggle Behavior..."    f.set_behavior
        no-label                f.separator
        "Restart..."            f.restart
    !   "Quit..."               f.quit_mwm
}
```

— VQ

13.20 *Using a Bitmap Image as a Menu Label*

Though most **Root Menu** items are generally identified by a text label, *mwm* does let you use a bitmap image instead. Use the bitmap filename in the first column of the menu definition *(13.19)* and precede it with an "at" symbol (@). The following line creates a **Root Menu** item identified by a bitmap image of a full mailbox (filename *flagup*); you can run *xbiff (7.10)* by selecting the mailbox image from the menu.

```
@flagup        f.exec "xbiff &"
```

Unless a full pathname is given for the bitmap file, *mwm* looks for bitmap files in a systemwide directory, generally */usr/include/X11/bitmaps*. (*flagup* is a standard bitmap *(22.15)* available in */usr/include/X11/bitmaps*. It's the image *xbiff* uses for its full mailbox window.) You can also specify an alternate standard bitmap directory for *mwm* using the `bitmapDirectory` resource variable *(17.03)*. See the *mwm* manpage for more information.

— VQ

13.21 Creating New Menus

mwm allows you to specify entirely new menus in your *.mwmrc* file. A new menu can be separate from all existing menus, or it can be a submenu of an existing menu *(13.22)*.

If you want to create a new, independent menu, the first step is to write a menu definition and include it in your *.mwmrc* file. Note that the definition must conform to the menu specification syntax *(13.19)*. Items must invoke predefined window manager functions; the online manpage describes all available functions.

The second step: in your *.mwmrc* file, specify how the menu will be displayed and in what context. This involves associating a key or button with the f.menu function. For example, suppose you've specified a new menu, titled **Games-Menu**, that runs various game programs, each in its own window. (The f.exec function would be used to define each item.) The following button binding specifies that pressing the second pointer button on the root window displays the **Games Menu**:

```
<Btn2Down>        root      f.menu    GamesMenu
```

— VQ

13.22 Cascading Menus

mwm allows you to create submenus, generally known as *cascading* menus because they are displayed to the right side of (and slightly lower than) another menu. You define a submenu using the syntax rules described for the Root Menu *(13.19)*.

The following lines create a **Utilities Menu** that invokes several desktop clients and one game:

```
Menu UtilitiesMenu
{
    "Utilities Menu"       f.title
    "Clock"                 f.exec "xclock &"
    "System Load"          f.exec "xload &"
    "Calculator"           f.exec "xcalc &"
    "Manpage Browser"      f.exec "xman &"
    "Tetris"               f.exec "xtetris &"
}
```

In order to make the **Utilities Menu** a submenu of the **Root Menu**, you need to add an f.menu function to the **Root Menu** definition. This f.menu function must be coupled with the correct submenu title:

```
# Root Menu Description
Menu DefaultRootMenu
{
    "Root Menu"              f.title
    "New Window"             f.exec "hpterm &"
    "Shuffle Up"             f.circle_up
    "Shuffle Down"           f.circle_down
    "Refresh"                f.refresh
    "Pack Icons"             f.pack_icons
    "Utilities"              f.menuUtilitiesMenu
  !  "Toggle Behavior..."  f.set_behavior
    no-label                 f.separator
    "Restart..."          f.restart
  !  "Quit..."            f.quit_mwm
}
```

After you specify the preceding menus in your *.mwmrc* file (and restart *mwm*), display the **Root Menu**. It will feature a new item, labeled **Utilities**. Since this item is actually a pointer to a submenu, it will be followed by an arrowhead pointing to the right, as in Figure 13-13.

Figure 13-13: An arrowhead pointing to the right indicates a submenu

If you drag the pointer down the **Root Menu** to the **Utilities** item, the submenu will appear to cascade to the right. Figure 13-14 shows it appearing.

If you release the pointer button, both menus will remain displayed and the **Utilities** item and the first item on the **Utilities Menu** will be highlighted by a box. You can then select an item from the **Utilities Menu** by moving the pointer to the item and clicking the first button.

Keep in mind that you can create several submenus beneath a single menu and that menus can cascade several levels, though such complexity is not necessarily desirable.

Note also that if you pair a label with an invalid function (or with f.nop, which specifies no operation), or with a function that doesn't work in the current context, the label appears in a lighter typeface. This "graying out" indicates that the menu item is not available for selection.

—VQ

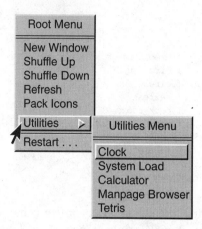

Figure 13-14: Utilities submenu of the Root Menu

13.23 *When You Don't Like Your Customizations*

Suppose you edit your *.mwmrc* file and specify some *mwm* resources, but the resulting environment is not what you'd hoped. In the worst case, suppose functions you've been using don't even work any more. Well, you do have an escape hatch. If you customize any feature of *mwm* (13.09) and decide you don't like the result, you can restart the window manager with the default settings for your system by typing the somewhat involved keystroke combination:

```
Shift-Control-Meta-!
```

(Shift, CTRL, and ! are actual keys, while Meta (18.14) is a function mapped to a particular key.) This keystroke combination invokes the pre-defined *mwm* function f.set_behavior, which is a toggle between your custom environment and the default. Thus, if you type the keystroke combination again, the window manager will be restarted using your previous customizations.

In either case, a dialog box will ask you to **OK** or **Cancel** the process. Click on the appropriate choice with the first pointer button or press **Return** to select the highlighted button (**OK**). Figure 13-15 shows the two possible dialog boxes.

The default **Root Menu** definition (in the *system.mwmrc* file) includes an item called **Toggle Behavior**, which invokes f.set_behavior; however, this item is commented out. If you want to make this available on the **Root Menu**, it's a simple matter of removing the exclamation comment mark from your *.mwmrc* file and restarting the window manager.

A final note: to be consistently useful, the **Toggle Behavior** menu item must be added both to your own *.mwmrc* file *and* to the *system.mwmrc* file. If it only appears in your own *.mwmrc* file, when you select it your environment will

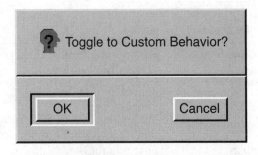

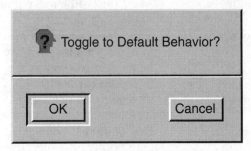

Figure 13-15: Dialog boxes to toggle custom and default mwm environments

be changed to reflect the standard **Root Menu**—which doesn't offer **Toggle Behavior!** Then the only way to toggle back is to use the **Shift-CTRL**-Meta-! keystroke combination.

—*VQ*

13.24 A Summary of mwm Functions

Table 13-8 summarizes the window management functions you can perform using the frame *(13.03)*, keys/buttons *(13.06)*, the Window Menu *(13.04)*, and the Root Menu *(13.05)*. The first column lists the desired function; the second, the pointer location; and the third, the required action (button-key combination, menu item, etc.). In this column, "click" means to press and immediately release the specified pointer button; "down" means to press and hold the pointer button, and "drag" means to move the pointer while holding down the pointer button.

The key combinations described in the table are valid for the default configuration of *mwm*, as specified in the *system.mwmrc* file. You can change them by editing your own *.mwmrc* file *(13.09)*. As always with Motif, the **Alt** and Meta *(18.14)* keys are equivalent.

Table 13-8: Summary of Window Manager Functions

Function	Pointer Location	Action
Window Menu	Window Menu button	First pointer button click; or first pointer button down
Window Menu	Frame	Third pointer button down
Window Menu	Icon	Third pointer button down
Window Menu	n/a	Meta-space bar or **Shift-Escape** displays menu for focus window.
Move	Titlebar	First pointer button down, drag
Move	Window or icon	**Alt-F7** (Meta-F7); move pointer; click to place window.
Move	Window Menu	Select **Move** item; move pointer; click to place window. (If **Move** item is boxed, can also select it by hitting the space bar or **Return**.)
Move	Window Menu	Type m; move pointer; click to place window.
Resize	Outer frame	First or second pointer button down; drag border or corner; release.
Resize	Window	**Alt-F8** (Meta-F8); move pointer to change border or corner; click to draw window in new size.
Resize	Window Menu	Select **Size** item; move pointer to change border or corner; click to draw window in new size.
Resize	Window Menu	Type s; move pointer to change border or corner; click to draw window in new size.
Raise window	Frame (not including title-buttons)	First pointer button click
Raise window	Window	First pointer button click (Keyboard-FocusPolicy must be explicit; FocusAutoRaise must be true; both are defaults.)
Raise window	Icon box	Double-click first pointer button on icon corresponding to active window you want to raise.
Lower	Window	**Alt-F3** (Meta-F3)
Lower	Window Menu	Select **Lower** item.
Lower	Window Menu	Type l.
Iconify	Minimize command button	First pointer button click

Table 13-8: Summary of Window Manager Functions (continued)

Function	Pointer Location	Action
Iconify	Window	Alt-F9 (Meta-F9)
Iconify	Window Menu	Select Minimize item.
Iconify	Window Menu	Type n.
Deiconify	Icon	Double-click first pointer button.
Deiconify	Icon	Alt-F5 (Meta-F5)
Deiconify	Window Menu	Select Restore. (If Restore item is boxed, can also select it by hitting the space bar or Return.)
Deiconify	Window Menu	Type r.
Root Menu	Root	Third pointer button down
New Window	Root Menu	Select New Window item.
Unfocus	Root Menu menu	Select Unfocus item; click any pointer button on target.
Shuffle window stack up	Root Menu	Select Shuffle Up item.
Shuffle window stack down	Root Menu	Select Shuffle Down item.
Refresh display	Root Menu	Select Refresh item.
Optimize icon box layout	Root Menu	Select Pack Icons item.
Restart window manager	Root Menu	Select Restart... item.
Stop window manager	Root Menu menu	Select Exit item.

— VQ

14

The olwm Window Manager

14.01 *A Word About OPEN LOOK and olwm*

OPEN LOOK is a GUI developed by AT&T and Sun Microsystems. Although OPEN LOOK has essentially lost the commercial GUI wars to Motif, the unencumbered availability of the XView toolkit ensures that it will remain popular among "freeware" users, particularly on the LINUX operating system. As well, its "minimalist" flavor appeals to many. Finally, Sun has committed to maintaining their X–based OPEN LOOK toolkits for several years.

The OPEN LOOK window manager is *olwm*. There are actually two versions of *olwm*: one for Sun OpenWindows, and the AT&T version. This chapter concentrates on the Sun OpenWindows version. Versions of OpenWindows up to 3.4 are OPEN LOOK–based; versions after 3.4 are expected to be Motif-based but include two OPEN LOOK toolkits (XView and OLIT) for backwards compatibility.

This chapter discusses some of the basics of using *olwm* (and in so doing, OPEN LOOK in general), and includes details about how to configure *olwm* to your liking. A warning: those of you with serious hacker mentalities will be disappointed in the potential to configure *olwm*, since OPEN LOOK is a fairly rigid standard.

There are many variations on details such as menu items among OPEN LOOK implementations and toolkits, but the general principles described here should work with any OPEN LOOK toolkit.

—IFD

14.02 olwm for the Impatient

Here's a quick tour of how to use the *olwm* window manager.

olwm has a look that distinguishes it from other window managers in X. Figure 14-1 shows a window decorated by *olwm*.

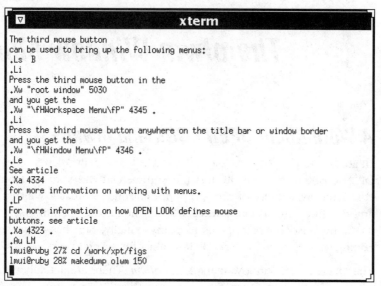
```
  ▽                         xterm
The third mouse button
can be used to bring up the following menus:
.Ls  B
.Li
Press the third mouse button in the
.Xw "root window" 5030
and you get the
.Xw "\fHWorkspace Menu\fP" 4345 .
.Li
Press the third mouse button anywhere on the title bar or window border
and you get the
.Xw "\fHWindow Menu\fP" 4346 .
.Le
See article
.Xa 4334
for more information on working with menus.
.LP
For more information on how OPEN LOOK defines mouse
buttons, see article
.Xa 4323 .
.Au LM
lmui@ruby 27% cd /work/xpt/figs
lmui@ruby 28% makedump olwm 150
```

Figure 14-1: Sample olwm window

In the figure, notice the following features:

- In each corner of the window is a small "corner" symbol, which reminds me of the sorts of black sticky tabs you'd use to keep pictures in an old-time photo album or scrapbook (and which never stuck very well and invariably left a yellow stain on your precious photograph of your great-great-grandparents on their wedding day).

  By holding the first mouse button down on any of the corners, you can resize the window. The cursor turns into a white bull's-eye symbol.

- At the upper-left corner is a small symbol with a triangle pointed downwards. By pressing the first mouse button down on this symbol, you can iconify the window. To restore an iconified window, double-click on the icon.

- You can move the window by dragging the titlebar with the first mouse button or by dragging the narrow frame surrounding the entire window.

This should be enough to get you moving around in *olwm*. The only other thing you need to know about is menus. The third mouse button can be used to bring up the following menus:

- Press the third mouse button in the root window *(6.02)* and you get the Workspace menu *(14.10)*.

- Press the third mouse button inside the main window of an OPEN LOOK application and you get an application-specific menu.

- Press the third mouse button anywhere on the titlebar or window frame and you get the Window menu *(14.08)*.

For more information on how OPEN LOOK defines mouse buttons, see Article 14.03.

—LM

14.03 *Using the Pointer*

Most mice used with X11R5 have three buttons. OPEN LOOK defines their use as follows; this is similar to (but not identical with) the commonly accepted uses in most X Window System applications. (Note in particular that the *xterm* terminal emulator is *not* OPEN LOOK–based, so it uses some buttons differently.)

- The first button is called SELECT, and is used for selecting, or telling the system what you want to do. You use SELECT both in a window's titlebar, to select that window to receive the input focus; and within a window, to select items of text or graphics, to push particular button items, and several other uses.

- The second button is called ADJUST, and is used for extending a selection.

- The third button is called MENU, and as you would expect, is used to work with menu choices.

If your mouse only has two buttons, then press both buttons together to get MENU.

In this chapter, we will ignore the OPEN LOOK style guide and documentation conventions, and continue to say "first mouse button" for SELECT, "second mouse button" for ADJUST, and "third mouse button" for MENU. This is because Linda thought it would be confusing to suddenly start using new terminology for familiar concepts. However, you should remember that the buttons in OPEN LOOK have distinct functions. This will help make *olwm* more intuitive to you.

—IFD, LM

14.04 Working with Menus

OPEN LOOK programs generally use pop-up menus. There are two ways to activate OPEN LOOK menus, the more traditional "pull-down sliding menu" style, and the "stay up" style.

- Pressing the third mouse button *and holding it down* pulls down the menu—it stays on the screen as long as you hold the mouse button down while you decide what to do. You can move the pointer to any of the menu items and release it. As you slide the pointer up and down, the item under the pointer is highlighted, and releasing the button selects the highlighted item.

- On the other hand, if you press the third mouse button and quickly release it, the menu appears in stay-up mode; that is, it stays up just until you select on one item. You can click the first mouse button on one of the menu choices to select that choice. Clicking the pointer button anywhere else on the screen (for example, in the root menu) dismisses the menu.

—IFD

14.05 Pinnable Menus

Important menus, such as the root menu or **Workspace** menu, are "pinnable," which means that you can pin them up and keep them on your desktop for future use. Pinnable windows have little pin symbols in the upper-left corner. You can activate the pin by moving the pointer over the pin and releasing the third mouse button. You'll see the pin move before you release the button, to show you that the pointer is in the right place. Figure 14-2 shows a pinnable menu.

Figure 14-2: Pinnable menu before pinning

Figure 14-3 shows the same menu once it has been pinned.

Figure 14-3: Pinnable menu after pinning

The menu stays up with the pin in. When you want to dismiss this menu, you can click the first mouse button on the pin to pull the pin out and make the menu disappear.

—IFD

14.06 *Working with Submenus*

When a menu item is followed by a small triangle pointing to the right, it means that it is a pointer to a submenu. (The small triangle is also called a *menu mark*). In Figure 14-3 you'll see a couple of items with menu marks in the Workspace menu. When you select one of these items with the third mouse button, you bring up a submenu. Figure 14-4 shows one such submenu.

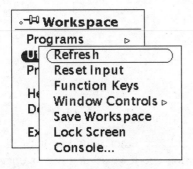

Figure 14-4: The Utilities submenu

Now, if you're new to *olwm* and OPEN LOOK applications in general, here's the part where you have to pay attention. Notice that one of the items–in this case the top item of the submenu–is highlighted. This item is the *default action* for the submenu. What it means is that if you select the Utilities button using the first mouse button instead of the third button, then the submenu doesn't come up, but its default action (**Refresh**) is performed. See Article 14.26 for information on how to change the default item.

Some people may prefer that the first mouse button to bring up a menu rather than default to an action. See Article 14.22 for information on how to change this behavior.

—LM

14.07 The Window Menu

The **Window** menu is the menu you get by holding down the third mouse button (aka the **MENU** button) on the titlebar or any part of the window frame. This menu allows you to perform common window operations, such as moving, resizing, and closing the window.

An advantage to *olwm* is that it lets you use the entire frame around the window to do these operations, so you don't have to have the titlebar visible (as you do for other window managers, such as *mwm* and *twm*).

The **Window** menu appears in Figure 14-5.

Figure 14-5: The Window menu

The most commonly used items are:

- **Close** iconifies (or "minimizes") a window.

- **Back** moves the window behind any other windows it overlaps. This is useful for finding a window when you have several that overlap.

- **Refresh** redisplays the window in case sections of it were overwritten or lost. (Notice that this only affects the X window itself; if you're using a character-based program within a terminal emulator, you may still have to use a different program-specific command to refresh its output, such as CTRL-L in *vi*.)

- **Quit** terminates the application. If the application has its own means of termination, such as logging out of a terminal emulator, that should be used instead of **Quit**. However, the presence of this item on the **Window** menu is the reason why most OPEN LOOK applications do not provide a **Quit** button of their own.

—IFD

14.08 *A Window Summary*

Table 14-1 shows the myriad of ways to open, close, iconify, bake, fry, and sauté your windows. It is a list of commands you can access on the **Window** menu, plus some handy shorcuts.

Table 14-1: Window Menu Commands

Command	Function	Shortcut
Close, Open	Closes or iconifies the window, i.e., it replaces the window with a tiny icon window. Clicking the third mouse button on the icon brings up a **Window** menu with the word "Close" replaced by "Open," which lets you open the window.	Click on triangle at left of titlebar to close. To open, double-click the first mouse button on icon.
Full Size, Restore Size	Expands the window to maximum size, usually the full height of the screen. If the window has already been set to "Full Size," this selection will read "Normal" and selecting it returns the window to its original size.	Double-click the first mouse button on titlebar.
Move	Sets up for mouseless **move** operation.	Click and drag the first mouse button on titlebar.
Resize	Sets up for mouseless **resize** operation	Click and drag the first mouse button on any resize corner.
Properties	Not available	—
Back	Moves the visible window to the back (bottom) of the window stack	—
Refresh	Redisplays the window	—
Quit	Terminates the window and the program or application controlling it	Client-specific methods (e.g., **CTRL-D** or exit in a shell window).

In addition, you can perform many of these operations on groups of windows using the Window Controls submenu of the Utilities menu. See Article 14.11.

—*IFD*

14.09 Closing Versus Iconifying

For those of you who are coming from a Microsoft Windows or Motif environment, the OPEN LOOK terminology of "closing a window" may confuse you. In Microsoft Windows and Motif, to close a window means to exit an application. In OPEN LOOK, however, "closing" is the equivalent of "iconifying." (Or "minimizing," in Microsoft Windows and Motif jargon.)

The Window menu *(14.08)*, therefore, has both Close and Quit functions. Don't let this confuse you: use Close to iconify and Quit to terminate the window.

—*IFD*

14.10 The Workspace Menu (or Root Menu)

The background screen area of your display is called the *workspace* in OPEN LOOK terminology, or the root window in X11 terminology. Moving the pointer into the background window and pressing the third pointer button brings up the Workspace menu (also called the Root menu. The normal content of this menu is shown in Figure 14-6.

Figure 14-6: Workspace menu

Both Programs and Utilities have a menu mark beside them, so selecting either one brings up a submenu *(14.06)*. The remainder of the menu items have ellipses (...) after them, to indicate that their selection brings up a pop-up window (such as the *props* client *(14.14)* or a confirming dialog).

Figure 14-7 shows the Programs submenu. This menu is used to start up new applications. For example, selecting Command Tool starts up a *cmdtool* terminal emulator. See Article 14.25 for information on how this menu is defined.

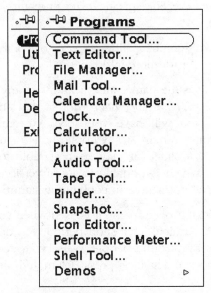

Figure 14-7: Workspace menu, Programs submenu

Figure 14-8 shows the Utilities submenu. This menu is used to modify the user's environment.

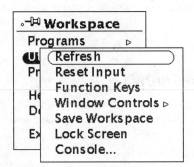

Figure 14-8: Workspace menu, Utilities submenu

The Programs submenu is fairly self-explanatory, but let's shine a little light on the Utilities submenu.

- The Refresh item redisplays your entire X display. (See Article 6.13 for more information on refreshing the screen.)

- The Reset Input item runs the Sun-specific *kbd_mode* program. It is sometimes needed when your keyboard starts acting like it's possessed. See Article 18.19 for more information.

- The **Function Keys** item runs the Sun-specific *vkbd* program, which gives you control of the function keys.

- **Window Controls** has its own submenu allowing you to iconify and close windows, etc. See Article 14.11 for more information.

- The **Save Workspace** item saves the names and locations of any pure OPEN LOOK applications in a file (*$HOME/.openwin-init*), so that any time you later start OpenWindows, you will have your own customized set of clients. However, it may miss certain MIT X applications or those developed with non-OPEN LOOK toolkits. It may be preferable to customize your startup script instead, which is portable to more versions of X. See Chapters 16 and 21 for more information on configuring startup scripts.

- **Lock Screen** starts a screenlock program *(6.19)*. It is used when you are away from your workstation or X terminal for a short period; you don't want to log out of X, but you don't want other people to use your account while you're away. To resume normal activities, press **Return** and then correctly type your login password.

- The last item, **Console**, starts up a terminal emulator with console output *(27.02)* directed to it (via the OpenWindows *cmdtool –C* client). This is useful to prevent further need for the **Refresh** item described above.

This is the default set of menu items. On Sun's OpenWindows, you can change the **Workspace** menu or even completely replace it. See Article 14.26 for more information.

—IFD

14.11 *Manipulating Lots of Windows*

olwm makes it easy to open, close, or iconify a single window several different ways (see Article 14.08). In addition, you can manipulate several windows at once using the **Window Controls** submenu of the Utilities menu *(14.10)*. Figure 14-9 shows the **Window Controls** submenu.

For a single window, it's easier to use the titlebar *(14.02)* or Window menu *(14.08)*; however, for working with several windows at once, the **Window Controls** menu can't be beat. You can select a group of windows in two ways:

- Sweep out a rectangle on the workspace that totally encloses the windows or icons you want;

- Click the first mouse button on the titlebar, frame, or icon of the first, and click on the second mouse button on the titlebars, frames, or icons of the rest.

As you select windows, each one of them has its border highlighted to show its selection.

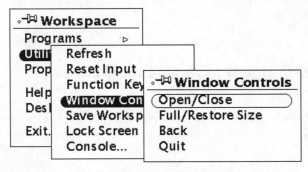

Figure 14-9: The Window Controls submenu

Once you've selected the windows, you can **Open/Close** them as a group, which opens any that are closed and closes any that are open. You can use the **Full/Restore Size** item, which makes any that are normal size occupy the full height of the display and any that are full height return to their normal height and position. You can move the whole group to the **Back**, and if you want to clean up your screen quickly, you can **Quit** a whole group of windows. Note that the group association is temporary; it is broken as soon as you use the first mouse button for any other purpose.

—IFD

14.12 *How Can I Change olwm?*

Some window managers have the flexibility to let you paint your root window sky blue, start an audio CD player *(6.25)*, and fire up their favorite game just by pressing the second mouse button in a titlebar while holding down the **Shift**, **CTRL**, and **Alt** keys...and the right foot pedal.... However, OPEN LOOK specifies the window system's behavior in such detail that the user can't be given this degree of flexibility. If permitted, users could (and some would) configure their systems in ways that would violate the OPEN LOOK spec. So *olwm* is considerably easier to configure (or less flexible, depending on your point of view) than some other X Window System window managers, such as the widely used *twm* and *mwm*. Customization of *olwm* is, in fact, limited to:

- Changing or replacing the **Root** menu or **Workspace** menu (and submenus thereof)

- Specifying options on the command line

- Specifying a number of X resources that control *olwm*'s behavior

In addition, the OpenWindows *props* client is a program for controlling OPEN LOOK applications without having to learn about X resources. Although it is not strictly part of *olwm*, it allows you to customize much of *olwm*'s behavior using a graphical interface. Article 14.14 describes what the *props* client can do for you.

—IFD

14.13   *Configuring olwm with Resources*

As with most X11 programs, there is a significant amount of configurable behavior built into the window manager, and much of it can be configured with X resources. For more information on using resources, see Chapters 17 and 20.

The class name *(20.05)* for Sun's version of *olwm* is OpenWindows, so the string OpenWindows* must be used as part of the name in the resource file. Thus, to enable automatic raising of the focus window *(14.17)*, you would put OpenWindows*AutoRaise: true in your X resource file. You can also use the *olwm* instance name (olwm), but it's generally better to use the class name.

The following articles give examples of resources you're likely to want to change. In addition to these, you should know that there are resources to tweak all sorts of behavior for calling up menus, dragging windows, etc. So if there's something esoteric you want to do and it isn't covered here, look through the *olwm* manpage before you give up: you may be pleasantly surprised.

—IFD, LM

14.14   *Configuring olwm with props*

The *props* client (also known as the **Properties Manager**) gives you a slick graphical interface for controlling resources for *olwm*. We talk about it here because it often seems to be part of *olwm*. But although *props* can be called from the default **Workspace** menu and can incorporate its changes directly into the running *olwm*, it is a separate client program.

Using *props*, you can manage:

• Placement of icons on your display

• Color of windows and the root window (workspace)

• Behavior of the first mouse button

• How the window manager uses the audio beep

• Focus policy (pointer focus or click to type)

• Behavior of scroll bars

• Behavior of the mouse

- Internationalization settings

To start *props*, you can either start it on the command line:

```
% props &
```

or you can start it by selecting **Properties...** from the Workspace menu *(14.10)*.

The initial *props* window depends on whether you're running on a monochrome or color display. On a monochrome display, *props* brings up a window for configuring icons, as shown in Figure 14-10.

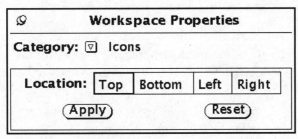

Figure 14-10: The props Icons category

You can use this window to specify where you want your icons to be arranged—at the top of the display, at the bottom, on the left, or on the right.

On a color display, the initial *props* window is one for managing your color scheme. (This category is disabled on monochrome screens.)

To move to a different category, hold the right mouse button over the word **Icons** (or over the triangle symbol to the left of it). This gives you a menu allowing you to select another category.

In addition to changing *olwm*'s behavior immediately, *props* also writes resources to your *.Xdefaults* file *(17.03)*. The idea is that the new behavior will take effect the next time you start up *olwm*. However, this depends on your using *.Xdefaults* to manage all your resources. Some X veterans will argue that this is a bad practice in general, since it means that every X program reads hundreds (maybe thousands) of resources at startup, and because *.Xdefaults* doesn't have the flexibility *xrdb* does for remote clients, and if you use *xrdb*, then *$HOME/.Xdefaults* isn't consulted at all.

For that reason, although *props* is very powerful, many users still prefer to set their resources manually.

—*LM*

14.15 Changing the Focus Policy

As a habitual *twm* user, I get nervous when I think I'm typing in one window and my keystrokes go into another. I'm used to pointer focus. With pointer focus, my keystrokes go into whatever window my pointer is in.

By default, the focus policy in *olwm* is click to type: that is, you have to click on a window before the keyboard focus follows there. So one of the first things I wanted to change was the focus policy. To do this, use the `SetInput` resource, which can be set to two values: `select` and `followmouse`. The default is `select`, i.e., click to type. In my case, I set it to `followmouse`:

```
olwm*SetInput:  followmouse
```

You could also get the same results by running *olwm* with the *–follow* or *–f* command-line option. In addition, you can use *props* (14.14) to change the focus policy (under the **Miscellaneous** category).

The decoration on the focused window is slightly different depending on which type of focus policy you're using. If you prefer one decoration to the other, you can switch them around using the `InvertFocusHighlighting` resource.

If you prefer to change the focus policy often, you can customize your **Workspace** menu to include the FLIPFOCUS function. (See Table 14-2 in Article 14.25.) This lets you change the focus policy dynamically without setting resources or having to restart *olwm*.

—*LM*

14.16 When the Focus Is Lost

As mentioned in Article 14.15, *olwm* provides two focus policies: pointer focus and click to type.

It may occasionally happen that the window manager will "drop out from under you." In this case, you will see a brief flurry of action as all the titlebars disappear and any iconified windows pop open. What happens to the focus under these circumstances? Well, fortunately, in most cases the input focus reverts to X11's native pointer focus mode, so you can just move the cursor into any terminal emulator window and type the command `olwm &` to get the window manager back.

Occasionally, however, the input focus is left in click-to-type mode and *not* in a terminal window. In that case, you can use the Secure Keyboard feature of *xterm* (11.17) to get the focus back: see Article 13.08 for an example of how this is done (using a different window manager).

If the **Secure Keyboard** method doesn't work for you (for example, if you don't have an *xterm* window running!), you can log in at another terminal and restart *olwm* from there. Remember to specify the *–display* command-line option *(19.02)*:

```
% olwm -display sunspot:0 &
```

—*IFD*

14.17 *Automatically Raising Windows*

Usually, windows are raised under *olwm* only when you click on its titlebar or border. This means that you might type into a window that's partially obscured.

Some people prefer to see the entire window in which they're currently typing. If this is your preference, then you should try out the AutoRaise resource. Under AutoRaise, the window is automatically raised when it receives the input focus. This is especially useful if your focus policy is set to click to type *(14.16)*. Then when you click anywhere in the window, not only can you start typing in it, the window is also raised above the rest.

```
OpenWindows*AutoRaise:    true
```

If you use pointer focus *(14.15)*, then AutoRaise might become a little bit annoying. Since the focus follows the mouse, you'll find that as you move your pointer around, windows raise all over the place in a flurry of activity that may drive you crazy. So if you use pointer focus, you might also like to specify the AutoRaiseDelay resource. This resource is set to the number of microseconds that *olwm* should wait between focusing on a window and raising it. This way, you can set it so that when your mouse sweeps across the screen, five different windows don't pop up in sequence.

```
OpenWindows*AutoRaiseDelay:      5000
```

Here, we've set it the delay to an arbitrary 5000 microseconds. These microseconds could be the difference between a pleasant working environment and a migrane headache. Play with the value of the AutoRaiseDelay until you come up with one you're comfortable with.

—*LM*

14.18 *If You Don't Want to Move an Outline*

I usually work at a NeXT workstation, and one of the things I've always bragged about is that when you move a window, the whole window moves, not just an outline. (Some people brag about how much money they make or about their celebrity friends, and then there are those of us who brag about our GUIs. Sad, eh?)

I thought I was such a hotshot. Well, *olwm* users can get the same effect by setting the following resource:

```
OpenWindows*DragWindow:   true
```

Now, when you move a window, the entire window is redrawn the entire way. I'm sure people will call me foolhardy for making your server work this hard just for a trivial effect, but it really makes a difference to me.

(Sigh, now I hear that even *twm* users can do this. So much for my moment of glory.)

—LM

14.19 Suppressing the Titlebar

Sometimes you just don't want that pesky titlebar. You can suppress the title-bar on a client by listing it under the MinimalDecor resource. For example, if you didn't want your *xcalc (5.05)* and *xclock (3.02)* windows to have titlebars, define the following resource:

```
OpenWindows*MinimalDecor: XCalc XClock
```

You can use either the client instance name or its application class name *(20.05)*. The resulting window doesn't have a titlebar or a iconify button. However, it does have resize corners *(14.02)*, and you can still get a Window menu *(14.07)* by clicking on the borders.

You might also want to suppress titlebars on all transient windows. To do that, set the TransientTitled resource to false.

—LM

14.20 olwm and the SHAPE Extension

Here's a nice feature of *olwm*. Under other window managers, you often have to suppress window decoration for clients that use the SHAPE extension, such as *oclock (3.02)*. However, *olwm* is smart enough to know automatically not to give these windows any decoration. No configuration is necessary. No assembly required.

Without decoration, you can still manipulate the window. To resize an undec-orated window, press the first mouse button on the window. The resize cor-ners *(14.02)* should appear, allowing you to resize the window as desired. To dismiss the resize corners, click the first mouse button anywhere on the root window. Figure 14-11 shows an *oclock* with temporary resize corners.

Figure 14-11: An oclock window with resize corners

To access the Window menu *(14.07)* for a window without decoration, just press the third mouse button in the window.

—LM

14.21 *Changing the Colors and Fonts*

If you want to change the way *olwm* looks, you'll want to fiddle with colors and fonts. I don't want to go into great detail on this, but here are the resources that you can play with to tweak your *olwm* environment to your liking:

Resource	Description	Default
Background	Background color of masked icons	*White*
BorderColor	Color for window and icon borders	*Black*
Foreground	Color for text in titlebars, menus	*Black*
PaintWorkspace	Whether to set the workspace background	*True*
WindowColor	Background color of windows, menus, notices	*#ccc (20% gray)*
WorkspaceColor	Color for workspace (root window)	*#40a0c0*

The colors starting with number signs (#) use hexadecimal notation for color. See Article 26.11 for more information.

You can also set up color schemes using the *props (14.14)* program. For many users, this will be the easiest way to manage colors under *olwm*.

The only one of these resources that may need special explanation is Paint-Workspace. With PaintWorkspace set to true (which is the default), the color specified with the WorkspaceColor resource is set as the root background color. Some users prefer to set their own backgrounds, so they may want to disable the workspace color and set PaintWorkspace to false. See Articles 6.02, 6.03, and 6.04 for more information on how to change your root background manually.

You probably shouldn't touch many of the font resources (such as `CursorFont` and `GlyphFont`). However, here are a couple that you may like to play with:

Resource	Description	Default
ButtonFont	Font for buttons in menus, notices	Lucida-Sans
IconFont	Font for icon names	Lucida-Sans
TextFont	Font for notices	Lucida-Sans
TitleFont	Font for titlebars, menu titles	Lucida-Sans

—*LM*

14.22 *Making Submenus the Default*

As described in Article 14.06, you invoke the default action of a submenu by pressing the first mouse button on that item. If this behavior makes you nervous, you can set the `SelectDisplaysMenu` resource to `true`. With this resource set, the first mouse button brings up the submenu just as the third mouse button would.

You can also change this behavior with *props (14.14).* under the **Menus** category.

Now, to be honest, the first time I encountered the OPEN LOOK submenu behavior, I was thrown for a loop. However, after a while I got used to it, and I realized how convenient it was to have reasonable "defaults" that you can call instantly without having to go through the Menu Shuffle. So although new users might be tempted to set this resource, I urge you to wait it out and see if you learn to like the status quo.

—*LM*

14.23 *Tweaking for Screen Dumps*

In making screen dumps for this chapter, *olwm* gave me a devilishly hard time. Here are some tips that will help you make screen dumps using *olwm*.

olwm attempts to give a three-dimensional look for multibit displays. This looks pretty nice on the screen, but it produces a hideous screen dump. You can turn off three-dimensional frames by using the *–Zd* command-line option or by using the `Use3DFrames` resource:

```
OpenWindows*Use3DFrames: false
```

or you can choose to make your screen dumps on monochrome displays (which is what I've done).

Another complication is that if you're taking screen dumps of menus, you run into the problem that *olwm* "grabs" the server when displaying menus and dialog boxes. This means that while you're displaying a menu, you can't run any other program, and if you want to take a screen dump of the menu using *xwd* *(23.01)*, you're stuck. The way to get around this is to turn off the Server-Grabs resource.

```
OpenWindows*ServerGrabs: false
```

—LM

14.24 *Using Multiple Screens*

On some Sun color workstations, you can use dual frame buffers (see Article 27.11 to see how to set this up). This means that there are two virtual screens accessible from a single physical monitor; screen 0 is color, and screen 1 is monochrome. You can scroll between them by moving the pointer off either side of the monitor.

By default, *olwm* supports all screens on a server. You can override this behavior using the *–single* command-line option. This way, you might run different window managers on different displays, or the same window manager but with different command-line options.

The opposite of *–single* is *–multi*, but since this is the default you will probably never have to use it.

—LM

14.25 *How olwm Menus Are Defined*

The OpenWindows version of *olwm* allows you to replace all the entries in the Workspace menu. To customize the Workspace menu in Sun's *olwm*, you need only edit text files. First, let's look at the default values so you can get your bearings.

The default configuration file for the Workspace menu is *$OPENWIN-HOME/lib/openwin-menu* (OPENWINHOME is usually defined as */usr/openwin*). The *openwin-menu* file on our system currently reads as follows (you may have a later version, or your system may have been customized locally):

```
#
# @(#)openwin-menu      23.15 91/09/14 openwin-menu
#
#       OpenWindows default root menu file - top level menu
#

"Workspace" TITLE

"Programs" MENU   $OPENWINHOME/lib/openwin-menu-programs

"Utilities" MENU   $OPENWINHOME/lib/openwin-menu-utilities
```

```
"Properties..."   "PROPERTIES

SEPARATOR

"Help..."   exec $OPENWINHOME/bin/helpopen handbooks/top.toc.handbook

"Desktop Intro..." exec $OPENWINHOME/bin/helpopen handbooks/desktop.intro.handbook

SEPARATOR

"Exit..."    EXIT
```

Note that the **Programs** and **Utilities** submenus are defined in separate files, which makes for simpler editing. The file that defines the **Programs** menu reads as follows:

```
#
# @(#)openwin-menu-programs      1.15 91/09/14 openwin-menu-programs
#
#         OpenWindows default root menu file - Programs submenu
#

"Programs" TITLE PIN

"Command Tool..."  DEFAULT exec $OPENWINHOME/bin/cmdtool
"Text Editor..."           exec $OPENWINHOME/bin/textedit
"File Manager..."          exec $OPENWINHOME/bin/filemgr
"Mail Tool..."             exec $OPENWINHOME/bin/mailtool
"Calendar Manager..."      exec $OPENWINHOME/bin/cm
"Clock..."                 exec $OPENWINHOME/bin/clock
"Calculator..."            exec $OPENWINHOME/bin/calctool
"Print Tool..."            exec $OPENWINHOME/bin/printtool
"Audio Tool..."            exec $OPENWINHOME/bin/audiotool
"Tape Tool..."             exec $OPENWINHOME/bin/tapetool
"Binder..."                exec $OPENWINHOME/bin/binder
"Snapshot..."              exec $OPENWINHOME/bin/snapshot
"Icon Editor..."           exec $OPENWINHOME/bin/iconedit
"Performance Meter..."     exec $OPENWINHOME/bin/perfmeter
"Shell Tool..."            exec $OPENWINHOME/bin/shelltool

"Demos" MENU                    $OPENWINHOME/lib/openwin-menu-demo
```

The file that defines the **Utilities** menu reads:

```
#
# @(#)openwin-menu-utilities      1.5 91/09/14 openwin-menu-utilities
#
#         OpenWindows default root menu file - Utilities submenu
#

"Refresh"                  DEFAULT REFRESH
"Reset Input"                      exec kbd_mode -u
"Function Keys"                    exec vkbd
"Window Controls" MENU
        "Open/Close"       DEFAULT OPEN_CLOSE_SELN
```

```
            "Full/Restore Size"      FULL_RESTORE_SIZE_SELN
            "Back"                   BACK_SELN
            "Quit"                   QUIT_SELN
    "Window Controls" END PIN
    "Save Workspace"                 SAVE_WORKSPACE
    #
    #  Uncomment the following if interested in colormap compaction
    #
    #"Save Colors" MENU
    #     "Save"            DEFAULT $OPENWINHOME/bin/cmap_compact save
    #     "Discard"                 $OPENWINHOME/bin/cmap_compact discard
    #"Save Colors" END
    #
    "Lock Screen"                    exec xlock
    "Console..."               exec $OPENWINHOME/bin/cmdtool -C
```

Each line consists of three fields: the name to appear on the menu, optional keywords, and either the action to take when the line is selected or the name of a file defining a submenu. Comment lines beginning with # in column one, and null lines are ignored.

The following is a full list of keywords you can specify. They must be written in uppercase.

Table 14-2:

Sun OpenWindows olwm Menu File Keywords

Keyword	Function
Defining menus	
MENU	Start a menu definition.
END	End a menu definition.
DEFAULT	Specify default case for menu.
PIN	Make menu pinnable (specify after END).
Working with the NeWS Server (Prior to OpenWin 3.3)	
POSTSCRIPT	Send rest of line to NeWS.
Configuring olwm	
FLIPDRAG	Invert the DragWindow resource.
FLIPFOCUS	Flip focus policy (click vs. follow-mouse).
SAVE_WORKSPACE	Save windows in *$HOME/.openwin-init*.
PROPERTIES	Start up the *props* client.
Formatting the Menu	
TITLE	Menu title
NOP	Does nothing (placeholder).
SEPARATOR	Produces a blank line.

Table 14-2:   (continued)

Keyword	Function
Restarting and Quitting	
RESTART	Rerun *olwm* (e.g., after changing the menu file).
REREAD_MENU_FILE	Reread the **Workspace** menu customization file.
WMEXIT	Exit window manager, but don't kill clients.
EXIT	Kill all clients and terminate (asks for confirmation).
EXIT_NO_CONFIRM	Kill all clients and terminate (no confirmation).
Manipulating Windows	
REFRESH	Refresh all windows.
BACK_SELN	Move selected windows and icons behind.
OPEN_CLOSE_SELN	Toggle open/closed states of windows and icons.
FULL_RESTORE_SIZE_SELN	Toggle full-sized/normal-sized states of windows.
QUIT_SELN	Quit the selected windows and icons.

—IFD, LM

14.26   *Configuring the Workspace Menu*

The easiest and safest way to change the **Workspace** menu is to copy the system configuration files into your home directory.

```
% cd $OPENWINHOME/lib
% cp openwin-menu $HOME/.openwin-menu
% cp openwin-menu-programs $HOME/.openwin-menu-programs
% cp openwin-menu-utilities $HOME/.openwin-menu-utilities
```

(Note that each file has the same name in your home directory but with a preceding dot *(2.10)*.)

olwm automatically looks for a file called *.openwin-menu* in your home directory, and only reads the systemwide *$OPENWINHOME/lib/openwin-menu* if it can't find one in your home directory. So if you make changes to your new *$HOME/.openwin-menu* file, they should automatically take effect the next time you restart *olwm*.

Now, notice that the configuration files for the **Programs** and **Utilities** submenus are pointed to by the master *.openwin-menu* configuration file. So if you want to make changes to your **Programs** or **Utilities** configuration files, you need to make sure that you change the appropriate lines in *.openwin-menu*, or else it will continue to use the systemwide versions. Change the following lines:

```
"Programs" MENU          $OPENWINHOME/lib/openwin-menu-programs

"Utilities" MENU         $OPENWINHOME/lib/openwin-menu-utilities
```

to:

```
"Programs" MENU          $HOME/.openwin-menu-programs

"Utilities" MENU         $HOME/.openwin-menu-utilities
```

Now edit away to your heart's content. In Article 14.27 are some menu configuration examples that you might want to try out.

The word MENU must be followed by either a filename or by an inline menu. Each menu or submenu must begin with MENU and end with an END with a matching label. END may be followed by PIN to make the menu pinnable. For example your *.openwin-menu* might contain this:

```
...
"Programs" MENU          $HOME/lib/.openwin-menu-programs
"Neat Stuff" MENU
   "Change Focus Policy"  FLIPFOCUS
   "Change Drag Policy"   FLIPDRAG
   "Aviator"              aviator
"Neat Stuff" END  PIN
"Utilities" MENU         $HOME/lib/.openwin-menu-utilities
...
```

If your menu file is huge, it can be hard to spot errors. *olwm* is pretty good at reporting many errors:

```
olwm: menu label mismatch in file /home/darian/ian/.openwin-menu, line 104
```

But make changes one at a time and keep track of your changes. Why? Because if you make a mistake, and your menu is incorrect, *olwm* may just ignore the menu file completely and use the system file. (Administrators: don't ever tamper with the system copy!) It's always easier to make changes in small doses so you can easily back up and see what you did wrong.

—LM, IFD

14.27 *Example Menu Configurations*

As an example of a simple change, if you'd prefer to start *xterm* instead of *cmdtool* from the **Programs** menu, change the line

```
"Command Tool..." DEFAULT exec $OPENWINHOME/bin/cmdtool
```

to these two lines:

```
"Xterm..." DEFAULT        exec xterm
"Command Tool..."         exec $OPENWINHOME/bin/cmdtool
```

The DEFAULT keyword is optional, but useful: it specifies what menu item will be selected when you click the first mouse button on the parent menu *(14.06)* (in this case, on the word **Programs** in the top-level **Workspace** menu). The word *exec (21.10)* is used for optimization. A copy of the UNIX shell is used to interpret the string that is given as the command, and the *exec* prevents this extra shell from sticking around waiting for the application (*xterm*, for example) to terminate.

As another example, if you get tired of the "Please confirm exit from window system" prompt, you can suppress it by changing:

```
"Exit" EXIT
```

to

```
"Exit!" EXIT_NO_CONFIRM
```

You can also just keep both commands available. The latter will exit without confirming.

Changing the Workspace Menu

Your changes aren't restricted to the **Programs** menu. You may not like the default **Workspace** menu, so another thing you can do is completely redefine it. My own **Workspace** menu looks like Figure 14-12.

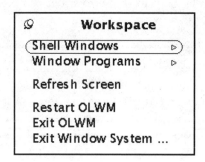

Figure 14-12: Ian's Workspace menu

The menu is defined in my *.openwin-menu* file like this:

```
# Sample Sun OLWM startup menu. The .openwin-menu file lets you
# change only the root menu (not the window menu). Many other things
# can be set by X Resources.
```

```
# The sub-menus must all exist (use touch(1) to create missing ones),
# or a simple dumb fallback menu will be used.

# Prepared by Ian Darwin, Learning Tree author/instructor.

"Workspace"              TITLE

"Lock Screen"            xlock -mode life

"Local Windows"          MENU  lib/owmenu-local

"Company-Ether Logins"   MENU  lib/owmenu-co

"Internet Logins"        MENU  lib/owmenu-in

"Desk Accessories"       MENU  lib/owmenu-deskacc

"Editors"                MENU  lib/owmenu-editors

"Games"                  MENU  lib/owmenu-games

"OpenWin Demos"          MENU  lib/openwin-menu-demo

"OpenWin Utilities"      MENU  lib/openwin-menu-utilities

# "Flip Focus Policy"    FLIPFOCUS

"Refresh Screen"         REFRESH

"Terminations"           MENU  lib/owmenu-terminate

"Workspace"              END PIN
```

Except for **Lock Screen** and **Refresh Screen**, all the items in my **Workspace** menu are pull-down menus. For example, the **Internet Logins** submenu lets me log in at any of several remote hosts. That menu is installed into a *lib* subdirectory of my home directory (*/home/darian/lib*), under the name *owmenu-in*, and it reads like this:

```
"Internet Logins"TITLE
        "ora.com"        xterm -T ora    -e rlogin gw -l myacct@ruby.ora.com
        "xyzzy.com"      xterm -T ora    -e rlogin gw -l ian@xyzzy.com
        SEPARATOR
        "FTP-GW" xterm -T FTP-GW  -e ftp gw
        "RLOGIN-GW"      xterm -T RLOGIN-GW -e rlogin gw
        "TN-GW"          xterm -T TN-GW   -e telnet gw
"Internet Logins"        END PIN
```

There is no limit to what you can put in this file.

—*IFD*

14.28 Finding the Menu Configuration Files

In addition to making sure that your search path *(2.05)* is set to include Open-Windows programs, there are a few other environment variables that you need to know about in using *olwm*.

The most important environment variable for OpenWindows is OPENWIN-HOME, which contains the root directory for your system's OpenWindows distribution. For Sun installations, OPENWINHOME should be set to */usr/openwin*. Many OpenWindows programs (such as *props (14.14)*) will give you an error message if you don't have OPENWINHOME set.

olwm itself will not give you an error message if OPENWINHOME isn't set properly, but it will behave differently. In particular, it won't find its default configuration files for its menus, so it will fall back on a "minimal" menu configuration. So if you are surprised by a different root menu from the one shown in our examples, it may be because OPENWINHOME is not defined. Running *olwm* without OPENWINHOME results in the nonstandard **Workspace** menu shown in Figure 14-13.

Figure 14-13: The fallback Workspace menu

See Articles 2.04 and 2.06 for information on how to set environment variables for OpenWindows.

Another environment variable that is used by *olwm* is OLWMMENU. Usually, *olwm* looks for a file in your home directory called *.openwin-menu*, then for the systemwide *openwin-menu*, and then finally the fallback shown above. However, you can use OLWMMENU to point to yet another configuration file, which overrides everything else. This comes in useful if you're testing a new **Workspace** menu but don't want to risk completely destroying your old one. It's also useful if you need to start *olwm* from some directory other than your home directory as some versions only look for the *.openwin-menu* in your current directory.

—LM

14.29 OPEN LOOK: Summary and Future

OPEN LOOK has some good features not in Motif, and many of these are being added to Motif as part of the Common Desktop Environment (CDE) *(1.05)*. But that still leaves some programs and some users as orphans. Or does it?

Not to worry: *olwm* and the XView toolkit will live forever, ensconced on tens of thousands of CD-ROMs and on LINUX and other publicly available distributions.

And on the Sun platform, expect to see XView maintained (and OLIT too) for a long time. Possibly even "as long as we ship X Windows," one Sun person was heard to say.

—IFD

15

The fvwm Window Manager

15.01 Now Playing on the Big Screen

How would you like several times the space of your current screen and the means to manage it all coherently? The user-contributed *fvwm* window manager provides just that.

fvwm

fvwm is built on a *twm (12.01)* foundation and some operations are clearly similar; *fvwm*'s window decorations and menus are somewhat reminiscent of Motif, though it is not quite as configurable as *mwm (13.01)*. But *fvwm* provides virtual screen power, in the form of multiple parallel desktops, that neither of the other window managers has yet incorporated. (The *tvtwm* window manager *(12.10)* offers *twm* with a single virtual desktop.)

Robert Nation, who developed *fvwm* from Tom LaStrange's *twm* code, claims he can't remember what the *fv* stands for. Maybe he can't, maybe he's protecting the guilty. Whatever. I like to think the letters mean "For Val."

— *VQ*

15.02 A Quick Tour of the fvwm Environment

The default *fvwm* environment is actually four environments, or desktops, in one. You might use different desktops for different projects or for different applications, whatever you like. You're also not stuck with four desktops. You can specify any number of desktops *(15.17)* you want (within reason). Personally, I find four desktops unnecessary; I'm happy with one or two.

The concept of multiple parallel desktops is the first one that you need to understand in order to work with *fvwm*. The second important concept is that each one of these desktops can be larger than the area of your screen. In the default *fvwm* environment, each desktop is actually the size of four adjacent virtual screens! These virtual screens, or "pages," are arranged two by two.

The number of pages in a desktop *(15.17)* is also configurable. In the default setup, there are 16 pages total, four on each desktop.

Of course, you can only look at one page/screenful at a time, but you can switch easily among these pages, run applications on each, and move applications between them. If you refer to a particular window all the time, you can even arrange for it to appear on every page of every desktop *(15.20)*. And you're not limited to viewing a page proper or keeping a window entirely on a single page.

How do you navigate such a large space? *fvwm* provides several ways (described in Article 15.04). The simplest way to navigate within a single desktop is just to move the pointer. When you first run *fvwm*, the pointer is in the first logical page—the upper-left one of a 2×2 page area. You can get to another page by moving the pointer off the current page, in whatever direction is logical. For example, from the first page, you switch to the next page to the right by moving the pointer off the right edge of the screen. Switch to the next page down by moving the pointer off the bottom edge. Once you get to the second column of pages, you won't be able to move the pointer any farther to the right: you cannot move the pointer from one desktop to another.

At startup, the default *fvwm* puts on a bit of a show, displaying a colorful pixmap of the letters "fvwm" on the root window and a large banner ("FVWM") in the center of the screen. Both announce, in effect, that *fvwm* is open for business. (I get the feeling it would sing "Hello, Dolly!" if it could.) If your system is configured differently, or you don't have the required system resources, you'll miss this production. The window manager also runs some *xterm* windows: one very large window that extends beyond the bottom edge of the first screen page and a standard-size window on top of the first.

When you restart the window manager, the fanfare is toned down, with a solid color root window background, no banner, and no additional windows. You can change what happens at startup and restart by editing the sections titled InitFunction and RestartFunction in your *fvwmrc* file *(15.14)*. See Article 15.23 and the *fvwm* manpage for guidelines. (Of course, you can run any client processes you like in your system startup file *(2.09)*.)

To help you get around and also remember what's going on in various parts of the multiple desktops, *fvwm* provides a small window called the *pager*, which appears on every page. Figure 15-1 offers a close-up (twice the actual size).

Think of the pager as a tiny mirror of your environment. The four headings correspond to the four desktops. The default headers (Misc, Maker, Mail, Matlab) are arbitrary; you can title your desktops anything you want.

Beneath each header, there are four partitions that correspond to the four virtual screen pages that compose each desktop, for a total of 16 pages. Each

Figure 15-1: The pager window mirrors the desktop and helps you navigate

application you run appears in miniature in the pager window. (The pager is not mirrored in itself, however.) Small windows like *xbiff* *(7.10)* and *xpostit* *(4.12)* will be fairly hard to spot in miniature, but a blip representing them is there if you look closely. The miniature version of a larger client, such as *xterm*, will even be labeled.

In the previous figure, the pager indicates that several *xterm* windows are running. The smaller blips represent icons and smaller clients. Since they're too small to be labeled, you'll have to remember what they are or be willing to go check. On the first desktop (labeled Misc), I remember that the tiny window in the first page on the second row is an *xcalc*. The tinier one in the upper-right corner of the same page is an icon. Notice that a window in the first desktop overlaps both the top-left and bottom-left pages. You're not limited to placing clients on a page proper, or viewing the screen in that way.

The title of the desktop you're working on will be highlighted by a different color in the pager; the same color will highlight the screen page you're on. The active window (or focus window) appears in a unique color. (A miniature application window is the same color as the border of the actual window.) In our figure, the active desktop is the first one, the active page is the upper-left one on that desktop, and the active window is the *xterm* in the center of that page.

If you move, resize, iconify, or otherwise alter a window, the corresponding miniature will be changed in the same way. Likewise, you can move the miniature versions and the actual windows will be moved. The pager is more than a mirror, it's also a tool. It can help you move windows between pages and desktops *(15.09)* and also select the screen area to be displayed on your monitor (Article 15.04).

In the *fvwm* environment, the pager is what is known as a "sticky" window. It is, in effect, stuck to the desktop, so that it appears on every virtual screen (in this case, in the lower-right corner). You can designate any number of the windows you run as sticky, using the Window Ops menu *(15.12)*, one of three root menus *fvwm* provides; or you can set up *fvwm* to make certain windows stick automatically *(15.20)*. A sticky window is distinguished from a window that appears on only one screen partition by a different border color. However, some sticky windows (including the pager) have their borders suppressed *(15.19)*, so you won't be able to rely on this feature. Note that sticky windows do not appear in the pager (so you won't see a pager within the pager).

In addition to the pager, *fvwm* provides one other default sticky window, known as GoodStuff. GoodStuff is sort of a menu of window manager functions in graphic form. In the latest incarnation of *fvwm*, the pager window has been incorporated into GoodStuff, in the lower-right corner of the GoodStuff window. (The combination GoodStuff/pager window appears on every virtual screen page.) The process of incorporating an application into the GoodStuff is known as "swallowing." In addition to the pager, the default GoodStuff window provides seven command buttons to perform window manipulations, run additional clients, and set environment characteristics. It also "swallows" an *xclock (3.02)*, which runs in miniature next to the command buttons.

Figure 15-2 shows a GoodStuff window for my current environment. The layout of the GoodStuff matches system defaults; obviously, the organization of windows within the pager reflects my system.

Figure 15-2: GoodStuff window offers command buttons, clock, and pager

Figure 15-3 shows the first page of the first desktop in my *fvwm* environment. Notice the GoodStuff/pager window in the bottom right.

The pager and the GoodStuff are actually separate programs that *fvwm* makes use of. Check out Article 15.03 for more information about this modular organization. You can modify the GoodStuff offerings *(15.23)* by editing your *.fvwmrc* file *(15.14)*.

Other than the GoodStuff and the pager, the *fvwm* environment is pretty much what you make of it. Of course, in addition to the higher-level desktop management, *fvwm* also provides basic window management functions *(15.05)*, as well as three root menus (one of which is also available in slightly different form as a window menu). The Utilities menu *(15.11)* lets you start other applications, run *fvwm* modules *(15.03)*, such as the GoodStuff, and stop and start various window managers. The WindowOps menu *(15.12)* provides a menu interface

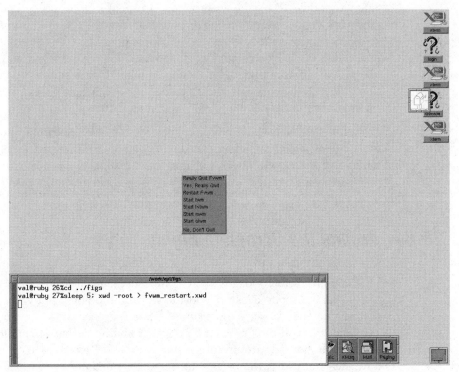

Figure 15-3: A typical virtual screen page under fvwm

to most of the standard window manager functions; slightly different versions of this menu can be accessed from the root window and from any application window. The FvwmWinList menu *(15.13)* provides a few functions, the most interesting of which lets you select the focus window; you can also navigate the desktops and move windows in the process. The same functionality is available via a desktop window that is identical to the menu.

— VQ

15.03 A Modular Approach

fvwm has been designed to allow the interested programmer or programmer wannabe to devise new components, known to insiders as *modules*. The pager and the GoodStuff window *(15.02)* are both modules, as is the FvwmWinList *(15.13)*, though it is also incorporated into *fvwm* as a menu. A module is actually a separate program from *fvwm*, but works in concert with it, passing commands to be executed to the window manager. The Utilities menu *(15.11)* offers a **Modules** submenu from which you can start any of the default *fvwm* modules.

Since a module is a separate program, a user can write his or her own modules without adversely affecting *fvwm*. Note, however, that you must configure *fvwm* to start the module process; you cannot start one from the command line. Some modules are intended to be used for the entire session (the pager and GoodStuff windows come to mind), while others simply perform a function and exit (FvwmClean and FvwmSave). See Article 15.11 for instructions on invoking the default modules.

From the speed at which new modules seem to be appearing, there must be quite a few *fvwm* enthusiasts out there. If you're interested in developing a module of your own, check out the *fvwm* manpage; since modules are programs in their own right, most of them have their own manpages, too.

— VQ

15.04 *Around the Screen in Eighty Ways*

Not quite eighty, but there are many ways to navigate *fvwm*'s multiple desktops and the screen "pages" that compose them. The simplest way to get around on a discrete desktop is just to move the pointer, but you can also use the pager window *(15.02)*, the FvwmWinList *(15.13)*, as well as many keyboard accelerators. You can't move the pointer from one desktop to another, but the other three methods are useful for this purpose. Each navigation method has advantages and disadvantages, but the sheer number of them should accommodate users of all habits.

Moving the Pointer by Hand (Within a Single Desktop)

You can move the pointer all around any discrete *fvwm* desktop. When you cross over from one page to another—by crossing an edge or corner of the screen—your monitor displays the new page. You can move up, down, and diagonally. Moving the pointer is the old reliable way of getting around.

Navigating a desktop in this manner takes nothing more than a little elbow grease and some common sense. Here's a fact that may not be immediately obvious but that will become so with very little practice: you can only move the pointer where there is space in the current desktop. For example, if you're in the first screen page (top left), you can move to the right or down or even off the bottom right corner, but that's it. There is no page to the left or above so you can't move the pointer there.

Once you move the pointer around for a while, navigating in this way should become second nature. Suppose you want to get from the first screen page (top left) to the last (bottom right). You can move the pointer diagonally (crossing onto a new page at the corner); or you could move over to the right and then down; down and then over to the right; or along any route you want that will also get you there.

Now, you may wonder, with all this real estate, how do you keep track of where you are? And how do you avoid bumping into walls that don't give? The only reliable way is to check the pager.

Switching the View Using the Pager

The pager window appears in the bottom-right corner of every page as part of the GoodStuff *(15.02)* module *(15.07)*. The pager provides a look at all of the desktops in miniature. (See Article 15.02 for an illustration and overview of the pager.) You can tell which page is being displayed on the screen because the corresponding partition in the pager window is highlighted. Thus, the pager is a necessary touchstone for getting around using the pointer, accelerators, etc.

But the pager is also a navigation tool in its own right. You can switch to any page on any desktop simply by clicking the first pointer button on the corresponding partition in the pager. I get around using the pager much more than I do by the pointer method. Why? Because I get tired of dragging the pointer all over that huge space; why walk when you can fly. The pointer method is better only when switching between two adjacent screens.

The pager also allows you to display an area that doesn't correspond to a page proper. In other words, you can view a screenful composed of parts of adjacent pages. This can be useful when you want to keep an eye on something happening on one page, but you're working on another; it's also handy when a window straddles more than one page (see Article 15.09).

Think of the pager as sort of a telescope onto the desktop(s); you use the pager to focus on a part of any desktop, and the magnified image of that area is displayed on the screen. To focus on an area "between" pages on a single desktop, place the pointer in the pager window at the point you want to be the upper-left corner of the screen; then click the third button. The screen displays the area you've selected. To get back to a page proper, click the first button on the corresponding pager partition.

In addition to changing the portion of the desktop(s) displayed on the screen, the pager allows you to move windows around any desktop and between desktops. See Article 15.09 for instructions.

Scrolling the Page Using Keystrokes

If you don't want to use the pointer to get around the current desktop, you can switch the screen page displayed using the **CTRL** key and an arrow key from the keypad. The pointer stays in the same place on the screen, but the view changes. The commands are summarized in Table 15-1. (There are no default keys to change the view to a different desktop, but Article 15.16 shows you how to configure some.)

Table 15-1: Key Combinations to Change the Page

Key Combination	Moves View
CTRL, right arrow key	One page to the right
CTRL, left arrow key	One page to the left
CTRL, up arrow key	One page up
CTRL, down arrow key	One page down

If you only want to scroll the screen one-tenth of a page at a time, you use the Meta key instead of **CTRL**. Why would you want to scroll less than a full page? Generally, you would do this if you have windows straddling two or more pages, but you might just want to look at windows on two different pages at the same time.

Scrolling in these small increments can be a little disorienting initially. Keep in mind that when you use the right arrow key, for instance, you'll see more of the screen to the right, but that means that everything is shifting to the left! You'll have to give it a try to see what I mean. Remember that the highlighted region in the pager will show you the part of the screen you're viewing. Table 15-2 summarizes the commands.

Table 15-2: Key Combinations to Scroll One-Tenth of a Page

Key Combination	Moves View
Meta, right arrow key	One-tenth page to the right
Meta, left arrow key	One-tenth page to the left
Meta, up arrow key	One-tenth page up
Meta, down arrow key	One-tenth page down

Moving the Pointer with Keystrokes

fvwm offers an unusual method of navigation. You can actually move the pointer (within a single desktop) using keystrokes. This capability is great for someone who doesn't like to use a mouse. When you move the pointer within the current screen page, the view remains the same; if you're using pointer focus (see focus policy), you can change the focus window in this way. But you can also use keystrokes to move the pointer beyond the bounds of the current screen (staying within the same desktop); when you do, the view changes to that page.

There are two sets of keystrokes, to move the pointer one-tenth of a page and one percent of a page, respectively. (The latter set is obviously for hardcore mouse haters.) Table 15-3 lists the first set.

Table 15-3: Key Combinations to Move the Pointer One-Tenth of a Page

Key Combination	Moves Pointer
Meta, **Shift**, right arrow key	One-tenth of a page to the right
Meta, **Shift**, left arrow key	One-tenth page of a to the left
Meta, **Shift**, up arrow key	One-tenth of a page up
Meta, **Shift**, down arrow key	One-tenth of a page down

Table 15-4 lists the keystrokes to move the pointer just a touch. (It takes one hundred actions to get across a single page.)

Table 15-4: Key Combinations to Move the Pointer One Percent(!) of a Page

Key Combination	Moves Pointer
CTRL, **Shift**, right arrow key	One percent of a page to the right
CTRL, **Shift**, left arrow key	One percent of a page to the left
CTRL, **Shift**, up arrow key	One percent of a page up
CTRL, **Shift**, down arrow key	One percent of a page down

Other Methods

The FvwmWinList module *(15.13)* provides yet another way to get around a single desktop and also to hop between desktops, but not the most intuitive way.

— VQ

15.05 *Basic Window Management Functions Using the Pointer*

fvwm was developed partly from *twm (12.01)* source code and it provides window decoration similar in appearance to Motif frames, but *fvwm* operates a bit differently than both of these window managers. Let's take a look at *fvwm*'s window decoration and some of the basic operations you can perform using the pointer.

The decoration *fvwm* provides begs to be called a frame, but it's actually called a border. And if you want to get technical about it, the border is composed of a titlebar, command buttons, four "sidebars," and four corner sections. To confuse matters further, the corner sections are collectively known as "the frame." The components are labeled in Figure 15-4.

As you've probably noticed, not all windows running under *fvwm* have this much decoration. The GoodStuff and pager windows have no window decoration at all. If you run an *xbiff (7.10)* window in the default environment, you'll find it has only a simple border, without either a titlebar or command buttons. The amount of decoration *(15.19)* is specified in the *.fvwmrc* file *(15.14)*.

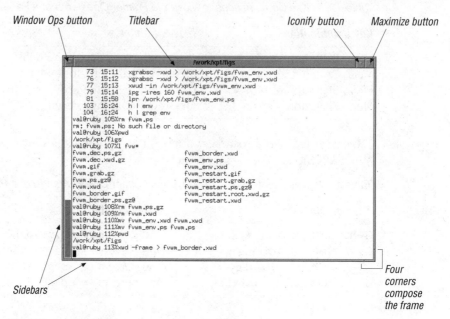

Window Ops button   *Titlebar*   *Iconify button*   *Maximize button*

Sidebars

Four corners compose the frame

Figure 15-4: The fvwm border

You can perform most basic window management functions by using the pointer on parts of the window border. Obviously, the border with titlebar offers more options. Table 15-5 summarizes the actions you can perform on a window (and its icon) using the pointer. For keyboard accelerators for most functions, see Article 15.06.

Table 15-5: Pointer Commands to Manage Windows and Icons

Function	Pointer Location	Action
Move	Titlebar or sidebar	First pointer button down, drag, release
Move	Icon	First pointer button down, drag, release
Raise	Any part of border except command buttons	First or third pointer button click
Raise	Icon	First or third pointer button click
Lower	Any part of border except command buttons	Third pointer button click
Lower	Icon	Third pointer button click

Table 15-5: Pointer Commands to Manage Windows and Icons (continued)

Function	Pointer Location	Action
Resize	"Frame" (i.e., corners)	First pointer button down, drag corner, release
Iconify	Iconify command button	Any pointer button click
Deiconify	Icon	Second pointer button click
Maximize vertically	Maximize command button	Any pointer button click
Window Ops menu	**Window Ops** command button	Any pointer button click
Window Ops menu	Any part of border except command buttons	Press second pointer button.

— VQ

15.06 *Keyboard Shortcuts for Window Management Functions*

If you'd prefer to rely on the keyboard rather than the mouse, all of the standard window management functions can be performed using keyboard accelerators, which are summarized in Table 15-6.

Table 15-6: Keyboard Accelerators

Function	Pointer Location	Action
Iconify	Window	Meta-F4
Move	Window or icon	Meta-F5, move pointer, click any button
Resize	Window	Meta-F6, move pointer to change border or corner, click any button
Utilities menu	Anywhere	Meta-F1
Window Ops menu	Anywhere	Meta-F2
CurrentDesk menu	Anywhere	Meta-F3
CirculateUp	Anywhere	Meta-F7
CirculateDown	Anywhere	Meta-F8

Once you begin a move or resize operation using Meta and a function key, you can complete it by moving the pointer (by hand or by keystrokes). Article 15.04 describes keyboard shortcuts for scrolling the screen page and moving the pointer. If you want to learn all the different keyboard accelerators, it's possible to perform every window management function from the keyboard.

—VQ

15.07 *Starting Windows on Different Desktops*

Depending on how your environment is set up, you might be able to start a window and have it automatically show up on the current screen in a reasonable location; you may choose to specify the location yourself using the *–geometry* option *(17.10)*, or perhaps you place the new window on the current screen using the pointer. But whatever you're used to doing, virtual desktops put you in a whole new ballgame.

The default *fvwm* environment *(15.02)* provides four parallel desktops of four pages each. Of course, the number and size of desktops *(15.17)* is configurable. But if you're using multiple desktops, you'll want to know how to start applications on different ones, as well as on different screen pages within the current desktop *(15.08)*.

There are three ways to start an application on a desktop other than the current one. The first is the most low-tech: you can switch the view to another desk (using the pager *(15.04)* or keyboard accelerators *(15.16)* you define yourself). Then you can open an *xterm* on that page using the Utilities *(15.11)* menu. Once you have an *xterm* going, the desktop is at your disposal. You can run any additional programs you like from the *xterm* and the windows will appear on that desktop (and page).

The second way to open windows on another desktop is to specify in your *.fvwmrc* file *(15.14)* that certain programs will appear on certain desktops automatically when you run them. You do this using *fvwm*'s `Style` variable *(15.19)*, which takes several arguments that determine the appearance and behavior of a particular client (or window manager component). One of the valid arguments, called `StartsOnDesk`, determines the default desk on which to display the named client(s). For example, the following line specifies that any time you run *xmh (7.06)*, the window appears on desk number 2:

```
Style "xmh"    StartsOnDesk 2
```

(Since the desks are numbered beginning with 0, this is actually the third logical desk.) This syntax is especially useful if you tend to use different desktops for different purposes. Perhaps you always read news *(8.05)* on the fourth desktop (number 3):

```
Style "xrn"    StartsOnDesk 3
```

It's more difficult to use this syntax with a common program such as *xterm*. Chances are you don't want to start every new *xterm* on a particular desktop.

You can get around this problem by giving different names to different instances of the program *(20.04)* and then using the different names with Style. For example, you might have:

```
Style "bigxterm"  StartsOnDesk 0
Style "smallxterm"  StartsOnDesk 1
Style "personalxterm"  StartsOnDesk 2
```

Or whatever you like.

When you are dealing with multiple instances of the same program, you might actually be better off using the third syntax, which allows you to specify the desk on the client's command line. The syntax requires you to use the *–xrm* command-line option *(17.05)*, which many of the common clients accept. (If a program doesn't understand this option, you're stuck using one of the previous two methods.) The following command runs an *xterm* window on desk number 1 (the second logical desk):

```
val@ruby 152% xterm -xrm "*Desk: 1" &
```

Note that the Style syntax runs a window on the first page of the desk in question. When you use the *–xrm* syntax, the destination page is related to the page you're on when you run the command. The new window appears on the analogous page of the desktop you specify.

Article 15.08 explains how to start windows on different pages within the current desktop.

— VQ

15.08 Starting Windows on Different Pages on the Current Desktop

Within the current desktop, how do you run a window on a page other than the first? There are a few ways. You might begin by switching the view to another page (using the pointer, the pager, **CTRL** and an arrow key, or any of the methods described in Article 15.04). Then you can open an *xterm* on that page using the Utilities menu *(15.11)*. Once you have an *xterm* going, you can run other clients on that page.

As an alternative, from the original page you can run a window with a *–geometry* option *(17.10)* and supply large enough coordinates to place it on another page in the desktop. In my environment, I sometimes use desktops of three pages square *(15.17)*. The following line places a window in the middle page:

```
xterm -geometry +1200+1200 &
```

It isn't easy to gauge distances of this magnitude. To educate yourself, you can try various coordinates on the command line and see where the windows pop up on the pager window. Or you can scroll to other pages, open windows using the Utilities menu *(15.11)*, and then determine their geometries. Sort of an intelligent cheat. *xwininfo* *(17.13)* won't help; you'll get coordinates relative to the page. But if you move the window around a bit using the pointer, a small box in the upper-left corner of the page will give you the coordinates relative to the desktop.

—VQ

15.09 Moving Windows Between Pages and Between Desktops

Within a single desktop, how do you move a window from one screen page to another? There are three ways:

1. Drag the window off the current screen page using the pointer.

2. Use the FvwmWinList *(15.13)*.

3. Move the corresponding tiny rectangle in the pager.

If you're moving a window from a page on one desktop to a page on another desktop, you're limited to the second and third methods. You can't drag the window itself beyond the bounds of the current desktop. (Because of this limitation, you may even choose to configure *fvwm* to provide a single, large desktop *(15.17)*.)

The first method is just an extension of a simple window manager move operation. You move the window in the regular fashion, but you keep going off the screen. Hold the first pointer button down anywhere on the window's border (the basic move operation), and drag the window outline off the edge of the current screen page.

When the pointer enters the next page, the view will switch to that page. You can drag the window in this manner across the entire desktop, but not beyond the current desktop. (The image in the pager will track the motion.) Release the pointer button to redraw the window in the new location.

Can you move a window so that it straddles two or more pages in a single desktop? Sure. Why you would want to is another question, but if you do, the pager allows you to switch the view to any screenful on a desktop, regardless of whether it coincides with a page. See Article 15.04 for instructions. (Note, however, that you cannot place a window or the view so that it overlaps two adjacent desktops; the portion that extends beyond the current desktop will be obscured.)

Among its various functions, the FvwmWinList provides a couple of methods for moving windows among pages and desktops. However, without giving distinctive titles to your application windows *(17.09)*, attempting to move them with the FvwmWinList can be confusing. See Article 15.13 to judge for yourself.

The third method of moving a window (from within the pager) is considerably more intuitive. It also offers more power than the first method, since you can cross from one desktop to another, and more precise control than the second method, since you're moving the window by hand. However, for shorter moves, the first method is the most precise. More about that later.

To move a window from within the pager, press the second pointer button on the small rectangle that represents the window. Then drag the image anywhere on the pager's desktop(s) and release in the location you want. The window is moved to the new location. You can move a window onto a page or let it intersect multiple pages in the same desktop; you can also move it to a different desktop.

Unlike the first method in which the view follows the window, a move operation using the pager can happen fairly invisibly. You always see the corresponding rectangle in the pager move, but that may be it. The view remains on the current screen. You see the actual window move only when it's on, or when it crosses, the current screen.

The pager method of moving windows is mainly useful for reorganizing the various desktops. It's also more suitable for longer moves. Though hypothetically you can use the pager to move a window around on a single screen page, the small scale of the pager makes it impossible to do this precisely.

If you try moving a window on the current screen using the pager, you'll find the move seems more like a jump—or a hiccup. For short moves, you're much better off dragging the window by the (first) pointer method. Even when you use the pager to move windows a long distance, you'll probably want to make fine adjustments using the pointer.

—VQ

15.10 GoodStuff

A sneak preview before we examine the GoodStuff window: If you have buttons labeled "Dopey," "Grumpy," and/or "Snoopy," don't bother pushing them, OK? I know it's tempting. More about this later.

The (unlabeled) window in the lower-right corner of every screen page is called GoodStuff. It provides several command buttons with spiffy pixmap labels, which perform window management operations, start other applications, and (in one case) configure the environment. The GoodStuff also incorporates (or *swallows*) the pager window *(15.02)*, which you can use to track what's going on in your environment, switch the portion of the desktop currently on screen, and move windows around.

The default GoodStuff window appears in Figure 15-5.

Figure 15-5: The default GoodStuff window

You can see the pager in the lower-right corner of the GoodStuff window. There are four headers to match the four default desktops.

The Kill button, in the upper-left corner of the GoodStuff, will give you a dot cursor that you can click on a window to zap it out of existence *(2.08)*. Use with caution. (The Kill button is analogous to the Destroy item on the Window Ops menu *(15.12)*.) If you can exit a window in a gentler way, it's not a bad idea. (The Window Ops menu Close item is kinder to underlying processes.)

At the risk of appearing heartless, I have to let you in on a little secret: Dopey, Grumpy, and Snoopy are dummies. By default, these buttons run remote *xterm*s (specifically the *rxterm* client) on dummy systems called—you guessed it—*dopey*, *grumpy*, and *snoopy*. In earlier releases of *fvwm*, if you selected one of these buttons and no one had customized them to reach actual sites, you could hang *fvwm*.

The latest and greatest *system.fvwmrc* file (15.14) (as of this printing, anyway) circumvents this problem by redirecting the commands to */dev/null*. Now, if you push one of those buttons, it will stay pushed and you may get an error message like:

```
grumpy: unknown host
```

(which sounds like a nerd title for Agatha Christie's *Ten Little Indians*), but no actual harm is done. If you do want to set up buttons to run remote terminal windows, make sure your system has *rxterm* or use an equivalent.

The Xcalc *(5.05)* button runs that program. The mail button runs *xmh (7.06)*. (You can also run *xcalc* from the Utilities menu *(15.11)*, which provides access to other clients as well.) Every system should have these clients.

The Paging button toggles whether or not you can scroll the pointer off the current page. Article 15.21 tells you all about it.

But my favorite part of the default GoodStuff window is the teeny-weeny *xclock (3.02)*, which appears between the Paging button and the pager window.

It may look like a clock icon, but it actually works. Besides being terribly cute, the mini-clock also saves me from having an *xclock* clutter my display.

The *xclock* button is analogous to the pager in that it's an entirely separate application that is incorporated into the GoodStuff using a function called Swallow. So, technically speaking, it isn't a button at all, but simply an *xclock* in miniature. (If you click on the clock button, you'll see that it can't be pushed.) The *system.fvwmrc* arranges this neat trick with the line:

```
*GoodStuff - clock.xpm Swallow "xclock" xclock -bg #908090 \
                     -geometry -1500-1 500 -padding 0
```

The hyphen appears in place of a text label, which is unnecessary in this case. The *clock.xpm* is the pixmap that decorates the button. Following Swallow is the name of the application (xclock), followed by the actual command line. (Since the pager is not a typical application, but an *fvwm* module *(15.03)*, it is incorporated using the function SwallowModule.)

You can edit the GoodStuff definition just as you would a menu definition. Article 15.23 examines the syntax and offers some tips, including a typical solution to the Dopey-Grumpy-Snoopy problem. For further information, see the *fvwm* manpage and the manpages of the relevant modules.

— *VQ*

15.11 *Utilities Menu: Start Clients and Other Window Managers*

If you hold the first pointer button down on the root window, you'll display the Utilities menu, which appears in Figure 15-6.

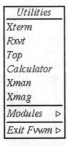

Figure 15-6: fvwm's Utilities menu

You can select Xterm *(11.01)*, Xman *(5.02)*, or Xmag *(25.05)* to run those programs. Calculator runs *xcalc (5.05)*. (You can also run *xcalc* from the GoodStuff window.)

When you display the menu by holding down the first pointer button, you drag the pointer down the menu and release to select the item you want.

Note, however, that you can also post the **Utilities** menu and keep it posted by typing Meta and the **F1** function key. While the menu is posted in this way, you can select an item either using the pointer or using the down arrow key to highlight an item and then hitting **Return**. Remove the menu without making a selection by clicking elsewhere or by hitting the **Escape** key.

Rxvt and **Top** won't work unless the *rxvt* terminal emulator is available on your system. Both of these menu items run this client; **Top** does so with a *–top* option. If you select either of these menu items and *rxvt* is not in your path, odds are you'll get an error message. (In earlier releases, it was possible to freeze the window manager in this way. I actually managed to crash my machine at the same time.)

The arrow symbols to the right of **Modules** and **Exit Fvwm** indicate that these items access submenus. If you release the pointer on **Modules**, you post a submenu with the same title (see Figure 15-7), which offers access to a variety of *fvwm* component programs, or modules *(15.03)*.

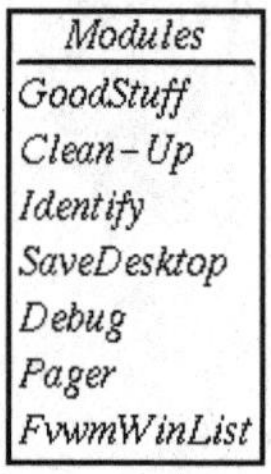

Figure 15-7: The Modules menu lets you initialize various fvwm module programs

The most important modules are the pager *(15.02)*, GoodStuff *(15.02)*, and FvwmWinList *(15.13)*.

While most environments provide a GoodStuff window that has swallowed *(15.10)* a pager on every screen page, you can use the menu to call them up if your system is configured differently.

The FvwmWinList is unique among the modules in that it is implemented both as one of the default menus and as a window proper. You call up the window version using the **Modules** submenu. By default, the FvwmWinList window appears in the lower-left corner of each screen page.

The downside of menu access to the window-based modules is that you can inadvertently run multiple instances of the same module. For example, if you select the **GoodStuff** item, you get another **GoodStuff** window, right on top of the default one (presuming you haven't moved it). This menu item is not a toggle, so selecting it again won't get rid of your duplicate window; it will add yet another one to the pile! This does no particular harm, but it is a waste of system resources. Keep in mind that you can remove an unwanted module window by using the **Close** item on the Window Ops menu *(15.12)*.

The other modules available on the **Modules** submenu are somewhat less useful. The **Clean-Up** item invokes the FvwmClean module, which iconifies windows you haven't used in a while so the desktop is less cluttered. **Identify** invokes the FvwmIdentify module, which lets you select a window about which to display some basic information, similar to that provided by *xwininfo* *(17.13)*. Click on the information window to pop it down.

Save Desktop starts the FvwmSave module, which attempts to create a session startup file *(2.09)* that will recreate your current window layout. It saves this file as *new.xinitrc* in your home directory. You may need a considerable amount of editing to really use the file (not to mention renaming the file itself), but the information you can gather from it about the clients you're running is somewhat interesting.

Only the serious programmer should consider selecting **Debug** (invoking the FvwmDebug module), which may give you far more information about the inner workings of *fvwm* than you bargained for. Note that the online source for the *fvwm* modules includes a manpage for each.

Now back to the **Utilities** menu. Selecting the ominous sounding **Exit Fvwm** item doesn't bump you out of the window manager, as you might imagine. If you release the pointer on **Exit Fvwm**, you post a submenu titled **Really Quit Fvwm?**, which makes sure you know what you're doing and offers several alternatives. You can quit, restart *fvwm*, start another window manager, or cancel the operation altogether. The menu appears in Figure 15-8.

Figure 15-8: The Really Quit Fvwm? menu provides a safety net

A few caveats: in some earlier releases of *fvwm*, if you try to start another window manager and it's not available on your system, you may hang *fvwm*. This problem should not occur in the latest version. Another issue: if you do start another window manager and it doesn't know anything about virtual screens, the windows scattered around any of the *fvwm* desktops will end up in strange and unusual positions, some on and some hanging way off the suddenly truncated screen. Some may be out of sight altogether. So, as a rule of thumb, it's a good idea to consolidate onto the first page of the first desktop before starting another window manager.

If you quit *fvwm*, all the windows scattered among the virtual screens will suddenly be crammed onto one. This shouldn't be a great problem for your system (unless you're a real window freak), but it can cause an awful, confusing mess. (This cramming effect also happens during a restart, but the windows are sorted out when *fvwm* comes up again.)

It's simple to change the Utilities menu by editing your *.fvwmrc* file. Article 15.23 describes how to edit menu definitions. Of course, whenever you make changes to the window manager startup file, you need to restart the program in order to activate the changes. You should be able to use the Utilities menu to do this. See Article 15.14 for contingency plans.

— VQ

15.12 The Ubiquitous Window Ops Menu

If you hold the second pointer button down on the root window, you display a menu of items that help you perform window management functions. You can display virtually the same menu (with one item replacing another and less the (Un)Maximize item) on various parts of a window's border. The longer version of the so-called Window Ops menu appears in Figure 15-9.

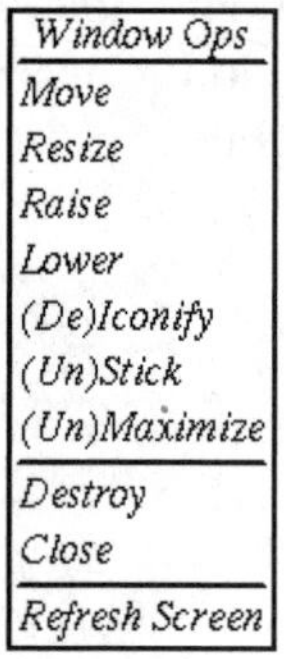

Window Ops
Move
Resize
Raise
Lower
(De)Iconify
(Un)Stick
(Un)Maximize
Destroy
Close
Refresh Screen

Figure 15-9: The Window Ops menu has some common and uncommon functions

Many of the functions on the Window Ops menu can also be performed simply by using the pointer on various parts of a window's border (or on an icon). The menu is a useful fallback for move, raise, lower, resize, iconify, and maximize functions that are difficult to perform using the pointer because the titlebar is obscured or the ultra-thin border is tough to get a handle on.

For instance, suppose you want to move a window whose titlebar is buried. You *can* press the first pointer button on any part of the border, but the border is very narrow and it's no party to grab. As an alternative, you might select

Move from the Window Ops menu. Then you can place the resulting dot cursor on any part of the window, press the first pointer, drag the outline, and release.

When you display the menu by holding down the second pointer button, you drag the pointer down the menu and release to select the item you want. Note, however, that you can also post the Window Ops menu and keep it posted by typing Meta and the F2 function key. While the menu is posted in this way, you can select an item either using the pointer or using the down arrow key to highlight an item and then hitting Return. Unpost the menu without making a selection by clicking elsewhere or by hitting the Escape key.

In addition to these standard functions, the Window Ops menu also offers some less common, highly useful functions. The most interesting of these items is (Un)Stick, which lets you toggle a window to be sticky or unsticky. As Article 15.02 explains, a sticky window is one that appears on every screen page. The combined GoodStuff/pager window is sticky by default. You can make a window follow you around temporarily by selecting (Un)Stick and then clicking on the window. Follow the same procedure to unstick the window.

The (Un)Maximize item is a toggle between a window maximized vertically toward the top of the screen page and its default size. *fvwm* is the only window manager discussed in this book that provides this vertical type of maximizing among its default powers, and it's actually fairly useful. (Note, however, that you can customize *twm* to do the same thing. See Article 12.19 for more information.) I often find myself in need of a longer *xterm* in which to write. Here I can have one in an instant. The maximize button on the titlebar performs the same function.

The Window Ops menu is also useful for removing unwanted windows. The Close item removes them in a gentle way; Destroy is predictably more brutal. See Article 2.08 for a discussion of the liabilities of killing a client.

The final item on the (unabridged) Window Ops menu is Refresh Screen, which lets you redraw the screen and remove any error messages, etc., that might be obscuring it. Article 6.13 describes another method, while Article 27.02 shows you how to avoid the problem altogether in certain environments.

You can display a slightly different Window Ops menu from any application window. In the window version, an item called ScrollBar replaces Refresh Screen. The ScrollBar item places the application window inside a special viewing window, complete with scrollbars. If you're running a larger application, your window may be severely truncated to fit into the viewing window. Since most decent applications provide ways for you to scroll, I've found this item to be virtually useless.

The easiest way to post the **Window Ops** menu on a window is to hold any pointer button down on the command button in the upper-left corner of the titlebar, as in Figure 15-10. Notice how the button appears to be pressed in.

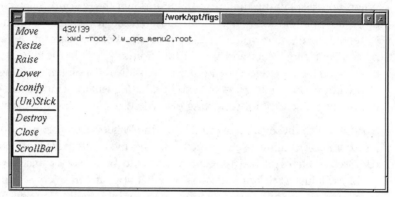

Figure 15-10: *Window Ops menu displayed from a window*

When you display the **Window Ops** menu from a window, the items operate slightly differently than when you display it from the root window. From the root window, when you select an item, you then always need to choose a window to act on. If you post the menu on a window, all commands apply immediately to that window.

You can also display the menu on a window by holding down the second pointer button on the titlebar or on a sidebar. When you post from a sidebar, notice that the pointer rests on the **Move** item. To unpost the menu without making a selection, you need to take the pointer off all choices before releasing. It's easy to call up a **Move** by mistake; just click again without moving the pointer to escape.

For the purposes of customization, the *.fvwmrc* file *(15.14)* refers to the root version of this menu as **Window Ops** and the window version as **Window Ops2**. Article 15.23 gives some tips on changing menu definitions.

— *VQ*

15.13 *The FvwmWinList: Switching the Focus*

The FvwmWinList is an *fvwm* module *(15.03)*, but you can access it in two ways: as one of the default root window menus. and as a window proper, via the **Modules** submenu of the Utilities menu *(15.11)*.

The FvwmWinList is a somewhat confusing tool. It allows you to switch the focus window, and also navigate the desktops and move windows in the process, but in a somewhat oblique way. (I prefer using the pager *(15.02)* to get around; that tool does not select a focus window, however.) The FvwmWinList also lets you iconify and deiconify windows around the desktops, without being on the same page.

When you hold the third pointer button down on the root window, the menu version is displayed, as in Figure 15-11. (The keystroke combination of Meta and the **F3** function key also posts this menu.)

Figure 15-11: The FvwmWinList details the current apps and helps you manage them

If you'd rather have the FvwmWinList appear as a sticky window *(15.02)* on each screen page, select it from the **Modules** submenu of the Utilities menu *(15.11)*. The window will appear in the lower-left corner of each screen.

Both incarnations of the FvwmWinList (the menu and the window) list all of the window-based applications you're currently running, with the exception of sticky windows. Since you're running different applications all the time, the contents are always changing. I find the list itself to be the module's most valuable feature. It helps me keep track of how many applications I'm running and may jog my memory about windows I haven't used for a while. (If you don't want to bother tracking this, you should be able to use the **Clean-Up** item on the **Utilities** menu to iconify neglected windows.)

The primary limitation is that it's somewhat difficult to tell which window in the list is which. Each entry in the FvwmWinList gives the text that appears in the corresponding window's titlebar (if the titlebar is suppressed, it gives the text that would normally appear). If a window is iconified, its FvwmWinList entry is surrounded by parentheses. Since there's a good chance you're running multiple instances of the same client, the titlebar text might not be enough to identify a particular window. If you become attached to the FvwmWinList, you might want to consider specifying different titles *(11.12)* for multiple instances of the same window. (One of the more useful variations is to specify the current directory in the titlebar.) With the number of windows I run, I would need to do this in order to use the FvwmWinList effectively.

In addition to information, the FvwmWinList provides some useful functions. Clicking the first pointer button on an entry in the FvwmWinList moves the input focus to the corresponding window. If that window appears on another desktop and/or page, the view is switched to that location. This action also raises the window to the front of the display.

If the FvwmWinList entry represents an iconified window, clicking with the first pointer button deiconifies it, transfers the focus to it, and raises it. The tricky (but also the neat) part is that the window is redisplayed on the page from which you make the request. Thus, you can use the FvwmWinList to move windows among the various desktops.

If you're using the default pointer focus, transferring the focus with the FvwmWinList causes the pointer to warp (or jump) to the corresponding window. If you've specified click-to-type focus *(15.15)*, the pointer stays in its current screen location, but the focus is transferred to the corresponding window.

Clicking the second pointer button on an FvwmWinList entry toggles the iconify/deiconify function for the corresponding window. You can tell if a window is iconified by the parentheses surrounding its FvwmWinList entry. When you iconify a window using the second pointer button, the icon stays on the same page the window was on, and the page currently viewed on the screen does not change. But when you deiconify a window on a different screen page (on any desktop), the deiconified window is moved to the current screen page. Voilà. If you extend your thinking about this, you'll realize that double-clicking the second pointer button on an entry that corresponds to an active window will move the window onto the current page (and give it the focus).

Pressing and releasing the third pointer button on an FvwmWinList entry displays a window containing information about the corresponding client. This is the same information that can be obtained using the **Identify** item on the **Modules** submenu of the Utilities menu *(15.11)*. Click on the information window to remove it.

The FvwmWinList has some fun features, particularly those that transfer the focus and move windows (and the view) around. But there are some limitations. First, it's easy to select the wrong window. Specifying different titles for your windows can help. Second, FvwmWinList is still under development. Until the code is more stable, you're liable to run into some bugs. If you're willing to organize your windows enough to use the FvwmWinList effectively, it's probably worth going up against the remaining bugs anyway.

You can change the behaviors of the various pointer buttons with FvwmWinList by editing the relevant lines in your *fvwmrc* file *(15.14)*. See the *system.fvwmrc* file, the *fvwm* and FvwmWinList manpages, and Article 15.23 for some guidelines.

— VQ

15.14 How Can I Change fvwm?

The operation of *fvwm* is largely controlled by a *system.fvwmrc* file. To modify *fvwm*, make a copy of this file and edit it in your home directory. Call your own file .*fvwrmc*.

The *system.fvwmrc* file is chatty in a very helpful way. It has lots of comments explaining what various lines mean and even gives tips on how to make certain customizations. The manpage provides additional information, as well as examples. Some of the more useful customizations are:

- Changing the number of desktops displayed in the pager and the number of pages per desktop (Article 15.17)

- Changing the focus policy *(15.15)*

- Placing new windows automatically *(15.22)*

- Raising the focus window automatically *(15.18)*

- Making a window appear on every virtual screen page *(15.20)*

- Defining keys to switch desktops *(15.16)*

- Limiting window decoration *(15.19)*

Whenever you edit your .*fvwmrc*, you need to restart the window manager in order to activate the changes. The easiest way to do this is to display the Utilities menu *(15.11)*, then select the Exit Fvwm submenu, which provides an item called Restart Fvwm. If menus are not an option, you can instead stop the window manager process and run it again.

— VQ

15.15 Selecting Click-to-Type Focus

By default, *fvwm* (like *twm*) works according to the pointer focus model. This means you need to move the pointer into a window in order to type in it, post an application menu, etc. However, *fvwm* is somewhat more versatile than *twm*[*] in this regard: you can change the focus policy to an explicit, or click-to-

---

[*] *twm* can mimic click-to-type focus for a single window at a time. See the Article "Keeping the Focus on One Window" (12.07).

type, model. The chatty *system.fvwmrc* walks you through this simple customization (as it does so many others):

```
# Normally, we'll be in focus-follows mouse mode, but uncomment this
# for mwm-style click-to-focus
#ClickToFocus
```

To change the focus to click-to-type, just delete the pound sign (#) comment symbol before ClickToFocus in your own *.fvwmrc* file *(15.14)* (assuming you've copied the *system.fvwmrc*) and restart the window manager.

There is a downside to using explicit focus with *fvwm*. If you like to move the pointer around using keystrokes *(15.04)*, you can't simply move it into a window and continue typing. You have to click before typing, which somewhat defeats the purpose of using keyboard accelerators to move the pointer in the first place.

—VQ

15.16 *Configuring Keys to Switch Between Desktops*

For some mysterious reason, the default *fvwm* does not provide keystrokes that allow you to switch from one desktop to another. (I imagine this support will be added in a not-too-distant release.) Currently, within a single desktop, you can easily switch between pages *(15.04)* using a number of methods. And you can switch between desktops using the pager *(15.04)* or the FvwmWinList *(15.13)*. But in order to hop between desktops using keyboard accelerators, you're going to have to add some lines to your *.fvwmrc* file *(15.14)* and restart the window manager.

Here are the key bindings I use in a four-desktop environment:

```
#SAMPLE KEYBOARD ACCELERATORS TO MOVE BETWEEN DESKTOPS
Key F11        A      N      Desk 0 0
Key F12        A      N      Desk 0 1
Key F13        A      N      Desk 0 2
Key F14        A      N      Desk 0 3
```

I've bound four function keys (having the keysyms F11 through F14 to the *fvwm* function Desk, which switches the view to the desktop identified by the numeric parameters following the function. The column following the keys specifies the *context*, that is, where the pointer has to be in order for the function to work. All of these accelerators specify a context of A for *any*. In other words, when you request the function, the pointer can rest anywhere on the screen. The next column specifies any necessary modifier keys (keys you need to use in combination with the initial key). I use N for *none*.

You can use the Desk function in either of two ways: to switch to a specific desktop or to switch to a desktop relative to the current one. I've chosen to use Desk in the former way. The numeric parameters following Desk determine what desk to switch to, but the syntax is a little confusing. Let's consider the syntax using the first binding I specified:

```
Key F11        A     N      Desk 0 0
```

This line maps the **F11** function key to switch to the first page. Why? Basically, when the first argument is 0, the second argument is the number of the desktop to switch to. The numbering scheme begins with 0 rather than 1, so the first desktop is 0 0, the second desktop is 0 1, the third is 0 2, etc.

When you have only one parameter after Desk and it's something other than 0, you're specifying a move relative to the current desk. Literally, the desktop you will be switching to will be the current desktop number plus the argument. You can also have a negative argument. For instance, you can map **F15** and **F16** to move to the next desktop and the previous desktop, respectively:

```
Key F15        A     N      Desk 1
Key F16        A     N      Desk -1
```

I don't use these relative commands myself because it's actually possible to advance beyond the desktops the pager displays *(15.17)*. You can run applications on these hidden desktops and the FvwmWinList *(15.13)* will know about them, but they'll be invisible to the pager. It's easy to forget about applications run outside the view the pager affords. Admittedly, however, it's a tempting place to play *spider (10.06)*.

— VQ

15.17 *But I Don't Need Four Desktops*

You can specify both the number of desktops the pager *(15.02)* displays and the number of pages per desktop in your *fvwmrc* file *(15.14)*. The default four desktops of four pages each are a little too much real estate even for me, and I'm a windowaholic.

Notice I said the "number of desktops the pager displays." That's because, technically speaking, multiple desktops exist, whether you display them in the pager or not. Thus, if you set up keyboard accelerators to move between desktops *(15.16)*, you can advance beyond the fourth desk. Keep in mind, however, that once you're outside the view of the pager, it's easy to lose track of applications. They will appear on the FvwmWinList *(15.13)*, but that might not be enough to really follow what you're doing. In any case, I avoid getting into this *fvwm* "Twilight Zone." How many desktops are hidden there? The manpage says up to four billion. I'm hoping the author used to work at McDonald's after school and is just a little confused.

So, you can't specify how many desktops exist, but you can specify how many appear in the pager. The default setup is determined by the lines:

```
*GoodStuff(4x1) - whatever SwallowModule "FvwmPager" FvwmPager 0 3

*FvwmPagerLabel 0 Misc
*FvwmPagerLabel 1 Maker
*FvwmPagerLabel 2 Mail
*FvwmPagerLabel 3 Matlab
```

The first line incorporates the pager into the GoodStuff window. The dimensions of the pager are given as 4x1 (which refer to the default layout of four parallel desktops). The 0 and 3 give the range of desktops visible. (The first desktop is number 0.)

In the subsequent lines, the first column contains the *fvwm* variable Fvwm-PagerLabel, which is used to specify a partition in the pager. The second column contains the number of the desktop. The third column contains the header you want to appear in the pager for the particular desktop. Misc, Maker, Mail, and Matlab are the (arbitrary) default headers. See Article 15.02 for an illustration.

Suppose you'd prefer two desktops, one for work and one for personal business (i.e., play). You might substitute the lines:

```
*GoodStuff(2x1) - whatever SwallowModule "FvwmPager" FvwmPager 0 1

*FvwmPagerLabel 0 Proj
*FvwmPagerLabel 1 Home
```

This works: The resulting GoodStuff window changes size to accommodate the pager's new layout. However, it suggests a minor complication that can arise because the pager is incorporated into the GoodStuff. If you experiment with the number of desktops (or with the other contents of the GoodStuff), you'll soon see that the GoodStuff window makes itself rectangular no matter what you put into it. Ideally, the various buttons and pager partitions should fit together in a reasonable way, as they do in the default arrangement. But if you radically change the size of the pager, the GoodStuff window may have to throw in some blank space to even itself out. Thus, if you redesign the pager, it's not a bad idea to edit the GoodStuff (15.23) to handle it.

Adjusting the variables GoodStuffRows, GoodStuffColumns, and GoodStuffGeometry can help as well. See the manpage and the *system.fvwmrc* file for guidelines. The default GoodStuff window has two rows and a geometry of -1-1. (You can specify either rows or columns, but not both.)

As an alternative, you can remove the pager window from the GoodStuff and run it as a separate module window. Once you specify the FvwmPagerLabels you want, comment out the line that swallows the pager into the GoodStuff by adding an initial pound sign (#). For instance:

```
#*GoodStuff(4x1) - whatever SwallowModule "FvwmPager" FvwmPager 0 3
```

Then make sure the pager is run as a separate window at startup and restart. You do this by adding the following line to the sections that begin InitFunction and RestartFunction.

```
Module "I"    FvwmPager
```

It's also a good idea to specify an alternate location (geometry) for either the pager or the GoodStuff because the default coordinates overlap. The following line will move the pager from its default lower-right corner (coordinates -1-1) to the lower-left corner:

```
*FvwmPagerGeometry +1-1
```

If you decide to leave the pager inside the GoodStuff, keep in mind another possible limitation: The pager has a smaller scale when it is swallowed into the GoodStuff than when it runs independently. Loosely speaking, the larger the area the pager has to cover, the less detail you'll see. This is another good reason to extricate the pager from the GoodStuff.

Now, what about the size of each desktop? You specify the size of the individual desktops using the variable DeskTopSize, followed by the dimensions in screen pages. (All desktops have to be the same size.) To be honest, the default 2×2 virtual screen pages per desktop is a little cramped for my style. I prefer:

```
DeskTopSize 3x3
```

Keep in mind that you're not limited to a square arrangement. For example, you could have three screens in one row:

```
DeskTopSize 3x1
```

Maybe you'd prefer a single large desktop. The following lines specify a desktop titled "TheBigScreen" composed of five screens square:

```
*FvwmPagerLabel 0 TheBigScreen
DeskTopSize 5x5
```

Of course, the larger the desktop, the harder it is to see the detail in the pager, particularly when it's part of the GoodStuff. It would be a good idea to run the pager separately from the GoodStuff in this case. "TheBigScreen" does not translate well to the little format the GoodStuff necessitates.

Of course, some people will be happy with the original layout they get.

—VQ

15.18 Raising the Focus Window Automatically

fvwm can't be configured to raise when you click on a window proper; you're limited to clicking on the border to raise. Since the border is so thin (with the exception of the titlebar) and the titlebar can be obscured, this limitation can make raising a window a bit of a pain.

I've simplified matters in my environment by specifying (in my *.fvwmrc* file) that a window be raised automatically when it becomes the focus window. The AutoRaise variable causes the focus window to be raised automatically after so many milliseconds, 750 in this case, a value the *system.fvmrc* file recommends:

```
AutoRaise 750
```

(That's three-quarters of a second to metric-resistant types like me.) The delay is important and makes the AutoRaise feature much more practical, especially in combination with the default pointer focus. Generally, when pointer focus is in effect, an auto-raise feature can make the display seem chaotic: when you move the pointer across the screen, the focus hits several windows and they are each raised in a distracting shuffle. With an auto-raise delay, you can avoid the shuffling by moving the pointer quickly to the window you want to focus on. Give it a try. (Don't forget to restart the window manager after editing your *.fvwmrc* file.)

Of course, those who can adapt to using the FvwmWinList module *(15.13)* to transfer focus will have their windows raised automatically, without having to edit *.fvwmrc.* But I'd rather not be dependent on the FvwmWinList myself.

— *VQ*

15.19 Modifying Window Manager Decoration

The default *.fvwmrc* file includes several lines that define the appearance and behavior of various *fvwm* components and some common clients. These lines all employ the variable Style, followed by the name of the module or client, and then by one or more parameters. For instance, the following line sets the decoration and also determines certain behaviors for the GoodStuff window *(15.02)*:

```
Style "GoodStuff" NoTitle, NoHandles, Sticky, WindowListSkip, BorderWidth 0
```

NoTitle, NoHandles, and BorderWidth 0 determine the GoodStuff window's level of decoration. NoTitle specifies no titlebar. The NoHandles and Border-Width parameters refer to the border of the window exclusive of the titlebar. NoHandles means no resize handles (the corners of the border), while Border-Width 0 speaks for itself. The resulting GoodStuff window has no window manager decoration.

You might choose simply to go without a titlebar for some applications, particularly those with very small windows, such as *xbiff* (7.10):

```
Style "xbiff" NoTitle
```

Then you'd get a window with a simple border instead. The default environment specifies `NoTitle` for several clock programs and *xbiff*.

The `WindowListSkip` parameter determines that the GoodStuff window will not appear in the `FvwmWinList` module (15.13). `Sticky` makes the window appear on every screen page. See Article 15.20 for more information.

— *VQ*

15.20 *Making the Same Window Appear on Every Page*

A window that appears on every virtual screen page is called a "sticky" window because it seems to stick to the glass. Some windows are designated as sticky in the *system.fvwmrc* file, among them *xbiff* (7.10), the GoodStuff module (15.02), and any program ending in the letters "lock" (in most cases, clocks). Sticky windows are distinguished from other windows by a different border color. (Since the default GoodStuff window has no border (15.19), you'll have to just trust me in that case.)

If you want a window to appear on the desktop no matter what page you're viewing, you need to specify that in your *.fvwmrc* file (15.14). The specification requires you to use the `Style` variable (15.19), followed by the client's name, and a hard-to-forget parameter, `Sticky`. I've added the following line, which specifies that *xpostit* (4.12) will stick to the glass:

```
Style "xpostit" Sticky
```

The `Style` variable can take either an application instance name (20.04) or class name (20.05) as an argument. In most cases, you'll only want small windows that you run a single instance of (and that you use frequently) to be sticky. Having an *xterm* appear on every screen is not as practical; it would take up too much space. If you do want a client like *xterm* to follow you around, be sure to name the client something distinctive using the *-name* option (20.04). Then use that name following `Sticky`.

For example, you could run an *xterm* you name "mailwindow":

```
% xterm -name mailwindow &
```

and then make it appear on every screen by adding the following line to your *.fvwmrc* file:

```
Style "mailwindow" Sticky
```

If you'd like to make a particular window sticky temporarily, the Window Ops menu (15.12) provides a toggle. Display the menu by holding the second pointer button down on the root window. Drag the pointer down to the (Un)Stick item and release. The pointer becomes a dot cursor. Click on the window you want to make sticky; the border color should change to indicate the new state. Select (Un)Stick again and click on the window to unstick it. The border color should change back to the original.

— VQ

15.21 *If You Keep Slipping onto Another Page*

I don't actually have this problem myself, but a few of my more energetic co-workers have complained that they'll be moving the pointer around near the edge of the current screen and accidentally bump themselves onto the next page. They find this rather irritating.

Well, there are two ways to improve this situation. The first option can make it more difficult to move the pointer onto the next page; the second option makes it impossible—at least temporarily.

You can set a resistance factor against moving the pointer onto another page using the EdgeResistance variable in your *.fvwmrc*. The variable takes two numeric parameters; the first is more relevant to the problem at hand: the number of milliseconds the pointer must be at the screen edge before you'll be moved onto the next page. The second parameter has to do with the way a window is moved between pages: it's the number of pixels over the edge of the screen a window's border must move before it moves partially off the screen.

The default settings are:

```
EdgeResistance 250 50
```

You can reduce the risk of slipping onto another page by mistake by increasing the first number. Something in the 500 to 1000 range should greatly improve matters. The maximum resistance is 10000, which makes it impossible to move over.

If you want to make it impossible for a limited time, *fvwm* offers a more practical method. The GoodStuff window *(15.10)* provides a somewhat mysterious command button labeled **Paging**. The vise image on the button gives a clue to its function, but not a very helpful one. The **Paging** button toggles whether or not you can move the pointer off of the current screen page. If you're going to work on one page for a while, it might be helpful to toggle **Paging** so that you can't move the pointer into another screen by mistake.

When you click on **Paging**, the button will appear to be pressed, indicating that it is toggled on. In this state, you are limited to working on the current screen page. When you toggle it on and try moving the pointer off the screen, you'll find yourself stuck, as if you were using a regular old X terminal.

In order to be able to cross into another page using the pointer, toggle Paging off. The button will appear to be raised to the same level as the other Good-Stuff command buttons and you can scroll over the edge normally.

— *VQ*

15.22 Placing New Windows Automatically

fvwm has a better plan for placing new windows than any other window manager I've used. There are two variables that control the placement of new windows. SmartPlacement, which is set in the default environment, causes a new window to be placed automatically in a smart location, that is, where it doesn't overlap any other windows.

If no smart location exists, *fvwm* falls back to having you place the window manually, which is less than ideal. If you add the RandomPlacement variable to your *.fvwmrc*, when *fvwm* can't find a smart location for a new window, it comes up with a reasonable random one.

The bottom line is that your *.fvwmrc* file needs to have both SmartPlacement and RandomPlacement. Once it does, just restart the window manager and you'll never have to place a window manually again.

— *VQ*

15.23 Customizing Menus and the GoodStuff Window

By now you probably appreciate that *fvwm* is slightly menu happy. You may not want to add a menu (to what key would you bind it, anyway), but you may want to customize one or more of the existing menus, or even the Good-Stuff window *(15.10)*.

How? Just by editing your *.fvwmrc* file *(15.14)* (and restarting the window manager, of course). The syntax of menus and modules *(15.03)* (like the GoodStuff) is fairly simple. Let's look at a couple of examples.

We don't have the *rxvt* terminal emulator on our system, so the Rxvt and Top items on the default Utilities menu *(15.11)* are useless. Let's do something about that. Here's the menu definition from the default startup file:

```
Popup "Utilities"
        Title   "Utilities"
        Exec    "Xterm"       exec xterm -e tcsh &
        Exec    "Rxvt"        exec rxvt &
        Exec    "Top"         exec rxvt -T Top -n Top -e top &
        Exec    "Calculator"  exec xcalc &
        Exec    "Xman"        exec xman &
        Exec    "Xmag"        exec xmag &
        Nop     ""
        Popup   "Modules"     Module-Popup
```

```
            Nop       " "
            Popup     "Exit Fvwm"       Quit-Verify
      EndPopup
```

The first line defines that **Utilities** is a pop-up menu. Each subsequent line defines a menu item. The first column of each item specifies the *fvwm* function to run. (The Exec function lets you run a system command.) The second column gives the menu item a label. The third column is only used when you need to provide a command to execute or a submenu to access. We can edit the lines corresponding to **Rxvt** and **Top** to run commands useful on our system:

```
      Exec      "Shelltool"      exec shelltool &
      Exec      "Hpterm"         exec hpterm &
```

After I restart *fvwm*, these items replace the useless ones on the default menu.

Now suppose you want to do something about the useless **Dopey**, **Grumpy**, and **Snoopy** buttons in the GoodStuff window. Here's the GoodStuff definition from the default startup file:

```
*GoodStuff Kill    rbomb.xpm  Destroy
*GoodStuff Dopey   rterm.xpm  Exec "dopey" rsh dopey "exec xterm \
                   -T dopey -display $HOSTDISPLAY </dev/null >&/dev/null & "&
*GoodStuff Grumpy  rterm.xpm  Exec "grumpy" rsh grumpy "exec xterm \
                   -T grumpy -display $HOSTDISPLAY </dev/null >&/dev/null & "&
*GoodStuff Snoopy  rterm.xpm  Exec "snoopy" rsh snoopy "exec xterm \
                   -T snoopy -display $HOSTDISPLAY </dev/null >&/dev/null & "&
*GoodStuff Xcalc   rcalc.xpm  Exec "Calculator" xcalc &
*GoodStuff mail    mail2.xpm  Exec "xmh" xmh &
*GoodStuff Paging  clamp.xpm  TogglePage
*GoodStuff -       clock.xpm  Swallow "xclock" xclock -bg \#908090 \
                   -geometry -1500-1 500 -padding 0
*GoodStuff(4x1) - whatever SwallowModule "FvwmPager" FvwmPager 0 3
```

The syntax for the GoodStuff is slightly different than menu syntax. Each line defines a button in the GoodStuff window or swallows a client or module into the GoodStuff. The first column contains *GoodStuff, which is followed by three columns that define the button's text label, the pixmap image that appears on it, and finally the action it performs. TogglePage, Swallow, and SwallowModule are predefined *fvwm* functions.

Exec is used slightly differently in this context than in the **Utilities** menu definition. Here it requires a quoted "name" that is more of a placeholder than anything else, but a necessary one. The important stuff—the command to be executed—follows this quoted name. We can change what the **Dopey**, **Grumpy**, and **Snoopy** buttons do by editing the associated commands:

```
*GoodStuff Ruby      rterm.xpm   Exec "xterm" xrsh ruby &
*GoodStuff Opal      rterm.xpm   Exec "xterm" xrsh opal &
*GoodStuff Obsidian  rterm.xpm   Exec "xterm" xrsh obsidian &
```

These lines replace the silly **Dopey**, **Grumpy**, and **Snoopy** buttons with useful ones labeled **Ruby**, **Opal**, and **Obsidian**, which open remote *xterm* windows on systems named—you guessed it—*ruby*, *opal*, and *obsidian*.

You can add an iconify button to the GoodStuff window by adding the line:

```
*GoodStuff (De)Iconify  -  Iconify
```

There's no obvious pixmap to use, so I'm going without. The manpage tells me `Iconify` is the function name. The label is truncated in the window, but it does work.

In previous versions of *fvwm*, the GoodStuff window also offered buttons to perform other common window manager functions, such as moving, lowering, and raising. Buttons like these can come in handy when the window border is not accessible. (You can also use the Window Ops menu *(15.12)* in this circumstance.) The following lines define three additional buttons:

```
*GoodStuff Move    arrows2.xpm  Move
*GoodStuff Lower   Down         Lower
*GoodStuff Raise   Up           Raise
```

`Move`, `Lower`, and `Raise` are predefined *fvwm* functions.

As Article 15.17 explains, when you modify the GoodStuff window, you may encounter problems with its layout and/or location. The variables `Good-StuffRows`, `GoodStuffColumns`, and `GoodStuffGeometry` can help you control these features. Figure 15-12 shows a modified GoodStuff window. I've kept the default two rows, added four command buttons, and removed the pager (as I suggested in Article 15.17).

Figure 15-12: A purer GoodStuff window: more commands, no pager

You may not want so many choices, but at least you get the idea. When you click on one of the buttons that performs a window management function, the pointer changes to a symbol appropriate for the function: **Lower** and **Raise** give you a dot; **Move** gives you cross-arrows. Move the pointer to the window you want to perform the function on. Complete a raise or lower simply by clicking. For a move, press a pointer button, drag the window, and release.

—VQ

Part Five

The User Environment

Some people think "X user" is an oxymoron, and only programmers can use X. Well, it's true that the X user environment can be a bit unwieldy ... but it's not *that* hard. You just need to know some things about shell programming, window manager configuration, X resources, fonts, keysym mapping, and a few minor details about UNIX networking. Once you know all that, it's a piece of cake!

Seriously ... the biggest hurdle for new X users is configuring their user environment. So this section of the book tries to identify some of the more tangible factors in the X user environment, and to steer users toward what they need to know in order to create or alter their own environment.

—LM

16

Simple Startup Scripts

16.01 Startup Scripts for the Masses

Occasionally, less technical users at our office ask me for advice. And very often, they regret it. Not because they don't get the results they want, but because I'm one of those people who tries to set things up in the most efficient, flexible manner, while I explain in great detail why things work the way they do. My theory is that if they understand the inner workings of UNIX and X, then they will be able to figure out what to do based on common sense. The reality is that not all people want to understand UNIX and X, they just want things to work.

In X, one area where users almost always need help is also one of the areas where all users should be able to do it by themselves. Every user's startup environment should be tailored to their personal needs. But in X, startup environments can be a tricky business, and a single mistake could become a disaster.

Thus this chapter. Yes, if you want to do something fancy, you need to learn a lot about UNIX and X. But for most users' needs, there are really only a few things you need to know about. So in this chapter, we describe the bare bones of what you need to know for a working X environment. For users who want more, see Chapter 21.

—*LM*

16.02 Which Is Your Startup Script?

Before you go any further, you need to know the name of your startup script *(2.09)*. There are several different ways to start your X session, and some of them are far too configurable for their own good. But in general, your startup script is either *$HOME/.xsession* or *$HOME/.xinitrc*. It all depends on how you log in.

If you log in using *xdm (28.02)*, your startup script is probably *$HOME/.xsession*. (I say "probably" because *xdm* can actually be configured to use a different startup script, but only a very perverse administrator (or vendor) might set you up that way.)

If you log in using *xinit* or *startx (1.03)*, your startup script is *$HOME/.xinitrc*.

Some people might look at their *$HOME/.xsession* and see a giant, unfathomable shell script. This may mean that you are running Vue, and this chapter is close to useless to you. Vue is an integrated user environment that provides its own user-friendly way of setting up your startup session. Under Vue, there is no way to manually edit a startup script; instead, click on the icon for the Style Manager, choose **Startup**, and from there you're on your own.

—LM

16.03 *Creating Your Startup Script*

If you don't have a startup script, the first thing you need to do is to create one.

Your startup script should be either *$HOME/.xsession* or *$HOME/.xinitrc (16.02)*. Open the file for editing, either in a UNIX-based editor like *vi* or *emacs (9.02)*, or using an X-based editor such as *xedit (9.03)* or *asedit (9.05)*.

The first line of the startup script should list the shell that it's written in. For simple scripts like yours, just use the Bourne shell, *sh.*[*] So using a special syntax specifying what program to run the script with, the first line should read #!/bin/sh.

Next, think about what programs you want to start. You have to start a window manager. You probably want to start at least one *xterm* window *(2.02)*. You might want to start a mailer or a calendar program. For now, just choose a few programs; you can always go back and add more afterwards (as shown in Article 16.05).

The next thing you need to decide is which program you want to be your *controlling process*. The controlling process is a program that, when you exit it, exits you out of your entire X session. It is also called the foreground process. There are two common programs to use as your controlling process: your window manager or an *xterm* window. Which you choose to use is up to you; see Article 21.11 if you want to hear some pros and cons of which program to use.

---

[*] The *.xinitrc* file must always be a *sh* script, but an *.xsession* script can be any executable program.

> **Note:** The controlling process isn't really magic or anything. It's just the way that programming in the shell works: the shell executes commands and then exits when all the commands have been executed. Unfortunately, in this instance, when the shell exits, so do you. So you have to keep a client in the foreground to make sure that the shell doesn't exit until that client is completed (i.e., exited). It's as simple as that.

Now just list all your programs on separate lines. For all programs except your controlling process, end the line with an ampersand (&) so the program is run in the background *(2.03)*. This is needed so you can have windows from several client programs running simultaneously.

The exception is the controlling process. List this program at the very bottom of your startup script, and make sure that you do *not* add an ampersand to the end of the line.

A simple startup script might read:

```
#!/bin/sh

xterm &
xmail &
xclock &

twm
```

Here, I've started *xterm*, *xmail (7.02)*, and *xclock (3.02)* clients, and then I've chosen to run my *twm* window manager *(12.01)* as my controlling process. When I exit my window manager at the end of the day (by selecting **Quit** or **Exit**), all my windows disappear and I am logged out.

Now you can exit the editor. If your startup script is *.xsession*, you need to take one more step and make the file executable before you can test it out. To do this, use the UNIX *chmod* command:

```
lmui@ruby % chmod +x $HOME/.xsession
```

Now you can log out and log in again. If you have trouble logging in, see Article 16.07 for ideas on where the problem lies.

In this example, all of the programs that I'm starting are local clients. That is, they all run on the same system as my startup script. See Article 19.15 for information about starting programs on remote systems from your startup script.

—LM

16.04 *Problems with Pathnames*

A common problem with startup scripts *(2.09, 16.03)* is that a program does not start up. If you use *xdm (28.02)*, then you might have an *.xsession-errors* file containing an error resembling:

```
xmail: Command not found
```

(If you use *xinit* or *startx (1.03)*, you probably won't get any errors.)

The first thing you need to do is to make sure the command exists. You can use the UNIX *which* command to see if it's in your path somewhere:

```
lmui@ruby % which xmail
/usr/local/bin/xmail
```

In this case, I've found out that *xmail (7.02)* does exist, and it's installed in a special *bin* area set aside on our system for local programs (i.e., programs that aren't part of the standard distribution from our vendor). Therein lies the problem.

Your *search path (2.05)* is a list of directories that your shell searches when you run a command. When you log in under a terminal emulator (like *xterm*) *(2.02)*, your search path is set automatically in either your *.profile* or n *.cshrc* file (depending on whether you use a Bourne shell or C shell derivative, respectively).

However, when you log in under X, your *.cshrc* or *.profile* file isn't run. So your startup script doesn't get your search path, and defaults to the value `bin:/usr/bin:/usr/bin/X11`. This means that it doesn't know how to find programs that don't live in one of those directories. So it can find commands like *xterm* and *xclock (3.02)* (which, being part of the standard X distribution, are installed into */usr/bin/X11*); but it can't find a command like *xmail*, which is tucked away into */usr/local/bin*.

There are several ways to deal with this problem:

- You can use the full pathname for the command. For example:

```
#!/bin/sh

xterm &
xclock &
/usr/local/bin/xmail &
      ...
```

(The main problem with this method is that some programs depend on some other programs that are installed in the same place. For example, *ical (4.03)* depends on finding a program called *calshellx* in the same directory.)

- If your shell is usually the Bourne or Korn shell (*sh* or *ksh*), you can source in your *.profile* file using the . command.

```
#!/bin/sh

. $HOME/.profile
```

- If you're a C shell user, and you have your path set properly in your *.cshrc* file, then you can just turn the startup script into a C shell script. As long as you don't include any Bourne shell-specific syntax (such as conditionals), a simple Bourne shell script can also serve as a C shell script. Just change the first line:

```
#!/bin/csh
```

The *.cshrc* file will now be automatically read in, and your search path will be set properly.

- You can set and export the PATH environment variable *(2.05)*. For example:

```
#!/bin/sh

PATH=$PATH:/usr/local/bin
export PATH

xterm &
xclock &
xmail &
        ...
```

- If you usually use the C shell but you want to keep your startup script as a Bourne shell script, you can use this trick to get the PATH from your C shell:

```
#!/bin/sh

PATH=`csh -c 'echo $PATH'`
export PATH
```

Another possibility is that if you log in using *xdm*, then administrators can also alter the value of PATH used for startup scripts on a systemwide level. This may be the best way of tackling this issue (see Articles 28.14 and 28.24).

—*LM*

16.05 *Adding a New Program to Your Startup Script*

Let's suppose you've discovered the *ical (4.03)* calendar program, you love it, you already have it installed, and you want to have it started automatically every day. How do you do this?

The line you want to add to your startup script *(2.09, 16.03)* is the following:

```
ical &
```

However, there are two major factors you need to take into account. The more serious thing you need to be careful about is that *you can't just put this command at the bottom of your script*. You need to add this line *before* the last controlling process *(16.03)*. For example:

```
#!/bin/sh

PATH=$PATH:/usr/local/bin
export PATH

xterm &
xclock &
xmail &

ical &

twm
```

If you put the `ical &` line after the `twm` line, then you'll never see the calendar since it won't start until you exit the window manager (and are logged out). Maybe you'll see it flicker by before you're logged out, but that's not really want you want.

The second thing you need to make sure of is that if *ical* has been installed into a non-standard place, then the startup script's search path needs to include that directory *(16.04)*. You can find out what directory a program is installed into by using the UNIX *which* command:

```
% which ical
/work/xpt/src/bin/ical
```

In this example, I had already set my PATH environment variable *(2.05)* to include */usr/local/bin*. However, *ical* is in a special directory I set up for programs to go into this book, */work/xpt/src/bin*. So I have to add this directory to my PATH environment variable:

```
PATH=$PATH:/usr/local/bin:/work/xpt/src/bin
export PATH
```

—LM

16.06 Placing Your Windows

After you have your initial startup session *(2.09, 16.03)* set up, you may want to set up initial window placements. Usually, windows are placed by your window manager, according to how you have your window manager configured. You may have your window manager set up so that windows appear stacked, one on top of another. You may have it set up so that new windows need to be explicitly placed when they appear. Or windows may be placed randomly. (For information on how to configure your window manager, see the appropriate chapter of Part 4.) However, if you explicitly set a window's geometry, it overrides the window manager and is placed in the specified position.

How to actually set the geometry is described in Article 17.10. But the hard part is often knowing exactly where to place the window.

One low-tech way of placing your windows is to just use trial and error until you have it placed exactly where you want it on the screen. For example, I might try a few positions for an *xterm* window *(2.02)*:

```
% xterm -geometry +500+1 &
```

I could continue experimenting with different positions until I find one I like, and then place its command in my startup script. After doing this for all my startup clients, my startup script might now look like the following:

```
#!/bin/sh

PATH=$PATH:/usr/local/bin:$HOME/bin
export PATH

xterm -geometry 80x24+409+8 &
xclock -geometry 164x164-15+13 &
xmail -geometry 698x744+0+0 &

twm
```

But a better idea is to just place the window where you want it and then use the *xwininfo* client to find out what its current position is. See Article 17.13 for information on *xwininfo*.

—LM

16.07 Problems Logging In

If you have trouble logging in: no fear, it's likely to be a very simple problem. Here are some of the more common situations:

- If you use *xdm* *(28.02)* and you didn't make your *.xsession* script executable using *chmod +x* *(16.03)*, then you might find that your login box *(28.02)* immediately returns.

- If the X session starts, launches all clients, and then disappears again (returning you to the login prompt under *xdm*, or returning you to your console prompt *(27.02)* under *xinit*), then it's likely that you didn't include a controlling process *(16.03)* properly.

- Remember that your controlling process needs to be an X client that will run concurrently with your other clients. If your startup script looks fine, remember that one possibility is that your startup script can't run your client at all because it isn't in your search path *(2.05)*. See Article 16.04 for more information.

- If you have an error in your startup script, the script may bomb out before it ever gets to start any clients. If you use *xdm* from X11R5 or later, look at the *$HOME/.xsession-errors* file for a list of errors; if you use X11R4 *xdm*, sort through */usr/lib/X11/xdm/xdm-errors* for error messages associated with your server. You might also try just running the script from the command line to see what sort of shell errors are reported. See Article 21.05.

—LM

17

Configuring Applications

17.01 Resources and Command-line Options

People have said many things about X (and they haven't always been polite about it!), but no one ever said that X wasn't configurable. Most X clients are customizable at startup time, using some combination of the following:

Resources
> Many applications have parameters set via X resources. Resources make it possible to configure the same application at the system level, at the server level, and at the user level.

Command-line options
> Like other UNIX commands, many X clients accept command-line options. Command-line options are useful for setting temporary behavior, e.g., if you want to see what *xterm (2.02)* looks like with a particular font. In most cases, command-line options have resource equivalents, so if you want certain behavior all the time, it's usually easier to just set a resource rather than use the command-line option every time.

Client-specific configuration files
> In addition, many clients use configuration files that are specific to their application. These files usually have names beginning with a dot (.), and are usually installed in the user's home directory. For example, a calendar application might look at a file called *.calendar* in the user's home directory, and a FTP client would use the user's *.netrc* file. Mailers use *.mailrc*. Window managers in particular usually have elaborate configuration files, such as *.twmrc*. (See Article 2.10 to find out more about filenames that start with a dot (.).)

When documenting a particular client in this book, we try to cover the ways to configure it in some detail. This chapter is an overview to configuring clients; we try to give examples of how to set resources, and we also describe some of the command-line options and resources that are common to many clients.

Resources are a hairy topic and aren't really appropriate for the unsuspecting user. But if you want to know more about managing your resources, you may want to supplement this reading with Chapter 20.

—LM

17.02 Simple Resource Syntax

Throughout this book, we tell you about what resources you can set to alter a client. A full resource name might have half a dozen fields and many different ways of specifying it. But the most basic syntax for a resource definition is:

```
client*resource: value
```

So if you want to set the blahBlah resource for the *gizmo* client to "true", the following definition will probably work fine:

```
gizmo*blahBlah: true
```

Here is a real example: suppose I always want to have a scrollbar in my *xterm* clients and I always want to scroll 200 lines of text. As described in Articles 11.02 and 11.03, I want to set the scrollBar resource to true, and I want to set the saveLines resource to 200. So I want to set the following resource definitions:

```
xterm*scrollBar:  true
xterm*saveLines:  200
```

To comment out a resource (i.e., to make sure that clients ignore it), just precede the line with an exclamation point:

```
!xterm*scrollBar:        true
```

Resources aren't always this easy. In particular, you might be confused by seeing some capital letters mixed in—such as "XTerm" in place of "xterm." But in most cases, "xterm" will work fine. (Article 20.05 explains this a bit more.) You might also see scrollbar instead of scrollBar. The asterisk that we use here is also a sort of shorthand that's explained in more detail in Article 20.15.

—LM

17.03 Installing Resources (the Easy Way)

Most people want to set up their resources so that they are automatically defined when they log in. There are many different ways to work this, but we'll try to simplify the procedure so that most anyone can do it.

Article 17.02 shows how to set a simple resource, but where do you set this resource? Well, in my opinion, the easiest way to set resources is to use one of the following two methods:

- Put all resource definitions in *$HOME/.Xdefaults*.

- Use the *xrdb* client, which loads resources directly into the X server.

Here's the rub. If you use *xrdb*, clients no longer look in *.Xdefaults*. *So you can't use both methods.* You need to choose one way and stick to it.

To use *.Xdefaults*, just put the resource definition in a file in your home directory called *.Xdefaults* and let her rip. Clients automatically look in *.Xdefaults* for resource definitions, so you don't need to do anything extra to have the resources take effect on all clients from now on.

To use *xrdb*, you need to put the resource in a file (such as *$HOME/.Xresources*) and then enter a line into your startup script to run *xrdb* on that file. Use the *–merge* command-line option *(20.18)*. You should put the *xrdb* line in your startup script *before* any other clients. Your startup script might read:

```
#!/bin/sh

xrdb -merge $HOME/.Xresources

xterm &
xclock &
    ...
```

If *xrdb* is already called in your startup script on a different file (such as *$HOME/.xrdb*, or even *$HOME/.Xdefaults*), just add your resource definition to that file.

If you use *xrdb* in this fashion, then the resource will be read automatically the next time you log in. If you want to make sure it's read immediately as well, run the *xrdb -merge* command now.

```
% xrdb -merge $HOME/.Xresources
```

—*LM*

17.04 *My .Xdefaults File Isn't Being Read!*

Here's a common complaint: resources are placed in your *.Xdefaults* file *(17.03)*, but then aren't making any difference to your client. What might be going on here is that you have some resources installed via *xrdb* and you don't know it! Try running:

```
% xrdb -q
```

If any resource definitions appear, then you are running *xrdb* and need to continue using *xrdb* for any subsequent resources. You aren't going crazy: it's possible that your system administrator has installed some resources for all users using *xrdb* without your knowledge.

If no resource definitions appear, then you're either setting the resource wrong, or the resource is being overridden from some other configuration file. See Articles 20.28 and 20.26 for hints on how to deal with this.

—LM

17.05 *Specifying Resources on the Command Line*

If you only want to set a resource temporarily for a single client, another very simple way of setting a resource is to set it on the command line. Xt-based applications accept a *–xrm* option for specifying resources on the command line. For example:

```
% xterm -xrm '*scrollbar:true' &
```

(Note that if your resource specification includes an asterisk (*) *(20.15)*, then it's a good idea to protect it using single quotes so that the shell doesn't try to interpret the asterisk.)

Many applications, however, also provide command-line shortcuts to resource specifications. For example, you might also get a scrollbar *(11.02)* by just entering:

```
% xterm -sb &
```

Other shortcuts are *–bg* and *–fg* for background and foreground colors *(17.06)*, *–title* for the title resource *(17.09)*, and *–fn* for the font name *(17.14)*. Although most of these options are standard with any Xt-based application, you should check the client manpage to see what command-line shortcuts are provided.

—LM

17.06 *Changing the Foreground and Background*

To change the foreground color for an application, use the *–fg* command-line option, or the foreground resource. For example, suppose I had a color display and wanted the type in my *xterm* windows *(2.02)* to be blue instead of black. I might do:

```
% xterm -fg blue &
```

or set the following resource:

```
XTerm*foreground:blue
```

To change the background color, use the *−bg* command-line option or background resource. For example, if I wanted the same *xterm* window on my color display to have a yellow background instead of white, I might do:

```
% xterm -bg yellow &
```

or set the following resource:

```
XTerm*background:yellow
```

See Article 26.04 if you want to know what colors are available to your server.
—LM

17.07 *Easy on the Eyes*

The white background of my display is a little harsh, so I create all my xterms with the following background color *(17.06)*:

```
xterm -bg lightyellow &
```

It creates a pleasant off-white background. Experiment with colors. A small difference can make a big difference. If you like one, you can set it as a resource *(17.03)*:

```
XTerm*background:lightyellow
```

— TOR

17.08 *Reverse-video Option*

The *−rv* (reverse video) command-line option specifies that a client be started with its foreground and background colors *(17.06)* swapped. In many cases, this means that a window will be white on black, rather than black on white. If other foreground and background colors have been specified (in a application-defaults file *(20.12)* or on the command line), reverse video will produce another combination.

In most cases, you would use reverse video purely for aesthetic reasons. Some people like to work with white text on black *xterm* windows *(2.02)*, for instance. You may also choose reverse video in cases where it enhances readability. I used both the standard reverse-video option and the client-specific *−transparent* option to create an interesting *oclock* *(3.02)* display; see Article 3.11.

Sometimes a program will specify reverse video to clue you in to a particular circumstance. For example, an *xterm* window will switch to reverse video to signal that you're in Secure Keyboard *(11.17)* mode.
— VQ

17.09 Changing the Title

Most window managers have a *titlebar*. The titlebar can be used to move and raise windows. It also has a string in it, which is usually the name of the program, but may also be changed using the *–title* command-line option or via the `title` resource.

There is also a *–name* command-line option (and corresponding `name` resource). When you change the name, the title is changed as well. The name of the application has other implications for application behavior, however, so it is discussed in full in Article 20.04.

—LM

17.10 Setting Your Geometry

The geometry of a window consists of its dimensions and its position on the screen.

The client has a default size built into the program, and the placement of the window is usually controlled by the window manager. The window manager might be set up to place clients randomly, to place them stacked on top of one another, or to require the user to manually place each new window. However, you can override the client defaults and window manager placement using the *–geometry* command-line option or the `geometry` resource.

For example, the *xclock (3.02)* client usually appears with a geometry of 164×164 pixels. You can get a clock that's almost twice as big using the following command line:

```
% xclock -geometry 300x300 &
```

If you want this clock to appear at the upper-left corner of the screen, you can type:

```
% xclock -geometry 300x300+0+0 &
```

The coordinates (0,0) represent the upper-left corner of the root window. The numbers following the plus signs (+) signify the horizontal and vertical offset (in number of pixels) from (0,0). So if you specify +0+0, there's no offset and your window appears at the upper-left corner. To have the window appear 400 pixels from the left and 600 pixels from the top, type:

```
% xclock -geometry 300x300+400+600 &
```

Two things to be aware of, however:

1. The *xterm* client *(2.02)* uses non-standard units for size specifications. Whereas most X clients use pixels as their units, *xterm* uses rows and columns. See Article 17.11 for more information.

2. Since the sizing and placement of windows is relative to the number of pixels on a display, a configuration that works on one server may not work on another. For example, a window may appear much too big on a display with a smaller resolution, or a window may be partially (or entirely!) off the screen on a display with smaller dimensions. Using negative offsets might help avoid the latter problem—see Article 17.12.

If you want to fiddle with different positions for a client, a useful program is *xwininfo* *(17.13)*, which tells you the geometry of a window currently on display.

—*LM*

17.11 *Sizing xterm Windows*

One thing about specifying window geometries *(17.10)* is that the client you're most likely to want to resize, *xterm* *(2.02)*, is also the one that is resized using non-standard syntax. Usually, the size of the window is specified in pixels, but not so for *xterm*. *xterm* uses lines and columns as its units for size for its *vt100* widget. This is actually very convenient, since you're more likely to care about how much text you can fit in an *xterm* window than you care about the actual size of the window; but it's not the way most clients work.

By default, *xterm* creates its windows in the size 80×24–that is, 80 columns across by 24 lines down. If you want a window that's 92 characters across and 40 lines long, enter:

```
% xterm -geometry 92x40 &
```

(The placement of the *xterm* window still uses pixels as units.)

The fact that *xterm* uses the rows and columns for sizing also means that the resulting size of the *xterm* window is dependent on what font it uses *(17.14)*. A window with a 10-point font will be smaller than one with a 14-point font.

And since the special geometry only applies to the *vt100* widget, you have to be careful when setting the geometry as a resource—see Article 20.17.

—*LM*

17.12 *Negative Offsets*

In addition to placing windows using positive offsets from the upper-left corner of a display, you can also use the *–geometry* command-line option and geometry resource *(17.10)* to place windows relative to the other corners of the display.

Each corner of the display can be addressed by special coordinates. In the same way that the upper-left corner is (0,0), you can think of the upper right corner as (-0,0), the lower left corner as (0,-0), and the lower right corner as

(-0,-0). (Don't try to make any sense out of this mathematically.) So to get an
xclock(3.02) window to appear at the upper-right corner of the display, type:

```
% xclock -geometry -0+0 &
```

Since displays differ in the number of pixels, a window may be placed differently depending on the size and resolution of your display. Using a negative
offset will guarantee that the window is always a certain distance from the
right side and bottom, regardless of the size. This is handy for startup scripts
(2.09, 16.03)* if you often move from one type of display to another, your windows
will always remain within the screen borders.

—*LM*

17.13 *Finding the Geometry with xwininfo*

The *xwininfo* client shows information about a specific window on your display. The most frequent use of *xwininfo* is to find out the geometry placement
(17.10) of a particular window, and apply that to your startup script (2.09, 16.03)*

```
% xwininfo
```

When you call *xwininfo* with no command-line arguments, it asks you to click
on the window you want information about, and then tells you its location,
dimensions, depth, etc. You can also use the *–name* command-line option, so
it will give you information about the window with the specified name rather
than asking you to select one by hand.

```
% xwininfo -name xclock

xwininfo: Window id: 0x1800009 "xclock"

   Absolute upper-left X:  922
   Absolute upper-left Y:  37
   Relative upper-left X:  0
   Relative upper-left Y:  0
   Width: 164
   Height: 164
   Depth: 2
   Visual Class: StaticGray
   Border width: 0
   Class: InputOutput
   Colormap: 0x22 (installed)
   Bit Gravity State: NorthWestGravity
   Window Gravity State: NorthWestGravity
   Backing Store State: NotUseful
   Save Under State: no
   Map State: IsViewable
   Override Redirect State: no
   Corners:  +922+37  -34+37  -34-631  +922-631
   -geometry 164x164-15+13
```

The last line gives you a *–geometry* specification. You can apply this value directly to the client command line in your startup script.

Note that *xwininfo* determines the geometry based on the current window manager. If you switch to another window manager later on, with different decorations, then the window's position may need to be tweaked again to compensate for the new frame.

—LM

17.14 *Specifying a Different Font*

You can run an application with a font different than the default by using the *–fn* command-line option or the `font` resource.

The hard part is knowing which font to use. Not all fonts will work well with all applications: for example, the *xterm (2.02)* client requires a constant-width font (such as Courier), so if you use a proportional font, your window will be difficult to read. See Article 11.13 for some guidelines as to what fonts to use with *xterm*.

You can use the *xlsfonts* client to get a listing of all fonts known to your server:

```
% xlsfonts
-adobe-courier-bold-o-normal--0-0-100-100-m-0-iso8859-1
-adobe-courier-bold-o-normal--0-0-75-75-m-0-iso8859-1
    . . .
-misc-fixed-bold-r-normal--13-100-100-100-c-70-iso8859-1
```

Suppose you decide to use the 13-pixel fixed-width font shown above with *xterm*. Supply this name using the *–fn* command-line option:

```
% xterm -fn -misc-fixed-bold-r-normal--13-100-100-100-c-70-iso8859-1 &
```

Or set this font in your resource file:

```
XTerm*font: -misc-fixed-bold-r-normal--13-100-100-100-c-70-iso8859-1
```

See Article 17.15 for information on using wildcards to abbreviate font names, and Article 17.18 for an explanation of the font-naming syntax. So-called scalable fonts *(17.16)* represent a special case in terms of specification. See Article 17.17 for guidelines.

—LM

17.15 Wildcards in Font Names

You could spend a lot of time typing in the absurdly lengthy X font names. Some of the more commonly used fonts have abbreviations, or aliases. Article 11.13 gives the aliases for some constant-width fonts you can use to display text in an *xterm* window.

If a font name does not have a predefined alias, you can instead create your own abbreviation using wildcard characters. You can use an asterisk (*) to represent any part of the font-name string (i.e., multiple characters). A question mark (?) can be used to represent any single character. (If you're familiar with the UNIX shell, you might recognize that wildcards in font names work just as they do for filename expansion in the shell.)

You can usually get the font you want by specifying only the font family, the width, the slant, and the point size, and wildcarding the rest. For example, to get Courier bold at 14 points, you could use the command-line option:

```
% xterm -fn '*courier-bold-r*140*'
```

(We use "140" instead of "14" because the font naming syntax *(17.18)* specifies points in tenths of a point.)

Though wildcarding definitely simplifies the matter of specifying a font, in practice it is slightly more complicated than it may initially look.

First of all, notice that the wildcarded font name is enclosed in single quotes. This is because the UNIX shell also has a special meaning for the * and ? characters, so the wildcarded font name needs to be "protected" from the shell if specified on the command line. (They do not need to be quoted when specified in a resource file.)

Second, if the wildcarded font name matches more than one font, the server will use the first one in the search path that it matches. If you aren't sure what font you'll get on your server, you can specify the wildcarded font to the *xlsfonts* client *(17.14)*, using the *–fn* command-line option. For example:

```
% xlsfonts -fn '*courier-bold-r*14*'
-adobe-courier-bold-r-normal--14-100-100-100-m-90-iso8859-1
-adobe-courier-bold-r-normal--14-140-75-75-m-90-iso8859-1
-adobe-courier-bold-r-normal--20-140-100-100-m-110-iso8859-1
```

Unless you're happy with the first font that *xlsfonts* reports, you need to make your font name more specific (e.g., *courier-bold-r-*-14-140-*).

If you want to specify a scalable font *(17.16)*, you have to be even more specific. The font name you construct has to make the size you're requesting completely clear. The safest way to do this is to include all the dashes of the name in the wildcard string:

```
-*-courier-bold-r-*-*-*-140-*-*-*-iso8859-1
```

Now there's no question that 140 is the size of the font in tenths of a point.

— VQ

17.16 What's a Scalable Font?

Most of the standard fonts provided with X11R5 are *bitmap fonts*; that is, each character is a bitmap image. Each bitmap font has a particular point and pixel size *(17.18)* (which are two components in the font's name). Note that each size of a bitmap font is stored in a separate font file—thus, they can take up a lot of space. Another liability: because of the different resolution of computer monitors, a bitmap font intended to be a particular point size might actually appear larger or smaller on various screens.

X11R5 introduced *font scaling* capability; that is, you can now specify an alternative size for any font and it will be scaled accordingly. X11R5 includes some *outline fonts*, which are suitable for scaling. An outline font stored in a single file can be scaled to any point or pixel size you request (though the scaling requires some system overhead). Though bitmap fonts can be scaled, they are not intended to be. The result is often jagged looking and less legible.

How do you tell a bitmap font from an outline font (besides by comparing the scaled result on a screen)? It's all in the font name. Article 17.17 examines the outline font naming syntax and gives tips on scaling these fonts.

— VQ

17.17 Specifying a Font to be Scaled

Any one of the outline fonts *(17.16)* included with X11R5 can easily be scaled to whatever point or pixel size you want. The *Speedo* directory in the standard X distribution provides eight scalable outline fonts, whose names are listed below:

```
-bitstream-charter-medium-r-normal--0-0-0-0-p-0-iso8859-1
-bitstream-charter-medium-i-normal--0-0-0-0-p-0-iso8859-1
-bitstream-charter-bold-r-normal--0-0-0-0-p-0-iso8859-1
-bitstream-charter-bold-i-normal--0-0-0-0-p-0-iso8859-1
-bitstream-courier-medium-r-normal--0-0-0-0-m-0-iso8859-1
-bitstream-courier-medium-i-normal--0-0-0-0-m-0-iso8859-1
-bitstream-courier-bold-r-normal--0-0-0-0-m-0-iso8859-1
-bitstream-courier-bold-i-normal--0-0-0-0-m-0-iso8859-1
```

Article 17.18 maps out the components in an X font name. For each outline font, the three name fields relating to size (pixels, points, and average width), plus the two resolution fields, have zeroes in them.

You can specify any one of these scalable outline fonts simply by adding a point size. The following name scales the Courier bold italic font to 24 points (on most screens, a huge font):

```
-bitstream-courier-bold-i-normal--0-240-0-0-m-0-iso8859-1
```

Note that you can also scale any of the bitmap fonts (to a different size than those offered) by taking the font name and:

1. Changing the pixel and average width fields to zero

2. Specifying the point size you want (in tenths of a point)

Note that every field must have something in it (even if you use an asterisk wildcard). Don't use an asterisk to replace multiple adjacent fields. The following name scales the Adobe Courier bold font (roman slant) to 15 points (a size not usually available).

```
-adobe-courier-bold-r-normal--0-150-75-75-m-0-iso8859-1
```

Remember, however, that scaling bitmap fonts may produce "jagged" results.

—VQ

17.18 A Font by Any Other Name. Please?

If my parents were X developers, they might have named me:

```
-quercia-val-6lbs-liberal-avg-classic-18in-2-28-61-open-std-Homosapiens-1
```

which would have effectively distinguished me from every other creature in the universe, not to mention grade school. Luckily for me, my parents think of X as just another letter. Fonts, on the other hand, have not been so fortunate. Most X font names have 14 components, which are strung together with hyphens, as in Figure 17-1.

A name like this leaves no room for confusion among fonts—that is its purpose—but it leaves plenty of room for confusion among users. And if you think it's time consuming to read, imagine typing it.

The good news is that if you don't want to experiment too much with fonts, you don't have to understand font names at all and you certainly don't have to type any. X provides nice, short aliases for most of the fonts you'll want to use. See Article 11.13 for pictures of some of the more readable fonts and instructions on using them. See Article 17.15 for information about using wild-cards in font names.

The bad news is that if you want to work with other fonts, create aliases, add font directories to your own machine, or access fonts from somebody else's, you probably have to understand a bit more about names. I could describe each of the font name components at great length, but my guess is that even

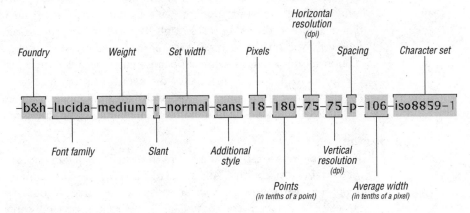

Figure 17-1: The X name for an 18-point Lucida font (written in the font itself)

people who are going to experiment a bit will need to know only a little about a few of the parts.

Our sample font is from the Lucida family of fonts. In this sense, a family is a group of related typefaces. Courier, Helvetica, and Times are other common families. The manufacturer may or may not be of interest to you. The Lucida font was created by Bigelow & Holmes (b&h). Other foundries or font providers include: Adobe, Bitstream, DEC, Schumacher, Sony, and Sun.

Some of the other characteristics it's helpful to understand are:

Weight The "heaviness" of the characters. The most common weights are medium and bold. Most of the text you read on the screen, or in books for that matter, is medium weight.

Slant

Just what you'd think. Common slants are roman (upright), italic, and oblique. Oblique fonts are generally just a slanted version of the upright font, while italic characters are reshaped to slant, some would say more elegantly.

Pixel and point size

Pixel size refers to the height of a character in the number of pixels it takes up on your screen. (Different characters vary somewhat in height; this size seems to be for the largest character.) Point size is a printer's measure; it's more arcane, but more people are probably aware of it. Most typewriters produce characters in either 10- or 12-point type. Notice that the X font name gives point size in tenths of a point—another complication. To gauge the point size, divide this figure by 10. How does this relate to using X fonts? Point and pixel sizes tell you which fonts are bigger or smaller than others, but they don't exactly tell you how big a font will look on your monitor. A font name may give the information that a 24-point font is 33 pixels high. But in practice, the resolution of the monitor affects the relative size of a font. Generally speaking, a higher resolution monitor makes a font appear smaller because there are more pixels per inch. What this means for the average user is that gauging sizes is largely a matter of trial and error. And if you understand something about geometry, the pixel size may be more meaningful than the point size.

Spacing

This characteristic is very important in terms of selecting appropriate fonts for certain applications. All standard X11R5 fonts are either: *p* (proportional, i.e., variable-width); *m* (monospace, i.e., fixed-width); or *c* (character cell). Character cell fonts are special monospaced fonts originally designed for computer displays. For *xterm* and other terminal emulators *(2.02)*, as a general rule you should use character cell fonts. Why aren't regular monospace fonts as good? In a character cell font, an invisible cell contains every character. Although monospaced fonts *can* be used for the text font in *xterm* windows, if you do so, you may notice that some "garbage" pixels are occasionally left on the screen. This happens because the characters are not clearly contained or divided from one another.

—VQ

17.19 Tips on Selecting Fonts with xfontsel

xfontsel (X font selector) allows you to preview fonts and select the name of the one you want. You can then paste the selected font name on a command line or in a resource file, or toggle it with the Selection item *(11.15)* on the *xterm* VT Fonts menu.

xfontsel

If you've used *xfontsel*, you know how the interface works. The window has 14 menus corresponding to the 14 components of a font name *(17.18)*. If you run *xfontsel* without any options, the 14-name components are initially represented by asterisk wildcards. Since an all-wildcard name could hypothetically match any font name, the upper-right corner of the *xfontsel* window displays the number of fonts available (586 on my system), and the window displays the first font in the font search path. You narrow the number of choices and change the font displayed by selecting font-name components from the menus.

If your system is using the standard X11R5 fonts, the *xfontsel* window initially displays a 12-point, constant width Hangul font (the Korean alphabet) from the *misc* font directory, the complete name of which is:

```
-daewoo-gothic-medium-r-normal--16-120-100-100-c-160-ksc5601.1987-0
```

This is the first font in the default font search path. (The foundry "daewoo" comes first alphabetically in the *misc* directory, the first directory in the default font path.) Figure 17-2 shows the initial *xfontsel* window.

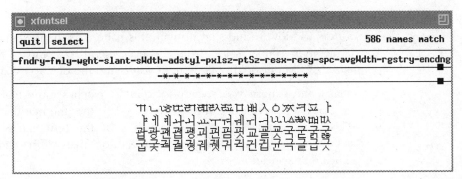

Figure 17-2: xfontsel window displaying Hangul font

This is how you should start if you have no idea what kind of font you're looking for. Run *xfontsel* without any options, and browse around using the menus. In order to make meaningful selections from the menus, you should know a little something about X font naming syntax *(17.18)*. You might begin by choosing a series of names from the fmly menu to preview a representative font from each family. It helps to be somewhat familiar with the more common font families, but if you aren't, you can still use *xfontsel*: browsing will just take a little longer.

Once you've chosen a family name, you can play with point size and other characteristics. Since the initial font you get may be very small or even be in a different character set than the one you anticipated, you may need to select from other menus just to get an idea what the family looks like.

Each selection narrows the possible font names you could be matching. For instance, if I select Courier from the family (fmly) menu, only 60 names match, and the window displays the first Courier font in the font path. In my environment, this happens to be a 10-point Courier bold with an oblique slant. This font is much too tiny give me a clear idea what the Courier family is like, so I can choose a larger point size from that menu.

If you're looking for fonts suitable for *xterm* (or another terminal emulator), you want the "fixed" family. In addition, choose "misc" from the fndry menu, unless you want Japanese characters (in which case you should choose "sony" or "jis").

In order to display a particular font, you'll probably have to make selections from several of the menus. Try explicitly selecting at least the font family, weight, slant, and point size. (Thus, you would make selections from the fmly, wght, slant, and ptSz menus.)

If you already have an idea what kind of font you'd like, you can start *xfontsel* with a more limited range of choices by using the *–pattern* option with a wild-carded font name *(17.15)*. For example, if you typed:

```
% xfontsel -pattern '*courier-bold-o-*'
```

the *xfontsel* window would start up with this pattern as the filename template. You could then simply select from the ptSz menu to compare the various point sizes of Courier bold oblique until you found the one you wanted.

Note that if the pattern you specify to *xfontsel* matches more than one font, the one that is displayed (the first match found) is the one that the server will use. This is in contrast to *xlsfonts*, which sorts the font names. You can always rely on *xfontsel* to show you the actual font that will be chosen, given any wildcard specification.

Once you've displayed the desired font using the menus, you can make the name of that font the PRIMARY text selection by clicking on the window's select button. You can then paste *(11.05)* the font name into another window using the pointer: onto a command line, into a resource file, etc. Making a font name the PRIMARY selection also enables you to choose that font using the Selection item on the *xterm* VT Fonts menu *(11.15)*.

— VQ

18

The Keyboard and Mouse

18.01 Input Devices

When working with X programs, you communicate with the program using your keyboard and your mouse (or pointer device). You might think of a key as just a key and a mouse button as just a mouse button, but the magic of software gives us the opportunity to reprogram their behavior and tailor it to our daily preferences.

In X, there are two levels where keys and pointers can be reprogrammed.

- At the server level *(1.02)*, you can change the mappings of keys and pointer buttons using the *xmodmap* client *(18.07)*. These changes will affect all X clients. You can also change mouse and keyboard behavior with the *xset* client *(6.18)*, such as the speed of the mouse *(18.02)*, or how loudly your keys click *(18.04)*. On some servers, you can alter the sensitivity of your keyboard *(18.03)*.

- At the client level, each X client can set special resources called *translations (20.29)* that define a special action when a particular key or pointer button is pressed. In addition, window managers have an opportunity to intercept keystrokes and pointer clicks via key bindings.

—LM

18.02 Pointer Too Fast?

xset is a powerful all-purpose client for changing a variety of server-controlled features. Among the parameters that can be controlled by *xset* is the pointer speed.

The *m* (mouse) option controls the rate at which the mouse or pointer moves across the screen. This option takes two parameters: *acceleration* and *threshold*. They must be positive integers. (The acceleration can also be written as a fraction, with the numerator and denominator separated by a slash, for example, 5/4.)

The mouse or pointer moves *acceleration* times as fast when it travels more than the *threshold* number of pixels in a short time. This way, the pointer can be used for precise alignment when it is moved slowly, yet it can be set to travel across the screen by a flick of the wrist when desired. If only one parameter is given, it is interpreted as the acceleration.

For example, the command:

```
% xset m 5 10
```

sets the pointer movement so that if you move the pointer more than 10 pixels, the pointer cursor moves five times as many pixels on the screen as you moved the pointer on the pad.

If no parameter or the value `default` is used, the system defaults will be set.

If you want to change the threshold and leave the acceleration unchanged, enter the value `default` for the acceleration parameter and then specify the threshold you want:

```
% xset m default 20
```

If you have a workstation, then another thing you can do is to start up the X server using the *−a* and *−t* command-line options. The *−a* option changes the acceleration and the *−t* option changes the threshold. See Article 18.05 for information on changing your server command.

— VQ, from the X Window System User's Guide

18.03 *Changing the Keyboard Auto-repeat*

Auto-repeat is the feature that allows the same character to be repeated over and over according to how long you hold down the key. By default, the auto-repeat is turned on. You can turn auto-repeat on or off by using the *xset* client:

```
xset r on|off
```

You can also control the auto-repeat using the *−r* and *r* command-line options to the X server. *−r* turns off the auto-repeat, and *r* turns it on. See Article 18.05 for information on how to change the command line to start your server.

Some servers also allow you to actually vary the auto-repeat rate. These servers may provide additional command-line options to set the rate at startup time. For example, you can start the *Xsun* server with the *−ar1 350 -ar2 30* options to reduce the sensitivity of the keyboard.

—LM

18.04 Keyclicks

The *c* option to *xset* sets the volume of the keyboard's keyclick—a sound generated by the server when you type each key (not to be confused with the noise the physical key makes). To specify a particular level of keyclick, use the option:

```
c volume
```

volume can be a value from 0 to 100, indicating a percentage of the maximum volume. For example:

```
% xset c 75
```

sets a moderately loud keyclick. The X server sets the volume to the nearest value that the hardware can support.

The *c* option also accepts the parameters on or off. If you specify xset c on, the system default for volume is used.

The keyclick can also be turned off with the −*c* option or by setting the volume parameter to 0 xset c 0).

On some hardware, a volume of 0 to 50 turns the keyclick off, and a volume of 51 to 100 turns the keyclick on. Note also that in some cases, the keyclick cannot be turned on.

If you want, you can control the keyclick using −*c* and *c* as command-line options to the X server. See Article 18.05 for more information.

— *VQ, from the* X Window System User's Guide

18.05 Changing Your Server Command

If you have a workstation, your X server is just a program that lives in */usr/bin/X11* with all the other standard X client executables. Usually the X server program has a name that indicates what sort of workstation it's for, such as *Xsun* or *Xnext*, but is then linked to just *X*.

Usually you don't think about your server program. But sometimes you might want to specify different command-line options. For example, if you have a workstation, then all the features shown in Articles 18.02, 18.03, and 18.04 can be set permanently through command-line options to your X server.

If you use *xinit* or *startx* to start your X session, the server is run by executing the command */usr/bin/X11/X*. You can change this by creating a file in your home directory called *.xserverrc*. For example:

```
/usr/bin/X11/X -r c 75 -a 5 -t 10
```

This turns off the auto-repeat *(18.03)*, sets the keyclick to 75% *(18.04)*, and turns the pointer acceleration and threshold *(18.02)* to 5 and 10, respectively.

If you use *xdm* *(28.02)* to log in, you need to edit the */usr/lib/X11/xdm/Xservers* file. (In most cases, this will require root permission.) The following line starts the X server for your local display:

```
:0 local /usr/bin/X11/X
```

Just add on the extra command-line options:

```
:0 local /usr/bin/X11/X -r c 75 -a 5 -t 10
```

See Articles 28.04 and 28.05 for more information on the syntax for the *Xservers* file.

—*LM*

18.06 Too Many xsets

After you've been editing your startup script *(2.09)* for a while, and taking advice (and snippets of files) from several people, you may find you have three or four calls to the *xset* *(6.18)* or *xmodmap* *(18.07)* programs. You can speed up the startup by merging these into a single call. For example, if you had

```
xset m 8
```

in one place,

```
xset r off
```

in another, and

```
xset b 60
```

in another, you could combine these into a single command:

```
xset m 8 r off b 60
```

Remember that the system can get quite busy when you are starting X and all its clients, so anything you can do to optimize the startup will be useful.

—*IFD*

18.07 Defining Keys with xmodmap

When the user types a key or presses a mouse button, the server is responsible for conveying this information to the appropriate X client. You can use the *xmodmap* client to change what key is reported to the client when certain keys or mouse buttons are pressed.

You probably wouldn't want to translate the alphanumeric keys on the keyboard, but you may want to translate others. For example, you might want to change the **Backspace** key to a **Delete**:

```
% xmodmap -e "keysym BackSpace = Delete"
```

(With the *xterm (2.02)* client, you might also be interested in ways to change the erase key using the UNIX *stty* command, or with the *xterm* ttyModes resource.)

If you are a DVORAK typist, you can use *xmodmap* to translate every key on the keyboard so your QWERTY keyboard behaves like a DVORAK keyboard.

The symbols such as Backspace and Delete are called *key symbols*, or *keysyms* for short. The mapping of a particular keysym to a hardware keycode is called a *keysym mapping*. If it ever seems that keystrokes are not working correctly, you can check current keysym mappings by running *xmodmap* with the *–pk* argument *(18.17)*. Article 18.12 shows how you can use the *xev* client to determine exactly what keycode each key generates on your display.

You can use *xmodmap* to add or remove keysyms, or even to redefine the keycode associated with that keysym. You can also use it to redefine the mouse buttons *(18.11)*.

If you find *xmodmap* too unwieldy for daily use, check out the *xkeycaps* client *(18.18)*, which is a graphical front-end to *xmodmap*.

—LM

18.08 *Faking Function Keys*

My keyboard doesn't have function keys. This poses a problem when I use *mwm (13.01)*, since it uses **Alt**–*function key* sequences to move, lower, open, and close windows.

My keyboard *does* have a keypad, though. And I don't use the keypad, so it occurred to me that I could use *xmodmap (18.07)* to map they keypad keys to function keys. I created a *$HOME/.Xmodmap* file, containing the following lines:

```
keysym KP_1 = F1
keysym KP_2 = F2
keysym KP_3 = F3
keysym KP_4 = F4
keysym KP_5 = F5
keysym KP_6 = F6
keysym KP_7 = F7
keysym KP_8 = F8
keysym KP_9 = F9
```

In my startup script, I call the *.Xmodmap* file like this:

```
xmodmap $HOME/.Xmodmap
```

... and applications are none the wiser.

—LM

18.09   *Problems with Sun Keyboards*

Some users on Sun keyboards have a problem where the middle set of cursor keys and function keys are useless. As a solution, you can use the following *xmodmap* *(18.07)* commands:

```
! up arrow
keycode 27 = Up
! down arrow
keycode 34 = Down
! left arrow
keycode 31 = Left
! right arrow
keycode 35 = Right
! page up
keycode 103 = Prior
! page down
keycode 130 = Next
! home
keycode 59 = Home
! end
keycode 81 = End
! insert
keycode 51 = Insert
```

You can place these commands in a file and then call the *xmodmap* client on that file, as shown in Article 18.08.

Since the keys aren't defined initially, you have to use the keycode command to map them for the first time. To find out the keycodes generated by a particular key, use the *xev* *(18.12)* client.

—LM

18.10   *That Pesky Caps Lock Key*

Do you ever hit **Caps Lock** accidentally? Do you ever do it within *vi*, and then you hit "j" repeatedly to go down a few lines, and suddenly you've joined 10 lines of text by accident?

There are times when I want to pry off my **Caps Lock** key and toss it in a drawer. My brother has actually done exactly that. He has a bowl at home filled with discarded **Caps Lock** keys, next to his jar of recycled paper clips. But there are better ways to defuse **Caps Lock**.

One of the easiest things to do is to disable **Caps Lock** entirely. Just use *xmodmap* (18.07) to remove its mapping (or more precisely, remap it to null):

```
% xmodmap -e "keysym CapsLock ="
```

Another thing is that when I use a Macintosh or PC X server, I find that I hit **Caps Lock** all the time. This is because the **Caps Lock** key on a Macintosh or PC keyboard is where I expect **CTRL** to be, and the **CTRL** key is where I expect **Caps Lock** to be. A solution is to just switch the two keys. Type the following into *$HOME/.Xmodmap*:

.Xmodmap

```
! .Xmodmap file
!
! Submitted by David Flanagan
!

remove Lock = Caps_Lock
remove Control = Control_L
keysym Control_L = Caps_Lock
keysym Caps_Lock = Control_L
add Lock = Caps_Lock
add Control = Control_L
```

Then run *xmodmap* on this file, either on the command line or on your startup script (2.09, 16.03)

```
% xmodmap $HOME/.Xmodmap
```

—*LM*

18.11 *Switching Mouse Buttons*

My server comes with a two-button mouse. Since many X programs expect three mouse buttons, the server has to make some adjustments. The first button acts like the first pointer button for X programs (as you'd expect), but the second button acts like the third mouse button for X programs. When running programs that want you to use the second mouse button, you have to press both buttons down at once. You also have to make sure you get the timing just right.

Now, the second mouse button is my favorite, and I rarely ever use the third. I use the second mouse button for scrolling (11.04), since it's so much easier to control. In *xterm* (2.02), I also use the second mouse button for pasting things I've selected with the first mouse button (11.05). Having to press both buttons down is a pain, especially since if you don't get the timing down exactly, you end up erasing whatever you were trying to paste.

The easiest solution for me was just to switch the second and third mouse buttons using *xmodmap* (18.07):

```
% xmodmap -e "pointer = 1 3 2"
```

This makes it a bit hard on those few occasions when I need to use the third mouse button, but it makes life much easier on the whole.

—LM

18.12 *Debugging Keysyms with xev*

xev

The *xev* client is essential for debugging keysym mappings. When you start up *xev*, a small event window appears (see Figure 18-1).

Figure 18-1: xev event window

All events that take place within that window are shown on standard output. This means screenfuls of output, but it also means that when you type a key, you can immediately trace the resulting event. For example, if you need to know what keysym is sent when you type the **Delete** key on the keyboard, just run *xev* and type the **Delete** key in the event window. Typical output might be:

```
KeyPress event, serial 13, synthetic NO, window 0x800001,
  root 0x8006d, subw 0x800002, time 1762968270, (50,36),
  root:(190,176), state 0x0, keycode 27 (keysym 0xffff, Delete),
same_screen YES,
  XLookupString gives 1 characters: "^?"

KeyRelease event, serial 15, synthetic NO, window 0x800001,
  root 0x8006d, subw 0x800002, time 1762968336, (50,36),
root:(190,176),
  state 0x0, keycode 27 (keysym 0xffff, Delete), same_screen YES,
  XLookupString gives 1 characters: "^?"
```

This tells you that the **Delete** key (keycode 27), is interpreted as keysym 0xffff (Delete) and character ^?. If you do an *xmodmap –pk*, you should see a line resembling:

```
27        0xffff (Delete)
```

If you redefine the **Delete** key as the **Backspace** key and do the same exercise (run *xev* and press the **Delete** key), you should see something like:

```
% xmodmap -e "keysym Delete = BackSpace"
% xev
      ...
KeyPress event, serial 13, synthetic NO, window 0x800001,
  root 0x8006d, subw 0x800002, time 1763440073, (44,39),
root:(240,235),
  state 0x0, keycode 27 (keysym 0xff08, BackSpace), same_screen
YES,
  XLookupString gives 1 characters: "^H"

KeyRelease event, serial 15, synthetic NO, window 0x800001,
  root 0x8006d, subw 0x800002, time 1763440139, (44,39),
root:(240,235),
  state 0x0, keycode 27 (keysym 0xff08, BackSpace), same_screen
YES,
  XLookupString gives 1 characters: "^H"
```

This tells you that now the **Delete** key (still keycode 27) is being interpreted as hexadecimal `0xff08`, keysym `BackSpace`, and generates character "^H." *xmodmap –pk* should show you:

```
27        0xff08 (BackSpace)
```

—*LM, from the* X Window System Administrator's Guide

18.13 *xev Under olwm*

If you're running *olwm (14.01)* and you can't seem to get *xev (18.12)* to respond to your keystrokes, set this resource in your *.Xdefaults* or *.Xresources* file *(17.03)*:

```
olwm*FocusLenience: true
```

What's going on here is that clients are supposed to tell the window manager when they want keyboard focus, but *xev* doesn't do this. So the `FocusLenience` resource tells *olwm* to let the renegade clients have their way. You also need to set up *olwm* to use pointer focus instead of click to type; see Article 14.15 for more information.

—*LM*

18.14 *I Never Meta Key...*

Many X clients provide commands that require you to use the so-called *Meta* key. The catch is that you won't find the name Meta printed on any existing keyboard.

Meta is the name of a function (recognized by X) that can be mapped to any physical key. Generally Meta is mapped to a convenient function key. The key that performs the Meta function might be labeled **Alt**, **Alternate**, **Compose**, **Left**, **Right**, or any number of names, depending on your keyboard and how it's configured. On the Sun3 keyboard, for example, Meta is either of the keys labeled **Left** or **Right**. For NCD X terminals, the Meta key is labeled **Alt**.

You can probably figure out which of the function keys on your keyboard is Meta with a little experimentation. For example, most window managers provide keyboard shortcuts involving the Meta key. *twm* users should try any of the commands described in Article 12.05.

To locate the Meta key more systematically, you need to use the *xmodmap* *(18.07)* and *xev (18.12)* clients.

The *xmodmap* client can tell you the current assignments of modifier keyname functions to physical keys and also allow you to change the assignments. To check the current mappings, run *xmodmap* without options. You should get output similar to:

```
xmodmap: up to 2 keys per modifier, (keycodes in parentheses):

shift       Shift_L (0x6a), Shift_R (0x75)
lock        Caps_Lock (0x7e)
control     Control_L (0x53)
mod1        Meta_L (0x7f),  Meta_R (0x81)
mod2
mod3
mod4
mod5
```

For each logical keyname (on the left), *xmodmap* lists one or more keysyms, each followed in parentheses by an actual hardware keycode inglorious hexadecimal. In this mapping, two keys are assigned as Meta (mod1) keys: keys having the keysyms Meta_L and Meta_R (for left and right, apparently one on each side of the keyboard). Unfortunately, this information doesn't pin down these keys on the physical keyboard.

You still need to know which physical keys (keycodes) have the keysyms Meta_L and Meta_R. Test this using *xev* as shown in Article 18.12.

```
% xev
```

To find the Meta key, direct focus to the *xev* window and leave the pointer within the central box. Then type a few keys you suspect might be the Meta key. The window from which you ran *xev* will be spewing output about your every action, including information about each of these keys. When you see output that includes the Meta keysym, you've found the key(s).

When I type the keys labeled **Left** and **Right**, I get the following output, which confirms they are the keys with the keysyms Meta_L and Meta_R:

```
KeyRelease event, serial 16, synthetic NO, window 0x3400002,
    root 0x2d, subw 0x3400003, time 3955291602, (28,26), root:(128,649),
    state 0x8, keycode 127 (keysym 0xffe7, Meta_L), same_screen YES,
    XLookupString gives 0 characters:  ""

KeyPress event, serial 16, synthetic NO, window 0x3400002,
    root 0x2d, subw 0x3400003, time 3955296162, (28,26), root:(128,649),
    state 0x0, keycode 129 (keysym 0xffe8, Meta_R), same_screen YES,
    XLookupString gives 0 characters:  ""
```

Type **CTRL-C** in the window from which you invoked *xev* to terminate the program.

— *VQ, TOR, from the* X Window System User's Guide

18.15 *Give Me Back My Backspace!*

One problem with using *xmodmap* *(18.07)* is that the mappings are maintained until the server is reset. This can cause a problem if you use a server that doesn't reset when each user logs out (as with some X terminals).

At our site, most of us want to use the key marked **Backspace**, which generates ^H, as our erase character. (**Delete**, or ^?, is the default.) We use *stty* to set up that up in our *.login* or *.profile* files:

```
stty erase ^H
```

But we have one occasional user (let's call him Bryan) who uses *xmodmap* to do the same thing. Instead of using *stty* to redefine what control sequence should be used for erasing, he just uses *xmodmap* to have the **Backspace** key generate the same control sequence as **Delete**.

```
xmodmap -e "keysym BackSpace = Delete"
```

What frequently happens is that Bryan uses someone else's terminal (generally someone who is out that day), and then the next day that person complains that their **Backspace** doesn't work anymore. This is because Bryan has set up the **Backspace** to generate ^?, but the user has *stty* commands to set the erase key to ^H, and that key doesn't exist anymore.

The low-tech solution is to just turn the X terminal off and then on again. But we'd prefer to find a way to fix it without having to log the person out. (Of course, the ideal situation would be if servers stored their default key mapping, so we could just say something like "xmodmap keysym reset".)

One way to fix it is to use .XET N .XE1 "xev command" .XE2 "determining Backspace keycode via" ./XET *xev* to find out the keycode for the Backspace key *(18.12)* and then remap that key to **Backspace**. Even if you remap a key, the keycode doesn't change and can be used to reassign it if necessary. For example,

```
% xev
        (type backspace key in xev window)
KeyRelease event, serial 15, synthetic NO, window 0x2400001,
    root 0x22, subw 0x2400002, time 786911518, (51,44), root:(1008,379),
    state 0x0, keycode 102 (keysym 0xffff, Delete), same_screen YES,
    XLookupString gives 1 characters: ""
```

From this, you find out that the **Backspace** key has keycode 102. Use this to reassign the mapping:

```
xmodmap -e "keycode 102 = BackSpace"
```

The difficult part is that you can't just automate this. Every server has different default keycode-to-keysym mappings. But you might be able to generate a single script for resetting keysyms for a specified server model. For example, since most of our users have NCD keyboards, we might set up a *resetncd* shell script that resets a series of keysyms for our NCD users.

An administrator might also tweak *xdm* to make sure that all X terminals are reset to their initial *xmodmap* settings when the user logs out. Article 28.26 shows how you might do this.

—LM

18.16 *Be Careful with X Terminals!*

Some X terminals are set up so that they don't actually reset their server between user logins. This means that some features are maintained between logins, including root-window backgrounds *(6.02)* and (you guessed it) keysym mappings.

The problem we describe in Article 18.15 is one byproduct of this "feature": the next user who logs in may be inconvenienced by your mappings. But there's an even more frustrating effect—when your keysym mappings prevent the next user from logging in at all!

One day, I was surprised when I tried to log in at an X terminal and kept on getting the **Login incorrect** message in my *xdm* login box *(28.02)*. After scratching my head for a while (and confirming with my manager that I still worked here!), I remembered that the last time I used this terminal, I had been playing around with the *xkeycaps* client *(18.18)*. I figured out that among the characters I redefined was one of the characters I use in my password!

Brilliant, aren't I?

I just rebooted the server and everything was fine again. But this is yet another reason why you should be very careful when changing keysyms on X terminals.

—LM

18.17 *Printing the Current Keysyms*

The *xmodmap* *(18.07)* client has a –*pk* option that prints the current keysym mappings:

```
% xmodmap -pk
There are 2 KeySyms per KeyCode; KeyCodes range from 8 to 103.

    KeyCode     Keysym (Keysym) ...
    Value       Value  (Name)   ...

      8
      9
     10
     11        0x005c (backslash)       0x007c (bar)
     12        0x005d (bracketright)    0x007d (braceright)
     13        0x005b (bracketleft)     0x007b (braceleft)
     14        0x0049 (I)
     15        0x004f (O)
                 ...
```

An even more useful option is –*pke*. As in –*pk*, all settings are printed; however, they are printed in syntax appropriate for *xmodmap* commands.

```
% xmodmap -pke
keycode   8 =
keycode   9 =
keycode  10 =
keycode  11 = backslash bar
keycode  12 = bracketright braceright
keycode  13 = bracketleft braceleft
keycode  14 = I
keycode  15 = O
           ...
```

What's this useful for? Well, one thing is that if you have your current keysyms set up just the way you like them, then you might run *xmodmap* –*pke* to copy them into a file, and then in your startup script *(2.09)* run *xmodmap* on that file. For example:

```
% xmodmap -pke > $HOME/.Xmodmap
```

And then in your startup script:

```
#!/bin/sh
   ...
xmodmap $HOME/.Xmodmap
   ...
```

This is slightly inefficient, since the –*pke* option saves all keymappings, not just the ones that are different from the defaults. But it works.

Another thing you can do is use *–pke* to save your mappings at the beginning of your X session, and then restore them when you log out. This avoids situations like that shown in Article 18.15. Your startup script might read:

```
#!/bin/sh

xmodmap -pke > $HOME/.Xmodmap.default
xmodmap $HOME/.Xmodmap

xterm &
xmail &
      ...
twm

xmodmap $HOME/.Xmodmap.default
```

What happens is that at the beginning of the X session, the current keysym settings are saved in a file called *.Xmodmap.default.* Then you load your own keysym preferences from a *.Xmodmap* file, and start clients (and a window manager) as usual.

When you exit your controlling process *(16.03)*, another *xmodmap* client is called, this time restoring the commands saved in *.Xmodmap.default* at the beginning of the X session. The result is that you leave the X terminal with the same keysym mappings as you found it in.

If you use *xdm (28.02)*, your administrator can also configure this on a systemwide level. See Article 28.26 for more information.

—*LM*

18.18 *xkeycaps: A Front-end to xmodmap*

One application you might find enormously useful is *xkeycaps. xkeycaps* is a graphical front-end to *xmodmap (18.07).* It shows you a keyboard and lets you remap keycodes to keysyms "on the fly."

If I were giving awards for most useful X programs, *xkeycaps* might make my Top 10 list. What makes it cool is that it takes some extremely esoteric syntax and makes it easy enough for any user. I wish other features in X had this sort of interface available.

xkeycaps

The first thing *xkeycaps* needs to do is to determine what sort of keyboard you have. If you know the *xkeycaps* code for your keyboard, you can specify it via the *–kbd* command-line option:

```
% xkeycaps -kbd sun4 &
```

You can get a listing of the accepted keyboards by calling *xkeycaps* with the *–help* command-line option:

```
% xkeycaps -help
xkeycaps: please specify -keyboard with one of the following names:
```

```
        Sun2            - Sun type2 (MIT layout)
        Sun3            - Sun type3 (MIT layout)
        Sun4            - Sun type4 (MIT layout)
        Sun4ow          - Sun type4 (OpenWindows layout)
        Sun5            - Sun type5 (MIT layout)
        Sun5OW          - Sun type5 (OpenWindows layout)
        Sun5SWFROW      - Sun type5 (Swiss-French OpenWindows layout)
        Sun5SW          - Sun type5 (Swedish MIT layout + patch)
        Sun5SWOW        - Sun type5 (Swedish OpenWindows layout)
        Sun5PC          - Sun type5/PC (MIT layout)
        Sun5PC2         - Sun type5/PC (MIT layout + patch)
        Sun5PCOW        - Sun type5/PC (OpenWindows layout)
        Sun5PCDEOW      - Sun type5/PC (German OpenWindows layout)
        Sun101A         - Sun 101A (MIT layout)
        NCD97           - Network Computing Devices N97
        NCD101          - Network Computing Devices N101
        NCD102          - Network Computing Devices N102 (US layout)
        NCD102F         - Network Computing Devices N102 (French layout)
        NCD102N         - Network Computing Devices N102 (Norwegian layout)
            ...
```

This is just the tip of the iceberg. I couldn't count them all, but it looked as if there were at least 70 keyboards supported in the latest version of *xkeycaps*. If you don't supply a keyboard type with the *–kbd* option, then a window usually appears for you to select a keyboard type. Supported keyboards include a variety of Sun, NCD, SGI, Tektronix, DEC, IBM RS/6000, SCO, Sony, SGO, and HP keyboards; plus Atari, PC and NeXT keyboards. *xkeycaps* examines your server's vendor display string and tries to make an educated guess of what sort of keyboard you use. It then asks you to either confirm the current keyboard type or select a new one. In some cases, it also gives you an opportunity to select between several different layouts of your keyboard.

As you select a keyboard, a small diagram of it shows up at the bottom of the **Select Keyboard** window (see Figure 18-2.) You should be very careful at this stage, since the success of *xkeycaps* relies entirely on it having the correct information about your keyboard; there is no way for it to get this information confirmed directly from the server. [*]

Once you've selected your keyboard, press **ok**.

Your keyboard appears in a window such as that in Figure 18-3. Each key appears with the character it's mapped to in bold. On the right of the key is the keycode that the key generates (in hexadecimal). As your pointer moves across the window, the **KeyCode**, **KeySym**, **ASCII**, **Modifiers**, and **AutoRepeat**

---

[*] On some Sun and HP workstations, *xkeycaps* can examine the keyboard hardware directly to figure out what sort of keyboard you're using. However, since this isn't supported by the X protocol, it only works if you are running *xkeycaps* locally.

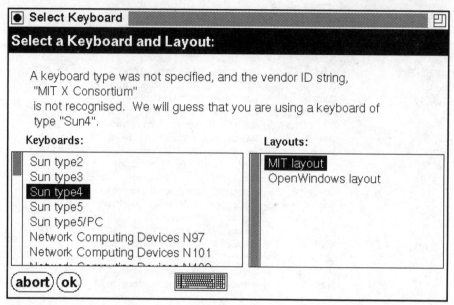

Figure 18-2: Selecting a keyboard type

fields at the top of the window are updated for that key.

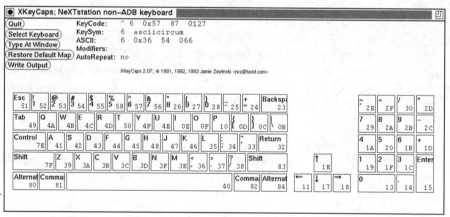

Figure 18-3: xkeycaps window

When you press on a key with the first mouse button, a keypress event for that key is generated. (This comes in handy with the **Type in Window** feature listed below.) When you press on a key with the third mouse button, a popup menu appears allowing you to edit the keysym, as shown in Figure 18-4.

If you select **Exchange Keys**, you're asked to select a second key to exchange it with. This may be useful in situations like that of Article 18.10, when the **Caps Lock** and **CTRL** keys need to be switched.

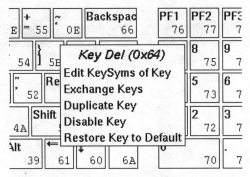

Figure 18-4: Editing the Delete key in xkeycaps

If you select **Duplicate Key**, it asks you to select a second key and makes the two keys identical. For example, if you want to have your **Backspace** key work the same as **Delete** (as shown in Article 18.07), you can now do this in just a couple of button clicks.

If you press **Disable Key**, this removes the key entirely. This might be another way to disable the **Caps Lock** key (see Article 18.10).

Restore Key to Default does just what it says.

If you select **Edit KeySyms of Key**, a window appears that allows you to redefine the key symbols with a bit more control, as shown in Figure 18-5. Each of the eight possible keysyms are shown on the far right of the window (although most keyboards only have one or two keysyms active). You can select one of the keysyms and then select a new symbol in the right column. You might also identify the key as a modifier *(18.14)* in the second column. (The third column gives you an opportunity to select another character set, but for most keyboards only Latin1 and Keyboard are relevant.)

At the upper left of the *xkeycaps* window are several command buttons.

Quit

Quit *xkeycaps*.

Select Keyboard

Brings up the **Select Keyboard** window, so you can select a different keyboard display.

Type at Window

This is a particularly cool feature. If you select **Type at Window**, your cursor becomes a crosshairs for selecting another window. Once you select the other window, the keys you select in the *xkeycaps* window are redirected to the new one. (If you use an *xterm* window for this, you have to remember to select **Allow SendEvents** from the *xterm*Main Options window *(11.14)*.)

The Keyboard and Mouse   **415**

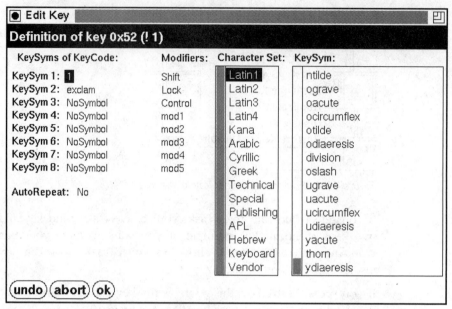

Figure 18-5: Editing keysyms in xkeycaps

Restore Default Map

This resets all keys to their defaults. It comes in very useful when you screw yourself over royally. The one thing to worry about is that you have to make sure that *xkeycaps* thinks you're using the correct keyboard; otherwise, you may end up with a completely useless keyboard.

Write Output

Now here's one of my favorite parts. You can have *xkeycaps* output your current settings to standard output. So if you redirect the output of *xkeycaps* to another file:

```
% xkeycaps > xkeycaps.out &
```

Then when you press **Write Output**, *xmodmap* commands are placed in the file. (You are asked whether you want all keys or just the ones that have been changed from the default.) This file can be applied later to the *xmodmap* client *(18.07)* in your startup script *(2.09)*, so you can have the same keyboard configuration every day:

```
xmodmap xkeycaps.out
```

—LM

18.19 Resetting the Keyboard

On Sun workstations, the abnormal termination of the X server may leave the keyboard in a weird state. (If you don't know what we mean by this, believe us, you'll know it when you see it.) The X distribution provides the command */usr/bin/X11/kbd_mode* to restore the keyboard on a Sun workstation. Since your keyboard is unusable, you'll have to use an alternative login to run the command (such as a *telnet* window, or running *rlogin (19.03)* from another machine).

```
# /usr/bin/X11/kbd_mode -a > /dev/console
```

—*EAP, from the* X Window System Administrator's Guide

18.20 Space Bar as CTRL

If you sometimes have trouble reaching your **CTRL** key, there's a patch available for using your space bar for **CTRL**. This patch requires that you have the source code for your server, so stop reading right here if you don't. For example, if you use a commercial X server (as you would if you use an X terminal), it's unlikely that you might have access to the source.

space-
bar_hack

You need to apply this patch to your server source code and then rebuild your server. The result is that your space bar is altered so that if you hold it down a bit, the space bar acts like the **CTRL** key instead. If you press the space bar normally, you just get a space.

This feature requires a bit of practice to get it right. For example, it's possible that you may try to type the string "two hands" and get "twoands", since if you hold down the space a bit too long, it gets combined with the "h" and you get a **CTRL-H** or **Backspace**. But with some practice, the space-bar patch may save you having to reach for the **CTRL** key all the time. This is especially useful for *emacs (9.02)* users.

—*LM*

The Keyboard and Mouse

19

Remote Clients

19.01 Why Run Clients Remotely?

Many X users run all their clients on a single host. They log on via *xdm* *(28.02)* to a host and start all their clients on that host. Or they log on via *xinit* *(1.03)* and run all their clients on their local workstation.

Occasionally, however, users have to run some clients on other machines. For example, my local workstation doesn't have a license for the commercial product FrameMaker. So I need to run FrameMaker on another machine. However, because FrameMaker is an X-based client, I can run it on the remote machine but display it on my server. This is an example of a *remote client*. A remote client is one that executes on one machine and displays to a server running on another.

In this instance, I'm running the client on a remote machine because of legal restrictions. There are other reasons to run remote clients. For example, my mail is not forwarded to my machine, but remains on a remote host, so when I run a mail client, I have to run it on the remote machine. As another example: for this book I've had some trouble building some programs on my local machine. So instead, I've had to build and test many programs on a remote SunOS host (which is a reference platform for almost all X-based software, so programs are more likely to build cleanly) and then display it onto my local server.

Once a remote client connects to your server, everything works transparently. However, in order to run remote clients, you generally have to do a little bit of preparation. This chapter covers what you need to know to get a remote client running on your server.

—LM

19.02 Over the Network and Through the Woods

We often define remote clients as clients that run "over the network." What does this mean?

The X server communicates with clients over *sockets*. Sockets can be loosely defined as a means by which programs can "listen" for requests on a given port and respond as appropriate. In the case of X, the X server listens for client requests on a designated port or socket (generally port 6000).

There are two protocols for communicating with a socket: UDP and TCP. UDP runs locally on the machine, so it can only be used by local clients communicating with the local server. TCP runs over an IP network (thus the familiar name TCP/IP), and can be used by any client that is connected to the host over the network.

As a rule, it's more efficient to communicate over UDP when you can and avoid the network. So local clients—that is, clients that run on the same machine as the machine running the server—generally run over UDP, also known as UNIX domain sockets. Remote clients, however, have to use TCP/IP.

How do we tell clients how to communicate with the server? Well, for that we use the DISPLAY environment variable *(2.04)* or the *–display* command-line option. For a local client, the display name can usually be set to unix:0 or just :0. For remote clients, the display name has to be set to the name of host followed by :0, e.g., *opal:0*. (The :0 part tells the client which port to use. :n tells the client to use port (6000+*n*), so :0 says to use port 6000. This is the port used by most servers. It's possible for servers to run on a different port, for example port 6001, in which case you would specify :1 instead.)

Usually, your DISPLAY environment variable is set up correctly for local clients when you first start your X session. However, if you want to run clients from a remote host, you may need to set your display differently for the remote clients. Articles 19.10 and 19.09 tell you more about setting DISPLAY for remote clients.

—LM

19.03 Remote Logins

Stop right there.

Probably the most commonly used client is *xterm (2.02)*. So it might make sense that one of the clients you're most likely to want to run remotely is *xterm*. I do this all the time since there are several different machines on our network that I work on.

However, does it really make sense to run remote *xterm* clients? Probably not. When you run a remote client, you have a client and server communicating over the network, conveying graphics requests. However, if you were to open a local *xterm* window and then *rlogin* or *telnet* (19.03) to the remote machine, then no graphics requests actually go over the network, only the characters you type.

```
lmui@opal% rlogin rock
Last login: Tue Jul 13 06:27:31 from opal.ora.com
SunOS Release 4.1.2 (ROCK) #2: Thu Jun 24 20:52:57 PDT 1993
lmui@rock 1 %
```

The other advantage of running local *xterm* clients for remote logins is that it prevents some serious security holes. Since your commands aren't going over the network, network snoops can't listen in on what you're typing. Also, if you don't intend to run any other clients from the remote system, you may not need to extend access control (19.12) to the remote system. If you don't mind typing in your password every time, you can even avoid editing your *.rhosts* file (19.06) and opening up that can of worms. For the security conscious, using *rlogin* or *telnet* is the much safer option.

The disadvantage is that a remote *xterm* client automatically defines some environment variables (2.04), such as DISPLAY. But when you just open a local *xterm* and use *rlogin* or *telnet*, then you have to explicitly set DISPLAY before you can run any remote clients.

If you're reading this chapter sequentially, then some of these arguments may not make sense yet. However, this is a big enough concern that we want to mention it straight off: use your head in running remote clients.

—*LM*

19.04 *Remote Logins with xterm -e*

If you want to use *telnet* or *rlogin* for a remote shell window (19.03), you can automate it by using the *-e* option to *xterm* (11.25). For example, I like to open windows on the machine *rock* using *rlogin*. To do that, I use the following command:

```
lmui@opal % xterm -name rock -e rlogin rock.west.ora.com &
```

You can use this command in your window manager's root menu or in your startup script (2.09, 16.03).

—*LM*

19.05 Running a Remote Client Manually

There are plenty of thorny details to worry about in running remote clients, but they aren't so bad once you figure out what you're trying to do and how to get UNIX and X to do it. This article introduces you to a few of the snags, with the follow-up articles explaining in more detail how to get around them.

Let's suppose a friend tells you that she has a great new X program built on her system. Rather than try to get it for your machine, you decide to try out the command first by running it as a remote client.

For example, I heard about the calendar program *plan (4.05)* from a co-worker of mine, who already had it installed on his workstation. Before going to the trouble of building it myself, I decided to try it out by running it remotely on his machine. Here are the few steps I needed to take to run *plan* on a remote machine and display it to my server.

1. First, I need to log onto the remote machine using either *rlogin* or *telnet*. If you cannot *rlogin* or *telnet* to the remote machine, you are not connected to it via TCP/IP *(19.02)* and cannot initiate a remote X connection. You can only run a remote client if it is connected to your server via TCP/IP.

   In my case, I want to run a client from a workstation named *jasper*, so I *rlogin* to that machine. (Note that I have to supply my password to *jasper* before I can log in. This is fine right now, but it will be a problem if I want to automate this process later on: see Article 19.06.)

   ```
   % rlogin jasper
   Password:
   Last login: Mon Mar 14 08:34:45 from ruby.ora.com
   SunOS Release 4.1.2 (JASPER) #1: Wed Aug 11 17:10:41 PDT 1993
   lmui@jasper %
   ```

2. All X clients need to be told what server to connect to. Usually, this information comes from the DISPLAY environment variable *(2.04)*, which is set automatically when you log in; but when you log in on a remote machine, the value of DISPLAY isn't transferred to the remote machine. I need to tell the *plan* program the name of my server.

   See Articles 19.09 and 19.10 for information on how to specify your display. In my case, I know that my server is opal:0. I can specify it to *plan* (and all other X clients started in this shell) by setting the DISPLAY environment variable.

   ```
   lmui@jasper % setenv DISPLAY opal:0
   ```

   (As an alternative to setting DISPLAY, I could use the *–display opal:0* command-line option for all clients. This may be preferable if you only intend to run one client from the remote system.)

3. The next thing I need to deal with is bypassing any security measures that may be in effect. The easiest (although not the most secure) way to get around access control is to allow access to the entire remote host. In a window connected to my local machine, I use the *xhost* command to extend access to *jasper*. This command *must* be run in a window running locally on my local machine *opal*.

```
lmui@opal % xhost +jasper
```

For more details about getting around access control, see Article 19.12.

4. Then there's your search path *(2.05)*. Your search path on the remote machine needs to include the directory containing the *plan* program. See Article 2.05.

```
lmui@jasper % whereis plan
plan: /usr/local/bin/plan /usr/local/bin/plan.help
lmui@jasper % set path=($path /usr/local/bin)
```

5. Now, in the window connected to *jasper*, I should be able to run the command successfully:

```
lmui@jasper % plan
```

Or, if you skipped step 2:

```
lmui@jasper % plan -display opal:0
```

—LM

19.06 *"Permission denied."*

If you want to run a remote client without having to manually log into the system (as we had to in Article 19.05), one issue you may have to deal with is the *$HOME/.rhosts* file. Bear with us; this information is very UNIX-y but quite essential if you want to run remote clients automatically.

First of all, you must have an account on the remote machine and be able to connect to it via *rlogin*. To run a remote shell, I use the *rsh* command. The simplest syntax is:

```
% rsh  host command
```

(If the *command* is omitted, you are logged in to the machine in an interactive shell, as you would be if you ran *rlogin* instead.)

For example, suppose I want to know who's logged in on the machine *jasper*. All I need to do is run the *who* command on *jasper*. Rather than log onto *jasper*, type out the *who* command, and log off again, I can do it all in one line using *rsh*:

```
lmui@ruby % rsh jasper who
norm     ttyp0   Mar 21 11:31   (:0.0)
norm     ttyp8   Mar 21 13:46   (:0.0)
```

However, in some cases you won't be able to run the command. From another machine, *opal*, I tried to run a *rsh* command on *jasper* and was rejected:

```
lmui@opal % rsh jasper who
Permission denied.
```

The `Permission denied.` message is another example of a common UNIX error that gives the novice user absolutely no clue as to the problem. The message is from *rsh*, and it's trying to tell you that you don't have permission to run the remote command.

In order to run a remote command from *opal*, *opal* must be listed in one of two places on *jasper*: in the */etc/hosts.equiv* file, or in the user's *$HOME/.rhosts* file. (If you list the machine in the */etc/hosts.equiv* file, then all users can run remote commands on the host.) For security reasons, it's better to use *$HOME/.rhosts* (and besides, you probably don't have write permission for */etc/hosts.equiv*.)

In *$HOME/.rhosts* on the remote host, just list the local machine's hostname. For example, in *$HOME/.rhosts* on *jasper*, I list *opal*'s hostname. It's better to use the fully qualified domain name (for security reasons):

```
opal.ora.com
```

If the *.rhosts* file already existed and there were other machines listed there, just add *opal* to the end of the list.

Next, make sure the *.rhosts* file is only readable and writable by you. Using the *chmod* command, give the *.rhosts* file permissions `600`:

```
lmui@jasper % chmod 600 $HOME/.rhosts
```

Now you should be able to run the remote command from *opal* with no problem:

```
lmui@opal % rsh jasper who
norm     ttyp0   Mar 21 11:31   (:0.0)
norm     ttyp8   Mar 21 13:46   (:0.0)
```

You'll also find that when you *rlogin* to the remote machine now, you're no longer prompted for your password. So be very careful with the *.rhosts* file! You need to add machines to *.rhosts* if you want to run remote X clients on them, but this also means that one more level of security is down. If someone breaks into your login account on *opal*, he or she can now automatically get into your account on *jasper* without having to crack your password.

Yes, this is a massive security hole, but it is the only way to automatically run remote X clients. Instead of a boring character-based command like *who*, you can now run X clients from the remote machine:

```
% rsh jasper xboard &
```

—LM

19.07 *"Command not found."*

Your search path *(2.05)* determines what commands you can run directly in your shell. Usually, this information is kept in your PATH environment variable *(2.04)*. However, in running remote clients, you need to remember that you're dealing with a whole new host, and your PATH environment variable on the local host isn't propagated to the remote host. So you need to take special care that the command you want to run is in your search path on the remote host. Otherwise, you might get an error message:

```
lmui@ruby % rsh jasper top
top: Command not found.
```

If you use *csh* as your shell on the remote host, then this is as easy as ensuring that your path is set correctly in your *.cshrc* file on the remote host. See Article 2.05 on how to do this.

If you use the Korn or Bourne shell, you have a special problem: the *$HOME/.profile* and *$HOME/.bashrc* files aren't read by *rsh* on the new system, so you have to use absolute pathnames.

```
bash$ rsh jasper /proj/local/bin/plan &
```

—LM

19.08 *"Error: Can't open display..."*

As we mentioned in Article 19.02, all X clients need to know what display to connect to. X clients get this information from the DISPLAY environment variable or *–display* command-line option. When you initally start your X session, DISPLAY is already set up properly for local clients, but when running remote clients, it's a whole new ball game.

When running a remote client, the value of DISPLAY (like PATH *(19.07)*) isn't propagated to the remote host. Furthermore, in some cases, you don't want it to be. Since local clients may connect differently than remote clients, you may need to use a different display value on the remote host than the one you use locally.

So in running a remote client, you have to make sure to pass it the correct value with a *–display* command-line option. Otherwise, the client has no idea what server to connect to, and you'll get an error message resembling:

```
Error: Can't open display:
```

The procedure for setting the display properly for a remote client depends on whether you are working on an X terminal or a workstation. See Articles 19.09 and 19.10.

—LM

19.09 *Setting DISPLAY on a Workstation*

If you log in at a workstation, it's likely that the value of DISPLAY used for local clients *cannot* be used for remote clients *(19.01)*. On a workstation, the value of DISPLAY may be either unix:0.0 or just :0.0. This means that clients will connect directly to the server running on the local workstation, bypassing the network *(19.02)*. This is fine for local clients (and probably works faster), but it means that you can't trust the value of $DISPLAY for remote clients since (being remote) they *must* use the network to connect to your server.

For example, in a local *xterm (2.02)* window on my workstation, my DISPLAY environment variable *(19.08)* is defined as :0.0:

```
lmui@opal % echo $DISPLAY
:0.0
```

To run a client from a remote host, however, I can't use the value of DISPLAY on an *rsh* command line *(19.06)*. Otherwise, the client would appear on the local server of the remote machine! Imagine my buddy Norm, working on *jasper*, being surprised by a new window appearing on his local display.

Instead, I need to use the *hostname*:0.0 syntax. To display an *xcalendar* client from *jasper* onto the local display on *opal*, I might type:

```
lmui@opal % rsh jasper xcalendar -display opal.ora.com:0.0 &
```

This can be shortened in two ways: since *jasper* is in my domain, I can omit the domain name, and since I'm using the default screen, I might also omit the trailing .0:

```
lmui@opal % rsh jasper xcalendar -display opal:0 &
```

If you use a workstation and start remote X clients automatically from your startup script *(2.09, 16.03)*, you can automate this using the UNIX *hostname* command.

```
#!/bin/sh

case $DISPLAY in
```

```
              unix:0*) REMOTE_DISPLAY=`hostname`:0;;
              :0*) REMOTE_DISPLAY=`hostname`:0;;
              *) REMOTE_DISPLAY=$DISPLAY;;

     esac

     xterm &
              ...
     rsh jasper xcalendar -display ${REMOTE_DISPLAY} &
              ...
```

We try to be careful to use the `hostname`:0 syntax only for remote clients, and only if the display name is currently unix:0.0 or :0.0. This way, we continue to use the simpler syntax for local clients, and the same startup script can be used with an X terminal.

—LM

19.10 *Setting DISPLAY on an X Terminal*

On an X terminal, the value of DISPLAY used for local clients can almost always be used for remote clients *(19.01)* as well. When a user logs in at an X terminal via *xdm (28.02)*, the DISPLAY environment variable *(19.08)* is set to the X terminal's hostname followed by :0.0.

For example, when I log in on an X terminal with hostname *ncd15* in domain *ora.com*, my DISPLAY environment variable is automatically set to ncd15.ora.com:0.0 in my startup script. Being an environment variable, this value is inherited by all clients started within the startup script, as well as all clients started from those clients, and so on. You can check the value of DISPLAY for your X session by using the UNIX *echo* command within an *xterm* window. (Some systems also support an *env* or *printenv* command that shows you *all* your environment variables *(2.04)*.)

```
lmui@ruby % echo $DISPLAY
ncd15.ora.com:0.0
```

At some sites, the domain name is omitted because it is not necessary within most local networks. So this may also read:

```
ncd15:0.0
```

The trailing .0 is also optional, so the entire display name may appear as just:

```
ncd15:0
```

But you shouldn't have to worry about this. If you're on an X terminal, just trust that DISPLAY is set correctly and run remote X clients with the *–display $DISPLAY* command-line option. For example, to run a remote *xcalendar* client from the machine named *jasper*, you might type:

```
lmui@ruby % rsh jasper xcalendar -display $DISPLAY &
```

The value of the DISPLAY environment variable is expanded within your local shell before the *rsh* command is executed. The *xcalendar* command on *jasper* is given the command-line option *–display ncd15.ora.com:0.0*, and therefore knows what server to display on.

—LM

19.11 *Complications with DISPLAY Names*

Occasionally, you may have trouble displaying a client on a particular server. When confronted with such a situation, we recommend trying the following:

- Make sure you are using the proper name of the display. A common mistake is for a workstation user to specify :0 or unix:0, forgetting that different hosts have different ideas of what these display names refer to. See Article 19.09 for more information.

- Make sure that TCP/IP *(19.02)* is properly configured by confirming that other connections work, using (for example) *rlogin* or *telnet.*

- Check the *name server.* The name server is responsible for properly translating hostnames to addresses. To determine if the problem is with your name server, substitute the IP address of the display for the hostname:

      lmui@ruby % xterm -display 140.186.65.35:0

  If this is your problem, it's out of your hands. Just tell your administrator that there's a problem with the name server, and let her deal with it.

- Make sure that access control *(19.12)* isn't the problem by temporarily allowing access from all hosts. (Remember to undo this after the experiment!)

      lmui@opal % xhost +

  If this is the problem, see Article 19.12 for information on how to deal with this correctly.

- Check your TCP/IP configuration. Some versions of TCP/IP, particularly on PCs, restrict the number of allowed connections. If you are using an X server on a PC, find out whether your PC is restricted to a certain number of TCP/IP connections and increase it as needed. (How you actually do this is dependent on the TCP/IP vendor.)

—LM, from the X Window System Administrator's Guide

19.12 "...Client is not authorized to connect to Server"

When running remote clients, you're likely to run into a problem with *server access control.* Server access control is a security measure that prevents every Tom, Dick, and Harriet on your network from running clients to your server. When you start your X session, you already have server access control set up so that you can run local clients. But for running remote clients, you might have to do a little tweaking.

The tip off that your problem is with server access control is that you get an error message that says something like "connection refused" or "client not authorized to connect to server". Or often, a whole bunch of errors:

```
Xlib:  connection to "opal:0.0" refused by server
Xlib:  Client is not authorized to connect to Server
Error: Can't open display: opal:0.0
```

There are several ways to adjust server access control so that you can run the remote client.

1. You can extend access to the remote host by using the *xhost* command on the local host. This is called *host-based access control.* For example, if I want to display a client from *jasper* onto my local display on *opal,* I might type:

   ```
   lmui@opal % xhost +jasper.ora.com
   jasper.ora.com being added to access control list
   ```

   Notice that I use the fully qualified domain name, not just the hostname. This is slightly safer, to prevent someone from doing harm from another machine named *jasper* in a different domain.

   For most servers, the *xhost* command can only be run on the local work-station. You cannot run it successfully from a remote host. A notable exception to this rule is X terminals: many X terminals allow you to run *xhost* from the client host.

2. The method shown above has a disadvantage: it allows all users on the remote machine to access yours. There is also a *user-based* method of access control, which needs to be set up in your startup script. You can tell if you are set up for user-based access control by seeing if you have a *$HOME/.Xauthority* file, and if you do, checking the permissions on it:

   ```
   % ls -l $HOME/.Xauthority
   -rw-------  1 lmui       53 Mar 23 15:37 /home/lmui/.Xauthority
   ```

   If the timestamp listed corresponds to the last time you logged in, it's likely that you're set up to use user-based access control. This means that clients need to provide the server with a special key from this file before they can connect to the server.* If this is the case, you need to run the following command from the local host:

```
% xauth extract - display | rsh remote_host xauth merge -
```

For example, if I want to run remote clients from the host *ruby* onto my server *opal:0*, I might type:

```
lmui@opal % xauth extract - opal:0 | rsh ruby xauth merge -
```

This method is harder to remember and a bit confusing, but it gives you much better control over who can access your server. And if you just put it in your startup script *(2.09, 16.03)* (before starting the actual remote clients, of course), you don't have to remember it.

—*LM*

19.13 *Extending Access Control to Another User*

As outlined in Article 19.12, there are two common ways of preventing other users from accessing your server: host-based access control (i.e., using the *xhost* command), and user-based access control (i.e., using the *xauth* command). That article explains how you can circumvent access control for yourself. But what if you want to extend access to other users?

If you use host-based access control, it isn't a big deal at all. Just use *xhost* to extend access to the host that the other user will be running clients on. For example, if I want someone on the host named *obsidian* to be able to run clients on my server *opal:0*, I do:

```
lmui@opal % xhost +obsidian
```

The only thing to remember is that the *xhost* command must be run on an *xterm* window *(2.02)* on *opal* (or for an X terminal, on the host that controls its *xdm (28.02)* session). And of course, you need to be aware that not only can your friend connect to your server, so can anyone else with an account on that host. So it's always better to use user-based access control, if you don't mind dealing with its difficulties.

If you are set up with user-based access control, extending access to another user is a bit harder. Suppose I want Val to be able to run clients from the system called *ruby* to display on my server. Somehow we have to get a special key from my *.Xauthority* file to hers. My *.Xauthority* is read/write only to me, and her *.Xauthority* file is read/write only to her. There's no way for me to

---

* The key is usually called a "magic cookie," but I can't say that with a straight face.

just say "let Val connect," so instead we have to do a little bending over backwards. There are many ways of doing this; here are a couple:

- Plan Number 1 is that I copy my key (or "magic cookie") to a file that's readable by Val, she reads the file, and then I remove the file.

  1. First of all, what I do is use the *xauth* command to extract my key into a file called *xauth.tmp* in my home directory:

     ```
     lmui@ruby % xauth extract ~/xauth.tmp opal:0
     ```

  2. Next, I make sure Val can read the file by changing permissions with the UNIX *chmod* command. I know Val is in my default group, so I just extend read access to my group:

     ```
     lmui@ruby % chmod g+r ~/xauth.tmp
     ```

  3. Now it's Val's turn to read the file. She uses the *xauth* command to merge the code back in:

     ```
     ruby:val % xauth merge ~lmui/xauth.tmp
     ```

  4. Finally, as soon as I know Val's done, I remove the file:

     ```
     lmui@ruby % rm ~/xauth.tmp
     ```

- Plan Number 2 is that I email the code to Val. This is a little less secure, but so what.

  1. First, I get the code in a numeric format. Usually the code is shown in an unreadable format, but if I'm going to be sending it in email, I need it in ASCII format. Use the *nextract* command to get the code in numeric format:

     ```
     lmui@ruby % xauth nextract - opal:0 | mail val
     ```

  2. When Val gets the email, she uses the ASCII code with the *nmerge* command. She might copy the mail message into a file (e.g., one called *lmui.code*), edit out the header and signature, and then apply it directly to *xauth*:

     ```
     ruby:val % xauth nmerge lmui.code
     ```

  3. Finally, Val deletes both the *lmui.code* file and the mail message (she better!).

Okay, this isn't the easiest thing in the world. But if you're on the Internet, you should be using all the security you can. Being on the Internet is sort of like having an apartment in a dangerous section of town: it may be a pain to have to deal with a dozen locks on your door, but you can never be too careful.

—LM

19.14 Running Remote Clients with xrsh

xrsh

xrsh is a shell script that simplifies starting clients on a remote machine. In Article 19.01, we talked about the various steps you need to go through if you want to run a remote client. *xrsh* takes care of some of the more troublesome details.

- One issue we discuss is setting your DISPLAY environment variable *(19.08, 19.09, 19.10)* for the client on the remote system. *xrsh* is smart enough to do this automatically.

- Another issue is passing environment variables *(2.04)* to the remote system. *xrsh* automatically passes your DISPLAY environment variable, but in some cases you might also want other environment variables passed along, such as PATH and PRINTER. For that, *xrsh* provides an environment variable called XRSH_ENVS_TO_PASS, which allows you to list environment variables to pass on to the remote system.

- *xrsh* also takes care of access control issues *(19.12)* for you. By default, *xrsh* assumes that you use host-based access control, so it figures out which is your host system and runs a *xhost* command on that system.

  This procedure doesn't really make sense for X terminals, however, which require you to run *xhost* on other machines. So to support X terminals and other methods of access control, *xrsh* uses an XRSH_AUTH_TYPE environment variable. If you use an X terminal with *xhost*-type access control, set XRSH_AUTH_TYPE to xhost-xterminal. Using xhost-xterminal, *xrsh* runs *xhost* on the host that you run *xdm (28.02)* from.

  If XRSH_AUTH_TYPE is set to xauth, then *xrsh* tries to copy the code in *$HOME/.Xauthority* to your account on the remote system.

  One unusual value for XRSH_AUTH_TYPE is environment. This is for when you want to run the client on another machine that has your home directory NFS-mounted. In this case, *xrsh* propagates the XAUTHORITY environment variable.

  If you prefer to deal with access control on your own, you can set XRSH_AUTH_TYPE to none, and then you're on your own.

One thing that *xrsh* cannot deal with is allowing remote shells on the remote machine. This is a detail that you have to set up yourself, as shown in Article 19.06.

Here's the beauty of it. To use *xrsh*, just specify the name of the remote host and the name of the command:

```
lmui@opal % xrsh ruby xmail
```

You don't even have to put the command in the background *(2.03)*.

—*LM*

19.15 *Running Remote Clients from a Startup Script*

Often, you want to run remote clients *(19.01)* every day, automatically. For example, when I log in I like to start an *xmail* client *(7.02)* from a remote host, *ruby*. In order to do this, you need to set things up both on the remote host and in your startup script *(2.09, 16.03)* on the local machine.

On the remote host, you need to be able to run commands from your local machine, as described in Article 19.06. Also on the remote host, the search path needs to include the remote command, as described in Article 19.07.

In your startup script, you can just run *xrsh (19.14)*:

```
xrsh ruby xmail
```

Or if you choose to do things the long way (which I do), you need to take care of access control *(19.12)* and then run the command using the correct value of DISPLAY *(19.08)*.

```
#!/bin/sh
    ...
xauth extract - opal:0 | rsh ruby xauth merge -

rsh ruby xmail -display opal:0 &
```

Since I prefer to use user-based access control, I use the *xauth* command to extend access control to the remote host. *opal* is the name of my local workstation. If I were content with host-based access control, I might have replaced the *xauth* line with the simpler command:

```
xhost +ruby.ora.com
```

Another alternative is that if you use host-based access control, you can just enter *ruby.ora.com* into a file called */etc/X0.hosts* (assuming you have *root* permission, of course). Then you'll always be able to connect to your server from *ruby*. (As can anyone else with an account on *ruby*....)

—*LM*

20

More About Resources

20.01 Resources for the Intrepid

Resources are integral to the function (and design) of X programs. They allow X programs to be configured differently under practically every possible circumstance. You can have different resources on different servers, different resources when using different hosts, etc.

Most readers don't need to know very much about resources, and if you're one of those readers, we respectfully encourage you to turn to the next chapter. However, if you want to do something fancy with resources, it's quite possible you can do it.

Resources are actually a pretty neat idea. Think of it this way: on a Macintosh or PC, the machine is "single-user:" that is, the computer runs programs that connect to exactly one monitor with exactly one keyboard and mouse. So any preferences—such as default fonts—can be built into the program, or configured at a systemwide level. There's no reason to have multiple layers of configuration, because there's always one user, one monitor, or one keyboard.

X, however, runs on multiuser systems. Many different users can be running the same program at the same time. The program can be used on monitors of varying dimensions, and depth. Because the same binary program can be shared among multiple hosts via NFS, a program can even be executed on different machines at the same time. Meanwhile, the administrator needs to maintain at least one copy of systemwide defaults, and in many cases may also need to maintain multiple copies, for different languages, for color displays, and so on.

Resources in X are designed to allow clients to be configured at each of these levels, so that you can tweak your preferences to run a client slightly differently depending on what host you're using or what server you're logged in on. For this reason, resources are not for the faint of heart; with all the different layers, configuring resources can become quite confusing. Article 20.02

gives you a hint of that: it outlines what resource files are read by programs to give you some context for the rest of the chapter.

—LM

20.02   *Quick Guide to Resource Files*

When a program is first started, it runs an initialization procedure which, among other things, reads the resources that apply to the program. Here's an approximate list of where resources are found when a client starts looking for a resource definition.

1. Most clients have systemwide application defaults *(20.12)* installed on the system. If the XFILESEARCHPATH environment variable *(20.25)* isn't set, the client looks in a built-in path. In most cases, */usr/lib/X11/app-defaults* is one of the directories used. For internationalization support, the client also looks for a LANG environment variable *(2.04)*; if set, the client first looks in a subdirectory named for the value of LANG.

2. The client looks for the user's application-specific resource files *(20.13)*. These files are expected to have the name of the client's application class *(20.05)* (e.g., XTerm for the *xterm* client). To determine which directory these files are in, it checks first the XUSERFILESEARCHPATH environment variable *(20.14)*, and if XUSERFILESEARCHPATH isn't set, it looks for the XAPPLRESDIR environment variable *(20.14)*. If neither variable is set, the client looks for these files in the user's home directory. If the LANG environment variable is set, then the client looks in a subdirectory named for the value of LANG.

3. Resources loaded into the server via *xrdb* are next. If no resources are loaded via *xrdb*, then resources set in the *.Xdefaults* file in the user's home directory are used instead. See Article 17.03.

4. If the XENVIRONMENT environment variable *(20.10)* is set, the client looks for the resources in the file pointed to by XENVIRONMENT. If it is not set, the client looks in a file with the name *.Xdefaults-* followed by the name of the host *(20.09)*. For example, if you're working on a machine called *ruby*, the program looks in *.Xdefaults-ruby* if the XENVIRONMENT environment variable is not set.

5. Resources specified with the *–xrm* command-line option *(17.05)* override any other resources set for that client.

6. If the client was called with any command-line options that coincide with resource values, the command-line option overrides all resources.

7. Finally, the application usually has some fallback resources to use.

All in all, the sequence looks sort of like Figure 20-1.

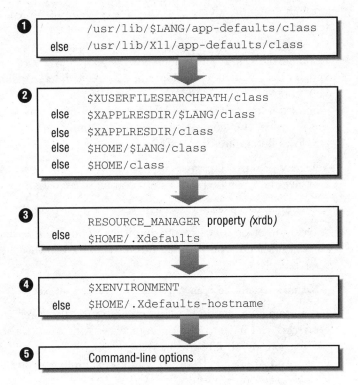

①

/usr/lib/$LANG/app-defaults/class

else /usr/lib/X11/app-defaults/class

②

$XUSERFILESEARCHPATH/class

else $XAPPLRESDIR/$LANG/class

else $XAPPLRESDIR/class

else $HOME/$LANG/class

else $HOME/class

③

RESOURCE_MANAGER *property (xrdb)*

else $HOME/.Xdefaults

④

$XENVIRONMENT

else $HOME/.Xdefaults-hostname

⑤

Command-line options

Figure 20-1: Resource merging

You might have an idea now why most people just use *xrdb* or *.Xdefaults* and forget about the rest of the resource possibilities.

—LM

20.03 *Why Aren't There Any Error Messages?*

Each client may end up reading hundreds of resources. However, it only processes the ones that actually apply to it, and ignores the rest! This means that if you make a mistake, it's very likely that the client won't tell you.

If you think about it, it makes sense that things are set up this way. You can set up resources so that they are read by all clients that recognize it, e.g., you can set a global background *(17.06)* color in your *xrdb* settings or *.Xdefaults* file *(17.03)* so that all your clients use the same background color. If a client doesn't recognize this resource, you don't want it to complain every time it starts up, but to just gracefully ignore it.

However, this means that if you just misspelt the name of a resource, you'll absolutely never find out until you notice that it didn't work.

Another common source of confusion is when a resource is set correctly but is redefined later on. You might set a new resource correctly in your *.Xdefaults* file or *xrdb* settings, but then forget that you also defined it in another resource file (e.g., one pointed to by your XENVIRONMENT *(20.10)* environment variable). So your new resource never takes effect. Again, this makes sense if you consider that resources are *supposed* to override each other, e.g., an administrator might choose a blue background for most users, but you might prefer green. Or you might wish to use one font in most of your *xterm (2.02)* windows but a different font in your login window *(21.12)*.

You may get error messages if a resource is correctly set to a "bogus" value. If you give the wrong type of value, you may get a "Cannot convert string" error:

```
Warning: Cannot convert string "yeah" to type Boolean
```

A common error concerns missing fonts. If your server doesn't have a particular font installed, you may get errors warning you that the font you requested wasn't available:

```
xterm:  unable to open font "helv10", trying "fixed"....
```

But all in all, clients don't tell you very much about resources, so when things go wrong you have to rely on your wits. Article 20.28 shows you how to find out what resource files are being read so you can track down possible problems. And Article 20.27 shows you an example of using the *editres (20.26)* client to solve a resource mystery.

—LM

20.04 *Different Resources for Different Instances*

Suppose you run several *xterm* windows *(2.02)* and you want some windows to appear (or behave) slightly differently. There are many different ways of doing this, and in describing them we get to explain several different ways of setting up resources.

For example, suppose you keep one large *xterm* window for editing text files. You also have another *xterm* window that's set up as a console window *(27.02)* (using the *−C* option to *xterm*). At minimum, you may want the titlebars *(17.09)* of the windows to indicate which are the special *xterm*s. You might want the console window to appear in reverse video *(17.08)* and to appear in the *fixed* font.

One way of dealing with this situation is to use the *−name* command-line option. The *−name* command-line option is supported by all Xt-based applications. What it does is effectively change the name of the client. The new name appears in the titlebar, in the icon name, and it also affects what resources apply to the client. Technically, it creates a new *instance* of the application.

The possibilities available with the *–name* option are best illustrated by example. You might define the following resources:

```
bigxterm.vt100.geometry:  80x40
bigxterm*font:    lucidasanstypewriter-14
CONSOLE*reverseVideo:      true
CONSOLE*font:     fixed
```

and then start up the windows with *–name* options corresponding to the first field in the new resource names. (If you don't know how to install the resources, see Article 17.03.)

```
% xterm -C -name CONSOLE &
% xterm -name bigxterm &
```

The bigxterm window appears with the string *bigxterm* in the titlebar and in the icon name. The window itself appears with an extra-large font and with 40 lines (instead of the default of 24). The console window also has the titlebar and icon names changed to CONSOLE, and appears in reverse video with the small *fixed* font.[*]

So the *–name* command-line option alters what resources affect this instance of the client. The default "name" of a client is generally the client name itself, e.g., xterm for an *xterm* window. One result of using *–name* is that resources that start with the string xterm no longer apply to either the bigxterm or CONSOLE windows, but only to windows with the default name xterm. See Article 20.05 for information on how to extend resource definitions to all instances of a client.

—LM

20.05 *Application Classes*

In Article 20.04, we showed you how to create a new instance of an application using the *–name* command-line option. The new name is used in the window's titlebar and icon title. It is also used for determining what resources are read by that instance. Resources with the string xterm in the first field will only be read by client instances with the name xterm, and not by any clients that are given a new name with the *–name* command-line option.

However, there is a way to specify resources that apply to all instances of the client. Each application has what we call an *application class*, and resources written with the application class will apply to all instances of the application.

For example, if you are running a console window (started with the *–C* option to *xterm*), you might want to name that window CONSOLE. Similarly, if you are

_____
* If all you want is to have the titlebar changed, you can just use the *–title* command-line option *(17.09)*. However, this will not affect the icon title or the resources used for that client.

20.05

running a window with a particularly large geometry, you might want to name it bigxterm. You can use these names in resource specifications, such as:

```
CONSOLE*reverseVideo:           true
bigxterm.vt100.geometry:  80x40
```

and then start the clients with the *–name* option shown above:

```
% xterm -name CONSOLE &
% xterm -name bigxterm &
```

Resources written with the name CONSOLE only apply to windows with the name *CONSOLE*, and resources with the name bigxterm only apply to windows with the name *bigxterm*. However, although the *bigxterm* and *CONSOLE* windows have different names, they can both be considered instances of the larger class, XTerm.

All windows begun with the *xterm* client belong to the class XTerm, and any resources written for the name XTerm will apply to all *xterm* windows, whether their name is *CONSOLE*, *bigxterm*, or just plain *xterm*. That is, the following resource definitions:

```
XTerm*scrollBar: true
XTerm*saveLines: 200
```

would apply to all *xterm* windows, regardless of their actual name.

—*LM, from the* X Window System Administrator's Guide

20.06 What If the Application Class Name Is Missing?

And what if the first field of the resource name is omitted entirely? This field usually has either the application class name *(20.05)* or the name of an instance *(20.04)*. If missing, then all applications that can access the resource will try to process it. That is, the following resource:

```
*font: fixed
```

will essentially cause all applications to use the *fixed* font. Fortunately, this sort of syntax is generally used only in either systemwide application defaults files *(20.12)* or in user application defaults files *(20.13)*, where only a single client is likely to read it.

—*LM*

20.07 Learning the Application Class with xprop

Knowing the application class name *(20.05)* for a given client is important in setting client-specific resources. The application class name is used in the name of the *app-defaults* resource file *(20.12)* (e.g., *XTerm* for the *xterm* client). It is

440 															**X User Tools**

also used in resource specifications to apply to all instances *(20.04)* of a particular client.

The name of the application class is usually the name of the client with either the initial letter or the first two letters in uppercase. Don't take this for granted, though; occasionally, other letters will also be in uppercase, and sometimes the application class is totally different from the client name. The manpage should also tell you the class name, but you can also use the *xprop* client or the f.identify function of *twm*.

To use *xprop*, call it on the command line:

```
% xprop
```

Your cursor becomes a set of crosshairs. Use the cursor to click on the desired window.

Those properties are then displayed to your screen.

```
% xprop
WM_STATE(WM_STATE):
                window state: Normal
                icon window: 0x20005d
WM_PROTOCOLS(ATOM): protocols  WM_DELETE_WINDOW
WM_CLASS(STRING) = "ruby", "XTerm"
WM_HINTS(WM_HINTS):
                Client accepts input or input focus: True
                Initial state is Normal State.
WM_NORMAL_HINTS(WM_SIZE_HINTS):
                user specified location: 0, 400
                user specified size: 739 by 364
                program specified minimum size: 28 by 19
                program specified resize increment: 9 by 15
                program specified base size: 19 by 4
                window gravity: NorthWest
WM_CLIENT_MACHINE(STRING) = "ruby"
WM_COMMAND(STRING) = { "xterm", "-display", "opal.ora.com:0", "-sb",
"-geometry", "80x24+0+400", "-name", "ruby" }
WM_ICON_NAME(STRING) = "ruby"
WM_NAME(STRING) = "ruby"
```

You can also use the *–name* option to *xprop*, in which case it will show you the properties of the client with the specified name.

```
% xprop -name bigxterm
```

Among other things, the *xprop* client lists a WM_CLASS category. In that category, the first string listed is the instance name, and the second string is the name of the class.

—LM

20.08 Learning the Application Class with twm

twm (12.01) users can also use the `f.identify` function to learn the application class name *(20.05)* for a window. To use this, you need to make the `f.identify` function available through a pop-up menu item. For example, I might enter into my root menu *(12.22)*:

```
"Identify"        f.identify
```

and then restart *twm.* To identify a window, just select `Identify`, and then select the window you want information for. A window pops up similar to that in Figure 20-2.

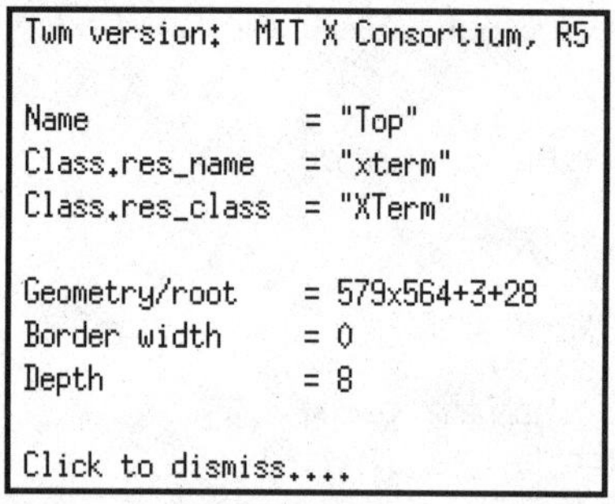

```
Twm version:  MIT X Consortium, R5

Name           = "Top"
Class.res_name  = "xterm"
Class.res_class = "XTerm"

Geometry/root  = 579x564+3+28
Border width   = 0
Depth          = 8

Click to dismiss....
```

Figure 20-2: The twm f.identify display window

Once you have the information you want, click on the window to dismiss it.

—*LM*

20.09 .Xdefaults-hostname Files

The *$HOME/.Xdefaults-hostname* file is searched for resources specific to the host that the client is running on. For example, I might have a home directory that's shared among several hosts and want slightly different resources loaded depending on which host I'm running clients from. If nothing else, I might want my *xterm* windows to have the hostname in the titlebar *(17.09)*.

I can do this by setting up a different resource file for each host. If the hosts I use are *ruby, rock,* and *rubble,* I might create *.Xdefaults-ruby, .Xdefaults-rock,* and *.Xdefaults-rubble.* Among other things, these files would contain an *xterm*title* resource. For example, the *.Xdefaults-rubble* file might contain:

```
xterm*title:      rubble xterm
```

When a client starts up on *rubble,* it looks for *.Xdefaults-rubble* and sets the `title` resource as specified.

—*LM*

20.10 The XENVIRONMENT Environment Variable

In Article 20.09, we showed how you can use a *.Xdefaults-hostname* file to define different resources for different hosts. Well, a nice feature is that you can use the XENVIRONMENT environment variable *(2.04)* to point to a resource file to be used instead of *.Xdefaults-hostname*.

Although XENVIRONMENT is designed for use with hostnames, you can also use it to change resources according to other features of your environment. For example, suppose there are several different X servers that you might log in with, and you have different resources that you want to set according to which server you're currently using. You might set up your startup script with lines resembling the following:

```
#!/bin/sh
    ...
case DISPLAY in
        unix:0.0|:0.0)  ;;
        opal*)   XENVIRONMENT=$HOME/.Xdefaults-opal ;;
        harry*|artemis*)  XENVIRONMENT=$HOME/.Xdefaults-sun360 ;;
        jasper*|obsidian*|jade*)  XENVIRONMENT=$HOME/.Xdefaults-sparc ;;
        ncd*)    XENVIRONMENT=$HOME/.Xdefaults-ncd ;;
esac
```

—LM

20.11 Defining New Resources Temporarily

Using XENVIRONMENT *(20.10)* is also one of the simpler ways of changing your resources on a temporary basis. I use XENVIRONMENT most frequently when I'm testing out a new application before installing it. The easiest way to access the resource file without having to rename it or mess with your other resource files is to set XENVIRONMENT. For example, when testing some new resources for the *asedit (9.05)* client, I typed:

```
% setenv XENVIRONMENT ./asedit.resources
% asedit &
```

Since I don't generally use *.Xdefaults-hostname* files, this doesn't conflict with any other part of my resource environment.

—LM

20.12 Application Defaults

Sometimes defaults are built into the application itself. But many applications also depend on a systemwide resource file that's installed at the same time as the application.

When installing a new program, one file that's frequently provided is an *application defaults* file. This file is usually installed in */usr/lib/X11/app-defaults*, and is named after the application class *(20.05)*. For example, the standard application default file for *xterm* is installed as */usr/lib/X11/app-defaults/XTerm*. Most of the resources in an *app-defaults* file are things that you're unlikely to change. For example, here are a few lines from the *XTerm* file:

```
*SimpleMenu*menuLabel.vertSpace:  100
*SimpleMenu*HorizontalMargins: 16
*SimpleMenu*Sme.height:  16

*SimpleMenu*Cursor: left_ptr
*mainMenu.Label:  Main Options
*mainMenu*securekbd*Label:  Secure Keyboard
*mainMenu*allowsends*Label:  Allow SendEvents
     ...
```

You may be surprised by the type of behavior specified in an *app-defaults* file. A lot of things you might have thought were built into to the application are actually controlled by resources. Here, you see that labels for menus are specified in the *app-defaults* file; this makes it easy to change the labels for another language. Also, often certain keystrokes and button presses are defined in *app-defaults* files, using a special type of resource called a translation table *(20.29)*. For example, the *xcalc* client *(5.05)* lets you type numbers on the keyboard as well as press the appropriate button with the pointer, but that behavior is all specified in the resource file.

An administrator can also use the *app-defaults* file to set systemwide preferences for the application. For example, if the administrator thinks that all *xterm* windows should have a scrollbar *(11.02)*, he or she can specify this in its app-defaults file:

```
*scrollBar:      true
```

Since all *xterm* clients started on this host will read its defaults from the */usr/lib/X11/app-defaults/XTerm* file, all users will have scrollbars from now on (unless they explicitly disable them).

You might notice that the resources shown in this article omit the name of the actual application (or its class *(20.05)*) at the beginning of each line. We can do this because the *app-defaults* file is guaranteed to be read only by the application in question. Note, however, that if we specified this same resource definition globally (e.g., in your *$HOME/.Xdefaults* file or by using *xrdb*, as shown in Article 17.03), then *all* X clients that support scrollbars would have one by default. So be careful.

Some clients use *app-defaults* files for just a few cosmetic features (such as what font to use, default colors, etc.). But other clients are very dependent on the resources specified there, and may be totally crippled without their *app-*

defaults file being properly installed. For example, our *xwebster* *(5.04)* *app-defaults* file provides us with a space to list the name of our Webster server host, so our users don't need to know about it themselves. This means, however, that without an *app-defaults* file to tell it the name of the Webster host, *xwebster* is close to useless. The *xcalc* program mentioned above is completely unusable (and unrecognizable) without its *app-defaults* file.

Although most *app-defaults* files are in */usr/lib/X11/app-defaults*, there are actually a whole series of directories that are searched. These directories can be altered by defining the XFILESEARCHPATH environment variable *(20.25)*. Most people don't have any use for defining of XFILESEARCHPATH; however, if you find that an application isn't working correctly, check that XFILESEARCHPATH isn't defined.

(Another possible problem might be that the *app-defaults* file isn't properly installed or that it isn't readable by all users. See your system administrator if this is the case.)

—LM

20.13 *Application Resource User Files*

In addition to the resource files in */usr/lib/X11/app-defaults*, applications also look for personalized user resources. By default, the application looks for these resources in your home directory. Like the systemwide *app-defaults* files *(20.12)*, these personal files are named after the application class *(20.05)*. For example, after reading */usr/lib/X11/app-defaults/XTerm*, the *xterm* client then consults *$HOME/XTerm* for any additional resource definitions you might have.

A disadvantage of using *xrdb* or *.Xdefaults* files *(17.03)* is that all applications have to read all the resources loaded into your server. Application resource files, on the other hand, are read only by the client in question. Using application resource files, you can structure it so that you never have to use *xrdb* or *.Xdefaults* at all.

The disadvantage is that it can clutter up your home directory to have a separate resource file for each of the applications you run. See Article 20.14 for information on how to place application-specific resources in a directory other than your home directory.

—LM

20.14 *Specifying a New Resource Directory*

In Article 20.13, we described how you can place resource files in your home directory that are only read by the client in question. But this can really crowd up your home directory. So one possibility is to use the XAPPLRESDIR environment variable *(2.04)* so you can put the resource files in a directory other than your home directory.

For example, I might create a *$HOME/Resources* directory:

```
% ls ~/Resources
XTerm
Xarchie
Xwebster
Zmail
```

and then set XAPPLRESDIR:

```
% setenv XAPPLRESDIR $HOME/Resources
```

Any clients started from this shell window will now use the resource files in the *$HOME/Resources* directory.*

If you want all clients to use the resources in *$HOME/Resources*, make sure to set them in a startup script *(2.09, 16.03)* For example, you might place the following lines at the beginning of the script:

```
XAPPLRESDIR=$HOME/Resources
export XAPPLRESDIR
```

The above example ensures that all clients started on that host will inherit the value of XAPPLRESDIR.

There is another environment variable, XUSERFILESEARCHPATH, which will override XAPPLRESDIR if it is set. XUSERFILESEARCHPATH is actually much more flexible than XAPPLRESDIR. However, it is also more difficult to use.

If you choose to tackle XUSERFILESEARCHPATH, then it gives you a bit more power because it lets you specify a series of pathnames to search for resource files. For example, as a simple example, you might enter:

```
% setenv XUSERFILESEARCHPATH $HOME/%N:$HOME/Resources/%N
```

This way, you can have resource files in both *$HOME* and in *$HOME/Resources*. Applications will search in *$HOME* first, and if no resource file is found, it will look in *$HOME/Resources*. This is clearly more flexible, but it's much more confusing. All you need to know for now is that the string %N in the path is expanded into the name of the client's application class.

---

* XAPPLRESDIR applies only to the application-specific resource files in your home directory (such as *$HOME/XTerm*). It does not affect the use of other files in your home directory, such as *.Xdefaults*, *.Xresources*, or *.Xdefaults-hostname* files.

XUSERFILESEARCHPATH actually just uses a subset of the syntax used for the XFILESEARCHPATH environment variable; see Article 20.25 for more information.

—LM

20.15 *More About Resource Syntax*

In Article 17.02, we showed examples using asterisks (*) in resource definitions. The asterisk is actually a sort of "wildcard" representing several fields of the resource name. The real name of a resource might be longer (and much more complicated).

The actual name of each resource follows the *widget hierarchy* for the application. This can reach a dozen levels down, and each level represents another field in the resource name. So the "real" names for resources can get pretty unwieldy, with a series of fields separated by periods (.). See Article 20.27 for examples of some truly hideous resource names, e.g.,

```
xarchie.color.outerPaned.browserForm.browserUpButton.background: gray90
xarchie.color.outerPaned.browserForm.browserDownButton.background: gray90
```

Furthermore, you often want to group several of the resources together; if you change the font *(17.14)* for one widget, you generally want to change it for each of the others as well. For these reasons, resources support the asterisk (*) as a wildcard for many fields at once, so you don't have to specify each of them individually. The above resources might both be set with the following line:

```
xarchie.color.outerPaned.browserForm*background: gray90
```

Or even just:

```
xarchie*background: gray90
```

When you use an asterisk as a wildcard within a resource specification, it is called a *loose binding*. If you use a period, it is a *tight binding*. (Tight bindings take precedence, so in fact, the last of these resource settings might easily be overridden for many of the interim widgets.)

Another thing to know about resources is that in the same way applications have class names and instance names (as described in Article 20.05), so do resources. If you look at a client manpage, you may see that the font resource is part of the Font class. Again, this makes it easy to group several resources together.

—LM

20.16 The Asterisk Only Replaces Complete Fields!

As demonstrated in Article 20.15, you can use the asterisk (*) as a wildcard within resource specifications. However, you should be aware that the asterisk only represents complete fields. That is, if you set:

```
xmail*background: yellow
```

Only the *xmail (7.02)* program is affected, not *xmailtool (7.05)* or *xmailbox (7.09)*.

— LM

20.17 When Loose Bindings Are Bad News

In most circumstances, it's better to use loose bindings *(20.15)* in resource files. However, there are exceptions. One example is with setting the geometry *(17.10)* for *xterm* windows. Whereas the *vt100* widget for *xterm* uses character size for window geometry *(17.11)*, other widgets within *xterm* use pixels. So if you were to explicitly set all widgets used within *xterm* to use a size of 80x24:

```
xterm*geometry:          80x24
```

The *vt100* widget would come out 80 columns by 24 lines, which is fine (and, in fact, the default!) But meanwhile, each of the **Options** menus would come out in 80×24 pixels, which is much too small (see Figure 20-3).

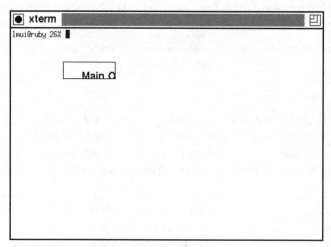

*Figure 20-3: xterm window with *geometry resource set*

What you want to do is to make sure you only set the geometry resource for the *vt100* widget:

```
    xterm*vt100*geometry:      80x24
```

—LM

20.18 Merging Options with xrdb

When using *xrdb* to install resources *(17.03)*, you need to be careful about whether to use the *–load* or the *–merge* options.

By default, *xrdb* replaces all resources loaded into the server. In some cases, this is exactly what you want, e.g., suppose you usually read your resources from your *.Xresources* file. When you add a new resource to *.Xresources*, you may want the new resource to take effect right away. Since all your resources came from *.Xresources* to begin with, you might as well reload the entire file:

```
% xrdb -load .Xresources
```

Using *–load* is actually the default, so this might also read:

```
% xrdb .Xresources
```

However, suppose you want to try out a new resource just this once. You might want to see what happens if you set the `*foreground` resource, but you don't want to install it into your *.Xresources* file yet. You can merge it into your resource database without overriding your other resources, using the *–merge* command-line option:

```
% xrdb –merge
*foreground:     yellow
^D
```

If you did not remember to use *–merge* in this instance, then all your other resources would have been destroyed.

I like to use *–merge* for all my *xrdb* needs, actually. The reason is that administrators might set users up with resources when they first log in (see Article 28.15). Unless you use *–merge*, you lose all of the resources set by the administrator.

—LM

20.19 Using xrdb with Conditionals

If you use *xrdb* for loading resources, you get an added bonus of being able to use C preprocessor directives in your resource definitions. Since *xrdb* *(17.03)* runs its input through *cpp*, you can use `#include` and `#ifdef` directives to control the flow of resource files. If you don't know anything about *cpp*, the most important point is that it gives you a way to have some parts of the resource file read only under certain conditions.

We haven't completely exhausted our example of putting hostnames in the titlebar *(17.09)*. Another way to do it might be to use *xrdb* with the –*D* option. The –*D* option defines a variable for *cpp*. If you use the –*D* option with *xrdb*, it is passed to *cpp*. Here's another way to have the name of hosts *ruby* and *rock* in the titlebar.

```
% xrdb -D'hostname' .Xresources
```

And then have in *.Xresources*:

```
#ifdef ruby
XTerm*title: ruby
#endif /*ruby*/

#ifdef rock
XTerm*title: rock
#endif /*rock*/
```

—LM

20.20 Predefined xrdb Variables

In X11R5 *xrdb*, some *cpp* variables *(20.19)* are already predefined. For example, the CLIENTHOST variable is predefined to the name of the host that *xrdb* is running on, so if you wanted to put the name of the host in the titlebar *(17.09)*, you can also do it this way:

```
% xrdb
XTerm*title:      CLIENTHOST
```

Other variables that are predefined by *xrdb* are SERVERHOST, COLOR, HEIGHT, WIDTH, and PLANES.

For example, you might set up a certain set of resources when you're logged in at a color display and a whole different set on a monochrome display:

```
#ifdef COLOR
! Place your own color resource specifications here
*Background:    whitesmoke
*Foreground:    darkorchid
xclock*background:  lightseagreen
xclock*foreground:  navy
#else
! Place your own monochrome settings here
xclock*reverseVideo:  True
#endif
```

The *cpp* command #ifdef says to process the lines before #else or #endif if the specified variable (COLOR) is defined. So the color resources are set only if I'm working on a color display. If I'm not working on a color display, the color resources are skipped and the resources after the #else statement and before #endif are processed.

—LM

20.21 Color App-defaults Files

Some X11R5 clients come with two *app-defaults* files *(20.12)*, one with resources appropriate regardless of the display hardware and another with additional resources appropriate only for a color screen. Among the clients that come with multiple *app-defaults* files are *bitmap (22.01)* and *xcalc (5.05)*. The idea is that both files are installed, and users can set a special customization resource variable if they want to use the color versions. For example:

```
% bitmap -xrm "*customization: -color" &
```

The naming convention for a color *app-defaults* file is the name of the standard *app-defaults* file (generally the class name *(20.05)*, e.g., *Bitmap*) followed by a hyphen and the word "color" (i.e., *Bitmap–color*).

If you think you might want to use the *–color* versions of all applications that supply one, you can set the customization resource in your resource file. You can set it permanently in your *.Xdefaults* or using *xrdb (17.03)*:

```
*customization: -color
```

Or if you use X11R5 *xrdb*, you can get fancy using the #ifdef COLOR syntax described in Article 20.19. This way, you can use color *app-defaults* files for all clients that supply one.

```
#ifdef COLOR
*customization: -color
#endif
```

The color defaults for *xcalc* are particularly uninteresting—all black, white, and gray! Run the following command if you want to see for yourself.

```
% xcalc -xrm "*customization: -color" &
```

—VQ

20.22 Other Customization Ideas

A system administrator with a creative bent (and some spare time) might use the customization resource *(20.21)* to come up with *app-defaults* files for other situations. For example, it's possible to create files with defaults intended specifically for monochrome screens. These files should be named after the application class name *(20.05)* with a *−mono* suffix. You can then supply *−mono* as the value to the customization resource:

```
% bitmap -xrm "*customization: -mono" &
```

Another possibility is to set up special app-defaults files for other situations. For example, you might make a special version of *xterm (2.02)* for servers with only two mouse buttons, or for servers with (gasp!) only one mouse button. But the potential is limited, if only by the fact that you can only specify one value for the customization resource. Since you can only use one special-case resource file at a time, you can't combine them, e.g., if you had a color display with only one mouse button.

—*VQ, LM*

20.23 *So Many Resources, So Many Files*

So how do you know where to put resources? Can they just all be lumped together in any of the places we mentioned?

Yes, and if you only have a few resources to change, that will work fine. But as you add more customization, one of several things happens:

- Your *.Xdefaults* file *(17.03)* gets too big

- The server database gets too large to easily handle with *xrdb (17.03)*

  or

- Your home directory gets too cluttered with class files *(20.13)*.

A little judicious partitioning will make life easier.

First, you need to decide which resources you want to treat as common to all clients. This list will be read by all clients, so it should contain only the truly common resources, and any resources that for some reason may need to override resources set elsewhere (see Article 20.02 for the rules on the order that resource locations are searched).

Typical candidates for these resources are background and foreground colors *(17.06)* and default fonts *(17.14)*:

```
*Background:          SandyBrown
*quit*Background:Red
*Foreground:          Black
*Font:                -bitstream-courier-medium-r-normal--*-110-*-*-m-*-*-*
```

Then you have to decide where to put these. You can place them in a file to be loaded via *xrdb* (such as *.Xresources*), or in the file that gets read when each client starts up (typically *.Xdefaults*). (See Article 17.03 for information on how to do this.) The former should be quicker in most instances, since it doesn't involve file-system access, and since all clients will always get these resources, regardless of what host they are executing on.

This latter fact means window manager resources might go here as well:

```
!
! mwm - I hate many of the mwm defaults...
!
Mwm*KeyboardFocusPolicy: pointer
*FocusAutoRaise:         False
*ClientAutoPlace:        True
*PassButtons:                    True
```

or if you use *xrdb*, you could just include your *Mwm* class file:

```
# include "/u/meo/app-defaults/Mwm"
```

Now any resources specific to a client can go into class files *(20.13)* for that client. For instance, as a developer, I spend much of my time staring at *xterm* *(2.02)* windows. I use the following defaults in my *XTerm* class file:

```
#ifdef COLOR
    XTerm*Foreground:      Wheat
    XTerm*Background:      MidnightBlue
    XTerm*cursorColor:     Yellow
    XTerm*pointerColor:    Green
#else
    XTerm*Foreground:      Black
    XTerm*Background:      White
#endif
!
aixterm*pointerShape:      XC_gumby
XTerm*pointerShape:        gumby
XTerm*fullCursor:true
XTerm*appcursorDefault:    True
!
XTerm*savedLines:1000
XTerm*scrollBar: false
!
XTerm*iconPixmap:/usr/include/X11/bitmaps/terminal
XTerm*Font:                -*-courier-medium-r-normal--*-100-*-*-m-*-*-*
```

While I like the Sienna/Black combination for occasional use (*xman (5.02)*, *xcalc (5.05)*), I find the MidnightBlue/Wheat combination less tiresome for constant use. The contrasting colors for the terminal cursor and the X pointer make life easier, too, if you have a color display.

Finally, environment-specific resources go in a separate file (XENVIRONMENT *(20.10)* or *$HOME/.Xdefaults-hostname (20.09)*). You might need these because of drastic (or at least annoying) differences in colors between different vendors' systems, monitor aging, screen resolution differences, or perhaps because you usually use a particular system for a specific task set different than your normal set. I normally work on a NeXT with a reasonable resolution (1120×832)

---

but sometimes test on a PC (with the hostname *hope*) with a typically PC resolution (800×600). The *xterm* sizes I normally use on the NeXT (80×40) will not fit on the PC screen in a useful font. Additionally, MidnightBlue displays lighter than I like on this particular monitor. The *.Xdefaults-hope* file takes care of this:

```
XTerm*Geometry:          80x30
XTerm*Background:#000044
```

Too Many Class Files

Actually, my home directory is full enough without any class files. But by the time I added a couple of dozen class files, it really got annoying. So I created a directory and put them there. A common directory name, derived from the standard systemwide location, is *$HOME/app-defaults*. You simply add this to your XUSERFILESEARCHPATH variable *(20.14)* like so:

```
setenv XUSERFILESEARCHPATH $HOME/app-defaults/%N:$HOME
```

Some Sample Files

RRU_resources

On the CD we include some sample files: an *.Xresources* file, and class resource files for many of the clients. These are all based on a common appearance for the clients, as much of the net software comes with no, or widely varying, resource files. We also include samples of other color combinations you can try; if you prefer one of them, simply use that *.Xresources* file instead, and modify the class files accordingly.

—MEO

20.24 A Complete Client Environment

In writing this book, I continuously downloaded and built new software. But since I'm not the administrator, I didn't actually install programs systemwide, but in my own private area. This is standard procedure for personal programs on UNIX systems—to use a *$HOME/bin* directory for non-standard programs—but for X programs, you also have to make sure that each program's *app-defaults* file *(20.12)* is installed someplace where you can read it.

So what I did was create my own *bin*, *man*, *app-defaults*, and *lib* areas under the directory we were writing the book in, */work/xpt*. The binaries, manpages, application defaults, and any other files required for running the program were placed in those directories as needed, either by hand or by editing the *Imakefile* or *Makefile* (depending on how much energy I had to wrestle with *imake* or *make (31.16)*):

Once the files were installed, I needed to make sure that they could be accessed easily by everyone who wanted them, as follows:

bin

Any executables were placed in the *bin* directory. This directory then has to be placed in my shell's search path *(2.05)*.

```
setenv path=(/work/xpt/src/bin $path)
```

I put the new directory at the beginning of the path because some of the programs need to override identically named programs in the systemwide *bin* directories. For example, the version of *xmessage* with a scroll bar *(29.08)* needs to be found before the standard systemwide *xmessage (4.09)*.

man

Any manpages were put in an appropriate subdirectory of *man*. The manpages usually appear with *.man* suffixes; they need to be renamed according to what section I put them in. For example, a manpage for an application like *xmail* would become *man/man1/xmail.1*. A manpage for a game like *spider* would become *man/man6/spider.6*. My MANPATH *(5.02)* then needs to include the parent *man* directory:

```
setenv MANPATH /work/xpt/src/man:$MANPATH
```

lib The kind of files that go into my *lib* are configuration files, help files, bitmap files, etc. Some of this should probably have gone in an *include* directory if I'd thought to make one. To be honest, my *lib* is a mess. Getting the program to look in *lib* isn't always simple: sometimes you can just change a few lines in the *app-defaults* file, but often you have to edit the *Imakefile* or *Makefile* and build the program all over again.

app-defaults

The application defaults files are usually distributed with the suffix *.ad*. You need to remove that suffix and then move these files to a directory where the application will find them. I use the XAPPLRESDIR environment variable *(20.14)*, which overrides using *$HOME* as the root of personal *app-defaults* files. (I should probably have used XUSERFILESEARCHPATH *(20.14)* or XFILESEARCHPATH *(20.25)*, but I got lazy.)

```
setenv XAPPLRESDIR /work/xpt/src/app-defaults
```

Now I can put my application defaults in */work/xpt/src/app-defaults* and all applications will find them. It also means that others can access these defaults just by setting the same environment variable *(2.04)*.

Using this scheme, I can put myself into a working environment by just running the following commands in my *.cshrc*:

```
set path=(/work/xpt/src/bin $path)
setenv XAPPLRESDIR /work/xpt/src/app-defaults
if ($?MANPATH) then
        setenv MANPATH "/work/xpt/src/man:${MANPATH}"
else
        setenv MANPATH /work/xpt/src/man:/usr/man:/usr/local/man
endif
```

I can also put these commands in a file and use the C shell *source* command to read it later on. This is an easy way to let others use this testing environment without having to install it into a global area.

—LM

20.25 Changing What App-defaults File Is Used

The XFILESEARCHPATH environment variable *(2.04)* contains a path that applications use for finding default resources. This may be tiresome to hear again in this chapter, but I'll say it again: users hardly ever need to think about this. */usr/lib/X11/app-defaults* is the directory that's almost always used for application defaults *(20.12)*.

So why do you need to know this? Well, the main reason for XFILESEARCHPATH is for internationalization support. It gives you a way to have multiple versions of application defaults depending on what language or "locale" you're using. Furthermore, once you figure out XFILESEARCHPATH, you can use it to point to application defaults that aren't installed in a standard place. In Article 20.24, we showed how I used XAPPLRESDIR to point to privately installed application defaults. The proper way to do this is to use XFILE-SEARCHPATH, but first you need to know more about it.

The syntax for the XFILESEARCHPATH environment variable is similar to PATH, but also includes some special variables using percent signs (%). The default path might look like the following:

```
/usr/lib/X11/%L/%T/%N%C%S:/usr/lib/X11/%l/%T/%N%C%S:/usr/lib/X11/%T/%N%C%S:\
/usr/lib/X11/%L/%T/%N%S:/usr/lib/X11/%l/%T/%N%S:/usr/lib/X11/%T/%N%S:
```

This isn't nearly as bad as it looks, it's just set up so that the application looks for defaults in order of decreasing specificity.

1. The %L symbol expands to your current language, locale, and codeset. If you don't know what locales and codesets are, you probably don't have to. But the idea is that the application defaults for *xcalc* in French might appear under */usr/lib/X11/fr_FR.88951/app-defaults/XCalc*.

2. The %l symbol expands to your current language. So French application defaults for *xcalc* might also appear in */usr/lib/X11/fr/app-defaults/XCalc*.

3. The %T symbol expands to the type of file. When used for resources, this string is expanded to the string *app-defaults*.

4. The %N symbol expands to the filename. When used for resources, this string is expanded to the application class name, such as *XCalc*.

5. The %C symbol expands to the value of an optional customization resource. See Article 20.21 for more information.

6. The %S symbol expands to an optional suffix. This feature is not used for application defaults.

If you take another look at the default application file search path shown above, it should make more sense now. It's just a way of making sure that if there's an *app-defaults* file that's more specific to your language or other customization, it'll use that one instead of the standard files in */usr/lib/X11/app-defaults*.

The most common reason to define XFILESEARCHPATH (overriding the default path) is if you have some application defaults in a nonstandard place. A common situation is if you're running both OpenWindows and X11R5, you might have application defaults in both */usr/lib/X11/app-defaults* and in */usr/openwin/lib/app-defaults*. You can set XFILESEARCHPATH in your startup scripts like this:

```
setenv XFILESEARCHPATH /usr/lib/X11/%T/%N:/usr/openwin/lib/%T/%N
```

(Note that this example circumvents the locale-specific defaults and customization features, out of laziness.)

Although you can probably get away with hardcoding the string "app-defaults" in place of %T, you really have to use %N or it won't find the proper resource files.

In the example introduced in Article 20.24, we could replace the line defining XAPPLRESDIR with the following line:

```
setenv XFILESEARCHPATH /work/xpt/src/%T/%N%C:/work/xpt/src/%T/%N:\
/usr/lib/X11/%T/%N%C:/usr/lib/X11/%T/%N
```

This makes sure that the *app-defaults* files in my private directory are looked at before the ones in */usr/lib/X11/app-defaults*.

—LM

20.26 When Do I Use editres?

editres is a *resource editor*. What does that mean? Basically, *editres* helps you examine a client's widget hierarchy and devise correct resource specifications. It also lets you test resource specifications dynamically. From a user's perspective, *editres* is most handy when a client's widget hierarchy is very complicated—when the window has lots of buttons, panes, menus, subwindows, etc.—and the resources you want to set are very specific.

For instance, suppose you're using an application with a menu and you want to change the font of only a single menu item. (A co-worker once asked me to help him do just that.) Or you want each of a client's command buttons to be a different color. OK, so you need to be a bit of a resource nut. But in cases like this, *editres* is invaluable. You could also use *editres* to unknot less tangled webs. However, you can probably accomplish the same thing by checking out the manpage and doing a little experimenting with the *−xrm* command-line option *(17.05)*.

So, those of you who might want to use *editres* know who you are. Don't be embarrassed. You are not alone. But be warned: it isn't easy. If you persevere, *editres* can help you:

- Display and scan through the client's widget hierarchy.

- Find the correspondence between widget names and the actual components.

- Display what resources may be set for a particular widget.

- Create resource specifications.

- Dynamically apply the new specifications to a client already running on the display!

- Write the new definitions to your own resource file.

Article 20.27 walks you through solving a real-life resource problem with *editres*. The article should give you an idea what *editres* can do, but it doesn't attempt to cover all the many features. You'll have to experiment on your own for that.

Note that the usefulness of *editres* will be limited somewhat by your understanding of widgets and the resources that can be applied to them. *editres* will show you *all* the resources that can be set for a widget, but it will not differentiate between those you can set at the user level and those that must be set by programming routines. Use the client manpages to get a better idea of what resources you can set yourself. And, of course, there's the old reliable method of setting resources and seeing if they work.

Note also that *editres* can only work with certain clients—those that understand the so-called *editres protocol*. Most clients built using the Athena widget
set will work with *editres*. A client built using another toolkit (e.g., the Motif
Toolkit) may not be compatible. If you try to use *editres* with an incompatible
client, you'll get an error message to that effect.

—VQ

20.27 *Solving a Resource Mystery with editres*

This section walks you through a situation in which *editres* (20.26) helped a co-
worker and me solve a resource problem. Depending on your purpose, you
can take a great number of paths through a client's widget hierarchy using
editres. This section walks you only one way through one application, and it
moves pretty fast. It should give you an idea of the powers and flexibility of
editres, but the only way to learn to use the program effectively is to use it,
preferably to solve a real problem.

So let's look at one. One of my co-workers, Len, was having trouble using his
xarchie window (8.04). The background and foreground colors (17.06) on part of
the application were both so dark that he couldn't distinguish them. In the rest
of the window, the colors contrasted adequately. He was using the default colors on a color monitor. On my color workstation, *xarchie* looked fine. Len's
monitor was interpreting the device-specific RGB colors differently. It looked
like he should be able to solve the problem by setting a different background
color for the part of the application that was illegible.

But what widget or widgets were we talking about? *xarchie* has many menus,
buttons, and panes. How would we name the parts in question in a resource
file? And was background really the correct resource variable? Here's where
editres came in.

In order for *editres* to examine a client's widget hierarchy, the client must be
running, so we ran both *xarchie* and *editres*:

```
% xarchie &
% editres &
```

Looking at Figure 20-4 should give you a better idea of Len's problem. Notice
that the horizontal bar under *xarchie*'s status line is virtually black. If you've
worked with *xarchie*, you may remember that this area provides two controls,
to shift text in the panes below backward and forward. Each control is indicated by a series of three angle brackets, left for back (<<<) and right for forward (>>>). But on Len's display, you can't see them.

Using *editres*, we determined the widget names for these controls and the
proper resource specifications to change their background color. How? No
matter what you want to do with *editres*, the usual first step is to display the

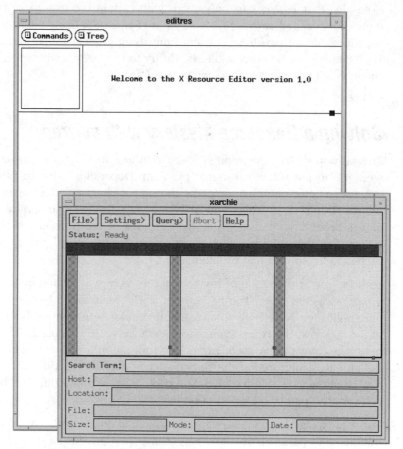

Figure 20-4: xarchie and editres

widget hierarchy of the client in question in the *editres* window. Select the item **Get Widget Tree** from the *editres* **Commands** menu. You will be prompted to

```
Click the mouse pointer on any Xaw client.
```

in the message window below and to the right of the menu buttons. Then click the cross pointer anywhere on the *xarchie* window and the client's widget hierarchy is displayed in tree format in the *editres* window. *xarchie* has a very complex hierarchy and only part of the tree can be viewed in the *editres* window, as shown in Figure 20-5.

Notice that the box beneath the menu command buttons has become smaller. This box is called the *panner* and it is actually a tool that allows you to scan the entire tree. The size and location of the panner in the larger square surrounding it suggests the portion of the widget tree that is visible—in this case, a very small portion. To view the rest of the tree, place the pointer on the

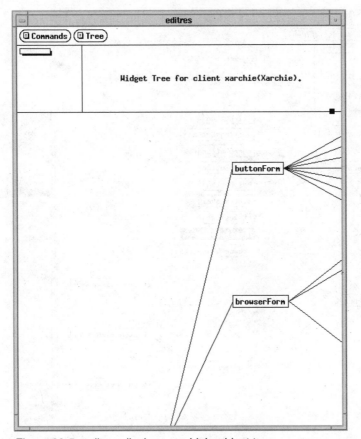

Figure 20-5: editres displays xarchie's widget tree

panner, hold the first pointer button, and drag. The *editres* window scrolls to reveal the remaining widgets.

The quickest way to find out the name(s) of the widget(s) we're interested in is to choose **Select Widget in Client**, the first item on the *editres* **Tree** menu. We're instructed to

```
Click on any widget in the client.
Editres will select that widget in the tree display.
```

Click on the left portion of the dark bar in the *xarchie* menu. The *editres* window highlights the corresponding widget in the tree display and moves the panner to reveal that portion of the tree, as in Figure 20-6.[*]

---

[*] The **Tree** menu item **Flash Active Widgets** lets you determine this correspondence in the opposite way. You begin by clicking on entries in the widget tree to highlight them. When you select **Flash Active Widgets**, the corresponding components in the application will be repeatedly highlighted.

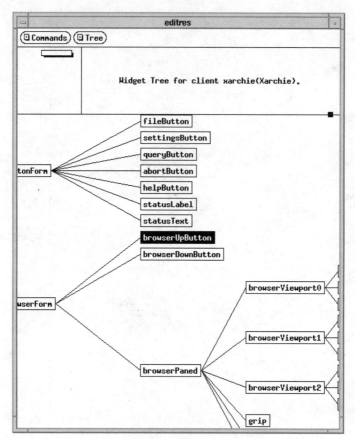

Figure 20-6: editres identifies the widget you click on

The widget corresponding to the backwards control is browserUpButton. We can infer that the right half of the bar, the forward control, is browserDownButton, which is adjacent on the tree.

Now we need to come up with some resource specifications to make these buttons legible. With one of the widgets selected in the tree, we select **Show Resource Box** from the **Commands** menu. The resource box subwindow appears on top of the main *editres* application window, as in Figure 20-7.

Across the top of the resource box is a template resource specification for the selected widget, which at this stage shows the tightly bound instance name ending with an unknown resource variable:

    .xarchie.color.outerPaned.browserForm.browserUpButton.unknown:

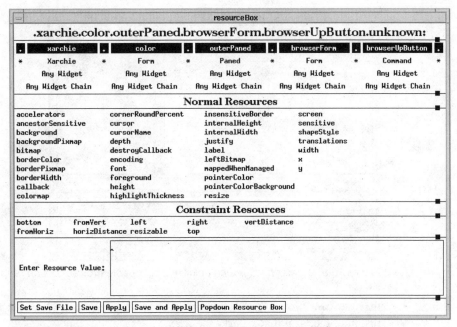

Figure 20-7: editres resource box for xarchie's browserUpButton widget

You can select the resource you want from the list in the box by highlighting it in the same way you did a widget in the tree: simply click the pointer on it. To solve the problem at hand, background seems a likely choice. When we click on it, the unknown variable in the template is changed to background.

Now we must enter a value for this resource (a color) in the text window near the lower right corner of the *editres* window. The phrase "Enter Resource Value:" appears to the left of the text window. To enter a value, place the pointer in the text window and type. (The text window is an instance of the Athena Text widget. To learn the valid editing commands, see Article 9.03.) We enter a pale gray shade called gray90.

Here's where *editres* comes in very handy. We can test our specification on the currently running *xarchie* client. Just click on the **Apply** command button on the bottom of the resource box. If the template resource can be applied successfully to the client in question, the message area to the right of the panner will display:

    SetValues was Successful.

And sure enough, the command button displays in the lighter background color, as in Figure 20-8.

Clearly, we've only solved half of Len's problem. If he uses only this resource specification, the browserDownButton will still be too dark. It's a fairly safe bet

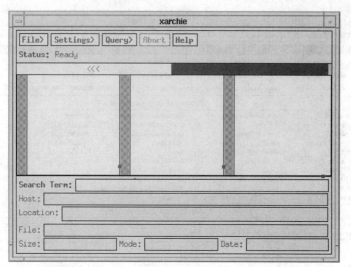

Figure 20-8: Lighter background color makes xarchie browser button readable

that we can copy our successful resource and substitute Down for Up in Len's resource file, and that will do the trick:

```
.xarchie.color.outerPaned.browserForm.browserUpButton.background: gray90
.xarchie.color.outerPaned.browserForm.browserDownButton.background: gray90
```

The command buttons at the bottom of the resource box help you either **Apply** the custom resource specification to the running client or **Save** the specification in a resource file. We can add the original specification we've come up with to Len's resource file by clicking on **Save**. We're prompted for the file-name to which the resource will be appended:

```
Enter file to dump resources into:
```

We enter:

```
/home/len/.xrdb
```

You can avoid this prompt by specifying a filename with **Set Save File**.

At this stage, the simplest way to add the second resource is to edit the resource file by hand. To use *editres* for this purpose, you'd have to **Popdown Resource Box**, select the Down widget in the tree, display another resource box, etc. For more complicated specifications, it might be worth it, but not in this case.

However, if you know a bit about resources, you know it's very possible that we can change both the Up and Down sides using a single specification. *editres* provides a way for you to edit the template resource specification to deal with situations like this. Notice that below the template are four lines of text, the first one of which matches the full instance name in the template, with each component (including connectors) highlighted. The next line down shows the full class name with loose bindings. As you can see, the four lines are spaced so that the components and connectors fall into columns.

These lines provide four sets of alternatives for each of the components in the template resource specification. As you move the pointer around among the various choices, notice that a box highlights each one in turn. You can change any part of the template specification by clicking on an alternative in the same column.

For instance, to switch any tight binding in the template to a loose binding, you would simply click on the corresponding loose binding on the class name line. The highlighting for that column will be switched to loose binding on the class name line, and the template will be redrawn to include the asterisk.

You can also replace any component in the template by clicking on the alternative component you want. Since we want to specify a background resource that applies to both browser buttons, perhaps we should select the class name that corresponds to the `browserUpButton` widget: `Command`. When we click the pointer on `Command`, that class name is highlighted and replaces `browserUpButton` in the template line, as in Figure 20-9.

If we move the resource box away from the main *editres* window, we'll see that all of the widgets covered by this specification—in this case, both buttons—are now highlighted. We can test this specification by clicking on **Apply**. It looks like we've got it:

— VQ

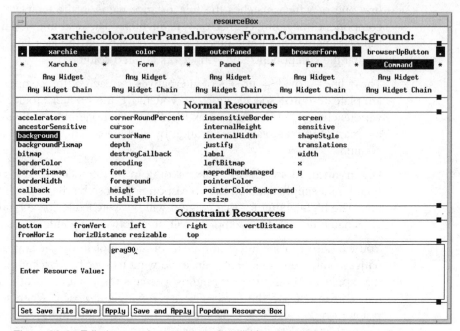

Figure 20-9: Edit the template resource by clicking on another component

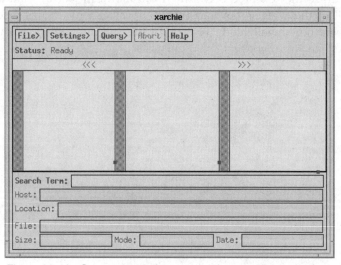

Figure 20-10: One resource line sets background for both of xarchie's browser buttons

20.28 Seeing What Resources Are Read

To see what resource files are read on client startup, try using the *trace* command on a SunOS machine, or the *truss* command on a Solaris 2.0 or SVR4
machine. For example:

```
% trace xterm >& /tmp/xterm.trace
```

Then examine the resulting file:

```
gethostname ("", 1002) = 0
open ("/home/lmui/.Xdefaults-ruby", 0, 017777777) = -1 ENOENT (No such
file or directory)
access ("/home/lmui/XTerm", 04) = -1 ENOENT (No such file or directory)
access ("/usr/lib/X11/app-defaults/XTerm", 04) = 0
stat ("/usr/lib/X11/app-defaults/XTerm", 0xf7ffed90) = 0
open ("/usr/lib/X11/app-defaults/XTerm", 0, 036734323664) = 4
stat ("/usr/lib/X11/app-defaults/XTerm", 0xf7fff200) = 0
read (4, "*SimpleMenu*BackingStore: NotUse".., 2800) = 2800
close (4) = 0
```

In the example, note that the user had resources loaded into the server, so
$HOME/.Xdefaults was not opened. The only resource file in its path that it
found and opened was the systemwide *app-defaults/XTerm* file.

—*EAP, from the* X Window System Administrator's Guide

20.29 Translation Tables

For many clients, you can modify the keys and buttons used to invoke an
action by specifying a type of resource called a *translation table*. Using translation tables, you can define certain keys or buttons to invoke an action.
(Note that this is distinct from redefining keystrokes and button presses at the
server level, which is controlled by the *xmodmap* client *(18.07).*)

Translations are best described by demonstrating their use in a common application. A client that defines a lot of translations is *xcalc*. The *xcalc* window
generally resembles the window shown in Figure 20-11.

Each of the buttons shown in the *xcalc* window is defined using a translation
table. For example, the *app-defaults* file for *xcalc* defines the fourth row of
keys on the standard *xcalc* keypad with the lines:

```
XCalc.ti.button16.Label:PI
XCalc.ti.button16.Translations:#override<Btn1Up>:pi()unset()
XCalc.ti.button17.Label:x!
XCalc.ti.button17.Translations:#override<Btn1Up>:factorial()unset()
XCalc.ti.button18.Label:           (
XCalc.ti.button18.Translations:#override<Btn1Up>:leftParen()unset()
XCalc.ti.button19.Label:           )
XCalc.ti.button19.Translations:#override<Btn1Up>:rightParen()unset()
```

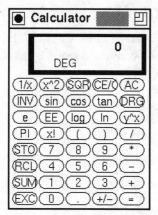

Figure 20-11: xcalc window

```
XCalc.ti.button20.Label:              /
XCalc.ti.button20.Translations:#override<Btn1Up>:divide()unset()
```

Each button is given its label (e.g., PI for the first button), followed by the event translation when it is pressed. In the case of the 16th button, the internal function *pi()* is called, presumably returning the value of π. (Since the foreground and background colors are reversed on the button when it is initially pressed, the widget action *unset()* is then called, returning the button colors to the default.) For the 20th button, "\" is the label, and pressing it calls the *divide()* function. Clearly a user could easily redefine the behavior of each button on the *xcalc* keypad by switching the translations in their own resource files. (Be sure to switch the labels too, though!)

Also in the *XCalc* application defaults file is a full translation table for interpreting keystrokes within the *xcalc* window:

```
XCalc.ti.bevel.screen.LCD.Translations:#replace\n\
              Ctrl<Key>c:quit()\n\
              Ctrl<Key>h:clear()\n\
              None<Key>0:digit(0)\n\
              None<Key>1:digit(1)\n\
                    ...
              <Key>KP_0:digit(0)\n\
              <Key>KP_1:digit(1)\n\
                    ...
              <Key>KP_9:digit(9)\n\
                    ...
              <Key>KP_Divide:divide()\n\
                    ...
              <Key>.:decimal()\n\
              <Key>+:add()\n\
              <Key>-:subtract()\n\
              <Key>*:multiply()\n\
              <Key>/:divide()\n\
```

```
<Key>(:leftParen()\n\
<Key>):rightParen()\n\
<Key>!:factorial()\n\
    ...
<Key>p:pi()\n\
    ...
<Btn1Down>,<Btn1Up>:toggle()selection()\n
```

These definitions allow you to type a "1" on the keyboard (either on the keypad or on the main part of the keyboard) rather than clicking the correct button in the *xcalc* window. They also allow keyboard shortcuts to many of the functions. You can access the `divide()` function by pressing a slash on either keyboard or keypad. You can get the value of π by pressing a "p," and get the factorial of a number by pressing an exclamation mark. As you could expect, this translation table can also be redefined at the user level.

Beware that translations are very specific about their syntax. A single space after one of the trailing backslashes will cause the resource manager to ignore all subsequent translations, with no error message reported.

A more complicated example is with the *xterm* client. As described in Article 11.05, selecting text with the first pointer button saves that text into memory. Selecting text is actually three separate X events:

1. Pressing the first pointer button.

2. Moving the pointer while holding down the first button.

3. Releasing the button.

Each of these input events performs a part of the action of selecting text:

1. Unselects any previously selected text and begins selecting new text.

2. Extends the selection.

3. Ends the selection, saving the text into memory (both as the PRIMARY selection and CUT_BUFFER0).

The event and action mappings are expressed in a translation table as:

```
<Btn1Down>: select-start()\n\
<Btn1Motion>: select-extend()\n\
<Btn1Up>: select-end(PRIMARY,CUT_BUFFER0)
```

where each event is enclosed in angle brackets (<>) and produces the action that follows the colon (:). A space or tab generally precedes the action, though this is not mandatory:

```
<event>: action
```

A translation table must be a continuous string. In order to link multiple mappings as a continuous string, each event-action line should be terminated by a newline character (\n), which is in turn followed by a backslash (\) to escape the actual newline. The basic syntax for specifying a translation table as a resource is:

```
... *translations:   #override\
      [modifier]<event>:  action
```

The first line is basically like any other resource specification with a few exceptions. First, the final *argument* is always translations. Second, the #override string says that what follows should override any default translations. You only literally override a default translation when the event(s) of the new translation match the event(s) of a default translation *exactly*. If the new translation does not conflict with any existing translation, it is merely appended to the defaults.

In order to be specified as a resource, a translation table must be a single string. The #override is followed by a backslash (\) to indicate that the subsequent line should be a continuation of the first.

The following *xterm* translation table shows multiple event-action mappings linked in this manner:

```
*VT100.Translations:    #override\
    <Btn1Down>:    select-start()\n\
    <Btn1Motion>:  select-extend()\n\
    <Btn1Up>:      select-end(PRIMARY,CUT_BUFFER0)
```

To learn how to specify your own resources in translation table format, see Articles 11.18, 11.21, and 20.30.

— VQ

20.30 *Translations for the Athena Text Widget*

You can specify event translations as resources to modify the operation of the Athena Text widget used by *xedit (9.03)*, *xmh (7.06)*, and other X Toolkit applications. Keep in mind, however, that the default Text widget recognizes dozens of commands. It may not be practical or desirable to modify them all.

If you choose to modify the Text widget, you can do so for all relevant clients by introducing the translations with the line:

```
*Text*Translations: #override\
```

Place this line in your *.Xdefaults* file, or load it into your server with *xrdb* (as shown in Article 17.03).

You can also specify different translations for different clients that use the widget by prepending the client's name. To affect the operation of the Text widget only under *xedit*, introduce the translation table with the line:

```
Xedit*Text*Translations: #override\
```

In modifying the operation of the Text widget, keep in mind that insert mode is the default. In other words, like *emacs* (9.02), most of the individual keystrokes you type are added to the text file; an exception is **Backspace**, which predictably deletes the preceding character. The commands to move around in a file, copy and delete text, etc., involve a combination of keys, one of which is generally a modifier key. If you want to modify a command, you should use an alternative key combination, rather than a single key.

For example, the following table offers two suitable translations:

```
*Text*Translations: #override\
        Meta<Key>f:      next-page()\n\
        Meta<Key>b:      previous-page()
```

The first translation specifies that pressing the key combination Meta-f moves the cursor ahead one page in the file (scrolls the file forward one window); the second translation specifies that Meta-b moves the cursor back one page. The actions performed are fairly obvious from their names. For a complete list of actions recognized by the Text widget, see the *xedit* manpage.

— *VQ*

21

More About
Startup Environments

21.01 More About Environments

Most users are happy with basic user environments that just work. For them, it's easiest to copy someone else's startup script *(2.09, 16.03)* and fire away. If you're one of those, then Chapter 16 probably tells you everything you want to know. However, some people are always more interested in making things a little more automated or a little more efficient.

So this chapter gives a few more details about configuring user environments.

- Invariably, it happens that your startup script doesn't work the way you intend it to. So we talk about some escape hatches *(21.02, 21.03)* and ways to find error messages *(21.05, 21.06, 21.07)*

- One of the least structured parts of the X user environment is how to log out of your X session. We include a few articles about which client to use as your controlling process *(16.03)*.

- Finally, we show you a few tools you may want to use in your user environment, and give you examples of things we've done to build environments the way we like them.

There are countless ways to configure and tweak your startup script. Since most startup scripts are written in the shell, shell fanatics can go wild with hundred-line scripts that test for every possible eventuality. I prefer simplicity myself, in theory at least, but sometimes I get a funny little idea that only becomes realized four hours and 200 lines of code later.

So if you're interested in twiddling with your startup script, read on.

—*LM*

21.02 Bypassing Your Startup Script from xdm

If you use *xdm* *(28.02)* to log in, a very useful feature lets you bypass the *.xsession* startup script *(2.09, 16.03)* entirely. You might want to do this if you're having trouble logging in, and you think something might be wrong with your startup script.

To bypass your startup script, type in your name and password as usual, but then type **CTRL-Return** or **F1** instead of **Return**. You are logged in with a single *xterm* window, which is not particularly appealing, but sufficient to edit your *.xsession* file. See Article 16.07 for hints about common problems you might have with your startup script.

—LM

21.03 Running xinit Automatically

If you are on a workstation and use *xinit* or *startx* *(1.03)* to log in, you might be tempted to put the *xinit* or *startx* command in your shell startup file (such as *.login* or *.profile*). The advantage is that it saves you the step of having to wait for a prompt before you can type the command to start your X session.

Be aware that this can be a very dangerous thing to do. One possible problem is that if your X session is corrupted for some reason, you may not be able to log in. Also, if you run *xterm* as a login shell *(21.09)*, you may end up in a loop.

—LM

21.04 Safeguards for xinit

If you do choose to start X automatically from your *.login* or *.profile* *(21.03)*, you should take a few safeguards. A good way to do this is to have the X startup in your *.login* or *.profile*, but surround it with *sleep 5* commands so that you can interrupt it. This not only gives you an escape hatch (so that your login doesn't become unusable), it also means that if you interrupt the script during the *sleep* (for example, using **CTRL-C**), then you'll be able to circumvent the X server. This is useful if you want to log in and do one non-GUI-based task (like send a short mail message) and log out again, without waiting for the window system to lumber awake.

Here is an example, patterned after Sun's default user environment's *.login* script:

```
echo "Starting X Windows (Interruptible for 5 seconds...)"

sleep 5

# if on a SunOS machine , start OpenWin, else start X
if ( -f /usr/openwin/bin/openwin ) then
```

```
          openwin -escape -includedemo

else
          xinit                   # or startx, or whatever.
endif

echo "Logging out automatically (interruptible for 5 seconds..)"

sleep 5

logout
```

The reason for the *sleep 5* and *logout* at the end of the previous example is to automatically log out when you are done. This is to spare you the embarrassment of shutting down the window system but forgetting to log out (this always happens when you're in a hurry), and having somebody walk in and erase or modify your files.

An even safer method is to use the command:

```
exec xinit
```

in the *.login* or *.profile* file. This causes your login shell to be replaced by the window system; when the window system terminates, you will be logged out immediately, and a new login prompt will appear. This is a bit less convenient if you are experimenting with different configurations, but it is much more secure.

—IFD

21.05 *Finding Error Messages in .xsession-errors*

If your startup script *(2.09, 16.03)* doesn't work properly, you can examine your script for errors. But it also helps to look at error messages...if you can find them.

If you use X11R5 *xdm (28.02)*, error messages are saved in a file in your home directory called *.xsession-errors*. For example:

```
% cat $HOME/.xsession-errors
/home/lmui/.xsession: xmail: not found
/home/lmui/.xsession: ical: not found
```

I got this error because my *xmail (7.02)* and *ical (4.03)* commands aren't in *xdm*'s default path. By default, *xdm* uses *:/bin:/usr/bin:/usr/bin/X11:/usr/ucb* as its search path *(2.05)*. See Article 16.04 for information on how to change that within your startup script, and Articles 28.24 and 28.14 for information on how to change *xdm*'s defaults at the system level.

Another possible error is this one:

```
/usr/lib/X11/xdm/Xsession: /home/lmui/.xsession: Permission denied
```

In this case, I forgot to make my *.xsession* script executable *(16.03)*.

```
% chmod +x $HOME/.xsession
```

You might also get errors from individual applications in your *.xsession* file. For example:

```
xterm:  bad command line option "-fontname"

usage:  xterm [-help] [-display displayname] [-geometry geom] [-/+rv]
        [-bg color] [-fg color] [-bd color] [-bw number] [-fn fontname] [-iconic]
        [-name string] [-title string] [-xrm resourcestring] [-/+132] [-/+ah]
        [-b number] [-/+cb] [-cc classrange] [-/+cn] [-cr color] [-/+cu]
        [-fb fontname] [-/+im] [-/+j] [-/+l] [-lf filename] [-/+ls] [-/+mb]
        [-mc milliseconds] [-ms color] [-nb number] [-/+aw] [-/+rw] [-/+s] [-/+sb]
        [-/+sf] [-/+si] [-/+sk] [-sl number] [-/+t] [-tm string] [-tn name] [-/+ut]
        [-/+vb] [-/+wf] [-e command args ...] [%geom] [#geom] [-T string]
        [-n string] [-C] [-Sxxd]

Type xterm -help for a full description.
```

In this case, I accidentally used a bogus *–fontname* command-line option to *xterm.* I meant to use *–fn.*

—LM

21.06 *Finding Error Messages in xdm-errors*

If you use *xdm* from X11R4, you can still get error messages, but they're sent to the systemwide file */usr/lib/X11/xdm/xdm-errors.* This file is cluttered with the rest of *xdm*'s messages, as well as the errors from anyone else's X session. You have to weed through these errors for your own.

One possibility is to have a terminal connection (independent of your X server) in which you use the UNIX *tail –f* command to monitor the *xdm-errors* file and then watch what messages pop up when you try to log in on the X server.

```
% tail -f /usr/lib/X11/xdm/xdm-errors
error (pid 163): server unexpectedly died
error (pid 163): Server for display :0 can't be started, session disabled
error (pid 24041): Hung in XOpenDisplay(ncd13.ora.com:0), aborting
error (pid 24041): server open failed for ncd13.ora.com:0, giving up
error (pid 163): Display ncd13.ora.com:0 cannot be opened
error (pid 163): Display ncd13.ora.com:0 is being disabled
```

—LM

21.07 Try Just Running the Script!

Here's another idea to find error messages from your startup script *(2.09, 16.03)*, regardless of whether you use *xdm (28.02)*, *xinit (1.03)*, or whatever. Just run the startup script like a regular command! The worst thing that will happen is that you'll start up a whole lot of extra clients (and your window manager will complain that it's already running), but you might also catch some errors.

```
% $HOME/.xinitrc
/home/lmui/.xinitrc: xpostit: not found
Wed Jun 22 11:32:08 1994: Cannot read newsrc file
(/home/lmui/.newsrc): Permission denied
xrn: Can not read the .newsrc file
mwm: Another window manager is running on screen 0
mwm: Unable to manage any screens on display.
```

Here, I've found out that my *xpostit* client *(4.12)* isn't installed correctly. I've also found out that my *xrn (8.05)* news reader didn't start because it couldn't read my *.newsrc* startup file. (I also get an error that another window manager is already running, but this is expected, so you can ignore this message.)

This method won't find errors because of environment variables *(2.04)* (such as PATH *(2.05)*) that aren't set right, since they are likely to be set properly in your current shell but may not be in the shell usually that runs your *.xinitrc*. However, it will find shell programming errors in your startup script, and it will give you errors from the clients themselves.

Admittedly, this is an act of desperation. But if you're an *xinit* user, you're not left with much of a choice!

—LM

21.08 Don't Set DISPLAY for Local Clients!

One of my pet peeves is startup scripts *(2.09, 16.03)* that explicitly set the DISPLAY environment variable *(19.02)*.

First of all, your DISPLAY environment variable is already set up correctly for local clients. You may have to do some fiddling to set it for remote clients (as shown in Article 19.08), but you should never have to adjust it for local clients.

Now the dangers. Once, a user here complained that he didn't get any of his clients when he logged in at someone else's X terminal. Sure enough, it was because his DISPLAY was set explicitly. While he was logging in at someone else's terminal, all his windows were displaying at his usual desk!

Another time, a new user couldn't log in. She had copied her startup script from a co-worker. Sure enough, the startup script she copied had DISPLAY set explicitly. When she logged in, all her clients appeared on the other user's server!

—LM

21.09 *Login Shells*

Many users who are new to X are surprised when they learn that their *xterm* windows *(2.02)* don't run their interactive shell startup files (such as *.login* and *.profile*).

The reason for this is that *.login* and *.profile* are meant more as batch files (for when you first log in) than for shell configuration. When we all logged in on character terminals, we used only one interactive shell at a time; hence each shell represented exactly one login, and the distinction between shell configuration files and batch files was largely academic. Not so now.

If you use the C shell, the idea is that your *.cshrc* file set up your shell environment (i.e., set variables like PATH *(2.05)* and your prompt, define aliases, etc.) while the *.login* file contained commands that you wanted to run every morning when you logged in. *.login* might be used to show the message of the day or run a mail program (or both).

```
cat /etc/motd
mail
```

Now that I use X every day, however, I have multiple *xterm* shell windows. And it doesn't make any sense for me to run all these commands every time I start a new shell window. For that reason, *xterm* by default doesn't run the *.login* or *.profile* file. The *.cshrc* file is expected to contain all the shell configuration commands that you need.

If you do want to run *.login* or *.profile*, *xterm* provides an *−ls* command-line option. What many users do is to start one of their *xterm* clients with *−ls* in their startup script.

```
xterm -ls &
```

This way, the commands in *.login* or *.profile* are run only once when you log in every morning.

My preference is to reexamine the usage of the *.login* file. Since I still occasionally log in on a character-based terminal, I keep *.login* for running a few crucial commands. But I've also translated these commands into X equivalents when possible, and placed them in my X startup script, *.xinitrc* or *.xsession* *(2.09, 16.03)* My startup script now contains these lines:

```
xmail &
xmessage -file /etc/motd &
```

I get my mail application *(7.02)* and I get my message of the day using *xmessage* *(4.09, 4.10)*, only as X clients now.

—LM

21.10   *Using exec with Your Controlling Process*

Here's a very small tip that might make a very big difference: when you call your controlling process *(16.03)*, use the *exec* command. For example, if you use the *twm* window manager *(12.01)* as your controlling process, then instead of:

```
twm
```

Use:

```
exec twm
```

Why do this? Because it's just a little bit more efficient. Usually when you run a command within a shell, the new command spawns its own shell, while the first shell continues to run. This is what you usually want, so that the first shell is still available for executing new commands. However, in a startup script, the controlling process is the last thing you're going to run anyway. So the original shell is waiting around for no good reason.

If you use the UNIX *ps* command to tell you your processes, you'll see that your startup script is running aimlessly, with no controlling terminal:

```
% ps -x
    ...
23395 ? IW  0:00 /bin/sh /home/lmui/.xsession
    ...
```

The *exec* command is used to tell the current shell to replace itself with the new one. By using it, you prevent the *.xsession* script from waiting around all day for you to finish working and go home. It's just one less process to clog up your machine, but when things get slow, every process helps.

—LM

21.11   *What Should You Use as Your Controlling Process?*

In Article 16.03, we mentioned the controlling process for an X session. The controlling process is an X client that appears at the end of your startup script. When you exit the controlling process, the entire X session exits. In most cases, people choose either an *xterm* window *(2.02)* or their window manager as their controlling process.

Now, I'm a firm believer in using a window manager as your controlling process. What I do is label the exit button on my window manager with the string **Log Out**. In your *.twmrc* file *(12.22)*:

```
menu "defops"
{
"twm Root Menu"  f.title
        ...
"Restart twm"    f.restart
"Log Out"        f.quit
}
```

Or in your *.mwmrc* file *(13.19)*:

```
Menu RootMenu
{
        "Root Menu"              f.title
                ...
        "Restart..."      f.restart
        "Log Out"                f.quit_mwm
}
```

My feeling about this is that most users don't view the window manager as a discrete component of their X environment, so it makes sense that when you exit your window manager, your entire X session exits. By relabeling the quit item as **Log Out**, you make this functionality clear.

Now, some people might disagree with me, and they certainly have a right to do so, no matter how misguided they might be. See Article 21.12 for a second opinion.

—LM

21.12 xterm Takes Control

Linda thinks whatever window manager you're using should be the controlling process *(21.11)*, and I think the controlling process should be a terminal emulator like *xterm*. Now, Linda knows that I think this, and she knows that I know what she thinks. She also thinks that I think she's crazy for thinking what she thinks. But if you've gotten this far, you know by now that we're both a little nutty. Still the question remains, which one of us goofballs is right?

Well, I may be touched, but I'm not stupid. I think it's a lot safer to have an *xterm* window as your controlling process. Why? Let me count the ways. First of all, I've never used a window manager that didn't up and die once in a while. *mwm, twm, olwm, fvwm*—as useful and pretty as they can be—have all been known to go south unexpectedly. (I personally have never used *olwm*, but even devotees acknowledge this.) As a matter of fact, it seems that the more intricate and interesting a window manager becomes, the more loopholes exist for you to hang yourself.

Now Linda points out that her window manager has never died, and she thinks I do stupid things with mine for the sole purpose of having something to write about. In my defense, I just want to say that I do plenty of other stupid things I could write about.

Another reason to stay away from using the window manager as the controlling process is that sometime you may want to change window managers. I do this all the time. Now you may say: "Who cares what you do? You've already admitted that you're a nut." Well, you have a point. If you always use the same old window manager, day after day, year after year—well, you get the picture—then you don't care about this. But if you do change window managers occasionally, and the window manager is the controlling process, the only way to do this requires you also to log out of X.

Even if you stick with the same window manager all the time, might you occasionally want to customize it? In order to activate changes to a window manager startup file or a resource file, you have to restart the window manager. (In the case of resources, you must first load the new resource settings *(17.03)* as well.)

Now you might think that restarting means stopping first (which in effect it does), so that restarting the controlling process will bring the whole house down. But that isn't the problem. Virtually any window manager will have a restart function that preserves the actual process—so even if the window manager is the controlling process, restarting it shouldn't make X go away. The danger lies in the fact that most window managers tend to group restart and exit options together, often on a root menu. It's easy to select exit when you really mean restart, and then X is hosed.

Of course, you can reorganize your menus by editing the window manager startup file, and alleviate the danger. Linda also suggests renaming the Exit or Quit option as **Log Out**. This is a good idea. (If you set this up for someone else, you might want to explain that the only reason exiting the window manager can log you out is because the X session file has been modified for this to happen. The window manager otherwise holds no special power.)

But rather than dwelling on the negatives of using a window manager as the controlling process, let's consider why *xterm* might be a better choice. Using an *xterm* basically lets you hide the trap door. You can start the window as an icon, making it hard to kill by mistake, and give it a distinctive name that discourages you from killing it, like "DIE." (I actually use "LOGIN," but that isn't as dramatic.) The line in the X startup script might read:

```
xterm -name LOGIN -iconic
```

This name is consistent with the fact that the controlling *xterm* is commonly called the login window, since it controls the login session. When you exit the window, you exit X.

Note that if you're using a workstation, you might have the login window double as a console window (with the $-C$ command-line option *(27.02)* supported on many systems). However, since you'll have to deiconify the window to read the console messages, you increase the risk of killing the *xterm* and your session in the bargain.

Of course, when it comes right down to it, what you use as a controlling process is simply a matter of personal preference. If you're likely to exit the window manager inadvertently, use another process. If you'll excuse a joke even older than some of mine: "Doctor, it hurts when I go like this." Doc: "Then don't do that."

— *VQ*

21.13 *A Logout Client*

Here's another idea: since you can use any client as a controlling process *(16.03)* (not just a window manager or an *xterm* *(2.02)*), you can make up a special logout client and use that as your controlling process. There are many ways to do this, but the easiest might be to just use the *xmessage* client *(4.09)* as your foreground process:

```
#!/bin/sh

xterm &
twm &

    ...

xmessage -iconic -name "Log Out" "Press here to log out" -buttons "Log Out"
```

The *xmessage* window is iconified at startup. When you want to log out, just de-iconify it and you'll see a window resembling Figure 21-1.

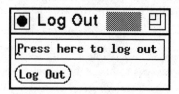

Figure 21-1: Using xmessage for a logout client

When you press **Log Out**, the *xmessage* client quits. Since it's your controlling foreground process, the entire X session quits simultaneously.

If you might also give yourself a few more safeguards:

```
#!/bin/sh

xterm &
twm &

    ...

logout="No";
```

```
while [ "$logout" = "No" ]
do
        xmessage -iconic -name "Log Out" "Press here to log out" \
-buttons "Log Out"
        logout=`xmessage -name Confirm "Are You Sure You Want to Log Out?" \
-buttons "Yes,No" -print`
done
```

Now, when you press **Log Out**, yet another *xmessage* window appears asking if you really mean it. If you press **Yes**, then you're logged out; but if you press **No**, the original *xmessage* **Log Out** window reappears (iconified), and you can keep on working as usual.

—LM

21.14 *Restarting a Window Manager*

Article 21.12 points out that using your window manager as your controlling process means that you can't easily change window managers. Well, here's an idea: you can set up your script so that when you exit your window manager, you can either log out or start a new window manager.

```
#!/bin/sh

xterm &
xclock &
        (many other clients started in the background)

WM="twm";

while [ "$WM" != "Log Out" ]
do
        $WM
        logout=`xmessage -name "Log Out" "Do you really want to log out?" \
-buttons "Yes,Restart" -print`
        if [ "$logout" = "Restart" ]
        then
                WM=`xmessage -name "Choose" "Choose a Window Manager" \
-buttons "mwm,twm,fvwm" -print`
        else
                exit
        fi
done
```

OK, this is admittedly a hack. But what it does is give you a chance to restart your window manager, and even choose a different window manager. It also protects you against situations when your window manager might crash. When you exit your window manager, the script doesn't exit right away, but goes into a loop in which you're asked whether you really want to exit, as shown in Figure 21-2.

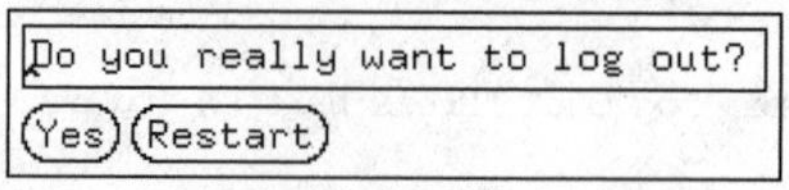

```
┌─────────────────────────────────┐
│ Do you really want to log out?  │
│ (Yes) (Restart)                 │
└─────────────────────────────────┘
```

Figure 21-2: Prompting to log out

(Since there is no window manager currently running, this window appears unadorned in the upper left corner of the screen.)

If you select **Yes**, you're logged out. But if you press **Restart**, you're allowed to choose between several window managers, as shown in Figure 21-3. (If there are other window managers that you might want to include, you can just add them to the list of buttons in the second *xmessage* command.)

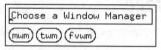

Figure 21-3: Prompting for a new window manager

This probably isn't worth the trouble for most users, since only a few of us ever bother to change our window managers. But it's a way to use your window manager as your controlling process while still maintaining the window manager as an interchangable component of your environment.

—LM

21.15 *But Wait, There's More!*

There's another alternative to using a particular program (such as your window manager or *xterm* *(2.02)*) as your controlling process *(16.03)*. You can use the UNIX *wait* program at the end of your startup script.

The *wait* program says to wait until all processes have exited before continuing execution. So for example, your startup script might read:

```
#!/bin/sh

xterm &
xmail &
xclock &

twm &

wait
```

What happens is that you have to exit all four programs—*xterm*, *xmail*, *xclock*, and *twm*—before your X session terminates. (Unfortunately, *wait* will only wait for those four clients that are called directly in the startup script. It will not wait for any additional clients that you start after you are already logged in, i.e., children of the original four clients.)

The disadvantage of using *wait* is that it can become very tedious to have to exit every program one by one. But it's probably the safest way of making sure that you exit all programs cleanly before you go home for the day.

—LM

21.16 *Getting Command Lines Easily*

xplaces

You can get the correct geometries *(17.10)* for your windows using *xwininfo* repeatedly as shown in Article 17.13. But a nifty publicly available client that saves you some of these steps is *xplaces*. (*xplaces* gets its name from being vaguely remininscent of a SunView application called *toolplaces*.)

xplaces gets the current window and icon geometries of each of the clients currently on the display, and then translates them into command lines you can then copy into your startup script. For example:

```
% xplaces
DISPLAY=ncd13.ora.com:0.0; export DISPLAY
rcmd opal /usr/bin/X11/xterm -xrm "*iconGeometry: 62x79+0+0" -geometry
80x24+12+28 -name LOGIN
xterm -geometry 80x24+108+108 -xrm "*iconGeometry: 62x79+0+0" -display
opal.ora.com:0 -name ruby
xmail -geometry 763x590+167+124 -xrm "*iconGeometry: 62x79+4+750"
xterm -geometry 88x50+40+54 -xrm "*iconGeometry: 62x79+0+0" -display
opal.ora.com:0 -name ruby
xterm -geometry 80x24+261+264 -xrm "*iconGeometry: 62x79+0+0" -display
opal.ora.com:0 -name ruby
```

The window geometries are specified using *–geometry* command-line options, and the icon geometries are specified by using the *–xrm* command-line option to set the iconGeometry resource. (Note that *xplaces* depends on the window manager to get the icon geometry information, so it might have some trouble with some window managers. If you are using an icon manager, it may not return the icon geometry at all.)

One area where *xplaces* is a bit screwy is when it comes to remote clients. When a client is run from a remote host, *xplaces* tries to be smart enough to give you the command for starting the remote client. So you have to be careful that you run *xplaces* from the system that your startup script is run on. If you use *xinit, startx,* or *openwin* *(1.03)* to start your X session, you have to run *xplaces* from your local workstation. If you use *xdm* *(28.02)*, you have to run *xplaces* from the machine that you log onto via *xdm*. Otherwise, the commands will be backward!

Another issue is how remote commands are actually executed in the *xplaces* output. *xplaces* assumes that you use a script called *rcmd* for running remote commands, which is distributed along with *xplaces*. However, if you prefer you can just replace it within your script with *xrsh* *(19.14)* or some other method of running a remote client.

To supply the *xplaces* output to your startup script, you can copy the text and then place it using an editor; you can put the text in an output file; or you can just redirect the output to your startup script:

```
% xplaces >> ~/.xsession
```

Whichever you do, you'll have to edit the commands a little before you can actually use them. You'll have to add trailing ampersands so commands run in the background *(2.03)*, and you'll probably have other command-line options you'll want to use. Also, note that *xplaces* doesn't include a command line to start the actual window manager. So you can't just apply the *xplaces* output to a startup script verbatim. But *xplaces* gives you a good place to start.

—*LM*

21.17 *Starting Applications with bricons*

You can configure your window manager's root menu *(12.22, 13.19, 15.11)* so that you can select **xterm** and have an *xterm* window come up, or press **Calculator** and have an *xcalc* window come up, and so on. *bricons* is a natural extension of this: using *bricons*, you can just press an icon to start up an application. This is one more step towards a real GUI like the big boys have.

bricons

bricons needs to be configured using a configuration file called *.briconsrc*. I've configured mine so when I start up *bricons*, I get a window that resembles Figure 21-4.

Figure 21-4: My bricons window

When I press on the HELP icon, I get the *bricons* manpage. When I press on the icon of a terminal, I get an *xterm* window. When I press on the icon of letters, my mailer starts up, and when I press on the READ NEWS pixmap a newsreader starts up. When I press the TEXT EDITOR pixmap my favorite editor appears.

Under the Desktop submenu are several more applications, as shown in Figure 21-5. These are for calling up *xbiff* *(7.10)*, *xclock* *(3.02)*, *xload* *(27.03)*, *xcalendar* *(4.02)*, and *xcalc* *(5.05)*, respectively. Under the Edit Icons submenu are selections for sourcing and editing the *bricons* configuration file, another help window, and for quitting *bricons* altogether.

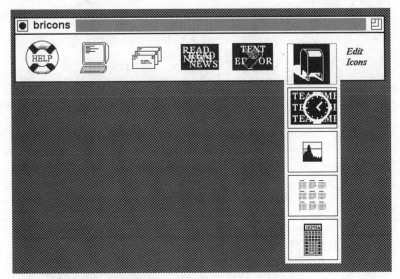

Figure 21-5: My desktop submenu

bricons is configured via a systemwide *.briconsrc* file, the location of which is specified at compile time. I didn't particularly like the *.briconsrc* file that comes with the *bricons* distribution, so I made my own:

.briconsrc

```
# <-- a line starting with a '#' is a comment line
#

# first line must have keyword %icon, %text or %pixmap

# "help" button -- opens up bricons manpage
%icon help.xbm
xedit /work/xpt/src/lib/bricons.txt

# "terminal" icon -- open up an xterm. "+" so you can open multiple
%icon+ terminal
xterm

# "letters" icon -- start mailer
%icon letters.xbm
xmail

# call up a news reader
%pixmap /work/xpt/src/lib/news.xpm
xrn

# call up an editor. "+" so you can call it multiple times.
%pixmap+ /work/xpt/src/lib/editor.xpm
xedit
```

```
# "desk accessories" submenu
%text Desktop\n (Submenu)
%sub_menu

        # xbiff app
        %pixmap /work/xpt/src/lib/mail.xpm
        xbiff

        # xclock app
        %pixmap /work/xpt/src/lib/clock.xpm
        xclock

        # xload app
        %icon load.xbm
        xload

        # calendar app (typo not mine)
        %icon calander.xbm
        xcalendar

        # calculator
        %icon calculator
        xcalc

%end_sub_menu
```

The basic structure for icon/command combinations is lines starting with %icon, %pixmap, or %text, followed by either the name of the bitmap *(22.01)*, the name of the pixmap *(22.01)*, or the text to be used. The next line is either the command to be executed when that icon is selected, or the %sub_menu command. Submenus follow the same format, ending with a line reading %end_sub_menu. Lines starting with # are ignored. Note that commands are *not* put in the background.

bricons assumes that in most cases, you don't want to select something twice—e.g., if you've already called up your mailer, you don't want to call it again. For that reason, the default is that icons are shaded gray when they are currently open, preventing them from being selected a second time. If you want to override this behavior, follow the %icon, %text, or %pixmap keyword with a plus sign (+). I've done just that for my terminal and editor icons, since I might want to open more than one terminal or editor window at a time.

You can invent your own icon/command combinations, as I did. For icons, you can use your own bitmaps or pixmaps, or take already existing ones. Pixmaps need to be specified with full pathnames, but *bricons* uses a bitmap-FilePath resource to determine where to look for bitmaps. My bitmapFilePath is set to */usr/include/X11/bitmaps:/work/xpt/src/lib/bricons*, so I can use both the systemwide bitmaps and the ones that were distributed with *bricons*. I use systemwide icons such as the calculator icon for *xcalc*, or the terminal icon for *xterm*.

If you want to use a different *.briconsrc* file other than the systemwide default, use the *–file* command line:

```
% bricons -file ~/.briconsrc &
```

Or set the icon_file resource:

```
bricons*icon_file:          /home/lmui/.briconsrc
```

—LM

21.18 *Making X Resemble My NeXT*

I have a NeXT workstation, and one thing I really like is the NeXT "application dock" on the right hand of the screen. The application dock gives you an icon for each of the commands you commonly run, and all you need to do is to click on it. So I configured *bricons(21.17)* to resemble the application dock.

First of all, I configured my *.briconsrc* file.

```
# "terminal" icon -- open up an xterm.
%icon+ terminal
xterm

# call up a news reader
%icon+ news.xbm
xrn

# mailer
%icon+ mail.xbm
xmail

# calendar app (typo not mine)
%icon+ calander.xbm
xcalendar

# dictionary
%icon+ webster-dict.xbm
xwebster

# manpages
%icon+ library.xbm
xman &

# calculator
%icon+ calculator
xcalc

# lock the display
%icon lock.xbm
xnlock
```

Next, I set up a few resources for *bricons* in my *.Xresources* file:

```
bricons*icon_file:          /home/lmui/.briconsrc
bricons*no_of_cols:         1
bricons*geometry:-1+1
bricons*bitmapFilePath:     /work/xpt/src/lib:/work/xpt/src/export/icons/bw-48:\
/work/xpt/src/export/icons/bw-64
```

I use my own *.briconsrc* file in my home directory. I set up *bricons* to use one column (so I'll get one long thin vertical column of icons, rather than a horizontal row of icons). I set up the geometry so that the *bricons* window appears at the upper-right corner of the screen *(17.12)*. And I define the bitmap-FilePath resource to include a few icon directories that I grabbed from the *AIcons* collection *(22.17)*.

Now I set up *bricons* to start automatically from my startup script *(2.09, 16.03)*. I use the *−default False* option because I don't want the Edit submenu. I also decide to also put up *xclock (3.02)*, *xload (27.03)* and, *xbiff (7.10)* windows underneath the *bricons* window, and I size them so they'll seem part of the same "environment."

```
#!/bin/sh

PATH=$PATH:/work/xpt/src/bin:/usr/local/bin

XUSERFILESEARCHPATH=/work/xpt/src/app-defaults/%N:$HOME
export PATH XUSERFILESEARCHPATH

xrdb -merge $HOME/.Xresources

xterm -geometry -100-1 &
xterm -geometry -100+1 &
bricons -default False &
xclock -geometry 80x80-1-1 &
xload -geometry 80x80-1-80 &
xbiff -geometry 80x80-1-160 &

exec twm
```

(Notice that since I set the geometry for *bricons* in the resource file, I don't need to do it in the startup script.)

Finally, I configure my window manager not to put any decoration around the *bricons* window. The way you do this depends on your window manager; if I used *mwm (13.01)*, I could set the following resource:

```
Mwm*bricons*clientDecoration:     none
Mwm*xload*clientDecoration:       none
Mwm*xclock*clientDecoration:      none
Mwm*xbiff*clientDecoration:       none
```

If I used *twm* *(12.01)*, I set it directly in the *.twmrc* file *(12.16)*:

```
NoTitle {
"bricons"
"xload"
"xclock"
"xbiff"
}
```

The resulting environment looks something like Figure 21-6.

Figure 21-6: My application dock

— LM

21.19 *Don't Ignore the Benefits of Tiling*

Many people strew windows at random around their screen and then find that they need virtual rooms or a more powerful window manager like *fvwm* *(15.01)* to make up for the clutter.

I still use *twm* *(12.01)*, but I find that I can do most of my work handily on a single screen by laying out in advance several working windows, neatly side by side to make maximum use of screen real estate. For example, on my Sun workstation, I use my startup script *(2.09, 16.03)* to set up an initial configuration like this:

```
xterm -geometry 79x32+0-0 -bg lightyellow -n isla2 -title isla2 &
xterm -geometry 79x32-0-0 -bg lightyellow -n isla3 -title isla3 &
xterm -geometry 79x26+0+85 -bg lightyellow -n isla1 -title isla1 &
xclock -digital -chime -update 1 -geometry -0+0 &
xcalc -bg lightyellow -geometry -0+30 &
xclipboard -iconic -g 300x100+550+0 &

xterm -title POSTITNOTES -g 33x33+580+0 -bg '#ffff95' -e vi $HOME/.postit &

exec xterm -C -bg lightyellow -n console -title console -geometry 80x4+0+0
```

I use light yellow for my window backgrounds *(17.07)* because it's a little easier on the eyes. Rather than use *xpostit (4.12)*, I have my own dedicated window for reminders *(4.13)*. And as a controlling process *(16.03)*, I call my final *xterm* as a console window *(27.02)*. Here's what my screen comes out looking like:

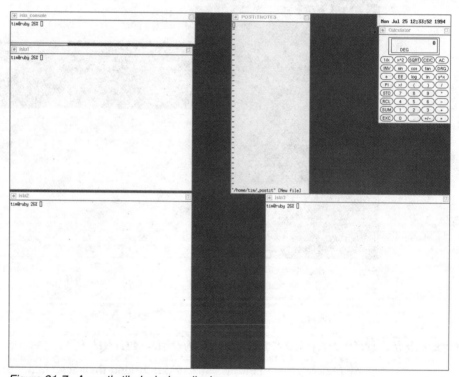

Figure 21-7: A neatly tiled window display

—TOR

21.20 A Neat Screen Makes Me Nervous

Within the next month I'm moving into a new apartment. It's kind of an odd place with floors that have settled into funny angles and crooked door jambs that have inexplicably settled the other way—the house is 150 years old. There's a staircase that goes nowhere and another staircase that's twisted enough to give you vertigo. One of the bedrooms has a window so close to the floor that I expect the Mad Hatter to come through at any moment.

But to tell you the truth, it's the very oddball nature of the place that I like about it. There's something about uniformity that I find very constricting. So I don't like regular old houses with three rooms up and four down. And I don't like to work with a screen that has a few neat windows all in a row. In other words, the benefits of tiling *(21.19)* are lost on me.

Now don't get me wrong. Tiling is a perfectly functional screen layout strategy for some very fine people, including the nice man who signs my checks. It just isn't for everybody. Give me a whole bunch of windows overlapping every which way and a bunch of virtual rooms, or desktops, any time. The *fvwm* window manager *(15.02)* makes navigating this apparent chaos a breeze. I'm organized by virtual desktops and I'm (reasonably) organized in my head. Most importantly, I'm happy in my little mess. (Since everyone knows what a mess looks like, I'll forego the illustration.) Best of luck finding the right screen setup for you.

—*VQ*

21.21 Sharing Screen Real Estate

With the help of the icon manager *(12.09)*, you can outdo even tiling *(21.19)* in making efficient use of screen real estate.

I typically keep *xterm* windows open on several of our networked systems, but I don't often need to access any of them. In my startup file *(2.09, 16.03)* I simply put three windows in exactly the same space:

```
xterm -geometry 79x26+0+85 -bg lightyellow -n rock -title rock -iconic \
-e rsh rock &
xterm -geometry 79x26+0+85 -bg lightyellow -n ruby -title ruby -iconic \
-e rsh ruby &
xterm -geometry 79x26+0+85 -bg lightyellow -n isla1 -title isla1 &
```

The window on *isla*, my home system, is tiled onto the screen, but the windows on *rock* and *ruby* are iconified. But if want to get to those systems, all I need to do is click on their buttons in the icon manager box to bring whichever one I want to the front.

I do the same thing with the commercial mailer I use—*zmail*—except that I don't overlay it on any particular window. Because it takes up a lot of screen real estate and has multiple subsidiary windows, I basically figure out how to tile its windows (which I do in its resource file) as a second layer over my normal *xterm* windows. I start it out iconified, and pop it up or down as I need it:

```
zmail -gui -geometry 575x550+575+320 -iconic &
```

Ditto for other "big window" programs like mosaic *(8.10)*.

—*TOR*

Part Six

Graphics

X is a *graphical* windowing system.

The standard version of X comes with a few graphics programs, notably the *bitmap* editor, *xmag*, which magnifies a screen image, and *xwd*, which makes a window dump file. But the public domain is brimming over with other programs that let you create and display graphic images in a variety of formats, as well as programs to convert images from one format to another.

This section covers the different X graphics formats: how to view them, convert them, capture them, and even draw them by hand.

—VQ

22

Bitmaps and Pixmaps

22.01 Bitmaps and Pixmaps in Their Natural Habitat

The image on your screen is composed of many tiny dots, or pixels, which are
not unlike the picture elements that produce a television image. You can't distinguish these individual pixels. Depending on the type of monitor, a screen
area one-inch square might actually be composed of more than a thousand of
them. To give you an idea of the scale we're talking about, Article 22.17
shows some typical icons and the accompanying text gives their dimensions in
pixels. If you're running the *twm* window manager *(12.01)*, the tiny iconify and
resize buttons *(12.03)* on the titlebar are 16×16 pixels.

If you have a monochrome monitor each pixel on your screen is either black
or white. Grayscale monitors display black and white, and also multiple
shades of gray, but no color, while color monitors enable you to have pixels
of several different colors. These different display capabilities are obviously
due to hardware differences. In the case of grayscale and color monitors, both
the display type and the available memory limit the number of colors that can
be displayed at once *(26.07)*.

A bitmap is a picture in which each pixel is described by a single bit in the
system's memory. This bit can be turned on or off. Thus, you can choose
between two states for every pixel: black or white on a monochrome display,
two shades of gray (or black or white) on a grayscale monitor, or two colors
on a color display. So, from a slightly less technical perspective, a bitmap is a
simple, two-color screen image.

Many of the images on an X display are actually bitmap images. For example,
most of the standard fonts are bitmaps *(17.16)*. The details of many applications,
such as command buttons, menu bars, etc., are often bitmap images. For
instance, bitmaps decorate the command buttons *(12.20)* on the titlebar *twm* provides *(12.03)*. The various cursor symbols representing the pointer on the
screen, such as the arrow, crosshairs, and I-beam, are bitmaps (in this case,

incorporated into the cursor font). Some application icons are bitmap images (though most clients will provide a more detailed icon if your screen can display it).

So, you encounter all kinds of bitmaps while working in the X environment. In addition, some applications allow you to specify alternate bitmaps for various purposes. For instance, you can specify a pointer symbol for the root window *(6.14)*. Often a window manager will let you specify your own icon symbols, though the average user probably has more pressing things to do. (See the online window manager manpage for details.) There are also purely fun or aesthetic ways to use bitmaps. For example, you can decorate your root window *(6.02)* with bitmap images.

Now, where do you get the images to use for these customizations? Well, most X environments provide some standard bitmap images *(22.15)* you can use. You may run across other bitmaps in your network travel. I have a bunch of pictures of cartoon characters all gathered from the Internet, which come in handy for root window decoration. You can also draw bitmaps of your own.

The *bitmap* client *(22.03)* lets you create and edit bitmap files that can then be used as backgrounds, icons, pointer symbols, etc. The current chapter reviews the basics of using *bitmap*, gives some tips about some of the trickier functions, and shows you how to create your own cursor *(22.12)*, and draw a bitmap to decorate a *twm* command button *(22.14)*. (You might also use the *xmag* client *(25.05)*, which magnifies a portion of the screen, to assist you in creating images with *bitmap*.) This chapter also describes an available bitmap viewing program called *xbmbrowser (22.16)*, and displays some publicly available images *(22.17)*.

Bitmaps work well for a variety of purposes, but they don't take advantage of the display capabilities of grayscale and color monitors. That's where pixmaps come in. A *pixmap* is an image in which multiple bits are used to define each pixel. Monochrome monitors provide only one bit per pixel and thus are limited to two-tone (also black-and-white) images. Thus, they can only display bitmaps. Grayscale and color monitors have the capacity to dedicate multiple bits towards displaying each pixel. Many such monitors have 8 bits per pixel, but some have 2, 4, or even 24 bits per pixel. (Article 26.07 explains how this information translates into color displaying capabilities.) Pixmap images are similar to bitmaps, but are designed to be displayed on color or grayscale monitors; thus, pixmaps use more than two tones. The more elaborate application icons are pixmaps. The *xbmbrowser (22.16)* can also display pixmaps; several appear among the "System icons" being previewed in Article 22.17.

Admittedly, the best programs with which to edit graphics are commercial offerings, which are beyond the scope of this book. But the publicly available *xpaint* program *(24.02)* is a lot of fun and can produce its output in pixmap format. The somewhat more primitive *pixt* program *(24.04)* will let you draw some basic pixmaps as well. Use the *xloadimage* utility *(24.05)* to display a pixmap image in a window, or to use as a root window background.

Now you understand something about the graphical building blocks of X. But if you're going to be working with graphics, it would also be helpful to know a bit more about the various types of graphics files *(22.02)*.

— VQ

22.02 *Graphic File Formats: Bitmaps, Pixmaps, and Others*

Bitmaps and pixmaps *(22.01)* are two generic names for types of graphic images. But technically speaking, every graphic image adheres to a particular file format. In the X Window System, bitmaps adhere to a format called *X bitmap*. (For this reason, many bitmap files have the mnemonic suffix *.xbm*, e.g., *flower.xbm*.) Most X users will only have to deal with this type of bitmap image, but you should be aware that there are other types of bitmaps, as well as entirely different image types.

For example, some bitmaps are *portable bitmaps*. Portable bitmap (pbm) images adhere to a slightly different file format than X bitmaps, and thus, have different uses. For example, you can't use the *bitmap* editor *(22.03)* to read a portable bitmap; it only understands the X bitmap file type. The portable bitmap format is primarily intended to convert graphics files from one type to another. Among the user-contributed X clients (see contrib) are dozens of graphic-conversion utilities collectively known as the Portable Bitmap Toolkit *(23.05)*. Most conversions you'll perform using the PBM Toolkit utilities require you to convert the file to a portable format, such as pbm, and from there convert it to the format you want.

As you might expect, most of the pixmaps you encounter in the X environment adhere to *X pixmap* format, and X pixmap files often have the suffix *.xpm*. There is also a *portable pixmap* (ppm) format, which the PBM Toolkit handles. The *xloadimage* utility *(24.05)* lets you display both X pixmap and portable pixmap images, among others.

The various flavors of bitmaps and pixmaps are just a few of the types of graphics files you may encounter. *X window dump* (xwd) files contain images of application windows captured with the *xwd* client *(23.01)*. There are also many formats intended for more complex images. Colorful, photo-like pictures may be stored in any one of several formats, including GIF, TIFF, and JPEG. You should be able to display these graphics using either *xloadimage* *(24.05)*, or *xv* *(24.06)*. FaceSaver is a unique and highly memorable file type that stores a digitized version of a video camera shot of someone's face. You can convert a FaceSaver to more universal formats using the PBM Toolkit. You'll undoubtedly read about other formats throughout this section of the book. Consult the Glossary for additional information on particular formats.

— VQ

22.03   *The bitmap Editor*

Virtually every flavor of X should come with *bitmap*, which is part of the standard X distribution. The *bitmap* client lets you create new bitmap images or edit existing ones. To bring up an empty *bitmap* window in which to edit, type:

```
% bitmap &
```

If you're using X11R5, no filename argument is necessary. (Earlier releases of *bitmap* require one.) The default *bitmap* window is shown in Figure 22-1.

The window that *bitmap* creates has three sections: a menu bar, a column of editing command buttons, and the actual editing area.

Menu Bar

The menu bar across the top of the application window provides two menus, Edit and File, which help you edit the image in the window and manage bitmap files, respectively. You display a menu by placing the pointer on the appropriate command button and pressing and holding down any pointer button. Article 22.06 reviews the menu items.

The menu bar also displays the name of the bitmap file. When you run a new instance of the program, this name will be *none*.

Editing Command Buttons

Below the menu bar, on the left side of the window, is a list of editing commands in buttons. Place the pointer on a command button and click the first pointer button to invoke the command. These commands help you draw the bitmap image. See Article 22.05 for an overview of these functions.

Editing Area

To the right of the command buttons is a grid in which you create/edit the bitmap. Each square in the grid represents a single pixel on the screen. The default size of the grid is 16×16 squares, representing an area of the screen 16×16 pixels—a fairly tiny spot *(22.01)*. The grid affords a close-up look at this area and allows you to edit an image that would otherwise be too small to work with.

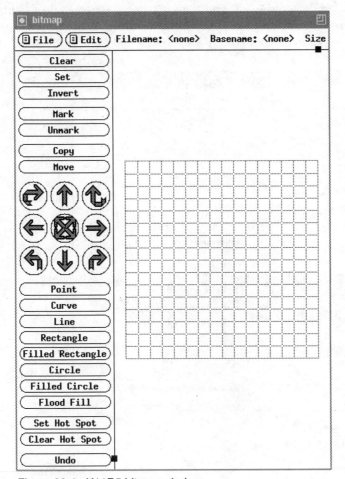

Figure 22-1: X11R5 bitmap window

Once you begin playing with *bitmap*, you may find the 16×16 space too restricting. You can specify another grid size using the *–size* command-line option, which has the syntax:

```
-size widthxheight
```

The following command line opens a *bitmap* window with a 32×32 grid, a more workable space:

```
% bitmap -size 32x32 &
```

The *–size* option was introduced in Release 5. In prior releases, you could supply the dimensions simply as a command-line argument, without a preceding option.

Figure 22-2 shows a 40×40 grid with a bitmap we created of Gumby. Since the *xsetroot* client lets you specify a bitmap as your root window pattern *(6.02)*, you could populate your screen with Gumbys.

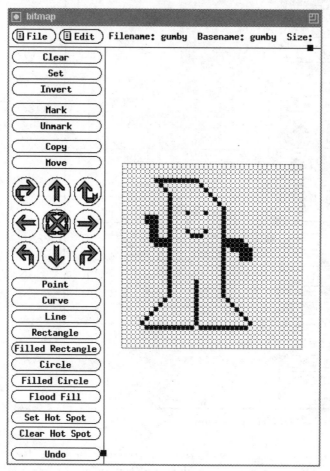

Figure 22-2: Gumby bitmap

Note that the standard cursor font also contains a Gumby character. You can specify the Gumby cursor as the root window pointer using the *xsetroot* client, as described in Article 6.14. We could also take our own Gumby bitmap (or any bitmap for that matter) and make it into a cursor *(22.12)*.

— VQ

22.04 *Image Size and the Size of the bitmap Window*

There is a relationship between the size of the bitmap image being edited and the size of the *bitmap* window. By default, the editing grid has 16×16 cells and each cell is 13 pixels square. You can specify another grid size using the *–size* command-line option *(22.03)*:

```
% bitmap -size 40x40 &
```

Keep in mind that if you specify grid dimensions of 40×40, the editing area alone will be 520 pixels square. Specifying a very large editing area may even result in an application window larger than the screen. (Since *bitmap* does not provide a scrollbar, a large window makes it very difficult to edit!)

You can change the size of the editing area (not the number of squares) by: specifying an explicit size for the overall application using the *–geometry* option; or resizing the application window using the window manager. In either case, *bitmap* will automatically adjust the size of each square in the grid to fit the overall window size. (If the bitmap image is very large and the *bitmap* window cannot incorporate it, the image will appear truncated. If you resize to a larger window, more of the image should be revealed.)

A mild caution about using the *–geometry* option: when you specify a size for the overall application window, it may be difficult to estimate what size the editing squares will be. So if you use *–geometry*, there's a reasonable chance you'll have to resize anyway.

You can control the size of the editing grid even more precisely by using the *–sw* and *–sh* command-line options, which set the width and height of each square in pixels. We find that we need at least 10×10 pixel grid squares to edit comfortably, but this is clearly an individual preference.

As you're probably realizing, the number of factors that can determine the size of the application window and the editing grid make specifying the size on the command line rather complicated. Your best bet may be to confine yourself to the *–size* option for a while and make any necessary adjustments using the window manager. (You may never need to use *–geometry*, *–sw*, or *–sh*.)

Once you run *bitmap*, you can adjust either the size of the squares in the grid, or the actual number of squares. You change the size of squares in the grid by resizing the *bitmap* window using the window manager. For example, if the cells in the grid aren't large enough for comfortable editing, make the window larger. Each square on the grid will be enlarged proportionally. Alternatively, you might have a grid with large dimensions and make the window smaller so it takes up less space. The squares will be made smaller proportionally. (Note, however, when the squares are made very small, the grid lines are suppressed. Though editing is still possible in such circumstances, it is difficult.)

You can change the number of squares in the editing grid using the **Resize** option on the File menu *(22.06)*. Of course, if you want, you can also change the dimensions of each square using the window manager.

You can open an existing bitmap file to edit by supplying the filename on the *bitmap* command line. Keep in mind that if no size is specified and the image you display is larger than 16×16, *bitmap* will try to fit the image into an editing area the same overall size as the default. However, to accomplish this, each pixel in the image will be scaled down and the grid lines will be suppressed. In this case, you can still use all the editing commands, but chances are the image will be too small to work with precisely. If the image is large enough, one pixel in the image may actually be represented by a single pixel in the editing area. Some images may even be too large to fit under this circumstance, in which case the image will appear truncated. If you resize to make the window larger, more of the image should be revealed. As a general rule, if you know the dimensions of the image in pixels, it's a good idea to give them with *–size*.

— VQ

22.05 *bitmap Command Button Summary*

Several command buttons appear in a column to the left of the *bitmap* editing grid. The following tables summarize the command button functions, grouping them in a logical rather than actual order.

The seven command buttons in Table 22-1 let you draw particular shapes using the pointer. First click on the command button. Then use the pointer to draw in the editing grid. In all cases except **Point**, hold down the pointer to begin the shape, drag, and release the button to finish drawing the shape.

Table 22-1: Drawing

Command Button	*What It Does*
Point	In effect when you start *bitmap*. First pointer button changes pixel to the foreground color *(17.06)*. Second pointer button inverts. Third pointer button changes to background color *(17.06)*. Click to change one pixel at a time; drag for multiple pixels.
Curve	Lets you draw a continuous curve. A good idea, but clumsy in execution.
Line	Lets you draw the straightest line possible.
Rectangle	Lets you draw a hollow rectangle.
Filled Rectangle	Lets you draw a solid rectangle.
Circle	Lets you draw a hollow circle.
Filled Circle	Lets you draw a solid circle.

Table 22-2 lists four command buttons that affect whether an area appears in the foreground (bits are set to 1) or background (bits are set to 0) color. All but Flood Fill affect the entire grid.

Table 22-2: Filling Shapes and the Grid

Command Button	What It Does
Flood Fill	Changes all pixels within a closed shape. To fill with the foreground color, click with the first pointer button; background color, third pointer button. Be careful that the shape is closed!
Clear	Changes all the grid squares to the background color and sets the bits to 0. Typing c while the pointer rests inside the grid has the same effect.
Set	Changes all the grid squares to the foreground color and sets the bits to 1. Typing s while the pointer rests inside the grid has the same effect.
Invert	Inverts all the grid squares and bitmap bits, as if you had clicked the second pointer button over each square. Typing i while the pointer rests inside the grid has the same effect.

The two command buttons in Table 22-3 help you mark an area for subsequent editing (including copying, cutting, and pasting) and unmark it again.

Table 22-3: Marking an Area for Editing

Command Button	What It Does
Mark	Lets you highlight an area. Certain editing commands will then apply only to that area. Article 22.08 explains how to use Mark.
Unmark	Removes highlighting.

Several buttons allow you to copy, move, or rotate the image (or a marked portion of it) within the current bitmap window. See Article 22.11 for instructions on copying between windows.

Table 22-4: Copy, Move, or Rotate Whole or Partial Image (in Current Window)

Command Button	What It Does
Copy	Copy the image (or part) within current window.
Move	Move the image (or part) within current window.

Table 22-4: Copy, Move, or Rotate Whole or Partial Image (in Current Window) (continued)

Command Button	What It Does
Nine arrow buttons	The nine circular buttons marked with some sort of arrow correspond to functions that allow you to flip or move the bitmap image in various ways. All of the buttons, except the central one (Fold), can act on a part of the image, if it has been marked. See Article 22.07 for a diagram of the correspondence between the arrow buttons and their functions.

The Undo button undoes the last action. Typing u while the pointer rests in the editing area has the same effect.

— VQ

22.06 bitmap Menus Revisited

The X11R5 *bitmap* editor provides two menus, a File menu and an Edit menu. Place the pointer on a menu command button and hold down the first pointer button to display the menu. The current article summarizes the functions available on each menu.

The File Menu

True to its name, the File menu helps you manage bitmap files. Table 22-5 lists the File menu items, their keyboard shortcuts, and gives a brief description of what each item does. You can probably figure out how to use most of the items simply by trying them. See Article 22.10 for a tutorial on using the somewhat less intuitive Insert command, which lets you insert another bitmap image into the current file.

Table 22-5: File Menu Items

Menu Item	Keyboard Shortcut(s)	What Item Does
New	CTRL-N	Clears the window so you can create a new image; prompts for a name for the new file. If you haven't saved the current file, the changes will be lost.
Load	CTRL-F	Dynamically loads another bitmap file into the editing window; if you haven't saved the current file, prompts you as to whether to save before loading the next file.

Table 22-5: File Menu Items (continued)

Menu Item	Keyboard Shortcut(s)	What Item Does
Insert	CTRL-I	Inserts a bitmap file into the image currently being edited. See Article 22.11 for instructions.
Save	CTRL-S	Saves the current image using the filename in the menu bar.
Save As	CTRL-W	Saves the current image but prompts for the filename. That name is subsequently displayed in the menu bar.
Resize	CTRL-R	Changes the dimensions of the editing grid to match dimensions you supply (*width*x*height*), without changing the size of the image. Thus, specifying a larger grid gives you more room to edit. Specifying a smaller grid may cause part of the current image to be truncated.
Rescale	CTRL-X	Changes the dimensions of the grid to match dimensions you supply (*width*x*height*) and changes the image so that the proportions (the ratio of the image to the grid) remain the same. Thus, if you specify a grid twice the size of the current one, the grid and the image will both be doubled. Specifying a smaller grid may cause part of the current image to be truncated.
Filename	CTRL-E	Lets you change the filename of the current file without changing the basename (which appears in the header lines of the file) or saving the file.
Basename	CTRL-B	Lets you change the basename (if you want one different from the filename). The basename appears in the bitmap file, as part of the C code.
Quit	CTRL-C, q, Q	Exits the application. If changes have been made and not saved, a dialog box will ask whether to save before quitting.

The Edit Menu

The *bitmap* Edit menu is divided into two sections by a horizontal line. The top portion contains items that determine characteristics of the editing area, such as its dimensions, whether or not grid lines are used, etc. Most of these items turn a characteristic on and off (i.e., the items are toggles). The bottom portion contains commands to Copy, Cut, and Paste images within the same *bitmap* window, between *bitmap* windows, or between *bitmap* and *xmag*.

Table 22-6 lists the Edit menu items and their keyboard shortcuts, and gives a brief description of their functions. You can probably figure out how to use most of the items simply by trying them. See Article 22.11 for a discussion of "Transferring Images Using bitmap's Edit Menu."

Table 22-6: Edit Menu Items

Menu Item	Keyboard Shortcut(s)	What Item Does
Image	Meta-I	Displays a window showing what the bitmap being edited looks like at its actual size (both as it appears and in reverse video). Clicking the first pointer button on this window pops it down.
Grid	Meta-G	Toggles grid lines. If the grid spacing is below the value specified by the gridTolerance resource (8 by default), the grid will be automatically turned off. You can turn it on by selecting this menu item.
Dashed	Meta-D	Toggles stippling in the grid lines. On by default when the grid lines are activated.
Axes	Meta-A	Toggles diagonal axes. The axes simply assist in drawing; they are not part of the image. Off by default.
Stippled	Meta-S	Toggles a stipple pattern to be used for highlighting within the editing area. (This stipple is a subtle shading; if toggled off, marking is done in the foreground color.) On by default.
Proportional	Meta-P	Toggles proportional mode, which forces proportional grid squares, regardless of the dimensions of the bitmap window. On by default.
Zoom	Meta-Z	Toggles zoom mode, which focuses in on a marked area of the image. (You can mark before or after selecting Zoom.)

Table 22-6: Edit Menu Items (continued)

Menu Item	Keyboard Shortcut(s)	What Item Does
Cut	Meta-C	Cuts the contents of any marked area into the application's local buffer. The marked area is deleted from the current image, but is available to be pasted from the local buffer. (If this was the last area marked, it is also available to be pasted into other applications via a global buffer.)
Copy	Meta-W	Copies the contents of any marked area into the application's local buffer. The marked area remains a part of the current image and is also available to be pasted from the local buffer. (If this was the last area marked, it is also available to be pasted into other applications via a global buffer.)
Paste	Meta-Y, CTRL key, mouse button click	Pastes the contents of the global buffer (the marked area in any bitmap or xmag application), or if the global buffer is empty, the contents of the local buffer, into the current image. To place the copied image, press and hold the first pointer button in the editing area, drag the outlined image to the position you want, and then release the button.

— VQ

22.07 *Rotating or Moving a bitmap Using Arrow Command Buttons*

Halfway down in the column of *bitmap* command buttons are nine circular buttons each marked with some sort of arrow. These buttons correspond to functions that flip or move the bitmap image in various ways. The developer of the *bitmap* client associates each of these buttons with a text name (though the name does not appear on the button). Figure 22-3 shows the button images on the left and their corresponding symbolic names on the right.

Note that all of the buttons (except **Fold**) will act on a part of the bitmap, if it has been marked. See Article 22.08 for instructions on marking an area.

When you mark an area, the commands to move (**Left**, **Right**, **Up**, **Down**) do so *only within that area*. Thus, if you have a square 3×3 pixels and you want to move it 5 pixels to the right, you must mark an area larger than the square itself.

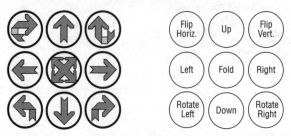

Figure 22-3: Arrow command buttons and their functions

Note also that to use a keyboard shortcut, the pointer must rest inside the editing grid or the surrounding whitespace (not in the menu bar or the command button column).

Flip Horizontally
Flips the image with respect to the horizontal axis. Pressing **h** inside the editing area has the same effect.

Up Moves the image up one pixel (grid square) at a time. Pressing the up arrow on your keypad has the same effect.

Flip Vertically
Flips the image with respect to the vertical axis. Pressing **v** inside the editing area has the same effect.

Left
Moves the image to the left one pixel (grid square) at a time. Pressing the left arrow on your keypad has the same effect.

Fold
A confusing command. Technically, it "folds" the image so that opposite corners become adjacent, but this explanation is just about as topsy-turvey as the reality. To get a better idea, imagine that the bitmap image is divided into four parts (along the vertical and horizontal axes of the editing area); then the diagonally opposite quadrants are swapped. Since it's much easier to see this for yourself, we provide an example in Figure 22-4. Note that pressing **f** inside the editing area has the same effect.

Right
Moves the image to the right one pixel (grid square) at a time. Pressing the right arrow on your keypad has the same effect.

Rotate Left
Rotates the image 90 degrees to the left (i.e., counterclockwise). Thus, selecting this command four times in a row brings the image around 360

degrees, to its original position. Pressing I inside the editing area has the same effect.

Down

Moves the image down one pixel (grid square) at a time. Pressing the down arrow on your keypad has the same effect.

Rotate Right

Rotates the image 90 degrees to the right (i.e., clockwise). Thus, selecting this command four times in a row brings the image around 360 degrees, to its original position. Pressing r inside the editing area has the same effect.

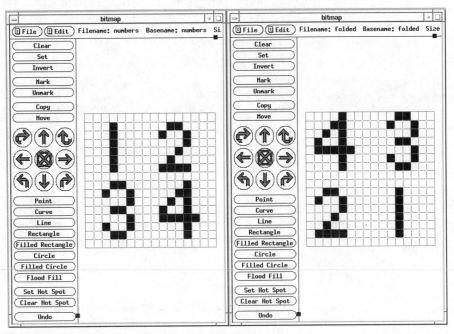

Figure 22-4: Folding an image: before and after

— VQ

22.08 *Marking an Area of a bitmap for Editing or Pasting*

When you Mark a part of the grid, many subsequent editing commands apply to that area only. For instance, you might mark a portion of a bitmap and then delete (cut) it. If you mark a part of a bitmap, you can then use the arrow buttons to move that part within the editing area one square at a time.

Mark requires you to select a rectangular area (a line counts); no irregular areas can be marked. The smallest area you can mark is a line composed of two squares.

The most important aspect of marking is that any marked area is available to be pasted from a global buffer via the selection mechanism. The main limitations of the selection mechanism are:

- Copying and pasting must be performed between clients that interpret data in the same format, e.g., *bitmap* and *xmag* (25.05).

- Since there can only be one PRIMARY selection on a display at any time, any area you mark in a *bitmap* window supersedes the previous selection—whether the previous selection is text or graphics. (*Only one area on the display can be marked at any time.*)

To mark part of a bitmap image:

- Click the first pointer button on the **Mark** command button. The button displays in reverse video.

- Move the pointer into the editing area. It changes to a crosshair symbol.

- Place the crosshair pointer on the upper-left square of the area you want to mark. (Upper left is easy for a right-handed person, but you can actually drag from any corner.) Press and hold down any pointer button. A gray shading covers the square the pointer is on.

- Drag the pointer away from that square. The area you cover with the pointer will be outlined in gray. In Figure 22-5, we drag the pointer diagonally to the right, highlighting an area 9 squares wide by 11 squares high.

- When you've marked the area you want, release the pointer button. The entire area will be highlighted in gray.

An area remains marked until you explicitly **Unmark** it or until you mark another area (or make a selection in any application).

Having a marked area does not interfere with any drawing you do in the window (using the pointer, command buttons such as **Point**, **Line**, etc.). However, if an area is marked, the following commands will act only on that area:

- **Copy** command button.

- **Move** command button.

- **Cut** item on **Edit** menu (and its keyboard shortcut, Meta-C).

- **Copy** item on **Edit** menu (and its keyboard shortcut, Meta-W).

- The arrow command buttons to flip, move, etc., and the corresponding keyboard shortcuts. The center arrow button, which performs the Fold function, is the exception. It acts on the entire bitmap image.

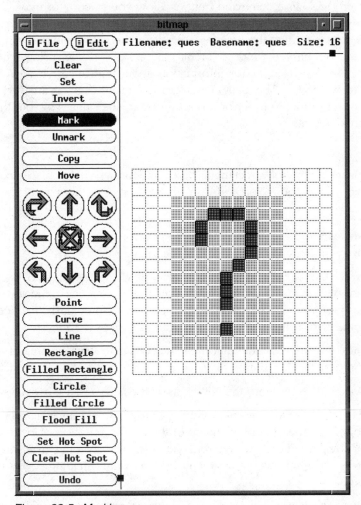

Figure 22-5: Marking an area

Keep in mind that if you select a copy or move and an area is already marked, you will be copying or moving that area. Note, however, that you don't have to select Mark before selecting the Copy or Move command buttons. These functions have "marking" built into them. See Article 22.09 for details. If you want to move part of a bitmap using the arrow command buttons, on the other hand, you *must* Mark it first.

— VQ

22.09 Copy/Move Within bitmap Window (Using Command Buttons)

The Copy and Move command buttons allow you to copy or move a rectangular area you select to another position within the current *bitmap* window. (Note, however, that the area you select for the copy or move can be pasted into another *bitmap* window, or into an *xmag* window, using other mechanisms. See Article 22.11 for information about transferring images from window to window.) The Copy and Move command buttons are very useful, if slightly confusing. You perform both functions the same way, but the result is slightly different:

Copy
> Makes a copy of a rectangular area and allows you to place it on another part of the grid. (You end up with two copies of that part of the image.)

Move
> Moves a rectangular area from one part of the grid to another. (You end up with one copy of that part of the image.)

The first step in either function involves marking the area to be copied or moved. Marking is built into both functions. To Copy or Move part of an image, perform the following steps. (If you've previously marked an area using the Mark command button, you can skip steps 2-5.)

1. Click the first pointer button on the Copy or Move command button, as appropriate. The button displays in reverse video.

2. Move the pointer into the editing area. It changes to a crosshair symbol.

3. Mark the area you want to copy or move. To do so, place the crosshair pointer on the upper-left square of the area in question. (Upper-left is easy for a right-handed person, but you can actually drag from any corner.) Press and hold down any pointer button. A gray shading covers the square the pointer is on.

4. Drag the pointer away from that square. A gray rectangle will surround the area you indicate with the pointer.

5. When you've surrounded the area you want, release the pointer button. The entire area will be highlighted in gray.

6. Then you can move the area or a copy of it, depending on which command you selected initially. To do so, place the pointer on the gray rectangle and hold down any pointer button.

7. Then move the pointer to position the copy/original. An outline of the rectangle follows the pointer's movement. When the outline is positioned

where you want it, release the pointer button. The image is redrawn in the place you indicated.

Notice that the area remains highlighted until you select another command. You can continue to move/copy the highlighted area by following steps 6 and 7 above. Note that if you copy an area and place the copy overlapping the original, the next copy will incorporate that image. In other words, when you perform steps 6 and 7, you're copying or moving what you see at the moment (not necessarily the same image you originally marked).

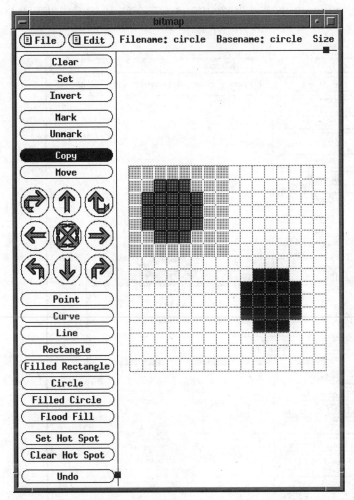

Figure 22-6: Copying an image

Figure 22-6 shows a circle being copied. Remember: if you previously high-lighted an area using the Mark command, you can move or copy that area by selecting either Move or Copy (step 1) and then performing steps 6 and 7.

—VQ

22.10 Inserting a File Within the bitmap Editor

One of the more useful but tricky operations you can perform using *bitmap's* File menu is to insert another image into the current one. To insert a bitmap file into the image you're editing, select Insert from the *bitmap* File menu. A dialog box will prompt you for a filename, as in Figure 22-7.

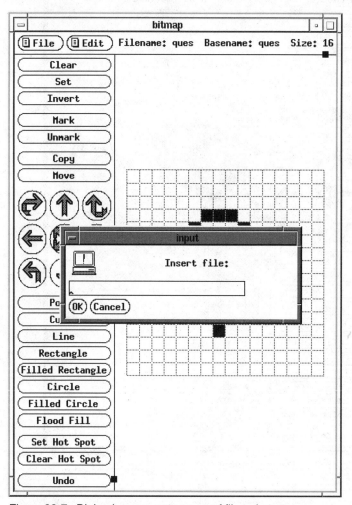

Figure 22-7: Dialog box requests name of file to insert

The pointer will be warped to the dialog box, enabling you to enter the path of the file you want. Use the editing commands for the Athena Text widget (described in Article 9.03). Once you type the filename, click on **OK** or press **Return** to request the file.

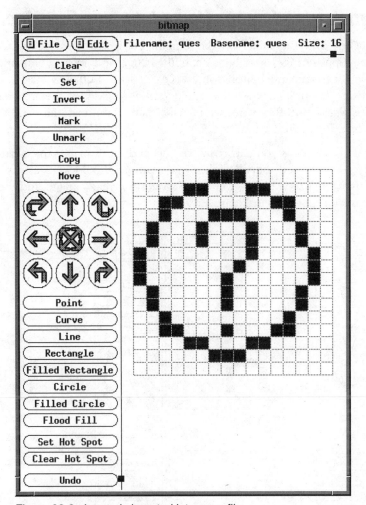

Figure 22-8: Image is inserted into open file

If the file exists, the pointer will change to the crosshair symbol. Move the pointer onto the *bitmap* editing grid, and press and hold down the first pointer button. You should see a gray outline that represents the image to be inserted. Drag the image to the position you want and release the pointer button. The image is inserted into the current file. In Figure 22-8, we've inserted a large circle into the arrow file.

— *VQ*

22.11 *Transferring Images Using bitmap's Edit Menu*

The Copy and Cut items on the *bitmap* Edit menu provide more powerful image transferring capabilities than the Copy and Move command buttons. While the command buttons only access a local buffer (which limits you to copying and pasting within a single *bitmap* window), the Edit menu items access a global buffer: when you "mark" part of an image, it can be pasted to any *bitmap* or *xmag* window.

The different ways you can copy (or cut) and paste makes transferring images a little complicated, but the following example should help clarify. First, we run two *bitmap* windows, one with a question mark image and the other an exclamation point, as in Figure 22-9.

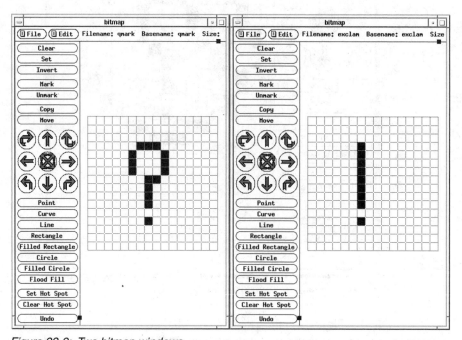

Figure 22-9: Two bitmap windows

Suppose we want to copy the exclamation mark from the right *bitmap* window into the left window, so that it appears after the question mark. There are a few ways to do this. We could:

1. Mark the exclamation using the procedure outlined for the **Mark** command button. While the exclamation is highlighted in this way, it is available to be pasted via the global buffer. In Figure 22-10, we've marked an area encompassing the exclamation and one additional pixel on all sides. (The entire area will be pasted.)

2. To paste the marked area into the question mark window, select **Paste** from the **Edit** menu in that window. Then move the pointer into the editing area. The crosshair pointer represents the upper-left pixel of the image to be pasted. Place the image where you want and click the first pointer button. The image is pasted, as in Figure 22-10.

Rather than selecting the **Paste** menu item, you could instead direct the focus to the question mark window and use either of the two keyboard/pointer shortcuts for the item: Meta-Y or **CTRL** and any mouse button click. Note that in the latter case, the click places the image. Until you mark another image, invoking the paste function in any *bitmap* or *xmag* window will paste the exclamation.

There are other ways to place the exclamation image in the question mark window. You could also highlight the exclamation image, then select either **Copy** or **Cut** from the **Edit** menu in the same window. (These items are only available for selection when a image is marked in the window.) Obviously, the former menu item makes a copy of the marked image, while the latter makes a copy but deletes the original from the window. In both cases, the image is available globally. Once you've selected **Copy** or **Cut** from the **Edit** menu, you can transfer the exclamation by invoking the paste function in any *bitmap* or *xmag* window.

If you run multiple *bitmap* windows and cut and paste frequently, the contents of the global and local buffers will often be different. In trying to determine what image you'll be pasting, the following rules of precedence apply:

1. If an image is currently marked (highlighted) in any *bitmap* window, that image will be copied to any *bitmap* or *xmag* window in which you invoke a paste command.

2. If no image is currently marked, the image that is pasted will be: the last image cut, copied, or pasted in any currently running *bitmap* window (using the analogous **Edit** menu options or their keyboard accelerators); or the last image selected in a currently running *xmag* window.

3. Whatever image you **Copy** or **Move** using the command buttons can only be pasted within the same *bitmap* window, *unless it remains highlighted*. In this case, the image is available via the global buffer and will be pasted according to rule 1 above.

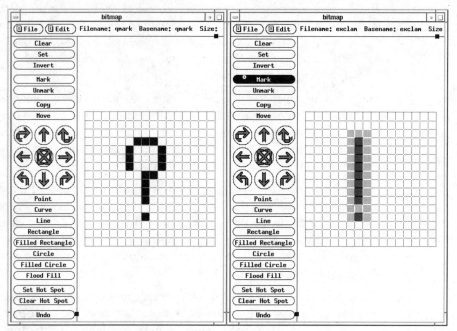

Figure 22-10: Marking the exclamation so that it can be pasted

The *xmag* client *(25.05)* can also access the global image buffer, so you can paste between *xmag* windows and also between *bitmap* and *xmag*.

— VQ

22.12 Creating Your Own Cursor

We've all seen and many of us have become bored with the X that is used as the default root window pointer. The *xsetroot* client lets you specify an alternate root window cursor *(6.14)*. If you don't want to use a cursor from the standard cursor font, you can create one of your own.

To create your own cursor, you need both a bitmap file and a *mask* file. The cursor is a composite of these two images. You can use the *bitmap* program *(22.03)* or a similar editor to create the bitmap image that will serve as the basic cursor shape; or you can borrow any publicly available bitmap image you like.

Once you have a bitmap for the face of the cursor, you need to create a mask file, which is placed behind the bitmap. The purpose of a mask file is to set the cursor off from certain backgrounds.

Generally, the mask file is a copy of the bitmap file with all the bits set (i.e., the mask file is black or whatever foreground color you're using); the mask

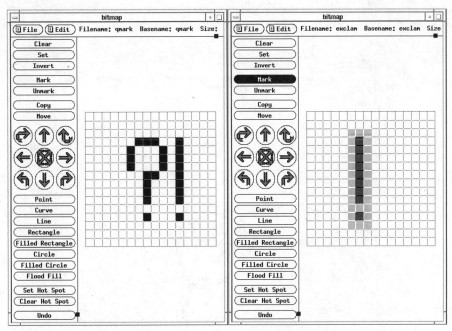

Figure 22-11: Pasting the exclamation next to the question mark

file is also edited to be at least one pixel wider than the bitmap file in all directions. Technically speaking, the mask determines the pixels on the screen that are disturbed by the cursor. It functions as a sort of outliner or highlighter for the cursor shape. The mask appears as a white (or background color) border around the cursor (black or another foreground color), making it visible over any root window pattern. This is especially important when a black cursor appears on a black root window. Without a mask file to highlight it, the cursor would disappear!

With the default root window pattern and cursor, you can observe the effect of a mask. When you move the X pointer onto the dark-gray root window, the X should have a very thin white border, which enables you to see it more clearly.

Every standard cursor has an associated mask. To get an idea of what masks look like, display the cursor font using *xfd*, the X font displayer:

```
% xfd -fn cursor
```

If you are using your own bitmap for a cursor, it's simple to create a mask file. First, make a copy of the bitmap file. Then use the *bitmap* editor *(22.03)* to change all the pixels in the mask file to the foreground color (which is generally black).* Finally, edit the image to be at least one pixel wider in all directions. Figure 22-12 shows a bitmap I created of a rose.

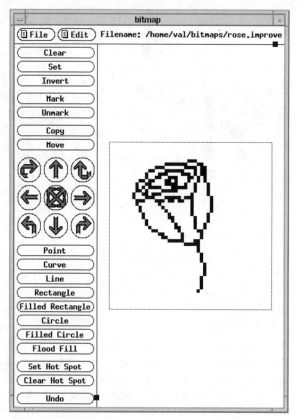

Figure 22-12: Rose bitmap to be used as a cursor

To create a mask file for the rose cursor, make a copy of the bitmap file:

```
% cp rose.xbm rose.mask
```

Use *bitmap* to edit the mask file. The **Flood Fill** command button lets you set all the pixels within a closed shape simultaneously. Click on the **Flood Fill** button, then click on every white partition within the rose to turn it black. Figure 22-13 shows the rose with the two outer petals filled.

Once the entire rose is black, select the **Point** command button to enable the pointer's drawing capabilities (see Figure 22-14). Then extend the black rose

---

* Don't be confused by the idea of a black cursor with a black mask on a black root window. Remember, the mask determines the pixels that are disturbed by the cursor, in effect creating an outline around the cursor. The outline appears in white (or specified background color), regardless of the color of the mask file.

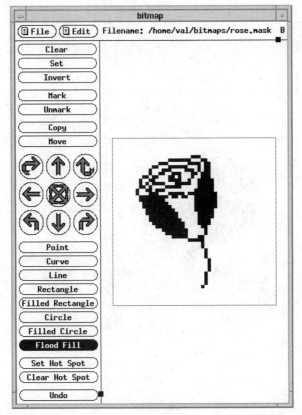

Figure 22-13: Select Flood Fill and then click to fill partitions

by one pixel in all directions by clicking the first pointer button around the outline.

Once you have both a cursor and mask file, you can use *xsetroot* to change the root window pointer *(6.14)*.

Every pointer needs to have a *hot spot*, the actual pixel that is used to point. Some cursor symbols have an obvious point that should serve as the hot spot: the tip of an arrow, the intersection of an X, the tip of a finger, etc. You can specify a hot spot *(22.13)* using the *bitmap* editor.

— *VQ*

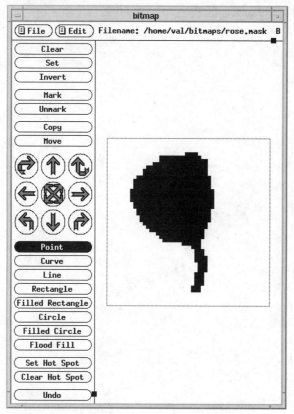

Figure 22-14: Mask file for the rose cursor

22.13 *Setting a Cursor's Hot Spot*

Every cursor symbol needs a spot with which you literally do the pointing. On the default X-shaped root window pointer, the hot spot is the intersection of the X. For arrow-shaped pointers, the spot is usually the arrow's tip.

When you use your own bitmap file as a cursor, you can specify a hot spot using the *bitmap* editor *(22.03)*. (If you don't specify a hot spot, by default the spot will be as close as possible to the center of the bitmap.) The rose bitmap I created for Article 22.12 doesn't have an obvious point that could serve as the hot spot. You might use the tip of the stem, but I prefer a spot on the left-most edge of the flower.

To add the hot spot, I run *bitmap*:

```
% bitmap rose.xbm &
```

I click on the **Set Hot Spot** command button. Then I select the hot spot by clicking the first pointer button on a pixel within the rose image. A hot spot is indicated by a small diamond symbol. Figure 22-15 provides a closer look at the rose. Notice the diamond on one of the leftmost pixels.

Figure 22-15: Rose cursor with diamond symbol indicating hot spot

To remove a hot spot, click on the **Clear Hot Spot** command button. The diamond will go away.

— VQ

22.14 *Bitmap to Decorate a Command Button*

The *twm* window manager *(12.01)* lets you add command buttons to the titlebar *(12.18)* it places on application windows. *twm* provides a few stock bitmap images to use as button decoration *(12.20)*, but you can also create an image of your own using *bitmap (22.03)*.

We customized *twm* to add a command button that performs the function of maximizing a window vertically. Article 12.19 describes how to do this, and also illustrates the new titlebutton, which is decorated with one of the default bitmaps *twm* includes.

The default bitmap is OK, but it doesn't particularly suggest the function of the button. Figure 22-16 shows a *bitmap* window containing an image I drew to represent the function of maximizing a window vertically. It's just two nested rectangles—sort of a before and after. Note that you need an image that fits within *bitmap*'s default size editing grid *(22.03)*. I used the **Rectangle** command button *(22.05)* to do the drawing. I've named the bitmap file *max*.

Article 12.20 shows how we used this bitmap as a *twm* titlebutton decoration. Granted, the image is on the primitive side. But those more artistic than myself (a very large group) might easily come up with a better design.

— VQ

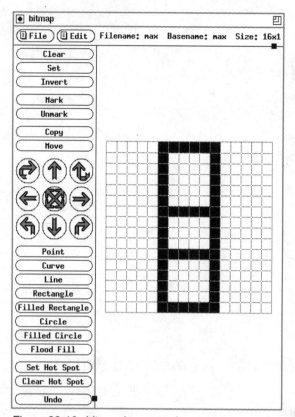

Figure 22-16: bitmap image to decorate twm maximize button

22.15 Standard Bitmap Images

A number of bitmaps are included with the standard distribution of X. These bitmaps are generally located in the directory */usr/include/X11/bitmaps*. Each image is in X bitmap format in its own file. You can use the *bitmap* application *(22.03)* to view these bitmaps in larger scale and to edit them (though their permissions normally do not allow overwriting). Or take a look at all of the images in the directory at once using *xbmbrowser (22.16)*.

Note that the bitmaps that come in pairs, such as *cntr_ptr* and *cntr_ptrmsk*, are intended for creating cursor shapes *(22.12)*. You can use *xsetroot* to specify a bitmap as the root window pointer *(6.14)*.

The 86 bitmaps pictured in Figures 22-17, 22-18, and 22-19 are included in X11R5.

— VQ

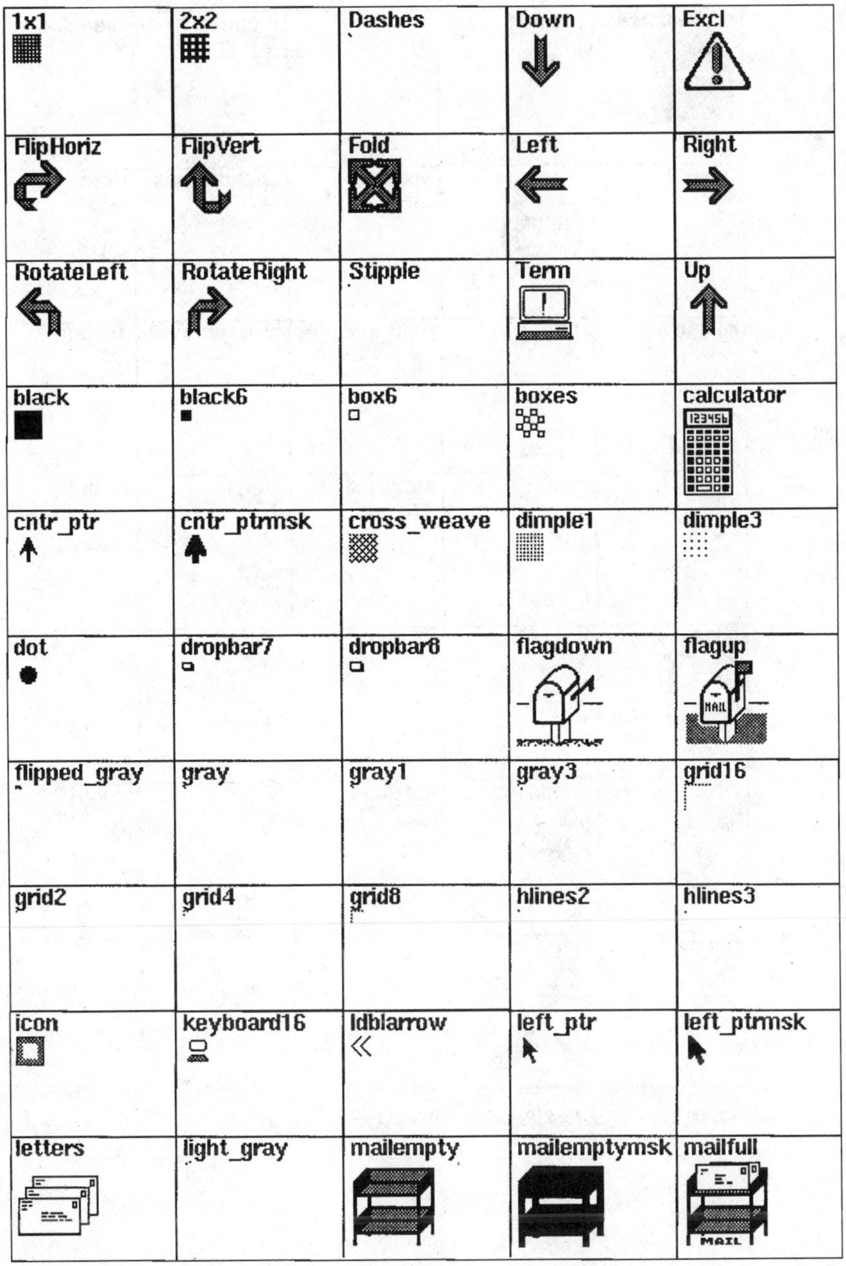

1x1	2x2	Dashes	Down	Excl
1x1	2x2			
FlipHoriz	FlipVert	Fold	Left	Right
RotateLeft	RotateRight	Stipple	Term	Up
black	black6	box6	boxes	calculator
cntr_ptr	cntr_ptrmsk	cross_weave	dimple1	dimple3
dot	dropbar7	dropbar6	flagdown	flagup
flipped_gray	gray	gray1	gray3	grid16
grid2	grid4	grid8	hlines2	hlines3
icon	keyboard16	ldblarrow	left_ptr	left_ptrmsk
letters	light_gray	mailempty	mailemptymsk	mailfull

Figure 22-17: The standard bitmaps—1

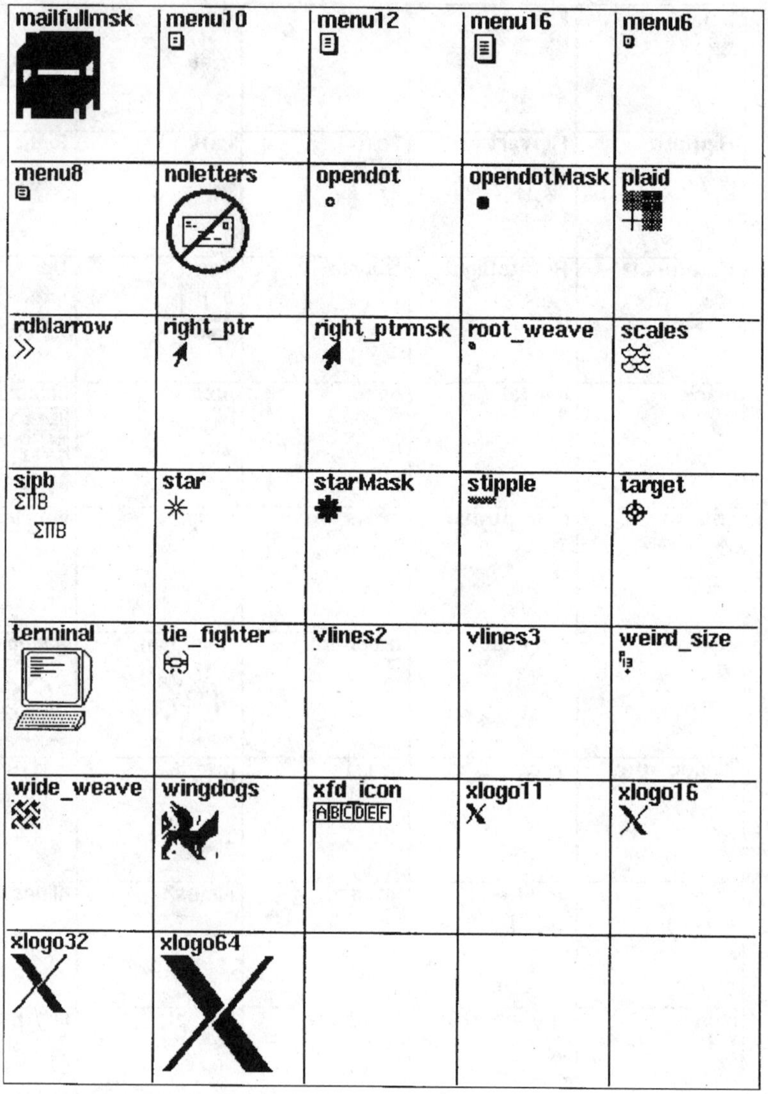

mailfullmsk	menu10	menu12	menu16	menu6
menu8	noletters	opendot	opendotMask	plaid
rdblarrow	right_ptr	right_ptrmsk	root_weave	scales
sipb ΣΠΒ ΣΠΒ	star	starMask	stipple	target
terminal	tie_fighter	vlines2	vlines3	weird_size
wide_weave	wingdogs	xfd_icon ABCDEF	xlogo11	xlogo16
xlogo32	xlogo64			

Figure 22-18: The standard bitmaps—2

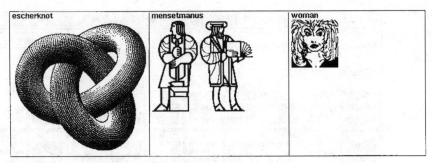

Figure 22-19: The standard bitmaps—3

22.16 Browsing Bitmaps

xbmbrowser

xbmbrowser is primarily a utility for displaying all the bitmaps *(22.01)* in a directory at once, but it also provides some bitmap management capabilities. You specify the directory of bitmaps to browse on the command line. If no directory is specified, *xbmbrowser* defaults to the current directory. Figure 22-20 shows *xbmbrowser* called on a directory of flag bitmaps (only slightly out of date).

If you hold the first pointer button down on a bitmap image in the browser window, you'll display a short menu of options. **Rename** pops up a dialog box in which you can enter a new name for the bitmap file. **Copy** gives you a dialog in which to enter a filename to copy the bitmap to. **Delete** removes the image from the window and the file from the directory. **Edit** opens up a *bitmap (22.03)* window containing the image so you can edit it. The **xsetroot** and **xsetroot rv** menu options let you decorate the root window *(6.02)* with the bitmap image. The latter causes the image to be displayed in reverse video *(17.08)*.

Note that you need the proper permissions for the relevant files and directories in order to **Rename**, **Copy**, **Delete**, or **Edit**. If you do edit an image, click on the **Rescan** button to update the contents of the *xbmbrowser* window.

—*LM, VQ*

22.17 A Collection of Icons

Applications like *bricons (21.17)* and *xbiff++ (7.11)* let you be inventive in using X bitmap and pixmap icons *(22.01)*. But where do you find appropriate icons? You can create your own icons using *bitmap (22.03)*, or another editing program, but before you go through that ordeal, check out the icons on our CD.

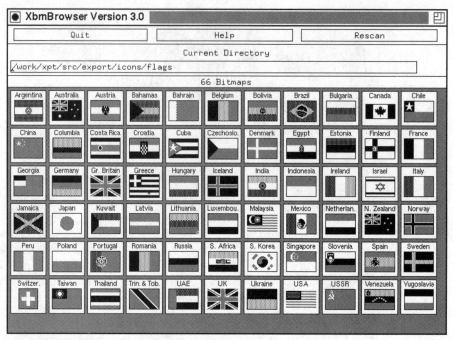

Figure 22-20: Browsing a flag bitmap directory

Alcons

The extensive *Alcons* collection was compiled by Anthony Thyssen, mostly for use by programmers. They include not only X bitmap icons, but also X pixmap icons for use with color machines. Some of these icons are really cool and useful. Others are just cute, some are kind of lame, while others are downright offensive. We aren't' going to show you all of the images, but here's a sampling. For viewing these icons, we recommend using *xbmbrowser* *(22.16)*.

One of my favorite collections is the flags collection (see Figure 22-20).

Figure 22-21 shows icons that make nice backgrounds; you might use these with the *–bitmap* option to *xsetroot (6.02)*.

```
% xsetroot -bitmap Fish.xbm
```

These are just a taste of what the *Alcons* collection includes. There are icons just for use for mailers and programs like *xbiff (7.10)*. There are icons for use with the *twm* icon manager. There are icons for "movies" that you might use with the *xancur* cursor animator client *(6.16)*. And there are just "bits" of icons for incorporating into new pictures.

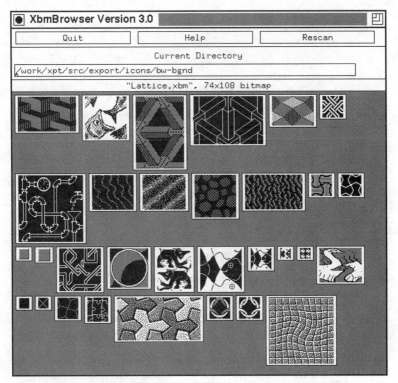

Figure 22-21: Background icons

The *AIcons* collection also includes several pixmaps for use with color displays. Since these color images are in GIF format, you can't use *xsetroot* (6.02) to decorate your root window with them. Instead, try *xcsetroot* (6.03), *xloadimage* (24.05), or *xv* (24.06).

So browse through the *AIcons* collection; you're likely to find a bitmap that you didn't know you couldn't live without.

—LM

23

Screen Dumps

23.01 Making a Window or Screen Dump: xwd

xwd is a utility for creating a "dump" of a window in X. This lets you capture an image of a single application window or of the entire root window. We commonly use window dumps created with *xwd* (and converted to PostScript) as illustrations for our books. In fact, almost all of the figures in this book started out as *xwd* output files.

An image captured using *xwd* is in X window dump format. You can redirect the image to a file and use it in various ways:

- Redisplay it using *xwud (23.03)* (window undumping utility).

- Use xpr *(23.04)* to convert the image to a format suitable for printing (such as PostScript).

- Convert the image to another graphic format (such as TIFF or X bitmap) using a utility like the Portable Bitmap Toolkit *(25.01)*. (You can edit graphic images in certain formats using a variety of editing programs. The bitmap *(22.03)* program allows you to edit X bitmap files.)

If you run *xwd* without any options, the program asks you to select the window you want using the crosshair pointer. Be sure to direct the output to a file:

```
% xwd > mywindow.xwd
```

When the window dump process begins, the keyboard beeps once. When the process finishes, you should hear two beeps. (The audio effects will vary depending on your system defaults. You can adjust the bell using the xset *(6.24)* client.)

Rather than using the pointer to select the window to be dumped, you can specify the window on the command line by supplying the window ID or the program name *(20.04)*.

```
% xwd -id 0x180000e > xterm.xwd
```

or

```
% xwd -name bigxterm > bigxterm.xwd
```

To capture the entire screen (root window):

```
% xwd -root > myscreen.xwd
```

Note that *xwd* is really only useful for capturing an image of a single application window or of the entire root window. If you want an image that shows only a part of one window or one that includes multiple screen features, you'll have to use another program, such as *xgrabsc (23.05)* or *asnap* (**UNKNOWN XREF**).

—*VQ*

23.02 A Good Root Window Background for Screen Dumps

When I have to dump an image that includes a few windows, I generally specify a whitish root window color. It helps the contrast.

```
val@ruby 39% xsetroot -solid snow
```

I like the color called snow, but there are plenty of other whites to choose from. Check out the RGB database *(26.04)*.

—*VQ*

23.03 Displaying an xwd Window Dump: xwud

To check that an X window dump file is readable, you can display it using the *xwud* (X window undumping) program.

```
% xwud -in  xwdfile
```

The window dump is displayed in an *xwud* window. To remove the window, click the pointer on it.

You can also use *xwud* to look at a file captured using *xgrabsc (23.05)* (with the −*xwd* or −*xwdxy* option). It's a good idea to use *xwud* to check what you've captured with these programs before bothering to convert the image to another format.

—*VQ*

23.04 Printing a Window Dump: xpr

xpr takes as input an X Window System dump file produced by *xwd (23.01)* and converts it to a printer-specific format, which can be printed on a PostScript printer, the Digital LN03 or LA100 printer, the IBM PP3812 page printer, the HP LaserJet (or other PCL printers), or the HP PaintJet. By default, output is formatted for PostScript. Use the *–device* option to format for another printer. For example, to format a window dump file for the DEC LN03 printer, type:

```
% xpr -device ln03    file file.ln03
```

Other options allow you to change the size, add headers or footers, and so on. See the *xpr* manpage for more information.

You can use *xwd* and *xpr* together, using the standard UNIX pipe mechanism. For example:

```
% xwd | xpr -device ln03 | lpr
```

And of course, you can write simple shell scripts if you want to save and to print the same figure. For example, here's a simple shell script that keeps a copy of both the original window dump and the converted PostScript file, and also prints a copy of the figure.

The *–portrait* option specifies that the figure will be oriented with the top edge of the picture parallel to what's generally considered the top edge of the page. The default is *–landscape*, which places the longer edge of the picture along the longer side of the paper, not the orientation you're likely to have in a book.

```
#!/bin/sh
# Usage: makefig filename

xwd -frame > $1.xwd
cat $1.xwd | xpr -portrait -scale 2 -device ps > $1.ps
lpr $1.ps
```

On the command line, all I have to do is type the command

```
% makefig    filename
```

and click on the window I want to capture.

—VQ, TOR

23.05 *Capturing a Window or a Partial Screen: xgrabsc and xgrab*

xgrabsc

xwd (23.01) is really only useful for capturing an image of a single application window or of the entire root window. If you want an image that shows only a part of one window or one that includes multiple screen features, take advantage of the user-contributed *xgrabsc* utility, or the graphical front end to it, *xgrab*. Either of these programs lets you grab the image of any rectangular screen area (as well as a window proper or the root window if you want) and save it in a number of formats.

xgrabsc provides these functions via the command line. For instance, you might enter:

```
% xgrabsc -xwd -o dump1.xwd
```

This command says let me grab a screen image and save it in X window dump format (*–xwd*) in an output file (*–o*) called *dump1.xwd*. Rather than use *–o*, you could instead direct the output to a file:

```
xgrabsc -xwd > dump1.xwd
```

Once you run the command, the cursor changes to an upper-left corner symbol to allow you to select a screen area. Place the corner cursor at the upper-left point of the area you want to grab. Then hold down the first pointer button and drag to surround the area you want. An elastic-like outline surrounds the area you select. Release the pointer button to complete the dump. (You should hear one beep when the capture begins and another two when it's finished.)

If we didn't specify *–xwd* for XWD output, we'd get PostScript, which is the default. Use *–eps* for Encapsulated PostScript; or *–bm* for either X bitmap (if the image is black and white) or X pixmap (if the image is gray or color). See the online client manpage for more information about output formats.

If you want to capture a single window, you can skip the step of using the pointer. Instead, specify the window you want to grab using its window ID:

```
% xgrabsc -id 0x580000e > window1.ps
```

If you need to capture a window in a shell script, *xgrabsc* works well. (*xwd* can also come in handy in a script, as in our sample one to dump, save, and print a window image *(23.04)*.) But if you're not writing a script and you're not married to the command line, you might do yourself a favor and use the much more friendly *xgrab*. *xgrab* provides a window in which you can set parameters using command buttons. It also automatically saves your images to files with names that vary by a single number; the names are settable if you choose. To begin, just run the command without any options:

```
% xgrab &
```

and you'll get a window in which to configure the grab function, as shown in Figure 23-1.

The various categories of options are labeled. The currently active option in each category appears in reverse video. To select another option, simply click on it.

Since I generally use *xgrab* to capture odd parts of the screen rather than a window proper, the default **Stretch Rectangle** works well for me in the input option category. For output format, I often switch the default **PostScript** to

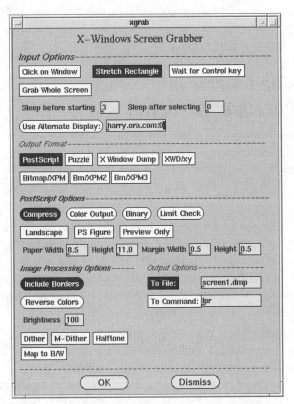

Figure 23-1: xgrab window lets you set parameters for capture and output

XWD format. (Presuming I stick with a file as the output method, I can perform conversions on the XWD format file.)

xgrab will automatically save the first image you capture in a file named *screen1.dmp* and increment the number for successive images. You can change the filename for the next image you save by editing the text field following **To File:** in the output options category. If you prefer to pipe the output to a command, select **To Command** in this category and edit the adjacent text field for the command you want. (The default command is *lpr(1)* to send the output directly to a printer.)

Once you've selected the configuration options you want, click on the **OK** button at the bottom of the window, and the *xgrabsc* function will be initiated. If you've stayed with **Stretch Rectangle**, this means that you'll get the upper-left-corner cursor with which to grab an image. If you haven't touched the output options, the image you grab will be saved in the file *screen1.dmp*; once the save is complete, that text window will be changed to *screen2.dmp* to prepare for the next capture. Click on **OK** again to grab the second image; and so on.

Dismiss exits the program. You can opt out in this way without capturing a single image, if you choose.

—VQ

23.06 Snapshot: The On-screen Photographer (OpenWindows)

Like xgrabsc *(23.05)*, *snapshot* can take a picture of a single window, the entire screen, or any part of the screen, just as if you had taken a photograph. The advantages of *snapshot* over a camera are that it's always in focus, never runs out of film (until your disk is full), and it's easy to limit the area you're capturing.

I ran *snapshot* in a few different environments, mostly hybrid, and mostly non-OpenWindows. I encountered quite a few irritating features that might or might not happen under purer conditions, but I cannot testify conclusively. Among the more annoying problems was an occasional unexplained hanging of the program, which also grabbed the server. In these cases, I logged on at another terminal and killed *(2.08)* the *snapshot* process.

The other notable irritation is that the program didn't seem to track accurately what images had been saved. I *was* prompted to save when I had to, which is good. But I was also prompted to save when I already had. (The *—n* command-line option stops all this prompting, but if you use it, you'll have to stay on your toes.)

There are some other limitations, which are discussed in a later section. Suffice it to say that I encountered enough problems that I'll always opt for *xgrab* over *snapshot*. But if you're an OpenWindows user, you may find *snapshot* to be quite sufficient.

When you run *snapshot*, you get an initial window, called the *control panel* as in Figure 23-2.

snapshot's control panel provides an interface that is somewhat less than intuitive. The basic principle to keep in mind is that the acts of taking a snapshot and viewing it are quite distinct from those of saving the image and accessing an image that has previously been saved. In other words, you can't just capture an image and save it into a file in one fell swoop, the way you can with *xgrabsc* and *xgrab (23.05)*.

The positive aspect of this arrangement is that you can verify that you've gotten the image you want before you bother to save it to a file. On the other hand, this very slight security comes with the hassle factor of having to snap and then save. It's a mixed bag. Anyway, the theory is a little confusing. We'll run through a couple of examples to give you a better idea how *snapshot* works.

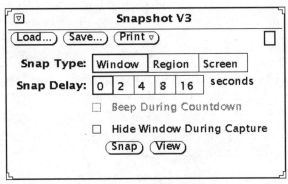

Figure 23-2: snapshot's control panel

Capturing and Viewing an Image

The buttons to the right of Snap Type determine whether you capture a single Window, a rectangular Region, or the entire Screen. The button of whatever type is active will be highlighted. Window is the default.

To initialize a snapshot, click on the Snap button at the bottom of the window using the first pointer button (or the SELECT button *(14.03)*, in OpenWindows parlance). If you're capturing a window, you then click the first pointer button on the window you want. An instruction to this effect will appear along the bottom of the *snapshot* window. Clicking the third pointer button (called MENU *(14.03)*) will cancel the snapshot.

Select Screen as the Snap Type to capture the entire screen. Then the snapshot simply happens when you click on Snap. If you would like a delay before the snapshot happens, choose a number of seconds following Snapshot Delay. The mutually exclusive choices are 0, 2, 4, 8, and 16 seconds. When a delay is set, you will have the option of selecting a Beep During Countdown. A nice feature is that there's a way to exclude the *snapshot* window itself from the root window image. Just click on the box preceding the line Hide Window During Capture. Note that the Hide feature automatically sets the Delay to eight seconds.

The trickiest function, and perhaps the one you'll use most frequently, is capturing a Region. To do this, first select Region as the Snap Type, then click on Snap. The pointer changes to an arrow symbol, and you will be prompted:

```
SELECT-Position rectangle. ADJUST-Snap image.
```

In OpenWindows applications, ADJUST *(14.03)* refers to the second pointer button. Again, you can use the third pointer button to cancel the operation (though this part of the instruction may be truncated from the window). So, to capture a rectangular screen area, move the arrow to the upper-left corner of the area you want. (The left corner is arbitrary; actually you can drag in any direction.) Hold down the first pointer button and drag to enclose the area in a rectangular outline. Click the second pointer button to complete the snap. The message "Snap succeeded" will appear along the bottom of the *snapshot* window.

OK, so now we have an image. You'd expect that image to be automatically saved in the *snapshot.rs* file, but I'm afraid that isn't the case. Once you capture an image, you *can* display it using the **View** button. But you need to save it explicitly in order to get a copy in a file.

Just click on **View** to take a look at the image. Figure 23-3 shows a **View** window containing a partial *xterm* I captured.

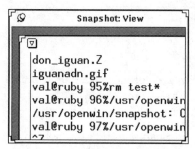

Figure 23-3: snapshot View window lets you see what you captured

View brings up the last image snapped. If you want to look at a previously saved image, you need to **Load** it first. More about this later.

You pop the image down by clicking on the pushpin in the upper-left corner. You may notice that sometimes the head of the pushpin appears to be sticking up (as you'd expect) and sometimes it appears in a side view. One click on the upright pin should pop the window down. But you may need a few of clicks on the sideways pin to get rid of the window. As an alternative, you can hold the third pointer button down on the titlebar and select **Dismiss** from the Window menu *(14.07)*.

Saving an Image

Let's save the image we've snapped to a file. If you click on the **Save** button, you'll reveal a dialog box that lets you specify a filename for the image and the directory in which to save (see Figure 23-4).

The defaults for these are the filename *snapshot.rs* (where "rs" is short for raster) and the current directory. You can change the directory or filename by clicking after the text in question, backspacing over, and retyping. I've specified a subdirectory of my home directory, called *figs*.

To make life easier on yourself, you might want simply to specify a default directory name on the *snapshot* command-line, using the *−d* option. The *−f* option lets you provide a default filename. Of course, if you save multiple

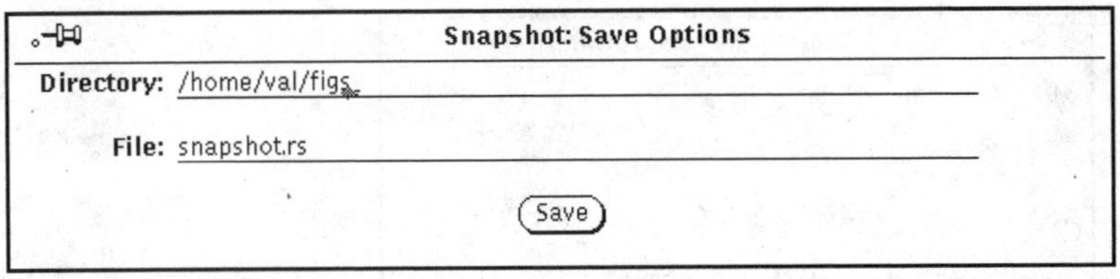

```
 ._-[ꢀ]                    Snapshot: Save Options
  Directory: /home/val/figs
      File: snapshot.rs
                         ( Save )
```

Figure 23-4: Save dialog lets you set directory and filename and then save

images, you'll need to pop up the **Save** dialog and change the filename each time anyway, so we'll stick with the default for now.

Once you're happy with the directory and filename, click on the **Save** button at the bottom center of the dialog box. When the image is saved, you'll see the message "Save succeeded" along the bottom of the initial *snapshot* window; the **save** dialog will pop down on its own when the save is successful. If the directory is wrong, you'll get a message to that effect in the *snapshot* window and you should edit the directory field in the dialog box. If the file you are saving into already exists, you will be prompted to confirm overwriting it, or to cancel the save. (Since you need to explicitly change the filename each time, or you will overwrite, this is an important check.)

Printing an Image

Once you snap an image, you should be able to print it. Hypothetically, clicking on **Print** using the first pointer button should send the image to your default printer. (As we'll see, you can set printer specifications before printing.) Note, however, that if you've saved an image to a file, and that file is named in the **Save** dialog, the saved image will be the one to print, even if you've subsequently snapped another.

Notice the down arrow symbol on the **Print** button; this signals a menu. You can set certain print specifications using this menu and its submenu. Clicking on **Print** using the third pointer button reveals a two-item menu. The first item, **Print Snap**, prints the image named in the **Save** dialog, or if no such image exists, the last snapped image. The **Options...** item signal yet another menu, a submenu of the current one. Click on **Options** with the third pointer button to pop up a dialog box (see Figure 23-5) containing printer options and specifications, including the printer to be used, size, scale, and orientation of the image.

Edit the fields in the dialog box however you like. When you print subsequently, these options will be valid.

Note that when you print a file, a shell script called *snapshot.print* is run. It normally converts the raster file to PostScript and pipes it to the UNIX *lpr* command to print. But if you're proficient at shell programming, you may want to

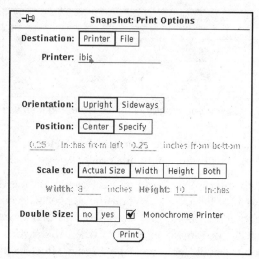

Figure 23-5: Print Options dialog box

write your own script, possibly using the conversion utilities provided with the Portable Bitmap Toolkit (25.01).

Loading Files for Viewing

When you select **View**, you display the file named in the **Load** dialog (and also the **Save** dialog) in a special window. Enter the directory and file you want in the **Load** dialog before clicking on **View**. (You may have to respond to an additional dialog box in order for the new image to be loaded.)

The image you view might be one you've captured. But you can actually use this method to display any file in Sun Raster format, as long as the directory name and filename in the **Load** dialog are correct.

Taking a Snapshot of a Transient Window

If you try to take a snapshot of a program that has popped up a transient window, such as a menu or a dialog box, you'll find that it doesn't work. This is because pop-up menus and dialogs grab the X server. In layman's terms, the menu, dialog, etc., takes exclusive control of the X server. Input events such as mouse-button clicks are passed to the associated client program. Thus, there's no way to use the pointer to select the window you want a snapshot of.

There are two ways to deal with a situation like this. Article 23.07, gives what I think is one of the better ways to capture a transient window, using other graphics utilities. (That's what I recommend.)

However, if you're determined to stick with *snapshot*, there may be a crude workaround, depending on the application and on your environment. What you need is a way to make the program you want to capture run without grabbing the server. Some applications may allow you to restart them in a special non-grab mode. You then pop up the menu or dialog you want to show. The sloppy part is that you then usually have to kill *(2.08)* the application because it cannot work without the grab.

If the program was written with the XView toolkit, use the *–Wfsdb* (window full-screen debug) command-line option. For example, you might run the File Manager program in this way:

```
% filemgr -Wfsdb &
```

to allow it to pop up dialog boxes without grabbing the server. This frees the pointer so you can click on a dialog box to capture a snapshot.

Of course, if the client isn't friendly to this no-grab idea, head for Article 23.07.

—*VQ, IFD*

23.07 Capturing a Screen That Includes a Transient Window

Suppose you want to capture an image that includes a transient window, such as a menu or dialog box. In most case, when a transient window is displayed, a grab takes place. This means that the X server sends all information, such as keyboard and pointer input, to the application that made the grab. Practically speaking, when a grab is in effect you can't use the pointer—except to respond to the transient window (i.e., select a menu item, answer the dialog).

This circumstance complicates making a screen dump that includes a transient window. For instance, you certainly can't pop up a menu, run *xwd*, and then click on the menu to capture the image. All that the click will do is select a menu item or possibly pop the menu down.

However, there's actually a fairly simple, if not immediately obvious way to get around this problem. For example, suppose you want a picture of the Twm pop-up menu *(12.04)* on the screen. The command *xwd -root* takes a picture of the entire root window, so that you can see the menu in context. Note also that with *xwd –root*, no pointer selection is necessary. If you combine *xwd* with the UNIX *sleep* command, you should have time to display the menu before the *xwd* process starts up. In summary, the steps are:

1. Run *sleep* with a reasonable time argument followed by *xwd –root*. Redirect the dump to a file.

```
% sleep 5; xwd -root > menu.root.xwd
```

2. Quickly move the pointer to the root window and post the Twm menu. When the *sleep* is over and the *xwd* process begins, the menu will be included in the image.

You can vary the sleep time depending on the circumstances. For instance, if you're trying to capture a dialog box, you may need more time to pop it up.

Now you have an image of the root window. If you want only a portion of the root, you can then use *xgrabsc (23.05)* to capture a part of that image. First use *xwud* to display the original image you captured:

```
% xwud -in menu.root.xwd
```

Then follow the steps outlined for *xgrabsc (23.05)*.

—*VQ*

24

Drawing and Viewing Pictures

24.01 *Still a Pretty Picture*

Let's face it. If you're very serious about producing computer graphics, you're going to get hold of some commercial software. The free software available on the Internet just doesn't provide the resources a real artist (or architect or mechanical engineer) needs. But plain old users like you and me can still have a lot of fun, and even produce usable bitmaps, pixmaps, and other images. Chapter 22, *Bitmaps and Pixmaps*, gives some tips about using the *bitmap* editor *(22.03)*, which is shipped with most flavors of X. The current chapter looks at some of the user-contributed graphic editors. In addition, this chapter reviews the most useful programs for displaying images in a variety of formats.

— VQ

24.02 *A Fun Paint Program*

xpaint

xpaint is a cut above most of the user-contributed drawing/painting utilities, which are primitive, to say the least. It provides fairly sophisticated graphic editing capabilities, allowing you to open several drawing windows simultaneously, and it handles color well. You can also create/edit pictures in several formats, including X bitmap, X pixmap, X window dump, and TIFF. Take advantage of the extensive online help, which can be accessed from top-level menus, as well as individual application features.

The initial *xpaint* window, which is known as the *toolbox*, appears in Figure 24-1.

The toolbox isn't an editing window; instead it provides a number of command buttons for operations to be performed in any number of separate editing windows you subsequently open. In *xpaint* parlance, these windows are known as *canvases*. Selecting New Canvas from the File menu opens a blank canvas window, as in Figure 24-2.

Figure 24-1: xpaint toolbox provides operations to be used in any paint window

To draw something in the canvas window, you first need to select the type of operation from the toolbox window. Whatever function you select applies in every editing window open at the time.

If you've ever used MacPaint or a similar paint program, the image on each toolbox command button should provide a reasonable clue as to its function. The first button in the upper-left corner shows a paint roller that appears to be spreading dots of color, which is just what the command allows you to do in a canvas window. If you press the third pointer button on any command button, you'll display a menu that provides help about the function, as well as variations you can select. The menu that accompanies the roller or "brush" button, as it's called, lets you select a different style and shape of brush with which to paint.

There's more to the eraser than meets the eye. Yes, it erases, but it also lets you retrieve the original image! Use its menu to choose which of these functions you want. Erase and unerase to your heart's content.

The dotted box allows you to highlight a rectangular area for subsequent editing. The scissors provide one of the less obvious functions: they let you highlight an irregular area for editing.

The first pencil draws a connected line; the second draws a dotted line. The spray can sprays. (A submenu lets you change the type of spray.) The bucket fills closed shapes. The letter A lets you type, in any of the fonts you choose, from a dialog box accessed from its menu.

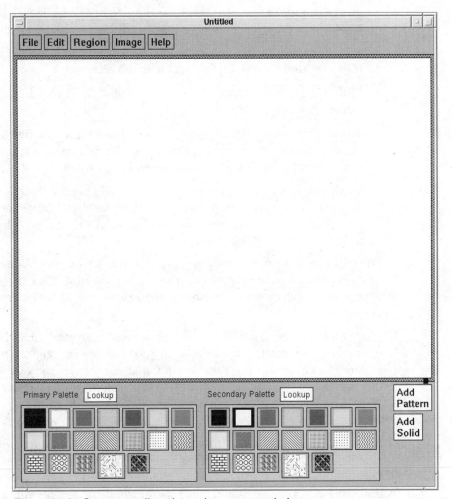

Figure 24-2: Create or edit a picture in a canvas window

Each of the remaining command buttons lets you draw something: a straight line, a series of connected rays, an arc, an empty rectangle, filled rectangle, empty oval, filled oval, connected lines, empty polygon, filled polygon, empty irregular shape, and filled irregular shape. Display the menu associated with any of these drawing functions and select Help to learn how to draw the shape in question.

A few general guidelines and tips:

- The first pointer button paints in the color or pattern selected under the **Primary Palette** in the canvas window, which is black by default. The second pointer button paints in the **Secondary Palette**, white by default.

- To select another color or pattern as the primary or secondary palette, simply click on the corresponding square using the first pointer button.

- When you draw a filled shape using the first pointer button, the perimeter is in the primary color and the inside in the secondary.

- In drawing, you can constrain an oval to be a circle or a rectangle to be a square by holding the **Shift** key.

- To clear the entire editing area, choose **Select All** from the **Edit** menu in the canvas window. Then choose **Clear** from the **Edit** menu. (You can get the same result by choosing **Cut**; the last cut image is also available to **Paste**.)

- To clear a part of the editing area, first select either the dotted box or scissors command button in the toolbox. Then highlight the region you want to delete. Finally, choose **Clear** or **Cut** from the canvas window's **Edit** menu.

The best way to learn to use *xpaint* is just to use it. You should hit upon some of the more fun features pretty quickly. I get a (small) kick out of drawing shapes filled with patterns. In Figure 24-3 I've drawn my version of an Easter egg.

The easiest way to draw this picture is to select the filled circle button from the toolbox. Then select the fill pattern you want by clicking on it in the secondary palette area of the canvas window. Finally, draw the oval by holding the first pointer button down, dragging the shape out, and releasing. Ta-da. The shape is automatically filled using your selection from the second palette choices.

Let's look at another typical operation. Suppose you want to move the egg image up higher in the canvas window. First, select the dotted box command button in the toolbox. Then highlight the image in the canvas window: hold down the first pointer button, drag to surround the image with a rectangle, and release. Notice the dotted rectangle around the image. Now you can move the highlighted area. Just press and hold the first pointer button anywhere on the rectangle. Drag it where you want and release the pointer button; the image is moved. Click outside of the rectangular area or select another toolbox function to remove the dotted rectangle.

Use the **File** menu on the canvas window to save the image or to close the current editing window without saving. Use the **File** menu on the toolbox to open additional canvases, either for new images or existing ones; also use the toolbox's **File** menu to quit the application, closing all editing windows.

Consult the online help for the use of other menus and features. And paint away!

—*VQ*

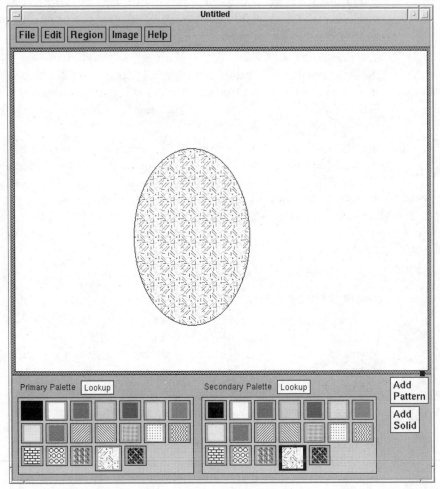

Figure 24-3: A filled oval contains the pattern/color selected as the secondary palette

24.03 *The xfig Drawing Utility*

xfig

xfig is a user-contributed line-drawing program, which provides several functions to create and edit simple figures. *xfig* accepts input and can create output in a number of formats, including PostScript, encapsulated PostScript, and XBM (X bitmap). *xfig* also one of the few publicly available editors that works with pictures created under LaTeX. (LaTeX is an extension to the TeX typesetting software package.)* *xfig* won't help you produce slick graphics, but it's a serviceable editor for simple line drawings and bitmaps. The current article

---

* For everything you always wanted to know on this subject, see the Nutshell Handbook *Making TeX Work*, by Norman Walsh, also published by O'Reilly & Associates Inc.

should help you get started in a productive way, but *xfig* has too many features to document in this format. To learn more, see the manpage on the accompanying CD-ROM.

The default size window is BIG: in the neighborhood of 12 inches square, with the editing area 10 inches square. You can specify smaller dimensions for the editing area using the *−pw* (width) and *−ph* (height) command-line options. (The units are either inches or centimeters, inches by default. Use *−me* to specify metric.)

It really isn't practical to have an editing area smaller than six or seven inches square; too many of the command buttons and other features can be obscured. So, if you do opt for a smaller editing area, you should also reorganize the draw command buttons (along the left side of the window) into additional columns. There are two columns by default; use the *−but* option to specify an alternative. I use an editing area seven inches square with three columns of buttons:

```
% xfig -pheight 7 -pwidth 7 -but_ 3 &
```

The resulting window appears in Figure 24-4.

Even these dimensions could still be a bit more generous. Notice the second button along the top of the window, **Delete AL**. This is not a National League scheme to rub out the American. A second L has been truncated due to lack of space. The command buttons along the top edge of the window provide editing and file manipulation functions.

So, how do you draw with *xfig?* First, you need to select a drawing mode. Notice the command buttons to the left of the editing grid. The upper half of the buttons provide drawing functions. When you click on one of these buttons, a text description of the function it provides is displayed in a small window above the ruler that spans the top of the editing area. For instance, if I select the first button, which is labeled with a circle and radius, the window displays:

```
CIRCLE drawing: specify radius
```

This function allows you to draw a circle by clicking on the two points that will become the ends of a radius (the center and a point on the perimeter). Try it. Click the first pointer button once where you want the center of the circle. A tiny cross marks the spot, and the cursor becomes a larger cross. Drag the cross cursor away from the center point, and a circle outline radiates out from that point. When the circle is the size you want, click the first pointer button again to complete the drawing, as in Figure 24-5.

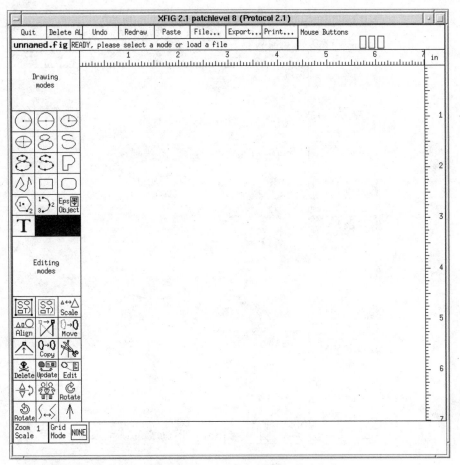

Figure 24-4: A slightly smaller and more manageable xfig window

The various drawing modes allow you to create all sorts of different lines and shapes. You can combine these simple figures to make more complex ones, known to the program as *compound objects*. We'll see how to join multiple figures into one when we discuss editing modes.

Notice that when you select a drawing function, several additional command buttons are displayed in a row below the editing grid. This area is known as the *indicator panel*; it provides commands that allow you to set drawing parameters such as line thickness, grid lines, rotation angle, how objects are filled, justification of text, etc. The possible parameters change depending on the drawing function selected.

To browse the possible settings for any parameter, click on the corresponding button. A dialog box listing the possible choices will be displayed. Within the

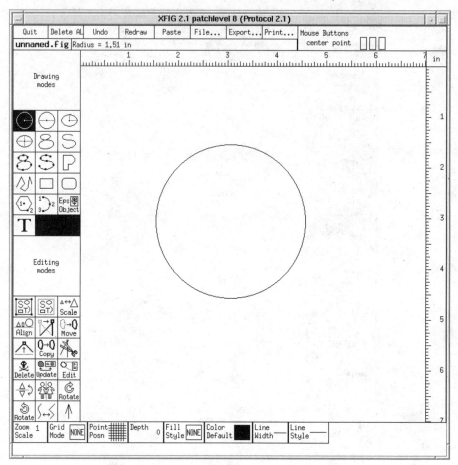

Figure 24-5: Drawing a circle

dialog, you can opt for another setting by clicking on its button or **cancel** the operation.

Some of the indicator panel settings are obvious: **Color**, for instance. If you pop up the color dialog, you can choose among several colors in which to draw; black is the default. If you have some experience with drawing or painting programs, **Fill Style** might also be fairly obvious. **Fill Style** determines what's inside closed figures. The default is none; the dialog lets you choose among twenty increasingly dark patterns, all the way to solid. If we change the fill style to solid and then draw another circle, the second circle will be filled in.

Among the less intuitive parameters is **Point Posn** (point position), which lets you determine whether objects can be placed anywhere or must be positioned to be aligned at certain intervals on the rulers (that border the grid). In addition to **any** position, the possible intervals are 1/16 inch (2mm in metric mode), ¼ inch (5mm), or ½ inch (10mm). In the dialog box, these intervals are represented by pictures of grids where the lines are separated by the equivalent distance.

Keep in mind that different drawing modes have different parameters. For instance, if you click on the button with the capital T, to enter text in the grid, the parameters will include such features as point size, font, and justification.

To the left of the editing grid, below the drawing modes, are several editing modes. The first editing mode, represented by a box with some shapes and letters inside, lets you combine multiple graphic objects into a single, compound object. First, click on the command button. Then click the first pointer button on each individual object you want to join into the compound object. (You can't click just anywhere on the figure; you have to click on a point marked by a tiny square.) Finally, click the third pointer button to join the objects. An outline will surround the group; each corner will be a tiny square. In Figure 24-6, I've drawn three circles and then joined them to create a familiar face.

If you select another drawing mode, the corner squares won't be visible, but the objects should still be linked. You can tell if the individual objects continue to form a compound object by selecting virtually any of the editing modes. If you select copy, move, rotate, etc., the corner squares should again outline the compound object, indicating the editing function will be operating on the whole. You need to use the pointer on one of these corner squares in order to perform these editing operations.

To ungroup a set of objects, select the second edit mode, the button to the right of the first. Then click on one of the corners of the group. See the manpage for more about the various editing modes.

The buttons along the top edge of the *xfig* window provide the *command panel functions*, many of which, like **Quit**, **Delete ALL**, and **Undo**, are obvious. (**Undo** is actually a toggle.) **Redraw** refreshes the window. Use the **File . . .** button to pop up a dialog that lets you load another file, save the current one, etc. The very important **Export** button pops up a dialog that lets you specify characteristics of the output file, which is in encapsulated PostScript by default. Hold the pointer down on this setting to choose from a menu of other formats. See the manpage for more information about menus.

— VQ

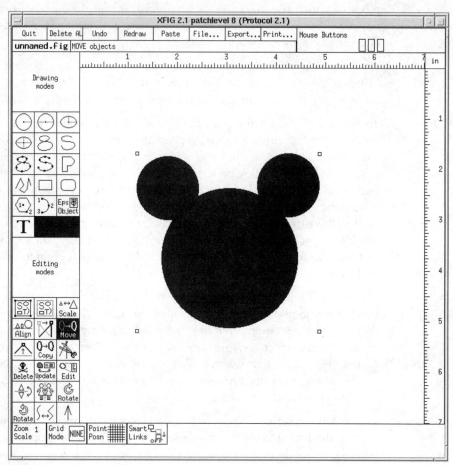

Figure 24-6: A familiar compound figure

24.04 *The pixt Pixmap Editor*

pixt lets you draw and edit X pixmap images. It has some useful features, but for the most part, it isn't nearly as versatile or powerful as *xpaint*, which can also produce pixmap files. You start it up by running the command:

pixt

```
% pixt &
```

There's only one option, −*s*, which lets you set the dimensions of the editing grid. By default, you'll get a 60×60 grid, which represents a 60×60 pixel region, in which to create a pixmap image. The following command would create an editing grid 30 squares wide and 40 high:

```
% pixt -s 30x40 &
```

Avoid dimensions much larger than the defaults because the default window is fairly big. Figure 24-7 shows a 30×30 grid. Anything bigger is impractical for illustration purposes.

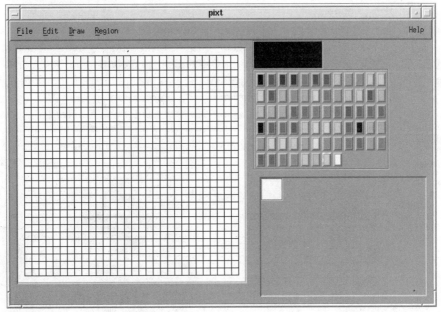

Figure 24-7: A pixt editing window

Notice the palette of colors to the right of the editing grid. You can draw in any one of these colors, or in another color from an image you import from an existing file or grab off your screen. The currently active drawing color appears in the larger box above the palette selections. The default is black.

To switch the current color, click the first pointer button on a color in the palette, or select a color from the image in the grid by clicking the third pointer button on an appropriate pixel. In either case, the selected color will fill the large square above the palette and become the active drawing color.

The rectangular area below the palette represents the potential pixmap size. (A grid of this size would not be practical, however.) The box within that area shows the actual pixmap. Currently the box is empty, but the edits made in the grid will be mirrored here.

pixt is not much of a drawing program. You can draw pixel by pixel using the pointer, but it only offers one time-saving drawing function. The **Draw** menu has a single option to allow you to **Draw a Line**. (Typing 1 while the window has the focus also invokes this function.) Once you select the line function, you click on the two end points to draw it.

The freehand drawing functions are:

- The first pointer button paints in the currently selected color.

- The second pointer button clears the pixels selected.

So, if *pixt* is not much of a drawing tool, what is it good at? The neatest thing that *pixt* lets you do is select an image from the screen that is then displayed in the grid for editing. Click on the **Edit** menu tag or type Meta-E to display the relevant menu. Then select **Capture Image From Screen**. The cursor changes to a wavering box outline. Move the box to the area of the screen you want to capture and click the first button. A magnified version is displayed in the editing grid. If you capture a non-pixmap image, you're effectively converting it to XPM (X pixmap) format when you save the *pixt* file. In Figure 24-8 I've captured part of the *xbiff* mailbox image.

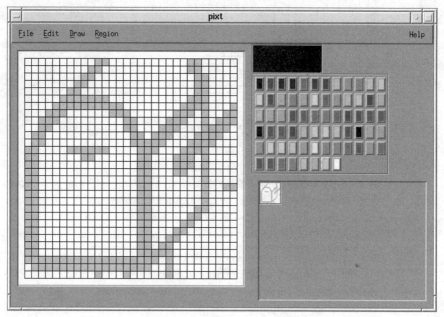

Figure 24-8: pixt lets you import an image from the screen

The mailbox is actually light blue. If I want to continue to draw in that color, I can click on one of the blue pixels with the third pointer button and the current color box will be changed to blue.

Note that *pixt*'s menus work like menus in a Motif application. You can post a menu and keep it posted by clicking on its tag with the first pointer button. The key combination Meta and the first letter of the menu name also posts the menu.

Notice that some of the menu options have mnemonic shortcuts, i.e., a single letter that invokes the function, in this case, without having to post the menu. The letter r, for example, is a shortcut for **Read XPM Pixmap** on the **File** menu. This item pops up a dialog box in which you can enter the name of a pixmap file to read into the editing window.

In addition to reading in an existing file, the **File** menu lets you save the current one (shortcut: **s**), or to quit the application (**CTRL-X**). As we've seen, the **Edit** menu lets you capture a screen image; it also lets you clear the editing area and make global color changes. The **Draw** menu provides the feeble **Line** drawing option. The **Region** menu allows you to mark and manipulate a part of the pixmap image.

— *VQ*

24.05 *Displaying Pictures with xloadimage*

The *xloadimage* client will load nearly any graphic image and display it on your X screen, either in a window or on the root window. You can also use *xloadimage* to perform some image manipulation and to save the transformed image to a file.

xloadimage

To use *xloadimage* to view a file, say *mom.xbm*, enter the command:

```
val@ruby 30% xloadimage mom.xbm &
```

If the file is a picture in any of the valid formats, you will get a message similar to:

```
mom.xbm is a 100x100 X11 bitmap file titled 'mom'
```

and then a window displaying that image (see Figure 24-9):

Figure 24-9: xloadimage window displaying mom.xbm

In some bitmap formats, a title is stored with each image, while in other formats, it is not. If your bitmap file has a title, it will be printed in the message (as it was in these examples) and displayed in the window's titlebar (though it will be truncated if the image is small). If there is no title, the filename of the image will be used.

To remove an image window, type q (for "quit"), or CTRL-C, when the window has the input focus.

If you want an image to be displayed on the root window, use the *–onroot* option. The following command creates a root window decorated with a bevy of birthday cakes that would make a mother proud:

```
val@ruby 31% xloadimage -onroot mom.xbm
```

You can display a series of images sequentially in an *xloadimage* window by giving more than one filename on the command line, in the order you want them to appear. To move from one image to another, type a letter n (for "next") in the *xloadimage* display window.

For example:

```
val@ruby 32% xloadimage mom.xbm minx.xbm max.xbm &
```

This command would first display the bitmap from *mom.xbm*; to view the second bitmap, you'd move the pointer into the image window and type n.

The number of formats supported by *xloadimage* is impressive, and it grows regularly because the program source code is structured to make it easy for C programmers to add code for new file types. Here is a recent list of the more common formats.

- X window dump (23.01

- X bitmap *(22.01)*

- X pixmap *(22.01)*

- Portable bitmap (PBM), portable pixmap (PPM), and portable graymap (PGM) *(25.01)*

- Sun Raster

- Sun Icon

- FaceSaver

- GIF

- Group 3 and Group 4 FAX formats

- MacPaint

- JPEG

- TIFF

Note that there are some additional proprietary formats. Run *xloadimage* with the *–supported* option for a complete list; see the online manpage for additional information.

xloadimage accepts several command-line options, like *–supported*, that affect the operation or appearance of the client. The *–geometry* option *(17.10)* would fit into this category.

In addition, *xloadimage* recognizes several options that alter an image in a variety of ways. You can choose either to display the modified image or to dump it into a file. Let's look at a couple of examples.

–zoom is one of the more useful options. It lets you change the size of the image. For example, the command:

```
val@ruby 33% xloadimage -zoom 300 mom.xbm &
```

displays the birthday cake bitmap in *mom.xbm* at triple the original size (that is, 300 percent as in Figure 24-10):

Figure 24-10: Zooming an image to 300%

Using an argument of **50** would create an image half the size of the original:

```
val@ruby 34% xloadimage -zoom 50 mom.xbm &
```

The resulting image is a little small (see Figure 24-11), but it is cute.

You can convert a color image to monochrome by using the *–dither* option. This process happens by default when you display a color image on a monochrome monitor. Thus, if all you want to do is view the image, you don't

Figure 24-11: The same image but small and cute

have to specify *–dither.* You need to use this option only when you want to convert the image and then dump it into a file.

xloadimage can read many more file formats *(22.02)* than it can write (that is, dump to a file). If you run *xloadimage –supported* to review the formats the program can display, you'll notice a column with the header "Can Dump." A "Yes" beside a particular format means that *xloadimage* can convert an image to that format and save it in a file. The formats *xloadimage* can save are TIFF, JPEG, PBM *(22.02)*, and a format local to the application called NIFF (Native Image File Format).

To save a converted image, you need to supply the *–dump* option, followed by an acceptable file format and the new filename. For example, to change a color pixmap *(22.01)* of a tiger to black and white, use *–dither,* then use *–dump* with a valid format, say *pbm,* followed by a reasonable output filename:

```
val@ruby 35% xloadimage -dither tiger.xpm -dump pbm tiger.pbm &
```

This command creates a monochrome portable bitmap file called *tiger.pbm.* You might then use one of the Portable Bitmap Toolkit *(25.01)* utilities to convert the file to an X bitmap format *(22.02)*. *pbmtoxbm* converts portable bitmap files to X bitmap format:

```
val@ruby 36% pbmtoxbm tiger.pbm > tiger.xbm &
```

You'll find that many more programs can handle X bitmap format than can deal with portable bitmap, which is more of a stepping stone between formats. An obvious example is *xsetroot (6.02)*, which lets you decorate your root window. *xsetroot* coughs on portable bitmap files, but our conversion to X bitmap lets us have a whole jungle of tigers:

```
val@ruby 37% xsetroot -bitmap tiger.xbm
```

Depending on the file format you specify with *–dump,* there may be additional arguments you can supply to perform further adjustments to the image. The JPEG format lends itself to fine tuning. See the online manpage for more information.

—VQ, IFD

24.06 A Powerful Graphics Package: xv

xv

The *xv* program can't read quite as many graphic file types *(22.02)* as *xloadimage*, but it can perform a much wider range of operations. Like *xloadimage*, *xv* can display an image in a window or on the root window (*–root*), and it can transform images. But *xv* can also capture images as *xgrab* and *xgrabsc* *(23.05)* do. It also offers considerable color editing capabilities, which we won't even try to get into here. One of *xv*'s more interesting and useful capabilities is in helping you manage your image files. *xv* offers an image management window, similar to many file manager applications, called the *visual schnauzer.* (You heard right.) More about that later.

xv is a heavyweight graphics application. The author of the program, John Bradley, has also written a sizeable manual covering *xv*'s many functions. Obviously, we cannot hope to approach teaching such a variety of skills in this context. The current article demonstrates some of *xv*'s basic image displaying powers and deals a bit with the visual schnauzer. From that point, you're on your own.

Unlike most of the programs we've been writing about, the sources for which are available free via the Internet, *xv* is classified as *shareware*, a concept somewhat better known in the personal computer world. If a program is shareware, you're welcome to use it, but the author requests that you pay him or her a reasonable sum for a "license." For an *xv* license, the suggested "donation" is $25. (Actually something of a bargain when you consider the market prices for graphics software.) Of course, this is an honor system. For more information about licensing a copy of *xv* from John Bradley, click on the **License** button in the *xv* control screen (which is described in a minute). If you decide to license the product, you will get a bound copy of the manual as well.

xv as distributed can read the GIF, PBM/PGM/PPM *(25.01)*, X bitmap *(22.02)*, Sun Raster, JPEG, and TIFF formats, as well as a format called PM, which is local to the program. Let's run *xv* on the sample bitmap we used with *xloadimage*, Mom's birthday cake:

```
% xv mom.xbm
```

The window appears in Figure 24-12.

This bitmap is a readable size (100×100 pixels). But if you wanted a larger (or smaller) image, you could resize the window, and *xv* would rescale the image accordingly. For a large full-color image, rescaling can take some time, but for such a simple image, it's virtually instantaneous. You can resize just for viewing purposes, or you can save a resized image, under the same filename or a new one. (The section "Saving an Image" shows you how.)

Figure 24-12: xv mom.xbm

The xv Controls Window

You can access most every *xv* feature from the *xv controls* window. With the input focus directed to any *xv* window, you can pop up the *controls* window by either pressing and releasing the third pointer button or typing a question mark (?) (see Figure 24-13).

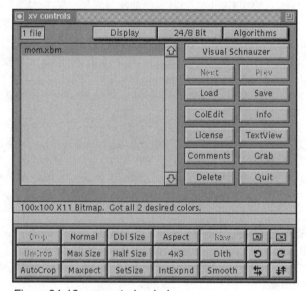

Figure 24-13: xv controls window

Both the third pointer button and the question mark are toggles; performing either action a second time pops down the *xv controls* window.

Notice the large, nearly empty window within the *controls* window. This window contains the list of filenames you're working with; currently it contains only *mom.xbm*. (The small box above the upper-left corner of the filename window displays "1 file" to confirm this.) If you run *xv* with a list of files on the command line, all of the names will appear in the filename window, and you can work with the images simultaneously. If the list of names is too long to fit in a single window, you can use the scrollbar, along the window's right edge, to view and work with the additional names.

The command buttons to the right of the filename window perform some general functions. They allow you to:

- **Load** image files into the file list so they can be displayed, altered, etc.

- **Save** image files (in any of the valid formats)

- Access **License** information, as well as **Info** about the image being displayed

- Bring up a color editor window (**ColEdit**)

- View the code used to produce the current image, i.e., the contents of the image file. The **TextView** command allows you to do this. (The code is mostly gibberish to some of us.)

- Display the **Comments** included in an image file, if any

- **Grab** or capture an image from the display

- **Delete** a filename from the list and/or from the system

- Display the images from the list sequentially (**Next** and **Prev**, i.e., previous)

- Open a **Visual Schnauzer** window with which to manage the image files in the current directory

- **Quit** out of *xv*

The format of this book precludes explaining every function in detail. Among the functions you'll want to know about right away are **Next** and **Previous**, which let you browse through multiple files. In our earlier example, they are grayed out because there is only one file to access. You can also display any image file in the list by double-clicking on its name using the first pointer button.

Info pops up a window containing information about the currently displayed image, as in Figure 24-14. The most useful information is probably the image size and file format. To pop down the info window, click on it using the first pointer button, or click on the **Info** button a second time.

Altering an Image

Two menus and an additional 21 command buttons are provided to assist you in altering the image; that's not to mention the color editor (accessed using the **ColEdit** command button). The *xv* manual describes these functions in detail. This article deals with some of them, in briefer terms. Note that unless you save the altered file, these changes affect only the displayed image.

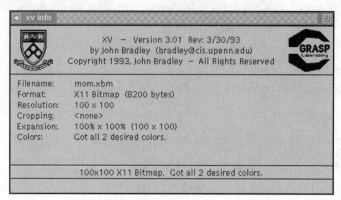

Figure 24-14: xv info window

First, let's look at the command buttons along the bottom of the *controls* window. (Figure 24-13 should refresh your memory.) These buttons are arranged in seven columns of three buttons each, for a total of 21.

Eleven of these command buttons allow you to change the size of the image. Nine of the resizing buttons are located in the second, third, and fourth columns (from **Normal** to **IntExpand**); the first button in each of the sixth and seventh columns is also for resizing (these buttons are labeled with a diagonal arrow).

Some of these resizing buttons have names that make the function they perform obvious: **Half Size** and **Dbl Size** (double size), for instance. Others are less obvious. The two buttons labeled with an arrow allow you to increase and decrease the image size by 10 percent. **4×3** makes the ratio of the width to the height (the *aspect ratio*) 4 to 3. This stretches our birthday cake a little in the horizontal dimension, as in Figure 24-15.

Figure 24-15: The 4×3 button gives an image a width-to-height ratio of 4 to 3

The **Aspect** button restores the default aspect ratio. At any point in resizing the image, you can recover the original size by pressing **Normal**.

Below the arrow buttons in the sixth and seventh columns are four buttons that allow you to rotate and flip the image in various directions. Play with them to get an idea.

The buttons in the fifth column help you deal with distortions and problems in displaying color. You can **Smooth** out an image that has been resized. The **Dith** button tries to approximate colors that might have been lost from the image because of display limitations; this process is generally called *dithering*. The **Raw** command undoes any smoothing or dithering you've performed.

The buttons in the first column allow you to crop the image, or remove parts of it. **AutoCrop** takes off any solid border, including whitespace, surrounding the image. This is fairly mindless, but useful. If you want to be more deliberate about what portion of the image to crop, you first need to mark the area you want to keep. You select what is known as a *cropping rectangle* using the second pointer button. You can then push the **Crop** button to remove everything outside the rectangle. **UnCrop** reverses any cropping you've done, returning the image to its original state.

In addition to the command buttons along the bottom of the *controls* window, *xv* provides image altering capabilities via two menus, **24/8 Bit** and **Algorithms**. You display a menu by holding the first pointer button down on the corresponding command button. The **24/8 Bit** menu determines in what form the image data is stored. The **Algorithms** menu performs more obvious and visually interesting manipulations. See the *xv* manual for more information.

Saving an Image

The **Save** button (to the right of the file list) lets you save the file under its current name, or a new name, in any of several formats. Pushing the button pops up a save window, as shown in Figure 24-16.

Notice the vertical list of graphics file formats in the lower-left corner of the window. The filled circle in front of **X11 Bitmap** indicates that this is the current format. The save window allows you to select another format simply by clicking on the corresponding circle using the first pointer button.

The column to the right of the file formats lists four color types; the choices available are limited by the current file format.

You can edit the filename in the small text window in the center of the window. If you've altered an image, you might want to save it under a different filename.

Once you've specified the filename, format, and color type you want, click on the **OK** button to save the file or on **Cancel** to abort.

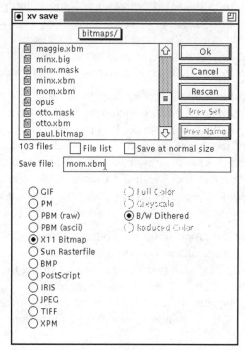

Figure 24-16: xv save window

Displaying an Image on the Root Window

You can display an image on the root window using the *–root* command-line option. The following command covers the screen with birthday cakes:

```
val@ruby 42% xv -root mom.xbm
```

If you have a *controls* window open, however, *xv* provides another fast and easy way to display an image on the root window, which also includes more varied methods of display: the **Display** menu. To post the menu, hold the first pointer button down on the command button marked **Display**, along the top of the *controls* window. The menu appears in Figure 24-17.

The first eleven choices determine how the image you're working with is displayed. A check mark precedes the current method of display. The default choice is in a **window**, as we got when we specified:

```
val@ruby % xv mom.xbm &
```

The other menu items let you display the image on the root window in a variety of configurations. Try some to get an idea. All of the items that include the word "tiled" come close to simulating the root window decoration that can also be performed using *xsetroot –bitmap (6.02)*.

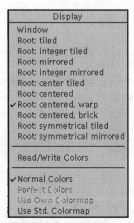

Figure 24-17: The Display menu

The **Root: centered, brick** menu item places a single image in the center of the screen and surrounds it with an image of a brick wall. Likewise, **Root: centered, warp** surrounds a single image with a "warp" pattern, which looks a bit like a '60s T-shirt pattern.

The rest of the **Display** menu deals with how colors are interpreted; but you'll need to use the internal color editor to change individual colors. See the *xv* manual for more information.

A Visual WHAT?

Some of *xv*'s capabilities will interest only the most serious image hacker, but the visual schnauzer can be useful even for dilettante artists like me. The visual schnauzer is a window that allows you to view and also manage the image files in a particular directory. Display it by clicking on the **Visual Schnauzer** button in the *xv controls* box, or by typing **CTRL-V** while the input focus is on any *xv* window.

The first time you run the schnauzer in an image directory, the image files will be represented by text, rather than icons. This is more economical with system resources, but basically no fun. You can generate icon symbols for all images in the directory by selecting two commands from the **Misc. Commands** menu, which is accessible from the command button in the upper-right corner of the window.

Hold the first pointer button down on the command button to display the menu. Then drag the pointer down the menu and choose **select All files**; then display the menu again and choose **Generate icon(s)**. The text labels in the schnauzer window will be replaced by icons of the images themselves (presuming *xv* can interpret the formats), accompanied by the filename. These icon images will be stored in a subdirectory (called *.xvpics*) of the current directory, so you only need to perform this conversion once. The next time you run the schnauzer in the image directory, the icons will be available and will be displayed automatically.

Figure 24-18 reveals the contents of my own bitmap directory, which encompasses fact and fantasy: somewhat fuzzy versions of my co-author and friend Linda Mui and her husband Paul Kleppner; a bitmap of one of my kitties, Minx; and one of Linda and Paul's kitties, Pesto; several cartoon characters; Mom's birthday cake, of course; and for a little species variety, a pterodon dinosaur. I have quite a collection of images; the scrollbar allows me to review them.

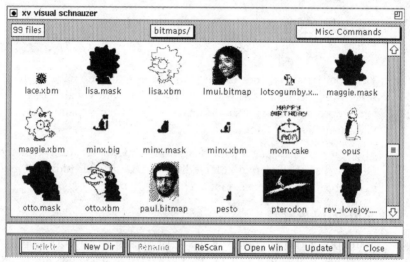

Figure 24-18: The visual schnauzer lets you manage the image files in a directory

Some of these images were gathered from the Internet. Linda drew Pesto using the *bitmap* editor *(22.03)* and I used the same program to fatten up Pesto to be the spitting image of my kitty Minx. The bitmaps of Linda and Paul were converted from FaceSaver images *(25.02)*. (And I actually get paid for this.)

The buttons along the bottom of the schnauzer window allow you to manage the files in the directory. If you click on one of the images in the schnauzer window, you'll highlight it and also enable the **Delete** and **Rename** buttons along the window's bottom edge. Once an image is highlighted, you can remove it from the directory (and also the visual schnauzer window) by clicking on **Delete**.

You can highlight more than one file by holding the **CTRL** key while you click on the image; thus you can remove multiple files in the directory at once. A dialog box will ask you to confirm any deletion.

The **Rename** button lets you rename a single highlighted image. **Rescan** checks to see if files have been added to or deleted from the directory (from a source other than the schnauzer) and updates the schnauzer window accordingly. **Update** performs a similar function, but takes it a bit farther by also looking for files that may not have had icons created and performing that action.

Close pops down the schnauzer window. See the *xv* manual for more information about the menus and other features.

— VQ

24.07 *See Any Good Movies?*

We aren't exactly at the point where we can see the latest Scorsese film on our workstation, but we're getting there. MPEG is a graphics format for animated movies, and *mpeg_play* is a program for viewing MPEG movies. All this is experimental, of course, but it's amazing enough that it works at all.

mpeg_play

To show movies, you need an 8-bit display. And of course, these are silent films. But Figure 24-19 shows a demonstration MPEG file (with *.mpg* suffix) as played by *mpeg_play*.

Figure 24-19: Playing an MPEG movie

— LM

24.08 *ghostview & ghostscript*

ghostview

In the book biz, we deal with PostScript files all the time. ("Did she just say 'book biz'?" Well, I'm tired.) If you're running X, you can preview documents and/or images in PostScript format using a program called *ghostview*, which opens a window in which the formatted file is displayed.

ghostscript

Underlying *ghostview* is a PostScript interpreter called *ghostscript*. While *ghostview* creates the viewing window, *ghostscript* draws in it. But you don't have to invoke *ghostscript*; *ghostview* will take care of that for you.

Typically, you run *ghostview* with no options and a single argument, the name of the PostScript file to be viewed. The following command previews a PostScript file I created by formatting the *ghostview* manpage:

```
val@ruby 13% ghostview ghostview.ps
```

The resulting preview window appears in Figure 24-20.

Notice that our sample window has both horizontal and vertical scrollbars bordering the viewing area. A *ghostview* window has a vertical scrollbar if the contents go on for more than a single screen page, and a horizontal scrollbar if the contents are wider than the window. To view text (or images) beyond the bounds of the window, you can drag the scrollbars using the pointer. You can also use any of several keyboard shortcuts: k moves the view up to reveal the top of the page; j moves the view down to show the page bottom; use h to shift the contents to the right; and l to shift to the left. (Users of the vi text editor will recognize the k, j, h, and l sequence of commands to navigate text.)

Notice the vertical list of page numbers to the left of the viewing area. You can view any page in a document by clicking on its number using the second pointer button. You can highlight one or more pages by holding down the first pointer button, dragging, and then releasing the button. This becomes important in terms of invoking menu functions, which we'll get to in a moment. You can also advance the page by hitting the **Return** key while the pointer rests in the viewing area, or go back a page by hitting **Backspace** or **Delete**.

When you begin working with *ghostview*, you may notice that the pointer can take on two different shapes within the window: a crosshair symbol and a target. The pointer looks like a target only when *ghostview* is "thinking"—in other words, when the program is working to update the window, bring up a dialog box, etc. You might get a target pointer symbol while scrolling to a new page, for instance. The pointer looks like a crosshair when the program is idle. It's generally a good idea to wait for the crosshair pointer before attempting to invoke a new action.

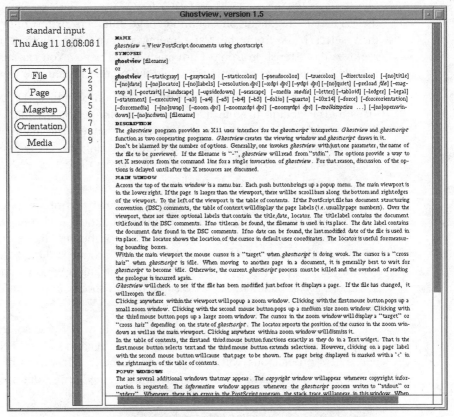

Figure 24-20: The ghostview window lets you preview a PostScript file

To the left of the page number list are five menu buttons. Use the **File** menu to **Open...** another PostScript file in the preview window. A dialog box will prompt you for the name. You can supply a name by typing in the pathname or by selecting the various pathname components from windows within the box. The **reopen** menu item causes *ghostview* to open the current PostScript file again, which you might do if you make changes to the file and reformat. The **File** menu also lets you **Print** the file or **Print marked pages**. (More about marking pages in a moment.) You can also use this menu to **Quit** the program; the **q** keyboard shortcut should accomplish the same thing.

The **Page** menu lets you: scan through the various pages (**Next** and **Previous**); **Redisplay**, or redraw, the contents of the window; orient the contents so that they appear in the **Center** of the viewing area; **Mark** pages so they can be referenced for subsequent actions; and **Unmark** pages.

You might want to mark one or more pages so that you can print those pages (using **Print marked pages** from the **File** menu). When a page is marked, an asterisk appears before its page number in the number list. In our previous figure, page 1 is marked. There are a few ways to mark pages. You can use the pointer to highlight one or more page numbers in the number list and then select **Mark** from the **Page** menu, or type the shortcut **m**. **Unmark** removes the asterisk in front of any highlighted page. You can also mark the page being displayed by typing **m** while the pointer rests in the viewing area.

The **Magstep** menu determines the magnification at which the contents are viewed. The default magnification factor, or *magstep*, is 0, which means that the size on the screen should match the size on paper. The menu lists magstep choices from -5 to 5, the negative numbers making the contents smaller and the positive numbers making the contents larger. The low end of the scale may very well be too small to read.

On a related topic, you can zero in on a particular part of any page by taking the crosshair and clicking one of the pointer buttons. Each button displays a second window containing a magnified image of the area that surrounded the crosshairs when you clicked. The third button produces the greatest magnification; the first produces the least. If the magnification window has a titlebar, it will display the title "zoom." A **Dismiss** button should appear in the magnification window so you can get rid of it.

The **Orientation** menu determines the direction in which the contents are oriented in the window. **Portrait** is the standard orientation of text. There are several others orientations with which to experiment. Most are only useful for viewing images. Figure 24-21 shows a familiar crew turned **Upside-down**.

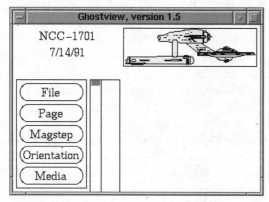

Figure 24-21: I'm a doctor, not a possum!

The **Media** menu lets you specify a page size. **Letter** is the default. The other available sizes should satisfy the needs of everyone from Shakespeare (**Folio**) to Rupert Murdoch (**Tabloid**).

— *VQ*

25

Conversions

25.01 *The Portable Bitmap Toolkit*

So once you have a window dump in *xwd* format, what do you do with it? Well, the answer is...practically anything you want!

pbmplus

The Portable Bitmap Toolkit (distributed under the name *pbmplus*) provides dozens of utilities for converting graphics files *(22.02)* between different formats. Rather than supporting direct conversions, though, the PBM Toolkit is designed to convert each format to a common, portable format, such as *portable bitmap* or *portable pixmap* format. From this portable format, you then convert the file to any of the other supported formats.

One of the supported formats is *xwd* format. Using the PBM Toolkit, you can convert *xwd* files to or from any of the other supported formats, such as GIF, TIFF, PostScript, Sun Raster, etc. During the file type conversion, you can also perform manipulations on the image, such as rotating, inverting, expanding, contracting, etc.

Developed by Jef Poskanzer, the Toolkit is composed of four parts, three of which correspond to a particular portable format:

- PBM: utilities to convert files to and from portable bitmap format.

- PGM: utilities to convert files to and from portable graymap format (grayscale images).

- PPM: utilities to convert files to and from portable pixmap format (color images).

The fourth part of the toolkit, PNM, provides utilities to manipulate images in any of the three formats. (The "NM" in PNM stands for "anymap," a term coined to serve as a collective for portable bitmaps, graymaps, and pixmaps.) For example, the program *pnmenlarge* enlarges a portable "anymap" by a factor you supply. *pnminvert* inverts an image in any of the three portable formats.

The available utilities and the conversions they perform are summarized in the *README* file in the source directory. Table 25-1 lists some representative conversion utilities and their functions.

Table 25-1: Some PBM Toolkit Conversion Utilities

Utility	Converts
giftoppm	GIF to portable pixmap
ppmtogif	Portable pixmap to GIF
pnmtoxwd	Portable anymap to X11 window dump
xwdtopnm	X10 or X11 window dump to portable anymap
ppmtopgm	Portable pixmap to portable graymap
fstopgm	Usenix FaceSaver file to portable graymap
pnmtops	Portable anymap to Encapsulated PostScript
pgmtopbm	Portable graymap to portable bitmap
pbmtomacp	Portable bitmap to MacPaint
macptopbm	MacPaint to portable bitmap
pbmtoxbm	Portable bitmap to X11 bitmap
pbmtox10bm	Portable bitmap to X10 bitmap
xbmtopbm	X10 or X11 bitmap to portable bitmap
pnmtoxwd	Portable anymap to X11 window dump
xwdtopnm	X10 or X11 window dump to portable anymap

As the table indicates, some of the available utilities come in pairs; they can be used to convert a file to a portable format and back to its original format again. (The table also includes a group of three related utilities to convert X10 and X11 bitmaps to portable bitmaps and back again.)

Certain conversions can only be performed in one direction. For example, you can convert a portable graymap to a portable bitmap (using *pgmtopbm*), but you can't convert a bitmap to a graymap. The one-way conversions generally involve changing a file to a simpler format.

You'll probably be most interested in converting graphics files to formats suitable for use with X: X bitmaps or window dump files. Keep in mind that a portable bitmap has a different format than an X bitmap. The program *pbmtoxbm* converts a portable bitmap to a bitmap compatible with X11.

The conversions you may want to perform can be simple (directly from one format to another) or complex (through several intermediate formats). An example of a simple conversion is changing a portable pixmap to a portable graymap using *ppmtopgm*:

```
% ppmtopgm pixmap > graymap
```

— VQ

25.02 *Converting a FaceSaver File to an X11 Bitmap*

The Portable Bitmap Toolkit source directory includes a file called *TIPS* that provides helpful hints on using the PBM utilities *(25.01)*. Based on these suggestions, we performed a fairly complex conversion: a FaceSaver image to a bitmap suitable for use with X. The following command performed the conversion on the file *myface* to create *myface.bitmap*:

```
fstopgm myface | pnmenlarge 3 | pnmscale -yscale 1.125 | pgmnorm |\
         pgmtopbm | pbmtoxbm > myface.bitmap
```

Notice that this particular conversion requires seven utilities! This procedure is by no means intuitive. We relied heavily on the *TIPS* provided.

The six conversions performed are:

- Convert FaceSaver image to portable graymap (fstopgm).

- Enlarge a portable anymap three times (pnmenlarge 3).

- Scale pixels in y dimension; x dimension is adjusted accordingly (pnmscale -yscale 1.125).

- Normalize contrast of portable graymap (pgmnorm).

- Convert portable graymap to portable bitmap (pgmtopbm).

- Convert portable bitmap to X11 bitmap (pbmtoxbm).

Be aware that the command:

```
pnmscale -yscale 1.125
```

may not be necessary on all systems or the necessary arguments may vary. If you omit *pnmscale* and the command is necessary, the system should return a message to that effect and also tell you what arguments to use.

Once you have a bitmap image of someone's face, there are plenty of fun and/or fiendish things you might do with it. One of the former is illustrated in Article 3.11.

The possible uses of the PBM Toolkit programs and the ways in which they can be combined are extremely varied. You'll have to do some experimenting.

To orient yourself, read the files *README*, *TIPS*, and *FORMATS* in the source directory. The source directory also includes manpages for each utility.

—*VQ*

25.03 *Converting xwd to TIFF*

We often have to make our screen dumps available to our graphics department for altering. This might be so that we can crop out parts of the figure. Or sometimes we need to show the pointer in the figure, and since X window dumps don't support that, we have to resort to drawing it in by hand.

So what we often have to do is to convert our *xwd* files to TIFF format, so our graphics department can read them onto their Macintosh computers. To make this easier, I wrote up an *xwdtotiff* shell script using the *pbmplus (25.01)* utilities. This script appears below:

xwdtotiff

```
#!/bin/sh

# xwdtotiff -- just combine a couple of pbm programs to make
#   things easier for our unix-illiterate Mac people.

#   All options except -d are passed to tifftopnm.

PATH=$PATH:/usr/local/pbmplus
export PATH

TIFFOPTS="-none "
FILELIST=""
OUTDIR="."
MYNAME=`basename $0`
zcat=/usr/local/bin/zcat      # GNU version; handles .gz and .Z

if [ $# -eq 0 ]
then
        echo Syntax:    $MYNAME [-d directory] [tiffoptions] file.xwd ...
        exit 2
fi

while [ $# -gt 0 ]
do
    case $1 in
    -d)  shift; OUTDIR=$1;;
    -*)  TIFFOPTS="$TIFFOPTS $1";;
    *.xwd|*.xwd.gz)  FILELIST="$FILELIST $1";;
    *)   echo Syntax: $MYNAME [-d directory] [tiffoptions] file.xwd ...
         echo "  where each xwdfile ends with a .xwd suffix"
         exit 2;;
    esac
    shift
done

if [ ! -d $OUTDIR ]
```

```
then
        echo "$OUTDIR isn't a directory.  Create a new
directory using \"mkdir $OUTDIR\".  Aborting."
        exit 2
fi

if [ ! -w $OUTDIR ]
then
        echo "  Error!  No write permission for $OUTDIR
  Use
        $MYNAME -d directory ...
  to change tiff file target directory.  Aborting ..."
exit 2
fi

for file in $FILELIST
do
        case $file in
        *.xwd)
        BASE=`basename $file .xwd`
        echo -n "Creating $BASE.tiff ... "
        xwdtopnm $file | pnmtotiff $TIFFOPTS > $OUTDIR/$BASE.tiff;;
        *.xwd.Z)
        BASE=`basename $file .xwd.Z`
        echo -n "Creating $BASE.tiff ... "
        $zcat $file | xwdtopnm | pnmtotiff $TIFFOPTS > $OUTDIR/$BASE.tiff;;
        *.xwd.gz)
        BASE=`basename $file .xwd.gz`
        echo -n "Creating $BASE.tiff ... "
        $zcat $file | xwdtopnm | pnmtotiff $TIFFOPTS > $OUTDIR/$BASE.tiff;;
        esac
    done
```

The script first sets the PATH environment variable to include the directory containing our *pbmplus* programs. The only real option used by *xwdtotiff* is −*d*, for specifying another directory in which to place the converted TIFF files. Any other options are taken as options to *tifftopnm*. (One of the default options that we use is −*none*, for no compression.)

You can then specify the names of the *xwd* files that you want converted. The script assumes that these files have an *.xwd* suffix, with or without a trailing *.Z* or *.gz* suffix for compressed *xwd* files.

We use a similar method for converting files to GIF format, MacPaint format, or any other format that's supported by *pbmplus*.

—*LM*

25.04 Viewing Photo CD Files

hpcdtoppm

The *hpcdtoppm* program lets you convert Photo CD files to portable pixmap *(22.02)* format. From that point, you can use the utilities in the Portable Bitmap Toolkit *(25.01)* to convert the portable pixmap into a format suitable for displaying, such as GIF or X pixmap *(22.02)*.

Here's a sample conversion. Let's take a Photo CD file of an exotic animal called the tapir and convert it to a GIF file. First, we need to convert the Photo CD file to a portable pixmap:

```
val@ruby 43% hpcdtoppm tapir.pcd > tapir.ppm
```

Then we can use the PBM utility *ppmtogif* to convert *tapir.ppm* to GIF format:

```
val@ruby 44% ppmtogif tapir.ppm > tapir.gif
```

Now that we have a GIF file, we can use *xloadimage (24.05)* or *xv (24.06)* to view it.
—*LM, VQ*

25.05 Magnifying the Screen: xmag

The *xmag* client enables you to magnify a portion of the screen; this close-up look can assist you in creating and editing bitmaps and other graphics or in capturing screen images (with *xgrabsc (23.05)* or a similar program). You can also copy and paste images between *xmag* windows or between *xmag* and the *bitmap* editor.

One instance of the *xmag* program lets you magnify several different areas of the screen and display the images either sequentially (in the same window) or concurrently (in multiple windows). In addition to giving you a look at a magnified bitmap image, *xmag* also provides certain information about the individual pixels in the image.

When might you use *xmag*? Suppose you're running a program that creates a special image on the root window, and you'd like to create a *bitmap* file of a part of that image. You can display a magnification of the image you want with *xmag*. Then you can either try to recreate the image by editing in an open *bitmap* window or copy the *xmag* image and paste it into the *bitmap* editor.

xmag is also useful for capturing a screen image that can then be saved with the *xgrabsc* client. (If you used *xwd (23.01)*, you'd also capture *xmag*'s command buttons!) Like *xgrabsc*, *xmag* can represent portions of several windows at once.

—*VQ*

25.06 What Area to Magnify and How Much

If you invoke *xmag* without options:

```
% xmag &
```

you can interactively choose the area to be magnified (the *source* area). The pointer changes to an upper-left corner symbol from which extends a small, hollow square with a wavering border. (By default, the square is 64 pixels on each side.) Move the corner cursor, placing the square over the area you want to magnify, and click the first pointer button.

If the window manager is set up to place windows automatically, the bitmap image inside the hollow square is magnified and displayed in an *xmag* window, as in Figure 25-1.[*]

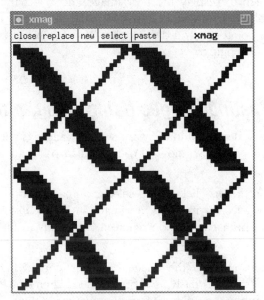

Figure 25-1: xmag window displaying magnified screen area

The default size *xmag* window shows an area 64 pixels square, magnified five times; thus, the image itself is 320 pixels on each side. This magnification enables you to see the individual pixels, which are represented by squares of the same color as the corresponding pixels in the source image.

---

[*] If interactive placement is specified, you'll have to place the magnification window using the pointer.

Rather than use the default source area and magnification, you can specify other values on the command line. The following command specifies that an area 100 pixels square be magnified twice:

```
% xmag -source 100x100 -mag 2 &
```

You can also select an alternative source area manually using the pointer. Press the second pointer button and drag to change the size of the hollow square. When you've covered the area you want, release the button. The area is magnified and displayed in an *xmag* window.

If you want to magnify another portion of the screen using the original source area size and magnification factor, you do not have to start *xmag* again. You can choose another source area and display it in the same *xmag* window by clicking on the **replace** command button. To display, open an additional *xmag* window in which to display the new image and select the **new** command button. Regardless of which button you pick, you then choose the source area using the pointer as you did initially. You can select any number of source areas during a single *xmag* session.

—VQ

25.07 *Copying and Pasting Images Using xmag, bitmap*

You can copy the image displayed in an *xmag* window and paste it in another *xmag* window or in a *bitmap* window. (You can also paste an image from *bitmap* into *xmag*.)

To copy the contents of *xmag*, click on the **select** command button. The *xmag* **select** function is analogous to "marking" an image in a *bitmap* window. The image is copied to the primary selection where it is globally available via the server.

There will be no indication that the image has been copied into memory, although the **select** button will flash in reverse video when you click on it. However, if you then move the pointer to another *xmag* window and click on **paste**, the image from the first window will be displayed in it.

Think of the **select** and **paste** buttons as accessing the same invisible graphics clipboard, which has room for only one image. The *bitmap* copy and paste mechanism accesses the same space in memory. Thus, you can select images from any *xmag* or *bitmap* window (by the mechanism appropriate to the particular client), but only the last image you copy remains in memory to be pasted elsewhere.

A note about pasting an *xmag* image into a *bitmap* window: the default *xmag* image represents a 64×64 pixel square while the default *bitmap* image is

16×16 pixels. If you intend to transfer images between these clients, it's a good idea to specify comparable dimensions. If you have the screen space, you might run:

```
% bitmap -size 64x64 &
```

However, this is a very large window. You can make the *bitmap* window smaller by specifying dimensions for the individual editing squares (using the –*sw* and –*sh* options), or you can specify another size for the *xmag* source area:

```
% xmag -source 16x16 &
```

Regardless of the area you want to work with, the important thing to remember is to keep the dimensions comparable.

— *VQ*

25.08 *What xmag Shows You*

If you move the pointer into the *xmag* window, the cursor becomes an arrow. Point the arrow at one of the magnified pixels and hold down the first pointer button. A banner across the top or bottom edge of the window displays information about the pixel, as shown in Figure 25-2.

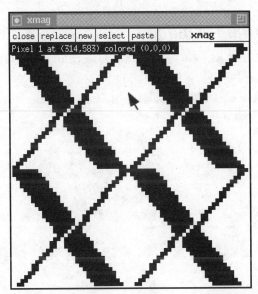

Figure 25-2: Displaying pixel statistics with pointer in xmag window

The banner displays the following information about the specified pixel:

- The pixel number. On a black-and-white display, this is either 0 if the pixel is in the background color or 1 if the pixel is in the foreground color. On a color display, the number corresponds to the position in the colormap.

- The positive x and y coordinates relative to the root window. These are the coordinates of the original image—not of the *xmag* window.

- The RGB color specification; a 16-bit value. The RGB spec is in three parts (of four hexadecimal digits each), corresponding to the three primaries in the RGB color model.

If you are trying to create a graphic image on a grid (such as the *bitmap* client provides), the x and y coordinates of each pixel can be especially useful. This RGB value is useful for determining what colors compose an image (though the definition is not portable). You can supply this hex value on the command line or in a resource file, or convert it to a portable format. (See Article 26.19).

xmag provides these pixel statistics dynamically. If you continue to hold down the first pointer button and drag the pointer across the window, the banner will display values for each pixel as the pointer indicates it.

—VQ

25.09 *Removing an xmag Window*

To remove a magnification window, select the **close** command button; or type **q**, **Q**, or **CTRL-C** while the window has the focus.

You can remove *all xmag* windows (started under the same instance of the program) using any applicable kill *(2.08)* method .

—VQ

26

Color

26.01 Colorizing Only Hurts the Movies

I'm glad to have a color workstation. I like having a root window the color of lilacs, or pebbles, or the ocean. It makes it a little easier to be inside.

If you have a color display, you can specify different colors for different applications, for window manager decorations, the root window, etc.—as much or as little as appeals to you. (A screen is limited to displaying a certain number of colors at a time, but this number is usually fairly high.) Be as tasteful or as garish as you want. Come up with a warm and fuzzy color scheme and leave it alone. Whatever. Article 26.03 reviews some of the ways you can use color.

X comes with a standard database of colors, described in Article 26.04, which should satisfy most users' needs. If you want to go further, you can mix your own colors using a color editor, like *xcoloredit (26.16)* or *xtici (26.17)*. I've had a lot of fun doing that. I've also paired my new color definitions with names in a database, so I can access them easily. (See Article 26.23.)

Of course, if you just want to deal with the barest strokes of color, the next article should suffice.

— VQ

26.02 Pick a Color, Any Color

In the X Window System, color can be a complicated business. But if you're like most people, you want to specify colors using names from your old Crayola box, without learning anything about the technology of color. Well, as foresight would have it, every X-based system comes with a pre-fab database of colors to choose from. How do you access these colors? Just name them on the command line or in a resource file. The clients and server work out the rest.

Most of the color names you can think of, plus many esoteric names, are included in the standard color database. So, odds are you can just pick a name out of your head, and the database will deliver. A case in point: the following command creates an *xbiff* *(7.10)* window with a bold midnight blue foreground *(17.06)* (for the mailbox picture) and an elegant orchid background *(17.06)*. (Oooo!)

```
% xbiff -bg orchid -fg midnightblue &
```

Article 26.03 surveys these and other typical uses of color. Note that whether you're running a command or adding a resource, you have to enter multiple-word color names like "midnight blue" as single words or surround them with quotes.

Article 26.04 gives you a better idea of the colors available in the standard database and shows you how to browse the names. Keep in mind, however, that there is an inherent limitation in this system. The color definitions in the standard database are in so-called RGB format *(26.10)*, in which colors are created by combining red, green, and blue pixels. RGB colors are device-dependent, which means they can look very different on different types of monitors. My guess is that most users won't care if their "pink" is too "orangy" and will just experiment with other colors in the database to find shades they like. (The *xcol* program, described in Article 26.05, will help you preview the standard RGB colors for your monitor.)

If you want absolute precision of color regardless of the environment and hardware, things get more complicated. Begin by reading about the X Color Management System (Xcms) in Article 26.12.

—VQ

26.03 *How Can I Use Color?*

All applications written using an Xt-based toolkit *(1.05)*— that's most of the programs you'll encounter—accept both command-line options and resource variables that specify foreground and background colors. Specifically, these options and resources are: *–fg*, *–bg*, foreground, background. (See Article 17.06 for examples.) The *–bd* option lets you set a border color. However, since most window managers provide decoration that largely supersedes the client's own border, this customization is usually not very noticeable.

There are also many client-specific options that allow you to set colors for particular features of an application. For example, *xclock* provides options and resources to specify colors for the hands of the clock (*–hd*, hands) and the edges of the hands (*–hl*, highlight). If you were to use these in concert with the standard foreground and background options/resources, you could have different colors for the clock face (background) and tick marks (foreground), as well. *xterm* allows you to set different colors for the text cursor (*–cr*, cursorColor) and the pointer symbol (*–ms*, pointerColor, pointerColorBackground). You'd use foreground for the text color and background for the window itself. See a client's manpage for color options and resources.

Perhaps the most dramatic use of color is as a root-window background. The *xsetroot* (6.02) client allows you to specify a solid color for the root window. I use a very peaceful color I came up with myself using *xcoloredit* (26.16); I call it beach glass—kind of a washed-out gray-green:

```
% xsetroot -solid beachglass
```

You can also specify foreground and background colors with a bitmap pattern (*–bitmap*) or a grid of various dimensions (*–mod*). See the *xsetroot* article for additional examples.

For a screen of a different color, try the *floatbg* program (6.05). *floatbg* chooses a root window color at random and then very gradually changes it; another way over the rainbow.

Whatever window manager you use will certainly allow color customization as well. You can probably specify colors for window manager decorations, menus, dialog boxes, etc. Generally there's no point in getting carried away; it's just distracting. Article 12.26 describes some *twm* color features. Article 13.16 gives some guidelines for adding color to Motif window manager features. For more information, see the appropriate window manager manpage.

Keep in mind that some clients come with a special file of application defaults intended for a color screen (20.21). You can also specify resources that will only be applied if you're using a color screen, as described in Article 20.21.

— *VQ*

26.04 *Browsing the Standard Color Names*

As of X11R5, the standard (RGB) color database has 738 color names (and their numeric definitions). However, this number is slightly deceptive: some color definitions are listed multiple times with variant spellings and capitalizations; still others are shades of the same color. How many shades of sea green do *you* need?

```
light sea green
sea green
medium sea green
dark sea green
SeaGreen1
SeaGreen2
SeaGreen3
SeaGreen4
DarkSeaGreen1
```

```
DarkSeaGreen2
DarkSeaGreen3
DarkSeaGreen4
```

There are also more than 100 shades of gray! (This may seem like a bit of overkill, but it makes grayscale monitors hum.)

You can browse all of the available color names by entering the command:

```
% showrgb | more
```

showrgb scrolls through the list of color names and their numeric definitions (used by the server), which live in the file *rgb.txt*. (This file is generally located in */usr/lib/X11*.) The color names in the *rgb.txt* file are too numerous to list here. Although there are no literal dividers within the file, you can look at it as roughly falling into three sections:

Section 1:

A standard spectrum of colors (red, yellow, sea green, powder blue, hot pink, etc.), which seem to be ordered roughly as: off-whites and other pale colors, grays, blues, greens, yellows, browns, oranges, pinks, reds, and purples.

Section 2:

Subshades of Section 1 colors (such as SeaGreen 1 through 4). These subshades make up the largest part of the file.

Section 3:

One hundred and one additional shades of gray, numbered 0 through 100. This large number of precisely graduated grays provides a wide variety of shading for grayscale displays.

Here are some representative colors from each section of the database. To brighten your day, I've chosen some of the more esoteric color names. Naturally all of the primary and secondary colors are also available.

```
Section 1:

ghost white        peach puff         lavender blush     lemon chiffon
slate gray         midnight blue      cornflower blue    medium slate blue
dodger blue        powder blue        turquoise          pale green
lawn green         chartreuse         olive drab         lime green
khaki              light yellow       goldenrod          peru
sienna             sandy brown        salmon             coral
tomato             hot pink           maroon             violet red
magenta            medium orchid      blue violet        purple

Section 2:

snow1 - 4          bisque1 - 4        cornsilk1 - 4      honeydew1 -4
azure1 - 4         SteelBlue1 - 4     DeepSkyBlue1 - 4   LightCyan1 - 4
```

```
PaleTurquoise1 - 4    aquamarine1 - 4      PaleGreen1 - 4       DarkOliveGreen1 - 4
SpringGreen1 -4       gold1 - 4            RosyBrown1 - 4       burlywood1 - 4
chocolate1 - 4        firebrick1 - 4       DarkOrange1 - 4      OrangeRed1 - 4
DeepPink1 - 4         PaleVioletRed1 - 4   plum1 - 4            DarkOrchid1 - 4
```

Section 3:

gray0 (grey0) through gray100 (grey100)

To see how the various colors look on your monitor, you can use the *xcol* client *(26.05)*.

— *VQ*

26.05 *Previewing the Standard Colors: xcol*

The *xcol* client allows you to see how the standard RGB colors *(26.04)* look on your display before you specify the colors for a client. Once you've selected certain colors, *xcol* can also assist you in editing the color specifications in your resources file.

xcol

To run the *xcol* program, simply enter:

```
% xcol &
```

A window titled ColorView will be placed on your screen. The ColorView window displays the outline of a cube containing scattered pixels of the available colors, almost like a universe of colored stars. The position of each of the colored pixels in the cube represents its RGB value *(26.10)*.

In many cases, a primary shade is associated with several subshades, which are distinguished from the primary shade by a number appended to its name. For example, you can specify the color dark sea green, and also DarkSea-Green1 through DarkSeaGreen4. Within *xcol*'s ColorView window, colors with the same name but different RGB values (signaling different intensities) are represented by a single pixel.

The pixels are not labeled, but you should be able to distinguish basic colors on a good quality color monitor. If you place the pointer on any of the pixels, a small box containing the color name will be displayed. The color name appears in white and the border of the box appears in the color specified. If the pixel represents several associated colors of differing intensities, the box will also contain a spectrum of those colors (though the individual shades are lumped under the primary name). By moving the pointer onto various pixels, you should be able to get an idea of how certain colors look on your display.

Some areas of the window are more cluttered with pixels than others. In these areas, you may not be able to distinguish individual pixels. However, if you move the pointer slowly over these "bunches," the individual color names will be displayed, outlined in the color.

While the pointer focus is directed to the ColorView window, you may notice the rest of the display becomes slightly darkened. This darkening happens because *xcol* provides its own colormap, different from the default. It is a normal effect and will stop when you switch the focus to another window.

—VQ

26.06 Using xcol to Edit Resources

In addition to letting you preview colors, *xcol* can also be used to edit color resource specifications. If you want to edit the color specifications in your *.Xresources* file, start the client using the command line:

```
% xcol ~/.Xresources &
```

This time two windows will be displayed: the ColorView window and a second window titled TextView, which contains the specifications pertaining to color from the *.Xresources* file, as in Figure 26-1.

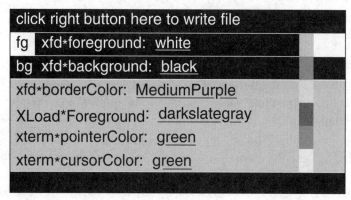

Figure 26-1: xcol's TextView window

The size of the TextView window depends on the number of color specifications in the *.Xresources* file. Though you can't tell from our black-and-white illustration, each specification in the TextView window appears in the color it names (the color is the foreground color of the text line). If you click the second pointer button on a specification line, a reverse video effect takes place: the named color becomes the background and the previous background color (gray by default) becomes the foreground (text) color. An "R" appears to the left of the text line, indicating that reverse video is enabled. Although reverse video is not necessary, it sometimes provides a better look at a color than the default display, and also a better look than the boxes surrounding color names in the ColorView window. Reverse video display is a toggle: if you want to return to the default display, click the second pointer button on the text line again.

By using the pointer on both the TextView and ColorView windows, you can change the colors specified in the *.Xresources* file. To select the resource to change, place the pointer on the corresponding line in the TextView window and click the first button. The selected line will be outlined in the current foreground color.

Once you've selected a resource, you can change the corresponding color value:

1. Place the pointer on a pixel in the ColorView window; wait until the color name box is displayed.

2. While the pointer rests on the pixel, click the first button.

The color value of the resource in the TextView window is changed to the color you select. The named color is also displayed as either the foreground or background color of the text line—background if reverse video was active. If you just want to look at some colors, you can change the color any number of times without saving changes to the text file.

Now let's consider a practical example. Suppose we want to change the following specification in our sample resource file:

```
XLoad*foreground: darkslategray
```

which makes the graph produced by *xload* (as well as the system name) appear in dark slate gray. First we select the resource by clicking on it with the first pointer button. Then we move the pointer to the ColorView window and search for an alternative color that would be good for the *xload* graph. Moving the pointer among the colored pixels in the ColorView window, we settle on medium orchid. While the pointer rests on the medium orchid pixel and the box enclosing the color name is displayed, we click the first pointer button. The resource in the TextView window changes to reflect our choice:

```
XLoad*Foreground: mediumorchid
```

and the color in which the line is displayed also changes from dark slate gray to medium orchid.

If the file displayed in the TextView window includes background and foreground specifications for the same resource, those resources are grouped together, and the letters "fg" and "bg" appear to the left of the foreground and background resources, respectively. These associated resources are displayed using the foreground and background color specifications they name. In our sample TextView window, the following resources are grouped:

```
xfd*foreground: white
xfd*background: black
```

These resources set the foreground and background colors for the *xfd* font displayer to white and black respectively. Thus, in the TextView window these specification lines appear in white with a black background.

To switch the colors specified by a foreground/background pair, place the pointer on either resource line and click the second button. Our sample resources would be changed to:

```
xfd*foreground: black
xfd*background: white
```

and the resources in the TextView window would also switch to black on white.

Keep in mind that you can change only one of the associated resources if you want, by using the method described previously.

Once you've selected colors you like, you can save the changes to the text file by placing the pointer in the horizontal bar at the top of the TextView window right below the titlebar and clicking the third button. The bar contains the message:

```
click right button here to write file.
```

When you click the third pointer button on this bar, *xcol* beeps and asks you to confirm the choice by displaying:

```
confirm writing with right button!
```

To write the file, click the third button on the bar again. The *.Xresources* file is saved and the following message is displayed in the horizontal bar:

```
file written with backup.
```

The previous version of the *.Xresources* file is saved as a backup and given the filename *.Xresources~*. To restore the old settings, simply rename the backup file *.Xresources*.

If you want to cancel writing the file, click any button other than the third on the horizontal bar and you will get the message:

```
writing aborted.
```

To quit the application, focus input on either the TextView or ColorView window and type q. Be aware that *xcol* will allow you to quit without saving changes and will not inform you.

—VQ

26.07 How Many Colors Can I Use at Once?

If you use color for your root window, window manager decorations, and even different applications, you'll probably still only be using a handful of colors. But if you display color pictures, using a program like *xv (24.06)* or *xloadimage (24.05)*, there's a good chance you'll come across an image that has too many colors for your display to handle. In most of these cases, the viewing program will compensate by reducing the colors of the image in an intelligent way. This technique will at least get the picture displayed, though some of the aesthetic quality may be lost.

There isn't much you can do in most of these situations. But it doesn't hurt to understand a little about where these limitations come from. The first concept you need to understand is that pictures on your screen are made up of lots of individual dots, or *pixels*. Each pixel corresponds to one or more bits in the workstation's memory. For a monochrome display, there is only one bit per pixel, and its value (0 or 1) determines whether the pixel is off or on (white or black).

Color and grayscale monitors use multiple bits to define each pixel. One way to think about this is to imagine that the flat thing you call your screen actually has *depth*. Think of the multiple bits that define each pixel as forming layers, each of which is known as a *plane*. If I run *xdpyinfo* on my color Sun 3/60, one of the display statistics I get is:

```
depth of root window:    8 planes
```

The number of different colors (or shades of gray) that can be displayed on the screen at any one time is a function of the number of planes, specifically the number 2 to the power of the number of planes. So, my 8-plane screen can display 2^8 colors, or 256 distinct colors. A 4-plane system can display 2^4 colors, or 16 distinct colors, while a 24-plane system can display 2^{24} colors (more than 16 million distinct colors).

So, does all this mean that I can use 256 colors at once? Come on. That would be too easy. Though hypothetically my screen can display that many colors at once, X can't necessarily handle that many. (Here's where the technology of color gets especially hairy. If you're just interested in screen decor, maybe mixing a few colors, it's time to go out for cigarettes.) Limitations stem from the method by which colors are translated from numeric definitions to the screen. This translation relies on what is known as a *colormap* (or *colormap table*).

On my screen, each pixel has eight bits (i.e., the screen has eight planes). Programs that draw in color use the value of these bits as a pointer to a lookup table called a colormap, in which each entry (or *colorcell*) contains the RGB values for a particular color.* For example, a pixel value of 16 will select the 16th colorcell. In Figure 26-2, colorcell 16 just happens to contain the RGB value 176, 226, and 208, the numeric definition of a color called "beach glass," which we mixed ourselves using *xcoloredit* (26.16).

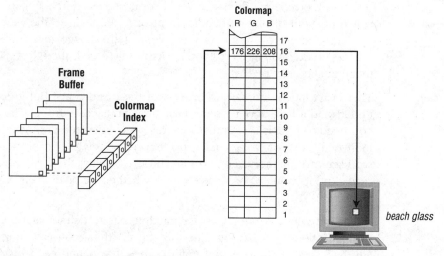

Figure 26-2: Multiple planes used to index a colormap

—VQ, TOR, AN

26.08 Running Out Of Colors

Why should you care about the colormap and how it works (26.07)? Because it limits the number of colors you can use at any one time. Your hardware may be able to handle 256 colors—or even 16 million!—but there isn't space for all of them to be stored in the colormap at one time. There isn't even a mechanism for them to be selected if they could be stored.

This limitation is made more significant by the fact that X is a multiclient environment. When X starts up, usually no colors are loaded into the colormap. As clients are invoked, certain of these cells are allocated. But when all of the free colorcells are used up, it is no longer possible to request new colors. When this happens, you will usually be given the closest possible color from those already allocated. However, you may instead be given an error message and told that there are no free colorcells.

---

* There is a type of high-end display in which pixel values are used directly to control the illumination of the red, green, and blue phosphors. But far more commonly the bits per pixel are used indirectly with the actual color values specified independently.

In order to minimize the chance of running out of colorcells, many programs use *shared* colorcells. Shared colorcells can be used by any number of applications, but they can't be changed by any of them. They can only be deallocated by each application that uses them, and when all applications have deallocated the cell, it is available for setting again. Shared cells are most often used for background, border, and cursor colors.

Alternatively, some clients have to be able to change the color of graphics they have already drawn. This requires another kind of cell, called *private*, which can't be shared. A typical use of a private cell would be for the palette of a color-mixing application, such as *xcoloredit*. This program has three bars of each primary color and a box that shows the mixed color. The primary bars use shared cells, while the mixed color box uses a private cell.

So, some programs define colorcells to be read-only and sharable, while others define colorcells to be read/write and private.

As an added complication, in order to deal with colormap limitations, some clients may temporarily swap in a private colormap of their own. You may have seen this happen; the effect isn't subtle. The client in question displays in the expected colors when you focus on it, while all other applications suddenly display in unexpected (and often unsavory) hues.

You can minimize the chance of having colormap conflicts by requesting unique numerical colors only when necessary. You're much less likely to run into trouble if you use a limited palette for most of your applications. In other words, pick some colors you like and use them (perhaps in different combinations) for all your clients.

— VQ, AN

26.09 *Determining the Colors in an Image*

When you display a picture created by somebody else, it's next to impossible to know exactly what colors are being used. A little known power of the *xmag* (25.05) magnification program is that it will give you the RGB color specification for a pixel in hexadecimal notation.

First use *xmag* to zero in on a part of the image. Then figure out the RGB value for any pixel (25.08). To use the hexadecimal RGB value on the command line or in a resource file, you have to remove the commas and also preface the hex number with a pound sign. To convert the hex number to a portable color space, see Article 26.19.

— VQ

26.10 *The RGB Color Model*

Most color displays on the market today are based on the RGB color model. Each pixel on the screen is actually produced by three phosphors: one red, one green, and one blue. Each of these three phosphors is illuminated by a separate electron beam, called a *color gun*. These color guns can be lit to different intensities to produce different colors on the screen.

When all three phosphors are fully illuminated, the pixel appears white to the human eye. When all three are dark, the pixel appears black. When the illumination of each primary color varies, the three phosphors generate an additive color. For example, equal portions of red and green, with no admixture of blue, make yellow.

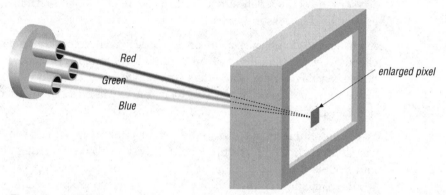

Figure 26-3: Red, green, and blue color guns

As you might guess, the intensity of each primary color is controlled by a numeric value. In the *rgb.txt* file, each color is associated with a decimal number between 0 and 255. Consider the following line from the *rgb.txt* file:

```
173 216 230            light blue
```

The three numbers make up what is known as an *RGB triplet*, which specifies the intensity of each of the three primary colors. The *rgb.txt* file contains 738 mappings of RGB triplets to color names. (Remember that the RGB system has an inherent limitation: the hardcoded intensities of red, green, and blue may look different on different displays.)

An RGB triplet can also be written in hexadecimal notation. You can use hex values to specify colors *(26.11)* on the command line or in a resource file.

—*VQ, TOR*

26.11 Using RGB Values in Hexadecimal Notation

The color values paired with names in the *rgb.txt* file *(26.04)* are in decimal (base 10) notation. You can specify a color from this file using the corresponding name. The decimal values themselves don't mean anything on the command line or in a resource file. However, you can specify an RGB color using a numeric value written in hexadecimal notation.

Why would you ever want to specify an RGB color using numbers? Well, for one thing, the base 16 hexadecimal numbering system affords greater precision than decimal values. So, if you're a real color jock, you can have the most precise shade of blue imaginable. (Of course, if you are so serious about precision, you'll probably opt for portable Xcms definitions *(26.12)* over the hardware-specific RGB variety, but that's another story.)

A more compelling reason to use hex RGB color values is that they plug readily into the command line or a resource file. Suppose, for instance, that you create a color of your own, using a program like *xcoloredit (26.16)*. *xcoloredit* outputs a color value in hexadecimal notation. You can use that hex definition as the equivalent of a color name by preceding it with a pound sign (#). (If you're going to use the color repeatedly, however, it's a good idea to pair the numeric definition with a name in a color database. See Article 26.23 for instructions.)

So, how do hex numbers describe an RGB color? Depending on the underlying hardware, different servers may use a larger or smaller number of bits (from 4 to 16) to describe the intensity of each primary. To insulate you from this variation, most clients are designed to take color values containing anywhere from 4 to 16 bits (1 to 4 hex digits), and the server then scales them to the hardware. As a result, you can specify hexadecimal values in any one of these formats:

```
#RGB
#RRGGBB
#RRRGGGBBB
#RRRRGGGGBBBB
```

where R, G, and B represent single hexadecimal digits and determine the intensity of the red, green, and blue primaries that make up each color.

When fewer than four digits are used, they represent the most significant bits of the value. For example, #3a6 is the same as #3000a0006000.

What this means concretely is perhaps best illustrated by looking at the values that correspond to some colors in the color name database. We'll use 8-bit values: two hexadecimal digits for each primary. The following definitions are the hexadecimal equivalents of the decimal values for some of the colors found in the *rgb.txt* file.

```
#000000      black
#FFFFFF      white
#FF0000      red
#00FF00      green
#0000FF      blue
#FFFF00      yellow
#00FFFF      cyan
#FF00FF      magenta
#5F9EA0      cadet blue
#6495ED      cornflower blue
#ADD8E6      light blue
#B0C4DE      light steel blue
#0000CD      medium blue
#000080      navy blue
#87CEED      sky blue
#6A5ACE      slate blue
#4682B4      steel blue
```

As you can see from the colors previously given, pure red, green, and blue result from the corresponding bits being turned on fully (FF in hex). Turning all three primaries off yields black, while turning all nearly full on produces white. Yellow, cyan, and magenta can be created by pairing two of the other primaries at full intensity. The various shades of blue shown previously are created by varying the intensity of each primary, sometimes in unexpected ways.

Of course, fiddling with the numbers is fairly unintuitive. If you want to play with color, use a color editor *(26.15)*.

—*VQ, TOR*

26.12 Portable Color: The X Color Management System

Until Release 5, you could ask for blue, red, lilac, peach, or any other color in the standard database, but the exact shade you got depended significantly on the display hardware (and to a lesser degree on the platform). To overcome this limitation, in X11R5 the X Consortium adopted the *X Color Management System* (*Xcms*), developed by Tektronix, which provides *device-independent* color. Under Xcms, colors are based upon internationally recognized standards. The idea behind Xcms is that color relies upon human vision. Simply put, red should look basically the same on any monitor, under any platform.

Xcms accepts color values in several different formats, called *color spaces*. Most of these color spaces describe color in a device-independent manner, using scientific terms and values commonly applied to color. Xcms will also recognize an RGB color space, but (as with the standard color database) the values are not portable.

From a user's standpoint, the primary advantages of Xcms are:

- It recognizes several types of color specification (color spaces), which can be supplied on the command line or in resource files.

- It enables you to make a database of colors you "mix" yourself, using a color editor. (While the server-side RGB color model allows for a single systemwide database, Xcms allows any user to have a private database.) In the Xcms database, you pair a name with a value in any of the accepted color spaces (formats). The Xcms database can then serve as an alternative to the default RGB database (you can specify colors from either).

- Xcms can "tune" colors to display more accurately on specific hardware. (Some X terminals are configured to do this automatically; on most other displays, you need to install a special file to perform this tuning.)

- Xcms allows users to take advantage of sophisticated color printer technology.

If you're at all interested in coming up with your own colors, it's worth reading more about Xcms (later in this chapter) and learning how to create your own database. Your system administrator might also want to create a system-wide Xcms database.

—VQ

26.13 *The HVC Color Model*

According to the RGB color model *(26.10)*, colors are created by mixing different intensities of three primaries, red, green, and blue. Each of the component colors is generated by the screen hardware, making RGB color definitions non-portable.

The alternative X Color Management System recognizes several portable color definitions (or color spaces *(26.18)*), among them a format called TekHVC, designed by Tektronix. A TekHVC color space defines color using three characteristics, known as *hue*, *value*, and *chroma*:

Hue
Generally speaking, the shade (e.g., red, blue, green).

Value
A range of the hue from light to dark. The lightest possible shade of any hue is white; the darkest is black.

Chroma
Also called *saturation*. The amount of the hue present (roughly speaking, the hue's intensity or vibrancy).

Like the red, green, and blue factors in an RGB definition, hue, value, and chroma are expressed in mathematical terms. The range of possible values for these three numbers are treated as coordinates for three axes, which together define a three-dimensional physical model, known as the HVC *color solid*.

Though the color solid results from pure mathematics, it is unfortunately not a simple, comforting symmetrical shape. On the contrary, it's disturbingly irregular. Though the HVC model is supposed to be intuitive, far denser books than this one have grappled with explaining it. Does that mean you can't understand it? Not at all. Does it mean you might prefer finger painting? Very possibly. But don't get discouraged. Let's look at a conceptual overview and see where we stand. Keep in mind, however, that you'll have a much better idea what the HVC color model is all about after you play with the *xtici* color editor *(26.17)*. *xtici* visually represents a slice of the HVC solid, which is known as a *hue leaf*, and lets you create colors by manipulating the hue, value, and chroma.

So, let's get down to the nitty-gritty. What does this phantasmagoric shape actually look like? And why should we care? Each of the defining characteristics (i.e., the hue, value, and chroma) provides one of the three dimensions. Technically speaking, each one defines an axis, with hue as the angle, chroma as the radius, and value the z-coordinate of a point. Clear as crystal, right? Figure 26-4 provides a visual aid. It shows a diagram of the TekHVC color solid, and a hue leaf, the cross section of the solid for a single hue.

If you spend some time working with *xtici*, you'll discover that hues near 0.0 are reds, hues near 60.0 are oranges and yellows, hues near 120.0 are greens, hues near 180.0 are blue-greens, hues near 240.0 are blues, and hues near 300.0 are violets. Because the hue coordinate is an angle, the reds near 0.0 "wrap around" to hues near 360.0.

For any given hue, the possible numbers for value and chroma define an approximately triangular area, the hue leaf. The hue leaf represents all the possibilities for the given hue, if you vary the chroma and value. For example, for the red hues around 10.0, colors with chromas near 0.0 are almost grey, and as the chroma increases, the range of possible values decreases, and the colors redden, passing through various reddish-brown shades, until around the maximum chroma (near 90.0) there are only a few possible values (near 50.0), and the colors are all bright red. At the same hue of 10.0, a chroma of 55.0 and the minimum possible value (near 30.0), the color is a deep maroon; it lightens as the value increases until at the maximum value (near 65.0) it is a salmon pink.

Any color that is visible to the human eye can be described by three coordinates in a device-independent color space such as this one. (Article 26.14 more clearly describes the relationship between the HVC color solid and

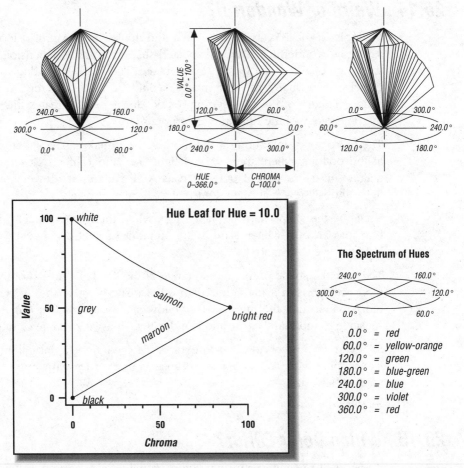

Figure 26-4: Three views of the TekHVC color solid and a single hue leaf from the solid

human vision.) But no given device can display all possible colors. This is, after all, the real world. Stated in another way, all colors visible to the human eye lie within the TekHVC color solid, but the colors that can be generated by any particular device lie within some subset of that solid. Thus, each monitor type has a *device gamut*—the set of colors it can display.

So, what happens if you request a color that is outside of the gamut for a monitor? Some form of *gamut compression* is used to map the requested color into a displayable color in a sensible way.

—VQ, AN

26.14 Weird or Wonderful?

Val looks at the HVC color solid *(26.13)* and thinks "how weird!" I look at it and say "how wonderful!" This unexpected shape is a three-dimensional graph of the range of colors the human eye can see. The shape for a dog's vision, or a camel's, or a snail's for that matter, would be quite different. It isn't some strange feature of the HVC system, or of *xtici* *(26.17)* that creates this shape, but the physiology of the human eye and brain.

The more you think about it, the more sense it makes. The shape is narrower at the bottom, where there is less light (i.e., the value is closer to 0). That makes sense in terms of our vision as well: we can see fewer colors at twilight, and still fewer at night. ("At night, all cats are black.")

Similarly, the shape narrows at the top, when there is too much light. Colors blur into an ever-whiter glare as the amount of light approaches the threshhold the eye can stand.

The irregular shape of the middle range of the solid is a revelation: we can see more variations in some colors than others. The fact that the hue leaf *(26.13)* for red is wider than the hue leaf for yellow simply means that our eye is more sensitive to red than yellow and can distinguish a wider range of saturation.

So, even if you feel no need to explore device-independent color, you might like to play with *xtici* *(26.17)* just because you want to learn more about how your eyes work!

—TOR

26.15 Which Color Editor?

If you want to create your own colors, you'll need to get hold of a color editing program. The two most popular user-contributed color editors are *xcoloredit* *(26.16)* and *xtici* *(26.17)*, which are just about as different as they could be.

xcoloredit is fun and easy to use, almost like a primary paint set. *xtici* is based on an extremely unintuitive color model. So you'd think the choice was obvious. Why make things complicated for yourself? Just use *xcoloredit* and have a good time. That's what I do.

The problem is that the friendly *xcoloredit* outputs an RGB color specification, which is not portable (i.e., the color will look somewhat different on different monitors). The more powerful and versatile *xtici* outputs values in several different formats, including some portable ones. Since most people work on the same monitor all the time, portability won't be an issue.

Users who are very serious about the technology of color will tackle *xtici*, regardless of the level of difficulty. If you'd like portable color definitions but don't want to work too hard, it is possible to coordinate *xcoloredit* and *xtici* in a rough way. You can use *xcoloredit* for the actual editing and then use *xtici* to convert *xcoloredit*'s results to a portable format. See Article 26.19 for this shifty workaround. Now, let's forget about formats and mix some colors.

— VQ

26.16 *Finger Painting for Nerds: xcoloredit*

xcoloredit

If you can deal with the minor limitation of having non-portable output *(26.15)*, try the *xcoloredit* program. *xcoloredit* lets you mix colors as easily as a kid mixes finger paints. Actually, using *xcoloredit* isn't quite as much fun as finger painting, but it is neater and it does let you remove color after you've added it. Once you've come up with a color you like, there are a bunch of ways to use it.

xcoloredit has a very intuitive interface. If you can remember sitting at a little desk and mixing red and blue to make purple, you should have no problem: *xcoloredit* works on the same principle. You can mix red, green, and blue to make a color that is displayed in the large central square. (I call this the mixing area, for lack of a name, better or otherwise.) Initially, the mixing area is black and displays some sample text, as in Figure 26-5.

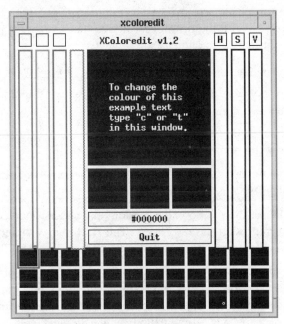

Figure 26-5: Initial xcoloredit window

Below the mixing area are three smaller squares, which will show you how much red, green, and blue you add. The red square is on the left, green in the middle, and blue on the right. To begin with, these three squares are also black.

Below the mixing area and the three component squares are 36 much smaller squares called color cells. The color cells allow you to save up to 36 colors (and their RGB values in hexadecimal notation *(26.11)*). More about this later. When you begin, all of the cells are black and the first cell (the upper-left one) is surrounded by a red dotted line.

To mix a new color in the large square (mixing area), you can use the three vertical bars on the left side of the window, which are outlined in red, green, and blue, respectively. These color sliders or scrollbars operate exactly like the Athena scrollbar (explained in Article 11.02). Though you can't tell immediately, each scrollbar has a "thumb" which can be dragged up from the base of the bar to add more of the color it represents.

To get an idea how this works, place the pointer at the base of the red scrollbar. When the thumb is accessible, the pointer changes to a vertical double-sided arrow. Press and hold down the second pointer button. The pointer again changes, this time to an arrow pointing right. Now drag the (pinkish) thumb toward the top of the scrollbar. As you drag up, you're in effect adding more and more red. As the thumb moves, notice that five other parts of the display are being constantly updated:

1. The mixing area is changing to reflect the amount of red you're selecting.

2. The red square beneath the mixing area also displays the amount of red you're selecting.

3. The hexadecimal window beneath the three color squares is being updated to show the numeric color value.

4. The dotted line surrounding the first color cell becomes a solid line. The color cell displays what is in the mixing area.

5. On the right side of the window, three additional sliders (labeled H, S, and V) move concurrent with the red slider. The H, S, and V sliders represent hue, saturation (also sometimes called chroma), and value. (See HVC in the Glossary.)

To mix a color, you'll probably want to play with the green and blue sliders as well. Note that if you also select green and/or blue, the mixing area and the first color cell display the new combination, while the smaller squares below the mixing area display the component colors in order to show you the amount of each color you're adding.

In Figure 26-6 I've mixed a color that reminds me of green "beach glass." (If you're landlocked, beach glass happens when the fragments of bottles and other bits of glass get worn smooth by the ocean.) Since these illustrations are black and white, I'm afraid this will take some imagination.

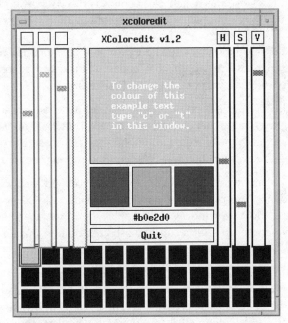

Figure 26-6: Well, it looks like beach glass to me

So, now we have a color. How do we use it? The key is the numerical definition in the hexadecimal window (beneath the three component squares). You can use this number on the command line or in a resource file the same way you'd supply a color name. Don't bother to type the number: *xcoloredit* provides an easy way to copy and paste. Just click the first pointer button in the hex window to copy (the hex window becomes reverse video to signal this); then paste the value into a terminal window by clicking the second pointer button.

For instance, after I click the first button on the hex window, I can type:

```
% xclock -bg
```

in an *xterm.* Then I click the second pointer button to paste the hex value for the new beach glass color (and add an ampersand to run the process in the background):

```
% xclock -bg #b0e2d0 &
```

This command line should create an *xclock* window with an elegant beach glass background. (Article 26.11 explains something about hexadecimal numbering and how it relates to RGB color definitions.)

We could also paste the hex value into a resource. The following line specifies that all *xclock* windows use the beach glass color as the background color.

```
XClock*Background: #b0e2d0
```

Once you've mixed one color, you can retain the image of that color in the first color cell and mix a second color that appears in the second cell. The hex values will also be saved so you can copy and paste them.

To begin, place the pointer on the second color cell (the one immediately to the right of the first) and click the first pointer button. The second cell becomes surrounded by a dotted outline; it also changes from displaying black to displaying the color in the first cell (and the mixing area).

Now you can begin mixing a second color, just as you did the first, by dragging the color sliders. The mixing area and the second color cell will display the new color, and the hex window will display its numeric value. For our second color we've come up with a sandy wash (remember: imagination) with the hex value #dfd5ab, as in Figure 26-7.

You can go back to the first color (display it in the mixing area) by placing the pointer on the first color cell and clicking the first button. All parts of the window go back to the state associated with the first color: the mixing area displays that color, the first color cell is outlined, the hex window displays its value (so you can copy and paste it), the sliders indicate the red, green, and blue components, etc.

To switch back to the second color, click on the second color cell. The display now reflects the second color.

If you want to use all of the color cells, you can actually mix and save 36 colors! Then you can browse through them by clicking on associated color cell. In effect, *xcoloredit* serves as a sort of color clipboard.

Moving on to the next color cell doesn't mean the previous one is frozen as it is. You can select any color cell and continue to edit it at any time. Or you can consider a cell to be static and move on to edit within another cell.

To quit the application, click the first pointer button on the **Quit** button, which is located just below the hex window.

—VQ

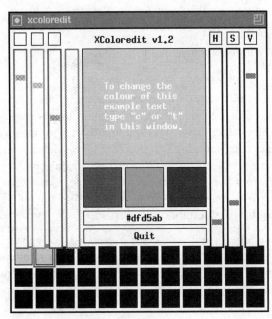

Figure 26-7: Mixing a second color

26.17 *An Editor with a Different Spectrum: xtici*

xtici

For many users, *xtici* (also known as the TekColor editor) will be somewhat unintuitive, but it offers a significant advantage over *xcoloredit*. It can provide color values in two of the Xcms portable color spaces *(26.18)* (as well as the non-portable RGB format).

You don't have to be a rocket scientist to use *xtici*. It's possible just to play with it and come up with some interesting colors. But using it intelligently requires understanding color in terms of a rather unusual model, one I at least have a lot of trouble visualizing. *xtici* interprets color in terms of three characteristics, called hue, value, and chroma. You create a color with *xtici* by manipulating these three factors.

Color defined according to these terms follows the so-called HVC color model *(26.13)*. Take a look at this article before proceeding. Since color model concepts can become fairly arcane, you might just want to check the definitions of hue, value, and chroma. Then come back and play with *xtici*.[*] The *xtici* program has an elaborate interface, complete with several menus. We'll just take a look at a few of the features you'll need to create your own colors. For more

---

[*] When mixing colors with *xcoloredit (26.16)*, you'll undoubtedly think in terms of red, green, and blue. However, the program does allow you to adjust the color based on hue, value, and chroma as well. Use the H, S, V sliders to the right of the mixing area.

information, see Tektronics' *TekColor Editor Reference Manual*, distributed with the *xtici* source code.

To run the program, simply enter:

```
% xtici &
```

Figure 26-8 shows a typical *xtici* window with some of the more significant features labeled. The color area shows an initial color, in this case the standard RGB color named sky blue. The boxes immediately to the right contain numeric values that correspond to this color. By default, the color is expressed as three numbers corresponding to hue, value, and chroma. This so-called TekHVC format (or color space) is portable. *xtici* also recognizes and can return values in another portable format, introduced by the prefix CIEuvY, as well as in the non-portable RGB format.

xtici allows you to change or edit this color in a variety of ways. Some of the editing methods involve dragging or clicking on graphical elements in the window, but you can also change the color in the color area by entering other numeric values in the boxes to the right. If you edit using the former style, the numeric values will change concurrently.

Because *xtici* provides many different ways to change the color in the color area, editing can be complicated. We'll show you some of the basic editing strategies in the next few sections, but regardless of the method you choose, you'll probably want to perform the following tasks:

1. Select a hue.

2. Adjust the value and chroma of the selected hue, if desired.

3. Select the numeric value of the color (using the Edit menu) in order to paste it on the command line, etc.

Choosing a Hue to Edit

When you first run *xtici*, the color in the color area will probably be a color that is currently being used elsewhere on the display. You can work from this initial hue—adjust its value (or lightness) and chroma (or intensity)—or select another hue and edit that. If you want to work from the hue in the color area (adjust its value and chroma), skip ahead to the section "Adjusting the Color with the Hue Leaf."

If you want to change the initial hue, first familiarize yourself with the so-called Colormap Scale area of the *xtici* window. Though it's difficult to tell in our black-and-white illustration, the hue in the color area also appears in the Colormap Scale area. The Colormap Scale area shows the current shade in relation to other shades in the spectrum.

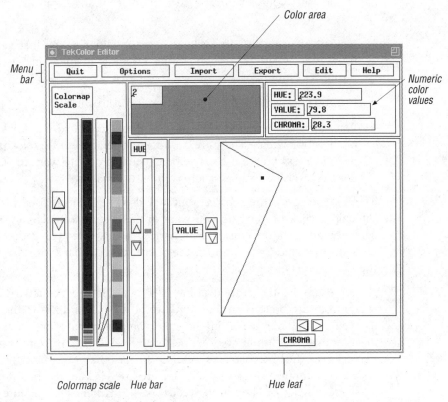

Figure 26-8: Initial xtici window

Notice the four parallel vertical bars. The first bar is a slider. (You can use the slider or the up and down arrows to its left to adjust the hue in the color area.) The second bar shows a spectrum of some of the possible colors.* The fourth vertical bar shows a magnification of part of the second bar— specifically, the shade that also appears in the color area and the shades that surround it in the colormap. (The third bar simply contains lines indicating what part of the second bar is being magnified in the fourth.)

If you want to change the initial hue, there are several ways to do it:

• Click the first pointer button on the color you want from either the second or fourth vertical bars in the Colormap Scale area.

• Click the first pointer button on either the up or down arrow (the slider in the first vertical bar echoes this motion). This action causes the color area to display the next shade above or below the current shade in the col- ormap. (If you press and hold down the pointer button, the motion is

---

* When you first run *xtici*, this second bar shows the colormap of the current screen— thus, the colors will be those the clients are using.

continuous; you can browse several adjacent shades in the colormap this way.)

- Instead of using the arrow keys, use the slider in the first vertical bar to browse adjacent shades. The slider operates in the same way the *xterm* scrollbar's "thumb" does.

- Use the hue bar. See the next section for instructions.

- Enter alternate numeric values in the three small text windows to the right of the color area. (These Text widgets operate as the xedit program *(9.03)* does.) Unless you're a color expert, you'll probably want to start with values from another source, such as the RGB database.

The first method is the simplest, but it is also the least precise. It's particularly difficult to click on the hue you want in the second vertical bar, which represents the adjacent hues using very narrow bands of color. It's much easier to click on the shade you want in the fourth vertical bar (with the liability that the spectrum is more limited).

In our example, the current color (sky blue) is represented by the second shade from the bottom on the fourth vertical bar. The lines in the third bar—as well as the number 2 in the color area—indicate this fact. (Though it appears that the current color is the third block from the bottom of the fourth vertical bar, the first block is actually blank—not a part of the colormap.) Let's select another color for the color area by clicking the first pointer button 12 shades higher on the fourth vertical bar (a darker blue). Figure 26-9 shows the resulting *xtici* window.

Notice that the number in the color area has been changed to 14, to indicate the fourteenth shade in the colormap. The slider in the first vertical bar has also moved. The numbers for hue, value, and chroma reflect the new shade. The other major change in the *xtici* window is the appearance of the hue leaf, which is discussed later on.

Changing the Hue with the Hue Bar

The hue bar allows you to view the hues the Colormap Scale offers in a wider spectrum of lightness and intensity—and to choose one of these shades to edit. The hue bar area contains arrow keys, a vertical bar with a slider, and the actual hue bar itself. When you first run *xtici*, the hue bar is blank. To fill the bar:

- Display the Options menu by clicking the first pointer button on the menu command box.

- Click on the Fill Hue Bar item.

The hue bar will display a range of hues. (A shorter representation of the same spectrum will also be added to the second vertical bar in the Colormap Scale area.) You can select one of the hues in the bar to edit in the color area in several ways:

- Click the first pointer button on the color you want in the hue bar.

- Click the first pointer button on either the up or down arrow (the slider echoes this motion). This action causes the color area to display the next shade above or below the current shade in the bar. (Press and hold down the pointer button to browse several shades.)

- Use the slider in the vertical bar to the right of the arrows to select a hue.

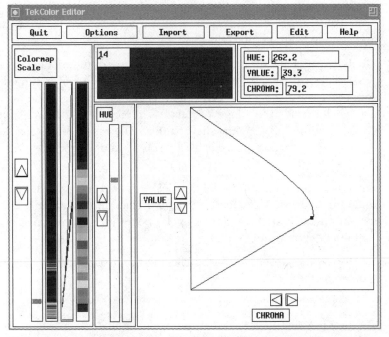

Figure 26-9: Changing the hue by clicking in the Colormap Scale area

Note that you don't have to fill the hue bar in order to adjust the hue using any of these methods. (You can even click on the blank hue bar, though this "blind" method is not particularly desirable.) The color area and the numeric values will be updated to match the shade you choose regardless.

If you select a hue by any of the mechanisms in the hue bar, you can then adjust the color using the hue leaf or by the less intuitive method of changing the numeric values.

If you fill the hue bar and then try to select a hue from the Colormap Scale area, there may occasionally be minor problems allocating color cells for the *xtici* application. In such cases, a dialog box will request your input. See the section "Problems Allocating Color Cells" for more information.

Adjusting the Color with the Hue Leaf

The hue leaf is intended to represent all possible variations of the current hue—a dramatic range. A hue can vary in value (lightness to darkness) and in chroma (the amount of the hue present; also known as saturation or intensity). The lightest possible shade of any hue is white; the darkest is black. (That is, the spectrum of possible values always spans white to black.) The range of chroma or saturation is more reliant on the actual hue. For example, in most cases, a red hue can exist in a wider range of intensities than a yellow hue. (This is a feature of human vision *(26.14)* , not *xtici*. You can adjust the value and chroma from the hue leaf.

The hue leaf is always triangular, but the shape of the triangle depends on the possibilities of varying the hue. The triangular hue leaf is turned on its side, so that the base is actually vertical—flush against the left side of the box containing the leaf. The range of value is represented along this vertical edge (white is at the top; black at the bottom). The range of chroma (saturation) is represented horizontally, with least to most saturation appearing from left to right.

When you first run *xtici*, the hue leaf appears blank and contains a small square dot cursor. This cursor marks the place in the leaf that corresponds to the current version of the hue. To get a better idea of the range of possibilities for the hue, you can fill the leaf:

1. Display the **Options** menu by clicking the first pointer button on the menu command box.

2. Click on the **Fill Leaf** item.

The hue leaf will display the range of possibilities for the current hue. Variations between shades create a sort of striped or checkerboard pattern.

The hue leaf allows you to fine tune the hue in question. Notice the arrow keys beside the Value and Chroma labels bordering the leaf. You can adjust the value and chroma by clicking on these arrows. For example, you would click on the up arrow next to Value to make the hue lighter (white is at the top of the value range). The dot cursor will move up within the leaf and the color area and numeric values will be updated to reflect the changes.

Click on the right arrow next to Chroma to get a more intense hue. The dot cursor will move to the right within the leaf and the color area and numeric values will be updated to reflect the changes.

As an alternative to using the arrow keys, you can use the pointer to move the square dot within the leaf. Either click on the shade you want within the leaf or hold down the pointer on the dot and drag it within the leaf.

As is the case with the hue bar, you don't have to fill the hue leaf to adjust the color using any of these methods. The color area and the numeric values will be updated regardless.

If you fill the hue leaf and then try to select a hue from the Colormap Scale area, *xtici* may have trouble allocating color cells and a dialog box with be displayed. See "Problems Allocating Color Cells" for more information.

Selecting and Pasting the Numeric Color Value

Once you have the color you want in the color area, you can select the numeric description of that color to paste on the command line, in a resource file, in a color database file, etc. To select the color value:

1. Display the **Edit** menu by clicking the first pointer button on the menu command box.

2. Select the **Copy Color** submenu.

3. Click on the format (color space) you want. The **TekHVC** and **CIE u'v'Y** items select portable color values; the **RGB** item selects the non-portable RGB color format.

TekHVC is a good choice. You can then paste the color value using whatever paste command is appropriate to your terminal emulator. I'm using *xterm*, so I click the second pointer button. For example, I can enter:

```
% xbiff -fg
```

and then click the second button to specify the color (adding an ampersand to run the process in the background):

```
% xbiff -fg TekHVC:223.93036/72.45283/29.67013 &
```

On my display, this color value produces a deeper version of the sky blue from the original example. If you intend to use a color repeatedly, it's a good idea to pair the numeric value with a name in an Xcms database *(26.23)*.

Note that *xtici* handles RGB values in an unusual way. The window displays RGB values in decimal notation; however, if you select **RGB** from the **Edit** menu, the output is in hexadecimal notation! This can be a bit confusing, particularly if you want to place RGB values in an RGB or Xcms database. An RGB database requires decimal values; an Xcms database recognizes RGB values (among others), but they must be in hexadecimal notation. If you have the decimal numbers to input to *xtici*, the editor can, in effect, perform the conversion to hex; or you can use the UNIX *bc*(1) utility to convert numbers from one notation to another. See Article 26.19 for instructions on using *bc*.

Working with the Numeric Color Values

When you change a color using one of *xtici's* graphic elements, the numeric values corresponding to the color are updated dynamically. However, you can also interact with *xtici* by entering numeric values yourself.

Thus far we've only seen the default Hue, Value, and Chroma number displays. (These provide a number in the portable TekHVC color space.) But *xtici* can interpret and output in two additional color spaces: the portable CIE u'v'Y format and the non-portable RGB format. To display the specification for the current color in any of these formats:

1. Display the **Options** menu by clicking the first pointer button on the menu command button.

2. Select the **Coordinates** submenu.

3. The two menu items, **RGB** and **CIE u'v'Y**, are toggles between the color space named and the default TekHVC color space. Thus, selecting **RGB** once toggles the decimal values for RED, GREEN, and BLUE. Selecting RGB a second time recalls the TekHVC values. Click on the format (color space) you want.

Let's consider a couple of ways you might work with *xtici* using numbers. Keep in mind that all of the numeric values are contained in small text windows which respond to the same commands as xedit *(9.03)*.

Suppose you want to edit a color from the standard RGB database. To place that color in the *xtici* color area:

1. Check the RGB decimal values in *rgb.txt*.

2. Using the **Coordinates** submenu of the **Options** menu, toggle the **RGB** numeric values.

3. Place the values from *rgb.txt* in the RED, GREEN, and BLUE text windows to the right of the color area.

As soon as you move the pointer out of the text window area, a dialog box will prompt:

```
Apply last keyboard input?
```

If you've entered the correct figures, select **OK** and the color area will be updated; otherwise, **Cancel** and continue editing.

As another example, say you've created a color using another editor, such as *xcoloredit*, that outputs values in the non-portable RGB format. If you enter the decimal versions of these values in the *xtici* window (as described in the previous example), *xtici* provides the portable color space equivalents.

Problems Allocating Color Cells

Because of the nature of colormaps *(26.07)* and the way color cells are allocated, certain problems may arise in working with *xtici*. One is a simple, albeit confusing "technicolor" effect. Depending on where the input focus is, applications may appear to swap colors and the shade in the *xtici* color area may not appear accurate. You're liable to get a more precise picture when the *xtici* window has the input focus, however.

Another potential problem: you may not be able to select a color in one area of the *xtici* window if it is being used in another area. If such a conflict arises, a dialog box will inform you. For example, say you select a color in the Colormap Scale area that is also being used in the hue bar, you may get a dialog to the effect that:

```
This color cell is used to fill the hue bar.
Hues will be removed to edit this cell.
```

The box provides the possible responses **OK** and **Cancel**. The safest course of action is to click on **Cancel** and then try to select the hue by another method. Clicking on the shade you want in the hue bar should work; or you might turn the hue bar off (the menu item is a toggle) and try to select the color by dragging the hue bar slider; or you could enter the appropriate numeric values, etc.

If you click on **OK**, the hue bar (and possibly the leaf and part of the Colormap Scale area) will be blanked out and the colors *xtici* is displaying will be changed. In such a case, try clicking on any visible color in the Colormap Scale area to begin editing again.

A similar conflict can arise if you select a hue in the Colormap Scale area that is also being used in the hue leaf:

```
This color cell is used to fill the leaf.
Fill will be removed to edit this cell.
```

Again, it's a good idea to click on **Cancel** and then try to select the hue by another method. Clicking on the shade you want on the hue bar or leaf should work; or you might turn either or both the bar and leaf off (the menu items are toggles) and try to select the color by another method.

Selecting **OK** will blank out the leaf (and possibly the bar and part of the Colormap Scale area) and change the colors the *xtici* window is displaying. Again, try clicking on any visible color in the Colormap Scale area.

Various other colormap conflicts can arise. Use the dialog boxes and your own experience for guidance.

— *VQ*

26.18 Using the Xcms Color Spaces

The X Color Management System recognizes color specifications in many different formats called *color spaces*, most of which describe color in a device-independent manner. Xcms also recognizes RGB decimal values *(26.10)*, though these remain device-specific. You can supply the Xcms color spaces on the command line and in resource files. You can also create a custom color database *(26.23)*.

Under Xcms, each color specification has a prefix (some shorthand for the color space) and a numeric value. Table 26-1 summarizes the valid color spaces and their prefixes.

Table 26-1: Xcms Color Spaces

Name	Prefix
Tektronix HVC	TekHVC
Various CIE formats	CIEXYZ, CIEuvY, CIExyY, CIELab, CIELuv
RGB	RGB
RGB Intensity	RGBi

Tektronix is the developer of the X Color Management System. The initials HVC refer to hue, value, and chroma, three characteristics of color (which are defined mathematically). CIE stands for *Commission Internationale de l'Eclairage* or *International Commission on Illumination*, an international standards organization.

Of the valid color spaces, all but the RGB formats specify color in a portable (i.e., device-independent) manner. Xcms recognizes RGB specifications for compatibility with the older RGB color model.

When you create a shade with a color editor, such as *xcoloredit* or *xtici*, the program supplies you with a numeric color value in one or sometimes multiple formats. To specify the color under Xcms, you combine the numeric value with the appropriate prefix for the color space/format. The syntax is:

```
prefix:value1/value2/value3
```

The following are sample Xcms color specifications:

```
CIEuvY:0.15259/0.40507/0.44336
TekHVC:223.93036/72.45283/29.67013
RGB:6a/bb/d8
```

These three sample values were derived from *xtici* (being run on a Sun 3/60 workstation); the values all define the deeper version of sky blue from Article 26.17, each using a different notation. Keep in mind that the RGB value is specific to the monitor used, while the TekHVC and CIEuvY values are portable.

I can supply *any* of these color spaces on my Sun 3/60 and get the same color. Thus, the following command lines should produce identical *xbiff* windows:

```
xbiff -fg CIEuvY:0.15259/0.40507/0.44336 &
xbiff -fg TekHVC:223.93036/72.45283/29.67013 &
xbiff -fg RGB:6a/bb/d8 &
```

(Note that the Xcms color spaces are case insensitive. Thus, rgb:6a/bb/d8 and RGB:6A/BB/D8 are equivalent.) If we want to display this shade of blue on another monitor, we would have to use either of the portable specifications:

```
CIEuvY:0.15259/0.40507/0.44336 &
TekHVC:223.93036/72.45283/29.67013 &
```

You can also use any valid color space as the value of a resource variable:

```
xbiff*foreground: TekHVC:223.93036/72.45283/29.67013
```

It's handy to be able to plug these numbers into a command line or resource specification, but if you want to use your own colors on a regular basis, it's a good idea to pair them with names in your own Xcms database. First read a bit more about Xcms later in this chapter. Then see "Creating an Xcms Color Database" for instructions.

— VQ

26.19 *Converting an RGB Color Definition to a Portable Format*

I like to use *xcoloredit* because it's fun and easy and because I'm basically childlike at heart. (Come on, I bet you like toys too.) The (somewhat minor) downside of *xcoloredit* is that it produces RGB color definitions, which aren't portable.

Well, I prefer to have portable definitions, so I cheat. First, I use *xcoloredit* to mix colors. Then I let the more versatile (and much less fun) *xtici* color editor convert the values to a portable syntax. Here's an example.

I play with *xcoloredit* and I come up with a color I really like, which reminds me of beach glass. (The exciting details of this discovery appear in Article 26.16.) *xcoloredit* outputs the hex RGB value of #b0e2d0.

The biggest cheat I can possibly pull here is to set the root window color to this value:

```
% xsetroot -solid #b0e2d0
```

Then simply run *xtici*. The initial color *xtici* displays should be the dominant one in your local color map, so it should pick up my beach glass color automatically, as it does in Figure 26-10.

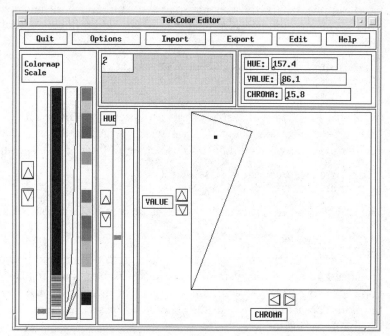

Figure 26-10: xtici automatically displays root window color

Notice the numeric values corresponding to hue, value, and chroma. These numbers represent a portable definition of the color. To output this definition in the correct syntax or color space, I click on *xtici*'s **Edit** menu button. Then I click on the **Copy Color —>** menu item. Finally, I click on the **TekHVC** item on the color submenu. The correct color space is copied into global memory; I can now paste it using whatever pointer button command my terminal emulator recognizes. In this case, I'm using *xterm* and I click the second pointer button to paste the color value saved in memory:

```
TekHVC:157.38392/86.05422/15.80653
```

This should be all I need to do. I can supply this color space on the command line, in a resource file, or pair it with a name in an Xcms database *(26.23)*. The color should look the same on any screen.

If this strategy doesn't work, converting an RGB value to a portable format becomes a bit more complicated. Rather than letting *xtici* do all the work, you have to manually supply *xcoloredit*'s numeric output to *xtici*. This is a pain in and of itself. But further difficulties arise because *xcoloredit*'s RGB output is in hexadecimal notation, but *xtici* expects regular old decimal input.

So, I need to convert the hex value (base 16) to a decimal value (base 10). Article 26.20 describes how to perform this conversion is with the UNIX *bc*(1) program.

Once I have a decimal definition for the RGB color, I can enter those numbers in the *xtici* window. First, I click on the **Options** menu button. Then I select the **Coordinates ->** submenu and choose **RGB**.

Until now, whatever color is in the *xtici* window has been represented by statistics for hue, value, and chroma. Once I select **RGB**, the numeric definition is switched to the RGB version, i.e., the red, green, and blue components replace hue, value, and chroma.

If I edit these numbers, the *xtici* window will display the color indicated. Notice the caret cursor in each of the numeric display windows. Click the pointer after the number to move the cursor there. Then backspace over the number and enter the one you want. I enter 176, 226, and 208, the decimal RGB specs for my beach glass color.

When you then move the pointer out of the numeric windows, *xtici* will pop up a dialog box asking if you want to:

```
Apply last keyboard input?
```

Once you've changed all the numbers as you want, click on **OK**. (Before then, click on **Cancel**.) The *xtici* window will display the color you want.

Now to get an equivalent portable definition (phew!), switch back to displaying the hue, value, and chroma. (Select the **Options** menu, the **Coordinates ->** submenu, and pick the **RGB** item again, which toggles back to the HVC values.) That was easy, huh? It's actually a lot simpler in practice. Give it a try if the first method fails.

—*VQ*

26.20 *Converting Hex Numbers to Decimal*

Article 26.19 describes how to convert the non-portable color definition exported by *xcoloredit* (in hex) to a portable format by supplying the output to the *xtici* program. This situation may require you to convert the hex value (base 16) *xcoloredit* understands to a decimal value (base 10) that *xtici* can interpret. So, how do we do that?

An easy way to perform this conversion is with the UNIX *bc* (1) program.

- Enter *bc* and press **Return**.

```
% bc
```

- Now enter the commands to do the conversion. Set the base of input to 16 (hex); *bc*'s output defaults to base 10, i.e., decimal.

```
ibase=16
```

- Then enter the hex numbers to convert, separated by semicolons; the letters in the hex values must be in uppercase.

  `B0;E2;D0`

  When you press **Return**, *bc* gives the decimal values for the three color components (RGB):

  ```
  176
  226
  208
  ```

- Type **CTRL-D** to quit *bc*.

— VQ

26.21 *Changing the Standard RGB Color Database*

If you come up with your own colors using *xcoloredit* or *xtici*, you can make them available to all users on the system by pairing them with names and adding them to the standard database of RGB colors. (Of course, these definitions are non-portable.)

In order to change the database, you need write permission for the *rgb* source files (located in *mit/rgb* in the source tree) and for the directory where the database will live, generally */usr/lib/X11*. If you want to use portable definitions, create an Xcms database *(26.23)* in */usr/lib/X11* instead. (If you don't have write permission for that directory, you can still create a private Xcms database for yourself.)

Each color in the RGB database has a name and a three-component numeric value, in decimal form. If you've used *xtici* to come up with a color, you can select RGB output in the necessary decimal form.

The simpler *xcoloredit* program outputs an RGB value in hexadecimal notation. You must convert the numbers to decimal before adding the color to the *rgb.txt* file. An easy way to perform this conversion is with the UNIX *bc* (1) program, as described in Article 26.19.

Once you have the decimal values for red, green, and blue, you pair them with a color name and add the color definition to the *rgb.txt* source file. The format of a line in the *rgb.txt* file is:

```
red green blue    color_name
```

where *red*, *green*, and *blue* are integers in the range 0 to 255; the *color_name* is case insensitive but must not include any special characters or symbols. There must be a tab separating the values from the name.

If the color name is composed of two or more words, the color should have two entries, one as multiple words and one as a single word. For example:

```
124 252   0     lawn green
124 252   0     LawnGreen
```

These entries allow you to use either a one- or two-word color name on the command line or in a resource file. When you use multiple words, they must be surrounded by double quotes.

To update the RGB database, use the following steps:

1. Edit the *rgb.txt* source file to add the new color specification(s) (or change existing ones). The new line(s) can go anywhere in the file. For example, if you want to add a color called tropical blue, you'll need the entries:

    ```
    9 229 251     tropical blue
    9 229 251     TropicalBlue
    ```

    If you used a one-word name, a single line would do:

    ```
    9 229 251     caribbean
    ```

2. Run the *rgb* program using the makefile also located in the *mit/rgb* directory. This program converts the text file (*rgb.txt*) to the UNIX *dbm*(1) format files (*rgb.dir* and *rgb.pag*), which are the files actually used as the color database. Just type:

    ```
    % make
    rm -f rgb.pag rgb.dir
    ./rgb rgb < rgb.txt
    ```

3. Then install the new files in */usr/lib/X11* by typing:

    ```
    % make install
    install -c -m 0644 rgb.txt /usr/lib/X11
    install -c -m 0644 rgb.dir /usr/lib/X11
    install -c -m 0644 rgb.pag /usr/lib/X11
    install -c -s showrgb /usr/lib/X11
    install in ./rgb done
    ```

Any colors you've added (or edited) should now be available by name.

—*VQ*

26.22 *Fixing a Corrupted RGB Database*

If the color name database gets corrupted in some way (e.g., written to accidentally), the server may not be able to find any colors with which to display. On a monochrome display, you may get error messages similar to those in the following list.

```
X Toolkit Warning:  Cannot allocate colormap entry for White
X Toolkit Warning:  Cannot allocate colormap entry for Black
X Toolkit Warning:  Cannot allocate colormap entry for white
X Toolkit Warning:  Cannot allocate colormap entry for black
```

If you get errors of this sort, perform steps 2 and 3 in the procedure described in Article 26.21. This will overwrite the corrupted *rgb* database files.

—VQ

26.23 *Creating an Xcms Color Database*

If you mix your own colors using a color editor and would like to use them multiple times, it's a good idea to pair the numeric definitions with names and put them in a database. (An Xcms dataase supplements the standard database of RGB colors, which remain available.) Then you can access your own colors simply by using the names.

Setting up an Xcms database is easy. The format of the database file is:

```
XCMS_COLORDB_START 0.1
color_name<tab>color_space
          .
          .
          .
XCMS_COLORDB_END
```

The first and last lines are literal. Don't forget the 0.1 at the end of the first line; it's important. Between the first and last lines you can put any number of color definitions. The text name goes in the first column, followed by a tab (this is also important), and then a valid color space *(26.18)*.

By default, Xcms expects the database file to be named *Xcms.txt*. Here is a sample *Xcms.txt* file:

```
XCMS_COLORDB_START 0.1
beach glass     TekHVC:158.2/86.0/15.6
cobalt   TekHVC:238.3/68.3/30.6
mustard         CIEuvY:0.227/0.538/0.608
orchid   TekHVC:315.8/83.8/24.5
sahara   TekHVC:77.9/84.8/22.7
tropical blue   CIEuvY:0.140/0.412/0.615
XCMS_COLORDB_END
```

The color names are case insensitive (for example, cobalt, Cobalt, COBALT, and CObaLT are equivalent).

In our sample database, we've used all portable color specifications, but you can include RGB color spaces as well. (Of course, the RGB specifications will be subject to hardware differences.)

An Xcms database file requires no compilation; you can begin to use the color names immediately. But where do you put the database and how do you let the server know that it exists?

The answer depends on whether you want the colors to be available systemwide, and whether you have the necessary permissions to do this. The server automatically looks for *Xcms.txt* in the directory */usr/lib/X11*. So, if you have write permission for that directory, and you place the file there, you're all set. All other users on the system will also be able to access the colors.

If you don't have write permission for */usr/lib/X11* or you would prefer to make the database private, you can specify an alternative file by setting the XCMSDB environment variable. The XCMSDB variable enables every user to have a private database. Note, however, that the server will check only *one* Xcms database. So, if someone creates a systemwide database file (*/usr/lib/X11/Xcms.txt*), and then an individual user sets XCMSDB to another file, the server will not check the systemwide file. (In other words, you cannot specify your own private colors and also take advantage of systemwide Xcms definitions.)

You can call your private Xcms database any name you like; then set the XCMSDB environment variable to the full pathname of the file. For example, say you create some colors you like to use in your normal X session (for the root window, window titlebars, etc.). You might put these into an Xcms file called *.xcolors*. Then specify:

```
% setenv XCMSDB ~/.xcolors
```

If you're going to be logging on to the same machine consistently, you can put this line in your startup script *(16.01)*. Of course, you can set XCMSDB to another file any time you like.

Once *Xcms.txt* is set up, you can immediately specify any of the color names it contains:

```
% xsetroot -solid beachglass &
```

Multiple word color names must be specified as a single word or be surrounded by quotes.

—VQ

26.24 *Fine Tuning Xcms for Specific Displays*

The X Color Management System provides for display-specific fine tuning in the form of a *Device Color Characterization* (DCC) file (also known as a *Device Profile*). The data provided in this file should be specific to the manufacturer, model, size, and screen type of your color monitor. For most users, this fine tuning will be unnecessary. You would probably need two adjacent monitors to perceive the fine adjustments DCC can provide. However, an application developer might choose to install a DCC file.

The DCC data is stored in properties on the screen's root window. Some servers are able to automatically load the properties with data appropriate to the attached display(s). For servers that are built from MIT source, you will probably have to load the DCC data by hand. The *xcmsdb* client that comes with the MIT source distribution will load the DCC data from a text file you specify.

There are two sample DCC files in the directory *mit/clients/xcmsdb/datafiles*, for two types of Tektronix monitors. If you have the MIT X11R5 user-contributed source code available, the directory *contrib/clients/xcrtca/monitors* contains additional DCC files for many commercially available displays:

```
Apollo19.dcc    NWP-513.dcc     Sparc2-19.dcc   VR290.dcc       VR299.dcc
Apple13.dcc     SGI-PI19.dcc    Sun3-60.dcc     VR297-0.dcc
HP98782A.dcc    Sparc1-19.dcc   Trini19.dcc     VR297-1.dcc
```

In addition to these DCC files, the directory contains files with *.ca100* extensions. These files represent an intermediary step between raw color data and the actual DCC files.

The top portion of a DCC file (following some comments) gives a description of the monitor. The following lines appear in the file *Sparc1-19.dcc*:

```
SCREENDATA_BEGIN        0.3

    NAME                Sun SPARCstation 1 19" color monitor
    PART_NUMBER         3
    MODEL               Hitachi HM-4119-S-AA-0, July 1989
    SCREEN_CLASS        VIDEO_RGB
    REVISION            2.0

                .
                .
                .
```

The remainder of the file provides data about the monitor's color capabilities. This data is loaded into the root window properties and then plugged into Xcms functions, allowing each device-independent color value to be converted into a device-specific value. You load a DCC file using the program *xcmsdb*. For example, if you have a Hitachi 19-inch color monitor on your Sun SPARCstation 1, you would use the command:

```
% xcmsdb Sparc1-19.dcc
```

If you need this type of color correction, you would probably load the DCC file in your startup script *(16.01)*.

—*VQ, adapted from the* X Window System User's Guide

Part Seven

System Administration

This part of the book is geared toward administrators. However, many non-administrators may also get a lot out of it. We have a chapter on programs for monitoring the system which is useful not only to administrators, but also to all those people who like to be the first to tell administrators bad news. We talk about some programs you can use in shell scripts, and about the current darling of the X community, Tcl/Tk. We also include more information than anyone wants to know about the X Display Manager, *xdm*.

Finally, this part of the book includes a chapter about installing programs from the CD-ROM.

—LM

27

Tools for Administrators

27.01 Administrative Front-ends

This chapter is about general tools that may help to make the administrator's life easier. Not all of these tools are strictly for administrators; most of them may be useful to unprivileged users as well. But administrators are the ones most likely to be interested.

We include programs for watching the system load *(27.03, 27.04)*, for monitoring disk space *(27.05)*, managing processes *(27.07)*, etc. We also snuck in a few articles about procedures that administrators often end up doing: configuring a workstation to use multiple framebuffers *(27.11)*, etc.

—LM

27.02 Console Messages

The *console* is a special device to which many UNIX system messages are written. In UNIXland, the console is the terminal addressed as */dev/console*; for a workstation running X, however, */dev/console* often has an X server running on it, so console messages become more of a distraction than anything else. Unless they are suppressed or diverted, the console messages strew across the workstation's display, disrupting windows and requiring the user to refresh the display on a regular basis.

Rather than leave you to clean up screen garbage after it happens (using the *xrefresh* client *(6.13)*, for example), X provides two ways to divert console messages. You can either run the *xconsole* client; or run *xterm* with the *−C* option. The only requirement is that the user needs to own */dev/console* (i.e., be logged in on the console).

xterm −C gives you an *xterm* window that receives console messages. Many users choose to use this window as their login window *(21.12)* and keep it iconified. The *−C* option is not supported on all systems.

xconsole just displays a window with console messages, as shown in Figure 27-1.

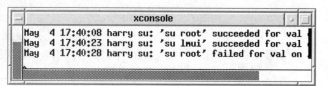

Figure 27-1: Getting console messages on an xconsole window

Scrollbars let you move up and down, or right and left. There are a few command-line options, e.g., *–daemon* (to place itself in the background), *–exitOn-Fail* (so if it can't grab the console, it exits right away), and *–verbose* (for line at the top giving an "informative message").

When you iconify *xconsole*, any new messages will result in an asterisk (*) being appended to the name of the client. (This doesn't always work, e.g., it doesn't work if you're using an Icon Box *(13.11)* under *mwm*). You can turn off this feature using the *–nonotify* command-line option.

—LM

27.03 Seeing the System Load: xload

Administrators and users alike may find use for the *xload* client. *xload* shows you the system load average, as shown in Figure 27-2.

Figure 27-2: The load average for a machine named ruby

xload

Every 10 seconds, *xload* queries the system for the load average and draws a new spike. You can use this to gauge whether this would be a good time to start that giant build, or whether it's a good time to go for lunch.

There are a few command-line options for *xload*. The *–update* option can be used to change how often to poll the system. The default is 10 seconds, but I think this is a little too often; I use 60 seconds instead:

```
% xload -update 60 &
```

You can use the *–label* command-line option to change the string that *xload* shows above the system load (usually this is set to the hostname). *–nolabel* says to use no string.

When the lines reach the right edge of the window, *xload* generally shifts over half the width of the window. You can set *xload* to shift a certain number of pixels using the *–jumpscroll* option. (A value of 1 results in "smooth" scrolling.)

Horizontal lines (tick marks) appear on the graph, each representing one load average point. You can change the scale using the *–scale* command-line option. For example, for each line to represent two load average points, use *–scale 2*.

Here's the most interesting command-line option. The *–lights* option suppresses the *xload* window, and instead uses the keyboard LEDs to show the current load average. I think this is Very Weird, but someone must have thought it was a good idea, so maybe I'm missing something.

—LM

27.04 *xload Across Machines*

System administrators often want to monitor system load on more than one machine at once. They might just run remote *xload (27.03)* clients from each of the machines, but an alternative might be to use the *xnetload* program.

xnetload

xnetload is a program for monitoring the loads on several machines at once. When starting *xnetload* on the command line, just list the names of whatever remote machines you want to monitor in addition to the current host. (The current host, i.e., the host on which the *xnetload* client is running, is reported by default. In my case, my workstation's name is *opal*.)

```
% xnetload ruby rock &
```

The initial window is mostly blank with just the system names on top, but after a few minutes you'll see a window similar to Figure 27-3.

For determining the system load for the local machine, *xnetload* needs to belong to group *kmem*, like *xload*. If you can't install *xnetload* under group *kmem* (i.e., if you are an unprivileged user), you should start *xnetload* with the *–nolocal* command-line option, or it will crash and burn.

—LM

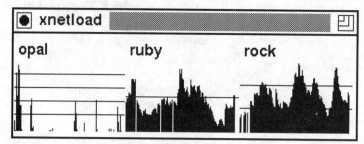

Figure 27-3: Multiple system loads

27.05 Monitoring File Systems

xfsm

If we made a list of a UNIX system administrator's least favorite sentences, "No space left on device" would certainly be included. *xfsm* is a client for monitoring file systems.

So what's the idea here? Just start *xfsm* and you'll see a display of each of the file systems mounted on your machine. Figure 27-4 shows what it looks like right now on our system.

For each file system, you'll see a horizontal bar that's partially shaded. The entire length of the bar vaguely reflects the size of the file system in proportion to the others. The shaded part of each bar shows how much of the disk space is currently in use. The percentage at the right also reflects disk space usage.

xfsm automatically updates this information for you. By default, it updates every 60 seconds, but you can specify another interval using the *-i* command-line option.

This is pretty useful on its own, but *xfsm* also includes a few other bells and whistles. You can use the *-w* command-line option to tell *xfsm* to warn you when a file system is above a certain percentage of use. Usually it just warns you by placing an exclamation point next to the percentage, but if you also use the *-e* option, then it also gives you a beep every time the display is updated. For example, to be beeped if a file system goes over 95% capacity, updating the information every 30 seconds, try:

```
% xfsm -w 95 -e -i 30 &
```

If you don't want to see all the file systems listed, you can use the *-d* option to omit specified file systems. You might want to do this if you don't really care about disk usage on file systems that are NFS-mounted from another

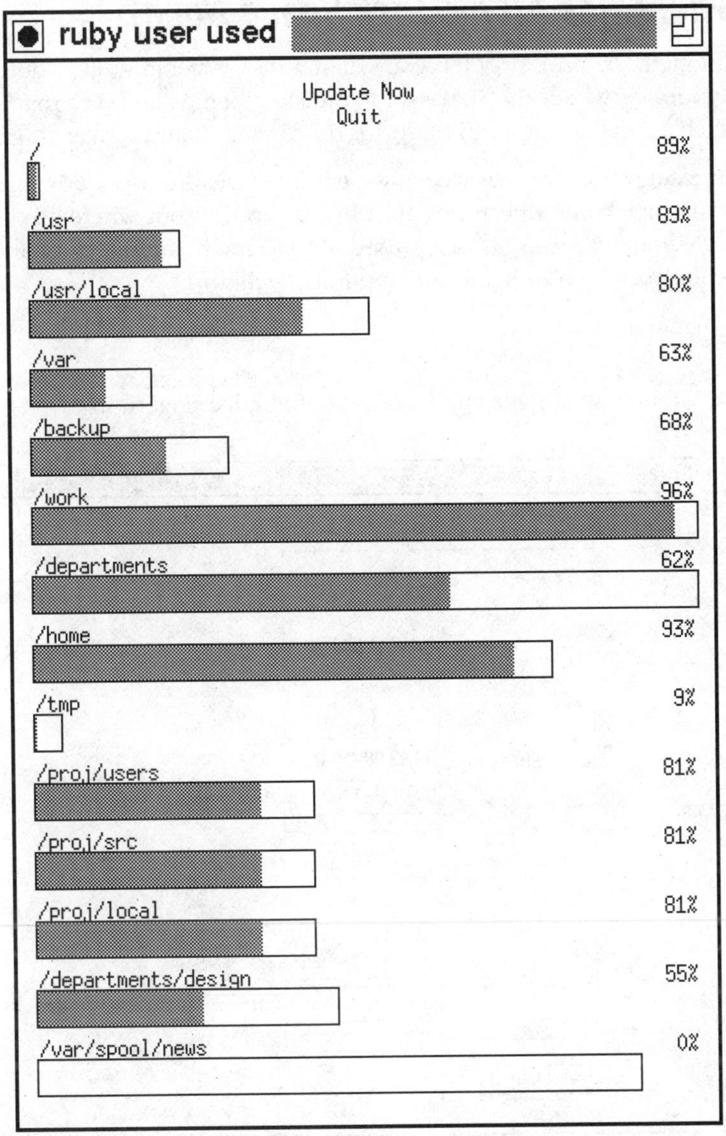

Figure 27-4: File system display

machine. For example, I might omit all file systems mounted from the *rock* and *amber* machines:

```
% xfsm -d /rock/home /rock/work /amber/online /amber/usr/local &
```

—LM

27.06 Where Has All the Disk Space Gone?

Although *xfsm* (27.05) may tell you when a disk is getting full, it doesn't give you any idea of where the space on that disk is being used. For that, we use *xdu*, which takes the output of the UNIX *du* command and formats it graphically.

xdu

For example, every few weeks we get messages from our administrator telling us that our home directories are too big. To find out where all the disk space in my home directory is being used, I *cd* to my home directory and use the *du* command. I then pipe the *du* output through *xdu*.

```
lmui@ruby % cd
lmui@ruby % du | xdu &
```

The window that comes up looks something like Figure 27-5.

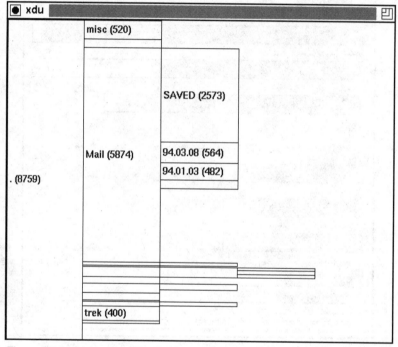

Figure 27-5: Disk space distribution in my home directory

xdu creates a box for each directory. The name of the directory appears in the box (when it can fit, that is), followed by the size of the directory. The size of the box is relative to the amount of the parent directory that it uses up. So for example, in the figure, *Mail* is the largest subdirectory of my home directory, so it's the largest subrectangle under the parent directory (.). In fact, most of my home directory is saved mail messages.

To focus in on a directory, click on the corresponding rectangle with the first mouse button. The window is redrawn with the selected directory as the topmost rectangle, so you can see its subdirectories in more detail. You can move upwards in the directory tree again by clicking on the leftmost rectangle; you can also press the slash (/) key to return to the "root" (i.e., the topmost directory in this tree).

To quit out of *xdu*, press q, or click the third mouse button. There are also keystrokes for ordering the directories in different ways and for setting the number of columns shown.

It would be nicer if *xdu* could get its data by itself, so you can have it rescan after removing or compressing some files. However, it's still a nice tool for showing you disk space at a glance.

—*LM*

27.07 *Process Display*

xpd is a program for displaying the processes of all users, and then allowing you to kill *(2.08)* the processes that you have permission to kill.

xpd

The *xpd* window shows three columns (see Figure 27-6). The first column contains a listing of all users currently logged in. When one of the users is selected, the second column shows all processes reported for that user, and the user's UID, user name, and full name are reported in the fields at the bottom of the screen. When you select a particular process, its command-line arguments are shown in the third column, and its process ID, parent process ID, process group, current process state, and associated *tty* (if any) are shown in the bottom fields.

Here's the neat part. To kill a process, you can just select it and then press the Kill button. The *kill* command appears in the top right field of the window. To alter the *kill* command, pull down the Kill Level menu. If the process is not killed, a pop-up window appears explaining why (for example, if you're an unprivileged user and you don't own the process).

Now, obviously you can't just kill anybody's processes. So *xpd* is meant to be installed *setuid* to *root*, and has two permission modes: you can run the command as *root* or run as a particular user. Unprivileged users can only run as themselves, whereas users who are in the group *wheel* can run as *root* if they choose (on BSD UNIX derivatives, that is).

xpd does not prompt for the root password. Any user on group wheel can run *xpd* as root and kill other users' processs, regardless of whether they know the root password. This is a serious security hole, so administrators might want to think twice about installing *xpd setuid* root.

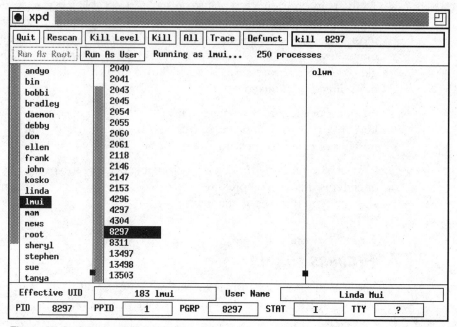

Figure 27-6: A process display via xpd

As an alternative, *xpd* might be installed so that it isn't *setuid* to *root* but simply *setgid* to *kmem* (otherwise it can't read the process table!). This is safer, but not as powerful for administrators since you can only run as yourself. Either way, you must have root permission to install *xpd*.

Another useful feature is the **Trace** button. This button brings up a window showing all ancestors of the process and all known children.

The **Defunct** button shows all defunct processes. If you select one of the processes, the main window automatically displays the process table for its owner. This is an easy way for administrators to find all defunct processes.

—LM

27.08 crontab Control

crontab is a *very* useful feature of UNIX. It allows you to set up commands to be run on a regular basis. For example, in managing the articles that comprise this book, I have a script called *updatetopics* that recalibrates my cross-reference lists. This script runs automatically at 7:54 each morning.

Now for the bad part about *crontab*. The syntax is atrocious. To run my command, I have to type in the following entry:

```
54 7 * * * /work/xpt/updatetopics
```

tkcron

I don't know about you, but every time I have to write up a new *crontab* entry, I have to pull out the %$!#@ manual again. Luckily for us, there's a Tcl-based *(30.01)* front-end to *crontab*.

tkcron takes some of the headache out of *crontab*. It shows you your current *crontab* entries and lets you add new ones easily. For example, suppose I have a *$HOME/tmp* directory and want to regularly clear out all files in there that are seven days old. Figure 27-7 shows how I might do this with *tkcron*.

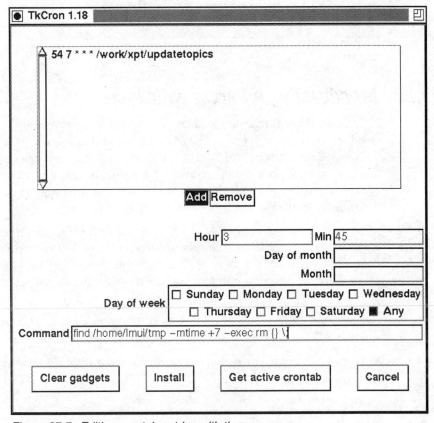

Figure 27-7: Editing crontab entries with tkcron

cron jobs that are already logged for your account appear in the scrollable field at the top of the window. To add a new job, specify when you want the job done using the fields below (Hour, Min, etc.), and then enter the command below. Unfortunately, the command still needs to be phrased as a UNIX command.

I choose to run this command at 3:45 A.M., since it's always better to use up cycles when no users are around (or at least, no sane users). To remove the

---

files, I use the *find* command—itself with its own bizarre collection of syntax rules, but I'm afraid *tkcron* can't help you here.

When you press **Add**, the entry is inserted into the list of *crontab* entries at the top of the window. The line reads:

```
45 3 * * * find /home/lmui/tmp -mtime +7 -exec rm {} \;
```

(You can also use *tkcron* to remove entries. Just select the line and press **Remove**.)

Notice that just pressing **Add** or **Remove** isn't sufficient to update your *crontab* entry; you need to press **Install** before the entries shown are installed and *tkcron* exits. Your *crontab* entries are shown on the standard output of the shell you started *tkcron* on.

—*LM*

27.09 *Broadcasting a Server with xmx*

Right now, I'm typing at one display, but my entire screen is also being duplicated on several other servers on our network. This is using the magic of *xmx*, an X-based multicasting application. *xmx* is pretty neat and may even be useful. For example, in a training course, the instructor might demonstrate a procedure on his/her X terminal, while students watch the progress at each of the X terminals on their desks.

xmx

xmx works by assigning one X server as a master X server, and then assigning any number of additional X servers as "slaves." *xmx* assigns a pseudo-display name for each of the servers, for example ruby:1. This pseudo-server becomes the connection point for each of the slave X servers.

First, you need to make sure that each of the X servers is in a "clean" state. Probably the easiest way to do this is to reboot them. You should also make sure the X servers are not configured to connect to a host via XDMCP *(28.03)*.

Next, run the following command from a remote terminal connection to the host running *xmx*:

```
ruby % xmx :1 -p -display ncd12 ncd25 ncd9
```

What this does is set up :1 or ruby:1 as the pseudo-display name for servers *ncd12*, *ncd25*, and *ncd9*. *If there is a real server named* ruby:1, *then use another value!* As the initial server listed, *ncd12* is taken as the master server. (The –*p* option says to echo the pointer motion of the master to the slaves as well.)

Now start an initial *xterm* to the pseudo-display:

```
ruby% xterm -display ruby:1
```

This *xterm* window should now appear on each of the servers. Only the person sitting at *ncd12* should be able to type into this window, however.

From now on, anything done at *ncd12* will be broadcast onto the other displays. Note that any new windows started from the initial *xterm* window will inherit *ruby:1* as the display name and will appear on all the screens. *xmx* is now a perfect tool for teaching a classroom of students.

Now for the bugs and restrictions: the X servers should probably all have the same depth and dimensions. The README warns that some window managers might have problems, and sure enough, *mwm (13.01)* crashes it completely. Also, if you do have any problems, make sure to kill *all xmx* processes, or else you may have some unexpected results.

—LM

27.10 *Using a Sun3 as an X Terminal*

Val still works on a Sun 3/60, despite the ridicule of all her tech writer friends.* Her 3/60 (named Harry) has a 19-inch color display, a nice keyboard, and an optical mouse, and it can run the latest X server, hot off the presses from the X Consortium. The only problem with the 3/60 is that it's Slow As Molasses.

If you have an old Sun3 on your site, and you can't find a sucker like Val who's happy with an outdated machine, then one thing you can do with it is to convert it into an X terminal. You'll end up with a machine that only knows how to run an X server, but it will be much, much faster. A more powerful host on the network can run *xdm (28.02)* and manage the workstation as if it were an X terminal.

XKernel

What you need to do is to strip down the UNIX kernel. Luckily for you, someone's already done this, all you need to do is to grab the binary off this book's CD-ROM.

Another possibility is that you can set up the Sun3 to boot diskless from another machine. (As the *README* says, why waste a disk on an X terminal?) The CD-ROM also includes *bootparams* for booting the Sun3 from a Sun4, NeXT, RS/6000, and even a (gasp) i486 running Interactive 4.0.

There is no reason why you could not do this with other hardware. The only reason the Sun3 series is singled out is because it is considered underpowered by today's standards.

—EAP, LM

---

* Val wants me to amend this, by saying she still uses the 3/60 because she's loyal and wants to save money for the company.

27.11 *Using More Than One Frame Buffer Under SunOS*

The X server for the Sun platform can support more than one frame buffer at a time. It is possible to have two separate monitors on the same host or to use separate frame buffers within the same monitor. The *cgfour* device driver has an 8-bit color frame buffer and 1-bit monochrome frame buffer. The *Xsun* X server will not use both unless you modify the default workstation configuration.

To use the multiple frame buffers:

1. Become *root* and change directories to */dev*:

    ```
    % su
    # cd /dev
    ```

2. Remove the default monochrome device:

    ```
    # rm /dev/bwtwo0
    ```

3. Create the new monochrome device:

    ```
    # MAKEDEV bwtwo1
    ```

4. Make sure the kernel contains the *bwtwo1* device and is not commented-out. For example, on a Sun 3/60 with a kernel named HARRY:

    ```
    # grep bwtwo1 /usr/sys/sun3/conf/HARRY
    device      bwtwo1 at obmem 7 csr 0xff300000 priority 4    # 3/60
    device      bwtwo1 at obmem 7 csr 0xff400000               # 3/60
    ```

    If the device is missing, add it to the kernel config file and build a new kernel.

If this procedure works, you should be able to toggle back and forth between the frame buffers just by moving the mouse pointer to the edge of the display.

Some systems support multiple physical monitors. The Sun color IPC comes with a monochrome frame buffer built onto the CPU board and a *cgthree* card in one of the SBus slots. If you connect a monochrome monitor to a CPU and a color monitor to the *cgthree* device, you can run the X server on both. Moving the mouse pointer to the edge of the screen will move it onto the adjacent monitor.

—*EAP, from the* X Window System Administrator's Guide

28

Configuring the
X Display Manager

28.01 How I Learned to Stop Worrying and Love xdm

The X Display Manager provides a way for users to log on and start initial clients. Using a special protocol, XDMCP, X servers can request login boxes *(28.02)* from host machines running the *xdm* daemon. X users can log in, their configured X sessions are started automatically, and at the end of the day they can log out and a new login box immediately appears. In my opinion, this is the most "elegant" way to use X.

In fairness to our readers, I should confess right now that I love *xdm*. Val thinks I'm nuts. She says, "Sure, print that . . . and they'll come for you with a straightjacket." Val believes that *xdm* should be avoided at all costs, and she's not alone. There are many seasoned X users out there who have never used *xdm* and are proud of it. If you have a single-user workstation and are happy starting your X session manually (with a command like *xinit, startx, openwin (1.03)*, etc.), then we encourage you to keep working that way and leave this chapter for us *xdm* fanatics.

However, if you're a system administrator, we recommend that you stick with this chapter. What I like about *xdm* is that in the spirit of X itself, *xdm* is vastly configurable. Using *xdm*, administrators have the opportunity to enforce global behavior among users and to impose security measures. It lets administrators control many aspects of the user's startup procedure, while leaving users some room to configure their own environments as needed. If you have X terminals at your site, you can't get along without *xdm*.

There are lots of fancy things you can do with *xdm*, and this chapter explores quite a few of them. I figure that any administrator interested in developing a well-crafted, seamless environment is a potential disciple to the cult of *xdm*.

—*LM*

28.02 What xdm Looks Like to Users

If your X server is set up to use *xdm*, then your X server is always running. Before you log in, you'll see either a "login" window or a "chooser" window. The login window may look like the one shown in Figure 28-1, allowing you to supply a username and password.

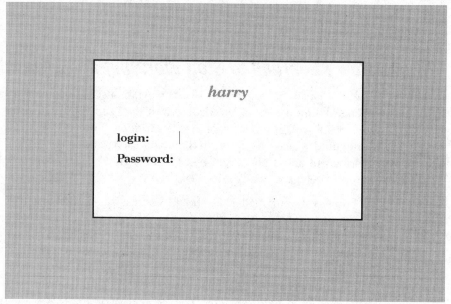

Figure 28-1: xdm login window

The login window lets you log in and start an X session on a particular host. Sites that want to give users a choice of hosts might configure users to receive a chooser window instead. The chooser window just lets the user choose between several hosts, as shown in Figure 28-2. The user then gets a login box (similar to Figure 28-1) from whichever host was chosen.

Once you log in successfully, a startup script *(2.09, 16.03)* is executed that defines your initial environment. This script is usually called *.xsession*, and lives in your home directory. See Chapters 16 and 21 for information on configuring your *.xsession* script.

If you have trouble logging in, try pressing **F1** after your password in place of **Return**. See Article 21.02 for more information.

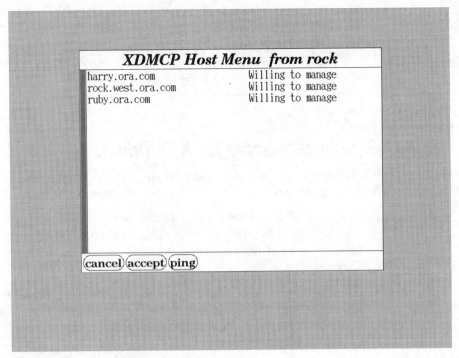

Figure 28-2: xdm Chooser window

Your login and chooser windows may look different from the ones shown here, depending on your vendor or on how your administrator has configured your site. See Articles 28.11 and 28.22 for more information on configuring the login and chooser boxes.

—LM

28.03 *Establishing the Connection*

As you can see from Article 28.02, *xdm* is pretty easy from a user's standpoint. However, underneath the simple facade is a maze of twisted passages involving protocols, configuration files, and shell scripts.

The X server first needs to establish connection with *xdm*. The connection can be initiated by either the *xdm* host or the X server. For most X terminals, the terminal itself initates the connection, using a protocol called XDMCP. The terminal uses XDMCP to request a connection from a host (which the host may actually refuse: see Article 28.18). There are three possible types of XDMCP connections: Direct, Indirect, and Broadcast; Article 28.17 talks about the different types of connection.

If the *xdm* host initiates the connection, then *xdm* needs to be configured to know what hosts to connect to. For the most part, this only applies to workstations that run *xdm* locally. In addition to initiating the actual *xdm* connection, *xdm* also assumes the extra responsibility of starting the server (which it can do, since the server runs locally). See Article 28.08 for more information on controlling the local display server.

—LM

28.04 *Simple xdm Setup for X Terminals*

If you want to use *xdm* only for managing several X terminals, then setting it up is relatively easy.

1. First of all, choose a central host to manage the X terminals. In most cases, the choice will be obvious: you should use your fastest and most robust host, since all X terminal users are likely to run all their remote clients from this host.

2. Check the *Xservers* file *(28.08)* in the *xdm* configuration directory. This file is usually set up correctly when you install *xdm*, but not always (especially if it has been copied from another host). What you want to watch for is a line reading:

   ```
   :0 local /usr/bin/X11/X
   ```

   or any other line starting with the string :0. If all you want to use *xdm* for is to manage some X terminals, you want this line commented out with an initial #. It should read:

   ```
   #:0 local /usr/bin/X11/X
   ```

3. Start *xdm* on the command line, for testing. You must be *root* to start *xdm*. For example:

   ```
   root # /usr/bin/X11/xdm
   ```

4. At an X terminal, configure it to make a Direct XDMCP query to the host running *xdm*, and then have it initiate that query. How you do this is dependent on your X terminal, but any X terminal that is X11R4 or later will support this functionality. If your X terminal does not support XDMCP, say "Oy!" and see Article 28.08.

5. The X terminal should receive a login box *(28.02)* from the host running *xdm*. Any user with an account on this system should be able to log in with their username and password.

6. When the user has logged out, the login box should return, awaiting another user.

To set this up permanently, you need to enter *xdm* into the system's *rc* startup files (as described in Article 28.30).

—*LM*

28.05 Simple xdm for Workstations

If you want to use the local *xdm* for managing the console display of a workstation, follow these steps:

1. Check the *Xservers* file in the *xdm* configuration directory. This file is usually set up correctly when you install *xdm*, but not always (especially if it has been copied from another host). What you want is a line resembling:

    ```
    :0 local /usr/bin/X11/X
    ```

    This line tells *xdm* that you want it to manage the console display, and that you want it to start the X server on that display as well. The last string, `/usr/bin/X11/X`, is the command that *xdm* will use to start the server; change this string if needed (see Article 18.05).

2. If you are already running an X server, exit it. This should bring you to a full-screen console terminal display.

3. Start *xdm* on the command line, for testing. You must be *root* to start *xdm*. For example:

    ```
    # /usr/bin/X11/xdm
    ```

4. The X server on the console should take over the display, and should receive a login box to the local host. Any user with an account on this system should be able to log in with their user name and password.

5. When the user has logged out, the login box returns, awaiting another user.

To set this up permanently, you need to enter *xdm* into the system's *rc* startup files (as described in Article 28.30).

• A workstation running *xdm* can also manage X terminals at the same time. All you need to do is to configure the X terminal to query the workstation for a login box.

—*LM*

28.06 Managing Another Workstation's Display

It's common to use *xdm* to manage X terminals *(28.04)*, but what if you want it to manage the display server on another workstation? This can be done; it just needs a little coordination between the two hosts. For example, if you want to set up a host *rock* to manage the display of the workstation *scribe*, you have to do the following:

1. First of all, if *xdm* is being run on the workstation *scribe*, make sure the local server isn't listed in the *Xservers* file on *scribe*, that is, if *xdm* is running, make sure the following is commented out in *Xservers*:

   ```
   #:0 local /usr/bin/X11/X
   ```

2. Start the X server with an active XDMCP query.

   ```
   % /usr/bin/X11/X -query rock.west.ora.com
   ```

   If you want to set it up permanently, put this command in */etc/rc.local* on *scribe*.

   The *–query* option tells the X server to place a Direct XDMCP query to the specified host. Use the *–indirect* option in place of *–query* for an Indirect query to the specified host, e.g., to get a *chooser* box *(28.20)*. You can also use the *–broadcast* option for a Broadcast query, in which case the first *xdm* host who replies to the query gets control of the server. (The *–broadcast* option is not followed by a hostname.) See Article 28.17 for more information on Direct, Indirect, and Broadcast queries.

—*LM, from the* X Window System Administrator's Guide

28.07 Just This Once

At our site, we have a few workstations and a lot of X terminals. Occasionally a workstation user will go off for vacation, and then an X terminal user wants to know how they can use the vacationer's "terminal" to log in. If the workstation user doesn't use *xdm*, it isn't obvious how to do this.

This happens to us all the time. One thing to do is try to set up the user with *xinit (1.03)* and then run remote clients *(19.01)* from the host they usually log in on, but this is really a lot of trouble for a single day's work. So instead, I like to have users run a "one-shot" *xdm* query to the remote *xdm* host. Then the user logs in the way she usually does, gets her usual environment, and at the end of the day everything's fine again.

First, I have the user log in at the console. Next, at the prompt, I have her start the X server *(18.05)* with a query to the remote *xdm* host *(28.06)*. In this case, the remote *xdm* host is named *ruby*:

```
% exec /usr/bin/X11/X -query ruby -once
```

The *–once* command-line option is very important in this context. As we saw in Article 28.06, the *–query* command-line option requests a login box from the specified host. The workstation effectively becomes an X terminal, and the only way to terminate the server or sever the *xdm* connection is to kill it manually. But if you use the *–once* option, the X server will automatically exit as soon as the X session is over.

The *exec (21.10)* is so the user will be automatically logged out after the X session is over. (People here never remember to log out.)

—LM

28.08 Configuring the Xservers File

In addition to listing the local display server *(28.05)*, the *Xservers* configuration file is used for X servers that don't support XDMCP, and therefore can't request *xdm* connections on their own. By listing a server in *Xservers*, *xdm* knows to send a login box to the server upon startup (*xdm*'s startup, that is).

To list a remote X server in the *Xservers* file, list the server name followed by the word foreign:

```
xterm1:0 foreign
```

Since the remainder of the line after foreign is ignored, you can also list a comment if you want:

```
xterm1 foreign  Public X terminal in printer room
```

Another feature is that you can specify a display class *(28.27)* for the server. For this, just enter a string between the name of the server and the word foreign:

```
xterm1 VISUAL-X19TURBO foreign  Public X terminal in printer room
```

(See Article 28.27 for more information on display classes.)

In general use, however, the *Xservers* file is only used for the local display server, where it has the advantage of letting you start and manage the X server "seamlessly" *(28.05)*. For any X terminal that supports XDMCP, the *Xservers* file should not be used because it has some serious logistical problems.

The main problem with depending on the *Xservers* file to manage X terminals is that if the X terminal is rebooted, *xdm* has no way of knowing it needs a new login box *(28.02)*. To get a new login box under that circumstance, you have to restart *xdm*. This was a serious problem before XDMCP was developed. It was so serious that some administrators set *cron (27.08)* jobs to restart *xdm* every five minutes!

—LM

28.09 Stopping the X Server from a Workstation

If you use a workstation and your server is started and managed directly by the *xdm* host (that is, via an entry in the *Xservers* file), then you can disable *xdm* control and return to a console terminal emulation using the **CTRL-R** sequence in the login box *(28.02)*. As shown in Article 28.11, the **CTRL-R** sequence aborts *xdm*'s control of this display and also kills the server that *xdm* started. Your login box disappears, and you can then press **Return** to retrieve the console prompt.

This feature is in X11R5 and later. It's nice because it gives workstation users an escape hatch from *xdm* control without having to resort to heroic measures. However, notice that it depends on *xdm* having control over the session. If you started the X server manually, initiating the XDMCP connection from the server side (as shown in Article 28.06), then *xdm* cannot sever the connection since the server will just request a new login box and continue on its merry way.

—*LM*

28.10 xdm Configuration Files

xdm is configured through a set of editable ASCII files in a central *xdm* configuration directory. (This directory is usually */usr/lib/X11/xdm*.) Before we talk about how to configure *xdm*, we should introduce you to the files that appear in the default configuration.

xdm-config
> Resources specified for *xdm*. Note that the location of all other files listed below can be redefined with resources specified in *xdm-config*. (The location of the *xdm-config* file itself can be reassigned using the *-config* option to *xdm*.) See Article 28.24 for the syntax of *xdm-config*.

Xservers
> A list of servers to be explicitly managed by *xdm*. If you want *xdm* to control the local display server, it should be listed here. For managing X terminals, however, this file is all but obsolete. See Articles 28.05 and 28.08 for more information.

Xsession
> The initial startup script used by each individual X session. See Article 28.12.

Xresources
> Resources to be loaded via *xrdb* *(17.03)* by servers managed by *xdm*. This file generally contains resources for the login box *(28.02)*, the *xconsole* client *(27.02)*, and the Chooser *(28.20)*. See Articles 28.11 and 28.22.

xdm-pid

> A file containing the process ID of *xdm*. Use this file for restarting *xdm*:

```
# kill 'cat /usr/lib/X11/xdm/xdm-pid'
```

xdm-errors

> The error log file for *xdm*.

Xaccess

> A file for configuring access control for XDMCP, specifying different behavior according to the sort of query used. See Articles 28.18, 28.19, 28.20, and 28.21 for information on configuring *Xaccess*.

GiveConsole

> A shell script that changes the ownership of the console to the user. See Article 28.23.

TakeConsole

> A shell script that changes the ownership of the console back to *root*. See Article 28.23.

Xsetup_0

> A shell script used for display setup specific to the local console server. See Article 28.23.

The names of the files used to configure *xdm* are defined in the *xdm-config* file. See Article 28.24 for details about *xdm-config*.

—LM

28.11 Configuring the Login Box

One of the first things people want to configure in *xdm* is (shock of shocks) also one of the easiest things to configure. The *xdm* login box runs as a widget and can be altered by changing a few lines in the *Xresources* configuration file. Article 28.02 shows a picture of a login box.

In its default configuration, that file contains the following lines:

```
xlogin*login.translations: #override\
    Ctrl<Key>R:  abort-display()\n\
    <Key>F1:  set-session-argument(failsafe) finish-field()\n\
    Ctrl<Key>Return:  set-session-argument(failsafe) finish-field()\n\
    <Key>Return:  set-session-argument() finish-field()
xlogin*borderWidth: 3
xlogin*greeting:  CLIENTHOST
xlogin*namePrompt:  login:\
xlogin*fail:  Login incorrect
#ifdef COLOR
```

```
xlogin*greetColor:  CadetBlue
xlogin*failColor:  red
*Foreground:  black
*Background: #fffff0
#else
xlogin*Foreground:  black
xlogin*Background:  white
#endif
```

Note that the first resource for *xlogin* is a translation table *(20.29)*, used for defining how special keystrokes might be used within the client.

- The first translation is to allow you to use **CTRL-R** to stop *xdm* from managing your display entirely *(28.09)*. This feature is only useful for a local console display that is not using XDMCP *(28.06)*. Otherwise, **CTRL-R** may abort the current *xdm* connection, but the server remains running annd a new login box will instantly replace the old one.

- The second and third translations allow you to log in without running your *.xsession* file *(21.02)*, by pressing **F1** or **CTRL-Return** after your password instead of **Return**. Pressing **F1** or **CTRL-Return** tells *xdm* to run a failsafe X session *(28.12)* (usually just a single *xterm* window). This is important, since otherwise you may have no way of logging in if your *.xsession* is corrupted.

- The last translation simply says to interpret **Return** as the end of each field.

How might you change these translations? Well, you might decide that it makes more sense to use **Escape** instead of **CTRL-R** to abort the display. You might also want to add some other special-case situations (other than *failsafe*, that is; see Article 28.16).

The remainder of the resources set for *xlogin* are fairly straightforward, used largely to specify the messages used for prompts and error messages. Note that since this resource file is loaded into the server via *xrdb (17.03)*, *cpp* preprocessor commands *(20.19)* (i.e., #ifdef, #else, and #endif) and several predefined variables recognized by *xrdb (20.20)* can be used.

Using these resource definitions, the border width for the login box is set to three pixels. The greeting is set to the name of the host, and the prompt is set to login:. If the login fails, the error message is Login incorrect.

The most common thing to change is the login box title. For example, when I'm testing *xdm* on my workstation, I sometimes worry that people will somehow get a login box from my workstation (e.g., through a Broadcast request *(28.17)*), log in, and then when I crash my machine through my testing, they'll lose their work. So I always add a little warning:

```
xlogin*greeting: CLIENTHOST--LOG IN AT YOUR OWN RISK
```

Finally, the resources set what colors to use for the login box, depending (naturally) on whether the display has color support.

—LM

28.12 *The Xsession Script*

When the user logs in, the *Xsession* script is executed. This script is responsible for starting initial clients for the user, primarily through calling an *.xsession* script in the user's home directory; but it also does a few extra things for getting things running smoothly. The standard *Xsession* script reads as follows:

```
#!/bin/sh
# $XConsortium: Xsession,v 1.7 92/08/06 11:08:14 gildea Exp $

# redirect errors to a file in user's home directory if we can
for errfile in "$HOME/.xsession-errors" "/tmp/xses-$USER"
do
        if ( cp /dev/null "$errfile" 2> /dev/null )
        then
                chmod 600 "$errfile"
                exec > "$errfile" 2>&1
                break
        fi
done

case $# in
1)
        case $1 in
        failsafe)
                exec xterm -geometry 80x24-0-0
                ;;
        esac
esac

startup=$HOME/.xsession
resources=$HOME/.Xresources

if [ -f $startup ]; then
        exec $startup
else
        if [ -f $resources ]; then
                xrdb -load $resources
        fi
        twm &
        exec xterm -geometry 80x24+10+10 -ls
fi
```

The first thing that the *Xsession* script does is to send error messages to a file in the user's home directory called *.xsession-errors (21.05)*. If that file doesn't exist or isn't writable, it writes to a file in */tmp* with the prefix *xses-* followed by the name of the user.

The next thing the X session does is take care of the failsafe situation. In Article 21.02, we showed you that using **F1** or **CTRL-Return** in the login box was a way to bypass your *.xsession* script. This is implemented partly through the login box translations in the *Xresources* file *(28.11)*, which sets a failsafe argument for this *Xsession* script. This is where the failsafe condition is checked for. If true, the script just runs an *xterm (2.02)* using the *exec* command *(21.10)* and never gets to the part of the script that executes *.xsession.*

Finally, the script looks for a startup script and executes it. (Note that since it calls *exec*, the script must be executable.) If the script doesn't exist, it looks for a resource file *(17.03)* in the user's home directory and starts a *twm* window manager *(12.01)* and an initial *xterm* window.

—LM

28.13 *Seeing the Message of the Day*

The *Xsession* script *(28.12)* gives administrators an opportunity to run some global clients. For example, one of the most common requests is to have the "message of the day" appear on everyone's display when they log in.

One way to do this is to use the *xmessage (4.09)* client. *xmessage* has a *–file* option *(4.10)* for taking the message from a file. You can use this to show the message of the day:

```
% xmessage -file /etc/motd
```

Administrators can put this command in the *Xsession* script, so that all users who log in under *xdm* see the message of the day. This is an easy way to make sure that everyone gets an important message:

```
if [ -f /etc/motd ]
        xmessage -file /etc/motd
fi

if [ -f $startup ]; then
        exec $startup
            ...
```

You might see something like the window shown in Figure 28-3.

Note that we choose not to put the *xmessage* command in the background. This is to ensure that the user sees the message and presses **okay** before any other clients can run. Otherwise, the message window might be obscured behind other windows and never seen.

—LM

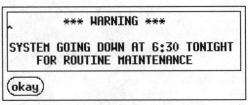

Figure 28-3: Xmessage and the message of the day

28.14 *Setting Environment Variables in Xsession*

One thing that many *xdm* users complain about is that their *.login*, *.profile*, or *.cshrc* scripts are not automatically run. Among other things, this means that their environment variables *(2.04)* like PATH *(2.05)*, MANPATH *(5.02)*, etc. aren't properly set. This affects any commands run directly from the startup script *(2.09, 16.03)*, as well as any scripts started from the user's root menu.

Users can take care of this individually, as described in Article 16.04. But administrators can also do something about it, by configuring the systemwide *Xsession* to set environment variables properly for running some popular programs.[*]

For example, on our system we have some X programs installed in */usr/local/bin*. We also have manpages for these programs in */usr/local/man*, and application defaults *(20.12)* in */usr/local/lib/X11/app-defaults*. If users want to use a program that's installed into one of these directories, then they'll need to do some fiddling with PATH if they try to call it from their startup script or window manager menu. If they start a program like *xman (5.02)* in their startup scripts or window manager menu, then they need to make sure that MANPATH is properly set, or else *xman* won't know about any of the local programs. And if they want to access the application defaults for any of these programs at startup, then they need to set a resource environment variable (for example, XFILESEARCHPATH *(20.25)*).

So if users want to use these programs, then their *.xsession* scripts need to be properly configured—requiring the users to know something about the shell, or making them dependent on system administrators to set up their environments. Article 16.04 gives you an idea of how irritating this can be. This is a job for *xdm*.

What we can do is set up the environment variables in the *Xsession* script.

```
#!/bin/sh
    ...
startup=$HOME/.xsession
```

---

[*] Administrators can also try setting the userPath and systemPath environment variables in the *xdm-config* file *(28.24)*, but this won't help MANPATH or the resource path.

```
resources=$HOME/.Xresources

PATH="$PATH:/usr/local/bin"
MANPATH="/usr/man:/usr/local/man"
XFILESEARCHPATH="/usr/lib/X11/%T/%N%C%S:/usr/lib/X11/%T/%N%S:\
/usr/local/lib/X11/%T/%N%C%S:/usr/local/lib/X11/%T/%N%S"
export PATH MANPATH XFILESEARCHPATH

if [ -f $startup ]; then
        exec $startup
            ...
```

We set PATH, MANPATH, and XFILESEARCHPATH to include */usr/local,* and then export all three variables. The result is that the users' startup scripts can all include programs in */usr/local/bin* without ending up with "Command not found" errors in *.xsession-errors.*

—*LM*

28.15 *Setting Global Resources*

Here's another way administrators may want to use the *Xsession* script.

Administrators might want to set some global resources for all users. In most cases, global resources should be set in the systemwide *app-defaults* files *(20.12),* but there are a few cases when administrators might want to set them in each user's environment.

A good example is when you'd want different behavior from a client depending on the server's properties. The client's *app-defaults* file isn't sufficient since you can't use the predefined variables such as COLOR or PLANES *(20.20);* these features are only available through *xrdb (17.03).*

For example, you can get special color *app-defaults (20.12)* files with clients that support them, but only if you set the customization resource *(20.21).* So one thing an administrator might do is to configure *xdm* to run *xrdb* on every server at startup time. Create a file called *UserResources* in the *xdm* configuration directory, reading something like this:

```
#ifdef COLOR
*customization: -color
#endif
```

And then in *Xsession,* run *xrdb* on this file:

```
#!/bin/sh

xrdb -merge /usr/lib/X11/xdm/UserResources
        ...
```

You can add any other global resources here as well. However, it's probably better to use *app-defaults* files when you can. One problem with this

procedure is that it depends on each user using *xrdb* with the *–merge* option
(20.18) when they apply their own resources to the server; otherwise, any new
resources that are loaded will override the ones set in *Xsession*. Another possible problem that you may run into is that if users are accustomed to using
their *.Xdefaults* file rather than loading resources with *xrdb* (see Article 17.03),
then loading resources with *xrdb* will mean that the resources in *.Xdefaults*
will be ignored.

—LM

28.16 Other "Failsafe"-like Translations

If you press **F1** or **CTRL-Return** after entering your username and password,
you get just a single *xterm* window, appropriate for editing your *.xsession*.
(See Article 21.02). This is called a failsafe session, and it is implemented
using a translation in the *Xresources* file *(28.11)*:

```
xlogin*login.translations: #override\
        . . .
        <Key>F1: set-session-argument(failsafe) finish-field()\n\
        Ctrl<Key>Return: set-session-argument(failsafe) finish-field()\n\
        . . .
```

and a few lines in the *Xsession* file *(28.12)*:

```
case $# in
1)
        case $1 in
        failsafe)
                exec xterm -geometry 80x24-0-0
                ;;
        esac
esac
```

There's nothing very magical about this. The `failsafe` argument is specified
right there in the *Xresources* file and then is processed in the *Xsession* file.
There's nothing stopping us from making other "special-case" translations.

For example, there might be some times when you don't want to start an
entire X session. All you may want is a mailer, so that you can check your
mail and get the heck out of there. For that, you can add a new translation in
Xresources:

```
<Key>F2: set-session-argument(mailer) finish-field()\n\
```

and then add a new value to the `case` statement in *Xsession*:

```
case $1 in
failsafe)
        exec xterm -geometry 80x24-0-0
        ;;
mailer)
        exec xmail
```

```
        ;;
    esac
```

(You may have to do a bit more fiddling to make sure *xmail* *(7.02)* is in your search path *(2.05)*, as shown in Article 28.14.)

Here's another example. I do a lot of testing with *xdm*, requiring me to mess around with my startup script *(2.09)* a lot. But I also occasionally log in just to do some work, and often what happens is that I can't log in because I've completely garbled my startup script. Another scenario is that it takes me a year and a day to log in because of all the junk I'd incorporated into my startup script for testing. I could just log in and use the failsafe *(28.12)* session, which gives me an *xterm*, but then I have to start a window manager, load resources *(17.03)*, etc.

So I made a "test" construct, which I implement using **F2** (although I could have used practically any other key that doesn't appear in my username or password). First, I enter the following line in *Xresources*:

```
xlogin*login.translations: #override\
        ...
    <Key>F1: set-session-argument(failsafe) finish-field()\n\
    Ctrl<Key>Return: set-session-argument(failsafe) finish-field()\n\
    <Key>F2: set-session-argument(test) finish-field()\n\
        ...
```

Second, I entered a "test" case in my *Xsession*:

```
case $# in
1)
        case $1 in
        failsafe)
                exec xterm -geometry 80x24-0-0
                ;;
        test)
                if [ -f $HOME/.Xresources ]; then
                        xrdb -merge $HOME/.Xresources
                fi
                if [ -f $HOME/.xsession-test ]; then
                        exec $HOME/.xsession-test
                else
                        xterm &
                        exec twm
                fi
                ;;
        esac
    esac
```

Now I can keep my usual *.xsession*, while I do all my testing in an *.xsession-test* file. All I have to do is remember to press **F2** instead of **Return** after typing my password.

—*LM*

28.17 *Direct, Indirect, and Broadcast Requests*

When an X server initiates an XDMCP connection *(28.03)*, there are three types of requests that can be made: Direct, Indirect, or Broadcast. When setting up an X terminal to use *xdm*, you usually need to specify what sort of request you want (and to what host, if applicable) before an XDMCP connection can be made. The actual response of the host *xdm* process can be controlled by the administrator using the *Xaccess* configuration file *(28.18, 28.19, 28.20)*.

The Direct query is the simplest and most commonly used. With a Direct query, you list the name of a host, and (if the query succeeds) you get an *xdm* login box *(28.02)* from that host. Whether or not the query succeeds depends on whether the specified host is currently running *xdm*, and on whether the host *xdm* is configured to send *xdm* login boxes to the server's host.

With a Broadcast query, you do not list a specific host but simply ask for a login box from whichever host on your subnet responds first. In our experience, this makes the most sense if there's only one host running *xdm* on your network, or if it really doesn't matter which host a user logs in on so they might as well use the one that has the fastest response time. Which host responds (if any) depends on several factors: which hosts are currently running *xdm*, which hosts are configured to send *xdm* login boxes to the server's host, and which host responds the quickest.

See Article 28.18 for more information on how to restrict *xdm* login boxes from responding to Direct and Broadcast queries from a server.

Indirect queries are a little harder to explain. As with a Direct query, you specify the name of the host with which you want an Indirect connection. However, the host does not necessarily respond with a login box but can forward the request to another host. An Indirect query can also be responded to using a utility called the Chooser, which gives the user a choice of several hosts currently running *xdm*. Articles 28.19 and 28.20 describe different *xdm* responses to Indirect queries.

Figure 28-4 diagrams the different types of queries.

—LM

28.18 *Who's Allowed a Login Box?*

In X11R5 and later, you can control which X servers receive login boxes *(28.02)* from your host. You do this using the *Xaccess* file in your *xdm* configuration directory.

You might well ask why you'd want to do this. Certainly, if the user on the remote host doesn't have an account on your host, they can't log in anyway.

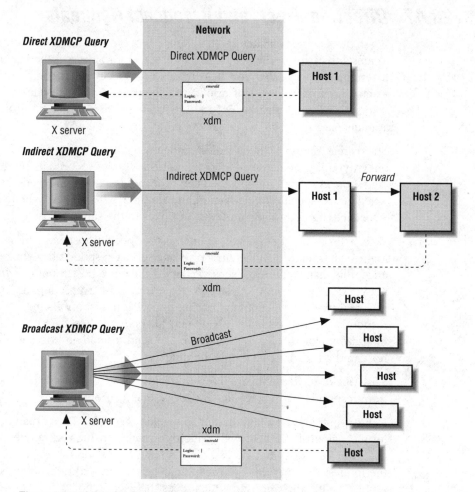

Figure 28-4: XDMCP Direct, Indirect, and Broadcast queries

In my opinion, the *Xaccess* file isn't so much a security measure as a control feature. It gives the administrator more control over which server connects to which *xdm* host. For example, on a site filled with workstations running *xdm*, you don't want a Broadcast request *(28.17)* to get login boxes from every work-station on the local network. So instead, you can configure each host's *Xaccess* file to specify which servers it will give login boxes to.

The *Xaccess* file is also used for configuring Indirect access to the host. But for simply restricting which hosts get login boxes, just list hostnames (or patterns), one each line. In the default distribution, all hosts are allowed to receive login boxes.

```
    *                              #any host can get a login window
```

When would you want to play with this? Well, suppose you have a single-user workstation on a site that also has X terminals. You may want to make sure that the X terminals don't end up getting a login box from the workstation. The easiest way to do that is to restrict *xdm* on the workstation to the local host. For example, on my workstation *opal*, I might replace the line above with:

```
    opal.ora.com              # Allow access to local workstation
```

This way, I can play with *xdm* configurations without having to worry about someone logging in by accident. Occasionally I also do some testing with a local NCD X terminal. So I might add that host to my list.

```
    opal.ora.com              # Allow access to local workstation
    ncd11.ora.com             # Allow access to ncd11
```

I might also decide that I want all hosts in the current domain to be able to connect *except* for the server on a machine named *nutmeg*. I can reject *nutmeg* by specifying it with an initial exclamation point (!). (I can't come up with a good reason to do this; for the purposes of the example, let's just say I'm doing it for spite.)

```
    *.ora.com                 # Allow access to everyone in ora.com
    !nutmeg.ora.com           #  ... except for that no-good nutmeg!
```

—*LM*

28.19 *Forwarding an XDM Request*

When *xdm* receives an Indirect XDMCP request, it can forward this request to another host. This is configured in the *Xaccess* file (available in X11R5 and later). For example, you can specify that requests from an X terminal named *ncd11* should be forwarded to the host named *jasper*.

```
    ncd11.ora.com             jasper.ora.com   # forward ncd11 to jasper
```

Why would you want to do this? Well, you might have an environment where there are a hundred X terminals. Naturally, you don't want to have them all using the same *xdm* host; instead, you might have several different *xdm* hosts distributed among the X terminals. One way you can do this is to hardcode each X terminal to make a Direct query to its allotted host. However, it's better not to hardcode this sort of information since it's subject to change. Instead, you can have all X terminals make Indirect requests to one central host, and this host becomes responsible for forwarding the terminals to the appropriate machines. For example, if the central host is *ruby.ora.com*, and the X terminals are named *xterm00* through *xterm99*, the central host's *Xaccess* file might read something like the following list.

```
xterm0?.ora.com            ruby.ora.com
xterm1?.ora.com            jade.ora.com
xterm2?.ora.com            rock.ora.com
xterm3?.ora.com            opal.ora.com
       ...
```

When *ruby* receives an Indirect request from one of these X terminals, it forwards it as a Direct request to the specified host. Notice that some of the terminals are redirected back to *ruby*. Even though each X terminal is set up to make an Indirect request to *ruby*, this is done behind the scenes, and all the user ends up seeing is a login box from their allotted host.

—LM

28.20 *Setting Up the Chooser*

In addition to responding to an Indirect query by forwarding the request to another host *(28.19)*, you can set up *xdm* to respond to Indirect queries with a Chooser box *(28.02)*. This gives the user the opportunity to choose between several hosts. To allow all X servers in the *ora.com* domain to choose from *harry.ora.com*, *ruby.ora.com*, and *rock.west.ora.com*, enter into *Xaccess*:

```
*.ora.com       CHOOSER harry.ora.com ruby.ora.com rock.west.ora.com
```

The CHOOSER keyword means to put up a *chooser* client. This client queries each of the named *xdm* hosts and asks if they will accept connections from the server. Then it gives the client a *chooser* box to select a host to log in on, as illustrated in Figure 28-5.

Yet another possibility might be to set up the *chooser* client so it just does a broadcast among all hosts on the network and allows the user to choose among them. To do this, type the keyword BROADCAST after the CHOOSER keyword.

```
*.ora.com       CHOOSER BROADCAST
```

Article 28.02 shows an example *chooser* box.

In our bicoastal environment, we use the *chooser* to allow East Coast employees to access their environments from the West Coast without having to do contortions: they simply choose the East Coast *xdm* host and they are greeted by the same friendly login box they're used to at home.

Like all the other *Xaccess* features, the *chooser* is only available with X11R5 and later. One restriction with using the *chooser* is that due to a bug in X11R4 *xdm*, it can be used only to transfer *xdm* control to another host running X11R5 *xdm* or later.

—LM

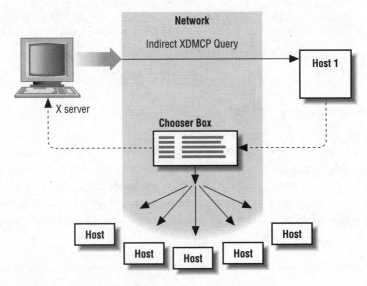

Figure 28-5: The chooser

28.21 Using Macros in Xaccess

The *Xaccess* file *(28.18, 28.19, 28.20)* allows you to define *macros* to group together a set of hosts. A macro definition starts with a percent character (%), followed by the macro name, followed by a list of hostnames. A backslash at the end of the line signifies that the definition continues onto the next line.

```
%NCDHOSTS        harry.ora.com ruby.ora.com rock.west.ora.com\
                 opal.ora.com jasper.ora.com
```

The macro is then called later on, preceded by the %.

```
ncd*.ora.com     CHOOSER %NCDHOSTS
```

Using macros comes in useful on sites with many hosts. It makes it easy to transfer control of an X server from one group of hosts to another.

— LM

28.22 Customizing the Chooser

To customize the appearance of the *chooser* client, use the *Xresources* file. The default *Xresources* file defines the following resources used by the *chooser* client:

```
Chooser*geometry:             700x500+300+200
Chooser*allowShellResize:     false
Chooser*viewport.forceBars:   true
Chooser*label.font:           *-new century schoolbook-bold-i-normal-*-240-*
```

```
Chooser*label.label:          XDMCP Host Menu  from CLIENTHOST
Chooser*list.font:      -*-*-medium-r-normal-*-*-230-*-*-c-*-iso8859-1
Chooser*Command.font:         *-new century schoolbook-bold-r-normal-*-180-*
```

The `geometry` resource is the first one I wanted to change. Since we only offer three or four hosts, there's no reason to have such a large window. I reduce the vertical size of the window:

```
Chooser*geometry:             700x500+300+200
```

The `viewpoint.forceBars` resource makes sure that there's a scrollbar *(11.02)*, so that if you have more than one screenful of hosts, you can scroll around until you reach the one you like. I don't know why this is turned on by default—probably to fix some bug which I haven't encountered yet—but I prefer not to have a scrollbar if I don't need one. (*chooser* seems smart enough to provide a scroll bar when needed anyway.) So I turn this resource off (`false`).

```
Chooser*viewport.forceBars:  false
```

The `label` resource is the only other one I'd be tempted to change. I changed it to:

```
Chooser*label.label:          Pick a Host, Any Host
```

After a little customization, my *chooser* now resembles Figure 28-6.

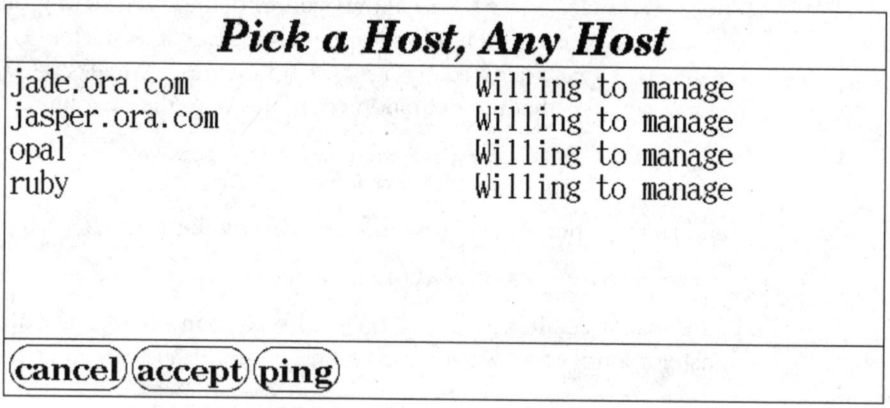

Figure 28-6: Altered chooser box

—*LM*

28.23 Dealing with Console Messages

Of the 10 configuration files that are currently part of the standard *xdm* distribution, three of them are included just to deal with console messages.

On the console display, messages are strewn across the screen (disrupting any X windows currently displaying to the server) unless they are diverted elsewhere. Usually, you want them diverted to an X window on the console. So on the console display of a workstation running *xdm*, the *xconsole* client *(27.02)* needs to be running to preserve the elegance of a pristine *xdm* login box *(28.02)*.

For this, the *Xsetup_0* script is called. This script is only run on the console display, and reads:

```
#!/bin/sh
xconsole -geometry 480x130-0-0 -daemon -notify -verbose -fn fixed -exitOnFail
```

When the user logs in, the console window disappears.

Now, once the user logs in, he or she is likely to either start his or her own *xconsole* client, or call an *xterm* with the *−C* command-line option *(27.02)*. The only problem with this is that since the X server on the console is usually started by *xdm*, which is run by *root*, then */dev/console* belongs to *root*. Neither *xconsole* or *xterm −C* can be run by a user who does not own the console.

To run *xconsole* or *xterm −c*, the *GiveConsole* script is needed. It simply changes permissions on */dev/console* when the user logs in.

```
#!/bin/sh
# Assign ownership of the console to the invoking user
#
# By convention, both xconsole and xterm -C check that the
# console is owned by the invoking user and is readable before attaching
# the console output. This way a random user can invoke xterm -C without
# causing serious grief.
#
chown $USER /dev/console
```

When the user logs out, another script called *TakeConsole* is executed. It returns ownership back to *root*.

```
#!/bin/sh
# Reassign ownership of the console to root, this should disallow
# assignment of console output to any random users's xterm
#
chmod 622 /dev/console
chown root /dev/console
```

If this seems sort of silly to you, you're not alone. But it works.

—LM

28.24 The Master Configuration File (xdm-config)

The *xdm-config* file is a resource file for *xdm*. You can use it for setting *xdm* preferences, but what interests me the most is that *xdm-config* defines each of the other configuration files used for *xdm*. By wrestling with *xdm-config*, you can set up different configuration files for different servers, and do some seriously tricky contortions to end up with a very elegant configuration.

The syntax for *xdm-config* follows standard resource specification syntax *(17.02, 20.15)*. The following is the sample *xdm-config* file as it appears in X11R5:

```
DisplayManager.errorLogFile:   /usr/lib/X11/xdm/xdm-errors
DisplayManager.pidFile:        /usr/lib/X11/xdm/xdm-pid
DisplayManager.keyFile:        /usr/lib/X11/xdm/xdm-keys
DisplayManager.servers:        /usr/lib/X11/xdm/Xservers
DisplayManager.accessFile:     /usr/lib/X11/xdm/Xaccess
DisplayManager._0.authorize:   true
DisplayManager._0.setup:       /usr/lib/X11/xdm/Xsetup_0
DisplayManager._0.startup:     /usr/lib/X11/xdm/GiveConsole
DisplayManager._0.reset:       /usr/lib/X11/xdm/TakeConsole
DisplayManager*resources:      /usr/lib/X11/xdm/Xresources
DisplayManager*session:        /usr/lib/X11/xdm/Xsession
DisplayManager*authComplain:   false
```

The keyword `DisplayManager` starting each resource name is the application class name *(20.05)* for *xdm*. *xdm* uses some resources for configuring *xdm* itself, and other resources for configuring its behavior once individual X display servers have connected to it. In particular, resource specification in *xdm-config* follows one of the following forms:

```
DisplayManager.variable: value
```

or

```
DisplayManager.DISPLAY.variable:
value
```

or

```
DisplayManager*variable: value
```

- In the first form, the `DisplayManager` keyword is separated from the variable name by a single period, meaning that this is a resource that makes sense only when applied to *xdm* proper. An example of a resource like this is `DisplayManager.servers`, which specifies what file should be used for listing the X servers to be managed by *xdm*. You can think of this sort of resource name as applying to *xdm*'s behavior independent of its connection to any particular X server: which servers to connect to, where to copy its process ID, where to put error messages, etc.

- The second form is used to specify a resource that should apply to a single display server only. Here's where the tricky part to resource naming rules for *xdm* comes into play: since the colon (:) has special meaning in resource specification syntax, the underscore (_) is used where these would normally occur in a display name *(19.02)*. For example, the display name xterm1:0 becomes xterm1_0 if it appears in a resource name. Without an underscore to specify that a particular server is being referred to, the name is taken to represent a group of X servers, called a display class *(28.27)*.

  The server which is most often used for defining a specific resource is the local console display (:0, specified as _0 in resource specifications). An example of one of these is the DisplayManager._0.setup resource, for running console windows on console displays *(28.23)*.

- The third form of an *xdm* resource specification is really just a generalization of the second form. By putting an asterisk between the DisplayManager keyword and the variable name, where a display name would normally be, you can define this value for all servers not specifically defined otherwise. As a common example, you could use the following lines:

```
DisplayManager*authorize:      false
DisplayManager._0.authorize:   true
```

  and only the local display server will use access control *(19.12)*. (In resource lingo, these are called *loose* and *tight* bindings *(20.15)*.)

See the *xdm* manpage for a description of other resources that can be specified in the *xdm-config* file. Among the other resources you may find interesting are userPath and systemPath. userPath can be used to define a value for PATH for the *Xsession* and *.xsession* scripts (see Article 28.14 for a more convoluted (if more robust) way of doing this). systemPath is the value of PATH used for running programs in the *Xsetup*, *Xstartup*, and *Xreset* scripts. For example:

```
DisplayManager*userPath: :/bin:/usr/bin:/usr/bin/X11:/usr/ucb:/usr/local/bin
```

The DisplayManager.autoRescan resource controls whether *xdm* automatically rereads the configuration files after they have been changed. If set to true (the default), *xdm* will reread the *xdm-config* file the next time a server connects to *xdm*.

—*LM, from the* X Window System Administrator's Guide

28.25 *Managing Multiple Hosts from the Same Directory*

You can use the *–config* option to *xdm* to point to a different configuration file than *xdm-config*. This is useful for testing new configuration files. In addition, the *-config* option can be used to set up a single configuration directory for multiple hosts.

Using a single NFS-shared directory to configure *xdm* for several hosts makes maintaining *xdm* very convenient for administrators. However, all hosts can't use the same *xdm-config* file. This is because among other things, *xdm-config* defines files to place log entries and the *xdm* process ID. It's better to use different log and *–pid* files for each host.

So on our site, we have three hosts that regularly run *xdm*, and correspondingly, there are three *xdm* master configuration files: *xdm-config-jade*, *xdm-config-jasper*, and *xdm-config-ruby*. In the boot files *(28.30)* for *ruby*, *xdm* is called with the *–config xdm-config-ruby* command-line option:

```
if [ -f /usr/bin/X11/xdm ]; then
    /usr/bin/X11/xdm -config /usr/lib/X11/xdm/xdm-config-ruby
fi
```

Similarly, the boot files on both *jade* and *jasper* call the appropriate *xdm-config-HOST* file.

At minimum, these files are identical except for the `errorLogFile` and `pidFile` resources. In addition, we also have separate *Xservers* files for each host. *ruby* doesn't have a local display, whereas *jade* and *jasper* do. So the *Xserver-ruby* file doesn't list a local display. *Xserver-jasper*, meanwhile, starts the server as usual:

```
:0 local /usr/bin/X11/X
```

The user on *jade*, meanwhile, prefers a slower keyrepeat *(18.03)*. This is only controllable on the server's command line, so we made a few adjustments for her. In *Xservers-jade*:

```
:0 local /usr/bin/X11/X -ar1 500
```

So *xdm-config-ruby* contains the following lines:

```
DisplayManager.errorLogFile:    /usr/lib/X11/xdm/xdm-errors-ruby
DisplayManager.pidFile:         /usr/lib/X11/xdm/xdm-pid-ruby
DisplayManager.servers:         /usr/lib/X11/xdm/Xservers-ruby
```

Whereas *xdm-config-jade* specifies:

```
DisplayManager.errorLogFile:    /usr/lib/X11/xdm/xdm-errors-jade
DisplayManager.pidFile:         /usr/lib/X11/xdm/xdm-pid-jade
DisplayManager.servers:         /usr/lib/X11/xdm/Xservers-jade
```

And *xdm-config-jasper* has:

```
DisplayManager.errorLogFile:    /usr/lib/X11/xdm/xdm-errors-jasper
DisplayManager.pidFile:         /usr/lib/X11/xdm/xdm-pid-jasper
DisplayManager.servers:         /usr/lib/X11/xdm/Xservers-jasper
```

If you choose to use this sort of setup, the only other thing we have to warn you about is to make sure that *root* on each host has permission to write to the *xdm* configuration directory. For example, the files are NFS-mounted from *ruby* onto *jasper* and *jade*. So in */etc/exports* on *ruby*, we need to extend *root* permission to *jade* and *jasper*.

```
/usr/lib/X11 -access=xterms:local_nodes,root=jade.ora.com:jasper.ora.com
```

If you prefer not to take this security risk, you can also configure *xdm* on each of the remote hosts to write to files in */tmp* or some other local file system. Beware that the error log and *pid* files aren't the only files that *xdm* needs to write: it also needs to write to the files pointed to by the keyFile, lockPidFile, and authFile resources, as well as to the directory pointed to by the authDir resource.

—LM

28.26 *Restoring Keysyms*

One annoying thing about key mappings in X is that there's no easy way to return to a default. We have some X terminals that are "public", and occasionally a user comes in and complains that the keys aren't working right. This is usually because a previous user (like me!) messed up the keysyms and didn't put them back. (This is only a problem on X servers that don't do a full reset when ending an X session. Most of our X terminals are set up this way.)

For example, as described in Article 18.08, since I don't have function keys and I don't have a keypad on my usual display, I reset my keypad keys to function keys. Occasionally I use a public X terminal, and imagine the surprise of the next user!

One way to deal with this is for each user to be a Good Citizen and reset keysyms when they log out, as shown in Article 18.17. But here's an even better idea. Rather than leaving it up to the user to do the right thing, administrators can use the *xdm* configuration files to have all keysyms restored at the end of the X session.

Here's what to do. First, the current keysyms need to be saved before the X session. To do this, create a file called *Xstartup* in */usr/lib/X11/xdm*, reading:

```
#!/bin/sh
xmodmap -pke > $HOME/.xmodmap-$DISPLAY
```

Next, the keysyms need to be reset at the end of the X session. For this, create the file *Xreset* in */usr/lib/X11/xdm*:

```
#!/bin/sh
xmodmap $HOME/.xmodmap-$DISPLAY
rm $HOME/.xmodmap-$DISPLAY
```

Finally, add the following lines to the system *xdm-config (28.24)* file:

```
DisplayManager*startup:        /usr/lib/X11/xdm/Xstartup
DisplayManager*reset:          /usr/lib/X11/xdm/Xreset
```

All X terminals from now on will run the *Xstartup* file before the user logs in, and will run the *Xreset* file after the user logs out. A file is created in the user's home directory containing its default X settings—for example, if I log in on *ncd11*, I might end up with a file called */home/lmui/.xmodmap-ncd11.ora.com:0*.

```
lmui@opal 49% ls -l ~/.xmodmap*
-rw-r--r--  1 root        4097 Apr 20 11:41  /lmui/.xmodmap-ncd11.ora.com:0
```

Notice that this file belongs to *root*. Remember, the *Xstartup* and *Xreset* files are run as *root*, so be very careful about what you put there!

The result is that X terminal users can go around remapping keys to their hearts' content, and the keysyms are guaranteed to be reverted to the default when they log out.

One more detail: the `startup` and `reset` resources are already set in the default *xdm-config* for the local server, `:0`. They are used for allowing the *xconsole* client to be run on the local server *(28.23)*. So this scheme will not work for the local server. This is fine, however, because *xdm* already resets the local server between sessions, which among other things reverts keysyms to their defaults.

—LM

28.27 *Display Classes*

Display classes provide a way to group together several X servers connecting to the same host.

The display class is built into the X server, and is presented to *xdm* when the X server connects via XDMCP. To find out the display class for a given X terminal, you can look it up in the documentation or ask the manufacturer; or, if it won't disturb any users, kill *xdm* and then restart it at a high debug level:

```
# /usr/lib/X11/xdm -debug 9
```

Running *xdm* at this level of debugging is likely to give you far more information than you really want. It also takes you out of daemon mode, so it's usually not a good idea to run *xdm* this way for very long. However, among its stream of messages is information about any X server that connects to *xdm*, including its display class:

```
Starting display visual5.ora.com:0,VISUAL-X19TURBO
```

This tells you that the Visual X terminal you're experimenting with is in the display class VISUAL-X19TURBO.

Display classes allow you to fine-tune your *xdm* configuration differently according to the display type.

For example, the Visual X19TURBO terminal has 2-bit grayscale support. This is nice, except that it confuses FrameMaker into thinking it has color support. FrameMaker therefore tries to show menus with its color defaults of black text on blue background; the X terminal tries to display that blue and comes up with a dark gray; and all menus are subsequently unreadable.

Using display classes, you can set up a separate *Xsession* file to be used only for the Visual X19TURBO by editing the *xdm-config* file *(28.24)*:

```
DisplayManager*session:                    /usr/lib/X11/xdm/Xsession
DisplayManager.VISUAL-X19TURBO.session: /usr/lib/X11/xdm/X19TURBOsession
```

And then edit the new *X19TURBOsession* file to include the required resource:

```
    ...
if [ -f $startup ]; then
        echo "Maker*Background:              white" | xrdb -merge -
        exec $startup
else
        if [ -f $resources ]; then
                xrdb -load $resources
        fi
        echo "Maker*Background:              white" | xrdb -merge -
        twm &
        exec xterm -geometry 80x24+10+10 -ls
fi
    ...
```

This will force the *X19TURBOsession* script to be run only by users logging on the X19TURBO X terminals, while users on all other X servers will continue to run the default *Xsession* script. The X19TURBO users become the only ones to have the new resource loaded into their servers.

(Note that this example depends on users using *xrdb–merge* *(20.18)* in their own *.xsession* scripts, or the Maker*Background resource will be lost.)

—*LM, from the* X Window System Administrator's Guide

28.28 Putting a Picture Behind the Login Box

One nice way to personalize your X display is to display a picture on your root background *(6.02)*. So one of the most trivial yet most popular questions that comes up is, how can you get a nice picture behind your login box *(28.02)*?

I must confess, I don't entirely understand why so many people want to do this. But if you must, there are a couple of ways to do it. My preferred way is to use the resource pointed to by the setup resource in *xdm-config*. This resource points to a program that is run alongside the login box. It is used in the default configuration to run the *xconsole* client for the console display *(28.23)*. However, it can also be used for any other program, so you might as well use it for *xsetroot*.

In *xdm-config*, define the setup resource for all servers:

```
DisplayManager*setup:    /usr/lib/X11/xdm/Xsetup_all
```

And then in the *Xsetup_all* file, enter the *xsetroot* command that you want:

```
#!/bin/sh
xsetroot -bitmap /usr/local/bitmaps/squiggle.xbm
```

Or if you want to get fancy, you can use a command like *xloadimage (24.05)* for more elaborate images:

```
#!/bin/sh
xloadimage -onroot /usr/local/gifs/babyducks.gif &
```

(It's probably better to stick to bitmaps *(22.01)* for monochrome displays, though.)

Remember that the console (:0) already has the setup resource set, generally to the *Xsetup_0* file *(28.23)*. So if you want to extend your picture to the console display, you should add the line to that file as well. *Xsetup_0* might read:

```
#!/bin/sh
xconsole -geometry 480x130-0-0 -daemon -notify -verbose -fn fixed -exitOnFail
xsetroot -bitmap /usr/local/bitmaps/squiggle.xbm
```

So what's my non-preferred way? Well, you might also use the xrdb resource *(28.29)* (which is what the *comp.windows.x* FAQ suggests). However, this is a serious hack, and for something this trivial, the setup resource works fine. The only reason you might use the xrdb resource is if you want the picture to appear behind a *chooser* box as well.

Whichever you do, *BE VERY CAREFUL*! The scripts pointed to by the xrdb and setup resources are run by *root*. So don't do anything there that might compromise your system.

—LM

28.29 Chooser and the System Loads

In Article 28.20, we showed you how you might have a *chooser* box display on an X terminal, allowing the user to choose any of several hosts. Well, I started thinking: what if your choice of host depended on which host had the lightest load? Wouldn't it be cool if you could show *xload* windows *(27.03)* from each of the hosts, so the user could see at a glance which host was least busy?

The problem was that there seemed to be no easy way to run a client alongside the *chooser*. The script pointed to by the Xsetup resource in *xdm-config* *(28.24)* can be run alongside the login box (it is used for showing a *xconsole* client with the login box), but there was no equivalent resource for running clients alongside the *chooser*.

At least, that's what I thought. The one thing that is done before the *chooser* box is displayed is that resources are loaded via *xrdb (17.03)*. This is necessary because these resources define *chooser (28.20)* preferences. I discovered that *xdm* provides a DisplayManager*xrdb resource, and that this resource can be set to an alternate program to load resources. First, set the xrdb resource to a script in the *xdm-config* file. Name that script *Xload*, and put it in the standard *xdm* configuration directory (e.g., */usr/lib/X11/xdm*):

```
DisplayManager*xrdb:          /usr/lib/X11/xdm/Xload
```

Next, create the *Xload* script.

```
#!/bin/sh
# called with arguments
#    "-display [DISPLAY] -load /usr/lib/X11/xdm/Xresources"

/usr/local/bin/xnetload ruby jasper jade -geometry -0-0 &
xrdb $*
```

I dug out the *xnetload* client *(27.04)* for this, which shows the network load on multiple hosts. Here, you need to know that the *chooser* box will show the current host (*opal*), *ruby, jasper,* and *jade*. After calling *xnetload* (in the background), run *xrdb* so that the resources are properly loaded.

The resulting window is shown in Figure 28-7.

If all four systems are otherwise equal, then this *xnetload* display allows you to select the host that has the lowest load (definitely not *ruby!*).

—LM

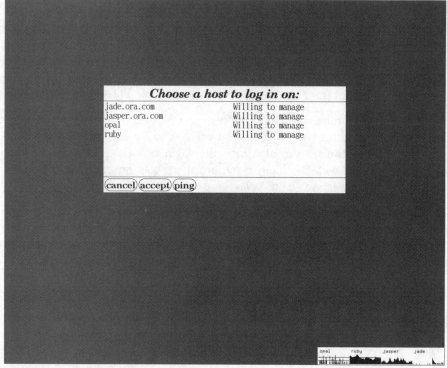

Figure 28-7: A Chooser box with the system loads

28.30 *Permanent Installation of xdm*

When you are happy with your *xdm* setup, it is time to install it so it will start automatically when the system boots. The way you do this is system dependent, but it is the same procedure as adding any other kind of daemon. In a typical BSD system, you would modify the */etc/rc.local* script. Under System V, edit */etc/inittab*. (Remember to keep backup copies of any system files you modify!)

Here are a few examples of installing *xdm* on various platforms:

Installing *xdm* on SunOS 4.1.1
    Add *xdm* to */etc/rc.local*:

```
if [ -f /usr/bin/X11/xdm ]; then
        /usr/bin/X11/xdm; echo -n "XDM"
fi
```

Then reboot the system.

Installing *xdm* on Ultrix 4.2
Add *xdm* to */etc/rc.local*:

```
[ -f /usr/bin/X11/xdm ] && {
        /usr/bin/X11/xdm & echo -n \`xdm \` > /dev/console
}
```

Then reboot the system.

Installing *xdm* on a System V Machine (IRIX 4.0)
(Your system may already be set up for running *xdm* as shipped. Check before continuing.)

Add *xdm* to */etc/inittab*:

```
xw:23:respawn:/usr/bin/X11/xdm -nodaemon
```

Then reboot the system.

Installing *xdm* on AIX 3.1
Add *xdm* to */etc/rc.tcpip*:

```
start /usr/bin/X11/xdm "$src_running"
```

Then reboot the system.

—*EAP, from the* X Window System Administrator's Guide

28.31 *Troubleshooting xdm*

Problems with logging in via *xdm* might be traced using *xdm* error messages. Many errors are placed in the file */usr/lib/X11/xdm/xdm-errors*, but if you are using X11R5 *xdm* or later, the first place to look is in the file *$HOME/.xsession-errors*. *$HOME/.xsession-errors* contains errors generated only under your user account. In addition, some of the more common situations are listed here:

- If the server doesn't start or if you don't get the login box, there is probably something wrong with your *xdm* configuration files. Look in the file */usr/lib/X11/xdm/xdm-errors* for hints. Good candidates for mistakes of this magnitude are the *Xservers (28.05, 28.08)*, *xdm-config (28.24)*, and *Xaccess (28.18, 28.19, 28.20, 28.21)* files. If you'd rather not deal with it, try to restore the files to the defaults and try again.

- If you get a "Login incorrect" error, you might have just typed your login name or password wrong. For the most part, *xdm* uses the same login authentication as the *login* program does, so if you can log on at the console or at any other terminal window, then you can log on using *xdm*. One possible snag is that if your server doesn't perform a full reset after each X session, then it's possible that some keysyms might be confusing the issue—see Article 18.16 for a real-life example.

- If you log on and the login box returns instantly, something's wrong with your environment. Either the */usr/lib/X11/xdm/xdm-errors (21.06)* file or *$HOME/.xsession-errors (21.05)* (under X11R5 or later) will contain error messages that can help you track the problem.

  One possibility is that your *.xsession* file isn't executable *(16.03)*. Try pressing **F1** (or in X11R5, **CTRL-Return**) after your password instead of the **Return** key to access the failsafe *(28.12)* session. If your problem is that your *.xsession* isn't executable, the error message in *.xsession-errors* (or *xdm-errors* in R3 and R4) will read something like:

  ```
  /usr/lib/X11/xdm/Xsession: /home/judy/.xsession: Permission denied
  ```

  If this is your problem, type:

  ```
  % chmod +x .xsession
  ```

  This commonly needs to be done when you've just created your *.xsession* file, or if you've just copied it from another machine using *ftp*.

- If you log on, windows flicker on your screen, and then the login box reappears, you probably put all your clients in the background *(2.03)* in your *.xsession* script. Press **F1** after your password to access the failsafe *(28.12)* session and edit your *.xsession* file. You need to put the last interactive client in the foreground by omitting the trailing "&." See Article 16.03 for more information.

  (Note that if this is your problem, *xdm* will not generate an error message since as far as *xdm* is concerned, everything was executed successfully.)

—LM, from the X Window System Administrator's Guide

29

Tools for Shell Scripts

29.01 UNIX Scripting

I'm one of these people who likes to automate anything I can, and UNIX is tailor-made for me. What I love about UNIX is that there are plenty of utilities for me to wrestle with for hours on end, without ever having to write a line of C code. Just working on this book, I wrote shell scripts to update outlines every day, to report when articles weren't properly included in any chapters, to manage cross references, etc.

This chapter is about writing your own tools with X interfaces. We assume that you already know how to write simple shell programs. If not, see our sister book, *UNIX Power Tools* (O'Reilly & Associates Inc. and Random House), to get a taste of the power of UNIX shell scripts.

—LM

29.02 Quick Xlib!

The tragedy of my career is that I'm not a programmer. Well, maybe "tragedy" is a strong word, but there are plenty of times when I know that what I want to do is easy in a C program, but I wouldn't know where to start.

dox

Well, my savior is the *dox* program. *dox* is a cheapo way of executing Xlib functions without having to know C. For example, if you want to make the screen go blank immediately:

```
% dox activatescreensaver
```

This calls the Xlib *XActivateScreenSaver( )* function. Just press a key or move the mouse to disable the screensaver again. (See Article 6.18 for information on how to do this with the *xset* client.)

Use the command *dox* = to get a full listing of all the functions available using *dox* on standard error. You'll still have to learn a little bit about how to use the Xlib functions, but that's not nearly so bad as having to learn how to program in C!

Admittedly, a lot of what you might do with *dox* can be done by fiddling with other X programs already available. *dox* comes with example shell scripts showing how you can rewrite *xkill* (2.08) and *xev* (18.12) as shell scripts that use *dox*; I'm afraid to say that in each of these cases, you might as well just use the X program already designed for the purpose. But in some cases, *dox* comes in pretty handy—see Articles 29.03 and 29.04.

—LM

29.03 *Resizing from the Command Line*

Among its many uses, the *dox* program *(29.02)* also allows you to resize any window to dimensions you specify on the command line. This precision can be extremely useful. In setting up screens for illustrations, for example, I've spent a lot of time futzing around with window sizes. After figuring out I need a window 100 pixels square, I can use a window manager to resize it, but I still need a steady hand. *dox* zaps any window you specify to the exact size you specify, and you don't have to fiddle with the pointer. (I might also run a new instance of the window and specify the dimensions using *–geometry* *(17.10)*, but sometimes I've worked on the contents of the window too!)

Suppose I have a text window I want to capture as a screen dump for a new book. To be consistent with other images, I'd like to have a window 350 pixels square. The *dox* program allows me to change the current window dynamically. First I need to find out the window ID using the *xwininfo* client *(17.13)*. I run the following command and then click on the window:

```
% xwininfo | grep id
```

The *xwininfo* output that contains the string "id" is:

```
xwininfo: Window id: 0x140000e text_widget
  Width: 222
  Border width: 1
  Override Redirect State: no
```

The first line of the output provides the window ID, 0×140000e. I can then resize the window using the resizewindow option to *dox*, also providing the window ID and the width and height in pixels:

```
% dox resizewindow 0x140000e 350 350
```

The window is immediately redrawn using my new dimensions. The upper-left corner stays at the original coordinates.

In rare cases, an application may not support resizing—regardless of how you try to do it. If you can't resize a window, the manpage should say so.

— VQ

29.04 Changing the Cursor with dox

Here's an example of how to use *dox (29.02)*.

Suppose I want to change the cursor to something different in each of my windows. By skimming my favorite Xlib programming manual, I learned that to assign a cursor you first need to initialize it with XCreateFontCursor and capture the cursor ID. Then you apply the cursor ID and the window ID to XDefineCursor.

So first I need to create a cursor. I can get a list of the cursor names by looking in my trusty Xlib reference manual, or by just giving a bogus cursor name to *dox*:

```
% dox createfontcursor help
dox: wild cursor name value
dox: usable values are: X_cursor arrow based_arrow_down based_arrow_up boat
bogosity bottom_left_corner bottom_right_corner bottom_side bottom_tee
box_spiral center_ptr circle clock coffee_mug cross cross_reverse crosshair
diamond_cross dot dotbox double_arrow draft_large draft_small draped_box
exchange fleur gobbler gumby hand1 hand2 heart icon iron_cross left_ptr
left_side left_tee leftbutton ll_angle lr_angle man middlebutton mouse pencil
pirate plus question_arrow right_ptr right_side right_tee rightbutton rtl_logo
sailboat sb_down_arrow sb_h_double_arrow sb_left_arrow sb_right_arrow
sb_up_arrow sb_v_double_arrow shuttle sizing spider spraycan star target
tcross top_left_arrow top_left_corner top_right_corner top_side top_tee
trek ul_angle umbrella ur_angle watch xterm
```

Let's try *gobbler*, which looks like a turkey. If you call *dox* to create the cursor, the cursor ID is returned:

```
% dox createfontcursor gobbler
0x4400002
```

Next, I need to get the window ID by using *xwininfo (17.13)*. *xwininfo* asks you to click on a window and then returns a plethora of information, including the window ID.

```
% xwininfo

xwininfo: Please select the window about which you
          would like information by clicking the
          mouse in that window.

      (click)

xwininfo: Window id: 0x1c0000d "xterm"
```

```
Absolute upper-left X:   121
Absolute upper-left Y:   44
      ...
```

Now I know that the cursor ID is 0x4400002 and the window ID is 0x1c0000d. I use this in my XDefineCursor function call:

```
% dox definecursor 0x1c0000d 0x4400002
```

This works as planned: I have a little turkey cursor. (And I already regret it.) Now, how do I automate it?

Well, the hard part is finding out the window ID. For *xterm* windows, you can take advantage of the WINDOWID environment variable (2.04). So from an *xterm* window, you can change the cursor of the current window with:

```
% dox definecursor $WINDOWID 'dox createfontcursor gobbler'
```

However, if you want to select a different window on your display, you're stuck with *xwininfo*. I wrote up a little front-end so that if I happen to know a window name or window ID, I can supply it on the command line.

wincursor

```
#!/bin/sh

# wincursor -- change cursor for a window.
#  syntax:  wincursor [-name NAME | -id ID] [-display DISPLAY] cursorname
#
# If ID not specified, uses xwininfo to find out, either through
#  -name or by letting you click on a window.


# Parse command line args.
while [ $# -gt 0 ]
do
        case "$1" in
                -id)      ID=$2
                          shift
                          ;;
                -display)
                          DISPLAY="$1 $2"
                          shift
                          ;;
                -name)
                          NAME=$2
                          shift
                          ;;
                *)        CURSORNAME=$1
                          ;;
        esac
        shift
done

# Must specify a cursor name.
if [ ! -n "$CURSORNAME" ]; then
```

```
                echo "Error:  No cursor specified!"
                exit 2
    fi

    # If no ID specified, use xwininfo to get it.
    if [ ! -n "$ID" ]; then

            if [ ! -n "$NAME" ]; then
                    echo "Please click on a window."
                    ID=`xwininfo |
                    sed -n '/xwininfo: Window id: \(0x[0-9a-f]*\) .*$/s//\1/p'`
            else
                    ID=`xwininfo -name $NAME |
                    sed -n '/xwininfo: Window id: \(0x[0-9a-f]*\) .*$/s//\1/p'`
            fi

    fi

    # Call dox to get cursor ID, then apply that to dox to define the
    # cursor on specified window.
    dox definecursor $ID `dox createfontcursor $CURSORNAME`
```

You can call this version with a *−name* command-line option:

```
% wincursor -name xterm heart
```

You can also use it with the *−id* command-line option, if you happen to know it off the top of your head. For example, you can change the cursor of the current *xterm*:

```
% wincursor -id $WINDOWID pencil
```

You can also call *wincursor* without identifying the window, and be prompted to click on a window.

—LM

29.05 *X Input for Shell Scripts*

There are several tools I use for prompting users within shell scripts: *xmenu* (29.06), *xpick* (29.07), and *xmessage* (4.09). It would seem that one of them would suffice, but actually they each have their strengths.

In addition to being useful for displaying output (see Articles 4.09, 4.10, 29.08 and 28.13), *xmessage* is ideal for creating simple dialog boxes for users. I might use it if I want to let the user select between Yes or No, or between OK or Cancel. I might also use it if I want to let the user to know why a script bombed before it exits.

xpick is nice for letting the user select several items from a list. In Article 29.10, we use it to have the user select files from the list of files on a *tar* archive.

xmenu is most useful for when the user has to select exactly one item of a list. See Article 29.09.

For getting text input from the user, I was surprised that I couldn't find any simple clients that took input from the user and sent it on to standard output. So I wrote one using Tcl/Tk: see Article 30.04 for information on *gettext*.

—*LM*

29.06 Menus in Shell Scripts with *xmenu*

xmenu

xmenu takes a list of arguments and provides them as "menu" items in a small window. For example:

```
% xmenu Coffee Tea Milk
```

gives you a small window resembling Figure 29-1.

Figure 29-1: xmenu example

The window appears directly underneath and to the right of the user's pointer. (You can change this using the *–geometry (17.10)* command-line option.)[*] When the user moves the pointer over one of the options, it is highlighted. By clicking on one of the options, the window disappears and *xmenu* returns the value of the specified string.

```
% xmenu Coffee Tea Milk
Tea
```

You can give the window a heading using the *–heading* command-line option. This is useful for prompting the user for what he/she is selecting.

Another useful command-line option is *–line*. If you specify *–line* between any two arguments, a line appears separating those arguments. This is nice for grouping menu options.

The return value for *xmenu* is usually whatever the user selects from the menu. If called on the command line, this return value is returned to standard output; or if you use *xmenu* within a shell script, the return value can be redirected as input to another command or saved in a variable.

However, you can also alter the return value by using equal signs (=) in the arguments. If an argument contains an equal sign, the portion of the argument

---

[*] I strongly recommend using *–geometry*. Otherwise, *xmenu* becomes almost impossible to use if the user's pointer happens to be near the bottom of the screen.

to the left of the equal sign is used in the menu, but the portion of the argument to the right of the equal sign is the resulting return value if that menu option is selected. This is probably the nicest feature of *xmenu*; it is particularly useful in shell scripts, since it lets you phrase a question to a user one way and then interpret it another without having to go through a case construct. For example, you might have a shell script that quizzes the reader on state capitals:

```
ANSWER=`xmenu -heading "What's the capital of Maine?" \
Portland=WRONG Freeport=WRONG "Bar Harbor"=WRONG Camden=WRONG -line \
"None of the Above"="RIGHT"`
```

The resulting window appears in Figure 29-2.

What's the capital of Maine?
Portland
Freeport
Bar Harbor
Camden
None of the Above
Don't know

Figure 29-2: An xmenu quiz

When the user selects an item, the $ANSWER variable is set to either RIGHT or WRONG. Depending on the value of $ANSWER, the programmer can commend or humiliate the user as appropriate.

—LM

29.07 *Selections Using xpick*

xpick

Like *xmenu (29.06)*, *xpick* is a utility to allow the user to select among several items. The strength of *xpick* is that it lets the user select more than one item, and that it provides some pattern-matching capabilities. For example:

```
% xpick anger envy gluttony lust pride sloth television
```

The resulting window resembles Figure 29-3.

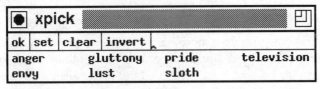

Figure 29-3: Choose your poison

(*xpick* doesn't support anything similar to the *–heading* option of *xmenu*. However, it's easy enough just to use the *–title (17.09)* option if you want to provide some instructions for the user.)

You can select among the listed items, using the first mouse button to select (or unselect) an item, and the third mouse button to extend a selection. Each item is highlighted as it is selected.

There are four buttons at the top, and one text field. You can use the text field to enter a pattern that you want to match. The patterns follow the same syntax as standard UNIX filename completion.

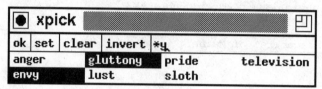

Figure 29-4: Matching a pattern

Pressing the **set** button or the **Return** key highlights the matching items. You can then select additional items or unselect some of the highlighted items using the first mouse button. The **invert** button reverses the selections. The **clear** button clears the entire listing.

When you are happy with the items selected, press **ok** and they are printed to standard output.

```
% xpick anger envy gluttony lust pride sloth television
envy
gluttony
```

xpick seems a little less trivial when you consider that you can run it on the listing of a directory:

```
% xpick 'ls /usr/bin/X11' &
```

You can use this sort of contruct to select command-line arguments within shell scripts. Article 29.10 shows an example of this method.

—*LM*

29.08 *Process Listing*

xps

I'm always forgetting my *ps* options, especially since they're different from system to system. Usually, all I want *ps* for is to show all my processes (whether or not it's associated with a tty), show all the processes for the current tty, or show all processes for all users. So I wrote up *xps* using *xmenu (29.06)* and *xmessage (4.09)* as follows:

```
#!/bin/sh

# xps -- just give a menu for the type of output you want.
#

# Get the tty for use by -t option:
TTY=`who am i | cut -c18-19`

# take xmenu output and supply to ps command line.
args=`xmenu -geometry +0+0 -heading "What do you want to get processes for?" \
"Processes associated with this tty"="-t$TTY" \
"All processes for $USER"="x" \
"All processes for all users"="agx"`

ps $args > /tmp/ps$$
xmessage -file /tmp/ps$$ -title "Output from  ps $args"
rm /tmp/ps$$
```

In this script, I let users choose what sort of output they want in human terms.
I use equal signs in the arguments to *xmenu* to represent the corresponding *ps*
command-line arguments and then set the args variable to the output of
xmenu. The args variable is then supplied to *ps*. I might have let the output
go to standard output, but I prefer to display it within a window using *xmessage*. To do this, I have to save the *ps* output in a file because *xmessage* won't
respect newlines otherwise.

When you start *xps*, you first get a menu to select what kind of *ps* output you
want, as shown in Figure 29-5.

```
What do you want to get processes for?
Processes associated with this tty
All processes for lmui
All processes for all users
```

Figure 29-5: *ps menu*

If I choose just processes for myself, I might get a window that resembles Figure 29-6.

As you can imagine, *ps* output for *all* users might get out of hand. So in this
script, I'm really using the variation of *xmessage* that includes a scrollbar *(11.02)*
if needed.

—LM

```
┌─────────────────────────────────────────────────────────────────────┐
│ ● Output from  ps agx ░░░░░░░░░░░░░░░░░░░░░░░░░░░░░░░░░░░░░░░░░      ▣ │
├─────────────────────────────────────────────────────────────────────┤
│   PID TT STAT   TIME COMMAND                                          │
│     0 ?  D     0:00 swapper                                           │
│     1 ?  S     0:19 /sbin/init -                                      │
│     2 ?  D     0:51 pagedaemon                                        │
│    63 ?  S     0:22 portmap                                           │
│    68 ?  S    14:56 ypserv                                            │
│    70 ?  I     0:00 ypbind                                            │
│    73 ?  I     0:00 /usr/etc/rpc.yppasswdd /var/yp/rawdata/passwd -m passwd│
│    75 ?  I     0:00 rpc.ypupdated                                     │
│    77 ?  I     0:00 keyserv                                           │
│    95 ?  S     7:54 in.named -b /var/named/named.boot                 │
│    98 ?  S     2:34 (biod)                                            │
│    99 ?  S     2:34 (biod)                                            │
│   102 ?  I     2:37 (biod)                                            │
│   103 ?  I     2:33 (biod)                                            │
│   107 ?  I     0:00 xterm                                             │
│   114 ?  S     2:55 syslogd                                           │
│   122 ?  I     0:19 sendmail: accepting connections                   │
│   128 ?  I     0:00 rpc.mountd -n                                     │
│   130 ?  S     3:03 (nfsd)                                            │
│                                                                       │
│ ( okay )                                                              │
└─────────────────────────────────────────────────────────────────────┘
```

Figure 29-6: ps output

29.09 Selecting a Printer

On our network, we have many printers, in several U.S. states. Most people prefer using a single printer, but occasionally they need to use a different one because of service, because of particular fonts, or because their favorite printer is being hogged by a beloved co-worker. When that happens, they just change their default printer using the PRINTER environment variable *(2.04)*:

```
% setenv PRINTER ibis
```

and then they're on their merry way.

Well, here comes Linda Mui, Trivial Scripter. It seemed to me that someone might forget how to use *setenv*, or might forget the names of the printers. Why not complicate the situation by writing a front-end? ("Why not indeed?")

printer_hack

I put the following lines in my *.cshrc*:

```
set printers=`grep '^[^<SPACE><TAB>#].*\|' /etc/printcap | sed 's/|.*$//'`
alias setprint 'setenv PRINTER `xmenu -geometry +0+0 -heading \
    "Choose a printer:" $printers`'
```

The first line sets a variable named printers to the list of printers known in */etc/printcap*. (If you type this in, note that the strings *<SPACE>* and *<TAB>* should be written as a literal space and tab, respectively.) The second line defines an alias called setprint, which calls *xmenu (29.06)* to give you a menu of printers. When you want to change your printer, type:

```
% setprint
```

A menu comes up at the top of your screen resembling Figure 29-7.

```
Choose a printer:
emu
kiwi
ibis
rheas
dodo
auk
moa
```

Figure 29-7: Choosing a printer

(Don't ask why we name our printers after extinct or endangered birds.)

The PRINTER environment variable is now changed in the shell that called *set-print*.

—*LM*

29.10 *Help with tar*

I'm always working with *tar* archives. One of my pet peeves is that *tar* is unwieldly to use when you don't want the entire archive, but only want a few files. So I wrote *xtar*, a quickie front-end to *tar*.

xtar

```sh
#!/bin/sh

if [ $# = 0 ]
then
        files=`ls *.tar *.tar.Z *.tar.gz *.tar.z 2>/dev/null`
        tarfiles=`xpick -title "Choose a tar source file:" $files`
else
        tarfiles=$*
fi

for file in $tarfiles
do
        case $file in
        *.tar)  PREPROC=""
                FILE=$file
                ;;
        *.tar.Z) PREPROC="zcat $file | "
                FILE="-"
                ;;
        *.tar.z) PREPROC="gzcat $file | "
                FILE="-"
                ;;
        *.tar.gz) PREPROC="gzcat $file | "
                FILE="-"
                ;;
        *)      echo "Error: $file has unexpected suffix!  Exiting."
                exit 2
```

```
            ;;

    esac

    listing=`eval $PREPROC tar -tf $FILE`

    target=`xpick -title "Unpack file:" $listing "ENTIRE ARCHIVE"`

    if [ "$target" = "ENTIRE ARCHIVE" ]
    then
            target=""
    fi

    eval $PREPROC tar xf $FILE $target
done
```

Any arguments to *xtar* are taken as names of *tar* files. However, without arguments, *xtar* prompts you for files in the current directory that have *.tar* suffixes (using *xpick (29.07)*), and asks you to choose among them, as shown in Figure 29-8. Note that *xtar* knows about compressed files with *.Z*, *.z*, or *.gz* suffixes, and knows how to uncompress them.

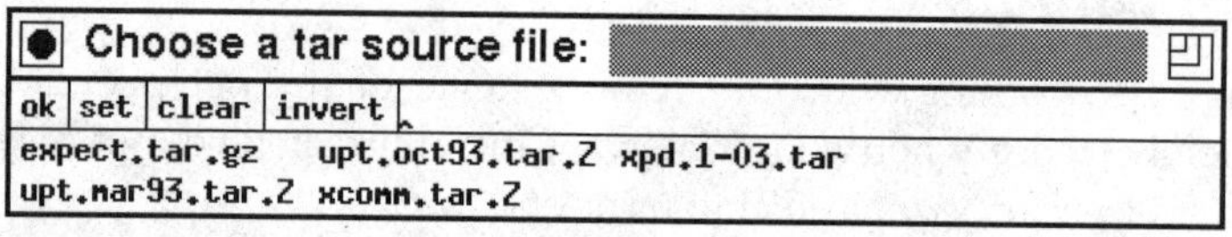

● Choose a tar source file: ▨
ok	set	clear	invert
expect.tar.gz   upt.oct93.tar.Z xpd.1-03.tar
upt.mar93.tar.Z xcomm.tar.Z

Figure 29-8: Choose a tar file, any tar file

For each of the files you choose, it then shows you a listing of its contents (with *xpick* again) and asks you to select files you want from the archive. (Alternatively, you can select the entire archive.) Figure 29-9 shows such a window.

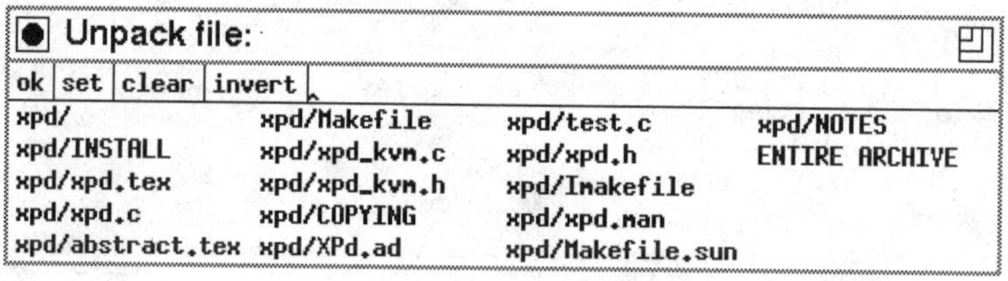

● Unpack file: ▨
ok	set	clear	invert
xpd/   xpd/Makefile   xpd/test.c   xpd/NOTES
xpd/INSTALL   xpd/xpd_kvm.c   xpd/xpd.h   ENTIRE ARCHIVE
xpd/xpd.tex   xpd/xpd_kvm.h   xpd/Imakefile
xpd/xpd.c   xpd/COPYING   xpd/xpd.man
xpd/abstract.tex xpd/XPd.ad   xpd/Makefile.sun

Figure 29-9: Listing of a tar file

As with all my scripts, *xtar* could use plenty of modifications. For example, it should know how to navigate directories, rather than only working with files in the current directory. It should also know how to deal with other *tar* options, or with errors. And it gets very confused when it encounters files that are linked. But it's good enough for my needs, and it demonstrates how handy *xpick* can be.

—LM

30

Writing Tools in Tcl/Tk

30.01 What Are Tcl and Tk?

Although innumerable utilities have been written in each of the shell programming languages using a host of indispensable utilities (*sed, awk,* and friends), there are still many tasks that seem just a little too complex to tackle in the shell and a little to trivial to warrant a "real" program (in C, Pascal, or what have you). These are tasks that can be efficiently solved with a language like Tcl.

Tcl is a general-purpose, interpreted programming language, developed by Dr. John Ousterhout. Tcl by itself isn't very exciting but because of its structure, some very interesting extensions have been built around it. The most exciting of these extensions is Tk. Tk is an X11 programming extension for Tcl that provides a simple mechanism for building applications with a Motif-like interface. Several programs in this book have been written with Tcl/Tk, such as *tkcron (27.08)*, *xelem (5.07)*, and *ical (4.03)*.

TclTk

Tcl/Tk is a flexible system that can be used several different ways. Programmers can link Tcl/Tk into their existing applications, allowing users to interact with their programs using Tcl. You can also write scripts without any C code, using the core Tcl interpreter *tcl,* or the extended Tcl/Tk interpreter *wish.*

We don't expect you to learn how to write polished applications in Tcl/Tk from this book: it is much too complex a language. However, you should be able to learn how to write some small programs. We hope to give you a taste of the power of Tcl/Tk, and perhaps feel empowered to start fiddling with it on your own. You probably need to know something about programming in X11 to get the most out of this chapter, but even if you don't, it's likely that you'll be able to follow examples and get a simple program running.

For more information on Tcl and Tk, we recommend *Tcl and the Tk Toolkit* by John Ousterhout (Addison-Wesley, 1994).

—*NW*

30.02 Hello, World!

"Hello, World" is the traditional name of a completely useless program that programming tutorials use at the very beginning of the book. Someone recently complained to me that the "Hello, World" example was one of his pet peeves, because it was unbearably dumb. This may be true, but in my opinion there's nothing like getting the user's feet wet in a new programming environment, and "Hello, World" is one of the quickest ways to do so. Using "Hello, World", any reader can type in the few lines and get a tangible example of how to get from a text file to a working program. New users aren't likely to learn much about the language from "Hello, World," but it helps to build their confidence. It demonstrates that there's no magic involved; you just need to learn the rules.

A "Hello, World" example, *world.tcl*, appears below. This program simply writes "Hello World!" onto standard output and then terminates. You can run this program by making it executable (with the UNIX *chmod +x* command) and adjusting the first line of the script to point to the *tcl* executable installed on your system. You can also just use the command:

```
% tcl -f world.tcl
```

The *world.tcl* script reads:

```
#!/usr/bin/tcl

puts stdout "Hello, World!"
```

What this script does is use the built-in `puts` command to print output. The first argument identifies the file that it writes to; `stdout` is the "special" name for the standard output device (i.e., your terminal shell). Technically, `stdout` is not required because that is the default output file. The second argument is the string to output. We wrote "Hello, World" because we're traditionalists, but any other string would do.

```
% world.tcl
Hello, World!
```

Wish Tricks

The Tk extension to Tcl adds a number of new commands for creating windows, buttons, and various sorts of data entry fields (entry fields, radio buttons, free-form text fields, etc.). We're going to repeat the "Hello, World" example, only this time with a windowing interface.

A simple Tk-based "Hello, World" example, *world.tk*, is shown below. This program creates a single window on the screen containing the string "Hello World!". You can run this program by making it executable and adjusting the first line of the script to point to the *wish* executable installed on your system. (*wish* is the windowing shell to Tcl/Tk.) You can also use the command:

```
$ wish -f world.tk
```

The *world.tk* script reads:

```
#!/usr/bin/X11/wish -f

label .hello -text "Hello, World!"

pack .hello
```

The resulting window appears in Figure 30-1.

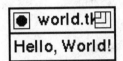

Figure 30-1: Hello, World! in Tk

Here, we have an example of creating a widget in Tk. The general form of a widget-creation command is

```
command .widget-name options
```

The `label` command in *world.tk* initializes a `label` widget with the name `.hello`. All widget names begin with a period. A `label` widget simply displays some text; other widget commands are `button` for a button widget, `scrollbar` for a scrollbar widget, `menu` for a menu widget, `frame` for a frame widget, etc.

Once a widget is created, it can't be displayed until it is placed in a top-level frame. You can create your own top-level frames, but the default top-level frame, called simply ".", is created for you automatically. There are several ways to place objects in the frame, but the *packer* is the simplest. The *packer* allows you to specify the relative placement of widgets and it resizes the top-level frame to fit around them. The `pack` command shown above packs the widget `.hello` in the default frame.

If you tried out the sample Tk-based "Hello, World" script shown above, then you may have noticed that there's no clean way to exit. You have to either interrupt the *wish* command shell, use the **Delete** option on your window manager's menu, or kill the window manually. This is because Tcl executes the commands in your script sequentially, but when Tk is being used, the script does not terminate when Tcl runs out of commands to execute. Instead, control is passed to an event handler that begins processing X11 events (button presses, text entry, key bindings, etc.) and responding to them.

The "Hello, World" example shown above only uses a `label` widget, which doesn't require any user interaction. So there is no way to exit. The following is another example of "Hello, World" in Tk, but this time a `button` is used instead of a `label` so the user can exit cleanly :[*]

```
#!/usr/bin/X11/wish -f

button .hello -text "Hello, World!" -command "exit"

pack .hello
```

The resulting window looks pretty much the same, but the string "Hello, World!" now appears within a button. If you place your pointer inside the button, it changes color; and if you press the **Hello, World!** button, the specified command will be executed—in this case, `exit`. This lets you exit from the program gracefully.

—NW, LM

30.03   *Quickie Tcl Syntax*

I've read innumerable introductory books teaching programming languages, and the part that takes forever is the part where they teach you the basic syntax of the language: how to set variables, data types, numeric operators, string operators, precedence, if/then/else structures, while loops, for loops, etc. Yawn. It's all information you need to know, but by the fifth time, I really don't need to be told that multiplication takes precedence over addition, and I don't need to have a conditional explained to me.

However, Tcl/Tk does things differently enough that we really do have to tell you something about its basic syntax. So this is my attempt at teaching "quick 'n dirty" syntax for people who are familiar enough with programming that they don't need to be told the basics. I include some examples, since I know that many readers (myself included) just skim to examples and don't read the text, but we'll try to keep this short and sweet.

You'll undoubtedly need a complete book on Tcl/Tk if you want to write any real applications, but these summaries should be enough for you to follow our examples, assuming you have some background in programming and know a little about programming in X. In addition, Tcl is installed with manpages for each of its commands.

---

[*] Yes, we love "Hello, World" so much that we're doing it three times.

Command Structure

A command has the structure:

```
command arguments ...
```

A semicolon (;) can be used to delimit the end of the command, but it is not required: a newline is sufficient.

Many commands are really several commands in one. For example, the string command can perform several different types of string manipulation, depending on its arguments.

Comments

Lines beginning with # are ignored in Tcl/Tk.

```
# This is a comment.
   #    Me too
set num1 10 ;   # Me three
```

Comments must be placed where Tcl expects a new command: they cannot be embedded within commands. That is, the # can be at the beginning of a line, or be the first non-whitespace character on a line, or it can come after a semicolon that ends a command; but if it appears in the middle of a command, Tcl will complain loudly.

Data Types and Declarations—Not!

There are no data types in Tcl. Characters, strings, decimal numbers, floating point, etc.; they're all equal under the law of Tcl. Everything is a string.

Variables do not need to be declared in Tcl, but they do usually need to be initialized if you want to avoid nasty error messages.

Setting Variables

Set variables in Tcl/Tk with the set command.

```
set num 128
```

The first argument to set is the name of the variable. The second argument is the value to set the variable with. In this case, we set the variable num to the value 128.

When the value of the variable is used later on, it is preceded by the dollar sign ($). For example, $num is interpreted as 128. You can delimit the names of simple variables using curly braces ({, }), as you can in the shell. So $num could also read ${num}. This is necessary when the name of the variable is not delimited by spaces or other punctuation. For example, if you want to print the value of $num inches as "128in," you cannot use $numin, you must use ${num}in so that the Tcl interpreter can tell where the variable name ends.

Command-line Arguments

Variable names are case sensitive (e.g., $num is different from $Num). The argv variable contains the command-line arguments to the Tcl script, and argc contains the number of arguments. The actual name of the script is not included in this listing; it is predefined as $argv0.

Numerical Expressions

Simple numerical expressions are performed using the expr command. expr takes an expression and returns its value. For example, the following expression returns the value of $num multiplied by 2:

```
expr $num * 2
```

There are also some special "shorthands." The incr command increments the variable, append appends a value to a variable, and unset deletes a variable.

Embedding Commands

In a script, you aren't likely to add a couple of numbers and let their sum go off into deep space (as shown above). You're more likely to use this value in another command. To do this, embed a command within another using square brackets ([,]). The return value of the embedded command can thus be used as an argument for the other. For example, to set the value of the variable num2 to $num times 2:

```
set num2 [ expr $num * 2 ]
```

Here, the return value of the expr command becomes the second argument to the set command. The $num2 variable becomes the value of $num times 2 (in our example, 256).

Backslash Escapes

As with many languages, backslashes can be used to represent special characters or to suppress interpolation of a character. For example, \n is a newline, and \$ gives you a literal dollar sign. A backslash at the end of a line suppresses the newline and compresses the whitespace surrounding it.

Quoting and Command Grouping

You can quote things two ways: using double quotes ("), or using curly braces ({, }). The big difference is that variables and special characters are interpreted within quotes, whereas within braces, what you see is what you get. (You might think of braces as being like single quotes in shell programming.)

If/Then/Else

The syntax for an `if` construct is: [*]

```
if { condition } {
    commands
} elseif { condition } {
    commands
} else {
    commands
}
```

(Enough said.)

While Loops

A `while` loop follows the syntax:

```
while { condition } {
        commands
}
```

While the *condition* is true, the *commands* are repeatedly executed. (Hopefully, the commands will alter the value of *condition*, so that it isn't true forever.) For example, to count down from 10:

```
#!/usr/local/bin/tcl

set num 10
while { $num >= 0 } {
    puts stdout $num
    set num [expr $num - 1 ]
}
```

The variable `num` is set to 10. The `while` continues to loop as long as `$num` is greater than 0. The `puts` command (shown in Article 30.02) prints `$num` to standard output. The `set` command decrements `num` by 1. Then the loop starts all over again.

For Loops

The syntax for a `for` loop is:

```
for { initialization } { condition } { iter_cmd } {
    commands
}
```

For example, to count down from 10 again:

---

[*] Tcl gurus may tell you that this isn't strictly true, since the curly braces aren't really a part of the required syntax. However, in practice, you will never write a construct like this without the curly braces.

```
for { set i 10 } { $i >= 0 } { incr i -1 } {
  puts stdout $i
}
```

Foreach Loops

The syntax for a foreach construct is:

```
foreach variable { list ... } {
        commands
}
```

Break and Continue

The break command terminates the current loop, and the continue command terminates the current iteration of the loop but continues with the next iteration. (Same as in C.)

Switch

The switch command performs the same function as a case statement in the Bourne shell. The syntax is:

```
switch $variable {
    value1 {
        commands
    }
    value2 {
        commands
    }
        ...
    default {
        commands
    }
}
```

The switch command will compare the specified variable against the specified values. When a match is found, it returns (i.e., executes) the corresponding commands. A default value at the end of the script is taken as the default option if no other matches are found.

switch supports arguments to specify different kinds of matches. See the manpage for more information.

Arrays

Tcl supports associative arrays. In the following example, the array is named child, and Monday and Wednesday are two indexes:

```
set child(Monday) "fair of face"
set child(Wednesday) "full of grace"
```

The individual array values are called by placing a dollar sign ($) before the array name:

```
puts stdout "Monday's child is $child(Monday)."
```

The `array` command supports many options for searching an array, returning the size of an array, etc.

Lists

A list is just a set of elements separated by spaces or tabs. For example:

```
{groucho harpo chico zeppo}
```

Tcl supports many list manipulation commands, too many to list here.

String Manipulation

The `string` command provides a multitude of string manipulation functions. The other commands that are useful are `format` and `scan`, which work sort of like the C functions `sprintf()` and `scanf()`.

Procedures

A *procedure* (or function, or routine, or whatever else you want to call it) is defined using the `proc` command. The syntax is:

```
proc name {args} {
        commands
}
```

Usually, one of the procedure's commands is `return`, to specify what the return value of the procedure should be. For example, here's a very simple procedure:

```
proc add3 {num1 num2 num3} {
        return [expr $num1 + [expr $num2 + $num3] ]
}
```

This creates a procedure named `add3` which accepts three arguments. It adds the three arguments and returns their sum. The procedure can be called anywhere later in the script:

```
set sum [ add3 1 2 3 ]
```

(The `$sum` variable becomes 6.)

The `global` and `upvar` commands can be used to juggle local and global variables.

Sourcing

The source command can be used to read Tcl commands from another file. This is most useful for including procedures that are in a different file.

Running System Commands

Tcl supports an exec command for running system commands. For example, if you wanted to put the output of the UNIX *date* command *(3.17)* in a variable:

```
set todaysdate [ exec date ]
```

Environment Variables

env is a predefined array containing environment variables *(2.04)* inherited from the shell that ran the script. For example, the user's login name is stored in $env(USER).

File I/O

Before you can read or write to a file, you need to open it with the open command, and place its file handle in a variable. You read lines using gets and you write lines using puts. Article 30.06 shows a robust example with file I/O.
—*LM*

30.04 Working with Widgets in Tk

Now that you've breezed through the dreary parts, here's the fun stuff.

In Article 30.02, we showed you how you can create a label widget in Tk, and then pack it into the top-level widget shell (.). There are other types of widgets you can create, and you can just as easily "pack" several of them together.

For example, you might have a couple of label widgets and then display them together:

```
#!/usr/local/bin/wish -f

label .label1 -text "The soup of the day is:"
label .label2 -text "NAVY BEAN"

pack .label1 .label2
```

The resulting display resembles Figure 30-2.

We neglected to include a way to exit. For that, we can just tack on an exit button, as we showed in Article 30.02:

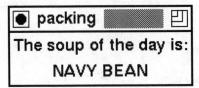

Figure 30-2: A couple of packed label widgets

```
#!/usr/local/bin/wish -f

label .label1 -text "The soup of the day is:"
label .label2 -text "NAVY BEAN"
button .button -text "OK" -command exit

pack .label1 .label2 .button
```

This one looks like Figure 30-3.

Figure 30-3: Adding an exit button

When the user (probably you) presses the **OK** button, the script terminates.

Entry Fields

So far, we've only used label and button widgets. What about getting input from a user? Well, for that we use the entry command. This creates a widget with an "entry" field, so you can prompt the user for input. The entry widget is generally used with a *–textwidget* argument to specify a variable that the input is placed into.

The following script allows users to type in a name, and then prints the name to standard output.

```
#!/usr/local/bin/wish -f

label .label -text "Enter your name:"
entry .info -textvariable name -relief sunken
button .button -text "OK" -command {
        puts stdout $name
        exit
}

pack .label .info .button
```

When the program is executed, the user sees a window resembling Figure 30-4.

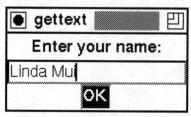

Figure 30-4: An example of an entry widget

Place the pointer inside the entry window, click the first mouse button, enter a name, and then press **OK**. The script returns the name to standard output. I use the *–relief* argument to specify the entry widget to appear "sunken"; this is to ensure that users can distinguish the entry field from a label field.

The button widget is worth looking at here. Instead of exiting immediately, I've grouped together two commands. This is to ensure that before exiting, the program prints the value of the name variable to standard output.

You can now generalize the script. It can be generalized to take the label from command-line arguments, using the predefined $argv variable. Even if you aren't interested in going any further with Tcl, you can use this script within shell scripts to get user input.

```
#!/usr/local/bin/wish -f

label .label -text "$argv"
entry .info -textvariable input -relief sunken
button .button -text "OK" -command {
        puts stdout $input
        exit
}

pack .label .info .button
```

For example, I might use this in a shell script that needs a zip code.

```
#!/bin/sh

zip=`gettext Enter your zip code:`
```

When the script is executed, users see something resembling Figure 30-5.

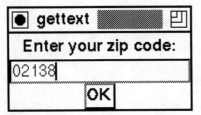

Figure 30-5: Prompting for a zip code

Bindings

There are plenty of other things to adjust in this script. You can use arguments to the entry widget to change the size of the entry field, for example. You can use arguments to pack to have the widgets stacked from left to right (rather than on top of one another), and to change how much space is between them. You can tweak things on this script forever if you wish. But the only thing that really drives me crazy is that if you press **Return** in the text field, you see a weird hex-like set of characters. This is Very Annoying, since it isn't unusual to think that **Return** can be taken as user input.

To allow users to press **Return**, set up a *binding* for the entry widget. To do that, use the bind command:

```
bind .info <Return> {
        puts stdout $input
        exit
}
```

bind is used to bind actions to widgets. In this case, bind the **Return** key in the .info widget to do the same thing as pressing **OK**. <Return> is only one of the actions that can be bound; you can actually bind any of the keys by specifying their key symbols within angle brackets (<, >) (use *xmodmap -pk (18.17)* for a quick listing of key symbols). You can also specify pressing each of the buttons (for example, <Button-1> or <1>).

gettext

Here is my modified version of *gettext*:

```
#!/usr/local/bin/wish -f

proc showinput {input} {
    puts stdout $input
    exit
}

label .label -text "$argv"
entry .info -textvariable input -relief sunken
button .button -text "OK" -command {
        showinput "$input"
    }
```

```
bind .info <Return> {
        showinput "$input"
}

bind .info <Escape> {
        set input {}
}

pack .label .info .button -side left
```

In this version, I not only used the `bind` command to do the same thing as pressing the **OK** button, I also created a tiny procedure for printing the exiting, called `showinput`. It doesn't save me much in typing; it's just a good practice that if you find yourself repeating code, then consolidate it. You never know when one little change may need to be repeated a hundred times.

I also added a second `bind` for the **Escape** key. This key empties out the `input` variable, so that the user can easily cancel the current input field and start over again.

In the actual `pack` command, I added the argument *–side left*. This means that instead of packing the widgets on top of one another, they pack side to side. This is just a matter of preference.

Here's an example of using the *gettext* script. Suppose you want to get a phone number within a script. In the script, use the following line:

```
phone=`gettext Enter your phone number:`
```

When this line is executed, the user sees the window shown in Figure 30-6.

Figure 30-6: Example gettext window

When the user fills in a phone number and presses the **OK** button (or presses **Return**), the `phone` variable is assigned that value.

—*LM*

30.05 *Using Functions*

Tcl makes it easy to install your own libraries of functions that are automatically loaded. When you install Tcl/Tk, many such libraries are automatically installed.

The *popupmsg* program is an example using one of the built-in functions. It displays a short message and waits for you to dismiss the window. (It's basically just a Tcl/Tk version of xmessage *(4.09)*.) This script uses tk_dialog, one of the routines provided in the Tk distribution. The appropriate source file is loaded automatically when you attempt to use the routine.

If you want to see the tk_dialog script, just look in your Tk library directory. On my system, I looked in */usr/local/lib/tk*. There are several files there, but the central file is *tclIndex*. This file points to the definitions of several functions, including tk_dialog:

```
set auto_index(tk_dialog) "source $dir/dialog.tcl"
```

This tells you to look for the definition of tk_dialog in a file called *dialog.tcl*. (The $dir variable points to */usr/local/lib/tk* in this instance.)

popupmsg

The *popupmsg* program reads:

```
#!/usr/bin/X11/wish -f

wm withdraw .

tk_dialog .d { Popup Message } $argv warning 0 { OK }

destroy .
```

The first thing to do is remove the default top-level frame from the screen. For this, use the wm command, which is the command that interacts with the window manager. The arguments withdraw . tell the window manager not to display the window named ".". (As mentioned in Article 30.02, "." is the name of the default top-level window provided by Tk.) This doesn't delete the window (you can still manipulate it with *tcl* commands, if you wish), but it is no longer displayed.

(We withdraw the . window because the tk_dialog function draws its own window, and it would look silly to have two windows on the screen.)

Next, call tk_dialog to create and display a new widget.

At the end of the script, we use destroy to delete the default top-level frame. When Tk is running, the event handler continues to search for events until the top-level frame is deleted, at which point control returns to the script. In this case, the exit command would have been just as effective.

To run the script, just call it with the text of the message:

```
% popupmsg Dentist appointment at 4:15 &
```

The window you get looks like Figure 30-7.

—NW

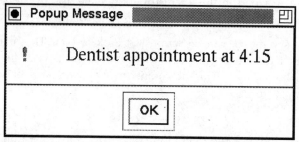

Figure 30-7: Pop-up message

30.06 A Simple Database Program

It's difficult to get a feel for a language by only looking at trivial programs. The next script that we will look at is considerably longer than the others, and it performs a real task.* Among other things, this script also shows you how to do simple file I/O in Tcl/Tk.

tkdb

The *tkdb* script is an editor for very simple, flat-file databases. In order to keep the script as simple as possible, you must create the database with an editor, providing a title and the specifications of the fields in the database. The *tkdb* program produces a window resembling Figure 30-8.

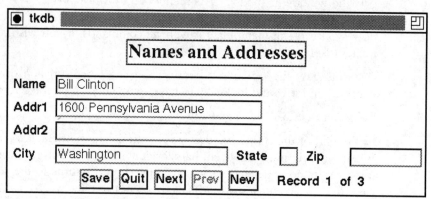

Figure 30-8: Example tkdb window

We'll discuss the script in pieces, referring to parts of the scripts using line numbers. If you want the complete script, however, just grab it off the CD-ROM.

---

* Granted, it's still a toy program, but it's not quite trivial ;-)

Opening the Database

First, *tkdb* gets the name of the database file from the command line. We use several list manipulation commands to break the $argv string into a list, so that it can access the command line arguments individually (in reality, *tkdb* expects a single argument, so this isn't strictly necessary).

```
40  # Get the dbName from the arguments, use ~/.tkdbfile if
41  # none is provided
42  set arglist [ split $argv " " ]
43  if { [ llength $arglist ] > 0 } {
44      set dbName [ lindex $arglist 0 ]
45  } else {
46      set dbName "~/.tkdbfile"
47  }
```

We use the $dbName variable to contain the name of the databse requested by the user, or *$HOME/.tkdbfile* if no database was specified. We use the file command to determine if the file exists. (file is just one of many functions that Tcl provides for querying the state of the system and the interpreter.) If the file exists, we open the file and store the file handle in the variable $f. If the file doesn't exist, we bomb out.

```
48  # Make sure the database exists
49  if [ file exists "$dbName" ] {
50      set f [ open "$dbName" ]
51  } else {
52      puts stderr "The database file $dbName does not exist."
53      exit 1
54  }
```

Next, we read the database title from the file, depending on the first line of the file to contain the database title. Then we build a label using the title. (Note how a backslash is used to allow a single command to span several lines.) Finally, we pack the .title label into the top of the default top-level frame.

```
55  # Read the database title and pack it into the frame
56  gets $f DatabaseTitle
57  label .title  -text "$DatabaseTitle" \
58      -font "-*-times-bold-r-*-*-*-180-*" \
59      -relief ridge

60  pack  .title -side top -padx 3m -pady 3m
```

Parsing the Field Specifications

The field specification determines the format of the database. The format is simple: Each field has a name and a length. The name is displayed next to the entry for the field. In the field specification, fields are separated by either semicolons or commas. Fields separated by commas appear next to each other on the same line, while fields separated by semicolons appear on separate lines.

So now we load the specification from the file, checking to make sure that a specification line exists. We initialize counters that are used to keep track of the fields.

```
61  # Load the field specification
62  if { [ gets $f FieldSpec ] < 0 } {
63      puts stderr "Cannot read field specification from $dbName."
64      exit 1
65  }

66  # In this context, linecount is lines in the window...
67  set linecount 0

68  set FieldCount 0
```

In order to construct the window, we create a frame for each line and pack the fields into it from right to left. Then we pack the lines into the window from top to bottom. In order to make the fields line up vertically, we have to calculate the width of the widest field name.

```
69  # Find the widest first field on the line
70  set ffWidth 0
71  # Parse the field specification
72  foreach line [ split $FieldSpec ";" ] {
73      set field [ lindex [ split $line "," ] 0 ]
74      if { [ regexp {(.*) ([0-9]+)} "$field" \
75             fmatch fname flength ] } {
76          if { [ string length $fname ] > $ffWidth } {
77              set ffWidth [ string length $fname ]
78          }
79      }
80  }
```

Line 72 splits the field specification into a list of line specifications and loops through each one in turn. Line 73 extracts the field specification for the first field on the line. Lines 74 to 79 extract the field name and increase ffWidth if the field name is longer than the longest name we've seen so far.

Now we can build the frame.

```
81  # Parse the field specification
82  foreach line [ split $FieldSpec ";" ] {
83      set linecount [incr linecount]
84      eval frame .line_$linecount

85      foreach field [ split $line "," ] {
86          set FieldCount [incr FieldCount]

87          if { [ regexp {(.*) ([0-9]+)} "$field" \
88                 fmatch fname flength ] } {
```

```
89              eval label .lf$FieldCount \
90                  -text {$fname} \
91                  -width $ffWidth \
92                  -anchor w
93              eval entry .ef$FieldCount -relief sunken \
94                  -textvariable Fields($FieldCount) \
95                  -width $flength

96              eval pack  .lf$FieldCount \
97                  -side left -padx 1m \
98                  -in .line_$linecount
99              eval pack  .ef$FieldCount \
100                 -side left \
101                 -padx 1m \
102                 -in .line_$linecount
103         } else {
104             puts stderr "Error: bad field: $field";
105             exit 1;
106         }
107     }

108     eval pack .line_$linecount -side top -pady .5m -fill x
109 }
```

Line 82 splits the field specification into a list of line specifications and loops through each one in turn. We then create a new frame, and eval is used to create a *dynamically named* frame. On the first iteration of the loop, a frame called .line1 is created, on the next .line2, etc.

Line 85 splits the fields on a single line into individual elements of a list and loops through them. Line 87 uses regular expression matching to break the field specification into a name and a length. In this form, the regexp function scans the contents of $field with the specified regular expression; it returns the complete expression in $matchf, and the first and second parenthesised sub-expressions in fname and flength, respectively. The regexp function returns true if and only if the expression is found.

Lines 89 through 102 construct a labeled entry for the field and pack it into the frame for the current line. Note the use of eval to build dynamically named fields. The entry field uses the *–textvariable* option to associate the contents of the displayed entry with the contents of the array Fields($FieldCount).

Line 108 packs the frame for this line into the top-level frame.

The Top-level Frame

Lines 112 to 137 (shown below) complete the initialization of the top-level frame. A frame is created for the buttons and for the message "Record n of m". Each button has an associated command, a Tcl procedure that performs the necessary action.

```
112   frame .crframe
113   frame .buttons
114   button .save -text "Save" -command "save"
115   button .quit -text "Quit" -command "quit"
116   button .next -text "Next" -command "next 1"
117   button .prev -text "Prev" -command "next -1"
118   button .new  -text "New"  -command "new_rec"
119   pack .save .quit .next .prev .new \
120       -in .buttons \
121       -side left -padx 1m
122   pack .buttons \
123       -side left \
124       -pady 1m \
125       -padx 5m \
126       -in .crframe

127   set RecNum 1
128   label .cr_record  -text "Record "
129   label .cr_current -textvariable RecNum
130   label .cr_of      -text " of "
131   label .cr_count   -textvariable RecordCount
132   pack .cr_record .cr_current .cr_of .cr_count \
133       -side left \
134       -in .crframe

135   pack .crframe -side top

136   # We begin at record 1, so disable the "prev" button
137   .prev configure -state disabled
```

Since we begin at record 1, the **Prev** button is initially disabled (line 137).

Dealing with Records

Lines 138 through 149, shown below, load the individual records of the database into the Records() array and close the file. If there is only one record in the file, the **Next** button is initially disabled (lines 145 to 147).

```
138   # Load all the records
139   set RecordCount 0
140   while { [ gets $f line ] >= 0 } {
141       set RecordCount [incr RecordCount]
142       set Records($RecordCount) "$line"
143   }

144   # If there's only one record, disable the "next" button
145   if { $RecordCount < 2 } {
146       .next configure -state disabled
147   }

148   # we don't need the database file anymore...
149   close $f
```

The `get_rec` procedure now copies the contents of the current record into the variables used for display.

```
150  proc get_rec { } {
151  # Copy the contents of the current record into
152  # the Fields()
153      global Records RecordCount RecNum
154      global Fields FieldCount

155      for { set fieldcount 1 } \
156          { $fieldcount <= $FieldCount } \
157          { incr fieldcount } {
158              set Fields($fieldcount) ""
159          }

160      set fieldcount 0
161      set line $Records($RecNum)

162      foreach field [ split $line "|" ] {
163          set fieldcount [incr fieldcount]
164          eval set Fields($fieldcount) { $field }

165          if { $fieldcount == $FieldCount } break
166      }
167  }
```

Lines 153 and 154 identify several variables as global. Unless a variable is explicitly made global, it is local to the currently executing procedure (Tcl provides other mechanisms for altering the scope of execution at runtime as well).

Lines 155 through 159 reinitialize the displayed fields and lines 162 through 166 copy the contents of the current record (`$Records($RecNum)`) into the display.

The remaining procedures are shown in the code sample that follows. These procedures are:

- `set_rec` performs the inverse of `get_rec`.

- `save` rewrites the database file.

- `quit` exits the program (first asking for confirmation if changes have been made).

- `next` moves forward or backward through the database.

- `new_rec` creates a new, empty record.

Detailed commentary is omitted since they do not use any new features of Tcl.

```
168  proc set_rec { } {
169  # Copy the contents of the Fields() into
170  # the current record
```

```
171        global Records RecordCount RecNum
172        global Fields FieldCount
173        global Changed

174        set fieldcount 0
175        set line ""

176        for { set fieldcount 1 } \
177            { $fieldcount <= $FieldCount } \
178            { incr fieldcount } {
179                if { "$line" != "" } {
180                    set line "$line|"
181                }
182                set line "$line$Fields($fieldcount)"
183            }

184    # Check to see if the record has been modified
185        if { "$Records($RecNum)" != "$line" } {
186            set Changed 1
187        }

188        set Records($RecNum) "$line"
189    }

190    proc save { } {
191    # Save the database
192        global DatabaseTitle FieldSpec
193        global Records RecordCount
194        global Changed
195        global dbName

196        set_rec

197        set f [ open "$dbName" "w" ]

198        puts $f "$DatabaseTitle"
199        puts $f "$FieldSpec"

200        for { set i 1 } { $i <= $RecordCount } { incr i } {
201            puts $f "$Records($i)"
202        }

203        close $f
204        set Changed 0
205    }

206    proc quit { } {
207    # Quit, making sure we don't accidentally lose
208    # any changes
209        global Changed

210        set_rec
211
212        set really_quit 1
```

```
213      if { $Changed } {
214            set really_quit [ confirm_quit ]
215      }

216      if { $really_quit } {
217          destroy .
218          exit 0
219      }
220  }

221  proc confirm_quit {} {
222  # Do you *really* want to lose those changes?
223      set reply [ tk_dialog .d "Are you sure?" \
224                  "There are unsaved changes that will be lost, \
225                   are you sure you want to quit?" \
226                      warning 0 "Save" "Cancel" "Discard changes" ]

227      if { $reply == 0 } {
228          save
229          return 1
230      }

231      if { $reply == 2 } {
232          return 1
233      }

234      return 0
235  }
236
237  proc next direction {
238  # Move forward or backward, updating the buttons
239      global RecNum RecordCount

240      set_rec

241      set nextrec [ incr RecNum $direction ]

242      if { $nextrec == 1 } {
243          .prev configure -state disabled
244      } else {
245          .prev configure -state active
246      }

247      if { $nextrec == $RecordCount } {
248          .next configure -state disabled
249      } else {
250          .next configure -state active
251      }

252      set RecNum $nextrec

253      get_rec
254  }
```

```
255   proc new_rec {} {
256   # Create a new record
257      global RecNum RecordCount Records
258      global Changed

259      if { $RecordCount > 0 } {
260          set_rec
261      }

262      set RecordCount [ incr RecordCount ]
263      set RecNum $RecordCount

264      set Records($RecNum) ""

265      get_rec

266      .prev configure -state disabled
267      .next configure -state disabled
268
269      if { $RecNum > 1 } {
270          .prev configure -state active
271      }

272      set Changed 1
273   }
```

Lines 274 through 280 complete the initialization of *tkdb* and then control passes to the event handler.

```
274   # If there are no records, create one
275   if { $RecordCount == 0 } {
276      new_rec
277   }

278   set Changed 0

279   get_rec

280   # "wish" will take over here...
```

Lines 275 through 277 assure that the database contains at least one record, line 278 initializes $Changed, which is used to keep track of changes to the database, and line 279 loads the first record into the display.

Extending tkdb

In an effort to keep *tkdb* simple, several features have not been implemented. If you are interested in learning more about Tcl, try adding these features to *tkdb*:

- The ability to delete a record

- The ability to search for a record (either by text anywhere in the record or by text in a particular field)

- The ability to sort records by field

- The ability to print records

The interpreted nature of *tcl* leaves the door open for many, more ambitious, changes. Many fields should only be able to contain specific, valid data. For example, state abbreviations should only be one of 50 two-letter pairs and the zip code should either be five or nine digits long. Similar checking can be performed for phone numbers (keep international numbers in mind, though!) and many other fields.

—NW

31

Working with the CD-ROM

31.01 The CD-ROM

This book comes with a companion CD-ROM that contains source code and binaries for the programs and utilities described in the book. The CD-ROM contains publicly available programs that we tested, liked, and wrote about in the book. Most of these programs are written in C and are distributed in both source and binary form. The binaries have been compiled for each of the supported platforms.

In selecting freely available software to put on the disk, we've tried to emphasize quality over quantity. Too many free software archives load you up with anything and everything they can find, without evaluating whether or not it's worthwhile. You're faced with the job of wading through everything to figure out whether it's worth using or not.

program name

Every program on the CD-ROM is introduced somewhere in this book. Near the first or most important of those mentions, you'll see a disk icon in the margin, with the name of the program underneath. Our idea was that as you read about a program you like, you could simply install it (as described in Article 31.08) and have it added to your private stock of X clients. (You can also add them all at once, and just use them as you read about them!) This chapter is designed to give you some background information about the software:

- A quick summary of what's on the disk (Article 31.03).

- A list of platforms for which precompiled binaries are included (Article 31.06)

- A detailed description of the installation procedure (Article 31.08)

- How to build the software from the source code if you don't have one of the supported platforms (Articles 31.14 through 31.19)

—TOR

31.02 "Free" Software vs. the Core X Distribution

Many of the programs that we discuss are already installed on your system. This is because X is distributed with a set of "core" clients—such as *xterm*, *xrdb*, *xclock*, etc. These clients are deemed important enough by the X Consortium that everyone should have them available. They are also fully supported by the X Consortium; that is, if you find a bug in *xterm*, you should report it to the Consortium, and they are responsible for addressing it.

X is also distributed with an area called "contrib." These are "contributed" clients, which are not supported by the X Consortium. Some of them have been written by the X Consortium, but are not considered important enough to support. Most are written by generous third-party individuals who are just happy to enhance the lives of X users everywhere. Some of the programs that were originally in "core" were downgraded to "contrib" in later releases. (In X11R6, many of the "classic" X programs such as *xbiff*, *xload*, and *xcalc* were downgraded.)

In addition, there are various collections of X programs that are available via Usenet and via *ftp*. Many of the programs in this book have come out of a Usenet group called *comp.sources.x*, where programmers submit their sources to the world at large.

When we talk about a program in this book, we include it on the CD-ROM only if it isn't part of the "core" distribution. If the program is part of "core," then we assume you already have it installed on your system.

—LM

31.03 Quick Descriptions of What's on the Disk

Alcons

A collection of bitmaps and pixmaps appropriate for use as icons. (Warning: some of these are in questionable taste.)

RRU_resources

A collection of resources for selected clients that provides a consistent "look and feel" among applications. Article 20.23.

TclTk

A scripting language (Tcl) and a toolkit (Tk) for writing X applications in Tcl. See Chapter 30.

.Xmodmap

A sample *.Xmodmap* file, for switching your CTRL key with your Caps Lock key. Article 18.10.

.briconsrc

A sample configuration file for *bricons*. Article 21.17.

asedit

A Motif-based editor. Article 9.05.

aXe

An Athena-based editor. Article 9.04.

bricons

A program launcher that allows you to start a client by clicking on its icon. Article 21.17.

capture

A version of the game Stratego for X11. Article 10.10.

cbzone

An arcade-like tank game. Article 10.09.

changepeg

A sample script that provides a useful front-end to the *xpeg* program. Article 4.17.

dclock

A digital clock, with numbers resembling the LED printout on familiar digital clock radios. Article 3.03.

dox

A command-line interface to Xlib. Article 29.02.

emacs

A full-fledged text editor with an X interface. Article 9.02.

exmh

An X interface to the MH mail handler system. Article 7.07

eyeball

A sample set of bitmaps, masks, and a script, which demonstrates how to make your own animated cursor for use with *xancur*. The *eyeball* example shows a dancing eyeball walking around your root window. Article 6.17.

floatbg

A program that changes your root window color incrementally. Article 6.05.

fvwm

A window manager with a virtual desktop. Chapter 15.

gettext

A sample script written in Tcl/Tk, for getting input from a user within a shell script. Article 30.04.

ghostscript

A PostScript interpreter used by the *ghostview* client. Article 24.08.

ghostview

A PostScript previewer for X11. Article 24.08.

gnuchess

A chess program used by the *xboard* client. Article 10.03.

hpcdtoppm

A program for converting Photo CD files to Portable Pixmap Format *(25.01)*. Article 25.04.

ical

A Tcl/Tk-based calendar program. Article 4.03.

ishido

A tile-based game for color displays. Article 10.08.

klondike

A popular solitaire game. This version is written in Tcl/Tk. Article 10.05.

meltdown

A program that "melts" your display; all your windows ooze down onto the bottom of the display before they are restored. Distributed with *xflip*. Article 6.12.

moxftp

The collective name for three X clients (*mftp*, *oftp*, and *xftp*) that use FTP (for Motif, OPEN LOOK, and Xt, respectively). The version that is already built on the CD is *xftp* (the Xt-based version). Article 8.02.

mpeg_play

A program for displaying *mpeg*-format movies. Article 24.07.

mxclock

A version of *xclock* that shows a cat with a swinging tail and shifty eyes. Warning: without its resources and the *–mode cat* command-line option, it looks just like boring *xclock*. Article 3.16.

oclock++

A version of *oclock* with sound support for SPARCstations. Article 3.09.

oneko

A program that changes your cursor to a mouse, and a cat runs across your display trying to catch it. Article 6.07.

pbmplus

A set of utilities for converting graphics files from one format to another. Article 25.01.

pegboard

A sample script that provides a useful front-end to the *xpeg* program. Article 4.17.

pixt

A program for creating and manipulating color pixmaps. Article 24.04.

plan

A spiffy calendar program. Article 4.05.

popupmsg

A sample Tcl/Tk program that simulates *xmessage*. Article 30.05.

printer_hack

A sample hack to facilitate selecting a printer for C shell users. Meant to demonstrate using *xmenu*. These commands should be placed in your *.cshrc*. Article 29.09.

spacebar_hack

A patch to the X server for using the space bar as your **CRTL** key. Only of use to people with X server source and the wherewithal to hack at it. Article 18.20.

spider

Our favorite solitaire game, involving two decks of cards and a lot of skill. Article 10.06.

sunclock

Shows a map of the world and what parts of the world are currently lit by the sun. Article 3.05.

swisswatch

A clock that's infinitely configurable, which can simulate a traditional Swiss railroad clock. Article 3.07.

t3d

A very odd clock that pulsates and gyrates. Article 3.15.

tetris

The traditional computer game. Article 10.02.

timex

A utility for helping you keep track of time during the workday. Article 4.18.

tkcron

A front-end to editing your *crontab* entry. Article 27.08.

tkdb

A sample program written to demonstrate writing tools in Tcl/Tk. Article 30.06.

tkman

A Tcl/Tk manpage browser. Article 5.03.

tkpostage

An *xbiff* variation that displays a postmark containing the number of mail messages you have. Article 7.12.

tvtwm

A "virtual rooms" version of *twm*. Article 12.10.

unclutter

A program that removes the cursor after it's been idle a few seconds, thereby "uncluttering" your display. Article 6.15.

wincursor

An example shell script using *dox* for changing your root window's cursor. Article 29.04.

xMovelt

A program that moves a window around the display according to the current time. Article 3.06.

xabacus

An abacus program. Article 5.08.

xancur

A cursor animation program. Article 6.16.

xarchie

An X interface to Archie, for finding files available via FTP. Article 8.04.

xascii

The ASCII chart. Article 5.06.

xasteroids

The arcade game Asteroids. Article 10.11.

xbiff

A program that indicates whether you have new mail. Article 7.10.

xbiff++

A version of *xbiff* with sound support for SPARCstations. Article 7.11.

xblackjack

The casino game Blackjack. Article 10.04.

xbmbrowser

A program for viewing all the bitmaps in a given directory. Article 22.16.

xboard

A chess game that's a front-end to GNU chess or the Internet Chess Server. It also includes *cmail,* a utility for playing chess via email. Article 10.03.

xcalc

A scientific calculator. Article 5.05.

xcalendar

A simple calendar program. Article 4.02.

xchrom

A color clock that shows the time by segmenting the clock into pie-shaped wedges. Article 3.14.

xchrono

A clock that displays multiple time zones. Article 3.13.

xcol

A program for viewing colors on your display. Article 26.05.

xcoloredit

A color editor that simulates fingerpainting. Article 26.16.

xcsetroot

A program for displaying GIF and XWD files on the root window. Article 6.03.

xcuckoo

A clock program that places the current time on the titlebar of another window. Article 3.08.

xdaliclock

A digital clock with numbers that "melt" into each other. Article 3.04.

xdu

A program that gives a graphical interface to the UNIX *du* program. Article 27.06.

xearth

A program that displays the Earth on your root background. Article 6.10.

xedit

An X-based editor. Article 9.03.

xelem

A Tcl/Tk-based program that shows the periodic table. Article 5.07.

xev

A program that reports events occurring within a window. Article 18.12.

xfig

A drawing program for creating and editing simple figures. Article 24.03.

xfishtank

A program that displays fish swimming around your root window. In addition to *xfishtank* itself, we include programs for converting fish images to and from GIF files and for converting PC and raster images into *xfishtank* fish. Article 6.11.

xflip

A program that "flips" your display over a vertical axis and then restores it. (distributed with *meltdown*). Article 6.12.

xfontsel

An interface for displaying X font names. Article 17.19.

xfsm

A program for monitoring disk space on each file system. Article 27.05.

xgetit

A quick way to FTP files without having to manually connect to the site. Article 8.03.

xgopher

An X interface to Gopher. Article 8.08.

xgrabsc

A program for taking screen dumps of a selected rectangle and outputting it in a variety of formats. Article 23.05.

xhchat

A program that provides a split-screen window on two servers, allowing the users to communicate. Article 8.07.

XKernel

A "stripped-down" UNIX kernel for administrators to convert Sun3 hardware into X terminals. Article 27.10.

xkeycaps

A front-end to *xmodmap*. Article 18.18.

xlbiff

Another version of *biff* that shows the subject line of each new mail messsage. Article 7.13.

xless

A program for viewing files. Article 9.07.

xload

A program that displays the system process load. Article 27.03.

xloadimage

A program for displaying graphics from a variety of formats. Article 24.05.

xlock

A program that locks your server while you're away from your desk, and also acts as a screensaver. Article 6.19.

xmahjongg

A mah-jongg-inspired tile game. Article 10.07.

xmail

An X-based mailer. Article 7.02.

xmailbox

A read-only mailer. Article 7.09.

xmailtool

Another X-based mailer, based on BSD mail. Article 7.03.

xman

A manpage browser. Article 5.02.

xmcd

A program that gives you an interface for playing audio CDs on your CD-ROM drive. Article 6.25.

xmcd_cddb

A set of audio CD databases for use with *xmcd*. Article 6.25.

xmenu

A utility for generating menus within shell scripts. Useful for prompting users to choose one of several options. Article 29.06.

xmessage

A program that displays a message on your display. This version includes a scrollbar. Article 4.09.

xmris

A game based on the arcade game "Mr. Do." Article 10.12.

xmx

A program for mirroring one server onto one or more others. Article 27.09.

xnetload

A program that displays the system process load for multiple machines. Article 27.04.

xnlock

A program that locks your server while you're away from your desk; also acts as a screensaver. Article 6.20.

xp

A program for viewing one or more files in a window, with split screens for comparing files. Article 9.08.

xpaint

A painting program for X. Article 24.02.

xpd

A program that shows the processes associated for each user. Article 27.07.

xpeg

A pegboard program. Article 4.16.

xphoon

A program that shows the current phase of the moon on the root window. Article 6.09.

xpick

A utility that allows users to choose one or more of several items within shell scripts. Article 29.07.

xplaces

A program for generating command lines that will duplicate the current configuration of the placement of clients. The output can be used to create or modify startup scripts. Article 21.16.

xpostit

A program for displaying and editing "sticky notes" on the display. Article 4.12.

xps

An example script that demonstrates using *xmenu* and *xmessage* in shell scripts. Article 29.08.

xrn

A Usenet news reader for X. Article 8.05.

xroach

Roaches hide behind windows, only to scurry around madly when you move or iconify the window. Article 6.08.

xrolodex

A rolodex program. Article 4.14.

xrolomatch

A Perl script for finding rolodex entries containing a specific string. Article 4.15.

xrsh

A shell script for running remote clients, correcting access control, and setting DISPLAY as needed. Article 19.14.

xscreensaver

A screensaver program. Article 6.22.

xsnow

A program that displays snowfall on your root window and shows Santa with his reindeer flying through the sky. Article 6.06.

xspread

A spreadsheet program, based on the UNIX program *sc*. Article 4.19.

xtalk

An X interface for the BSD 4.3 *talk* daemon. Article 8.06.

xtar

A (lame) script for selecting files from a *tar* archive. Article 29.10.

xtici

A program for editing colors under the HVC color model. Article 26.17.

xticktalk

A clock that gives you the time in English words...or in French, German, Spanish, Klingon, etc. Article 3.10.

xv

A program for displaying images of a variety of formats. Article 24.06.

xwais

An X interface to WAIS for finding on-line information. Article 8.09.

xwdtotiff

A shell script to convert *xwd* files to TIFF files, using the *pbmplus* toolkit. Article 25.03.

xwebster

> A dictionary client for X (assuming you have a Webster server available on your network). Note that some platforms have a Motif version (*xwebster_motif*), whereas others may have an older version based on Xw widgets. Article 5.04.

—LM

31.04 Using the CD-ROM

The *X User Tools* CD conforms to the ISO 9660 CD-ROM format. This is sometimes called "High Sierra," but there are differences between the two formats. The 9660 standard is what most CD-ROM drivers support (although some still read High Sierra disks).

For UNIX users, ISO 9660 may come as a shock. For example, a directory listing of an ISO 9660 disk might look like this:

```
% ls /cdrom
ALPHA           CONFIG2.REV;1    INSTINFO        RS6000         SUN3
BUILD.XUT;1     CONFIG3.Z;1      README.;1       SOURCE.XUT;1   SUN4C
COMMON          HP700            REVISION.1;1    SOURCES
CONFIG1.;1      INSTALL.XUT;1    RISC            SSOL2
```

ISO 9660 specifies that the filenames are mono-case, and limited to eight characters with three-character extensions. If the filename doesn't contain a dot, one is added at the end of the filename. A "version number" is also appended, following a semicolon (version numbers are used in some non-UNIX file systems such as VMS). Some systems do not use all these features, so there are several variations you will encounter.

For example, the file called *install.xut* may appear as any of the following, depending on which system you mount the CD on:

```
INSTALL.XUT;1 INSTALL.XUT install.xut;1 install.xut
```

Directory names are simply eight characters or less and mono-case. A directory called "SOURCES" can appear as *SOURCES* or *sources*.

ISO 9660 also limits directory depth to eight levels.

Note that the semicolon character (;) in version numbers needs to be hidden from the UNIX shell when you specify the filename in a UNIX shell. You can hide the semicolon either by surrounding the filename with single quotes, or by preceding the semicolon with a backslash (\). For example:

```
% more 'README.;1'
```

or

```
% more README.\;1
```

If you don't hide the backslash from the shell, you'll get a message like this:

```
README.: Command not found.
1: Command not found.
```

Luckily for you, we provide installation software that hides most of this ugliness.

Mounting the CD-ROM

In most cases, the standard UNIX *mount* command can be used to mount the CD. This usually has the form:

```
# mount  CD-ROM_device mount_point
```

The CD-ROM device name varies depending on the type of system. If you do not know the device name, consult the documentation that comes with your system. On some systems, the SCSI ID of the CD-ROM device can vary. The SCSI ID will be part of the device name; e.g., */dev/rz3c/* is the CD-ROM at SCSI ID 3 on a DECstation.

The mount point is simply a directory that will become the parent directory of the CD when it is mounted.

Most systems do not provide a way for unprivileged users to mount the CD. It is probably necessary to mount and use it as the superuser. For this reason, the bulk of this article assumes some knowledge of system administration and superuser commands. You may need to have your system administrator install the *X User Tools* software for you.

As the CD-ROM is read-only, you may have to specify this fact to the *mount* program or it will generate an error if it tries to open the CD-ROM device for writing. Some systems also need to be told the type of file system being mounted if it is not the default (usually ufs or nfs). There may be options to the *mount* program that control whether all the ISO 9660 features (such as version numbers) are turned on.

For example, the CD can be mounted on a SunOS 4.1.1 system with the command:

```
# /etc/mount -r -t hsfs /dev/sr0 /cdrom
```

This command mounts the CD (*/dev/sr0*) on the mount point (*/cdrom*) in a read-only fashion (*–r*). If you omit the *–r* option, *mount* will give the following error:

```
mount_hsfs: must be mounted readonly
mount: giving up on:
   /cdrom
```

If you omit the file system type of hsfs (High Sierra File System, which preceded the ISO 9660 format), you will get:

```
mount: /dev/sr0 on /cdrom: Invalid argument
mount: giving up on:
   /cdrom
```

The procedure for mounting a CD varies with each type of operating system. You should consult the manual pages for the *mount* command and look for a mention of CD-ROM, ISO 9660, or High Sierra:

```
% man mount
```

Some examples of *mount* commands for the supported systems are:

Sun4 and Sun3 SunOS 4.1.1

```
# /etc/mount -r -t hsfs /dev/sr0 /cdrom
```

Solaris 2.2

```
# /etc/mount -r -F hsfs /dev/dsh/c0t6d0s0 /cdrom
```

(If you have the Solaris volume manager enabled, this command is not necessary; the CD is automatically installed when inserted into the drive.)

IBM RS/6000 AIX 3.2.5

```
# /etc/mount -r -v cdrfs /dev/cd0 /cdrom
```

HP 700 HP-UX 9.01

```
# /etc/mount -r -s cdfs /dev/dsk/c201d2s0 /cdrom
```

DECstation Ultrix 4.2

```
# /etc/mount -t cdfs -o noversion /dev/rz3c /cdrom
```

(The *noversion* option will disable the version information on the filenames.)

OSF/1 for Alpha DecStation

```
# /usr/sbin/mount -t cdfs -o noversion /dev/rz3c /cdrom
```

Some examples of *mount* commands for other systems are:

SGI IRIX 4.x

```
# /usr/etc/mount -o ro,notranslate -t iso9660 \
    /dev/scsi/sc0d510 /cdrom
```

You can also start up the *cdromd* process:

```
# cdromd -o ro,notranslate -d /dev/scsi/sc0d510 /cdrom
```

To mount the disk, just insert it in the drive. To unmount it, use the *eject* command.

Once you have the CD mounted, you can run the installation program to copy precompiled binaries off the CD and onto your system's hard disk. The installation program is Ready-to-Run Software's "Smart Installation System."

Unmounting the CD-ROM

When you are finished with the installation, you can unmount the CD with the *umount* command, specifying the mount point as the argument:

```
# /etc/umount /cdrom
```

—*EAP, LM, adapted from* UNIX Power Tools

31.05 *Do You Need to Be Root?*

We've tried to set up the CD-ROM installation so that you can install the software as an unprivileged user. It's much safer to install software as an unprivileged user, and furthermore, many readers may not have *root* permission. However, there are a few instances when you need *root* permission. In those instances, you may need the assistance of your system administrator to help you install software from the CD-ROM.

An unavoidable situation is that on most systems, only the superuser can mount and unmount the CD-ROM as described in Article 31.04. However, after getting the CD-ROM mounted, you should be able to continue on your merry way without needing administrator assistance.

When it comes to actually installing the software, you have a few options. The default installation directory is */usr*, but an unprivileged user probably doesn't have permission for */usr* (and shouldn't). The advantage of using the default installation directory is that it places binaries in */usr/bin/X11*, manpages in */usr/man*, and application defaults in */usr/lib/X11/app-defaults*. Since these are already standard directories in most X distributions, users won't have to worry about setting their search path *(2.05, 31.11)* or using application defaults in a non-standard area *(20.25, 31.12)*. The disadvantage is that it's possible you'll overwrite software that already exists.

If you choose to run the installation as an unprivileged user, then you'll probably have to set up the installation with a different installation directory as described in Article 31.08. This is much safer than using the defaults, but it means you may have to do some juggling to make the software work for you. See Articles 31.11 and 31.12.

Users who are not using the prebuilt binaries but are building the software from source will have a special set of problems. When installing into a non-standard directory, some of the programs will need special configuration. Furthermore, the installation may have to be done by manually copying the files into the correct directories and then reconfiguring the programs as needed. See Article 31.20.

In addition, some clients need to be installed by *root* regardless of their target installation directory, because they need to be installed with special permissions. For example, *xload* *(27.03)*, *xnetload* *(27.04)*, and *xpd* *(27.07)* all need to be installed with special permissions. Some programs may also require special fonts to be installed, and if you use an X terminal, you may need *root* permission to install them.

—LM

31.06 *Installing Precompiled Binaries*

There are two software installation programs provided on the CD. The first program installs precompiled binaries. The second program builds programs from source code. If you have one of the supported platforms, you can install software off the CD-ROM and use it immediately. If your platform is not one of the supported platforms, or you wish to change the software in some way, you should be able to build it from source code *(31.14)*.

Binaries for the following platforms are on this CD-ROM:

- Sun4 Solaris 2.2

- Sun4 SunOS 4.1.*x*

- Sun3 SunOS 4.1.*x*

- DECstation Ultrix 4.2

- DECstation Alpha OSF1 V2.0

- IBM RS/6000 AIX 3.2.5

- HP 700 HP-UX 9.01

The precompiled binaries may work on operating system versions slightly older or newer than the ones listed here. Some programs take advantage of features that are not supported on all the platforms. The installation program will tell you if a program is not available for your platform.

If you are uncertain of your operating system version, the *uname* command may help:

```
% uname -a
SunOS ruby 4.1.3_U1 24 sun4m
```

If your platform is not listed, you should try building the programs from source code as described in Articles 31.14 through 31.19.

Starting the Installation

To begin the installation process, become the superuser and mount the CD-ROM. For example, on a Sun:

```
% su
Password:
# /etc/mount -r -t hsfs /dev/sr0 /cdrom
```

If you intend to install the software into areas that can be written by an unprivileged user, then you can quit out of being superuser at this point.

```
# ^D
%
```

Now change directories to the mount point you specified for the CD-ROM and see what is there. In our case, we specified */cdrom* as our mount point:

```
% cd /cdrom
```

One of the first things that the installation program will do when installing software is to copy the programs into a "staging" area. By default, this is the directory */tmp*. By setting the TMPDIR environment variable *(2.04)* to another directory, you can alter this location.

For example, if you want to use the directory */mondo* for the staging area:

```
% setenv TMPDIR /mondo      csh
$ TMPDIR=/mondo; export TMPDIR      sh
```

Running the Installation Program

Once you have the CD-ROM properly mounted, run the appropriate install command for your system. For example:

```
% ./install.xut
```

or:

```
% ./INSTALL.XUT\;1
```

(depending on how the *install.xut* file appears on your system).

The installation program will display menus and prompt you for input from now on. It will also try to guess the type of machine you are running on:

```
% ./install.xut
Assuming MACHINE is sun4c
            Welcome to Ready-to-Run Software's
```

* Smart Installation System *

> This installation system requires write permission in /tmp (or $TMPDIR if it's set) directory (for staging the install) and write permission in the installation directory for the actual install (these may be the same).
>   ...

At this point, the installation program may ask if you want to use a different *umask* value for the installation process:

> Use umask of 022 instead of 002 for install [y]?

This will affect the permissions of the software when it is installed. The suggested value of 022 will allow anyone to execute or read the programs, but gives write permission only to you.

The installation program will then present a list of the available software. First the shareable *(31.07)* files are shown:

```
The X User Tools package contains the following scripts:

.Xmodmap    .briconsrc              AIcons     RRU_resources        changepeg
eyeball     gettext     klondike    pegboard   popupmsg   printer_hack
tkdb        wincursor   xelem       xmcd_cddb  xps        xrolomatch
xtar        xwdtotiff

    ... hit RETURN to continue ...
```

After pressing **Return**, the nonshareable files are shown:

```
The X User Tools package contains the following packages:

TclTk      XKernel    aXe         asedit     bricons    capture    cbzone
dclock     dox        emacs       exmh       floatbg    fvwm       ghostscript
ghostview  gnuchess   hpcdtoppm   ical       ishido     libXpm     moxftp
    ...
```

After the names of all the software packages have been displayed, you are prompted for which ones to install:

> Enter the name of a package to install or choose Search, Quit or All
> <package>, S(earch), A(ll), Q(uit) [Search]?

You can now type the name of the package, search for packages, quit the installation program, or install all packages in one fell swoop.

—EAP, LM

31.07 *Shareable Files*

Shareable files are those files that are machine independent and can be shared across many machines in a network using NFS. These are typically text files, such as manual pages or special configuration files. Sharing files reduces the amount of disk space required by allowing several different systems to use the same set of files, as opposed to having to duplicate them for each machine. It also simplifies administration of the files by having only a single copy to maintain.

Non-shareable files are machine/architecture specific and may not be shared (except with other hosts of the same architecture). These are typically binaries or data files that depend on a certain architecture or byte order.

The installation program gives you the ability to split the shareable and non-shareable files into separate directories. Using this scheme, you could put shareable files onto a partition or directory that is mounted by multiple machines.

If you want to store shareable and non-shareable files at the same directory level, the shareable directories can be preceded by a leading *s* to mark them as shareable. For example, *sbin* is shareable, while *bin* is non-shareable. See Article 31.08 for information on how to install shareable files into directories with "s" prefixes. By default, shareable and non-shareable files are installed into the same directory.

—*EAP, LM, adapted from* UNIX Power Tools

31.08 *Installing a Single Program*

Some of you might prefer to install selected programs instead of the entire distribution. For this example, let's assume you only want the *xarchie (8.04)* client. Type xarchie at the prompt, followed by **Return**.

```
<package>, S(earch), A(ll), Q(uit) [Search]? xarchie  Return
```

A description of the program is now displayed, as well as information on how much disk space the *xarchie* installation uses.

```
xarchie - version 1.3

Xarchie is an X11 browser interface to the Archie network information
service using the Prospero virtual filesystem protocol. Archie
provides information about files available for ftp anywhere on the Internet;
xarchie displays this information using an easy-to-use, point-and-click
interface.

The xarchie package is approximately 445Kb
    272Kb - Required
     74Kb - Shared: Formatted Man pages
```

```
36Kb - Shared: Other Shareable files
63Kb - Shared: Unformatted Man pages
```

```
Install xarchie [y]? Return
```

After pressing **Return**, any copyright information for the *xarchie* package is printed out:

```
xarchie was compiled and made "Ready-to-Run" by
    Ready-to-Run Software, Inc.
```

```
Copyright (c) 1989, 1990, 1991 by the University of Washington
```

```
Permission to use, copy, modify, and distribute this software and its
documentation for non-commercial purposes and without fee is hereby
granted, provided that the above copyright notice appear in all copies
    ...
```

After reading the copyright information, you are prompted with installation questions, with the default answers printed within square brackets ([ ]).

The first question is where to install the software. As described in Article 31.05, the installation program assumes */usr* as the default installation directory. If you want to change the default, type the name of a different directory here. This directory will now be used when you are prompted for the same information in all subsequent packages. Be sure that you have write permission for this directory!

```
Install package at dir [/usr]? /usr/local/xut   Return
```

The next question is where to install the shared files for the package. The default is to use the same directory you specified in the previous question.

```
Install shared files at [/usr/local/xut]? Return
```

Third, you're asked whether to remove the *s* prefix from the names of the directories in which you install the shared files. The default is "y" for "yes": remove the *s* prefix. (See Article 31.07 for more information about installing the shared directories.)

```
Convert slib->lib, sbin->bin, sspool->spool, sinclude->include [y]? Return
```

The fourth question is whether to install all the shared files, some, or none of them. The default is to install just some selected shared files.

```
Install Shared files (All, Some, None) [s]? Return
```

Now you're asked whether to install all, none, or some of the documentation. The default is to install all of it. You might choose not to install unformatted manpages if you are low on disk space or if you don't have the UNIX *nroff* command on your system to format them with:

```
Install Unformatted Man pages (Approx  63Kb) [y]? Return
Install Formatted Man pages (Approx  74Kb) [y]? Return
```

Finally you're asked about any other shareable files.

```
Install Other Shareable files (Approx  36Kb) [y]? Return
```

Some packages might have some additional questions, as appropriate.

After you answer all the questions, the installation script sets up its installation information and asks you once more if it's correct. If you change your mind about the current configuration, press **n** to get another chance to change some of your installation parameters or to abort the installation of this package entirely. If the current configuration is acceptable, press **Return** a final time and the package is installed.

```
Please wait....

About To Install: xarchie

    at /usr/local/xut
    with shareable files at /usr/local/xut
    slib->lib, sbin->bin, sspool->spool, sinclude->include

Are these correct [y]? Return
Proceeding with install...

2 directories added, 4 files installed, 0 symbolic links created.
Approximately 445Kb installed.
```

Once the *xarchie* installation is completed, the installation script returns to the main menu if this is the only package you have selected.

After all programs are installed, you can quit the installation program.

```
Enter the name of a package to install or choose Search, Quit or All
<package>, S(earch), A(ll), Q(uit) [Search]? q  Return

See /tmp/RTRinstall.log for a list of the packages and files processed.
```

A log file of the installation process is kept in */tmp/RTRinstall.log*. A typical entry looks like this:

```
Package: xarchie -- installed Thu Aug 11 17:10:34 EDT 1994

/usr/local/xut/bin/X11/xarchie
/usr/local/xut/lib/X11/app-defaults/Xarchie
/usr/local/xut/lib/X11/app-defaults: Making directory
/usr/local/xut/lib/X11: Making directory
/usr/local/xut/man/catn/xarchie.n
/usr/local/xut/man/mann/xarchie.n
```

```
2 directories added, 4 files installed.
Approximately 445Kb installed.


   ********************************
```

—EAP, LM

31.09 Searching for a Package

Suppose you don't know the exact name of a program. You can try the installation's searching feature: at the main menu prompt, press **Return** (or **S** for Search):

```
Enter the name of a package to install or choose Search, Quit or All
<package>, S(earch), A(ll), Q(uit) [Search]? Return
```

Now enter a string that you want to search for.

```
Search package descriptions for (? for help) []? ftp  Return
```

The installation program searches the descriptions of each of the packages for this string. The descriptions are usually adapted from the README files for the packages. Your results vary on the completeness of those descriptions and on the precision of your search string; however, if you're lucky, you might just find what you're looking for:

```
The descriptions for the following packages mention "ftp":
   1.  moxftp
   2.  xarchie
   3.  xgetit

   A.  ALL
   N.  NONE

Choose one please:
```

Now you can enter a number, A, or N, and the requested packages are installed.

```
Choose one please: 2  Return
xarchie - version 1.3

Xarchie is an X11 browser interface to the Archie network information
service using the Prospero virtual filesystem protocol. Archie
      ...
```

—LM

31.10 Installing Many Packages

If you're installing more than one package at once, you probably don't want to be bothered with being questioned for each package in the installation. Here are a few tips for bypassing the configuration questions.

If you answer the string ++ to any of the configuration questions, the installation script will use current settings for the remainder of the questions. If you just want to use default settings (e.g., using */usr* as your installation directory), you can specify ++ at the first question about your *umask*.

```
Use umask of 022 instead of 002 for install [y]? ++   Return
```

If you want to install packages into a different directory, you can wait until after you've specified a new installation directory and enter ++:

```
Install package at dir [/usr]? /usr/local/xut   Return
Install shared files at [/usr/local/xut]? ++   Return
```

You'll still be asked to specify packages, but you won't have to answer questions about each package.

If you want to install all the packages now without having to monitor the installation, specify A for All at the main menu:

```
Enter the name of a package to install or choose Search, Quit or All
<package>, S(earch), A(ll), Q(uit) [Search]? A   Return
```

Each program in the distribution is installed in turn.

Another thing you can do is answer a question in uppercase (e.g., "Y" instead of "y"). If an answer is written in uppercase, the installation script takes it as the default answer for all subsequent packages, and doesn't prompt you further.

—*EAP, LM*

31.11 Setting the Search Path

In order to run the software after installation, you will need to make sure that your PATH variable includes the directory or directories that the binaries were copied into. If you use the default installation directory (*/usr*), the programs will be installed into */usr/bin* and */usr/bin/X11*, which are probably already in your search path; however, if you specify a non-standard installation directory, you may need to change your search path.

For example, if you choose */usr/local/xut* as your installation directory, then binaries are installed in */usr/local/xut/bin* and */usr/local/xut/bin/X11*. You'll need to add these directories to your search path as described in Article 2.05. In the C shell, you'll want to add this line to your *.cshrc*:

```
set path=($path /usr/local/xut/bin /usr/local/xut/bin/X11)
```

In the Bourne or Korn shell, you'll want to add this line to your *.profile*:

```
PATH=$PATH:/usr/local/xut/bin:/usr/local/xut/bin/X11
export PATH
```

—LM

31.12 *What About the Application Defaults?*

Many programs depend on their application default files being installed before they will run properly. Application default files (familiarly known as *app-defaults* files) define resources that control how the client looks and behaves. You can recognize an *app-defaults* file by its name: generally, the name is the same as the name of the client, with at least the first character in uppercase, and often with several other letters in uppercase as well. For example, the *app-defaults* file for *xterm* is named "XTerm."

App-defaults files for the standard X clients are usually installed into the */usr/lib/X11/app-defaults* directory. All X clients are expected to look in that directory for application defaults.

When you install programs from the *X User Tools* CD, *app-defaults* files are placed under the same directory tree as the rest of the installation. For example, if you use the default installation directory tree of */usr*, the *app-defaults* are placed in */usr/lib/X11/app-defaults*, so they are automatically found by clients. However, if you choose to install the *X User Tools* software under a different directory tree, you may have to do some special work to access the application defaults.

The installation script does what it can to deal with this situation. If it has write permission to */usr/lib/X11/app-defaults*, it will attempt to put a second copy of the *app-defaults* file there (with the restriction that it won't overwrite existing files).

However, if you're not running the installation as *root*, it's unlikely you'll have write permission to */usr/lib/X11/app-defaults*. The only copy of the application defaults will be in the *lib/X11/app-defaults* subdirectory of the parent installation directory (e.g., */usr/local/xut/lib/X11/app-defaults*). In this case, you will have to do something special to tell X clients where to find their application defaults.

By far the easiest thing to do is to just copy the files to */usr/lib/X11/app-defaults* (or have your administrator copy them over, if you don't know the *root* password). But if this isn't a reasonable solution, you have several other options:

- Copy the *app-defaults* files to your home directory. If you don't have either the XUSERFILESEARCHPATH or XAPPLRESDIR environment variables set, then X clients will look for resource files in your home directory. So if you used */usr/local/xut* as your installation directory, you might copy the *Xgopher* file to your home directory using the following command:

```
% cp /usr/local/xut/lib/X11/app-defaults/Xgopher $HOME
```

  This creates a new file in your home directory called *Xgopher*. Be aware that if you are installing a lot of clients, your home directory can easily become very crowded this way.

- If you don't have the XUSERFILESEARCHPATH or XAPPLRESDIR environment variables set, you can set XAPPLRESDIR to the directory containing the application defaults files. For example, if you used */usr/local/xut* as your installation directory, you can set XAPPLRESDIR as follows. If you use the C shell:

```
% setenv XAPPLRESDIR /usr/local/xut/lib/X11/app-defaults
```

  If you use the Bourne or Korn shell:

```
$ XAPPLRESDIR=/usr/local/xut/lib/X11/app-defaults
$ export XAPPLRESDIR
```

  For many users, the best way to deal with this is to set the environment variable in your startup script *(16.03)*. For example, in your *.xsession* or *.xinitrc* file, enter the following lines near the beginning of the file:

```
XAPPLRESDIR=/usr/local/xut/lib/X11/app-defaults
export XAPPLRESDIR
```

  The caveat is that once you do this, any resource files in your home directory are no longer read.

- If you're feeling a bit reckless, try out the XUSERFILESEARCHPATH environment variable. Set XUSERFILESEARCHPATH in your startup script as follows:

```
XUSERFILESEARCHPATH=$HOME/%N:/usr/local/xut/lib/X11/app-defaults/%N
export XUSERFILESEARCHPATH
```

  This way, application defaults are read from either your home directory or from the *X User Tools* installation directory.

- If you're really ambitious and want to do things the Right Way, you can set your XFILESEARCHPATH environment variable. In a simplified form, you can set XFILESEARCHPATH to the following string:

```
/usr/local/xut/lib/X11/%T/%N:/usr/lib/X11/%T/%N
```

  For example, in your startup script, you might enter:

```
XFILESEARCHPATH=/usr/local/xut/lib/X11/%T/%N:/usr/lib/X11/%T/%N
export XFILESEARCHPATH
```

Users with a different language or locale, however, will need to use a more complicated form (as will users who want to take advantage of color *app-defaults* files). See Article 20.25 for more information, and good luck.

If you want to know more, see Chapter 20, which tells you everything you'd ever want to know about resources (and then some).

—LM

31.13 *Installing a Font*

Warning: This article may be hazardous to your mental health.

For most clients on the CD, no special fonts are needed so you don't have to worry about installing new fonts. In fact, the only one I know of that does require a new font is *xmahjongg* (10.07). So if you don't plan to install *xmahjongg*, you can probably live a very happy, carefree life without ever knowing how to install fonts in X. However, if you do want to use *xmahjongg* or any other client that requires special fonts, read on.

xmahjongg is distributed with a file called *xmahjongg.pcf.* This is a font distributed in *pcf* format, which probably means nothing to you, except that it's a format supported since X11R5. (Other font formats for distribution are *snf* and *bdf.* For more information about font formats, see O'Reilly & Associates' *X Window System User's Guide.*)

If you are on an X terminal, you may not be able to install a font without the help of the administrator. At any rate, X terminals can be configured to deal with fonts in several different ways. You're best off if your X terminal is X11R5-compatible and supports the font server; see your administrator or the O'Reilly book, *X Window System Administrator's Guide,* for more information, and good luck. If your server is X11R4 or (gasp) older, then you'll have to convert it to *snf* format, which is also beyond the scope of this book.

If you are on a workstation and wish to install the font, you should have a server that's at least X11R5 compatible in order to use the *pcf* format (or convert it to *snf* format, which as I already said a paragraph ago is beyond the scope of this book). Now, the most important thing to keep in mind is that the font is read by the server, not the client. So you should first make sure the font is in a directory that is accessible to your server. By "accessible," I mean that the directory is on a disk that is local to the same machine running your server, or on one that is NFS-mounted to that machine. If the installation directory is either on your local disk or NFS-mounted to your machine, you can probably just leave it there.

For example, when I installed *xmahjongg*, the font was installed into */usr/local/xut/lib/X11/xmahjongg*. Although I installed *xmahjongg* on a remote machine (*ruby*) and intend to run it as a remote client, the font needs to be accessible to my local machine (*opal*). So if */usr/local/xut* were NFS-mounted to my local machine, I'd be sitting pretty. However, as it turns out, this directory is not NFS-mounted to my local machine, so before I can even think about installing the new font, I need to copy the font somewhere that is locally accessible. The easiest place is my home directory. So I create a subdirectory of my home directory and copy the new font there:

```
lmui@ruby% mkdir $HOME/newfonts
lmui@ruby% cd /usr/local/xut/lib/X11/xmahjongg
lmui@ruby% cp xmahjongg.pcf $HOME/newfonts
```

Once you've copied the font into your chosen directory, go to the new font directory and run the *mkfontdir* command. For example:

```
lmui@ruby% cd $HOME/newfonts
lmui@ruby% mkfontdir
```

This creates a file called *fonts.dir* in the directory.

Now, run the *xset* command with the *fp+* option to add the new font directory to your font path. The only thing you need to be careful about is that you use the font path as it would be known to your local server. That is, if my home directory */home/lmui* on the machine *ruby* were NFS-mounted to my workstation *opal* under the name */ruby/home/lmui*, then I need to specify */ruby/home/lmui/newfonts* in my font path. Otherwise, if I use the wrong font path, the local server can't find the directory locally and gives me a very coherent error resembling the following:

```
lmui@ruby % xset fp+ /home/lmui/newfonts
X Error of failed request: BadValue (integer parameter out of range
for operation)
 Major opcode of failed request: 51 (X_SetFontPath)
 Value in failed request: 0x5
 Serial number of failed request: 4
 Current serial number in output stream: 6
```

For those of you who don't understand my sense of humor, I was kidding when I said this error was coherent. All the error really means is that it can't find the font directory, but does it say that? Noooo. If you look on *opal*, it begins to makes sense because */home/lmui* doesn't exist.

```
lmui@opal % ls -d /home/lmui
/home/lmui not found
lmui@opal % ls -d /ruby/home/lmui
/ruby/home/lmui
```

So you need to make sure the directory is specified as it appears on the local workstation:

```
lmui@ruby% xset fp+ /ruby/home/lmui/newfonts
```

If you don't get any error messages, then the installation worked, and you should be able to run the *xmahjongg* client without any trouble.

—LM

31.14 *Building Programs from Source Code*

The programs on the disk are supplied in binary form for the most popular UNIX platforms. But we also supply C source code for those of you who want to recompile programs for your platform or who are on unsupported platforms. The rest of this chapter concentrates on how to build the source code on the CD-ROM.

Now, don't run away. You don't have to be a C programmer to compile these sources. I've never written a C program in my life, and I compile software all the time. The CD-ROM provides build scripts for each of the packages, so many of you can just run the script and have everything built automatically. If you want to install the software into default areas, the software is installed as well.

The CD-ROM also has a script to copy the sources to your local hard disk, so you can build the sources manually. You may want to do this if you're not on one of the supported platforms, or if you want to do some special configuration to the binaries. Although we can't promise that you'll be able to build the sources on your own without a hitch, Articles 31.16 through 31.19 include some explanation of how to build sources without learning C programming.

Once the programs are built, you need to install them. Article 31.20 describes how to install software once it is built.

—LM

31.15 *Running the Build Scripts*

If you're on a supported platform, then before you do anything you should try out the build scripts.

The build script will copy the files off the CD into your current directory and compile the package. (It can also install the software for you, but only if you want the software installed into the default system areas.)

Since the build script needs to copy files and directories into your current directory, you can't build the source code on the same file system that the CD-ROM is mounted on (since the CD-ROM is read-only). Instead, you need to run the build from another directory in which you have write permission, such as your home directory.

For a list of the available packages, run the *build.xut* script in the CD-ROM mount directory. The actual name of the script depends on your platform, but assuming that the CD-ROM is mounted on */cdrom*, it is likely to be one of the following commands:

```
% /cdrom/BUILD.XUT\;1
% /cdrom/BUILD.XUT
% /cdrom/build.xut\;1
% /cdrom/build.xut
```

The command will print a list similar to the following:

```
% /cdrom/build.xut
BUILD script provided by Ready-to-Run Software, Inc.
Copyright 1994 Ready-to-Run Software, Inc. All Rights Reserved.
Assuming MACHINE is sun4c

BUILD is available for the following packages:

TclTk        XKernel     aXe        asedit      bricons      capture
cbzone       dclock      dox        emacs       exmh         floatbg
fvwm         ghostscript ghostview  gnuchess    hpcdtoppm    ical
     ...
```

To build one of these packages, run the same command followed by the package name.

```
% pwd
/home/lmui
% /cdrom/build.xut xgopher
BUILD script provided by Ready-to-Run Software, Inc.
Copyright 1994 Ready-to-Run Software, Inc. All Rights Reserved.
Assuming MACHINE is sun4c
Ignore any errors about directories already existing
mkdir: /usr/local/bin: File exists
mkdir: /usr/local/lib: File exists
mkdir: /usr/local/share/man: File exists
mkdir: /usr/local/share/man/man1: File exists
mkdir: /usr/local/share/doc: File exists
mkdir: /usr/local/share/bin: File exists
mkdir: /usr/local/share/lib: File exists
x xgopher.1.3/Documents/Changes, 8921 bytes, 18 tape blocks
x xgopher.1.3/Documents/Customization, 15585 bytes, 31 tape blocks
     ...
```

The build script first unpacks the entire archive. It then applies any patches that it can find for this package, and then runs *xmkmf* to create a Makefile. (See Article 31.16 if you want to know more about this process.)

```
     ...
x xgopher.1.3/version.h, 1522 bytes, 3 tape blocks
x xgopher.1.3/xglobals.h, 1400 bytes, 3 tape blocks
mv Makefile Makefile.bak
imake -DUseInstalled -I/usr/lib/X11/config
```

```
makedepend  -s "# DO NOT DELETE" --   -I/usr/local/X11/include
-DHELP_FILE=\"/usr/local/X11/lib/X11/xgopher/xgopher.help\"  --
xgopher.c item.c itemList.c dir.c dirList.c markList.c  util.c misc.c
net.c  gui.c resources.c help.c status.c jobs.c  panel.c save.c text.c
error.c cso.c index.c  bkmkfile.c options.c version.c single.c
itemInfo.c subst.c  sc_dir.c sc_index.c sc_telnet.c sc_tn3270.c
sc_cso.c sc_image.c sc_sound.c sc_text.c sc_binary.c  sc_extend.c
KeyWSink.c
```

Next, it runs *make* to create the program.

```
cc  -pipe   -I/usr/local/X11/include
-DHELP_FILE=\"/usr/local/X11/lib/X11/xgopher/xgopher.help\"   -target
sun4 -c  util.c
cc  -pipe   -I/usr/local/X11/include
-DHELP_FILE=\"/usr/local/X11/lib/X11/xgopher/xgopher.help\"   -target
sun4 -c  misc.c
        ...
cc  -pipe   -I/usr/local/X11/include
-DHELP_FILE=\"/usr/local/X11/lib/X11/xgopher/xgopher.help\"   -target
sun4 -c  KeyWSink.c
rm -f xgopher
cc -o xgopher xgopher.o item.o itemList.o dir.o dirList.o markList.o
util.o misc.o net.o  gui.o resources.o help.o status.o jobs.o  panel.o
save.o text.o error.o cso.o index.o  bkmkfile.o options.o version.o
single.o itemInfo.o subst.o  sc_dir.o sc_index.o sc_telnet.o
sc_tn3270.o  sc_cso.o  sc_image.o sc_sound.o sc_text.o sc_binary.o
sc_extend.o KeyWSink.o  -pipe  -L/usr/local/X11/lib -lXaw -lXmu -lXt
-lXext -lX11
```

Now the software is built, and the only thing left to do is to install it. In its default setup, the build script quits at this point. This is because software being built from source code gets its installation information from *imake* configuration files *(31.16)* that have already been installed on your system. The build script has no control over these defaults. If you want to install the software in the default system areas, and you have write permission for those areas, you can install the software with just a couple of commands. However, if you want to install the software in a non-standard area, you'll have to do it by hand. *cd* to the *xgopher* subdirectory and see Article 31.20 for more information on installing by hand.

(Beware that it's also possible that you'll need to reconfigure the software and build it again. In this case, you'll have to build the software by hand as described in Articles 31.18 and 31.19.)

If you have write permission to the default system areas, and you want to install the software there, another thing you can do is set the RM environment variable to "true" before starting the build script. This tells the build script to attempt to install the software into the default areas and then remove the build directory. You may want to do this if you are installing as *root*:

```
# setenv RM true
# /cdrom/build.xut xgopher
```

—LM

31.16 Compilation Basics

Compiling programs from source doesn't require you to be a C programmer, just that you understand the general procedure and that you have some common sense and luck. For many packages, you can just follow the instructions in the README or INSTALL file and do fine. But if things get tricky, you should really know some background about what you're trying to do.

Almost all UNIX binary programs are written in the C language. These programs are written in text files—the text files are referred to as the *source code*—and then converted to binary files using a *compiler*. The typical compiler on a UNIX system is called *cc*. Some machines also have a compiler called *gcc*, the GNU compiler, which is ANSI-compatible.

Although most people call *cc* a "compiler," it's really a front-end program. Unless you tell it not to, *cc* first runs a *preprocessor*. Next it runs the compiler. Then it runs the *linker/loader* to make the actual executable file. We'll gloss over that in this article and just say that "*cc* does it."

On top of *cc*, there's usually another front-end: almost all programs are designed to be built using the *make* program. And before you run *make*, most X packages want you to run a program called *xmkmf* to generate a file called a Makefile.

Although we can't prepare you for everything you might need to know to compile programs from the CD-ROM for your platform, this section should at least give you an idea of how it's *supposed* to work.

Functions, Libraries, and Header Files

To understand the compilation process, it helps to understand a little about libraries and header files.

C programs are written almost entirely using *functions*. C language functions group together a series of commands, give them a name, and you can then execute those commands, using that name whenever you want and as many times as you want. Functions are also sometimes referred to as *subroutines*, *library functions*, or just *routines*.

Now, you can define C functions in the same source file. But the operating system also provides a vast collection of function definitions; which is very nice, because otherwise you'd be building every program from scratch. The function definitions are kept in *libraries*, which are generally installed on your system in */usr/lib* with a *lib* prefix and a *.a* suffix (for example, */usr/lib/libc.a*).

Functions also have to be *declared* in the program. Function declarations are kept in *header* or *include* files, which are generally installed on your system in */usr/include* with *.h* suffixes (for example, */usr/include/stdio.h*).

If you use functions that are defined in libraries (and you most definitely will), you need to make sure that when the program is compiled, it is *linked* to the libraries it needs. You also have to make sure the proper header files are read by your program, since the program won't compile unless all functions have been declared.

For example, if you need to take the square root of a number in your program, you need to use the *sqrt()* function. This function resides in the Math library. This means that you need to link the program with *libm.a* and you need to read in the *math.h* header file (which declares *sqrt()*). So in the program, you need to have the following line near the top of the source file:

```
#include <math.h>
```

and when you compile the program, you need to use the *–l* command-line option to link with *libm*:

```
% cc -o    file file.c -lm
```

Note the following facts:

- Unless you name the executable file with *–o file*, *cc* will name it *a.out*.

- The source filename must end with a *.c* suffix.

- Since *math.h* lives in */usr/include*, you don't need to give its full pathname on the #include line; instead, just put the name of the header file between angle brackets as shown. Relative pathnames starting at */usr/include* can be used in angle brackets. For instance, <sys/foo.h> means */usr/include/sys/foo.h*. By default, *cc* looks for header files in */usr/include*. You can have it look automatically in other directories by specifying them with the *–I* command-line option. If you want to use a header file in directory that isn't searched by default, supply its absolute or relative pathname in double quotes instead.

- When linking with a library on the command line, you should put the *–l* options at the end. If you use more than one library, you'll need more than one *–l* option. The order of the *–l* options is important; check the documentation or look for a comment in the source code.

- The compiler found *libm.a* because it was in */usr/lib*, which it searches by default. If you want it to use a library in another directory, you may need to supply the directory using the *–L* command-line option.

As you can imagine, there's much more to know. But that's the general idea of compiling C programs on UNIX systems, and it's about as much as we can tell you without starting to teach you C.

The make Program

When you're writing a simple C program, you can simply compile the program using *cc*:

```
% cc test.c
```

But more complicated programs (like many of the programs on the *X User Tools* disk) require a bit more work. More complicated programs are easier to handle if you write them in *modules*.

So, for example, the *xgopher* source tree on the CD-ROM contains several *.c* files, such as *cso.c, help.c, options.c, panel.c,* and *xgopher.c*. Each of these source files needs to be compiled separately into *object files* (with *.o* suffixes). If you give the *–c* option, *cc* will compile ".c files" into ".o files" and stop without making the finished executable. When you run *cc* again (with the *.o* filenames *cso.o, help.o,* and so on), it will link all those object files with the libraries and make the executable file.

This makes compilation a bit harder to keep track of. There are a lot more steps. Furthermore, it means that whenever a file is changed, you have to remember not only to recompile it, but also to relink the entire program.

This is a job for the *make* program. *make* looks for a file called *Makefile*, which lists each of the modules and each of their dependencies. It also keeps track of any command-line options you might want passed to *cc*, including libraries to link to. The result is that when you want to build a program, all you need to do is type:

```
% make  program
```

Or, if the Makefile is set up properly, just:

```
% make
```

This is a lot easier than trying to keep track of all the modules and command-line options yourself.

So if you can't compile a program because the header file it needs is installed in a non-standard place, you'd specify that in the *Makefile*. You could add the appropriate *–I* option to the COPTS declaration line:

```
COPTS    = -I/usr/include/sys
```

Or if you want to use a different compiler than *cc*, you could redefine that variable:

```
CC       = /usr/local/bin/gcc
```

imake and xmkmf

make makes it easier to maintain software on a single machine, but once you start building programs on many different machines, you'll find you have to keep tweaking the Makefiles. *imake* is a utility for generating Makefiles differently depending on what system you're on, so that the same source distribution will work on many different platforms.

Programs distributed for use with *imake* will have a file called *Imakefile*. To generate a Makefile, just call *imake* via its front-end *xmkmf* (which stands for "X Make Makefile"):

```
% xmkmf
cp Makefile Makefile.bak
imake -DUseInstalled -I/usr/lib/X11/config
```

xmkmf first copies any existing *Makefile* to a backup version (*Makefile.bak*) and then calls *imake*. *imake* is told to look in the directory */usr/lib/X11/config* for configuration files that define things like what the default compiler should be, what command-line options are applicable, what installation directory to use, etc. It then generates a *Makefile* with these values.

Many packages distributed with *imake* have a *Makefile* as well as an *Imakefile*. This is so users who don't have *imake* installed can still build the package by adapting the sample Makefile. However, if you do have *imake*, you should regenerate the Makefile with *xmkmf* and avoid editing the actual Makefiles.

Some packages are a little more complicated. For example, they may have subdirectories containing programs or libraries that need to be built before the actual program. So for those packages, you run *xmkmf* with the *–a* command-line option:

```
% xmkmf -a
mv Makefile Makefile.bak
imake -DUseInstalled -I/usr/lib/X11/config
make Makefiles
make includes
make depend
makedepend  -s "# DO NOT DELETE" --   -I/usr/local/X11/include      -- xhchat.c
```

Again, this is only the tip of the iceberg. But a basic understanding of libraries, header files, *make*, and *imake* has helped me build many programs that wouldn't compile the first time. For help with *make*, see O'Reilly & Associates' Nutshell Handbook *Managing Projects with make* by Andrew Oram and Steve Talbott. For help with *imake*, see *Software Portability with imake* by Paul Dubois, also published by O'Reilly.

—LM, adapted from UNIX Power Tools

31.17 Getting and Preparing the Source Code

When building programs from source code, the first thing you need to do is get the build directory ready. Usually, you follow these steps:

1. Copy the source distribution file(s) to a local hard disk.

2. Unpack the source distribution.

3. Apply any patches.

Note: Alas, just as free sources themselves have traditionally been distributed without the intervention of UNIX operating system vendors, so have the tools used to distribute them. This means that the tools needed to prepare some of these sources may not be installed on your system. In some cases, we provide sources on the CD-ROM, but in other cases you may need to call for technical support as described in Article 31.21. In particular:

- *gzip* and *gunzip. gzip* is a GNU compression scheme, and is not usually part of a vendor's operating system distribution. If you don't have this package already installed, you can copy its sources from the CD-ROM.

- The *patch* command. If you don't have *patch* on your system, you'll need to get the sources from the CD-ROM.

- The *unshar* command. This is distributed as part of the *shar* package, as an easy and safe way to unpack *shar* archives. You can still unpack *shar* archives without it by using the Bourne shell (*sh*).

Copying the Sources

Before you can actually compile the sources, you need to copy the sources to your local hard disk. You can't just compile the sources directly on the CD-ROM partition because the CD-ROM is read-only.

First, decide where you want to install the sources, and then *cd* to that directory. For example, I like to build sources in a subdirectory of my home directory. Let's suppose I want to install the *xgopher (8.08)* program. I create the new directory and then *cd* there:

```
% mkdir $HOME/xgopher
% cd $HOME/xgopher
```

For installing the sources onto your local hard disk, the CD-ROM has a script called *source.xut.* Assuming that the CD-ROM is mounted on */cdrom,* the script can be called using one of the following commands:

```
% /cdrom/SOURCE.XUT\;1 package-name
% /cdrom/SOURCE.XUT package-name
% /cdrom/source.xut\;1 package-name
% /cdrom/source.xut package-name
```

package-name is the name of the package that you want to build. To get a listing of the packages, call *source.xut* without any arguments:

```
% /cdrom/source.xut
SOURCE script provided by Ready-to-Run Software, Inc.
Copyright 1993 Ready-to-Run Software, Inc. All Rights Reserved.

Usage: /cdrom/source.xut <package>
Available packages are:

    .Xmodmap    .briconsrc   AIcons     RRU_resources   TclTk
    XKernel     aXe          asedit     bricons         capture
    cbzone      changepeg    dclock     dox             emacs
    exmh        eyeball      floatbg    fvwm            gettext
                ...
```

In my case, I want to install *xgopher*, so I run the following command:

```
% /cdrom/source.xut xgopher
SOURCE script provided by Ready-to-Run Software, Inc.
Copyright 1993 Ready-to-Run Software, Inc. All Rights Reserved.

Copied /cdrom/sources/xgopher/sun4c/xgopher to sun4cpatch.xgopher
Copied /cdrom/sources/xgopher/ssol2/xgopher to SSol2patch.xgopher
Copied /cdrom/sources/xgopher/xgoph133.gz to xgopher.1.3.3.tar.gz
Copied /cdrom/sources/xgopher/hp700/xgopher to hp700patch.xgopher
Copied /cdrom/sources/xgopher/rtr/xgopher to rtrpatch.xgopher
5 file(s) copied successfully.
```

The *source.xut* script copies all the relevant files into your current directory.

What Are Those Files?

There are three kinds of files you might find after copying a source distribution from the CD-ROM:

- Compressed *tar* archives. These are files with a suffix of *.tar.Z*, *.tar.gz*, or *.tar.z*. The files need to be uncompressed and then unpacked with the *tar* command. *xgopher.1.3.3.tar.gz* is an example of a compressed *tar* archive.

- Compressed *shar* archives. The filename conventions for *shar* archives are less rigid than for *tar* archives, but they often appear in several parts, each of the form part0n.Z. For example, the *ishido* (10.08) game is distributed in three files called *part01.Z*, *part02.Z*, and *part03.Z*.

  Occasionally, *shar* archives deviate from this format with suffixes like *.shar.Z* or *.shar.gz*. The *dclock* (3.03) client, for example, is distributed under the name *dclock.shar.gz*.

Whichever filename conventions are used, you need to uncompress the distribution files and then unpack them with the *unshar* or *sh* command. If you use *sh*, you may have to edit the files before you can unpack them.

- Patch files. Patches appear with the string *patch*, *pch*, or *.p1* in the file- name. They need to be applied using the *patch* command after unpacking the source distribution.

Uncompressing the Sources

If you now list the directory, you'll find the files that were just copied there.

```
%ls
SSol2patch.xgopher    rtrpatch.xgopher    xgopher.1.3.3.tar.gz
hp700patch.xgopher    sun4cpatch.xgopher
```

The file called *xgopher.1.3.3.tar.gz* is the *xgopher* source package, in a tarred and compressed form. Before you go further, you should uncompress any compressed files.

There are many different compression schemes, but on UNIX systems, the most common methods are *compress* and *gzip*. Files that have been com- pressed with *compress* have a *.Z* suffix, and files that have been compressed with *gzip* have a *.gz* or *.z* suffix.

In this case, the file has a *.gz* suffix, so you need to use the *gunzip* command to uncompress it.

```
% gunzip xgopher.1.3.3.tar.gz
```

If you don't have the *gunzip* command, you can get it from the CD-ROM.

If the file had a *.Z* suffix, you would use the *uncompress* command. For exam- ple, many *shar* archives are distributed with *.Z* suffixes:

```
part01.Z    part02.Z    part03.Z
```

For packages with the *.Z* suffix, use the *uncompress* command:

```
% uncompress part01.Z part02.Z part03.Z
```

Untarring the Sources

After you have uncompressed the file, you'll see the file without the *.Z* or *.gz* suffix.

```
% ls xgopher*
xgopher.1.3.3.tar
```

The *.tar* suffix to the *xarchie-4.3.tar* file means that the file was packed using the *tar* command. To unpack the file, use *tar* with the *x* option for "extract" and the *f* option to specify a filename. (I also like to use *v* for verbose out- put.) My command line might read:

```
% tar xvf xgopher.1.3.3.tar
xgopher.1.3/Documents/
xgopher.1.3/Documents/Changes
xgopher.1.3/Documents/Customization
xgopher.1.3/Documents/Sun-names
xgopher.1.3/Documents/Porting
    ...
```

The files are unpacked into a subdirectory called *xgopher.1.3.*

If you are on a System V-based system, you may have to use *tar* with the *–o* option to make sure that you get ownership of the files.

Unsharring the Sources

If the package is distributed as a *shar* archive, then the filename may have the suffix *.shar*, or the package may be distributed as a series of files with the names *part01.Z, part02.Z,* and so on. Rather than using the *tar* command, you should unpack the files using the *unshar* or *sh* command. For example, the game *ishido* is distributed as a *shar* archive:

```
% mkdir ishido_src
% cd ishido_src
% /cdrom/source.xut ishido
SOURCE script provided by Ready-to-Run Software, Inc.
Copyright 1993 Ready-to-Run Software, Inc. All Rights Reserved.

Copied /cdrom/sources/ishido/part02.z to PART02.Z
Copied /cdrom/sources/ishido/part03.z to PART03.Z
Copied /cdrom/sources/ishido/part01.z to PART01.Z
Copied /cdrom/sources/ishido/ssol2/ishido to SSol2patch.ishido
Copied /cdrom/sources/ishido/sun4c/ishido to sun4cpatch.ishido
Copied /cdrom/sources/ishido/sun3/ishido to sun3patch.ishido
Copied /cdrom/sources/ishido/hp700/ishido to hp700patch.ishido
Copied /cdrom/sources/ishido/rtr/ishido to rtrpatch.ishido
8 file(s) copied successfully.
```

To extract the *ishido* sources, uncompress the "PART" files and then use the *unshar* program to unpack them.

```
% uncompress PART0?.Z
% unshar PART0?
unshar:  Sending header to PART01.hdr.
unshar:  Doing PART01:
shar: Extracting "README" (1961 characters)
shar: Extracting "Makefile" (904 characters)
shar: Creating directory "bitmap"
shar: Extracting "gl.c" (9528 characters)
shar: Extracting "gl.h" (3085 characters)
shar: End of archive 1 (of 2).
    ...
```

If you don't have *unshar*, it's on the CD-ROM; but the true beauty of *shar* archives is that you can always remove any headers and footers from the file and use the Bourne shell (*sh*) to unpack the files.

To unpack a file using *sh*, you just need to remove any lines at the top of the file that don't resemble Bourne shell syntax. Since many *shar* archives are distributed in mail or in newsgroups, the files might include the header of a mail message or news posting. The author might also precede the actual *shar* archive with some explanation of what the program does. A good bet is to look for a line reading #!/bin/sh and remove all lines preceding it. Even better, most shell archives contain directions right in the file:

```
        (text .... )

#! /bin/sh
# This is a shell archive.  Remove anything before this line,
# then feed it into a shell via "sh file" or similar.
# To overwrite existing files, type "sh file -c".
```

To remove the footer, look for anything resembling a user's mail signature. (*shar* archives usually have an *exit* message at the end, so editing out the footer isn't always needed, but it doesn't hurt.)

After editing out the header and footer, just run the files through *sh* individually:

```
% vi PART0?
        edit out headers
% sh PART01; sh PART02
        ...
```

Note that it's especially important to install and unpack *shar* archives in discrete, well-named directories (such as *ishido_src*, in this case). Since *shar* files are often given generic names of *part01*, *part02*, etc., it's easy to overwrite files or to get confused if you accidentally unpack more than one package in the same directory.

Applying Patches

When I copied the *xgopher* sources using the *source.xut* shell script, I also got several *patch* files. The patch with the prefix *rtrpatch* is a general-purpose patch that should be used for all platforms. Some of the patch files have the names of platforms in their filenames, such as *sun4cpatch.xgopher*. As the filename indicates, this is a patch specifically for compiling the *xgopher* package on the Sun4c platform. If you aren't on a Sun4c, you don't need this file; but if you are, you should apply this patch for a trouble-free build. Similarly, the *hp700.patch* file should be applied if you are on an HP 700 series machine, etc.

The *sun4cpatch.xgopher* file is one provided by Ready-to-Run Software for the *X User Tools* CD-ROM. When building other packages, you may see other platform-specific *patch* files, with prefixes like *risc*, *rs6000*, *hp700*, etc. Only use the patches that refer to your platform.

Other *patch* files may appear in the source directory once it is unpacked. Before you apply any of Ready-to-Run's patches, you should first make sure there aren't any *patch* files in the untarred source directory. If the sources include *patch* files you want to apply, they have to be applied before those of Ready-to-Run. In the *xgopher.1.3* directory, list the directory contents:

```
% ls
Documents          item.c           sc_image.c
Imakefile          item.h           sc_image.h
KeyWSink.c         itemInfo.c       sc_imageP.h
KeyWSink.h         itemInfo.h       sc_index.c
KeyWSinkP.h        itemList.c       sc_index.h
MIT-Xos.h          itemList.h       sc_indexP.h
MIT-Xosdefs.h      jobs.c           sc_sound.c
Makefile.NoNo      jobs.h           sc_sound.h
R6patch            listP.h          sc_soundP.h
README             markList.c       sc_telnet.c
       ...
```

A *patch* file generally has the string *patch* or *pch* in it. The file *R6patch* is the only one in this directory.

To find out what the patch is for, you can just use the *more* command to see whether the file is commented. In this case, it is:

```
% more R6patch
From @cannon.ecf.toronto.edu:steve@ecf.toronto.edu Thu May 12 16:05:13 1994
      ...
I could not build xgopher-1.3.2 under X11R6 because the file KeyWSink.c
was giving me compiler errors. I contacted the author, Allan Tuchman
      ...
The following patch changes 2 files (Imakefile and text.c) so that
xgopher can compile under X11R6.
```

If you are building *xgopher* under X11R6, then you should apply this patch. Otherwise, leave it alone. In my case, I'm still on an X11R5 machine, so I don't want this patch.

The patches I want to install are *rtrpatch.xgopher* and *sun4cpatch.xgopher* in the original parent directory. To apply patches, make sure you're in the source directory (in this case, the *xgopher.1.3* subdirectory created when I ran *tar*). Then run *patch* for each individual *patch* file, taking input from the *patch* files in the parent directory:

```
% patch < ../rtrpatch.xgopher
Hmm... Looks like a unified diff to me...
The text leading up to this was:
--------------------------
|--- ./Imakefile.orig   Fri May 13 10:49:43 1994
|+++ ./Imakefile        Wed Aug 24 14:23:54 1994
--------------------------
Patching file ./Imakefile using Plan A...
Hunk #1 succeeded at 113.
```

```
done
% patch < ../sun4cpatch.xgopher
Hmm... Looks like a unified diff to me...
The text leading up to this was:
--------------------------
|--- ./Imakefile.rtr    Fri May 13 10:49:43 1994
|+++ ./Imakefile        Tue Jul  5 10:25:18 1994
--------------------------
Patching file ./Imakefile using Plan A...
Hunk #1 succeeded at 13.
done
```

The patches are now applied.

—*LM*

31.18 *Configuring Source Code for Your Machine*

Up to now, all we've been doing is getting the source tree together. Now we're up to the part where we actually build the package.

First of all, if there's any universal rule about compiling sources, it's:

IF THERE'S A FILE CALLED README, READ IT!

README files often contain esoteric details about the history of the program and what improvements could be made, etc. But they might also contain details about how to build the package. Reading a *README* can save you hours of frustration trying to figure out what to tweak to make the program build on your platform. Occasionally, a file called *INSTALL* also appears in the directory; it usually behooves you to peruse the *INSTALL* file as well.

(Another file to look for is one called *Configure*. *Configure* is the name commonly used for a shell script that tries to figure out what sort of platform you're on and how to build the package for you, and it's remarkably effective. The sources for many Tcl/Tk-based programs come with *Configure* scripts.)

To look at the *README* file, use the *more* command:

```
% more README
              Installation Notes
                  on the
                Xgopher client


These notes describe Xgopher version 1.3, completed in May 1993.
         ...
```

Further down in the *README* are the instructions on how to actually install the program.

```
+---------------+
| Installation  |
+---------------+
```

The Xgopher program will likely be obtained as a Unix tar file.
After using tar to extract the contents of this file, perform
the following steps.

1. Modify the configuration file (conf.h). If you do not modify this
   file at all, then Xgopher will connect to the University of Illinois
   gopher server by default. The comments in the file tell you what
   is expected. Possibly little change will be necessary, but at least
   consider changing the default top-level gopher server host name to
   a server near you. These are just the compiled-in defaults, most
   can still be changed at run-time to accommodate individual preferences.

This brings us to Universal Rule Number 2: *FOLLOW DIRECTIONS*.

Now you'll look at the *conf.h* file and feel overwhelmed that you don't know
what you're doing. Don't worry about it. Just change the things that make
sense to you (if any) and continue on your merry way. For example, our
office has our own Gopher server, so I change the default host:

```
#define ROOT_SERVER     "gopher.ora.com"  /* default host server */
```

Editing the Imakefile

The directions don't really say it, but one thing you should always do is take a
look at the *Imakefile* and edit as needed. Sometimes the *Imakefile* is uninteresting (and unreadable!), but occasionally the programmer has placed comments in the *Imakefile* to make it easier for people to configure the program.
The *Imakefile* for *xgopher* is one that's well commented:

```
XGOPHERDIR = $(LIBDIR)/xgopher

/* You may add -O to the next line if you'd like.  There will
   not be too much difference for most machines. */

CDEBUGFLAGS =

/************************************************************************
 **      for compiling Xgopher with Sun's OpenWindows 3, uncomment    **
 **      the following 3 lines:                                       **
 **      You may (not certain) need to add -lresolv to second of these **
 **      two lines if you have trouble connecting to other hosts.     **
 **      In other words, maybe use:  EXTRA_LIBRARIES  = -lresolv -lm   **
 ************************************************************************/
MKDIRHIER       = BourneShell /pub/mousse/bin/mkdirhier
/*
  EXTRA_LIBRARIES = -lm
  XMULIB          = -lm -Bstatic -lXmu -Bdynamic
*/
      ...
```

This *Imakefile* has a lot of suggestions for building *xgopher* on different platforms. It's worth it to look through this listing to see if there's anything special about your platform.

—LM

31.19 Compiling the Source

Once the *Imakefile* is set up, compiling is usually a matter of just executing a few commands and hoping it works. In most cases, what you need to do is run *xmkmf* to create a *Makefile*, and then run the *make* command to build the distribution.

Prepare the Makefile

From the *README*:

```
2. xmkmf
   (this will turn the Imakefile into a Makefile, if X11R5
   is properly installed on your system.)
```

xmkmf is a shell script (usually kept in */usr/bin/X11*) that is designed to run *imake* to create Makefiles for third-party X11 software distributions. If a software distribution comes with a proper *Imakefile*, if your X distribution is set up properly, and if you're generally a lucky person, you can simply run *xmkmf* and your *Makefile* is all set.

```
% xmkmf
imake -DUseInstalled -I/usr/lib/X11/config
```

You now have a new *Makefile*. (If there was already a file called *Makefile*, then the old one is first moved to *Makefile.bak*.)

The next item in the *README* is to run *make depend*:

```
3. make depend
   (this will build the include file dependency information
   into the Makefile.)
```

Do as they say:

```
% make depend
makedepend  -s "# DO NOT DELETE" --    -I/usr/local/X11/include
-DHELP_FILE=\"/usr/local/X11/lib/X11/xgopher/xgopher.help\"  -- xgopher.c
item.c itemList.c dir.c dirList.c markList.c  util.c misc.c net.c  gui.c
resources.c help.c status.c jobs.c  panel.c save.c text.c error.c cso.c
index.c  bkmkfile.c options.c version.c single.c itemInfo.c subst.c
sc_dir.c sc_index.c sc_telnet.c sc_tn3270.c  sc_cso.c sc_image.c sc_sound.c
sc_text.c sc_binary.c  sc_extend.c KeyWSink.c
```

Some source distributions come with several subdirectories. Subdirectories might also have *Imakefiles*, so you have to run *xmkmf* in each subdirectory. As an alternative, you can run *xmkmf* with the *−a* command-line option, which works on subdirectories as well. *xmkmf -a* also automatically runs *make depend*, so it's a quick way of combining steps 2 and 3.

```
% xmkmf -a
imake -DUseInstalled -I/usr/lib/X11/config
make Makefiles
make includes
make depend
makedepend  -s "# DO NOT DELETE" --   -I/usr/local/X11/include
-DHELP_FILE=\"/usr/local/X11/lib/X11/xgopher/xgopher.help\"  -- xgopher.c
item.c itemList.c dir.c dirList.c markList.c  util.c misc.c net.c  gui.c
resources.c help.c status.c jobs.c  panel.c save.c text.c error.c cso.c
index.c  bkmkfile.c options.c version.c single.c itemInfo.c subst.c
sc_dir.c sc_index.c sc_telnet.c sc_tn3270.c  sc_cso.c sc_image.c sc_sound.c
sc_text.c sc_binary.c  sc_extend.c  KeyWSink.c
```

The Actual Build

Now that your *Makefile* is all set and you've done all the configuration that seems reasonable, it's time to run the actual build. From the *README*:

```
4. make
   (this will compile the 37 or so source files and link them
   with X11 to produce the executable file xgopher.)
```

Run the *make* command, and cross your fingers.

```
lmui@opal% make
cc  -pipe   -I/usr/local/X11/include     -DHELP_FILE=\"/usr/local/X11/lib
/X11/xgopher/xgopher.help\"  -target sun4 -c  xgopher.c
cc  -pipe   -I/usr/local/X11/include     -DHELP_FILE=\"/usr/local/X11/lib
/X11/xgopher/xgopher.help\"  -target sun4 -c  item.c
        ...
cc  -pipe   -I/usr/local/X11/include     -DHELP_FILE=\"/usr/local/X11/lib
/X11/xgopher/xgopher.help\"  -target sun4 -c  KeyWSink.c
rm -f xgopher
cc -o xgopher xgopher.o item.o itemList.o dir.o dirList.o markList.o  util.o
misc.o net.o  gui.o resources.o help.o status.o jobs.o  panel.o save.o text.o
error.o cso.o index.o  bkmkfile.o options.o version.o single.o itemInfo.o
subst.o  sc_dir.o sc_index.o sc_telnet.o sc_tn3270.o  sc_cso.o sc_image.o
sc_sound.o sc_text.o sc_binary.o  sc_extend.o  KeyWSink.o  -pipe
-L/usr/local/X11/lib -lXaw -lXmu -lXt -lXext -lX11
```

And now, believe it or not, the *xgopher* program is done.

```
% ls -F xgopher
xgopher*
```

Editing the Application Defaults

You might be tempted to try out the *xgopher* program now. However, first take a minute to look at the *app-defaults* file.

5. Modify the application defaults file (Xgopher.ad).
   Little change may be necessary. However, the entries in this
   file (e.g., for host name, port number, help file name, etc.)
   override those defaults compiled into xgopher through
   the configuration file (step 1).

Look at the file called *Xgopher.ad*. This is the app-defaults file for *xgopher*. In general, the app-defaults file for a program is distributed under the name of its application class name *(20.05)* followed by a *.ad* suffix. It is meant to be installed as */usr/lib/X11/app-defaults/Xgopher*, but you can install it elsewhere, and you can also try it out without installing it.

In this case, there aren't too many things you'll want to change right away (although some of them might need changing once you start using *xgopher* and begin nitpicking).

```
!=====================================================================
! Xgopher version 1.3 resources
!=====================================================================
Xgopher.title:                      Xgopher 1.3
! Xgopher.helpFile:                 /usr/lib/X11/xgopher/xgopher.help


!=====================================================================
! "Standard" extended types
!=====================================================================
Xgopher.extendedTypes:              4g

Xgopher.type4.sameAs:               9
Xgopher.type4.dataType:             ascii
     . . .
```

Further down, there are a few things worth noticing, in case you want to change them later. However, the defaults will do for now.

```
     . . .
!=====================================================================
! Application resources that a user may want to change.
! Several are commented out because the installer's choice in
! the file conf.h is most likely correct
!=====================================================================

! Xgopher.rootServer:               gopher.uiuc.edu
! Xgopher.rootPort:                 70
! Xgopher.mainTitle:                UIUC Gopher Information Service
! Xgopher.rootPath:
! Xgopher.helpFile:                 /usr/lib/X11/xgopher/xgopher.help
! Xgopher.bookmarkFile:             ~/.gopherrc

Xgopher.printCommand:      enscript -G -b"%n" -p - %f | lpr -Pgfx
Xgopher.telnetCommand:     xterm -n "telnet" -title "%h" -e telnet %h %P &
Xgopher.tn3270Command:     xterm -n "tn3270" -title "%h" -e tn3270 %h %P &
! Xgopher.tn3270Command:   aixterm -n "tn3270" -title "%h" -e tn3270 %h %P &
! Xgopher.tn3270Command:   x3270
Xgopher.imageCommand:      xloadimage -quiet
```

```
Xgopher.soundCommand:          cat > /dev/audio
! Xgopher.hasSound:                     True
      ...
```

The one thing to notice is that the program won't be able to find its help file, since you haven't installed it yet. You could set the `helpFile` resource to `./xgopher.help`, just for testing; or you could just trust that it'll work once installed and not worry about it.

Now try out the program. Set your XENVIRONMENT environment variable *(20.10)* to *Xgopher.ad* and start up the application.

```
% setenv XENVIRONMENT Xgopher.ad
% ./xgopher &
```

Play with *xgopher* a bit. Change its application defaults as needed. When you're happy with it, install it as described in Article 31.20.

Note that, for this example, you didn't need to know any C programming, you just needed to use some basic common sense. Not all compilations work this easily, but many do.

—LM

31.20 Installing the Software

Once you've built the software, you need to install it. If you're installing the software into a standard system area (as *root*, usually), then it's very easy. Otherwise, it takes a little bit of work.

Installing into a System Area

If you want to install the software in the default system area, and if you have write permission to do so, then the installation involves just a couple of commands.

First, before you install software for real, it's a good idea to make sure you know where it's going. Use the *make −n install* command to see where *make* intends to install the *xgopher* program. (The *−n* option to *make* says not to actually execute these commands but just describes what it would do. It's a good idea since you should never trust that you won't end up blowing away some system files.)

```
% make -n install
if [ -d /usr/local/X11/bin ]; then set +x; \
else (set -x; /bin/sh /usr/bin/X11/mkdirhier /usr/local/X11/bin); fi
install -c -s xgopher /usr/local/X11/bin
if [ -d /usr/local/X11/lib/X11/xgopher ]; then set +x; \
else (set -x; /bin/sh /usr/bin/X11/mkdirhier /usr/local/X11/lib/X11/xgopher);
fi
install -c -m 0444 xgopher.help /usr/local/X11/lib/X11/xgopher
```

```
if [ -d /usr/local/X11/lib/X11/app-defaults ]; then set +x; \
else (set -x; /bin/sh /usr/bin/X11/mkdirhier /usr/local/X11/lib/X11/app-defau
lts); fi
install -c -m 0444 Xgopher.ad /usr/local/X11/lib/X11/app-defaults/Xgopher
if [ -d /usr/local/X11/lib/X11/app-defaults ]; then set +x; \
else (set -x; /bin/sh /usr/bin/X11/mkdirhier /usr/local/X11/lib/X11/app-defau
lts); fi
install -c -m 0444 Xgopher-color.ad /usr/local/X11/lib/X11/app-defaults/Xgoph
er-color
echo "install in . done"
```

If you're satisfied with these locations, run the installation for real. (You may have to become *root* now.)

```
% su
Password:
# make install
    ...
```

To install the program's manpages, you can usually just run *make install.man*.

```
# make install.man
```

Now a few caveats: an installation procedure is only as good as it was configured to be. It sometimes happens that *make install* doesn't do everything you need it to (for example, the application defaults often aren't installed). In addition, if you want to install the program into a non-standard directory, you'll probably have to do it by hand. So if you're in any of these boats, read on.

Installing by Hand

If you want to install the program in a non-standard directory, then you'll need to address these issues:

- Installing the binary program. Usually, this is just a matter of moving or copying it to another directory. However, occasionally programs need to be installed with special permission, such as *xmcd, xload, xnetload,* and *xpd,* which need to be installed by *root*. In those cases, there's no escaping it: you need someone with *root* permission to install the program.

  In addition, sometimes the program depends on other programs. For example, the *ical* program is useless by itself. To get *ical* to work, you need to also install *calshell* and *calshellx,* and you need *tcl* and *wish* installed independently. Another example is *xscreensaver*, which requires each of its "module" programs to be installed as well, not to mention the *xscreensaver-command* program.

- Installing the application defaults. Many programs will not run without the application defaults. Others will run, but will be real ugly. See Article 31.12 for information on what to do with the application defaults.

- Installing the manpage(s). Most manpages are distributed with a *.man* suffix. To install them, you need to copy them into a *man* directory structure. If you're not familiar with the *man* directory structure, usually there's a parent *man* directory with subdirectories named *man1*, *man2*, etc. The manpage filenames within each directory correspond to the directory name, e.g., the manpage *xgopher.man* might be renamed as */usr/local/man/man1/xgopher.1*. Common suffixes are the digits *1* through *8*, *n*, and *l*.

- Installing other files, such as configuration files or help files. Programs will sometimes run without their help files, but often they crash and burn without their configuration files. In addition to installing these files properly, you also need to make sure that the program can find them once they're installed. Sometimes this is as easy as changing a resource in the *app-defaults*, but occasionally you need to do something more serious. Sometimes pathnames are built into the binary, and you'll have to reconfigure the sources and then run the build all over again.

So here's a sample installation by hand. Let's suppose I want to install *xgopher* into my home directory. I want the actual *xgopher* binary in *$HOME/bin*. First I make the new *bin* directory; I move the *xgopher* file there; and I put *$HOME/bin* in my search path:

```
% mkdir $HOME/bin
% mv xgopher $HOME/bin
% set path=($HOME/bin:$path)
```

Next, I want to install the manpages. I create a new *man* directory structure under my home directory, move the *xgopher* manpage there, and then set my MANPATH to include the new directory:

```
% mkdir $HOME/man
% mkdir $HOME/man/man1
% mv xgopher.man $HOME/man/man1/xgopher.1
% setenv MANPATH $HOME/man:/usr/local/man:/usr/man
```

By setting MANPATH, I ensure that my manpage browser (such as *xman (5.02)*, *tkman (5.03)*, or the standard UNIX *man* command) can find the *xgopher* manpage.

Now I have to deal with the application defaults. Since I'm lazy, and I know that my XAPPLRESDIR and XUSERFILESEARCHPATH environment variables aren't defined, I just copy the *Xgopher.ad* file into my home directory:

```
% mv Xgopher.ad $HOME/Xgopher
```

Now I can just start *xgopher* and see if it works.

xgopher seems okay, except that it gives me an error about not finding its help file. Looking at the manpage, I find out that the program looks for the help file in */usr/local/lib/X11/xgopher.help*. I find the file *xgopher.help* in the build directory; now my only problem is where to put it, and how to tell the program where it is.

I choose to copy the *xgopher.help* file into my home directory:

```
% cp xgopher.help $HOME
```

To configure *xgopher* to find the help file in its new home, I actually have a couple of options. I could go back to the build directory and edit the *Imakefile* and rebuild the program. Or I can just edit the following line in the *app-defaults* file:

```
! Xgopher.helpFile: /usr/local/lib/X11/xgopher/xgopher.help
```

I change it to:

```
Xgopher.helpFile: /home/lmui/xgopher.help
```

When I start the program again, I see that the help file is now found, and the program works like a dream.

—LM

31.21 *What To Do If You Have Problems*

Although we've tried to make it easy to install programs on the CD-ROM, platforms and sites vary. Any number of things can go wrong, some of which we have no control over. If you have problems with installing the *X User Tools* software, you can either call us at 1-800-998-9938, or email us at *bookquestions@ora.com*.

Before you call, here are a few things you should try first:

- Some programs may produce errors (or even completely fail) if you don't have any resources installed via *xrdb* or via your *$HOME/.Xdefaults* file. Try installing a bogus resource in *$HOME/.Xdefaults* and see if that makes a difference:

```
% cat > $HOME/.Xdefaults
xresource.phony: oh yeah
^D
```

- Tcl-based programs often need Tcl/Tk installed before they can work. In addition, these programs are often scripts with a first line resembling:

```
#!/usr/local/xut/bin/X11/wish -f
```

Some systems (e.g., SunOS) have a restriction of 32 characters for this line (not including the #!). If you have trouble running Tcl-based programs, the problem may be that the line is too long. For example, if you used

/usr/local/xusertools/ as your parent installation directory, the first line would read:

```
#!/usr/local/xusertools/bin/X11/wish -f
```

On systems with the 32-character restriction, only the first 32 characters are read (/usr/local/xusertools/bin/X11/wi), and you get the error:

```
Command not found.
```

—LM

Glossary

2-bit display

A 2-bit display is one that has only 2 bits per pixel. See depth.

8-bit display

An 8-bit display is one that supports 8 bits per pixel. See depth.

active window

You can't be in more than one place at a time, and you can't work in more than one window at a time. The window that is receiving input is know as the *active*, or *focus*, window. How you select an active window depends on the focus policy in effect.

Without a window manager running, the active window is simply the window your pointer is currently resting in. A window does not have to be *raised* in order to be active. If the pointer is resting on the corner of a partially buried window, your input will still go to that window.

It's possible for no window to be active. Without a window manager running, for instance, if the pointer does not rest on an application window—if it's on the root window—no window is active. If you type when no window is active, the input is lost. You'd think that X would be smart enough to know that if you only have one window open, then that's the one you want to be typing in, but you'd be wrong.

alias

A shorthand version of a command or font name. Many UNIX shells let you define aliases for system commands. The X Window System provides aliases for some of the more commonly used font names *(11.13)*.

alphanumeric

Alphanumeric characters are the uppercase letters A–Z, the lowercase letters a–z, and the numbers 0–9.

ASCII

ASCII is a character set that assigns numerical values between 0 and 127 to letters, numbers, special characters, and control characters. See Article 5.06.

ASCII file

An ASCII file is technically one that only contains ASCII characters. More commonly (in the United States at least) this is a file containing text that's printable, viewable, and has no "binary" (non-ASCII) characters.

Athena

Athena is a set of widgets for X, developed by the X Consortium for use with the Xt toolkit.

Athena Text Widget

The Athena Text Widget is a widget used by Athena-based clients for entering text.

background process

A background process is one that is called in the background, allowing the shell to continue processing new commands while the background process continues to run. Most X clients need to be called as background processes; see Article 2.03.

Berkeley

See BSD.

bin directory

A *bin* directory is a special directory containing binary programs and other executable files (such as shell scripts). This directory is expected to be installed into users' search paths *(2.05)*.

binary program

A binary program, or just *binary*, is a compiled executable program. The binary is generally installed into a directory with the name *bin* (such as */usr/bin*, */usr/local/bin*, etc.), which is expected to be in your search path *(2.05)*. See source code.

Alternatively, binary is also the name for a base-2 arithmetic system, using the numbers 0 and 1.

---

binding

See key and pointer bindings.

bitmap

A bitmap is a graphic image composed of individual dots or *bits*, one for each pixel on the screen. Each bit in a bitmap image is described as being either turned on or turned off. What this means is that each dot in the image can be either one of two states: on a monochrome display, each dot can be either black or white; on a color display, each dot can be either one of two colors. (Thus, regardless of the screen type, a bitmap image is composed of two colors maximum.) The bitmap editor *(22.03)* lets you create images of your own.

Bourne shell

The Bourne shell, *sh*, is a shell that's primarily used for programming. It has the advantage of being portable (since it's found on every version of UNIX), but it is a bit inflexible for complicated scripts.

BSD UNIX

The versions of UNIX developed at the University of California, Berkeley. BSD stands for Berkeley Standard Distribution.

C shell

The C shell, *csh*, is a shell that is sometimes used for programming, but more commonly used only as an interactive shell. The C shell prompt is usually the percent sign (%).

child process

A child process is one that is started by another process, also known as a *subprocess*.

client

Broadly speaking, an X client is any program that communicates with the X server. Your *xterm* program *(11.01)* is an X client, as are your *xclock* *(3.02)* and *xcalc* *(5.05)* programs. In most sentences, you can substitute "client" with the word "program" or "application."

Notice, however, that some programs are clients that you wouldn't think of that way. Your window manager *(1.04)* is an X client. The X Display Manager, *xdm* *(28.02)*, is an X client. While many (if not most) X clients open windows on your display, many do not—such as *xrdb* *(17.03)*, and *xset* *(6.18)*.

Meanwhile, some X-related programs might look like X clients, but aren't really. Examples of these are *xpr* (23.04), *xauth* (19.12), and *showrgb* (26.04), all of which are X utilities that never actually contact the X server.

comp.windows.x

comp.windows.x is a Usenet newsgroup, or bulletin board, that is devoted to the discussion of the X Window System.

comp.windows.x FAQ

The *comp.windows.x* FAQ list is a list of Frequently Asked Questions about X (with answers). It is an excellent source of information about X.

constant width fonts

In a constant width, or *monospaced*, font, every character has the same width. Courier is a typical constant width font. For the text in *xterm* windows, it's a good idea to use special constant width fonts, called character cell fonts (17.18), which are special monospaced fonts originally designed for computer displays. The idea behind a character cell font is that each character is surrounded by an invisible box, or cell.

Character cell fonts have simple aliases (11.13) that correspond to their dimensions in pixels. For example, in the font named 8×13, each character occupies a box 8 pixels wide by 13 pixels high.

contrib

Contrib is a phrase used to refer to "contributed" software for X. This software is made available for users by the X Consortium, but the Consortium doesn't accept any responsibility for maintaining the software. Many of the programs in this book are *contrib*.

crosshairs

"Crosshairs" is one of the cursor font symbols, generally provided by an application when you are requested to click on an item.

.cshrc

.cshrc is a file in your home directory that is executed every time you start a C shell (either for interactive use, or just for running a C shell script).

curses

curses is a programming library for manipulating character-based terminal emulators.

cursor font

A standard font in which the character set is composed of symbols used as screen cursors. You can specify any one of these cursor font characters as the root window pointer *(6.14)*. Some applications also allow you to specify your own cursor symbol.

cut buffer

Generically, a memory area in which selected text is stored, and from which it can be pasted to another application. In the X Window System, a cut buffer is a property of the root window, in which text copied from an *xterm* window is stored. However, the contents of the PRIMARY text selection generally take precedence over the contents of the cut buffer. See the definition of selection and the description of the text selection mechanism for additional information. Knowledge of cut buffers is useful when you're working with an application like *emacs* *(9.02)*, which doesn't interpret selections *(11.24)*.

daemon

"Daemon" is a UNIX term for a process that runs invisible to users and often unassociated with a particular terminal. A daemon waits for specific requests or events and then acts accordingly.

decimal

Our standard base-10 arithmetic system.

depth

The depth of the display (or server) is the number of bits per pixel that it supports. For example, a black-and-white display has 1 bit per pixel, since each pixel has only two choices: it can be either black or white. A color display might have 8 bits per pixel, in which case each pixel can support as many as $2^8 = 256$ colors. The black-and-white display therefore has a depth of 1, and the color display has a depth of 8. Displays might have depths as great as 24 or 32.

device driver

A device driver is a program that negotiates communication between the operating system and a particular "device" (such as a monitor, disk drive, tape drive, etc.).

dialog box

A dialog box is generally a small window a client pops up to get additional input from the user. For example, when you attempt to quit a text editor before saving changes, a dialog box may ask whether you want to save before exiting.

dimensions

The dimensions of a display refer to how many pixels it can address horizontally and vertically. These figures do not necessarily correspond to the size of the display, since one 19-inch display might have much greater resolution than another. The *xdpyinfo* command can tell you the dimensions of the display:

```
% xdpyinfo
name of display: opal:0.0
version number:  11.0
vendor string:   MIT X Consortium
      ...
screen #0:
   dimensions:   1120x832 pixels (309x229 millimeters)
   resolution:   92x92 dots per inch
      ...
```

From these numbers, I can figure out that I'm working on a display with a size of 12×9 inches, with a 15-inch diagonal.

display name

The full generalized syntax for a display name is:

```
[hostname]:[:]server#[.screen#]
```

Technically, the part of the display name up to and including the colons specifies how to connect to the host running the server. A hostname followed by a single colon indicates using TCP/IP to connect to that hostname. The special hostname unix (or omitting a hostname entirely) followed by a colon means using UNIX domain sockets (IPC) and bypasses the network at large. But a hostname followed by two colons indicates using DECnet instead of TCP/IP.

The portion of the display name after the colon(s) represents what server and screen to connect to on that host. Most hosts have only one server running, so :0 will suffice. Occasionally you'll see an implementation where several servers are running on the same machine, and in those cases you might need to specify a different server number (such as :1). When running an X terminal over a serial line, the X servers themselves often run on the host machine rather than on the X terminal itself, and in those cases you're likely to have multiple servers running on the same host.

Using the screen number is a little more common. Some X servers may have more than one screen—either literal screens (as in two monitors with one keyboard and one mouse), or virtual screens (as in having one monitor that reveals a second screen if you move your mouse off the edge.)

DVORAK keyboard

DVORAK is an alternative keyboard layout designed for ease of typing (as opposed to the QWERTY keyboard, which was designed to slow people down—no joke).

Encapsulated PostScript

A format created using a subset of PostScript and a process of "encapsulation," which allows the resultant data to be used with different applications and on multiple platforms. Encapsulated PostScript files commonly contain graphic images; these files may be included in a larger PostScript language document.

event

An X event is just something that the server needs to tell clients about. An event might be a character that you type on your keyboard, or the fact that you moved your pointer. Not all events have to be related to user action, e.g., if a window is killed, then windows that were obscured by it need to know that it's gone (in order to redraw).

extensions

An extension refers to an extension to the X protocol. Although the protocol itself has remained unchanged over the years, extensions allow enhancements to be added on easily. One of the most famous extensions is the SHAPE extension.

FAX formats

Since computers can now send and receive FAX (facsimile) images, and there's a world of hardware available with which to accomplish this, there are actually dozens of facsimile (FAX) file formats. Though a standard is still emerging, virtually every format consists of a header, followed by compressed image data. Group 3 and Group 4 FAX images *(24.05)* refer to two of the more popular types of compression.

focus policy

Refers to the method by which you select the window to receive input (also known as the focus or active window).

In some cases, the focus follows the pointer. In other words, you have to move the pointer into a window in order to enter text in that window, invoke commands on it, etc. This focus policy is known as "pointer focus," and is also described as "real-estate-driven" because it relates to the location of windows and the pointer.

In other cases, you have to select the window to receive input by clicking on it with the pointer. This focus policy is known as "explicit focus," or more commonly as "click to type."

The window manager generally specifies the focus policy. The window manager will provide a default policy, but many window managers also allow you to select an alternative. Without a window manager running, pointer focus is in effect.

focus window

See active window.

font search path

The X server has a *font path*, which is set initially at startup. The default font path for X11R5 is composed of the following directories in this order:

```
/usr/lib/X11/fonts/misc
/usr/lib/X11/fonts/Speedo
/usr/lib/X11/fonts/75dpi
/usr/lib/X11/fonts/100dpi
```

The *misc* directory includes many fonts suitable for terminal emulators *(11.13)*. The *Speedo* directory contains scalable outline fonts *(17.16)*. The *75dpi* and *100dpi* directories contain fonts for monitors with resolution of 75 dots per inch and 100 dots per inch, respectively.

You can change the font path using the *xset* command. See the *xset* online manpage for the appropriate options. See Article 31.13 for an example.

When a client wants to use a particular font, it requests the font from the X server. The fonts must either exist on local disk for the server or must be downloaded via the font server. When a font server is being used, the name of the machine and the directory on that machine are added to the font path.

foreground process

A process is called a foreground process if the shell waits for it to complete before executing another command. See background process.

frame

Many window managers provide decoration in the form of a "frame" that surrounds windows on the display. The frame is usually composed of a titlebar and a border. You should be able to perform most window management functions by using the pointer on various parts of the frame.

FTP

FTP stands for file transmission protocol. It is a method for downloading files from remote machines over the Internet. See Article 8.02.

GIF

GIF refers to the graphics interchange format, a graphics file format developed by CompuServe Inc., which is used on a variety of platforms and systems. GIF files typically contain multiple bit *(26.07)* color, or grayscale images. You're much more likely to find 16- or 256-color near-photographic quality images, or scanned grayscale images, than monochrome images, in a GIF file. GIF is one of the most widely used formats for storing complex graphics.

grayscale

A grayscale display is one that supports multiple shades of gray, with more than 1 bit per pixel but no color support.

group

Several users on a single UNIX system can be lumped together into a single "group," used primarily for maintaining an additional level of UNIX file permissions.

GUI

The programs that compose the basic X Window System are extremely simple, almost skeletal, in appearance; without the graphical niceties associated with commercial software. A GUI *(1.04)*, or graphical user interface, adds a particular "look and feel" to a basic environment such as X, determining how windows, menus, dialog boxes, etc., look and how you work with them. Motif and OPEN LOOK are two of the more popular GUIs available for X.

hexadecimal

A base-16 arithmetic system, which uses the digits A through F to represent the base-10 numbers 10 through 15. Hexadecimal notation (called hex for short) is frequently used with computers because a single hex digit can represent four binary digits (bits). X clients accept RGB color specifications in hexadecimal notation (prefixed by a # character).

home directory

Each user on a UNIX system has an assigned "home directory." Many UNIX programs and X clients look for configuration files in the user's home directory. When the user first logs in, users are placed in their home directory by default. To find out your home directory, look in the HOME environment variable *(2.04)*:

```
% echo $HOME
/home/lmui
```

If you use the C shell, you can also use the tilde character (~) to represent the home directory on the command line.

```
% echo ~
/home/lmui
```

HVC

A model by which color is described according to three characteristics: hue, value, and chroma. Generally speaking, hue is the shade (e.g., red). Value refers to the range of a hue from light to dark. The lightest possible shade of any hue is white; the darkest is black. Chroma refers to the intensity of a hue; i.e., the amount of the hue present. (Also called *saturation*.) Unlike the older RGB color model, the HVC model allows color to be described in device-independent terms.

I-beam

The I-beam is a cursor symbol that looks like a spidery capital letter I. It is the default symbol used to represent the pointer inside an *xterm* window.

iconify

When a window manager is running, you can convert any client window to an icon, or iconify it. An icon is basically a small symbol that represents a window in an inactive state. While a window is iconified, all processes that were happening in the window continue, but you cannot enter input or read output. The window manager also allows you to deiconify a window, that is, convert an icon back to its original state.

input focus

When you enter input (using either the keyboard or pointer), where the input goes depends on the focus policy in effect and where you choose to direct (or *focus*) the input. Chances are you will want to focus input on a particular application window. Whatever window is receiving the input focus is called the active window, or focus window.

interactive shell

An interactive shell is a shell that you use for typing your commands within a terminal window, as opposed to a shell used for programming.

Internet

The Internet is a massive network connecting thousands of machines over the world. Using the Internet, a machine in another hemisphere can be accessed as if it were in the next room.

IP address

"IP" stands for "Internet Protocol." The IP address for a given host is a unique string that identifies it to all other hosts on the Internet. This address is usually translated to a hostname by a special daemon called a *name server*. If you need to know an IP address for any reason (for example, if the name server is down), try using the *nslookup* command. For example, to find out the IP address for my workstation, *opal*:

```
% nslookup
Default Server:  ora.com
Address:  198.112.208.25

> opal
Server:  ora.com
Address:  198.112.208.25

Name:    opal.ora.com
Address: 198.112.208.35

> exit
```

My IP address is 198.112.208.35.

job control

Job control is a feature within some UNIX shells on some systems. With job control, users can stop processes and restart them easily.

---

key and pointer bindings

A binding refers to the association of some input action (such as a keystroke, pointer click, etc.) with a particular application command or function. For instance, with the *twm* window manager *(12.01)* the iconify function is "bound" to the combination of the Meta key and a second pointer button click. Note that a function may be bound to a simple keystroke, a key combination, a simple pointer action, or a key-pointer combination. Many clients let you customize which input actions invoke a function.

keyboard accelerators

While X is by and large a pointer-dominated environment, some people would prefer to keep their hands on the keyboard. Thus, many applications (particularly window managers) provide *keyboard accelerators*, or keyboard shortcuts, for application commands.

keycode

Each physical key on the keyboard can be identified by a number known as a keycode. (Technically speaking, a keycode is the actual value the key generates.) Keycodes cannot be mapped to other keys. No matter what functions you assign to various keys with *xmodmap (18.07)*, the keycode associated with each physical key remains the same.

keypress event

A keypress event happens when a user presses a key.

keysym

Each physical key on the keyboard is associated with a name known as a keysym, which stands for *key sym*bol name. A keysym corresponds to a key's function; generally it is reflected by the label on the physical key, though technically you can map a function to an entirely different physical key. The *xmodmap* client *(18.07)* allows you to map key functions to physical keys.

keysym mapping

A keysym mapping is the mapping of a keysym to a given hardware keycode (and thus to a physical key). See Article 18.07.

library

A library is an archive of function definitions that are used in programs. Many programs need to access library definitions in order to function properly; in these cases, the libraries must be available on the system. For example, in order for the *xloadimage* graphics utility *(24.05)* to handle image files of the JPEG format, it must have access to the JPEG library of routines. See also shared library.

local client

A local client is a program that runs on the same machine the server is running on, generally on a workstation. See remote client.

.login

.login is the name of a file in your home directory that is executed when you first log in under the C shell for interactive use.

lowering

Lowering a window means shuffling it below any windows currently underneath it in the window stack. Your window manager should provide commands for lowering, as well as raising windows.

manpages

Most UNIX programs are distributed with documentation called a "manual page," or "*manpage*" for short. To see a manual page at the UNIX shell prompt *(2.02)*, use the *man* command:

```
% man xterm
```

The format and syntax for manpages may seem hard to decipher at first, but after a while you'll learn how to skim for the information you want. Manual pages are most useful for learning the syntax for running a command, or for finding out what command-line options are supported. Some manpages also have some very good tutorial documentation for new users. However, many manpages are less thorough, so users often prefer other documentation sources (like this book!).

If you prefer, you can use the *xman* command *(5.02)* to view manpages.

Manpages are separated into "sections." This matters mostly because you might see a reference to a command with a number in parentheses following (e.g., *cat(1)*). This signifies the *cat* command, which is in Section 1 (User Commands).

maximizing a window

In window manager parlance, maximizing a window means enlarging it to maximum size. Generally, this is the size of the root window, but some applications specify their own maximum size. The *mwm* frame *(13.03)* provides a maximize button to toggle between regular and maximum size. Keep in mind that the graphic load involved in maximizing certain applications can impact system resources.

Certain window managers also allow you to maximize in one or more dimensions. For instance, you might be able to maximize vertically, to get the tallest window possible for your screen. This limited resizing is generally more useful.

Meta

In virtually every X environment, a particular keyboard key is configured to perform a function called "Meta." The key that performs the Meta function varies from keyboard to keyboard; often, the **Alt** key serves as Meta. The Meta key is basically a function key (similar to **CTRL**) that many X applications require you to use. See Article 18.14 for more information.

Motif

Motif is a toolkit and GUI specification for the X Window System; Motif was developed by the Open Software Foundation.

netiquette

What Miss Manners would advise her Gentle Users to follow, if they and she worked on the Internet.

newline

The character that marks the end of a line of text in most UNIX files. (This is a convention, not a requirement.)

NFS

NFS, or Network File System, is a system for sharing the same file system across several different hosts over TCP/IP. Under this system, one host may have a local file system but "export" it to other machines. For each of the remote machines, they can "mount" or "NFS-mount" the remote file system and use it as if it were on local disk.

octal

A base-8 arithmetic system.

OPEN LOOK

OPEN LOOK is a GUI specification supported by AT&T and Sun. See Article 1.05.

OpenWindows

See Sun OpenWindows.

parent process

A parent process is a process that spawned a child process.

patch

A patch to a program is basically a change to the source code that usually fixes a bug or adds a new feature, often distributed separately from the program itself. Patches are usually installed by using the UNIX *patch* program on the source code before compiling.

perl

perl is an interpretive programming language used primarily on UNIX systems. It combines the accessibility of shell scripts with much of the power of the C language.

Photo CD files

Photo CD is a image format developed by Kodak for storing photographic images in high-resolution digital format. The images are usually distributed on a CD-ROM.

pipe

In a UNIX shell, the output of one command can be applied as the input to another by using a pipe symbol (|). For example, output is often piped through the *more* command:

```
% xlsfonts | more
```

pixel

A pixel is the smallest graphical unit that can be addressed on a server's display. See depth and dimensions.

pixmap

A pixmap is an image in which multiple bits are used to define each pixel. See Article 26.07.

pointer

The pointer is the device used to point at and select windows, widgets, etc. on an X server. Generally, a pointer is a mouse, but X also supports trackballs, joy sticks, etc.

pop-up menu

While a pull-down menu must be accessed from a particular application feature (such as a menu bar), a pop-up menu is displayed wherever your pointer is positioned, when you press the appropriate keys/buttons. The *mwm* Root menu *(13.05)* is a typical pop-up menu.

---

pop-up window

An application may from time to time display a subwindow to allow you to specify parameters, etc. We sometimes refer to such a subwindow as a pop-up window. A dialog box is an example of what we call a pop-up window.

PostScript

PostScript is a standard language for printing documents. Documents and images are converted to PostScript before they can be sent to the printer.

process ID

The process ID is an identification number used by the operating system. You can use the process ID to kill *(2.08)* an X client.

.profile

.profile is the name of a file in your home directory that is executed when you first log in under the Bourne shell or Korn shell for interactive use.

property

A property is a piece of information associated with a font or a window (including the root window). Properties are stored in the server, where they can be accessed by any client. A typical root-window property is the PRIMARY text selection.

pull-down menu

A pull-down menu is one you access from a particular application feature, like a command button or menu bar. In effect, you pull the menu down from this feature. See also pop-up menu.

QWERTY keyboard

The QWERTY keyboard is the familiar keyboard with the letters "QWERTY" in the upper-left section. See DVORAK.

raising a window

Raising a window means bringing it to the front of the display, or the top of the window stack. Your window manager sets the policy for how windows are raised and lowered. Without a window manager, there is no easy way for a user to raise and lower windows.

Once you have a window manager running, you can almost always raise a window by clicking on its titlebar. In addition, some window managers can be configured to let you click anywhere in the window, or click on a window "border" (if available). In some window managers, raising a window often also makes the window the active window ; check the specific

---

window manager documentation because this may require some customization.

raster

Raster is a synonym for bitmap.

real estate

In the context of X, the phrase "real estate" often refers to your screen
(and the windows on it). If the focus policy for a window manager is "real
estate driven," for example, then that means that the focus follows wherever your pointer goes. If a window "takes up less real estate," it means
that it uses a smaller part of your screen.

remote client

A remote client is one that runs on a different machine than the one the
server is running on. Practically all clients running on X terminals are
remote clients. See Article 19.01 for more information.

resolution

The resolution of a display is the number of dots per inch (or pixels per
inch) supported by the display. The *xdpyinfo* command can tell you the
resolution of the display; see dimension.

resources

Resources are variables that define the default behavior of a client. See
Article 17.03 for information on how to set a resource easily.

RGB

An additive method for defining color in which the primaries red, green
and blue are combined to form other colors. In terms of X, the RGB color
model creates hardware-specific (thus, non-portable) color definitions.

root

root is the user name for the superuser. A user needs to be a member of
wheel and have the *root* password before he or she can gain superuser
privileges.

root menu

A root menu is generally a pop-up menu that you see by pressing the first
mouse button in the root window. The root menu is a function of your
window manager, and can be changed in your window manager's configuration file. See Articles 12.22, 13.19, 14.26, and 15.23.

root window

You can think of the root window as the background behind all your client windows. In OPEN LOOK, the root window is also called the *workspace*. See Article 6.02.

screen

A server may provide several independent screens, which may or may not have physically independent monitors.

selection

Text copied into memory using the pointer is saved in a global cut buffer and also becomes what is known as the PRIMARY text *selection*. The contents of the PRIMARY selection and the cut buffer are stored as properties of the root window, where they can be accessed by any client. The property mechanism permits "copied" text to be stored in memory and later "pasted" into the windows of other clients.

Both the contents of the cut buffer and the contents of the PRIMARY text selection are globally available to all clients. When you paste text into an *xterm* window, by default the contents of the PRIMARY selection are pasted. If no text is in the PRIMARY selection, the contents of the cut buffer (called CUT_BUFFER0), are pasted.

In most cases, the PRIMARY selection and cut buffer will contain the same text. Another root window property, the CLIPBOARD selection is used to save text you copy into the *xclipboard* window *(11.21)*.

Some clients (particularly those not updated to X11R5) may not understand the selection mechanism, and will interpret only the cut buffer contents. *emacs (9.02)* is one such client. Pasting from *xterm* to an *emacs* window can be problematic because they interpret text selections differently. Article 11.24 offers a modification that will enable you to paste from *xterm* to *emacs*.

server

The X server is the program that controls your display. Your display is your monitor, keyboard and mouse. See Article 1.02.

SHAPE extension

The SHAPE extension is an X protocol extension introduced with X11R4, allowing windows to take on irregular shapes (i.e., not just rectangles). See Article 3.02.

shared library

A shared library is a library that can be shared between many programs that link with it. Usually, each program that calls a library ends up with an entire copy of each of the functions it calls embedded within its binary. With shared libraries, several programs can link dynamically with a single copy of the function definition, thus reducing the amount of disk space and memory that a program uses.

shell

The UNIX command shell is a character-based program with which a user executes UNIX commands, including X commands on a UNIX system. (See Article 2.02.) The shell can also be used as a programming language. See shell script.

There are two basic types of shell: Bourne shell and C shell. The Bourne shell (*sh*) is more likely to be used for programming, whereas the C shell (*csh*) is more popular for interactive use. There are also popular variations of each of these shells: the Korn shell (*ksh*), which supports the power of the Bourne shell but is a easier to use interactively, and the T shell (*tcsh*), which is a superset of the C shell that includes command-line editing.

shell prompt

When typing commands on your interactive UNIX shell, your *prompt* is the string that appears to signify that the shell is ready for another command. Your prompt can be configured in your *.cshrc*, *.login*, or *.profile* file, but a general convention is that prompts in the C shell end in a percent sign (%) and prompts in the Bourne shell end in a dollar sign ($). See Article 2.02.

shell script

A *shell script* is a UNIX command that is written using one of the UNIX command shells (usually *sh*). It can be thought of as a "batch" script that combines several commands together for ease of use.

source code

Programs are written in "source code" in ASCII form, and then compiled (or *built*) into an executable binary. Programs that are distributed in source code can be rewritten and ported to other platforms, whereas a binary will only work for the platform it has been built for. See article 31.16.

stacking order

Stacking order is the order in which clients fall in the window stack. You can change the order with any window manager, e.g., raise a window to the top of the stack, or lower it to the bottom.

standard error

Standard error (*stderr*) is where a program sends error messages. Standard error is usually sent to the output device associated with the process that started it (e.g., your terminal or terminal emulator), but not on the same stream as standard output, so you can redirect standard output and still see error messages on your terminal.

standard input

Standard input (*stdin*) is where many UNIX programs read text if a filename is not specified (or if the filename is specified as "–"). When reading from standard input, the program reads input either from the user's keyboard, or from the output of another command (see *pipe*).

standard output

Standard output (*stdout*) is where a program sends any normal messages or responses to the user. It is generally sent to the output device associated with the process that started it (e.g., your terminal or terminal emulator). The user can redirect this output to a file, or as the input to another program. See pipe.

startx

startx is a way of starting both the X server and an initial X session on workstations. The user starts out with their workstation display in a "console" mode (i.e., like one big ugly terminal). After logging in, the user needs to type in the *startx* command:

```
% startx
```

The X server starts and a startup script *(2.09)* called *.xinitrc* is executed. *startx* is essentially a front-end to *xinit*, configured to be a little smarter about what to do if you don't have an *.xinitrc* file.

stty

The UNIX *stty* command defines some of the behavior of a terminal emulator, especially in terms of which keys may be interpreted as the "erase" character, as "interrupt," as "end-of-file," etc.

Sun Icon

Sun Microsystems' own file format used for icons under both the OPEN LOOK and SunView graphical user interfaces (see GUI).

Sun OpenWindows

Sun OpenWindows is a implementation of the OPEN LOOK GUI specification, maintained and distributed by Sun Microsystems.

Sun Raster

The Sun Raster image file format is Sun Microsystems' own bitmap format, designed for UNIX systems running the SunOS operating system. Sun Raster files can store black-and-white, grayscale, and color bitmap images of any depth.

superuser

The superuser is a privileged user on a UNIX system who can kill processes, read and write all files, and basically create havoc in the wrong hands. Generally, only the system administrator has superuser privileges on a multiuser system. On a workstation, however, it's common for the workstation user to have superuser privileges. See root.

System V

System V is the flavor of UNIX developed by AT&T.

tcsh

An extended version of the Berkeley C shell, which includes a command-line editor, command and filename completion, etc.

.tcshrc

If you have a *.tcshrc* file in your home directory, it will be executed when you start *tcsh*. If you don't have a *.tcshrc* file, and a *.cshrc* file is present, *.cshrc* will be executed.

telnet

telnet is a facility you can use to log in to a remote system over a TCP/IP network.

termcap

termcap is a terminal capability database.

terminal emulator

A terminal emulator is a program that simulates a character-based terminal connection to a host. The *xterm (2.02)* client is a terminal emulator.

terminfo

terminfo is a terminal capability database.

TIFF

TIFF refers to the tag image file format, a graphics file format developed by Aldus Corporation, which has become a standard format found in most paint, imaging, and desktop publishing programs. TIFF is both powerful and flexible, and allows for storage of multiple bit *(26.07)* images of any pixel depth.

tiling

Tiling refers to a style of screen layout whereby windows do not overlap; instead they fit beside each other, much as ceramic tiles do on a floor. You might want to create an X session startup script *(16.01)* that sets up your screen in a tiled fashion. Keep in mind, however, that tiling drastically limits the number of windows you can have on the screen at a time. Many people are happier with a window stack, in other words, windows that overlap each other.

titlebar

The titlebar of a client is the top part of the window manager decoration. It usually displays the name (or title) of the client.

toggle

A function or command that allows you to switch between two states. In a sense, a light switch is a toggle.

toolkit

A toolkit is a set of libraries and widgets for programming in X, coordinating a cohesive "look and feel" for all applications that are based on them. See Article 1.05. Xlib, XView, and Motif are all examples of X toolkits.

USENIX

USENIX is a non-profit professional membership organization of individuals and institutions with an interest in UNIX.

vi

vi (pronounced vee-eye) is the character-based editor found on all fine UNIX systems. Most new users are horrified by *vi*, but *vi* veterans defend it as being exceedingly efficient. The UNIX world can be thought of as being split into two camps, *vi* users and *emacs* *(9.02)* users.

wheel

wheel is a special group on many UNIX systems, set aside for users who have permission to become superuser.

widget

A widget is a graphical component that can be used in writing client programs. See Article 1.05.

window ID

Each window has a unique identification number associated with it. This number is commonly referred to as the *window ID* (or the *resource ID*). You can use the window ID as command-line argument with several clients. For example, you can specify the window to capture with the *xwd* window dump utility *(23.01)* by providing its ID number after the *–id* option.

The *xwininfo* client *(17.13)* provides many statistics about any window you select, including the window's geometry and its ID number. To determine a window's ID, just enter:

```
% xwininfo | grep -i "window id"
```

in any terminal emulator window. The pointer changes to a crosshair symbol and you are prompted:

```
xwininfo: Please select the window about which you
          would like information by clicking the
          mouse in that window.
```

You can select any window on the display, including the window in which you've typed the command and the root window. You should receive output similar to the following:

```
xwininfo: Window id: 0x540000e xterm
```

If you don't want to use the pointer, you can instead run *xwininfo* with the program's own *-name* option, followed by the intended window's title, or name if it has no title. See Article 17.09 for information about specifying a client's title or name.

In addition to *xwd*, the *xkill (2.08)* and *xprop (20.07)* clients also accept the window ID as an argument, both following an *-id* option.

window manager

A window manager is a program that controls how windows are moved, resized, and iconified. See Article 1.04.

window manager startup file

Each window manager has default settings and behaviors. In most cases, these features are determined by a systemwide defaults/startup script. This file often lives in */usr/lib/X11* or a subdirectory thereof, named for the window manager. This startup file itself usually begins with the word *system*, followed by a dot, then name of the window manager, and the letters *rc* (reminiscent of the UNIX *rc* startup script). Thus, the systemwide startup file for *twm* is (you guessed it) *system.twmrc*.

Why should you care about this? Because you can have your own window manager startup file, in which you can tailor the program for your needs. Often the startup file controls what menu options are available, what keys perform what functions, etc. To create a personal startup file, copy the systemwide file to your home directory, dropping the "system" prefix—for instance, *.twmrc, .fvwmrc, .mwmrc*. Then edit away.

window stack

Unless you're an advocate of tiling, windows may often overlap on your display, much like a stack of papers on your desk or a deck of cards. The "pile" of windows is commonly referred to as the *window stack*. Any window manager will let you change the stacking order. You can raise a window to the top of the stack, or lower it to the bottom.

workstation

A UNIX workstation can be loosely defined as a UNIX machine that can run both a server and clients (as opposed to an X terminal, which doesn't have the overhead of running UNIX; or a file server, which may run clients but often doesn't have an attached display to run a server on).

WYSIWYG

A WYSIWYG word processor is one in which what you see on the screen is what will print on the page. Literally, WYSIWYG stands for "what you see is what you get." Word processors like FrameMaker and Microsoft Word are both WYSIWYG editors, whereas markup languages like *TeX* and *troff* are not.

X Consortium

The X Consortium is a non-profit organization responsible for developing and maintaining X technology. The Consortium was formerly associated with the Massachusetts Institute of Technology.

X distribution

X is available in source code from the X Consortium, via magnetic tape, CD-ROM, or *ftp* access. X in this form is often called the "standard X distribution" (as opposed to a vendor's version of X, which would be based on the X Consortium's but then tweaked to the vendor's own liking).

X Protocol

The X protocol is the language used to communicate between the client and the server. See Article 1.05.

X terminal

An X terminal is a machine that is optimized to run an X server. Although some X terminals may include some local clients, the idea is that X terminals run all their clients remotely from another machine on the local area network.

X10

X10 was the version of the X protocol that preceded X11.

X11

X11 is the current version of the X Protocol.

X11R3

X11R3 refers to Release 3 of X. We're assuming in this book that no one is still running X11R3.

X11R4

X11R4 refers to Release 4 of X. Big changes in X11R4 were the SHAPE extension and the emergence of XDMCP.

X11R5

X11R5 refers to Release 5 of X. Big changes in X11R5 were the font server and scalable fonts, and the *xdm* "chooser" facility and *Xaccess* file.

X11R6

X11R6 refers to Release 6 of X. Most of the new functionality in X11R6 is at the programmer level and does not directly affect users.

XDMCP

The X Display Manager (*xdm*) Control Protocol. See Chapter 28 for more information about *xdm*.

xinit

xinit is a way of starting both the X server and an initial X session on workstations. The user starts out with their workstation display in a "console" mode (i.e., like one big ugly terminal). After logging in, the user needs to type in the *xinit* command:

```
% xinit
```

The X server starts and a startup script *(2.09)* called *.xinitrc* is executed.

Xlib

Xlib is the lowest-level library for writing client applications in X. It has a one-to-one correspondence with the X protocol. See Article 1.05.

Xt

Xt, or the *X toolkit*, is a "sample" toolkit distributed with the standard X distribution.

Xt options

Applications written with the same toolkit not only have the same "look and feel," they also inherit a core set of command-line options and resources *(1.06)*. The following are some of the widely used resources available to all applications written with Xt and Xt-based toolkits:

Resource	Option	Description	Article
foreground	*–fg*	Foreground color	17.06
background	*–bg*	Background color	17.06
reverseVideo	*–rv*	Reverse video	17.08
geometry	*–geometry*	Geometry	17.10
font	*–fn*	Font name	17.14
title	*–title*	Title name	17.09
name	*–name*	Application name	20.04

Other command-line options that are widely used are *–display* and *–iconic*.

XView

An OPEN LOOK-based toolkit for X, meant to provide backward compatibility with SunView. See Article 1.05.

Index

icons
    active (in xterm), 214
    collection of, 529
    in twm, 241
    starting applications by pressing, 486
<idx> string (Gopher), 154
if construct (Tcl), 689
images, 508
imake utility, 744
Imakefile, 744
    editing, 752
<img> (Gopher), 155
Indirect query to XDMCP
    protocol for, 653
    responding to (by forwarding
        request), 655
    responding to (with chooser box),
        656
information retrieval
    via WAIS, 154-155
    via WWW, 160
inheritance of environment variables, 16
input devices, 399
input focus, 771
inserting bitmaps into images
    using bitmap editor, 516
installation
    of single program, 729
    of fonts, 736-738
    of many programs from CD-ROM, 733
    of precompiled binaries, 726
    of software built from source code,
        756
instance of application, 438
interactive shell, 771
Internet, 137, 771
Internet Starting Points (Mosaic), 161
interrupting jobs, 13
IP (Internet Protocol) addresses, 771
ishido, 192
ISO 9660 CD-ROM format, 722

job control (UNIX), 771
JPEG files, 499
    viewing via xloadimage, 558
    viewing via xv, 86, 561
jumpScroll resource (xterm), 202

kbd_mode program, 417
    in olwm, 317
key and pointer button shortcuts (twm),
    238
key bindings, 772
key mappings
    restoring, 663
keyboard accelerators, 772
    for fvwm, 347
    in mwm, 285-287
keyboard layouts
    DVORAK, 767
    QWERTY, 776
    translating QWERTY into DVORAK,
        403
keyboards, 399-418
    auto-repeat on (changing), 400
    disabling Caps Lock key on, 404
    faking function keys on, 403
    keyclick adjustment for, 401
    listing of xkeycaps accepted, 412
    Meta key on, 407
    resetting (via kbd_mode), 417
    Sun (problems with), 404
    using space bar as CTRL key on, 417
keycode command, 404
keycodes, 217, 772
Keymap resource (xterm), 219
keymap() action (xterm), 219
keypress event, 772
keys
    defining via xmodmap, 402
keysyms (key symbols), 403, 772
    mapping of, 403, 772
    printing current (via xmodmap), 411
    restoring, 663
kill (emacs), 167
kill command (UNIX), 18
kill ring (emacs), 168
killing windows, 16
klondike, 187
kmem group, 627
Korean abacus program, 82
Korn shell
    setting search path in, 15, 734

^L (CTRL-L)
    in xedit, 172
label widget, 685
LANG environment variable, 436

About the Authors

Linda Mui started working for O Reilly & Associates in 1986. She was first hired as a production assistant, later became an apprentice system administrator, and is now a writer. Her first writing job was *termcap and terminfo*, which she co-authored with John Strang and Tim O Reilly. She later co-authored *The X Window System Administrator s Guide* with Eric Pearce.

Linda was raised in the Bronx, New York, and now lives in Cambridge, Massachusetts.

Valerie Quercia is a staff writer for O Reilly & Associates and co-author (with Tim O Reilly) of several editions of *Volume 3: X Window System User s Guide*. Her personal trainer and manager, Dr. Heinrich Bunsen, reports: Though X has been very, very good to her, Val would really like to try another letter, maybe a nice Q.

Val lives close enough to Boston to be upset by the Red Sox.

Colophon

Our look is the result of reader comments, our own experimentation, and feedback from distribution channels.

Distinctive covers complement our distinctive approach to technical topics, breathing personality and life into potentially dry subjects.

The history of the modern Swiss Army knife, pictured on the cover of this book, begins in 1884, when Karl Elsener, a Swiss cutler, discovered that the knives issued to members of the Swiss Army were made in Germany. Thinking that it would be more appropriate for the Swiss Army to carry Swiss-made knives, he formed the Association of Swiss Master Cutlers in 1891. That same year he developed a pocketknife that contained a blade, a screwdriver, a can opener, and a hole punch. He called this knife the Soldier's knife, beginning the tradition of giving the knives model names rather than model numbers. In 1897 Elsener discovered a way to use one spring to attach blades to both the back and the front of the knife, thus enabling him to add more implements to his knives without adding more bulk. He put an additional blade and a corkscrew on his original knife and called it the Officer's knife. Even today, the knives issued to Swiss officers have corkscrews, while those issued to non-officers do not.

The Swiss Army has traditionally split its orders for knives between the company that Elsener founded, Victorinox, which is based in the German-speaking part of Switzerland, and the Wenger company, which is based in French-speaking Switzerland. The knives purchased by the Swiss Army do not have the familiar red plastic handle, but one of a quilted gray aluminum. A small red shield with a white cross in it appears on the side of each knife.

The popular red knives, such as the one pictured on this book, are currently made by both Victorinox and Wengler for commercial use. The vast majority of these knives are sold in the United States, where they were popularized by soldiers returning from World War II.

Edie Freedman designed this cover and made the cover photograph. The cover layout was produced with Quark XPress 3.3 using Adobe Helvetica Black condensed fonts. Edie Freedman also designed the page layouts.

Text was prepared in SGML using the DocBook 2.1 DTD. The print version of this book was created by translating the SGML source into a set of gtroff macros using a filter developed at ORA by Norman Walsh. Steve Talbott designed and wrote the underlying macro set on the basis of the GNU gtroff -gs macros; Lenny Muellner adapted them to SGML and implemented the book design. The GNU groff text formatter version 1.08 was used to generate PostScript output. The body text of the book is set in the Adobe ITC Garamond typeface; the examples are set in Courier. Headings and captions are set in the Helvetica Condensed Bold Oblique typeface.

The figures were created in Aldus Freehand 4.0 and screenshots were processed in Adobe Photoshop 2.5 by Chris Reilley. This colophon was written by Clairemarie Fisher O'Leary.

BOOKS
From O'Reilly & Associates
SUMMER 1996

Linux Series

Linux in a Nutshell

By Jessica Hekman and the Staff of O'Reilly & Associates
1st Edition Fall 1996
650 pages (est.), ISBN 1-56592-167-4

Thedesktop reference for Linux, Linux in a Nutshellcovers the core commands available on common Linux distributions. This isn't a scaled-down quick reference of common commands, but a complete reference containing all user, programming, administration, and networking commands.

Many UNIX users who have GNU versions of standard UNIX tools will also enjoy this book because it documents a wide range of GNU tools.

This book includes all the essential commands you need to run your system and all the commands that historically have been included on UNIX systems. Specialized packages included in most distributions of Linux are not covered.

Linux in a Nutshellis a must for any Linux user; it weighs less than a stack of manual pages, but gives you everything you need for common, day-to-day use..

Contents include:

- Commands with complete lists of options
- Shell syntax for the bash, csh, and tcshshells
- Pattern matching
- emacs, vi, and exediting commands
- sed, gawk, and perlcommands
- Software development commands
- System administration commands

Linux Multimedia Guide

By Jeff Tranter
1st Edition Fall 1996
400 pages (est.), ISBN 1-56592-219-0

Linux is increasingly popular among computer enthusiasts of all types, and one of the applications where it is flourishing is multimedia. Take a low-cost hardware platform and add the Linux operating system, which really exploits its speed, and you have a great host for developing multimedia applications. These often can be ported to other UNIX systems, increasing their value. Another attraction comes in the form of a great variety of free software packages that support manipulation of graphics, audio, and video, the best of which are described in this book.

But it's not simple to put multimedia together on Linux. There are few packages that integrate everything for you, such as companies sell for other operating systems. Instead, you are handed a bunch of programming interfaces and stand-alone utilities that are each suited for a particular job. You could use some guidance to fit the pieces together, and that's what Jeff Tranter offers in this book.

Part of the book is aimed at C programmers. Handling sound cards and CD-ROMS is not too difficult if you understand the standard interfaces. The book also describes tools that nonprogrammers can use. Sample multimedia applications are also shown.

Contents include:

- Introduction to multimedia and the devices that Linux supports
- Configuration and use of sounds cards, CD-ROMs, and joysticks
- Applications for sound and music, graphics, video, and games
- Programming devices such as sound cards and CD-ROMs
- Overview of graphical toolkits and APIs

Running Linux, 2nd Edition

By Matt Welsh & Lar Kaufman
2nd Edition Summer 1996
650 pages (est.), ISBN 1-56592-151-8

Linux is the most exciting development today in the UNIX world—and some would say in the world of the PC-compatible. A complete, UNIX-compatible operating system developed by volunteers on the Internet, Linux is distributed freely in electronic form and for low cost from many vendors. Its software packages include the X Window System (X11R6); TCP/IP networking (including SLIP, PPP, and NFS support); popular software tools such as Emacs and TeX; a complete software development environment including C, C++, Perl, Tcl/Tk, and more; libraries, debuggers, multimedia support, scientific and database applications, and much more. Developed first on the PC, it has been ported to many other architectures, and a POSIX-compliant version has even been developed.

Running Linuxexplains everything you need to understand, install, and start using the Linux operating system. This includes a comprehensive installation tutorial, complete information on system maintenance, tools for document development and programming, and guidelines for network and Web site administration.

New topics in the second edition include:

- Printer configuration, management, and use
- Configuration of network clients for NFS and NIS
- Expanded information on configuring a wide range of hardware devices
- Updated configuration information for the kernel and XFree86

O'Reilly & Associates has collaborated with Red Hat Software, Inc. to produce the accompanying Running Linux Companion CD-ROM. With Running Linuxand the Companion CD-ROMyou have everything you need to install and run Linux on your personal computer. If you plan to obtain the Linux software through other means, Running Linuxcan be used alone.

"I received the book today, and am thrilled. As a fairly 'long time' linux user, I thought I'd not really get a lot from this book, but having it in my hands and skimming, I've found three or four commands, or tips that I wondered about in the past. Actually, I've found that it's a very good book, and well formatted. The text and subjects are, of course, quite timely, and written with a USERS viewpoint...always important to a reader. This isn't thrown together to take advantage of an incredible market, this book is written by a user, for users, with first hand knowledge of users problems. Ideal. Excellent."

—John L. Clarke,III, Linux Systems Administrator, March 1995

Running Linux Companion CD-ROM

By O'Reilly & Associates and Red Hat Software
2nd Edition July 1996

Includes two CD-ROMs
140 pages, ISBN 1-56592-212-3

LINUX is a multi-user, multi-tasking operating System that is in use around the world at research and development organizations as a fully functional, low-cost UNIX workstation. *Running Linux Companion CD-ROM* contains version 3.03 of Red Hat Linux, the most reliable, easy-to-install, and easy-to-upgrade version of the Linux operating system around. This software, together with the popular book, Running Linuxby Matt Welsh and Lar Kaufman, provides a complete software/documentation package for installing and learning to use the Linux operating system.

Linux Network Administrator's Guide

By Olaf Kirch
1st Edition January 1995
370 pages, ISBN 1-56592-087-2

Linux, a UNIX-compatible operating system that runs on personal computers, is a pinnacle within the free software movement. It is based on a kernel developed by Finnish student Linus Torvalds and is distributed on the Net or on low-cost disks, along with a complete set of UNIX libraries, popular free software utilities, and traditional layered products like NFS and the X Window System.

Networking is a fundamental part of Linux. Whether you want a simple UUCP connection or a full LAN with NFS and NIS, you are going to have to build a network.

Linux Network Administrator's Guideby Olaf Kirch is one of the most successful books to come from the Linux Documentation Project. It touches on all the essential networking software included with Linux, plus some hardware considerations. Topics include serial connections, UUCP, routing and DNS, mail and News, SLIP and PPP, NFS, and NIS.

Basics

Learning the UNIX Operating System

By Grace Todino, John Strang & Jerry Peek
3rd Edition August 1993
108 pages, ISBN 1-56592-060-0

If you are new to UNIX, this concise introduction will tell you just what you need to get started and no more. Why wade through a 600-page book when you can begin working productively in a matter of minutes? It's an ideal primer for Mac and PC users of the Internet who need to know a little bit about UNIX on the systems they visit.

This book is the most effective introduction to UNIX in print. The third edition has been updated and expanded to provide increased coverage of window systems and networking. It's a handy book for someone just starting with UNIX, as well as someone who encounters a UNIX system as a "visitor"via remote login over the Internet.

Learning GNU Emacs, 2nd Edition

By Debra Cameron, Bill Rosenblatt & Eric Raymond
2nd Edition Summer 1996
450 pages (est.), ISBN 1-56592-152-6

An introduction to Version 19.29 of the GNU Emacs editor, one of the most widely used and powerful editors available under UNIX. Provides a solid introduction to basic editing, a look at several important "editing modes"(special Emacs features for editing specific types of documents, including email, Usenet News, and the World Wide Web), and a brief introduction to customization and Emacs LISP programming. The book is aimed at new Emacs users, whether or not they are programmers.

Learning the bash Shell

By Cameron Newham & Bill Rosenblatt
1st Edition October 1995
310 pages, ISBN 1-56592-147-X

Whether you want to use bashfor its programming features or its user interface, you'll find Learning the bash Shella valuable guide. If you're new to shell programming, it provides an excellent introduction, covering everything from the most basic to the most advanced features, like signal handling and command line processing. If you've been writing shell scripts for years, it offers a great way to find out what the new shell offers.

Learning the Korn Shell

By Bill Rosenblatt
1st Edition June 1993
363 pages, ISBN 1-56592-054-6

This Nutshell Handbook® is a thorough introduction to the Korn shell, both as a user interface and as a programming language.

The Korn shell is a program that interprets UNIX commands. It has many features that aren't found in other shells, including command history. This book provides a clear and concise explanation of the Korn shell's features. It explains kshstring operations, co-processes, signals and signal handling, and command-line interpretation. The book also includes real-life programming examples and a Korn shell debugger called kshdb, the only known implementation of a shell debugger anywhere.

Using csh and tcsh

By Paul DuBois
1st Edition August 1995
242 pages, ISBN 1-56592-132-1

Using csh and tcsh describes from the beginning how to use these shells interactively to get your work done faster with less typing. You'll learn how to make your prompt tell you where you are (no more pwd); use what you've typed before (history); type long command lines with very few keystrokes (command and filename completion); remind yourself of filenames when in the middle of typing a command; and edit a botched command without retyping it.

Learning the vi Editor

By Linda Lamb
5th Edition October 1990
192 pages, ISBN 0-937175-67-6

A complete guide to text editing with vi, the editor available on nearly every UNIX system. Early chapters cover the basics; later chapters explain more advanced editing tools, such as excommands and global search and replacement.

"For those who are looking for an introductory book to give to new staff members who have no acquaintance with either screen editing or with UNIX screen editing, this is it: a book on vithat is neither designed for the UNIX in-crowd, nor so imbecilic that one is ashamed to use it."—;login, May/June 1989

sed & awk

By Dale Dougherty
1st Edition November 1990
414 pages, ISBN 0-937175-59-5

For people who create and modify text files, sed and awk are power tools for editing. Most of the things that you can do with these programs can be done interactively with a text editor. However, using sed and awk can save many hours of repetitive work in achieving the same result.

This book contains a comprehensive treatment of *sed* and *awk* syntax. It emphasizes the kinds of practical problems that sed and awk can help users to solve, with many useful example scripts and programs.

"Anyone who uses these two tools (whether regularly or infrequently), should have a copy on their shelves."—Sun UK User

SCO UNIX in a Nutshell

By Ellie Cutler & the staff of O'Reilly & Associates
1st Edition February 1994
590 pages, ISBN 1-56592-037-6

The desktop reference to SCO UNIX and Open Desktop®, this version of *UNIX in a Nutshell* shows you what's under the hood of your SCO system. It isn't a scaled-down quick reference of common commands, but a complete reference containing all user, programming, administration, and networking commands.

"A very handy desktop reference to have... faster than search[ing] through pages of man references. A valuable and handy guide."
—Rob Slade, alt.books.reviews

UNIX in a Nutshell: System V Edition

By Daniel Gilly & the staff of O'Reilly & Associates
2nd Edition June 1992
444 pages, ISBN 1-56592-001-5

You may have seen UNIX quick-reference guides, but you've never seen anything like UNIX in a Nutshell. Not a scaled-down quick reference of common commands, UNIX in a Nutshell is a complete reference containing all commands and options, along with generous descriptions and examples that put the commands in context. For all but the thorniest UNIX problems, this one reference should be all the documentation you need.

Covers System V, Releases 3 and 4, and Solaris 2.0.

What You Need to Know: When You Can't Find Your UNIX System Administrator

By Linda Mui
1st Edition April 1995
156 pages, ISBN 1-56592-104-6

If you're like most UNIX users, you have a job to do aside from exploring your operating system -- like analyzing that hot new stock, running another experiment, or typesetting another report. What happens when you have problems? What happens when the system slows to a crawl, when you can't get logged back in after a power failure, or when you've sent a file to the printer three times but have yet to find a printout?

When You Can't Find Your UNIX System Administrator, part of our new *What You Need to Know* series, gives you tools for solving problems. It offers:

Practical solutions for problems you're likely to encounter in logging in, running programs, sharing files, managing space resources, printing, and so on
Just enough background so that you can make sense of our suggestions, rather than simply memorizing keystrokes
An explanation of how to present problems to your sys admin so that you're more likely to get quick, accurate support
A list of the site-specific information to which you should have access, and a place to write it down
A quick-ref card summarizing what to try first, second, third for commonly encountered problems

The goal of this book is not to make you a guru, but to get you back to the job you'd rather be doing.

Volume 3M: X Window System User's Guide

By Valerie Quercia & Tim O'Reilly
2nd Edition January 1993
956 pages, ISBN 1-56592-015-5

The X Window System User's Guide, Motif Edition orients the new user to window system concepts and provides detailed tutorials for many client programs, including the xterm terminal emulator and the window manager. Building on this basic knowledge, later chapters explain how to customize the X environment and provide sample configurations.

This alternative edition of the User's Guide highlights the Motif window manager, for users of the Motif graphical user interface. Revised for Motif 1.2 and X11 Release 5.

Tools

Programming with GNU Software

By Mike Loukides & Andy Oram
1st Edition Summer 1996
250 pages (est.), ISBN 1-56592-112-7

This book and CD combination is a complete package for programmers who are new to UNIX or who would like to make better use of the system. The tools come from Cygnus Support, Inc., a well-known company that provides support for free software. Contents include GNU Emacs, gcc, C and C++ libraries, gdb, RCS, and make. The book provides an introduction to all these tools for a C programmer.

Applying RCS and SCCS

By Don Bolinger & Tan Bronson
1st Edition September 1995
528 pages, ISBN 1-56592-117-8

Applying RCS and SCCS tells you how to manage a complex software development project using RCS and SCCS. The book tells you much more than how to use each command; it's organized in terms of increasingly complex management problems, from simple source management, to managing multiple releases, to coordinating teams of developers on a project involving many files and more than one target platform.

Few developers use RCS or SCCS alone; most groups have written their own extensions for working with multiperson, multiplatform, multifile, multirelease projects. Part of this book, therefore, discusses how to design your own tools on top of RCS or SCCS, both covering issues related to "front-ending"in general, and by describing TCCS, one such set of tools (available via FTP). This book also provides an overview of CVS, SPMS, and other project management environments.

lex & yacc

By John Levine, Tony Mason & Doug Brown
2nd Edition October 1992
366 pages, ISBN 1-56592-000-7

Shows programmers how to use two UNIX utilities, *lex* and *yacc*, in program development. The second edition contains completely revised tutorial sections for novice users and reference sections for advanced users. This edition is twice the size of the first, has an expanded index, and covers Bison and Flex.

"Even after many years of using *lex* and *yacc*, this book showed me new things about them, and new uses for facilities I thought I knew. It will have an honoured position on my bookshelf"
—Pete Jinks, Sun UK User

Managing Projects with make

By Andrew Oram & Steve Talbott
2nd Edition October 1991
152 pages, ISBN 0-937175-90-0

make is one of UNIX's greatest contributions to software development, and this book offers the clearest description of makeever written. Even the smallest software project typically involves a number of files that depend upon each other in various ways. If you modify one or more source files, you must relink the program after recompiling some, but not necessarily all, of the sources.

makegreatly simplifies this process. By recording the relationships between sets of files, makecan automatically perform all the necessary updating. This book describes all the basic features of makeand provides guidelines on meeting the needs of large, modern projects.

"I use makevery frequently in my day-to-day work and thought I knew everything that I needed to know about it. After reading this book I realized that I was wrong!"—Rob Henley, Siemens-Nixdorf

Software Portability with imake

By Paul DuBois
1st Edition July 1993
390 pages, ISBN 1-56592-055-4

imake is a utility that works with maketo enable code to be compiled and installed on different UNIX machines. This Nutshell Handbook(R)--the only book available on imake--is ideal for X and UNIX programmers who want their software to be portable. The book covers a general explanation of imake, how to write and debug an Imakefile, and how to write configuration files. Several sample sets of configuration files are described and are available free over the Net.

Porting UNIX Software

By Greg Lehey
1st Edition November 1995
538 pages, ISBN 1-56592-126-7

This book deals with the whole life cycle of porting, from setting up a source tree on your system to correcting platform differences and even testing the executable after it's built. It exhaustively discusses the differences between versions of UNIX and the areas where porters tend to have problems.

X User Tools

By Linda Mui & Valerie Quercia
1st Edition November 1994
856 pages,(Includes CD-ROM), ISBN 1-56592-019-8

X User Tools provides for X users what UNIX Power Toolsprovides for UNIX users: hundreds of tips, tricks, scripts, techniques, and programs—plus a CD-ROM—to make the X Window System more enjoyable, more powerful, and easier to use. This browser's book emphasizes useful programs culled from the network, offers tips for configuring individual and systemwide environments, and includes a CD-ROM of source files for all—and binary files for some— of the programs.

UNIX Power Tools

By Jerry Peek, Mike Loukides, Tim O'Reilly, et al.
1st Edition March 1993
1162 pages, (Includes CD-ROM)
Random House ISBN 0-679-79073-X

Ideal for UNIX users who hunger for technical—yet accessible—information, *UNIX Power Tools* consists of tips, tricks, concepts, and freeware (CD-ROM included). It also covers add-on utilities and how to take advantage of clever features in the most popular UNIX utilities.

This is a browser's book...like a magazine that you don't read from start to finish, but leaf through repeatedly until you realize that you've read it all. You'll find articles abstracted from O'Reilly Nutshell Handbooks®, new information that highlights program "tricks"and "gotchas,"tips posted to the Net over the years, and other accumulated wisdom.

The goal of *UNIX Power Tools* is to help you think creatively about UNIX and get you to the point where you can analyze your own problems. Your own solutions won't be far behind.

Exploring Expect

By Don Libes
1st Edition December 1994
602 pages, ISBN 1-56592-090-2

Written by the author of Expect, this is the first book to explain how this new part of the UNIX toolbox can be used to automate Telnet, FTP, passwd, rlogin, and hundreds of other interactive applications. Based on Tcl (Tool Command Language), Expect lets you automate interactive applications that have previously been extremely difficult to handle with any scripting language.

Text Processing

Making TEX Work

By Norman Walsh
1st Edition April 1994
522 pages, ISBN 1-56592-051-1

TeX is a powerful tool for creating professional-quality typeset text and is unsurpassed at typesetting mathematical equations, scientific text, and multiple languages. Many books describe how you use TeX to construct sentences, paragraphs, and chapters. Until now, no book has described all the software that actually lets you build, run, and use TeX to best advantage on your platform. Because creating a TeX document requires the use of many tools, this lack of information is a serious problem for TeX users.

Making TEX Work guides you through the maze of tools available in the TeX system. Beyond the core TeX program there are myriad drivers, macro packages, previewers, printing programs, online documentation facilities, graphics programs, and much more. This book describes them all.

Understanding Japanese Information Processing

By Ken Lunde
1st Edition September 1993
470 pages, ISBN 1-56592-043-0

Understanding Japanese Information Processing provides detailed information on all aspects of handling Japanese text on computer systems. It brings all of the relevant information together in a single book and covers everything from the origins of modern-day Japanese to the latest information on specific emerging computer encoding standards. Appendices provide additional reference material, such as a code conversion table, character set tables, mapping tables, an extensive list of software sources, a glossary, and more.

"Creating multilingual software is a challenge in the growing global marketplace, and the task is especially daunting with Japanese—one of the world's most difficult languages. *Understanding Japanese Information Processing* is *the* resource for developers building the bridge between Japanese and Western languages."——Henry McGilton, Trilithon Software

Business, Career & Health

Electronic Publishing on CD-ROM

By Steve Cunningham & Judson Rosebush
1st Edition August 1996 (est.)
350 pages (est.), ISBN 1-56592-209-3

This book explores electronic publishing on CD-ROM and the World Wide Web. It discusses design, authoring, manufacturing, marketing, and distribution of CD-ROMs; electronic document authoring systems; document standards and formats; and the costs of CD-ROM publishing projects—staff, manufacturing, and phases of development. Includes an extensive resource list, glossary, and CD-ROM full of information resources and software.

Building a Successful Software Business

By Dave Radin
1st Edition April 1994
394 pages, ISBN 1-56592-064-3

This handbook is for the new software entrepreneur and the old hand alike. If you're thinking of starting a company around a program you've written—and there's no better time than the present—this book will guide you toward success. If you're an old hand in the software industry, it will help you sharpen your skills or will provide a refresher course. It covers the basics of product planning, marketing, customer support, finance, and operations.

The Future Does Not Compute

By Stephen L. Talbott
1st Edition May 1995
502 pages, ISBN 1-56592-085-6

This book explores the networked computer as an expression of the darker, dimly conscious side of the human being. What we have been imparting to the Net—or what the Net has been eliciting from us—is a half-submerged, barely intended logic, contaminated by wishes and tendencies we prefer not to acknowledge. The urgent necessity is for us to wake up to what is most fully human and unmachinelike in ourselves, rather than yield to an ever more strangling embrace with our machines. The author's thesis is sure to raise a controversy among the millions of users now adapting themselves to the Net.

Love Your Job!

By Dr. Paul Powers & Deborah Russell
1st Edition August 1993
210 pages, ISBN 1-56592-036-8

Love Your Job! is an inspirational guide to loving your work. In addition to providing solid practical advice to anyone who is dissatisfied with work and wants to get more out of it, this book challenges readers to look inside themselves—at what really motivates them at work and at what kinds of lives they want to lead. Love Your Job!consists of a series of one-page reflections, anecdotes, and exercises aimed at helping readers think more deeply about what they want out of their jobs. Each can be read individually (anyplace, anytime, whenever you need to lift your spirits), or the book can be read from start to finish.

The Computer User's Survival Guide

By Joan Stigliani
1st Edition October 1995
296 pages, ISBN 1-56592-030-9

The bad news: You canbe hurt by working at a computer. The good news: Many of the factors that pose a risk are within your control.

The Computer User's Survival Guide looks squarely at all the factors that affect your health on the job, including positioning, equipment, work habits, lighting, stress, radiation, and general health. It is not a book of gloom and doom. It is a guide to protecting yourself against health risks from your computer, while boosting your effectiveness and making your work more enjoyable.

This guide will teach you what's going on "under the skin"when your hands and arms spend much of the day mousing and typing, and what you can do to prevent overuse injuries. You'll learn various postures to help reduce stress; what you can do to prevent glare from modern office lighting; simple breathing techniques and stretches to keep your body well oxygenated and relaxed; and how to reduce eye strain. Also covers radiation issues and what electrical equipment is responsible for the most exposure.

Stay in touch with O'REILLY™

Visit Our Award-Winning World Wide Web Site

http://www.ora.com/

VOTED

"Top 100 Sites on the Web" —*PC Magazine*
"Top 5% Websites" —*Point Communications*
"3-Star site" —*The McKinley Group*

Our Web site contains a library of comprehensive product information (including book excerpts and tables of contents), downloadable software, background articles, interviews with technology leaders, links to relevant sites, book cover art, and more. File us in your Bookmarks or Hotlist!

Join Our Two Email Mailing Lists

LIST #1   NEW PRODUCT RELEASES: To receive automatic email with brief descriptions of all new O'Reilly products as they are released, send email to: listproc@online.ora.com and put the following information in the first line of your message (NOT in the Subject: field, which is ignored): **subscribe ora-news "Your Name" of "Your Organization"** (for example: **subscribe ora-news Kris Webber of Fine Enterprises)**

List #2   O'REILLY EVENTS: If you'd also like us to send information about trade show events, special promotions, and other O'Reilly events, send email to: **listproc@online.ora.com** and put the following information in the first line of your message (NOT in the Subject: field, which is ignored): **subscribe ora-events "Your Name" of "Your Organization"**

Visit Our Gopher Site

- Connect your Gopher to **gopher.ora.com**, or
- Point your Web browser to **gopher://gopher.ora.com/**, or
- telnet to **gopher.ora.com** (login: **gopher**)

Get Example Files from Our Books Via FTP

There are two ways to access an archive of example files from our books:

REGULAR FTP — ftp to: **ftp.ora.com** (login: **anonymous**—use your email address as the password) or point your Web browser to: **ftp://ftp.ora.com/**

FTPMAIL — Send an email message to: **ftpmail@online.ora.com** (write "help" in the message body)

Contact Us Via Email

order@ora.com — To place a book or software order online. Good for North American and international customers.

subscriptions@ora.com — To place an order for any of our newsletters or periodicals.

software@ora.com — For general questions and product information about our software.
- Check out O'Reilly Software Online at **http://software.ora.com/** for software and technical support information.
- Registered O'Reilly software users send your questions to **website-support@ora.com**

books@ora.com — General questions about any of our books.

cs@ora.com — For answers to problems regarding your order or our products.

booktech@ora.com — For book content technical questions or corrections.

proposals@ora.com — To submit new book or software proposals to our editors and product managers.

international@ora.com — For information about our international distributors or translation queries.
- For a list of our distributors outside of North America check out: **http://www.ora.com/www/order/country.html**

O'REILLY™

101 Morris Street, Sebastopol, CA 95472 USA
TEL 707-829-0515 or 800-998-9938 (6 A.M. to 5 P.M. PST)
FAX 707-829-0104

TO ORDER: **800-889-8969** (CREDIT CARD ORDERS ONLY); **order@ora.com; http://www.ora.com/**
OUR PRODUCTS ARE AVAILABLE AT A BOOKSTORE OR SOFTWARE STORE NEAR YOU.

Listing of Titles from O'REILLY™

INTERNET PROGRAMMING

CGI Programming on the
    World Wide Web
Designing for the Web
Exploring Java
HTML: The Definitive Guide
Web Client Programming with Perl
Learning Perl
Programming Perl, 2nd.Edition
    (Fall '96)
JavaScript: The Definitive Guide, Beta
    Edition (Summer '96)
Webmaster in a Nutshell
The World Wide Web Journal

USING THE INTERNET

Smileys
The Whole Internet User's Guide
    and Catalog
The Whole Internet for Windows 95
What You Need to Know:
    Using Email Effectively
Marketing on the Internet (Fall 96)
What You Need to Know: Bandits on the
    Information Superhighway

JAVA SERIES

Exploring Java
Java in a Nutshell
Java Language Reference
    (Fall '96 est.)
Java Virtual Machine

WINDOWS

Inside the Windows '95 Registry

SOFTWARE

WebSite™ 1.1
WebSite Professional™
WebBoard™
PolyForm™

SONGLINE GUIDES

NetLearning
NetSuccess for Realtors
NetActivism (Fall '96)

SYSTEM ADMINISTRATION

Building Internet Firewalls
Computer Crime:
    A Crimefighter's Handbook
Computer Security Basics
DNS and BIND
Essential System Administration,
    2nd ed.
Getting Connected:
    The Internet at 56K and Up
Linux Network Administrator's Guide
Managing Internet Information Services
Managing Usenet (Fall '96)
Managing NFS and NIS
Networking Personal Computers
    with TCP/IP
Practical UNIX & Internet Security
PGP: Pretty Good Privacy
sendmail
System Performance Tuning
TCP/IP Network Administration
termcap & terminfo
Using & Managing UUCP (Fall '96)
Volume 8: X Window System
    Administrator's Guide

UNIX

Exploring Expect
Learning GNU Emacs, 2nd Edition
    (Fall '96 est.)
Learning the bash Shell
Learning the Korn Shell
Learning the UNIX Operating System
Learning the vi Editor
Linux in a Nutshell (Fall '96 est.)
Making TeX Work
Linux Multimedia Guide (Fall '96)
Running Linux, 2nd Edition
Running Linux Companion
    CD-ROM, 2nd Edition
SCO UNIX in a Nutshell
sed & awk
Unix in a Nutshell: System V Edition
UNIX Power Tools
UNIX Systems Programming
Using csh and tsch
What You Need to Know:
    When You Can't Find Your
    UNIX System Administrator

PROGRAMMING

Applying RCS and SCCS
C++: The Core Language
Checking C Programs with lint
DCE Security Programming
Distributing Applications Across
    DCE and Windows NT
Encyclopedia of Graphics File
    Formats, 2nd ed.
Guide to Writing DCE Applications
lex & yacc
Managing Projects with make
ORACLE Performance Tuning
ORACLE PL/SQL Programming
Porting UNIX Software
POSIX Programmer's Guide
POSIX.4: Programming for
    the Real World
Power Programming with RPC
Practical C Programming
Practical C++ Programming
Programming Python (Fall '96)
Programming with curses
Programming with GNU Software
    (Fall '96 est.)
Pthreads Programming
    (Fall '96)
Software Portability with imake
Understanding DCE
Understanding Japanese Information
    Processing
UNIX Systems Programming for SVR4

BERKELEY 4.4 SOFTWARE DISTRIBUTION

4.4BSD System Manager's Manual
4.4BSD User's Reference Manual
4.4BSD User's Supplementary Docs.
4.4BSD Programmer's Reference Man.
4.4BSD Programmer's Supp. Docs.

X PROGRAMMING
THE X WINDOW SYSTEM

Volume 0: X Protocol Reference Manual
Volume 1: Xlib Programming Manual
Volume 2: Xlib Reference Manual
Volume. 3M: X Window System
    User's Guide, Motif Ed.
Volume. 4: X Toolkit Intrinsics
    Programming Manual
Volume 4M: X Toolkit Intrinsics
    Programming Manual, Motif Ed.
Volume 5: X Toolkit Intrinsics
    Reference Manual
Volume 6A: Motif Programming Man.
Volume 6B: Motif Reference Manual
Volume 6C: Motif Tools
Volume 8 : X Window System
    Administrator's Guide
Programmer's Supplement for Release 6
X User Tools (with CD-ROM)
The X Window System in a Nutshell

HEALTH, CAREER, & BUSINESS

Building a Successful Software Business
The Computer User's Survival Guide
Dictionary of Computer Terms
The Future Does Not Compute
Love Your Job!
Publishing with CD-ROM

TRAVEL

Travelers' Tales: Brazil (Summer '96 est.)
Travelers' Tales: Food (Summer '96)
Travelers' Tales: France
Travelers' Tales: Hong Kong
Travelers' Tales: India
Travelers' Tales: Mexico
Travelers' Tales: San Francisco
Travelers' Tales: Spain
Travelers' Tales: Thailand
Travelers' Tales: A Woman's World

International Distributors

Customers outside North America can now order O'Reilly & Associates books through the following distributors. They offer our international customers faster order processing, more bookstores, increased representation at tradeshows worldwide, and the high-quality, responsive service our customers have come to expect.

EUROPE, MIDDLE EAST AND NORTHERN AFRICA (except Germany, Switzerland, and Austria)
INQUIRIES
International Thomson Publishing Europe
Berkshire House
168-173 High Holborn
London WC1V 7AA, United Kingdom
Telephone: 44-171-497-1422
Fax: 44-171-497-1426
Email: **itpint@itps.co.uk**

ORDERS
International Thomson Publishing Services, Ltd.
Cheriton House, North Way
Andover, Hampshire SP10 5BE,
United Kingdom
Telephone: 44-264-342-832 (UK orders)
Telephone: 44-264-342-806 (outside UK)
Fax: 44-264-364418 (UK orders)
Fax: 44-264-342761 (outside UK)
UK & Eire orders: **itpuk@itps.co.uk**
International orders: **itpint@itps.co.uk**

GERMANY, SWITZERLAND, AND AUSTRIA
International Thomson Publishing GmbH
O'Reilly International Thomson Verlag
Königswinterer Straße 418
53227 Bonn, Germany
Telephone: 49-228-97024 0
Fax: 49-228-441342
Email: **anfragen@arade.ora.de**

AUSTRALIA
WoodsLane Pty. Ltd.
7/5 Vuko Place, Warriewood NSW 2102
P.O. Box 935, Mona Vale NSW 2103
Australia
Telephone: 61-2-9970-5111
Fax: 61-2-9970-5002
Email: **woods@tmx.mhs.oz.au**

NEW ZEALAND
WoodsLane New Zealand Ltd.
21 Cooks Street (P.O. Box 575)
Wanganui, New Zealand
Telephone: 64-6-347-6543
Fax: 64-6-345-4840
Email: **info@woodslane.com.au**

ASIA (except Japan & India)
INQUIRIES
International Thomson Publishing Asia
60 Albert Street #15-01
Albert Complex
Singapore 189969
Telephone: 65-336-6411
Fax: 65-336-7411

ORDERS
Telephone: 65-336-6411
Fax: 65-334-1617

JAPAN
O'Reilly Japan, Inc.
Kiyoshige Building 2F
12-Banchi, Sanei-cho
Shinjuku-ku
Tokyo 160 Japan
Telephone: 8-3-3356-5227
Fax: 81-3-3356-5261
Email: **kenji@ora.com**

INDIA
Computer Bookshop (India) PVT. LTD.
190 Dr. D.N. Road, Fort
Bombay 400 001
India
Telephone: 91-22-207-0989
Fax: 91-22-262-3551
Email: **cbsbom@giasbm01.vsnl.net.in**

THE AMERICAS
O'Reilly & Associates, Inc.
101 Morris Street
Sebastopol, CA 95472 U.S.A.
Telephone: 707-829-0515
Telephone: 800-998-9938 (U.S. & Canada)
Fax: 707-829-0104
Email: **order@ora.com**

SOUTHERN AFRICA
International Thomson Publishing Southern Africa
Building 18, Constantia Park
240 Old Pretoria Road
P.O. Box 2459
Halfway House, 1685 South Africa
Telephone: 27-11-805-4819
Fax: 27-11-805-3648

O'REILLY™

Here's a page we encourage readers to tear out...

Nineteenth century wood engraving
of a coatimundi from the O'Reilly
& Associates Nutshell Handbook®
C++ The Core Language.

BUSINESS REPLY MAIL

FIRST CLASS MAIL   PERMIT NO. 80   SEBASTOPOL, CA

Postage will be paid by addressee

O'Reilly & Associates, Inc.
101 Morris Street
Sebastopol, CA 95472-9902